Publications of the Algonquian Text Society
Collection de la Société d'édition de textes algonquiens

H.C. Wolfart, *General Editor*

ana kâ-pimwêwêhahk okakêskihkêmowina

ᐊᓇ ᑳ ᐱᒣᐧᐁᐧᐦᐊˣ ᐅᑲᑫᐢᑭᐦᑫᒧᐃᐧᓇ

The Counselling Speeches of Jim Kâ-Nîpitêhtêw

wâskahikaniwyiniw-âcimowina
ᐊᐧᐢᑲᐦ ᐃᑲᓂᐃᐧᔨᓂᐤ ᐊᒋᒧᐃᐧᓇ
Stories of the House People
Told by Peter Vandall and Joe Douquette.
Edited, translated and with a glossary by Freda Ahenakew, 1987.

The Dog's Children: Anishinaabe Texts Told by Angeline Williams
Edited and translated by Leonard Bloomfield. Newly edited and with a glossary by John D. Nichols, 1991.

kinêhiyâwiwininaw nêhiyawêwin
ᑭᓀᐦ ᐃᔮᐃᐧᐃᐧᓂᓇᐤ ᓀᐦ ᐃᔭᐁᐧᐃᐧᐣ
The Cree Language is Our Identity:
The La Ronge Lectures of Sarah Whitecalf
Edited, translated and with a glossary by H.C. Wolfart and Freda Ahenakew, 1993.

âtalôhkâna nêsta tipâcimôwina
Cree Legends and Narratives
from the West Coast of James Bay
Told by Simeon Scott *et al.*
Text and translation edited and with a glossary by C. Douglas Ellis, 1995.

ana kâ-pimwêwêhahk okakêskihkêmowina

ᐊᓇ ᑳ ᐱᒣᐧᐁᐧᐦᐊᕽ ᐅᑲᑫᐢᑭᐦᑫᒧᐃᐧᓇ

The Counselling Speeches of Jim Kâ-Nîpitêhtêw

Edited, translated and with a glossary by
Freda Ahenakew & H.C. Wolfart

The University of Manitoba Press
1998

Winnipeg, Manitoba R3T 2N2
Printed in Canada

Design and typography: Norman Schmidt and Arden C. Ogg
Syllabic typography: John D. Nichols and Arden C. Ogg
Printed on acid-free paper. ∞

All royalties from the sale of this book revert to the Society's Publication Fund.

The publication of this volume was made possible through the support of the Cree Language Project, University of Manitoba, and the Saskatchewan Indian Cultural College in Saskatoon.

The publisher gratefully acknowledges the support provided to its publishing program by the Canada Council for the Arts, the Department of Canadian Heritage, the Manitoba Arts Council and the Manitoba Department of Culture, Heritage and Citizenship. This book has been published with the help of a grant from the Humanities and Social Sciences Federation of Canada, using funds provided by the Social Sciences and Humanities Research Council of Canada.

Canadian Cataloguing in Publication Data

Kâ-Nîpitêhtêw, Jim, d. 1996

Ana kâ-pimwêwêhahk okakêskihkêmowina = The counselling speeches of Jim Kâ-Nîpitêhtêw

(Publications of the Algonquian Text Society)

Text in Cree (roman orthography and syllabics) and in English translation.
Includes bibliographical references and index.
ISBN 0-88755-648-5

1. Cree language – Texts. 2. Cree Indians – Religion. 3. Cree Indians – History. 4. Cree language – Dictionaries – English. I. Ahenakew, Freda, 1932–. II. Wolfart, H.C., 1943–. III. Algonquian Text Society. IV. Title. V. Title: The counselling speeches of Jim Kâ-Nîpitêhtêw. VI. Series.

PM989.K36 A65 1998 497'.3 C98-920162-7

Contents

Preface

The *kakêskihkêmowina* or 'counselling discourses' which make up this collection of Plains Cree texts were given between 1987 and 1989, while the speaker was senior member of the Council of Elders at the Saskatchewan Indian Cultural College in Saskatoon and Freda Ahenakew the Director of the Saskatchewan Indian Languages Institute.

They were all delivered on public occasions – at the College itself, at a retreat held by the College on Thunderchild's Reserve and, above all, at the Saskatchewan Indian Languages Institute – by *kâ-pimwêwêhahk*, known in English as Jim Kâ-Nîpitêhtêw or simply (but affectionately and respectfully) as 'Old Jim'. A widely respected orator from *wîhcêkaskosîwi-sâkahikanihk* 'at Onion Lake' and a monolingual speaker of Cree, *kâ-pimwêwêhahk* was almost ninety years old at the time of his death on 20 August 1996.

As public speeches, these formal discourses of exhortation and explanation were first of all addressed to a live audience of fellow elders, chiefs, College and Institute staff and visitors. At the same time, however, the speaker intended the recordings that were being made to be preserved for future educational use:

> *êwak ôm ôhci, nawac ê-miywâsik kîkway ka-nakatamahk, k-âpacihtât, tâpiskôc ômatowihk* [gesture] *ka-nitohtahk, êkota k-ôh-kiskisôhtot osk-âya.* (2-6)
> 'That is why it is better that we should leave behind good things for them to use, for example, that they might listen on this kind [*points to the audio-recorder*] and that the young might thereby remind one another.'

Together with the audio- and video-recordings, he obviously saw the written record as an important part of the collective effort at preservation and documentation:

> […], *mâka ka-nêhiyawastêk anim âcimowin,* […] (5-3)
> '[…], but that this story will be written down in Cree, […]'

êwak ôhci k-ôh-nanâskomoyân êwak ôma ê-wî-isîhcikâtamihk, k-âti-kiskinowâsohtahk ômis îsi kiwâhkômâkaninaw, êwak ôma tânis ê-itwêmakahk, êwak ôma 'oskiciy' k-êsiyîhkatêk. (5-2)
'That is why I give thanks that this [audio-recording] is being arranged, so that our relatives might learn by hearing about it in this way what this 'pipestem', as it is called, means.'

The historical and ritual passages which form part of these sermons demand proper attention to authenticity and authority, while the ritual material, in addition, must always be treated with propriety and respect:

â, êwak ôma kâ-wî-tâhkôtamân, matwân cî kwayask nika-kî-isi-tâhkôtên tânis ê-kî-itâcimostawit kâ-kî-oyôhtâwîyân, [...] (6-1)
'Well, this which I am about to discuss, I wonder if I will be able to discuss it with proper faithfulness, just as my late father had told me the story about it, [...]'

"pitanê, êkâ kîkway pâstâhôtotamân," nititêyihtên mân êwak ôm âyimôtamâni. (5-5)
' "I wish that I might not commit any sacrilege," I usually think when I talk about this.'

As the speaker stresses time and again, the most urgent task at the present time is the effort not to let the thread of transmission break:

mêkwâc kîkway kêhtê-aya kisêyiniw, nôtikwêw kîkway ê-kiskêyihtahk, êkos îsi ka-wîhtamawât ka-kâsispohtêmakahk êwako. êkâ êkosi tôtamihko, mêstohtêtwâwi kêhtê-ayak, pêyakwan iskotêw ê-âstawêk, êkos ôma k-êsi-kitimâkan kinêhiyâwiwininaw. [...] *êwak ôhci mâna mistahi ninanâskomâw ayisiyiniw kâ-nôhtê-kiskêyihtahk.* (7-14)

'While the elders, the old men and the old women, still know something, they should tell them [the young] in this manner so that it might be handed down. If this is not done, then our Cree culture will be miserable once the old people are all gone, like a fire that has gone out. [...] I am very grateful, therefore, when a person wants to know.'

Above all, then, we in turn are grateful to the late *kâ-pimwêwêhahk* for his permission to record and publish his texts. We also thank all those at the Saskatchewan Indian Cultural College and the Saskatchewan Indian Languages Institute who provided support and technical assistance, especially of course Alec Greyeyes and Ted Whitecalf. It is a pleasure, finally, to acknowledge the formal support of the Saskatchewan Indian Cultural College and its President, Linda Pelly-Landrie, for the publication of this book.

Thanks are also due to Arden C. Ogg, who helped construct the English Index to the Glossary and once again printed the syllabics designed by John D. Nichols, and to the Social Sciences and Humanities Research Council of Canada, without whose support the laborious task of transcribing, analysing and editing the audio-recordings and preparing the translation and the glossary would have taken even longer. The essay on the texts was written while the author held a Killam Research Fellowship. For their advice and encouragement, last but not least, we are indebted to all our colleagues in the Cree Language Project at the University of Manitoba.

ᐊᓇ ᑮ ᐱᒣᐧᐁᐧᐦᐊᕽ ᐅᑲᑫᐢᑭᐦᑫᒧᐃᐧᓇ

1 ᑲᑫᐢᑭᒫᐊᐧᓱᐃᐧᐣ

[1] ᐁᐊᐧᑯ ᐆᒪ ᑮᑳᐧᐩ, ᑳ ᓂᑕᐁᐧᔨᐦᑕᐦᑭᐠ ᐆᑭ ᑲ ᐄᐧᐦᑕᒪᐊᐧᑭᐠ, ᐁᐊᐧᑯ ᐆᒪ ᑳ ᒫᒋ ᐃᐦᑖᔮᐣ ᐆᑕ, ᑳ ᐴᓂ ᐊᔭᒥᐦᐁᐃᐧ ᑮᓯᑳᐠ, ᑳ ᐊᔭᒥᐦᐁᐃᐧ ᑮᓯᑳᐠ ᐆᑕ ᑳ ᑕᑯᐦᑌᔮᐣ. ᑮᑳᐧᐩ ᐅᐦᒋ ᑳ ᐆᐦ ᑮ ᐯ ᐃᑐᐦᑌᔮᐣ ᐆᑕ, ᐁᐊᐧᑯ ᐆᒪ ᑮᑳᐧᐩ ᑳ ᐊᐢᑖᐦᐃᑯᔭᕽ, ᑕᐦᑖᐧᐤ ᐁ ᑮᓯᑳᐠ ᐁᑳ ᑮᑳᐧᐩ ᑳ ᒥᔮᐧᓯᐠ. ᐁᐊᐧᑯ ᐊᓂᒪ ᐯᔭᐠ ᑭᓭᔨᓂᐤ ᐁ ᑮ ᓇᑭᐢᑲᐊᐧᐠ, ᐁᐊᐧᑯ ᐆᒪ ᐁ ᑮ ᐄᐧᒎᐦᑲᒪᐃᐧᐟ, ᑖᓂᓯ ᐁ ᐃᑕᐢᑌᔨᐠ ᐄᐧᐢᑕ ᐅᑲᑫᐢᑭᒫᐊᐧᓱᐃᐧᐣ, ᐁᐊᐧᑯ ᐆᒪ ᑳ ᑮ ᐄᐧᐦᑕᒪᐃᐧᐟ, ᑳ ᐯ ᐄᐧᐦᑕᒪᐊᐧᑭᐠ ᐆᑭ ᐆᑕ.

[2] ᓇᒨᔭ ᑭᓂᓯᑐᐦᑖᑯᓇᐤ ᑮᑳᐧᐩ, ᑭᑕᐋᐧᓯᒥᓯᓇᐤ ᑰᓯᓯᒥᓇᐤ ᐯᔮᐦᑎᐠ ᐋᑕ ᑮᑳᐧᐩ ᑲ ᐄᐧᐦᑕᒪᐋᐧᔭᕽ, ᓇᒨᔭ ᑭᓂᓯᑐᐦᑖᑯᓇᐤ. ᐱᑯ ᒣᒧᐦᒋ ᑲ ᓂᓯᑐᐦᑕᒨᐦᐃᐦᐟ, ᑖᓂᓯ ᐁ ᑮ ᐃᓯ ᑲᑫᐢᑭᒥᐦᐟ ᑲᔮᐢ ᐅᐢᑳᔭ, ᐅᐢᑭᓃᑭᐢᑫᐧᐤ, ᐅᐢᑭᓃᑭᐤ, ᑖᓂᓯ ᐁ ᑮ ᐯ ᐃᓯ ᑖᐯᐧᐦᑕᐦᑭᐠ ᑮᑳᐧᐩ ᐁ ᒥᔮᐧᓯᐠ ᑮᑳᐧᐩ ᑳ ᑮ ᐯ ᐄᐧᐦᑕᒫᑯᒋᐠ, ᐅᓃᑭᐦᐃᑯᐋᐧᐊᐧ ᐊᐦᐴ ᐅᒧᓲᒥᐋᐧᐊᐧ ᐆᐦᑯᒥᐋᐧᐊᐧ. ᒥᐢᑕᐦᐃ ᑮ ᓇᓇᐦᐃᐦᑕᒼ ᐅᐢᑭᓃᑭᐢᑫᐧᐤ, ᑮᑳᐧᐩ ᑫᑖᓲᒥᑯᐟ ᐆᐦᑯᒪ ᐅᑎ. ᒋᑫᒨ ᐯ ᓇᑲᒋᐦᑖᐤ ᓅᑎᑫᐧᓯᐤ ᑲ ᐃᓯᔩᐦᑳᓱᐟ, ᑲᐦᑭᔭᐤ ᑮᑳᐧᐩ ᑖᓂᓯ ᐁ ᐯ ᐃᓯ ᒪᓈᒋᐦᑖᐟ. ᐁᐊᐧᑯ ᐊᓂᒪ ᑳ ᑮ ᐋᓲᓇᒫᐊᐧᐟ ᐆᓯᓯᒪ, ᑖᓂᓯ ᑮᑳᐧᐩ ᑲ ᐃᓯ ᓇᐦᐁᔨᐦᑕᕽ, ᐅᑕᐋᐧᓯᒥᓯᒫᐤ ᐅᓵᓯᓯᒥᒫᐤ, ᑖᓂᓯ ᑲ ᐃᓯ ᓇᐦᐁᔨᐦᑕᒥᐦᐃᐦᐟ. ᓇᒨᔭ ᓈᓂᑕᐤ ᐃᑖᐸᑕᐣ, ᑭᔮᓇᐤ ᑎᐱᔭᐤ ᑭᑕᐋᐧᓯᒥᓯᓇᐤ ᑰᓯᓯᒥᓇᐤ, ᑭᔮᒼ ᐱᑯᔩᑯᕽ ᑲ ᑭᔩᐁᐧᐦᑲᐦᑕᐋᐧᔭᕽ ᑮᑳᐧᐩ ᐁ ᐸᑳᐧᑕᒪᐋᐧᔭᕽ, ᑲ ᐄᐧᐦᑕᒪᐋᐧᔭᕽ. ᒋᑫᒨ, ᑭᓴᐢᑲᒋᐦᑖᑯᓇᐤ, ᑮᑳᐧᐩ ᐊᓂᒪ ᑳ ᐋᑕ ᑲᑫᐧ ᑭᑖᓲᒫᔭᕽ, ᐁᑳ ᑮᑳᐧᐩ ᑲ ᑑᑕᕽ ᐊᓂᒪ, ᐁᑳ ᑮᑳᐧᐩ ᐁ ᒥᔮᐧᓯᐠ. ᑲᐦᑭᔭᐤ ᑮᑳᐧᐩ ᐊᑎ ᐁᐧᐱᓇᒼ ᐅᐢᑳᔭ ᐊᓄᐦᐨ, ᑲᐦᑭᔭᐤ ᑮᑳᐧᐩ ᐊᑎ ᓇᒨᔭ ᑖᐯᐧᐊᐧᑫᔨᐦᑕᒼ. ᐁᐊᐧᑯ ᐊᐊᐧ ᑲ ᐄᐧᐦᑕᒪᐊᐧᐠ ᐊᓄᐦᐨ ᐊᐊᐧ, ᐆᑕ ᑳ ᐄᐧᑕᐱᒪᐠ ᐊᐊᐧ, ᒥᓴᐋᐧᐨ ᐁᑐᑫᐧ ᑭᓂᓯᑕᐁᐧᔨᒫᐊᐧᐤ, Freda ᐃᓯᔩᐦᑳᓱᐤ, ᐁᑯᑕ ᐆᒪ ᐄᐧᐢᑕ ᐁ ᐊᑐᐢᑫᐟ ᐆᑕ, ᑖᐱᐢᑰᐨ ᐆᒪ ᐃᑌ ᒫᓇ ᑳ ᐯ ᐄᐧᑕᐱᒪᑭᐠ ᐆᑭ, ᓀᐦᐃᔭᐃᐧ ᑭᐢᑭᓄᐦᐊᒫᑐᐃᐧ ᑲᑫᐢᑭᐦᑫᒧᐃᐧᑲᒥᐠ ᐃᓯᔩᐦᑳᑌᐤ.

[3] ᐁᑯᑐᐊᐧᕽ ᐊᐊᐧ ᐄᐧᐢᑕ ᐁ ᐊᑐᐢᑳᑕᕽ ᐆᑕ, ᐁᐊᐧᑯ ᐅᐦᒋ ᑳ ᐆᐦ ᓂᑕᐁᐧᔨᐦᑕᕽ ᐊᐱᓯᐢ ᑮᑳᐧᐩ ᑲ ᐄᐧᐦᑕᒪᐊᐧᐠ, ᑖᓂᓯ ᑮᑳᐧᐩ

ᑫ ᐯ ᐃᓯ ᑭᐢᑫᔨᐦᑕᒫᐣ, ᑖᓂᓯ ᐁ ᑮ ᐯ ᐃᓯ ᐑᐦᑕᒪᐏᐟ ᑮᑿᐩ, ᑭᓭᔨᓂᐤ ᑳ ᑮ ᐯ ᐅᐦᐱᑭᐦᐃᐟ. ᐱᔨᐢ ᐁᑯᑕ ᐅᐦᒋ ᑳ ᑮ ᐅᐦᑕᐢᑌᐠ ᐁ ᐑᑕᑐᐢᑫᒪᑭᐠ ᑭᓭᔨᓂᐘᐠ, ᑕᐦᑭ ᐊᔨᐚᐠ ᑮᑿᐩ ᓂᑮ ᐊᑎ ᒥᔨᑿᐠ ᐁ ᒥᔻᓯᐠ, ᑮᒁᐩ ᐊᓂᒪ ᑲ ᒪᒥᓰᑐᑕᒫᐣ ᑕᐦᑘᐤ ᐁ ᑮᓯᑳᐠ. ᐁᐘᑯ ᐅᐦᒋ ᑳ ᐆᐦ ᐯ ᐅᑎᐦᑕᑭᐠ ᐆᑭ ᐆᑕ, ᓇᒨᔭ ᐁ ᒨᐦᒸᔨᒪᑭᐠ, ᓇᒨᔭ ᒦᓇ ᓅᐦᑕᐤ ᐁ ᐃᑌᔨᒪᑭᐠ ᑖᓂᓯ ᐁ ᐃᐢᐲᐦᑌᔨᒥᓲᔭᐣ, ᒫᑲ ᐁ ᓅᐦᑌ ᐑᒨᐦᑲᒪᐘᑭᐠ, ᑮᒁᐩ ᑭᑲ ᐋᐸᒋᐦᐃᑯᒋᐠ, ᐃᔨᑯᕽ ᐆᒪ ᐆᑕ ᐁ ᑯᓯᑿᓂᔨᐠ ᐅᑕᑐᐢᑫᐏᓂᐚᐤ, ᐁᐘᑯ ᐊᓂᒪ ᐅᐦᒋ ᑳ ᐆᐦ ᐯ ᐱᒧᐦᑌᔮᐣ. ᐁᑯᓯ ᓂᓇᓈᐢᑯᒧᐣ, ᐚᐸᐦᑭ ᐃᐢᑵᔮᐨ, ᐆᑕ ᑲ ᐑᒋ ᐲᐦᑘᒪᑭᐠ, ᑲ ᑳᑮᓯᒧᔭᕽ ᑮᑭᓭᐹ. ᐁᑯᓯ ᒥᐢᑕᐦᐃ ᓂᓇᐦᐁᔨᐦᑌᐣ, ᐁ ᓂᑐᐦᑕᐏᒋᐠ, ᐁᐘᑯ ᐆᒪ ᐁ ᓇᓈᐢᑯᑕᒷᐠ ᑖᓂᓯ ᐏᔭᐚᐤ ᐁ ᐃᓯ ᓂᓯᑐᐦᑕᐦᑭᐠ, ᒫᑲ ᒥᑐᓂ ᐁᑯᓯ ᐁ ᐃᓯ ᓂᓯᑐᐦᑖᑯᒋᐠ ᐅᑑᐢᐠ ᐋᔨᒥᐚᐘ – ᑮᒁᐩ ᐆᒪ ᒥᐢᑕᐦᐃ ᑳ ᒫᒥᑐᓀᔨᐦᑕᒥᐦᐃᑯᐟ ᐊᐘ ᐑᐢᑕ ᐅᑕᐚᓯᒥᓴ, ᐯᔭᐠ ᐋᓰᓀ –. ᐁᐘᑯ ᐊᓂᒪ ᒥᐢᑕᐦᐃ ᓇᔦᐦᑖᐘᐣ, ᐁᑯᓯ ᐃᓯ ᐁᑳ ᑎᐱᔭᐤ ᐁ ᑮ ᑭᑐᑕᐠ ᐊᓇ ᐅᐢᑳᔭ, ᒫᑲ ᐁ ᐃᓯ ᑲᐢᑭᐦᑖᔮᐣ, ᐃᔨᑯᕽ ᓂᓂᑐᑕᒫᑫᐢᑕᒪᐚᐤ ᐋᑕ, ᑕᐦᑘᐤ ᑲ ᐅᐦᐹᐢᑯᓇᐠ ᐅᐢᑻᑲᐣ. ᐁ ᐋᐸᐦᑲᐏᓂᔨᐠ ᒥᑐᓀᔨᐦᒋᑲᐣ, ᑲ ᑲᑵ ᒥᔨᑯᐏᓯᐟ ᐑᐢᑕ, ᑲ ᑵᐢᑭ ᐱᒫᑎᓯᐟ, ᑖᐱᐢᑰᐨ ᐊᐦᒫᐦᑯ ᐱᒫᑎᓯᐏᓂᕽ ᐃᑌᐦᑫ ᐃᓯ. ᐁᐘᑯ ᐆᒪ, ᐋᑕ, ᑳ ᐊᐦᑲᒣᔨᒧᑐᑕᒫᐣ, ᐁ ᑲᑵ ᐃᓯ ᐑᒨᐦᑲᒪᐘᐠ, ᒫᑲ ᓇᔦᐦᑖᐘᐣ, ᐁᑳ ᑎᐱᔭᐤ ᐁᑯᓯ ᐃᓯ ᐁ ᑮ ᑭᑐᑎᐦᐟ ᐅᐢᑳᔭ ᐊᐘ. ᒫᑲ ᑮᐦᑘᒼ, ᓇᐦᐃᐸᔨᑭ, ᐆᑕ ᑕᑯᐦᑌᔮᓂ, ᓂᑲ ᒥᔧᔨᐦᑌᐣ, ᐁᐘᑯ ᐊᐘ ᑲ ᑭᑐᑕᐠ ᐅᐢᑳᔭ.

[4] ᒥᐢᑕᐦᐃ ᒫᒥᑐᓀᔨᐦᑕᒼ, ᑭᑭᐢᑫᔨᐦᑌᓈᐚᐤ, ᑫᐦᑌ ᐊᔭ, ᐅᑑᐢᐠ ᐋᔨᒪ ᐁᑳ ᒁᔭᐢᐠ ᐁ ᐃᓯ ᐑᒣᐦᑐᔨᐟ. "ᐋᐤ, ᒥᐢᑕᐦᐃ ᒫᒥᑐᓀᔨᐦᒋᑲᐣ ᐁᑯᑕ ᒥᔨᐠ, ᑕᐦᑘᐤ ᐁ ᑮᓯᑳᐠ. ᐁᑯᓯ ᐁᐘᑯ ᐊᓂᒪ, ᐋᑕ ᑳ ᑲᑵ ᐑᐦᑕᒪᐘᑭᐠ ᐆᑭ ᐅᐢᑳᔭᐠ, ᑭᑲ ᓇᓈᐢᑯᒥᐦᐟ ᑰᐦᑖᐑᓇᐤ, ᐏᔭ ᑳ ᑎᐯᔨᐦᑕᕽ ᑭᐱᒫᑎᓯᐏᓂᓇᐤ, ᐁ ᒥᔨᑯᔭᕽ ᐯᔭᐠ ᑮᓯᑳᐤ ᐃᑕ ᑲ ᐱᒧᐦᑖᑕᒪᕽ ᑭᑮᓯᑳᒥᓇᐤ, ᐁ ᐃᓯ ᐘᓂᐢᑳᔭᕽ ᑲ ᓇᓈᐢᑯᒫᔭᕽ, ᑲ ᓇᓈᐢᑯᑕᒹᔭᕽ ᐅᑭᓭᐚᑎᓯᐏᐣ. ᐁᐘᑯ ᐁᑿ ᐋᑕ ᑳ ᐆᐦ ᑲᑵ ᐃᓯ ᐑᒨᐦᑲᒪᐘᑭᐠ ᐆᑭ, ᑖᓂᓯ ᐑᐢᑕᐚᐤ ᑲ ᑮ ᐃᓯ ᐱᑭᐢᑳᑕᒋᐠ, ᐁᑯᓯ ᐏᔭ ᐁᐘᑯ ᐁ ᐃᓯ ᐲᑭᐢᑳᑕᒫᐣ.

[5] ᐁᑲᐧ ᑯᑕᐠ ᐆᒪ, ᐁᐊᐧᑯ ᒫᓇ ᓅᐦᑖᐃᐧᐩ ᓂᑮ ᐄᐧᐦᑕᒫᐠ, ᐁᑲᐧ ᐊᐊᐧ ᐆᑌ ᑭᓭᔨᓂᐤ ᑳ ᓇᑭᐢᑲᐊᐧᐠ, ᐁᐊᐧᑯ ᐁᑲᐧ ᑳ ᑭᐢᑭᓲᒥᐟ ᓅᐦᑖᐃᐧᐩ ᐅᐲᑭᐢᑫᐧᐃᐧᐣ, ᐯᔭᑲᐧᐣ ᑳ ᑮ ᐃᓯ ᐄᐧᐦᑕᒪᐃᐧᐟ, ᐁᑯᓯ ᐁ ᐃᓯ ᐄᐧᐦᑕᒪᐃᐧᐟ ᐊᐊᐧ ᑭᓭᔨᓂᐤ, ᐊᔨᓈᓀᐃᐧ ᒥᑕᓇᐤ ᐊᔨᐋᐧᐠ ᐊᔨᓈᓀᐤ ᐁ ᐃᑕᐦᑐᐱᐳᓀᐧᐟ, «ᐋ, ᐁ ᐯ ᐄᐧᒎᐦᑲᒫᑖᐣ ᐆᒪ, ᐁ ᑭᐢᑫᔨᐦᑕᒫᐣ ᒥᐢᑕᐦᐃ ᐁ ᑯᓯᑲᐧᕽ ᑭᑕᑐᐢᑫᐃᐧᐣ ᑕᐦᑖᐧᐤ ᐁ ᑮᓯᑳᐠ, ᒫᑲ ᐁᑳᔭ ᐳᓂᐦᑖ. ᐋᐦᑲᒣᔨᒧ.» ᐁ ᐃᑌᐧᐟ ᐁᐊᐧᑯ ᐊᐊᐧ ᑭᓭᔨᓂᐤ. ᐁᐊᐧᑯ ᐆᒪ ᑳ ᐄᐧᐦᑕᒪᐊᐧᐠ ᐊᐊᐧ ᐆᑕ, ᐊᓅᐦᐨ, ᐆᑕ ᐁ ᐲᐦᑖᐧᔮᕽ, ᐁᑯᓯ ᓂᑕᐩ ᐋᒋᒧᐢᑕᐋᐧᐤ ᐆᒪ ᐁᐊᐧᑯ ᐅᐲᑭᐢᑫᐧᐃᐧᓂᔨᐤ. ᐁᑯᓂ ᐆᐦᐃ, ᑮ ᑖᐦᑰᒣᐤ ᓃᑳᐣ, ᑳ ᑮ ᐅᔫᐦᑖᐃᐧᔮᐣ, «ᐊᔭᒥᐦᐁᐃᐧᔨᓂᐤ ᑳ ᐃᓯᔩᐦᑳᓱᐟ, ᐊᑳᒪᐢᑮᕽ ᐄᐧ ᐅᐦᑐᐦᑌᐤ ᐋᐧᐱᐢᑭ ᐃᐧᔮᐢ, ᐊᔭᒥᐦᐁᐃᐧᔨᓂᐤ ᑲ ᐃᓯᔩᐦᑳᓱᐤ, ᒫᑲ, ᓂᔭ, ᓇᒨᔭ ᐁᑯᑐᐊᐧᕽ ᐁᑯᓯ ᓂᑎᓯᔩᐦᑲᑖᐤ,» ᓂᑮ ᐃᑎᐠ ᑳ ᑮ ᐅᔫᐦᑖᐃᐧᔮᐣ, «ᐁᐊᐧᑯ ᐊᐊᐧ ᐊᔭᒥᐦᐁᐃᐧᔨᓂᐤ ᑭᔦ ᐃᓯᔩᐦᑳᓱᐟ, ᐅᓂᑕᐊᐧᐦᑖᐤ ᓂᔭ ᓂᑲ ᐃᓯᔩᐦᑲᑖᐤ, ᒫᒋᑰᑎᑕᐣ ᐆᑌ ᑭᔦ ᐊᑎ ᓃᑲᓂᐃᐧᐠ, ᐁᐊᐧᑯ ᐊᐊᐧ ᑲᐦᑭᔭᐤ ᐁᑲᐧ ᑮᑲᐧᐩ ᑲ ᐯ ᓅᑎᓇᒡ, ᑳ ᑮ ᒥᔨᑯᔭᕽ ᐆᒪ ᒫᒪᐃᐧ ᐆᐦᑖᐄᐧᒫᐤ ᒪᐃᐧᒧᐢᒋᑫᐃᐧᐣ, ᐁᐊᐧᑯ ᐆᒪ ᐁ ᐄᐧ ᐯ ᓅᑎᓇᕽ. ᒫᑲ ᓇᒨᔭ ᑲ ᑮ ᑲᐢᑭᐦᑖᐤ ᐄᐧᐦᑳᐨ, ᐁᐊᐧᑯ ᐊᓂᒪ ᑲ ᑮ ᐱᑯᓇᕽ. ᒋᑫᒨ ᑭᑮ ᒥᔨᑯᓇᐤ ᑰᐦᑖᐃᐧᓇᐤ, ᑮᐢᑕᓇᐤ ᑳ ᓀᐦᐃᔭᐃᐧᔭᕽ, ᑮᑲᐧᐩ ᑲ ᓇᑖᒧᑐᑕᒪᕽ,» ᓂᑮ ᐃᑎᐠ ᒫᓇ ᑳ ᑮ ᐅᔫᐦᑖᐃᐧᔮᐣ.

[6] ᒌᑳᐦᑕᐤ ᐁᑯᓯ ᑳ ᐃᓯᐟ ᐊᐊᐧ ᑭᓭᔨᓂᐤ, ᒫᑲ ᐁᑲᐧ ᓂᑲ ᐋᑐᑌᐣ ᐅᐲᑭᐢᑫᐧᐃᐧᐣ, ᑳ ᐃᓯ ᐄᐧᐦᑕᒪᐊᐧᐠ ᐊᐊᐧ ᑮᑲᐧᐩ. «ᐱᑕᒫ ᐆᐦᐃ ᒥᑖᑕᐦᐟ ᑮᑲᐧᐩ, ᐁᑳ ᑲ ᑑᑕᒪᐣ, ᐁᐊᐧᑯ ᐊᐊᐧ ᐊᔭᒥᐦᐁᐃᐧᔨᓂᐤ ᑳ ᐄᐧ ᐯᑖᐟ, ᐄᐧᐢᑕ ᐅᑕᔭᒥᐦᐋᐃᐧᐣ ᐋᐧᐱᐢᑭ ᐃᐧᔮᐢ, ᐁᑯᓂ ᐆᐦᐃ ᑲᐢᑭᐦᑖᔭᓂ ᒥᑖᑕᐦᐟ ᐁᑳ ᑮᑲᐧᐩ ᑲ ᑑᑕᒪᐣ, ᐁᑯᓂ ᐹᐢᑖᐦᐅᐃᐧᓇ ᑳ ᐃᓯᔩᐦᑳᑕᕽ, "ᐋᐤ, ᐁᑯᑕ ᐁᑲᐧ, ᑲᐢᑭᐦᑖᔭᓂ ᐁᑯᓂ ᐁᑳ ᑲ ᑑᑕᒪᐣ, ᐁᑯᑕ ᐁᑲᐧ ᑭᑳᐦ ᑮ ᐄᐧᒉᐋᐧᐤ ᑖᓂᓯ ᐁ ᐃᓯ ᒪᐃᐧᒧᐢᒋᑫᐟ. ᐁᑯᓯ ᒫᑲ, ᐃᑕ ᐁ ᒪᐃᐧᒧᐢᒋᑫᐟ, ᒫᒪᐃᐧ ᐆᐦᑖᐄᐧᒫᐊᐧ ᐁ ᑖᐦᑰᒫᐟ, ᓂᑕᐃᐧ ᐸᑯᓯᐦ, ᓂᑕᐃᐧ ᓂᑐᐦᑕᐤ. ᒋᑫᒨ ᐄᐧᐢᑕ ᐯᔭᑲᐧᐣ ᐊᓂᐦᐃ ᑳ ᒪᒥᓰᐟ, ᐁᑯᓂ ᐆᐦᐃ. ᒫᑲ ᓇᒨᔭ ᐃᔭᐃᐧᐢ, ᐊᐦᒑᐦᑯ ᐱᒫᑎᓯᐃᐧᓂᕽ ᐃᓯ, ᐄᐧ ᐊᑐᐢᑲᑕᒡ ᐁᐊᐧᑯ ᐊᐊᐧ. ᒫᒋᑰᑎᑕᐣ ᐆᑌ ᑫ ᓃᑲᓂᐃᐧᐠ, ᓅᒪᓇᐠ ᐱᒫᑎᓯᔭᓂ, ᑲ ᐊᑎ ᐋᐧᐸᐦᑌᐣ, ᐁᐊᐧᑯ ᐊᐊᐧ, ᐊᔭᒥᐦᐁᐃᐧᔨᓂᐤ ᑭᔦ ᐃᓯᔩᐦᑲᑎᐦᐟ,

ᐁᐊᐧᑯ ᐊᐊᐧ ᐅᓂᑕᐊᐧᐦᑖᐤ ᓂᔭ ᑳ ᐃᓯᔩᐦᑳᑕᐠ, ᐱᔨᐢᐠ ᐊᓇ ᐁᑯᑌ ᑭᑲ ᐃᐢᐸᔨᐦᐅᐤ, ᑲ ᐋᐧᐸᐦᑕᐠ ᐄᐧᐢᑕ, ᐁ ᑖᐯᐧᒪᑲᕽ ᐃᑕ ᑰᐦᑖᐄᐧᓇᐤ ᐁ ᑮ ᒥᔨᑯᔭᕽ, ᑮᑳᐧᐩ ᑲ ᒪᐃᐧᒧᐢᑕᒪᕽ,» ᐁᑯᓯ ᒫᓇ ᑮ ᐃᑌᐧᐤ ᐊᐊᐧ ᑭᓭᔨᓂᐤ, ᑳ ᑮ ᐅᐦᐱᑭᐦᐃᐟ, ᐁᐊᐧᑯ ᐊᓂᒪ ᑳ ᐆᐦ ᑭᐢᑭᓲᒥᐟ ᐊᐊᐧ ᑭᓭᔨᓂᐤ. ᒫᒋᑲ ᐊᐊᐧ ᐊᓄᐦᐨ ᑳ ᑭᑐᑕᐠ, ᐁᑯᓂ ᐆᐦᐃ ᓂᑯᑖᐧᓯᐠ ᑮᑲᐧᐩ ᓂᑲᑫᐧᒋᒫᐤ, ᒪᐦᑎ ᐁ ᐄᐧ ᐊᑐᐢᑳᑕᕽ ᐁᑯᓂ, ᒫᒋᑲ ᐆᒪ ᓂᐢᑕᐠ ᐁ ᑲᑫᐧᒋᒪᐠ, «ᐋ, ᓇᒨᔭ,» ᐃᑌᐧᐤ, «ᓇᒨᔭ ᐁᐊᐧᑯ ᐁ ᐄᐧ ᐊᑐᐢᑳᑕᒫᐣ,» ᐃᑌᐧᐤ. ᐁᑯᓯ ᐅᐦᐱᒣ ᐆᒪ ᓂᑕᐢᑖᐣ, ᒣᐧᐦᒋ ᓃᓱ ᐋᓴᐩ ᒦᓇ ᐁᑲᐧ ᑮᑲᐧᐩ ᐁ ᑲᑫᐧᒋᒪᐠ, «ᐋ, ᓇᒨᔭ,» ᐃᑌᐧᐤ, «ᓇᒨᔭ ᐁᐊᐧᑯ ᐁ ᐄᐧ ᐊᑐᐢᑳᑕᒫᐣ.» ᒣᐧᐦᒋ ᓂᐢᑐ ᐁ ᑲᑫᐧᒋᒪᐠ, ᐁᐊᐧᑯ ᒦᓇ, «ᐋ, ᓇᒨᔭ ᒦᓇ ᐁᐊᐧᑯ ᐁ ᐄᐧ ᐊᑐᐢᑳᑕᒫᐣ,» ᐃᑌᐧᐤ.

[7] ᐁᑯᓂ ᐆᐦᐃ ᓂᑯᑖᐧᓯᐠ, ᐁ ᑮᓯ ᑲᑫᐧᒋᒪᐠ, ᑲᐦᑭᔭᐤ ᓇᒨᔭ ᐁᑯᓂ ᐄᐧ ᐊᑐᐢᑳᑕᐠ – ᒋᑫᒨ ᓇᒨᔭ ᐁᑯᓂ ᐁ ᒥᔮᐧᓯᑭ, ᑖᓂᑕ ᑲ ᑮ ᐅᐦᒋ ᓂᓯᑐᐦᑖᑯᐟ ᐆᐦᐃ ᐄᐧᐢᑕ, ᐅᑕᐋᐧᓯᒥᓴ ᐆᓯᓯᒪ. ᐁᑲᐧ ᐆᐦᐃ ᓀᐅᐧ ᑳ ᐃᐢᑯᓇᒫᐣ ᐆᐦᐃ, ᑯᒐᐋᐧᑲᓂᓴ ᐁᑯᓂ ᐁᑲᐧ ᓅᑎᓀᐣ, «ᐆᐦᐃ ᐃᑕ, ᑰᐦᑖᐄᐧᓇᐤ ᑳ ᑮ ᒥᔨᑯᔭᕽ, ᑖᓂᓯ ᑲ ᐃᓯ ᒪᐃᐧᒧᐢᒋᑫᔭᕽ, ᑳ ᓀᐦᐃᔮᐃᐧᔭᕽ, ᐁᐊᐧᑯᔨᐤ ᒌ ᑭᐄᐧ ᐅᑎᓀᐣ, ᑰᐦᑖᐄᐧᓇᐤ ᐅᑭᓭᐋᐧᑎᓯᐃᐧᐣ ᒥᔪ ᐄᐧᒉᐦᑐᐃᐧᐣ ᑭᑎᒫᑫᔨᐦᑐᐃᐧᐣ, ᐁᐊᐧᑯᔨᐤ ᒌ ᑭᐄᐧ ᐅᑎᓀᐣ,» ᐁ ᐃᑕᐠ, «ᐁᐦᐊ,» ᐃᑌᐧᐤ, ᐁᑯᓯ ᒥᐢᑕᐦᐃ ᓂᓇᓈᐢᑯᒫᐤ ᐁᐊᐧᑯ ᐆᒪ ᐁ ᓇᐢᑯᑕᕽ. ᐁᑯᓯ ᒫᑲ, ᑕᐦᑐ ᐆᒪ ᑫ ᑭᑐᑖᐟ ᐁᑯᓂ ᐆᐦᐃ, ᒥᐢᑕᐦᐃ ᓂᑲ ᓇᐦᐁᔨᐦᑌᐣ, ᑲ ᓇᓇᐦᐃᐦᑖᑯᐟ, ᑲ ᓂᑐᐦᑖᑯᐟ, ᑖᓂᓯ ᑮᑲᐧᐩ ᐁ ᐃᓯ ᐄᐧᐦᑕᒪᐋᐧᐟ. ᒋᑫᒨ ᐁᑯᓯ ᐱᑯ ᑲ ᑑᑕᒪᕽ, ᑮᑲᐧᐩ ᑲ ᒫᒪᐆᐧᐦᑲᒫᑐᔭᕽ ᐁ ᒥᔮᐧᓯᐠ ᑰᐦᑖᐄᐧᓇᐤ ᑲ ᓂᑐᑕᒪᐋᐧᔭᕽ, ᐃᑕ ᑮᓯᑳᐤ ᐁ ᒥᔨᑯᔭᕽ, ᑲ ᐱᒧᐦᑖᑕᒪᕽ ᐁ ᒥᔮᐧᓯᐠ ᑭᑮᓯᑳᒥᓇᐤ, ᐃᐧᔭ ᐊᔨᐢᐠ ᑳ ᐸᒥᐦᑖᐟ ᑭᐱᒫᑎᓯᐃᐧᓂᓇᐤ. ᐁᐊᐧᑯ ᐅᐦᒋ, «ᐁᑳᔭ ᐄᐧᐦᑳᐟ ᓂᑎᐯᔨᒥᓱᐣ ᐃᑌᐧ.» ᑳ ᐆᐦ ᐃᑎᐦᒋᐠ ᐅᐢᑳᔭᐠ, «ᐃᐧᔭ ᐊᓇ ᑳ ᑎᐯᔨᐦᑕᕽ ᑭᐱᒫᑎᓯᐃᐧᓂᓇᐤ. ᓇᒨᔭ ᐄᐧᐦᑳᐨ ᐊᑲᐋᐧᔨᕽ ᑲ ᑮ ᑮᑲᐧᐩ ᑑᑌᓈᓇᐤ, ᑖᐱᐢᑰᐨ ᐆᒪ ᐋᔨᒨᐦᑐᐃᐧᐣ. ᑳ ᐋᔨᒨᒫᔭᕽ ᑮᒋ ᐋᔨᓯᔨᓂᓇᐤ, ᐊᐦᐳ ᑲ ᐸᐦᐱᐦᐋᔭᕽ ᐁ ᑭᑎᒫᑭᓈᑯᓯᐟ, ᑭᔮᓇᐤ ᐊᓂᒪ ᑳ ᐋᔨᒨᒥᑯᔭᕽ,» ᐁᑯᓯ ᑲ ᑮ ᐯ ᐃᑌᐧᒋᐠ ᑫᐦᑌ ᐊᔭᐠ. ᐁᐊᐧᑯ ᐅᐦᒋ, ᑳ ᑮ ᑭᑕᐦᐊᒫᒋᐠ ᑫᐦᑌ ᐊᔭᐠ ᐆᑭ, ᑭᓭᔨᓂᐊᐧᐠ, ᒋᑫᒨ ᑮ ᐯ ᓂᓯᑕᐃᐧᓇᒪᐧᐠ

ᐃᐧᔭᐊᐧᐤ ᑮᑲᐧᐩ. «ᐁᑳᔭ ᐄᐧᐦᑳᐨ ᐸᐦᐱᐦᐃˣ ᓅᑎᑫᐧᓯᐤ ᐋᐧᐄᐧᐢ, ᐋᑕᔩᐦᑲᓇᑭᓱᐤ ᐊᓇ, ᓅᑎᑫᐧᓯᐤ, ᒋᑫᒨ ᐊᐊᐧ, ᐃᐧᔭ ᑳ ᐱᒥᐸᔨᐦᑖᐟ ᑭᑕᔨᓯᔨᓂᐃᐧᓂᓇᐤ. ᑮᐢᐱᐣ ᐁᑳ ᐅᐦᒋ ᐃᐢᑫᐧᐤ, ᓇᒌᔭ ᑭᑳᐦ ᐱᒫᑎᓯᓈᓇᐤ ᑳ ᐊᔨᓯᔨᓂᐃᐧᔭˣ,» ᑳ ᑮ ᐃᑌᐧᒋᐠ ᒫᓇ. ᐁᐊᐧᑯ ᐆᒪ, ᑌᐱᔮˣ ᐁᑯᓯ ᐁ ᐯ ᐃᑖᒋᒧᐢᑕᐊᐧᐠ ᐊᐊᐧ ᐆᑕ ᑳ ᐄᐧᑕᐱᒪᐠ ᐊᐊᐧ. ᐁᑯᓯ, ᐁᑯᓯ ᐁ ᐃᓯ ᓇᓈᐢᑯᒪᐠ ᐆᒪ, ᐁ ᓂᐳᐦᑕˣ ᐆᒪ ᑮᑲᐧᐩ ᑳ ᐄᐧᐦᑕᒪᐊᐧᐠ. ᒫᑳ ᒥᓴᐋᐧᐨ ᑮᐦᑖᐧᒼ ᑕᑯᐦᑌᔮᓂ, ᐍᑎᓇˣ ᐁᑯᑕ ᓂᑲ ᐋᒋᒧᓈᐣ.

[8] ᐁᑯᓯ ᓂᑳᐦ ᒥᔦᐧᔨᐦᑌᐣ, ᐁᐊᐧᑯ ᐆᒪ ᐄᐧ ᑖᐦᑰᑕᒪᐦᑭ ᑮᐦᑖᐧᒼ, ᒋᑫᒨ ᑫᐦᑌ ᐊᔭ ᐱᑯ ᑳ ᐊᐢᐱᐳᓈᒧᔭˣ, ᐃᐧᔭ ᐅᑎᐦᑕᒫᓱᐤ ᒫᒪᐃᐧ ᐆᐦᑖᐄᐧᒫᐊᐧ, ᐊᓂᒪ ᑮᑲᐧᐩ ᑳ ᑮ ᐃᓯ ᒥᔫᐱᑕˣ, ᑳ ᑮ ᐃᓯ ᒥᔫᓂᐢᑫᐦᑳᑕˣ, ᐁᑯᑌ ᑳ ᐆᐦ ᑕᐋᐧᑕᒫᑯᔭˣ, ᑳ ᐲᑭᐢᑫᐧᐢᑕᒫᑯᔭˣ, ᐁᑯᓯ ᐁ ᐃᑌᔨᐦᑕᒫᐣ ᒫᓇ, ᓂᔭ ᐆᒪ. ᐁᐊᐧᑯ ᐅᐦᒋ ᒥᐢᑕᐦᐃ ᓂᓇᐦᐁᔨᐦᑌᐣ, ᑳ ᐊᐢᐱᐳᓈᒧᔭˣ ᑮᑲᐧᐩ ᑫᐦᑌ ᐊᔭ, ᐊᐦᐴ ᐍᐱᓈᓱᐣ ᐊᐦᐴ ᑮᓯᑌᐤ. ᐁᐊᐧᑯ ᐅᐦᒋ ᑳ ᓂᐴᐢᑲˣ ᐊᐊᐧ, «ᑖᓂᓯ ᐊᓂᒪ ᐁ ᑮ ᐃᓯ ᑮᑲᐧᐩ ᐊᐧᐢᑲᐄᐧᐳᑕˣ» – ᓂᔭ ᐊᓇ ᐁ ᒥᐢᑲᐊᐧᐠ ᑮᑲᐧᐩ, ᐆᑌ ᐁ ᑮ ᐊᐧᐋᐧᓇᐢᑫᐦᑖᐟ, ᐁᑲᐧ ᑭᐢᑌᓯᓇᐤ ᐄᐧᓴᐦᑫᒑˣ. ᐋ, ᒋᑫᒨ ᐁᑯᓂᐠ ᑲᐦᑭᔭᐤ ᑮᑲᐧᐩ ᑭᑮ ᐊᐧᐋᐧᓇᐢᑫᐦᑕᒫᑯᓇᐊᐧᐠ, ᐁᐊᐧᑯ ᐊᐊᐧ ᑳ ᓂᑕᐍᔨᐦᑕˣ ᑭᑲ ᐋᒋᒧᐢᑕᐊᐧᐠ. ᒫᑲ ᑮᐦᑖᐧᒼ ᑕᑯᐦᑌᔮᓂ, ᐲᓵᑲᐧᐣ ᐊᔨᐢᐠ ᐁᐊᐧᑯ ᐋᒋᒧᐃᐧᐣ, ᑭᓭᔨᓃᐃᐧ ᐋᒋᒧᐃᐧᐣ ᐆᒪ, ᐁᐊᐧᑯ ᐱᑯ ᑭᑲ ᐋᐸᒋᐦᑖᔮᐣ, ᑭᑲ ᐋᒋᒧᐢᑕᐊᐧᐠ. ᐁᑯᓯ ᐁ ᐃᑖᒋᒧᐢᑕᐊᐧᐠ ᐊᓇ, ᒫᑲ ᒥᐳᓂ ᐊᔭ, ᑳ ᐋᐸᒋᐦᐃᑯᐟ ᐆᒪ ᑮᑲᐧᐩ ᑳ ᓂᑕᐍᔨᐦᑕˣ, ᐁᑯᓯ ᑕ ᐃᑖᒋᒧᐢᑕᐊᐧᐠ ᐊᓇ. ᓂᔭ ᑳ ᐲᑭᐢᑫᐧᔮᐣ ᐆᑌ ᐅᐦᒋ Onion Lake, ᑭᓂᓯᑕᐍᔨᒥᓈᐋᐧᐤ, ᑳ ᐱᒣᐧᐍᐦᐊˣ ᓂᑎᑎᑲᐃᐧᐣ ᐁ ᓅᐦᐃᔭᐤ ᐄᐧᐦᐃᑲᐃᐧᔮᐣ, ᐁᐊᐧᑯ ᐆᒪ ᓂᔭ ᑳ ᐋᒋᒧᔮᐣ ᐆᑕ.

[9] ᐁᑯᓯ, ᐁᐊᐧᑯ ᐊᓂᒪ ᐁᑯᓯ ᐁ ᐃᑖᒋᒧᐢᑕᐊᐧᐠ.

2 ᑮᑲᐧᐩ ᑲ ᐋᐸᒋᐦᐃᑯᓴᐠ

[1] ᐁᐊᐧᑯ ᐆᒪ ᑳ ᐄᐧ ᐄᐧᐦᑕᒫᑕᑯᐠ, ᓇᒨᔭ ᓂᔭ ᑮᑲᐧᐩ ᐁ ᑭᐢᑫᔨᐦᑕᒫᐣ, ᒫᑲ ᐁᑐᑫᐧ ᑰᐦᑖᐄᐧᓇᐤ, ᑳ ᑎᐯᔨᐦᑕᕽ ᐊᐊᐧ ᑮᑲᐧᐩ, ᐁᐊᐧᑯ ᐁᑐᑫᐧ ᐆᒪ ᐁ ᐃᑌᔨᒥᐟ, ᑖᓂᓯ ᑲ ᐃᓯ ᐄᐧᐦᑕᒪᐊᐧᐠ ᑮᑲᐧᐩ ᐅᐢᑳᔭ, ᐁᑳ ᑭᓀᐧᐢ ᐆᑕ ᑲ ᑮ ᐄᐧᒉᐊᐧᐠ ᐊᔨᓯᔨᓂᐤ, ᐁᐊᐧᑯ ᐅᐦᒋ. ᐁ ᐊᐧᓂᐢᑳᓴᐠ ᐃᑕ ᑮᑭᓭᐹ, ᑲ ᓇᓈᐢᑯᒫᓴᐠ ᑰᐦᑖᐄᐧᓇᐤ, ᐁ ᒥᔨᑯᓴᐠ ᑮᓯᑳᐤ, ᐁ ᒥᔮᐧᓯᐠ ᐃᑕ ᑲ ᐱᒧᐦᑖᑕᒉᐠ, ᐅᑭᓭᐋᐧᑎᓯᐃᐧᐣ ᐋᐦᒋ ᐱᑯ ᑲ ᓇᓈᐢᑯᑕᒉᐠ, ᓇᒨᔭ ᓈᓂᑕᐤ ᐃᑖᐸᑕᐣ ᑮᑲᐧᐩ, ᑖᐱᐢᑰᐨ ᐆᒪ, ᐄᐦ, ᐃᔫᑎᐣ ᐃᔨᑯᕽ ᑳ ᐱᒧᐦᑌᒪᑲᕽ, ᐁᑳᔭ ᐄᐧᐦᑳᐨ ᓭᑭᓯᐠ, ᐁᑳᔭ ᐄᐧᐦᑳᐨ ᒪᐃᐧᒧᐠ. ᑭᐢᑭᓯᐠ ᑰᐦᑖᐄᐧᓇᐤ, ᐃᐧᔭ ᐊᓇ ᑳ ᑎᐯᔨᐦᑕᕽ ᐆᒪ ᑭᐊᐧᐢᑲᐄᐧᐃᐧᓂᓇᐤ, ᑖᓂᓯ ᐃᑌᔨᐦᑕᐦᑭ, ᐁᑯᓯ ᑲ ᐃᐢᐸᔨᓈᐋᐧᐤ. ᑮᐢᐱᐣ ᐃᑌᔨᒥᑯᔭᐦᑯ, ᑭᑎᒫᑫᔨᒥᑯᔭᐦᑯ, ᑲ ᐄᐧᒫᐢᑳᑯᓇᐤ ᐊᓇ ᑳ ᐱᒧᐦᑌᐟ ᐃᔫᑎᐣ. ᐁᐊᐧᑯ ᐆᒪ, ᐄᐦ, ᑳ ᐆᐦ ᒪᑐᑎᓯᔮᕽ, ᑳ ᐆᐦ ᒪᑐᑎᓯᔮᕽ, ᐍᐱᓈᓱᐣ ᐁ ᐱᒥ ᐸᑭᑎᓇᒫᕽ.

[2] ᑖᓂᓯ ᐁ ᐃᑖᐸᑕᕽ, ᑯᑕᑲᐠ ᐆᑭ ᐊᐢᑮᐦᑳᓂᕽ, ᐁᑳ ᑮᑲᐧᐩ ᐁᑯᑐᐊᐧᕽ ᐁ ᓈᑖᒧᐢᑕᐦᑭᐠ, ᑳ ᑖᐦ ᑖᐃᐧᓂᑯᒋᐠ ᐆᒪ ᐁᐊᐧᑯ ᑮᑲᐧᐩ. ᐁᐊᐧᑯ ᐆᒪ ᓂᔭᓈᐣ ᐁ ᒪᒥᔩᔮᕽ, ᑕᐦᑐ ᓃᓱ ᑮᓯᑳᐤ ᐁ ᒪᑐᑎᓯᔮᕽ, ᐍᐱᓈᓱᓇ ᐁ ᐸᑭᑎᓇᒫᕽ, ᑖᓂᑕᐦᑖᐧᐤ ᐁᑲᐧ ᐁ ᐱᒧᐦᑌᐟ, ᓂᐄᐧᒫᐢᑳᑯᓈᐣ. ᐁ ᑖᐯᐧᒪᑲᕽ, ᑮᑲᐧᐩ, ᐅᑭᓭᐋᐧᑎᓯᐃᐧᐣ ᐃᑕ ᐁ ᓂᑐᑕᒫᐦᐟ ᑰᐦᑖᐄᐧᓇᐤ. ᓇᒨᔭ ᓈᓂᑕᐤ ᐃᑖᐸᑕᐣ ᑲ ᒪᐃᐧᒧᔭᕽ ᐆᑕ, ᓇᒨᔭ ᓈᓂᑕᐤ, ᓇᒨᔭ ᑭᔮᓇᐤ ᑭᑎᐯᔨᐦᑌᓈᓇᐤ ᐃᐧᔭ, ᐃᐧᔭ ᐃᑌᔨᐦᑕᐦᑭ, ᑭᑎᒫᑭᓈᑯᔭᐦᑯ, ᑲ ᓂᓯᑕᐃᐧᓀᓈᓇᐤ ᐅᑭᓭᐋᐧᑎᓯᐃᐧᐣ, ᐁᐊᐧᑯ ᐊᓂᒪ ᓂᔭ ᐁ ᐋᐸᒋᐦᑖᔮᐣ ᑕᐦᑐ ᑮᓯᑳᐤ. ᐄᐧᐦᑲᐢᑲᐧ ᑳ ᐅᐦᐸᐦᐸᐦᑌᓇᒫᐣ, ᑲ ᐃᑌᐧᐢᑕᒫᑯᔭᕽ, ᐁᑯᓯ ᐃᐧᔭ ᓂᔭ ᐁ ᐃᓯ ᒪᒥᔩᔮᐣ, ᐁᐊᐧᑯ ᐆᒪ, ᑮᐢᑕᐊᐧᐤ ᐁ ᐊᐧᓂᐢᑳᓴᐠ, ᓇᓈᐢᑯᒥᕽ ᑰᐦᑖᐄᐧᓇᐤ, ᐁ ᒥᔨᑯᓴᐠ ᑮᓯᑳᐤ ᐃᑕ ᑲ ᐱᒧᐦᑖᑕᒉᐠ. ᐋᐦᒋ ᐱᑯ ᓂᑐᑕᒫᕽ ᐅᑭᓭᐋᐧᑎᓯᐃᐧᐣ. ᑲ ᑭᑎᒫᑭᓈᑯᓇᐤ, ᐁ ᒫᒪᐆᐧᐦᑲᒫᑐᕽ ᑮᑲᐧᐩ, ᑖᓂᓯ ᐁ ᐃᓯ ᐸᑯᓭᔨᒧᕽ, ᐁᐊᐧᑯ ᐊᓂᒪ. ᓇᒨᔭ ᓈᓂᑕᐤ ᐃᑖᐸᑕᐣ, ᓇᒨᔭ ᓈᓂᑕᐤ ᐃᑖᐸᑕᐣ, ᑲ ᐊᐧᓂᑭᐢᑭᓯᔭᕽ, ᑰᐦᑖᐄᐧᓇᐤ ᑮᑲᐧᐩ, ᐃᐧᔭ, ᐁ ᑎᐯᔨᐦᑕᕽ ᑭᐊᐧᐢᑲᐄᐧᐃᐧᓂᓇᐤ, ᐱᑯᔨᑯᕽ, ᐱᑯ ᐃᑌ ᐃᑖᒧᔭᐦᑯ, ᐱᑯ ᐃᑌ ᒪᐃᐧᒧᔭᓂ, ᓇᒨᔭ ᓈᓂᑕᐤ ᑲ ᑮ ᓈᑕᒫᑯᐣ, ᐃᐧᔭ ᐃᑌᔨᐦᑕᐦᑭ, ᑲ ᓈᑕᒫᑯᓇᐤ, ᐁᐊᐧᑯ ᐆᒪ ᑳ ᐄᐧᐦᑕᒪᐊᐧᐠ ᐊᔨᓯᔨᓂᐤ, ᑳᑭᑫ, ᓇᒨᔭ ᓈᓂᑕᐤ ᐃᑖᐸᑕᐣ ᐁᐊᐧᑯ

ᐊᓂᒪ, ᑲ ᒪᐃᐧᒧᐟ ᐊᔨᓯᔨᓂᐤ. ᐋᐦᒋ ᐱᑯ ᑳ ᑭᐢᑭᓯᐟ ᑰᐦᑖᐄᐧᓇᐤ ᐆᐦᐃ, ᐃᐧᔭ ᑲ ᑭᑎᒫᑭᓈᑯᓯᕽ, ᐃᑕ ᑳ ᑮ ᐸᑭᑎᓂᑯᓯᕽ ᐆᒪ, ᐁ ᓂᐦᑖᐃᐧᑮᐢᑕᒪᕽ ᐊᐢᑭᐩ. ᑖᐱᐢᑰᐨ ᐄᐦ, ᑲᐦᑭᔭᐤ ᑮᑲᐧᐩ ᑮᓯ ᐅᒐᐋᐧᓯᒥᓯᐤ, ᑲᐦᑭᔭᐤ ᑮᑲᐧᐩ, ᑳ ᐸᐹᒥᐦᐋᐟ ᐊᐊᐧ, ᑳ ᐸᐹᒥᐸᐦᑖᐟ ᐆᑕ ᐊᐢᑮᕽ, ᑲᐦᑭᔭᐤ ᑮᓯ ᐅᒐᐋᐧᓯᒥᓯᐤ ᐁᐊᐧᑯ. ᐯᔭᑲᐧᐣ ᐆᒪ ᒪᐢᑭᐦᑭᐩ, ᑳ ᐄᐧᐦᑕᒫᑖᐣ ᐊᐊᐧ, ᑰᐦᑯᒥᓇᐤ ᐊᐊᐧ ᑳ ᓵᑭᑭᐦᑖᐟ ᐆᒪ ᐊᐢᑭᐩ, ᑲᐦᑭᔭᐤ ᐁᐊᐧᑯ ᐁᑲᐧ ᓵᑭᑭᐣ ᐄᐦ. ᐁᐊᐧᑯ ᐅᐦᒋ ᐊᓂᒪ, ᐁ ᐊᑎ ᑫᐧᐢᑭᓈᑲᐧᕽ ᐆᒪ ᐊᐢᑭᐩ, ᐁᐊᐧᑯ ᐅᐦᒋ ᐁᑳ ᑲ ᐴᓂᐦᑖᐟ ᐊᔨᓯᔨᓂᐤ, ᑲ ᓇᓈᐢᑯᒧᐟ ᑕᐦᑐ ᑮᓯᑳᐤ, ᑲ ᑳᑮᓯᒧᑐᑖᐦᐟ ᐁᐊᐧᑯ ᐊᐊᐧ ᑳ ᐱᒧᐦᑌᐟ ᐆᑕ, ᐁᐧᐱᓈᓱᐣ ᑲ ᒥᔨᐦᐟ, ᑲ ᒪᑐᑎᓯᕽ, ᑲ ᓂᑐᑕᒫᐦᐟ ᐁ ᒥᔮᐧᓯᐠ ᑮᑲᐧᐩ, ᐁᐊᐧᑯ ᐱᑯ ᑭᓭ ᐋᐸᒋᐦᐃᑯᓯᕽ, ᐁᐊᐧᑯ ᐱᑯ ᑭᓭ ᐋᐸᒋᐦᐃᑯᓯᕽ.

[3] ᑭᔮᒼ, ᐱᑯᔨᑯᕽ ᐁ ᐃᔨᓃᓯᐟ ᐊᔨᓯᔨᓂᐤ, ᒥᐦᒉᑖᐧᐤ ᓂᐄᐧᐦᑕᒪᐋᐧᐊᐧᐠ ᐅᑭᒫᐦᑳᓇᐠ, ᐁ ᑕᓭᐧᑭᓇᐦᑭᐠ ᒪᓯᓇᐦᐃᑲᐣ, ᐲᑐᐢ ᐊᐊᐧ ᑳ ᐃᓯ ᐊᔭᒥᐦᐋᐟ ᐊᔨᓯᔨᓂᐤ, ᐁ ᑕᓭᐧᑭᓇᕽ ᒪᓯᓇᐦᐃᑲᐣ ᐁ ᒪᒥᓰᐟ, ᓇᒨᔭ ᒪᓯᓇᐦᐃᑲᐣ ᑲ ᑮ ᓈᑕᒫᐠ, ᑰᐦᑖᐄᐧᓇᐊᐧ ᐱᑯ ᑲ ᓈᑕᒫᑯᐟ.

[4] ᐁ ᑮ ᐃᓯ ᐃᐧᔭᑭᒥᑯᓯᕽ ᐆᑕ ᑰᐦᑖᐄᐧᓇᐤ, ᐆᒪ ᐄᐦ ᑲ ᑮ ᐋᐸᒋᐦᑖᐟ, ᐆᒪ ᑮ ᐋᐸᒋᐦᑖᐤ ᐅᒥᓯ ᐁ ᐃᓯᓂᐢᑫᔨᐟ, «ᐁ ᐄᐧ ᐋᔨᒧᒥᔭᐣ ᐆᒪ, ᓂᔭ ᐆᒪ ᐆᒪ,» ᑮ ᐃᑌᐤ, ᐆᒪ ᐅᒋᐦᒋᐩ, «ᐆᐦᐃ ᓀᐅᐧ, ᐁᑯᓂ ᑳ ᒥᔨᑖᐣ ᑲ ᒪᐃᐧᒧᐢᒋᑫᔭᐣ. ᐆᒪ ᑫᐧᐢᑭᓂᐢᐠ, ᐁᐊᐧᑯ ᐆᒪ ᓇᓈᑐᕽ ᐊᔭᒥᐦᐋᐃᐧᐣ, ᒨᓂᔭᐃᐧ ᐊᔭᒥᐦᐋᐃᐧᐣ, ᓇᒨᔭ ᐁᐊᐧᑯ ᑭᒥᔨᑎᐣ,» ᑲ ᑮ ᐃᑖᐟ ᐁᓴ ᓀᐦᐃᔭᐊᐧ. «ᑖᓂᑕ ᑲ ᐆᐦ ᑖᐯᐧᐦᑕᐃᐧᔭᐣ, ᐁ ᒥᔨᑖᐣ ᐆᒪ, ᑮᑲᐧᐩ ᐁ ᐄᐧ ᑑᑕᒪᐣ, ᐆᒪ ᑲ ᐅᑎᓀᐣ, ᐄᐦ, ᐁᐊᐧᑯ ᑳ ᒥᔨᑖᐣ ᑭᓭᐋᐧᑎᓯᐃᐧᐣ.» ᐁᑯᓯ ᐁᓴ ᐁ ᑮ ᐃᑌᐧᐟ ᐊᐊᐧ ᑰᐦᑖᐄᐧᓇᐤ ᐆᑕ, ᑲ ᑮ ᐄᐧᐦᑕᒪᐋᐧᐟ ᑭᓭᔨᓂᐊᐧ. ᐁᑯᓂ ᐆᐦᐃ ᓀᐅᐧ ᒪᐃᐧᒧᐢᒋᑫᐃᐧᓇ, ᐁᐊᐧᑯ ᐆᒪ ᓃᑳᓄᕽ ᒪᑐᑎᓵᐣ, ᓂᐹᑫᐧᓯᒧᐃᐧᑲᒥᐠ, ᐲᐦᑖᐧᐃᐧᑲᒥᐠ, ᐁᑲᐧ ᐆᒪ ᐋᐧᓴᑳᒣᓯᒧᐃᐧᐣ ᐆᒪ, ᐁᑯᓂ ᐆᐦᐃ ᑳ ᑮ ᒥᔨᐦᐟ ᐊᔨᓯᔨᓂᐤ, ᑲ ᑳᑮᓯᒫᐧᑫᐟ. ᑖᐱᐢᑰᐟ ᐯᔭᑲᐧᐣ ᐆᒪ ᑳ ᑮᓯᑌᐳᔭᐣ, ᑳ ᓂᒥᓇᒪᐋᐧᐟ ᑫᐦᑌ ᐊᔭ, ᐋᓴᐩ ᐁᑯᑕ ᑲ ᐆᐦ ᑭᑖᐸᒥᑯᐃᐧᓯᐣ, ᐁᑯᓯ ᐊᓂᒪ ᐁ ᑮ ᐃᑕᑭᐦᑕᕽ ᐁᐊᐧᑯ ᐆᒪ. ᐁᐊᐧᑯ ᐅᐦᒋ ᐆᒪ, ᑳ ᐆᐦ ᑮ ᐃᑌᐧᒋᐠ ᑭᓭᔨᓂᐊᐧᐠ, «ᑲᐦᑭᔭᐤ

ᑮᑲᐧᐩ ᐁ ᑮᓯ ᓂᐦᑖᐃᐧᑭᐠ, ᐁ ᓂᐦᑖᐃᐧᑭᓈ ᐊᐧᓱᐟ ᑲᐦᑭᔭᐤ ᐱᓯᐢᑭᐤ, ᒫᒋᑯᑎᑕᐣ ᐊᐧᔭᐄᐧ. ᒥᑐᓂ ᐃᑌ ᐁ ᑲᓈᑕᐦᒑᐠ, ᐁᑯᑕ ᓇᐦᐊᐱ. ᐆᒥᓯ ᐃᓯ ᐹᐢᑭᓇ ᒪᐢᑯᓯᔭ. ᑲ ᐋᐧᐸᒫᐤ ᐁᑯᑕ ᐁ ᐱᒫᐦᑕᐄᐧᐟ ᒪᓂᒎᐢ, ᐁᐊᐧᑯ ᐊᓇ ᐁ ᐊᐢᑮ ᐃᐧᐢᑲᕽ ᐊᐢᑭᐩ, ᐁᐊᐧᑯ ᐅᐦᒋ ᑭᑎᒫᑫᔨᒥᕽ. ᐋᐧᐄᐧᐢ ᐊᐊᐧ, ᐱᓭᓰᓴ, ᐁᑯᓂ ᐁ ᑭᐦᒉᔨᒫᐟ ᑰᐦᑖᐄᐧᓇᐤ, ᐁ ᐅᒐᐊᐧᓯᒥᓯᐟ ᐁ ᐋᐧᐸᒫᓭᐠ, ᐁᑳᔭ ᐄᐧᐦᑳᐨ ᐱᓯᐢᑫᔨᒥᕽ ᐊᓇ.» ᑮ ᐃᑌᐧᐊᐧᐠ ᒫᓇ ᑭᓭᔨᓂᐊᐧᐠ, ᐁᐊᐧᑯ ᐅᐦᒋ ᑲ ᐆᐦ ᒪᓈᒋᐦᑖᕽ ᑮᑲᐧᐩ. ᐃᐧᔭ ᐊᓇ ᐁ ᑭᑎᒫᑫᔨᒫᐟ ᐁᑯᓂ. ᑖᐱᐢᑰᐨ ᐄᐦ, ᐯᐲᓯᐢ ᑭᒥᔨᑲᐃᐧᐣ, ᑲ ᑭᑎᒫᑫᔨᒫᐟ ᐊᓇ ᐁᐊᐧᑯ, ᑲ ᑭᑎᒫᑫᔨᒫᐟ.

[5] ᐊᓄᐦᐨ ᑳ ᑮᓯᑳᐠ ᑭᐱᐦᒋᐴᐦᐃᑯᓇᐤ ᐋᐧᐱᐢᑭ ᐃᐧᔮᐢ, ᐃᑕ ᐆᒪ ᑳ ᐱᒍᐦᑌᔭᕽ. ᑮᐦᑳᓈᑳᐧᐣ ᐋᑕ ᐁᐊᐧᑯ, ᒫᑲ ᓇᒎᔭ, ᐋᓴᐩ ᑭᐊᐧᓂᓯᒥᑯᓇᐤ ᐋᐧᐱᐢᑭ ᐃᐧᔮᐢ, ᐊᐧᓂᓯᒉᐤ ᑭᑕᐋᐧᓯᒥᓯᓇᐊᐧ. ᒫᒋᑯᑎᑕᐣ, ᑖᓂᑕ ᑲ ᐆᐦ ᑖᐯᐧᐦᑕᕽ ᐊᔨᓯᔨᓂᐤ, ᒥᓴᑎᒼ ᐊᐊᐧ ᑳ ᐃᓯᔩᐦᑳᓱᐟ ᓂᑲ ᐅᑎᓈᐤ, ᓂᑲ ᓴᑲᐦᐱᑖᐤ ᐆᑕ, ᓂᑲ ᓰᑭᐦᑕᑕᒪᐋᐧᐤ ᑭᐢᑎᑳᓇ, ᐃᔮᔭᐤ ᐁᑯᓂ ᑲ ᐱᒪᑯᒋᐣ, ᐁᑯᓯ ᒉᐧᐦᒋ ᐁ ᑑᑖᐦᒋᐠ ᐆᑭ, ᑭᑕᐋᐧᓯᒥᓯᓇᐊᐧᐠ ᑰᓯᓯᒥᓇᐊᐧᐠ, ᑕᐦᑐ ᓃᓱ ᐊᔭᒥᐦᐁᐃᐧ ᑮᓯᑳᐤ ᐁ ᒥᔮᐦᒋᐠ ᑲ ᒦᒋᓱᒋᐠ ᑮᑲᐧᐩ, ᐁᑯᓂ ᒉᑕᐋᐧᑫᐊᐧᐠ, ᐊᐧᓂᓯᒥᑲᐧᐠ ᐋᓴᐩ ᐁᑯᑕ ᒎᓂᔭᐊᐧ. ᐃᑌ ᓂᔭᓈᐣ ᑳ ᑮ ᐯ ᐅᐦᐱᑭᔮᕽ, ᓂᑮ ᓂᑐᓄᓈᐣ ᑮᑲᐧᐩ ᑲ ᐱᒫᒋᐦᐊᐧᑫᔮᕽ, ᓂᑮ ᐊᑐᐢᑳᓈᐣ, ᓇᒪ ᑮᑲᐧᐩ ᐁᑲᐧ ᐊᓄᐦᐨ, ᐁᑯᑕ ᐋᓴᐩ ᐁ ᐊᐧᓂᓯᒥᑯᔭᕽ. ᐁᐊᐧᑯ ᐅᐦᒋ ᐁᑳ ᑳ ᐆᐦ ᑖᐯᐧᐊᐧᑫᔨᐦᑕᕽ ᓄᐦᐃᔭᐃᐧ ᒪᐃᐧᒍᐢᒋᑫᐃᐧᐣ, ᐅᐢᑳᔭ ᐊᓇ. ᓇᒪ ᑮᑲᐧᐩ, ᐆᑌ, ᓈᐊᐧᐩ ᐊᐦᐁᐤ ᑫᐦᑌ ᐊᔭ, ᓄᑎᑫᐧᐊᐧ ᐆᑌ ᐊᐦᐁᐤ, «ᓂᔭ ᓇᐊᐧᐟ ᓂᑎᔨᓃᓯᐣ,» ᐁ ᐃᑌᔨᐦᑕᕽ, ᐁ ᐊᐧᓂᓯᒥᑯᐟ ᐊᓂᐦᐃ ᒎᓂᔭᐊᐧ. ᐁᑯᓯ ᐆᒪ ᐁ ᐃᓯᓈᑲᐧᕽ, ᒉᑳᐧᐟ ᐃᑕ ᑳ ᐱᒍᐦᑌᔭᕽ, ᐁᐊᐧᑯ ᐆᒪ ᐅᐦᒋ, ᐅᐢᑳᔭ, ᓇᒎᔭ ᒦᓇ ᓈᓂᑕᐤ ᐁ ᐃᑖᐸᑕᕽ ᑲ ᑭᓰᑭᑐᑕᐟ ᑭᑕᐋᐧᓯᒥᐢ, ᑰᓯᓯᒼ ᒦᓇ, ᓇᒎᔭ ᓈᓂᑕᐤ ᐃᑖᐸᑕᐣ ᑲ ᑭᓰᐁᐧᐦᑲᐦᑕᐊᐧᐟ ᑮᑲᐧᐩ ᐁ ᑭᑕᐦᐊᒪᐊᐧᐟ, ᓇᒎᔭ ᑲ ᑮ ᐋᐸᒋᐦᐃᐠ, ᐯᔮᐦᑎᐠ ᑭᑐᐢ. ᐯᔮᐦᑎᐠ ᑭᑐᐢ. ᓂᓯᑐᐦᑕᒎᐦ ᐆᒪ. ᑖᓂᓯ ᐁ ᐃᐢᐸᔨᐠ, ᑭᑎᒫᑫᔨᐦᑐᐃᐧᐣ, ᑖᐱᐢᑰᐨ ᐅᑭ, ᐄᐦ, ᑳ ᐃᑕᐱᒋᐠ, ᑭᑎᒫᑫᔨᐦᑐᐃᐧᐣ ᐁᑐᑫᐧ, ᐁ ᐅᐄᐧᒋᓵᓂᐦᑐᒋᐠ, ᐁᐊᐧᑯ ᑳ ᑮ ᒥᔨᑯᔭᕽ ᑰᐦᑖᐄᐧᓇᐤ, ᑲ ᑭᑎᒫᑫᔨᐦᑐᔭᕽ.
ᑭᔮᒼ ᐱᑯᔨᑯᕽ ᐁ ᑭᑎᒫᑭᓯᐟ ᑭᓭᔨᓂᐤ, ᓄᑎᑫᐧᓯᐤ ᐁ ᑭᑎᒫᑭᓯᐟ, ᑲ ᑭᑎᒫᑫᔨᒥᐦᐟ, ᐋᓴᐩ ᐆᑌ ᑭᑭᑖᐸᒥᑲᐃᐧᐣ. ᐋᐧᐄᐧᐢ ᒌ ᐁ ᑮᐊᐧᑎᓯᐟ ᐊᐋᐧᓯᐢ, ᐁ ᑭᒋᒫᑭᓯᐟ,

ᑲ ᐄᐧᒎᐦᑲᒪᐋᐧᔦᐠ, ᐊᓴᐩ ᐆᑌ ᑭᑭᑖᐸᒥᑲᐃᐧᐣ, ᑮᑲᐧᐩ ᐁ ᑮᐢᐱᓇᑕᒫᐣ. ᐄᐦ, ᓀᐅᐧᓵᑊ ᐁ ᐊᑎ ᐃᑕᐦᑐᐱᐳᓀᐧᔮᐣ ᐁ ᐅᐦᒋ ᐊᑐᐢᑲᐊᐧᐠ ᑭᓵᔨᓂᐤ, ᓇᒪ ᑮᑲᐧᐩ ᓅᐦ ᐋᐧᐸᐦᑌᐣ ᑲ ᑮᐢᐱᓇᑕᒫᐣ, ᐊᓄᐦᐨ ᑳ ᑮᓯᑳᐠ ᒫᓇ ᓂᓇᓈᐢᑯᒧᐣ, ᐁ ᒥᐦᒉᑎᒋᐠ ᓅᓯᓯᒪᐠ, ᐯᔭᑯᓵᑊ ᐃᐦᑕᓯᐊᐧᐠ ᓅᓯᓯᒪᐠ, ᒥᐦᒉᑎᐊᐧᐠ ᓂᑖᓂᐢᑯᑖᐹᓇᐠ, ᐁᑯᓂᐠ ᐁᒥᑲ ᐆᑭ ᐁ ᑮᐢᐱᓇᑕᒪᐊᐧᑭᐠ, ᐃᔨᑯᕽ ᐁ ᑮ ᐯ ᑲᑳᐧᑕᑭᐦᐅᔮᐣ, ᐁᐊᐧᑯ ᒫᓇ ᓂᓇᓈᐢᑯᒧᐣ ᐁᔮᐱᐨ. ᐁᐊᐧᑯ ᐅᐦᒋ ᐃᑌ ᑎᔦᐹᐧᑎᑲᐃᐧᔭᓂ, ᓂᐄᐧ ᑲᑫᐧ ᑕᑯᐦᑖᐣ, ᑮᑲᐧᐩ ᐁ ᒥᔮᐧᓯᐠ ᑲ ᑲᑫᐧ ᐄᐧᒎᐦᑲᒪᐊᐧᐠ ᐊᔨᓯᔨᓂᐤ. ᓇᒨᔭ ᐆᑕ ᐁ ᐅᑎᓇᒫᐣ, ᓇᒨᔭ ᐁ ᐃᔨᓃᓯᔮᐣ, ᐁ ᐃᑌᐧᔮᐣ, ᒫᑲ ᑰᐦᑖᐄᐧᓇᐤ ᐁᑐᑫᐧ ᐁ ᐃᑌᔨᒥᐟ, ᑲ ᑮ ᐄᐧᒎᐦᑲᒪᐊᐧᐠ ᐊᔨᓯᔨᓂᐤ. ᐁᐊᐧᑯ ᐅᐦᒋ ᒫᓇ ᓂᒥᔦᐧᔨᐦᑌᐣ ᑲ ᐄᐧᐦᑕᒪᐊᐧᐠ ᑮᑲᐧᐩ ᐁ ᒥᔮᐧᓯᐠ ᐊᔨᓯᔨᓂᐤ. ᒥᓴᐋᐧᐨ ᐆᑕ, ᐃᐢᐲ ᒉᐢᑐᐦᑌᑖᐧᐃᐧ, ᑖᐱᐢᑰᐨ ᐆᒪ ᑭᔮᓇᐤ ᑳ ᑫᐦᑌ ᐊᔨᐃᐧᔭᕽ, ᓇᑲᑕᒪᐦᑭ ᐆᒪ ᐊᐢᑭᐩ, ᐁᑳ ᑮᑲᐧᐩ ᐄᐧᐦᑕᒪᐋᐧᔭᐦᑭ ᐅᐢᑳᔭ, ᑖᓂᓯ ᐁᑲᐧ ᑫ ᑑᑕᕽ.

[6] ᐁᐊᐧᑯ ᐆᒪ ᐅᐦᒋ, ᓇᐊᐧᐨ ᐁ ᒥᔮᐧᓯᐠ ᑮᑲᐧᐩ ᑲ ᓇᑲᑕᒪᕽ, ᑲ ᐋᐸᒋᐦᑖᐟ, ᑖᐱᐢᑰᐨ ᐆᒪᑐᐃᐧᕽ ᑲ ᓂᑐᐦᑕᕽ, ᐁᑯᑕ ᑲ ᐆᐦ ᑭᐢᑭᓲᐦᑐᐟ ᐅᐢᑳᔭ. ᓇᒨᔭ ᓈᓂᑕᐤ ᐁ ᐃᑖᐸᑕᕽ ᐆᑕ ᐊᔨᓯᔨᓂᐤ ᑳ ᐋᔨᒨᐦᑐᐟ, ᐋᐧᐄᐧᐢ ᐁ ᐅᐄᐧᒋᓵᓂᐦᑐᐟ. ᓈᓂᑕᐤ ᐁ ᐄᐧ ᐃᑌᐧᐟ ᐊᔨᓯᔨᓂᐤ, ᐊᐦᐳ ᓂᔭ ᑎᐱᔭᐤ, ᓈᓂᑕᐤ ᐁ ᐃᓯᐟ ᐊᔨᓯᔨᓂᐤ, ᓂᔨᑲᑌᐦᑖᐣ, ᓇᒨᔭ ᓂᓅᐦᑌ ᓂᑐᐦᑕᐋᐧᐤ, ᓇᒨᔭ ᓈᓂᑕᐤ ᐃᑖᐸᑕᐣ ᐊᔨᐢᐠ ᑲ ᓂᑐᐦᑕᐊᐧᐠ, ᑯᓂᑕ ᑲ ᓇᐢᑫᐧᐊᐧᓯᒪᐠ, ᓇᐊᐧᐨ ᐊᓂᒪ, ᐁᑳ ᑲ ᓂᑐᐦᑕᐊᐧᐠ, ᐁᑯᓯ ᐁ ᑮ ᐃᓯ ᐄᐧᐦᑕᒫᑲᐃᐧᔮᐣ ᓂᔭ, ᐁᐊᐧᑯ ᐅᐦᒋ ᑭᑲ ᐋᐸᒋᐦᐃᑯᓈᐋᐧᐤ ᐁ ᐃᓯ ᐅᐄᐧᒋᓵᓂᐦᑐᔦᐠ, ᐁ ᐃᓯ ᐅᑕᐋᐧᓯᒥᓯᔦᐠ ᑰᓯᓯᒪᐠ, ᑲ ᑭᑎᒫᑫᔨᒥᐢᑭᐠ, ᒉᑳᐧᐨ ᐁ ᐄᐧᑫᐊᐧᒋᐠ, ᐁᐊᐧᑯ ᐊᓂᒪ ᐱᑯ ᑫ ᐱᒧᐦᑕᐦᐃᑯᒋᐠ, ᐁᑯᓯ ᐁ ᑮ ᐃᓯ ᐄᐧᐦᑕᒫᑲᐃᐧᔮᐣ ᓂᔭ. ᐁᑲᐧ ᐆᒪ ᐊᓄᐦᐨ ᑳ ᐆᐦ ᒥᔦᐧᔨᐦᑕᒫᐣ ᑲ ᐄᐧᐦᑕᒪᐊᐧᐠ ᑮᑲᐧᐩ ᐁ ᒥᔮᐧᓯᐠ, ᑮᑲᐧᐩ.

[7] ᑮᑳᐧᐩ ᐅᐦᒋ ᑳ ᐆᐦ ᐄᐧᐦᑕᒫᐣ, ᒪᐢᑭᐦᑭᐩ ᐆᒪ ᑳ ᐅᑎᓇᒫᐣ, ᐁ ᒥᔮᐧᓯᐠ ᐁ ᑮ ᓇᑲᑕᒫᑲᐃᐧᔮᐣ, ᐊᔨᓯᔨᓂᐤ ᐁᐊᐧᑯ ᐁ ᐋᐸᒋᐦᑕᒨᐦᐊᐠ ᒥᐦᒉᐟ, ᐁ ᐅᐦᒋ ᒥᔮᐧᔮᐟ ᐁᑯᑕ ᐅᐦᒋ. ᐯᔭᑲᐧᐣ ᑳᑮᓯᒧᐃᐧᐣ, ᐁᐧᐱᓈᓯᓇ ᑳ ᐲᑭᐢᑳᐧᑕᒫᐣ, ᐁ ᓂᓯᑕᐃᐧᓇᕽ ᐊᔨᓯᔨᓂᐤ, ᓂᓇᓈᐢᑯᒧᐣ ᒫᓇ ᐁᐊᐧᑯ. ᓇᒨᔭ,

ᓇᒎᔭ ᑮᑳᐧᕀ ᐁ ᒫᔦᔨᐦᑕᒫᐟ ᑲ ᑑᑕᒫᐟ, ᒫᑲ, ᑮᑳᐧᕀ ᑳ ᒪᒥᓰᐚᑎᑲᐏᔮᐟ, ᑖᐻ ᓂᑌᐦᐃᕽ ᓂᓂᑐᑕᒫᐟ ᑮᑳᐧᕀ ᐁ ᒥᔮᐧᓯᐠ ᑲ ᓂᓯᑕᐏᓇᒫᐟ, ᐁᑯᓯ ᐆᒪ ᐁ ᐃᐢᐸᓰᐠ ᐁᐘᑯ ᐆᒪ. ᐁᐘᑯ ᐅᐦᒋ ᒦᓇ, ᐆᒪ ᐚᐦᔭᐤ ᑳ ᐑ ᐃᑐᐦᑌᔭᐟ ᐆᒪ, ᐁᑳᔭ ᐑᐦᑳᐨ ᐘᓂᑭᐢᑭᓯ ᑭᑕᐚᓯᒥᓴᐠ ᐆᑌ ᐁ ᓇᑲᑕᒋᐠ. ᑰᐦᑖᐑᓇᐤ ᓂᑐᑕᒪᐤ, ᑲ ᑲᓇᐍᔨᐦᑕᒫᐢᐠ. – ᐁᐘᑯ ᐊᓂᒪ ᐱᑯ ᑫ ᐋᐸᒋᐦᐃᑯᔭᐟ.

[8] "ᐋᐤ, ᐁᑯᓯ ᐱᑯ ᐁ ᐃᓯ ᐑᐦᑕᒫᑕᑯᐠ, ᑲ ᐋᐸᒋᐦᐃᑯᔦᐠ ᐆᒪ ᑮᑳᐧᕀ.

3 ᓇᑲᑕᒪᐋᐧᐦᑳᐤ

[1] ᐁᐊᐧᑯ ᐆᒪ ᑫᐦᒋᓈ, ᐁ ᓅᐦᑌ ᐊᑎ ᐲᑭᐢᑲᐧᑖᐠ Alec ᐊᐊᐧ, ᐁᐊᐧᑯ ᐅᐦᒋ ᑳ ᐆᐦ ᑮ ᐯ ᓭᐁᐧᐱᑕᒪᐊᐧᐠ, ᐆᑌ ᐁ ᐅᐦᑐᐦᑌᔮᐣ ᐆᒪ, ᐃᑌ ᑳ ᑮ ᐯ ᓈᑎᑎᓴᐦᐅᑲᐃᐧᔮᐣ, ᒫᑲ, ᐱᑕᒫ ᐁᐊᐧᑯ ᐁ ᐄᐧ ᐋᒋᒧᐢᑖᑕᑯᐠ, ᐄᐧᐢᑕ ᐁᑐᑫᐧ ᐁ ᐃᑌᔨᒥᑯᐟ ᒫᒪᐃᐧ ᐆᐦᑖᐄᐧᒫᐊᐧ, ᐁ ᐄᐧ ᓇᑲᑕᕽ ᐊᐢᑭᐩ, ᐁᑯᑕ ᑳ ᑮ ᐲᑭᐢᑲᐧᑖᐟ ᐊᔨᓯᔨᓂᐊᐧ. «ᑖᓀᐦᑭ ᐁᑐᑫᐧ,» ᓂᑎᑌᔨᐦᑌᐣ, «ᐁ ᑭᑎᒫᑭᓯᔮᐣ ᓂᔭ, ᐁᑳ ᑮᑲᐧᐩ ᐁ ᑭᐢᑫᔨᐦᑕᒫᐣ, ᐃᑌ ᐋᐧᐦᔭᐤ ᑳ ᐆᐦ ᐯ ᓈᑎᑎᓴᐦᐅᑲᐃᐧᔮᐣ, ᑲ ᓂᑕᐃᐧ ᓂᑐᐦᑕᐊᐧᐠ ᐊᓇ ᐁ ᐄᐧ ᐲᑭᐢᑫᐧᐟ,» – ᐁ ᑭᐢᑫᔨᐦᑕᕽ ᐁ ᐄᐧ ᓇᑲᑕᕽ ᐊᐢᑭᐩ. ᐁᐊᐧᑯ ᐊᓂᒪ, ᓇᒨᔭ ᑲᑫᑎᕽ ᓂᑮ ᒫᒥᑐᓀᔨᐦᑌᐣ ᐁᑯᑌ ᐁ ᑕᑯᐦᑌᔮᐣ, ᐁ ᐋᐧᐸᒪᐠ, ᐁ ᐋᐢᐸᑎᓯᕽ ᐆᒥᓯ ᐃᓯ, «ᒪᑖᐧᐣ ᒌ ᐊᐊᐧ ᑖᐯᐧ ᐁ ᐄᐧ ᓇᑲᑕᕽ ᐊᐢᑭᐩ,» ᓂᑎᑌᔨᐦᑌᐣ, ᓇᒨᔭ ᒥᑐᓂ ᓂᑖᐯᐧᐊᐧᑫᔨᐦᑌᐣ ᐁ ᐄᐧ ᓇᑲᑕᕽ ᐊᐢᑭᐩ, ᑳ ᐄᐧ ᐲᑭᐢᑫᐧᐟ ᐆᒪ.

[2] "ᐋᐤ, ᐁᑲᐧ ᐅᐢᐹᐧᑲᐣ ᐁ ᑮ ᒥᔨᑲᐃᐧᔮᐣ, ᐁ ᑮᓯ ᐲᐦᑖᐧᔮᐣ ᓂᒫᒥᑐᓀᔨᐦᑌᐣ, «ᑖᐯᐧ, ᑖᐯᐧ, ᐃᐧᔭ ᑰᐦᑖᐄᐧᓇᐤ ᑳ ᑎᐯᔨᐦᑕᕽ ᑭᐱᒫᑎᓯᐃᐧᓂᓇᐤ, ᑖᐯᐧ ᐁᑐᑫᐧ ᐊᐊᐧ ᐁ ᑭᐢᑫᔨᐦᑕᒨᐦᐃᑯᐃᐧᓯᐟ ᑮᑲᐧᐩ ᑲ ᐄᐧᐦᑕᒪᐋᐧᐟ ᐊᔨᓯᔨᓂᐊᐧ,» ᓂᑎᑌᔨᐦᑌᐣ.

[3] ᐁᑯᓯ ᐁᑲᐧ, ᐁᐊᐧᑯ ᐆᒪ ᐁ ᒫᒥᑐᓀᔨᒪᐠ ᒣᑳᐧᐨ ᐁ ᐊᐱᐟ, «ᐋ, ᒥᑐᓂ ᑖᐯᐧ, ᑲᐧᔭᐢᐠ ᑭᒫᒥᑐᓀᔨᐦᑌᐣ ᐆᒪ ᑳ ᐃᓯ ᒫᒥᑐᓀᔨᐦᑕᒪᐣ,» ᑳ ᐃᓯᐟ, «ᒫᑲ, ᑭᔭ ᓃᑳᐣ ᐆᒪ ᐁ ᐄᐧ ᑭᑐᑎᑖᐣ,» ᓂᑎᑎᐠ. «ᐋᐦᐊ.» ᓂᑎᑖᐤ, «ᑖᐯᐧ ᒥᐢᑕᐦᐃ ᑲ ᒥᔮᐧᓯᐣ ᑮᑲᐧᐩ ᐁ ᒥᔮᐧᓯᐠ ᑲ ᐄᐧᐦᑕᒪᐃᐧᔭᐣ,» ᓂᑎᑖᐤ.

[4] «"ᐋᐤ. ᐆᒪ ᑳ ᐃᑕᐦᑲᒥᑭᓯᔭᐣ, ᐁᑳᔭ ᐄᐧᐦᑳᐟ ᓈᓂᑕᐤ ᐃᑌᔨᐦᑕ. ᐁᑳᔭ ᐄᐧᐦᑳᐟ ᓈᓂᑕᐤ ᐃᑌᔨᐦᑕ. ᐊᓄᐦᐨ ᒥᐢᑕᐦᐃ ᑭᒫᒥᑐᓀᔨᐦᑌᐣ ᐃᑕ ᑳ ᐊᐱᔭᐣ,» ᓂᑎᑎᐠ. «ᐁᐦᐊ,» ᓂᑎᑖᐤ, «ᑭᑖᐹᐧᐣ, ᓃᓱ ᑮᑲᐧᐩ ᐆᒪ ᒥᐢᑕᐦᐃ ᐁ ᒫᒥᑐᓀᔨᐦᑕᒫᐣ,» ᓂᑎᑖᐤ, «ᑭᔭ ᐆᒪ ᐁ ᒫᒥᑐᓀᔨᒥᑖᐣ,» ᓂᑎᑖᐤ. «ᐁᑲᐧ ᐆᒪ ᐃᑕ ᑳ ᐊᐱᔮᐣ,» ᓂᑎᑖᐤ, «ᐋᐧᐦᔭᐤ ᐆᒪ ᑳ ᐅᐦᑐᐦᑌᔮᐣ,» ᓂᑎᑖᐤ, «ᐁᑲᐧ ᐆᒪ ᐃᑕ ᑳ ᐊᐱᔭᐣ, ᒫᑲ ᓇᒨᔭ ᓈᓂᑕᐤ ᐁᔮᐱᐨ ᐁ ᐃᑌᔨᐦᑕᒫᐣ,» ᓂᑎᑖᐤ, «ᐁᑯᓯ ᐆᒪ ᐆᑕ ᐁ ᒥᒋᒨᐦᐅᔮᐣ,» ᓂᑎᑖᐤ, «ᐆᑕ ᐆᒪ ᑳ ᐋᐧᐸᒥᔭᐣ ᐁ ᐊᐱᔮᐣ, ᑲᑎᐢᐠ ᐆᒪ ᓂᐱᒧᐦᑌᐃᐧᐣ ᐆᑕ ᐁ ᑕᑯᐦᑌᔭᐣ ᐁ ᑌᐱᐸᔨᔭᐣ, ᐁᐊᐧᑯ ᐆᒪ ᒥᓇ

ᑳ ᒫᒥᑐᓀᔨᐦᑕᒫᐣ,» ᓂᑎᑖᐤ, «ᒫᑲ, ᑰᐦᑖᐄᐧᓇᐤ ᐃᑌᔨᐦᑕᐦᑭ ᐁᑐᑫᐧ, ᑳᐃᐧ ᓂᑲ ᐋᐧᔦᓃᐣ ᐆᑕ ᐅᐦᒋ,» ᓂᑎᑖᐤ, «ᐃᐧᔭ ᐊᔨᐢᐠ, ᑮᑲᐧᐩ ᑳ ᐱᒥᐸᔨᐦᑖᐟ,» ᓂᑎᑖᐤ.

[5] ᐁᐊᐧᑯ ᐅᐦᒋ, ᓇᒨᔭ ᐄᐧᐦᑳᐟ ᓈᓂᑕᐤ ᓂᑎᑌᔨᐦᑌᐣ, ᐊᔨᐢᐠ ᓂᑮ ᐃᓯ ᐄᐧᐦᑕᒫᐠ ᑭᓭᔨᓂᐤ. «ᐃᑕ ᑮᑲᐧᐩ ᐁ ᐊᐧᐋᐧᓀᔨᐦᑕᒪᐣ, ᐊᐦᐴ ᒥᓴᑎᒪᐧᐠ ᐁ ᐋᐸᒋᐦᐊᒋᐠ ᐁ ᐱᒥᑖᐹᓱᔭᐣ, ᑮᑲᐧᐩ ᐁ ᐲᑯᐸᔨᐠ, ᐁᑳᔭ ᐄᐧᐦᑳᐨ ᑲ ᑭᓯᐋᐧᐦᐃᐠ ᑰᐦᑖᐄᐧᓇᐤ, ᐃᐧᔭ ᐊᓇ, ᐁ ᐃᑌᔨᐦᑕᕽ ᐁ ᑯᑌᔨᒥᐢᐠ, ᒪᐦᑎ ᑖᓂᓯ ᐁ ᐃᑕᐢᑌᐠ ᑭᒥᑐᓀᔨᐦᒋᑲᐣ, ᐁᑯᓯ ᒫᓇ ᓂᑮ ᐃᑎᐠ ᓅᐦᑖᐃᐧᐩ,» ᓂᑎᑖᐤ, «ᒣᑳᐧᐨ ᐁ ᐱᒫᑎᓯᐟ,» ᓂᑎᑖᐤ. «ᐁᐊᐧᑯ ᒫᓇ ᓂᑭᐢᑭᓱᐸᔩᐣ,» ᓂᑎᑖᐤ, «ᐃᑌ ᑳ ᒥᒋᒨᐦᐅᔮᐣ, ᓇᒨᔭ ᓈᓂᑕᐤ ᓂᑎᑌᔨᐦᑌᐣ, ᐋᐦᒋ ᐱᑯ ᓂᓂᑐᑕᒪᐋᐧᐤ ᑰᐦᑖᐄᐧᓇᐤ ᐅᑭᓭᐊᐧᑎᓯᐃᐧᐣ. ᐁᑯᓯ ᐆᒪ, ᑳ ᐆᐦ ᓇᓈᐢᑯᒧᔮᐣ ᑕᐦᑖᐧᐤ ᐁ ᐊᐧᓂᐢᑳᔮᐣ, ᑕᐦᑖᐧᐤ ᐁ ᑮᓯᑳᐠ ᓂᓇᓈᐢᑯᒫᐤ ᑰᐦᑖᐄᐧᓇᐤ. ᐁ ᓇᓈᐢᑯᒪᐠ, ᐁ ᐄᐧᒋᐦᐊᐠ ᐊᔨᓯᔨᓂᐤ, ᐁ ᒥᐦᒉᑎᒋᐠ ᓅᓯᓯᒪᐠ, ᐯᔭᑯᓵᑊ ᐁ ᐃᐦᑕᓯᒋᐠ ᓅᓯᓯᒪᐠ, ᓂᑖᓂᐢᑯᑖᐸᓇᐠ ᐁ ᒥᐦᒉᑎᒋᐠ. ᐁᐊᐧᑯ ᐁᒋᑲ ᐆᒪ ᐁ ᑮᐢᐱᓇᑕᒫᐣ, ᓂᑎᑌᔨᐦᑌᐣ ᒫᓇ, ᐁᐊᐧᑯ ᒫᓇ ᑳ ᐆᐦ ᓇᓈᐢᑯᒪᐠ.» ᐁᑯᓯ ᓂᑎᓯ ᑭᑐᑖᐤ ᐊᐊᐧ. «ᑖᐯᐧ ᑲᐧᔭᐢᐠ ᑭᒫᒥᑐᓀᔨᐦᑌᐣ. ᒫᑲ ᐆᒪ, ᑲ ᑕᓯᐦᑲᒪᐣ, ᐁᑳᔭ ᐴᓂᐦᑖ.» ᓂᑎᑎᐠ. ᒪᑐᑎᓵᐣ ᐆᒪ, ᐁᐊᐧᑯ ᐆᒪ ᐱᑯ ᑲ ᐱᒧᐦᑕᐦᐃᑯᓴᐠ ᐆᑌ ᓃᑳᐣ, ᐁᑲᐧ ᐁᑯᓂ ᐆᐦᐃ — ᐄᐦ. ᑳ ᐃᑕᐢᑌᑭ ᐆᐦᐃ ᐁᐧᐱᓈᓯᓇ —, ᐁᑳᔭ ᑯᓂᑕ ᐲᐦᑎᑫᐧᑐᑕᒧᐠ ᒪᑐᑎᓵᐣ. ᐁᑯᓂ ᐆᐦᐃ ᐁᑯᑕ ᑲ ᐲᐦᑎᑫᐧᒪᑲᓇᐧ.

[6] ᐁᑯᓂ ᐆᐦᐃ ᑮᓯ ᐲᑭᐢᑳᐧᑕᒣᑯ, ᐁᑯᓂ ᐆᐦᐃ ᑫ ᑲᓇᐁᐧᔩᒥᑯᓴᐠ, ᐁᐧᐱᓈᓯᓇ ᑳ ᐃᓯᔩᐦᑳᑌᑭ, ᐁᐊᐧᑯ ᐅᐦᒋ, ᑳ ᐆᐦ ᑮ ᐯ ᒥᔭᐊᐧᑳᑎᓂᑫᐟ ᑭᓭᔨᓂᐤ, ᑮᑲᐧᐩ ᐁ ᓈᑖᒧᐢᑕᕽ, ᐁ ᓈᒋᓀᐦᐃᑫᕽ ᐆᐦᐃ. ᑰᐦᑖᐄᐧᓇᐤ ᐅᑑᐢᑭᓃᑭᒪ ᐅᑭᓭᐊᐧᑎᓯᐃᐧᐣ ᐁ ᓂᑑᐢᑲᒫᒥᐦᐟ, ᐁᑯᓂ ᐆᐦᐃ ᑳ ᐃᑕᐢᑌᑭ, ᐄᐦ, ᑭᐋᐧᐸᐦᑌᓈᐊᐧᐤ ᐁᑯᓂ ᐆᐦᐃ. ᑖᐱᐢᑰᐨ ᐊᐊᐧ ᐁᐊᐧᑯ ᐊᐊᐧ ᑳ ᐄᐧᐦᑕᒪᐊᐧᐠ ᐅᑖᑯᓯᕽ, ᒥᐢᑕᐦᐃ ᓂᒥᔦᐧᔨᐦᑌᐣ ᐆᒪ ᐃᑕ ᐁ ᑭᑲᐢᑌᐠ ᐆᒪ. ᐁᑯᑐᐊᐧᕽ ᐆᑕ ᑲ ᑮ ᐊᐢᑌᐠ, ᒫᑲ ᓇᒨᔭ ᓈᓂᑕᐤ, ᐯᔭᑲᐧᐣ ᐆᒪ ᑭᑳᐄᐧᓇᐤ ᐆᒪ, ᑳ ᐃᑕᑭᐦᑌᐠ ᐆᒪ ᐁᐧᐱᓈᓯᐣ, ᒣᐧᐦᒋ ᓂᔮᓇᐣ ᐁᐊᐧᑯ ᐆᒪ. ᒋᑫᒨ, ᐃᐧᔭ, ᐆᑕ

ᑳ ᐆᐦ ᐊᐱᔭᕽ, ᑭᑳᐄᐧᓇᐤ ᐊᐢᑭᐩ ᐊᐊᐧ, ᐁᑯᑕ ᐁ ᑮ ᐸᑭᑎᓈᐟ ᑰᐦᑖᐄᐧᓇᐤ, ᐊᐢᑭᐩ ᐆᒪ, ᐃᑕ ᑲ ᐅᐦᐱᑭᐦᐃᑐᔭᕽ.

[7] ᐁᐊᐧᑯ ᐅᐦᒋ, ᓂᐢᑕᑦ ᐁ ᑮᓭᑭᒫᐟ ᐊᔨᓯᔨᓂᐊᐧ ᐆᑕ ᑳ ᑮ ᑭᑐᑖᐟ – ᓈᐯᐤ ᑳ ᐃᓯᔩᐦᑳᓱᐟ –, ᐁᑯᓂ ᑳ ᑮ ᑭᑐᑖᐟ. «ᑭᐋᐧᐸᐦᑌᐣ ᒌ ᐆᐦᐃ» – ᐆᒥᓯ ᑳ ᐃᓯᓂᐢᑫᔨᐟ –, «ᑭᐋᐧᐸᐦᑌᐣ ᒌ ᐆᐦᐃ ᐁ ᐃᑌᐧᒪᑲᐦᑭ.» – «ᓇᒨᔭ, ᓇᒨᔭ.» – «ᑭᑲ ᐄᐧᐦᑕᒫᑎᐣ, ᑖᓂᓯ ᐁ ᐃᑌᐧᒪᑲᕽ.»

[8] ᐆᒪ ᐆᑕ ᐁ ᐃᑕᐦᑕᐧᐱᔭᕽ, ᐊᐄᐧᓇ ᐆᒪ ᒥᑐᓂ ᐁ ᓄᐦᐃᔮᐃᐧᐟ ᑕ ᐃᑌᔨᐦᑕᕽ, ᐆᒪ ᐆᑕ ᐁ ᐃᑕᐦᑕᐧᐱᓭᐠ. ᑮᑳᐧᐩ ᓄᐦᐃᔮᐃᐧᐃᐧᐣ ᒥᑐᓂ ᑲ ᑭᐢᑫᔨᐦᑕᕽ, ᑭᓭᔨᓂᐊᐧᐠ ᑳ ᑮ ᐯ ᓇᑲᑕᐦᑭᐠ. ᓇᒨᔭ ᐁᑳ ᐁᑐᑫᐧ ᐊᐃᐧᔭᐠ ᐅᐦᒋ ᐄᐧᐦᑕᒪᐋᐧᐤ – ᒫᒋᑰᑎᑖᐣ ᑭᑖᐸᐦᑕᒧᐠ ᓀᒪ ᑳ ᒪᓯᓇᐦᐃᑳᑌᐠ, ᓀᒪ. ᓀᒪ ᐊᐧᑎᐦᑳᐧᐣ ᑲ ᓈᑖᐧᐸᔩᐠ, ᐄᐦ, ᐱᓭᓯᐤ ᐊᓂᒪ ᐁ ᑮ ᑑᑕᕽ, ᐁᐊᐧᑯ ᐊᓂᒪ. ᐁᑯᓯ ᐁ ᐃᓯ ᐋᐧᐸᐦᑕᒣᐠ, ᑲ ᓈᑖᐧᐁᐧᐸᐦᐊᕽ ᐆᒪ, ᐁ ᐅᑎᓇᒥᕽ ᐊᓂᒪ, ᐅᑎᓂᑳᑌᐤ, ᐁ ᑮ ᐃᑑᑕᐦᑭᐠ ᑫᐦᑌ ᐊᔭᐠ, ᐁᑲᐧ ᐁᐊᐧᑯ ᐊᓂᒪ ᐁ ᑲᓇᐁᐧᔨᐦᑕᐦᑭᐠ. ᒥᑐᓂ ᐆᒪ ᑳ ᓃᐱᕽ, ᑳ ᒥᔨ ᒫᔨ ᑮᔨᑳᔨᐠ, ᒐᐸᓯᐢ ᑳ ᑭᑐᒋᐠ, ᐁ ᑮ ᒪᒍᐢᑌᐦᐊᐦᑭᐠ ᐊᓂᒪ. ᐃᐢᐹᐦᑫᑯᒋᐣ ᐊᐊᐧ ᐁᐊᐧᑯ ᑳ ᑭᑐᐟ. ᐁᑯᓯ ᐊᓂᒪ ᐁ ᑮ ᐃᑖᐸᒋᐦᑖᒋᐠ ᐁᐊᐧᑯ ᐊᓂᒪ. ᐁᑲᐧ ᒦᓇ ᐱᑐᐢ ᑮ ᐃᑖᐸᒋᐦᑖᐊᐧᐠ, ᒥᑐᓂ ᑳ ᐄᐧ ᓂᐸᐦᐃᑯᐟ ᐄᐧᐱᑕ ᐆᒪ ᐊᔨᓯᔨᓂᐤ, ᐁᑯᑕ ᒦᓇ ᐁᑯᑕ ᐊᓂᒪ ᐁ ᑮ ᐊᐢᑖᒋᐠ – ᐲᑲᐧᑐᐊᐧᓇᐧ ᐊᓂᐦᐃ ᒦᐱᑕ, ᐁᑯᓯ ᐆᒪ ᐁ ᑮ ᐃᑖᐸᒋᐦᑖᒋᐠ ᓀᒪ.

[9] ᐁᐊᐧᑯ ᐅᐦᒋ, ᒫᔭᐤ ᐁ ᐋᐧᐸᐦᑕᐦᑭᐠ ᐁᑯᑐᐊᐧᕽ, ᑮ ᐅᑎᓇᒪᐧᐠ ᑭᓭᔨᓂᐊᐧᐠ, ᐁ ᑲᓇᐁᐧᔨᐦᑕᐦᑭᐠ ᐁᐊᐧᑯ. ᐁᐊᐧᑯ ᐊᓂᒪ ᑳ ᑲᑫᐧᒋᒥᑕᑯᐠ, ᐄᐦ, ᓇᒨᔭ ᐊᐦᐴ ᐊᐃᐧᔭᐠ ᐁᑐᑫᐧ ᐆᐦ ᐯ ᓈᑲᑑᐦᑫᐤ ᐁᐊᐧᑯ.

[10] ᐁᑲᐧ ᐊᓂᒪ ᒐᐸᓯᐢ, ᐊᓇ ᑳ ᐱᒧᐦᑌᐟ ᐊᓇ, ᑖᐱᐢᑰᐟ ᐱᓭᓰᐢ ᑳ ᐃᓯᓈᑯᓯᐟ – ᐊᐄᐧᓇ ᐊᓂᐦᐃ ᑳᐦ ᑮ ᐄᐧᐦᐁᐤ, ᑲ ᓄᐦᐃᔭᐁᐧᐟ, ᑖᓂᓯ ᑳ ᐃᓯᔩᐦᑳᑖᐟ ᐁᑯᓂ. ᑮᐢᐱᐣ ᑮ ᐯᐦᑕᑦ, ᑖᓂᓯ ᐁ ᐃᓯᔩᐦᑳᓱᐟ ᐁᐊᐧᑯ ᐊᓇ.

ᑭᐯᐦᑖᐋᐧᐋᐧᐤ ᐁᐊᐧᑯ ᑳ ᐄᑲᐧᐢᑲᐧᕽ, ᐆᒪᑐᐃᐧᕽ ᐁ ᐯᐦᑖᑯᓯᐟ ᐃᐢᐱᒥᕽ, ᐆᒥᓯ ᐁ ᐃᓯ ᑕᐸᐦᒋᐸᓲᐦᐅᐟ ᐁ ᑭᑐᐟ, ᐁᐊᐧᑯ ᐊᓇ ᐊᓇ ᑳ ᒪᓯᓇᐦᐃᑳᓱᐟ. ᐁᑲᐧ, ᑳ ᐄᑲᐧᐢᑲᐧᕽ ᐆᒪ ᑳ ᐯᐦᑖᑯᓯᐟ, ᐊᐦᐸ ᑳ ᐊᑎ ᐋᐢᑌ ᑮᓯᑳᐠ, ᐋᓴᕀ ᐁᑯᑕ ᐯᐦᑖᑯᓯᐤ, ᐆᒥᓯ ᐁ ᐃᓯ ᑖᐦ ᑕᐸᐦᒋᐸᓲᐦᐅᐟ. ᐁᐊᐧᑯ ᐁ ᓀᐦᐃᔭᐁᐧᕽ ᐅᐸᒐᐢᑲᐦᐊᓰᐢ ᐃᓯᓲᐦᑳᓱᐤ, ᐆᒪ, ᑖᐱᐢᑯᐨ ᐊᐢᑭᕀ ᐁ ᑭᑖᐸᐦᑕᕽ ᐁᑲᐧ ᑮᓯᐠ, ᐁᐊᐧᑯ ᐊᓂᒪ ᑳ ᐆᐦ ᐃᓯᓲᐦᑳᓱᐟ, ᐅᐸᒐᐢᑲᐦᐊᓰᐢ, ᑖᐱᐢᑰᐟ ᐆᒪ ᑮᓯᐠ ᐁᑲᐧ ᐊᐢᑭᕀ, ᐁᐊᐧᑯ ᐊᓂᒪ ᑳ ᐆᐦ ᑕᐸᐦᒋᐸᓲᐦᐅᐟ, ᐁᐊᐧᑯ ᐊᓇ ᐊᓇ ᑳ ᒪᓯᓇᐦᐃᑳᓱᐟ. ᐁᐊᐧᑯ ᐊᓂᒪ, ᑳ ᐃᑕᒫᐣ, ᓇᒨᔭ ᑭᓂᑕᐃᐧ ᑭᐢᑫᓲᐦᑌᓈᓇᐤ ᑖᓂᓯ ᑮᑲᐧᕀ ᐁ ᐯ ᐃᐢᐸᓲᐠ ᐆᒪ, ᑳ ᓀᐦᐃᔭᐃᐧ ᐄᐧᐦᑕᒧᕽ.

[11] ᐁᐊᐧᑯ ᐅᐦᒋ, ᒥᐢᑕᐦᐃ ᑳ ᐆᐦ ᓇᓈᐢᑯᒧᔮᐣ, ᒣᑳᐧᐨ ᐆᑕ ᐁ ᐱᒫᑎᓯᔮᐣ ᑮᑲᐧᕀ ᑲ ᐄᐧᐦᑕᒪᐊᐧᐠ ᐊᓲᓯᓲᓂᐤ. ᓇᒨᔭ ᐃᐧᔦ ᑮᑲᐧᕀ ᐁ ᑭᐢᑫᓲᐦᑕᒫᐣ, ᒫᑲ, ᑮᑳᐧᕀ ᐊᓄᐦᐟ ᑲ ᐋᐸᒋᐦᐃᑯᐟ, ᐁᐊᐧᑯ ᑳ ᓅᐦᑌ ᐄᐧᐦᑕᒪᐊᐧᐠ ᐊᓲᓯᓲᓂᐤ. ᐁᐊᐧᑯ ᐅᐦᒋ ᐄᐦ, ᒪᔭᐤ ᑳ ᑕᑯᐦᑌᔮᐣ ᓀᑌ, ᓂᑕᐢᑮᕽ, ᐋᓴᕀ ᐁᑯᑕ ᐁᐧᐱᓈᓲᐣ ᐁ ᐊᐢᑌᐠ, ᒋᐢᑌᒫᐤ ᐁ ᐊᐱᐟ, «ᐦᐋᐤ, ᐁᑯᑌ ᐁ ᓂᑐᒥᑲᐃᐧᔭᐣ.» ᐦᐋ, ᑖᓂᓯ ᑫ ᑮ ᑑᑕᒫᐣ – ᐱᓲᐢᐠ ᒫᓇ ᐅᓯᐢᑫᐸᓲᐤ ᑖᓂᓯ ᐁ ᐃᓯ ᐱᒧᐦᑌᔮᐣ. ᐁᐊᐧᑯ ᑳ ᐃᑕᒫᐣ, ᓇᒨᔭ ᐄᐧᐦᑳᐨ ᓂᒥᐦᑖᑌᐣ, ᑲ ᓂᑕᐃᐧ ᐄᐧᒍᐦᑲᒪᐊᐧᐠ ᓇᐊᐧᐨ ᐊᓲᓯᓲᓂᐤ, ᒣᑳᐧᐨ ᐆᑕ ᐁ ᐱᒫᑎᓯᔮᐣ.

[12] ᐁᑳ ᐁᑯᓯ ᑑᑕᐦᑭ ᑫᐦᑌ ᐊᔭ, ᒥᐦᒉᐟ ᑫᐦᑌ ᐊᔭ ᑭᐯ ᐋᐧᐸᒫᐋᐧᐤ ᒫᒋᑰᑎᑕᐣ, ᓇᒪ ᑮᑲᐧᕀ ᐁ ᒥᔮᐧᓯᐠ ᑭᓇᑲᑕᒫᑯᐋᐧᐤ, ᓇᒪ ᑮᑲᐧᕀ. ᑮᑳᐧᕀ ᐊᓂᒪ ᐃᑕ ᑲ ᑮ ᐅᐦᒋ ᐱᒧᐦᑕᐦᐋᐟ ᐅᑖᐧᓯᒥᓴ ᐆᓯᓯᒪ, ᓇᒪ ᑮᑲᐧᕀ ᓇᑲᑕᑦ.

[13] ᐁᐊᐧᑯ ᐆᒪ, ᐱᑯ ᑫᐦᑌ ᐊᔭ ᐁᑯᓯ ᑲ ᑑᑕᕽ, ᑲ ᓇᑲᑕᒪᐋᐧᐟ ᐅᐢᑳᔭ ᑮᑲᐧᕀ ᐁ ᒥᔮᐧᓯᐠ, ᑖᐱᐢᑰᐨ ᐊᐊᐧ ᐅᐢᐹᐧᑲᐣ, ᐄᐦ, ᑖᓂᓯ ᑭᑲ ᐃᓯ ᐸᒥᓂᐦᐟ, ᐱᑯ ᑲ ᓇᑲᑕᒪᐋᐧᐟ ᐁᐊᐧᑯ – ᐊᐊᐧ ᒦᓇ, ᐄᐦ. –, ᐱᑯ ᑲ ᓇᑲᑕᒪᐋᐧᐟ – ᑖᓀᐦᑭ ᐊᐊᐧ, ᑳ ᐆᐦ ᐃᐦᑕᑯᐟ ᐆᑕ. ᓇᒨᔭ ᐊᓲᓯᓲᓂᐤ ᐆᐦᐃ ᐁ ᐅᐦᒋ ᐅᓰᐦᐋᐟ ᐆᐦᐃ, ᐆᑕ ᑳ ᑮ ᐃᐦᑕᑯᐟ ᐊᐊᐧ. ᑮᓯᑳᐃᐧ ᐱᓯᑦ ᐆᐦᐃ, ᐁ ᑮ ᐅᓰᐦᐋᐟ, ᐆᐦᐃ, ᐊᐊᐧ ᑳ ᐯ ᓵᑯᐦᑌᐟ ᐆᑕ ᑳ ᐱᒧᐦᑖᑕᕽ ᐆᒪ. ᐁᐊᐧᑯ ᐅᐦᒋ, ᒪᐧᔦᐢ ᐋᐸᑎᓯᐟ,

ᒥᔭᐚᑳᐨ ᐲᐦᑎᑲᐧᐦᐃᐦᐟ ᒪᑐᑎᓵᓂᕽ, ᐁ ᑳᑮᓯᒧᑖᐦᐟ. "ᐋᐤ, ᐁ ᑮᓰᐦᐋᐟ ᐆᐦᐃ ᐆᒥᓯ ᑮ ᐃᑌᐤ, «"ᐋᐤ, ᑭᔭ. ᑲ ᑌᐹᐧᑕᒪᐚᐤ ᐊᔨᓯᔨᓂᐤ, ᓂᐢᑕᐠ ᒪᑐᑎᓵᓂᕽ ᐲᐦᑎᑲᐧᐦᐃᑲᐏᔭᓂ, ᓭᐍᐱᓂᑲᐏᔭᓂ, ᐯᑌᐧᐍᐦᑕᒪᐚᐦᑳᐣ ᐅᑭᓭᐚᑎᓯᐏᐣ ᐊᔨᓯᔨᓂᐤ.» ᐁᑯᓯ ᐁᑲᐧ ᑮ ᐃᑎᐠ ᐊᐘ, «"ᐋᐤ. ᑮᐦᑖᐧᐠ ᐃᓯ ᐍᐱᓂᑲᐏᔭᓂ, ᐁᑲᐧ ᐁᑯᑕ ᐅᑭᓭᐚᑎᓯᐏᐣ ᑲ ᐯᑌᐧᐍᐦᑕᒪᐚᐤ ᐊᔨᓯᔨᓂᐤ. ᒣᐧᐦᒋ ᓂᐢᑖᐤ ᐃᓯ ᐍᐱᓂᑲᐏᔭᓂ, ᐱᒫᑎᓯᐏᐣ ᐁᑯᑕ ᑲ ᐯᑌᐧᐍᐦᑕᒪᐚᐤ, ᑲ ᐅᐦ ᐅᐦᐱᑭᓈᐘᓱᐟ ᑮᑲᐧᐩ. ᒣᐧᐦᒋ ᓀᐚᐤ ᐃᓯ ᐍᐱᓂᑲᐏᔭᓂ – ᑮᑲᐧᐩ ᑳ ᐊᐢᑖᐦᐃᑯᔮᐣ ᐁᑳ ᐁ ᒥᔮᐧᓯᐠ, ᐁᑲᐧ ᐁᑲᐧ ᑲ ᒦᑖᑫᐧᐏᔮᐣ,» – ᐁᑯᓯ ᐊᐘ ᐁ ᑮ ᐃᑕᑭᒥᐦᐟ ᐊᐘ ᓰᓰᑲᐧᐣ ᐊᐘ. ᒥᐦᒉᐟ ᓇᒨᔭ ᑭᐢᑫᔨᐦᑕᐠ ᑯᓂᑕ – ᑳ ᓂᐹᑫᐧᓯᒧᕽ, ᒥᐦᒉᑖᐧᐤ ᓂᐑᐦᑌᐣ ᐁᑯᑕ ᐁ ᐊᐱᔮᐣ, ᐆᒪᑐᐘᕽ ᐁ ᐋᐸᒋᐦᐋᐟ ᑭᓭᔨᓂᐤ ᐁ ᐯ ᑮᐦᑳᑕᐦᐊᕽ, ᐁ ᑮᓯ ᓂᑲᒧᐟ ᐆᑌ ᑳ ᐃᓯ ᐍᐱᓈᐟ, ᒥᐢᑎᑲᐧᐢᑭᐦᑲᐧ ᐁ ᐅᑎᓈᐟ –, ᓇᒨᔭ ᑭᐢᑫᔨᐦᑕᐠ ᐁᑯᑕ ᐁ ᑭᓯᐱᐸᔨᔨᐠ ᐅᓂᑐᑕᒫᐏᐣ, ᐁᐘᑯ ᐊᐘ, ᑯᓂᑕ ᐁ ᒣᑕᐚᑫᕽ ᐊᐘ ᓰᓰᑲᐧᐣ, ᐁᐘᑯ ᐊᓂᒪ, ᓇᒨᔭ ᒫᑲ ᐁ ᑭᐢᑫᔨᐦᑕᕽ, ᑯᓂᑕ ᐁ ᒪᒪᒋᑲᐢᑌᐟ, ᒥᐢᑎᑲᐧᐢᑭᐦᑲᐧ ᐅᑎᓀᐤ, ᐁᑯᓂ ᐁᑲᐧ ᐁ ᒪᑌᐧᐦᐚᐟ, ᐁᑲᐧ ᐆᐦᐃ ᐊᓭᓀᐤ.

[14] ᐯᔭᑲᐧᐣ ᐊᔨᓯᔨᓂᐤ ᑳ ᒥᔨᐦᐟ ᑲᓅᓯᒧᐣ ᑲ ᐋᐸᒋᐦᑖᐟ, ᐁᑳ ᐁ ᑖᐯᐧᐘᑫᔨᐦᑕᕽ ᑳ ᐊᓭᓇᕽ, ᐁ ᐊᓭᓇᕽ ᐊᓂᒪ ᑰᐦᑖᐑᓈᐤ ᐅᑭᓭᐚᑎᓯᐏᐣ, ᐊᓇ ᑳ ᑮ ᐅᔩᐦᑖᐟ ᑲᓅᓯᒧᐣ. ᑭᔩᑲᑌᓀᐣ ᐊᔩᐢ, ᐁᑯᑕ ᐁᑲᐧ ᑭᓯᐱᐸᔩᐤ ᑭᓂᑐᑕᒫᐏᐣ, ᐁᐘᑯ ᑳ ᑮ ᑯᐢᑕᐦᑭᐠ ᑭᓭᔨᓂᐘᐠ. ᐁᐘᑯ ᐆᒪ ᐅᐦᒋ, ᒥᐢᑕᐦᐃ ᓂᒥᔦᐧᔨᐦᑌᐣ ᑲ ᐑᐦᑕᒪᐘᐠ ᐊᔨᓯᔨᓂᐤ ᒣᑲᐧᐨ ᐆᑕ ᐁ ᐱᒫᑎᓯᔮᐣ, ᓂᑭᐢᑫᔨᐦᑌᐣ ᐆᑌ, ᓇᒨᔭ ᑭᓀᐧᐢ ᐊᔨᓯᔨᓂᐤ ᑮᑲᐧᐩ ᑲ ᑮ ᐑᐦᑕᒪᐘᐠ, ᓇᒨᔭ ᒥᓇ ᑮᑲᐧᐩ ᓂᔭ ᐁ ᑭᐢᑫᔨᐦᑕᒫᐣ ᐁ ᐃᑌᐧᔮᐣ, ᑖᓂᓯ ᐁ ᑮ ᐯ ᐃᓯ ᓇᑲᑕᒪᐏᐟ ᓅᐦᑖᐏᐩ, ᐁᐘᑯ ᐆᒪ ᐅᐲᑭᐢᑫᐧᐏᐣ ᑳ ᐋᐸᒋᐦᑖᔮᐣ. ᑖᓂᑕ ᑲ ᑮ ᐅᐦᒋ ᑖᐯᐧᐘᑫᔨᒥᐦᐟ ᑳ ᑮ ᐅᔫᐦᑖᐑᔮᐣ, ᐄᐦ, ᓀᐅᐧ ᑮᓯᑳᐤ ᐁ ᑮ ᓇᑲᑕᕽ ᐊᐢᑭᐩ – ᐁᐘᑯ ᐆᒪ ᑭᑭᐢᑫᔨᐦᑌᓈᐘᐤ, ᐁ ᓀᐦᐃᔭᐍᕽ ᐚᐘᐢᑫᓯᐘᒌᐢ ᐃᓯᔩᐦᑳᑌᐤ, ᒫᑲ ᐁ ᐋᑲᔮᓰᒧᕽ White Elk Hills ᐃᓯᔩᐦᑳᑌᐤ, ᐊᓂᒪ ᐆᒉᓈᐢ ᑲ ᐊᔮᐠ, ᐯ ᓯᐯᐧᒧᐣ ᒣᐢᑲᓇᐤ, ᓇᒨᔭ ᐚᐦᔭᐤ ᐁ ᐯ ᐃᑕᒧᐠ, ᐆᑕ ᒥᓇᐦᐃᑯᐢᑳᐤ, ᐆᑕ ᐅᓴᐦᒑᐤ, ᐁᑯᑕ ᐁ ᐑᑭᔮᕽ ᐁ ᒥᔫᐢᑲᒥᐠ, ᐁᑯᑕ ᑳ ᑮ ᓇᑲᑕᕽ ᐊᐢᑭᐩ. ᐊᓂᒪ

ᓵᑲᐦᐃᑲᐣ ᐆᑌ ᐃᑕᑳᒼ ᐁ ᐃᐢᐸᑎᓈᐠ, ᐁᑯᑕ ᑳ ᑮ ᓂᑕᐃᐧ ᐊᑯᑎᐦᐟ. «ᐦᐋᐤ.» ᐃᑌᐧᐤ, ᐁ ᐄᐧ ᓇᑲᑕᕽ ᐊᐢᑭᐩ, «ᒪᐦᑎ ᑫᔨᐁᐧᕽ, ᑮ ᓀᐅᐧ ᑎᐱᐢᑳᑭ, ᐊᐃᐧᔭᐠ ᑲ ᐯ ᓂᑕᐋᐧᐯᓂᑫᐤ, ᒫᑲ ᒥᓴᑎᒪᐧᔮᐣ, ᐆᒪᑐᐊᐧᕽ, ᐁᑯᑐᐃᐧᕽ ᑲ ᐁᐧᐁᐧᑲᐦᐱᓯᓈ ᐋᐧᐤ,» ᑮ ᐃᑌᐧᐤ. ᐁᑯᓯ ᑮ ᐃᓯ ᐸᒥᐦᐋᐤ.

[15] ᒉᑳᐧᐟ ᓂᐢᑌᐢ ᐁ ᐱᒫᑎᓯᐟ ᐁᑯᐢᐲ, ᐊᓇ ᒫᓇ ᑳ ᑮ ᑯᓵᐸᐦᑕᕽ, ᐁ ᑮ ᓀᐅᐧ ᑎᐱᐢᑳᐠ ᐁᑲᐧ, ᑲᓈᑕᓄᕽ ᑳ ᒫᓄᑫᒋᐠ ᒦᑭᐋᐧᐦᑊ, ᐁ ᒥᔭᐦᑲᓯᑫᒋᐠ ᐁᑯᑕ. «ᐦᐋ, ᒪᐦᑎ ᑫᔨᐁᐧᕽ, ᓂᔭ ᓂᑲ ᓂᑕᐋᐧᐯᓂᑳᐣ ᓅᐦᑖᐃᐧᐩ.» – ᑳ ᓴᑳᐯᑭᐸᐦᐋᐟ ᒥᓴᑎᒪᐧ. ᐁᑯᑕ ᐁᑲᐧ ᐁ ᐋᐦ ᐊᐱᕽ ᐁᑲᐧ, ᓂᔮᓇᐣ, ᐸᐸᑭᐊᐧᔮᓂᑲᒥᑲᐧ ᐁᑯᑕ ᐁ ᒋᒪᑌᑭ, ᐁ ᒥᔪᐢᑲᒥᐠ ᐆᒪ ᐁ ᓅᒋᐦᒋᑫᕽ, ᐆᒥᓯ ᐁ ᐃᑕᐱᒋᐠ ᐊᔨᓯᔨᓂᐊᐧᐠ – ᑫᑕᐦᑕᐁᐧ ᑳ ᐯ ᓅᑯᓯᒋᐠ, ᑮ ᐯ ᓃᓯᐊᐧᐠ, ᐆᑕ ᐁ ᑕᑯᐸᔨᒋᐠ, ᐁᑯᑕ ᑳ ᐯ ᐄᐧᒋᐦᐃᐁᐧᐟ ᓅᐦᑖᐃᐧᐩ ᐊᐊᐧ. ᐄᐦ, ᐁᑯᑕ ᐊᓂᒪ ᐁ ᐯ ᑮᓯ ᐃᑖᐢᑯᓂᑫᐟ, ᐁᐊᐧᑯ ᐆᒪ ᐁ ᑮ ᐄᐧᐦᑕᕽ ᐆᒪ, ᑮᑲᐧᐩ ᐁ ᑮ ᐄᐧᐦᑕᒪᐃᐧᐟ, ᑖᓂᓯ ᑲ ᐃᐢᐸᔨᐠ, «ᐦᐋᐤ. ᓅᒪᓇᐠ ᑭᐄᐧ ᐱᒫᑎᓯᐣ, ᓂᑯᓯᐢ. ᐁ ᒥᔮᐧᓯᐠ ᑮᑲᐧᐩ ᓇᑲᑕᒪᐋᐧᐦᑲᐣ ᐊᔨᓯᔨᓂᐤ. ᓇᒨᔭ ᑭᑲ ᑮ ᑭᑭ ᓯᐯᐧᐦᑖᐣ ᑮᑲᐧᐩ, ᓇᒨᔭ ᑭᑲ ᑮ ᑭᑭ ᓯᐯᐧᐦᑖᐣ ᐃᐢᐲ ᓇᑲᑕᒪᓂ ᐊᐢᑭᐩ, ᐁ ᒥᔮᐧᓯᐠ ᑮᑲᐧᐩ ᓇᑲᑕᒪᐋᐧᐦᑲᐣ. ᐁᐊᐧᑯ ᐊᓂ ᐱᑯ ᑲ ᑭᐢᑭᓄᐋᐧᐸᐦᑕᕽ ᐅᐢᑲᔨᓯᔨᓂᐤ. ᐊᔨᓯᔨᓂᐤ ᐆᒥᓯ ᐃᓯ ᑳ ᐋᔨᒧᒪᐟ, ᑮᒋ ᐊᔨᓯᔨᓂᐤ, ᐆᑕ ᑭᑲ ᐊᐱᐤ ᑭᑕᐋᐧᓯᒥᐢ, ᐆᑕ ᑭᑲ ᐊᐱᐤ ᑰᓯᓯᒼ, ᐁᐊᐧᑯ ᐊᓂᒪ ᐁᑳᔭ ᐁ ᒥᔮᐧᓯᐠ ᑮᑲᐧᐩ, ᑲ ᑭᐢᑭᓄᐋᐧᒍᐦᑕᕽ. ᒫᑲ ᐁ ᐊᐧᓂᐢᑳᔭᐣ, ᑯᐦᑖᐄᐧᓇᐤ ᓇᓈᐢᑯᒼ. ᐁ ᒥᔮᐧᓯᐠ ᑮᑲᐧᐩ ᓂᑐᑕᒪᐤ. ᑲ ᑭᐢᑭᓄᐋᐧᒍᐦᑕᕽ ᐊᐊᐧ ᑭᑕᐋᐧᓯᒥᐢ, ᑖᓂᓯ ᑭᑲ ᐃᓯ ᑭᑎᒫᑫᔨᐦᑐᐟ ᐊᔨᓯᔨᓂᐤ,» ᐁᑯᓯ ᒫᓇ ᓂᑮ ᐃᑎᐠ, «ᐋ, ᐁᐊᐧᑯ, ᐁᑳᔭ ᐄᐧᐦᑳᐨ ᑭᓯᐋᐧᐦᐃᕽ ᐊᔨᓯᔨᓂᐤ.»

[16] ᐁᑲᐧ, ᐁᑯᑕ ᐁᑲᐧ ᑳ ᑮ ᐊᑎ ᐲᑭᐢᑳᐧᓯᐟ ᓂᑳᐃᐧᐩ, «ᐋ, ᓂᑯᓯᐢ. ᐁ ᒥᔮᐧᓯᐠ ᑮᑲᐧᐩ ᑭᐄᐧᐦᑕᒫᑲᐃᐧᐣ, ᑲᑫᐧ ᑲᓇᐁᐧᔨᐦᑕ ᐆᒪ ᑳ ᐄᐧᐦᑕᒫᑲᐃᐧᔭᐣ. ᒫᑲ ᐁᑲᐧ ᓂᔭ ᑳ ᐄᐧ ᐄᐧᐦᑕᒫᑖᐣ, ᐁᑯᓂ ᐅᐦᐃ ᒪᐢᑭᐦᑭᔭ ᑳ ᓇᑲᑕᒫᑖᐣ, ᐁ ᐱᒫᑎᓯᐃᐧᓄᐃᐧᑭ ᐅᐦᐃ, ᑭᑎᒫᑭᐦᑕᐃᐧᐣ, ᐁᑯᓂ ᐅᑎᓇ. ᐆᒪ ᒪᐢᑭᐦᑭᐩ ᐊᐃᐧᔭᐠ ᐄᐧ ᒥᔨᐢᑭ, ᐁᑳᔭ ᐁ ᒥᔭᐧᑭᐦᑌᐠ, ᐁᑳᔭ ᐄᐧᐦᑳᐨ ᐅᑎᓇ, ᐁᑳᔭ ᐄᐧᐦᑳᐨ ᐅᑎᓇ. ᓇᒪ ᓈᓂᑕᐤ ᑭᑲ ᐃᑐᐦᑕᐦᐃᑯᐣ ᐆᒪ, ᑳ ᑮ ᐅᐦᒋ ᐱᒫᒋᐦᐋᐟ

ᐊᔨᓯᔨᓂᐤ,» ᓂᑮ ᐃᑎᐠ ᐁᐊᐧᑯ ᓂᑳᐃᐧᐩ. «ᒫᒋᑰᑎᑕᐣ, ᐁᐊᐧᑯ ᐆᒪ, ᑲᓇᐁᐧᔨᐦᑕ ᑳ ᐄᐧᐦᑕᒫᑖᐣ. ᐆᒪ ᓂᔭ ᑲ ᐃᐢᐲᐦᑎᓯᔮᐣ, ᐁ ᑮ ᒥᔨᑯᐃᐧᓯᔮᐣ ᒦᑲᐧᐣ ᑳ ᑲᓇᐁᐧᔨᒥᐟ ᑕᐦᑖᐧᐤ ᐁ ᑮᓯᑳᐠ. "ᐋᐤ, ᐊᐊᐧ ᒦᑲᐧᐣ ᑭᓇᑲᑕᒫᑎᐣ, ᑭᐄᐧ ᑫᐦᑌ ᐊᔨᐃᐧᐣ ᐆᒪ, ᑲᓇᐁᐧᔨᑦ ᐊᐊᐧ ᒦᑲᐧᐣ.» ᓂᑮ ᐃᑎᐠ ᒫᓇ. ᐄᐦ, ᑲᔮᐢ ᑳ ᓇᑲᓯᐟ ᓂᑳᐃᐧᐩ, ᐁᔮᐱᐨ ᓂᑲᓇᐁᐧᔨᒫᐤ ᐊᓇ ᒦᑲᐧᐣ. ᐆᐲᑭᐢᑫᐧᐃᐧᓇ ᐁᑲᐧ, ᑫᐦᑌ ᐊᔭ, «ᐁᐊᐧᑯ ᐆᒪ ᐅᑎᓇᒪᓂ, ᒪᐢᑭᐦᑭᐩ ᐁᑳᔭ ᐁ ᒥᔮᐧᓯᐠ – ᒪᐢᑭᐦᑭᐩ ᑮᑲᐧᐩ ᑭᑲ ᐋᐸᒋᐦᐃᑯᔭᐣ ᑳ ᓇᑲᑕᒫᑖᐣ, ᐁᐊᐧᑯ ᐊᓂ ᐱᑯ ᐋᐸᒋᐦᑖ. ᒪᔭᐤ ᐅᑎᓇᒪᓂ ᐁᑳᔭ ᐁ ᒥᔮᐧᓯᐠ ᒪᐢᑭᐦᑭᐩ, ᓇᒨᔭ ᓈᓂᑕᐤ ᑭᑲ ᐃᑖᐸᒋᐦᐃᑰᐣ ᐆᒪ ᒪᐢᑭᐦᑭᐩ,» ᐁᑯᓯ ᒫᓇ ᓂᑮ ᐃᑎᐠ. ᐁᐊᐧᑯ ᐆᐦᒋ ᒥᐢᑕᐦᐃ ᓂᒥᔦᐧᔨᐦᑌᐣ ᐊᔨᓯᔨᓂᐤ ᐁᑯᑐᐊᐧᕽ ᐁ ᓂᑑᐢᑲᕽ.

[17] ᐊᓅᐦᐨ ᑳ ᑮᓯᑳᐠ, ᓂᐋᐧᐦᑰᒫᑲᓂᑎᐠ, ᑭᑭᐢᑫᔨᐦᑌᓈ ᐋᐧᐤ – ᑖᐱᐢᑰᐨ ᐊᐊᐧ ᓅᓯᓯᑦ ᐊᐊᐧ Ted, ᐁ ᓃᑳᓃᐢᑕᕽ ᐆᑕ, ᐁᑲᐧ ᒦᓇ ᐊᐊᐧ, ᐆᒪ ᐆᑕ ᑳ ᐊᑐᐢᑫᔦᐠ, ᑮᑳᐧᐩ ᑳ ᓃᑳᓃᐢᑕᒣᐠ –, ᐆᑕ ᐊᓇ ᐁ ᐅᓵᐸᒥᑯᔦᐠ ᐊᔨᓯᔨᓂᐤ, ᐆᑌ ᑲ ᐆᐦ ᐅᓵᐸᒥᑯᐋᐧᐤ. "ᐋ, ᒪᐦᑎ ᑫ ᑮ ᑑᑖᐢᑭᐠ, ᐋᓴᐩ ᐁᑯᑕ ᐁ ᑯᑌᔨᐦᑕᕽ ᐆᒪ ᒪᐢᑭᐦᑭᐩ. ᓇᒨᔭ ᐊᓇ ᑭᔭᐋᐧᐤ ᐁ ᑭᑎᒪᐦᐃᑯᔦᐠ, ᓇᒫᐧ, ᐃᐧᔭ ᐊᓇ ᐁ ᑭᑎᒪᐦᐃᓯᐟ. ᐄᐧ ᓇᑲᑕᐦᑭ ᐊᐢᑭᐩ, ᐆᑕ ᐊᓇ ᐁᑲᐧ ᑫ ᑲᑳᐧᑕᑭᐦᑖᐤ ᐁᐊᐧᑯ, ᓇᒨᔭ ᐄᐧᐦᑳᐨ ᑲ ᑮ ᐱᐦᑯᐦᐁᐤ ᐅᒑᐦᒑᐦᑲᐧ.

[18] ᐁᐊᐧᑯ ᑭᓴᔨᓃᐃᐧ ᐲᑭᐢᑫᐧᐃᐧᐣ ᐁ ᐄᐧᐦᑕᒫᑕᑯᐠ, ᐊᔨᓯᔨᓂᐤ ᑳ ᐋᔨᒧᒫᐟ ᐄᐧᒋ ᐊᔨᓯᔨᓂᐊᐧ, ᐊᐦᐹ ᐅᑕᐋᐧᓯᒥᓴ ᓈᓂᑕᐤ ᐁ ᐃᑎᒥᐦᐟ, ᑳ ᓈᑕᒫᐊᐧᓯᐟ, ᓇᒨᔭ ᓈᓂᑕᐤ ᑲ ᐃᑐᐦᑕᐦᐃᐠ, ᓇᒨᔭ ᓈᓂᑕᐤ ᑲ ᐃᑐᐦᑕᐦᐃᐠ, ᐆᑕ ᐊᓇ ᐁᑲᐧ ᑫ ᑲᑳᐧᑕᑭᐦᑖᐟ ᐆᑕ ᐊᐢᑮᕽ. ᐁᐊᐧᑯ ᐆᒪ ᑕᐦᑐ ᑮᓯᑳᐤ ᓇᓈᐢᑯᒫᔭᐦᑭ ᑰᐦᑖᐄᐧᓇᐤ, ᐃᐢᐲ ᑌᐹᐧᑎᑯᔭᐦᑭ ᑲ ᓇᑲᑕᒪᕽ ᐆᒪ ᐊᐢᑭᐩ, ᑖᐱᐢᑰᐨ ᐁ ᑕᐋᐧᐠ, ᐃᑌ ᑭᑲ ᐃᑐᐦᑌᔭᕽ. «ᓂᐢᑎᓇᐧ ᐆᐦᐃ ᐃᐢᑳᐧᐦᑌᒪ,» ᑳ ᑮ ᐃᑌᐧᒋᐠ ᑭᓴᔨᓂᐊᐧᐠ, «ᑲᐧᔭᐢᐠ ᐱᒫᑎᓯᔭᓂ, ᑲ ᑕᐋᐧᐤ ᑭᑎᐢᑳᐧᐦᑌᑦ, ᐁᑳ ᑲᐧᔭᐢᐠ ᐱᒫᑎᓯᔭᓂ, ᓇᒨᔭ ᑲ ᑮ ᑕᐋᐧᐤ ᑭᑎᐢᑳᐧᐦᑌᑦ, ᒣᐧᐦᒋ ᓂᐢᑐ ᐆᒪ ᑭᑎᐢᑳᐧᐦᑌᑦ, ᑭᑭᐢᑫᔨᐦᑌᐣ ᒌ ᑖᓀᐦᑭ ᐆᒪ ᓂᐢᑐ ᑭᑎᐢᑳᐧᐦᑌᑦ.» – «ᓇᒨᔭ, ᓇᒨᔭ ᓂᑭᐢᑫᔨᐦᑌᐣ.» – «ᐁᐊᐧᑯ ᐆᒪ ᐃᐢᑫᐧᔮᐨ ᑭᑎᐢᑳᐧᐦᑌᑦ ᐆᒪ, ᐋᐧᑎᐦᑳᐣ ᐁ ᑮᓰᐦᑕᒫᑲᐃᐧᔭᐣ ᐁ ᐸᑭᑎᓇᒫᑲᐃᐧᔭᐣ,

ᒣᐧᐦᒋ ᓂᐢᑐ ᑭᑎᐢᑳᐧᐦᑌᒪ, ᐁᑯᑕ ᐊᓂᒪ ᑭᔦ ᑕᓯ ᑲᑳᐧᑕᑭᐦᑖᔭᐣ, ᐁᑳ ᑲᑕᐋᐧᕽ ᐁ ᐃᓯ ᐊᔨᓯᔨᓂ ᐃᐧᔭᓂ,» ᐁᑯᓯ ᒫᓇ ᐁ ᑮ ᐃᑌᐧᐟ ᓅᐦᑖᐃᐧᐩ, ᐁᐊᐧᑯ ᐆᒪ ᒫᓇ ᓂᒫᒥᑐᓀᔨᐦᑌᐣ.

[19] ᒥᐢᑕᐦᐃ ᓂᒥᔦᐧᔨᐦᑌᐣ ᐊᓄᐦᐨ, ᐁ ᐃᓯ ᐯᐦᑕᒫᐣ ᐅᑖᑯᓯᕽ, ᐁᐊᐧᑯ ᐊᐊᐧ ᑳ ᐊᐱᐟ, ᐄᐦ, ᑳ ᐄᐧ ᐸᓯᑰᓇᕽ ᐊᓄᐦᐨ ᑳ ᑮᓯᑳᐠ, ᐁ ᐄᐧ ᓇᓈᐢᑯᒧᐟ, ᒪᑐᑎᓵᐣ ᐆᒪ ᑳ ᐄᐧ ᐅᓰᐦᑖᐟ. ᑭᐋᐧᐸᐦᑌᓈᐋᐧᐤ ᑲᐦᑭᔭᐤ ᐁᑲᐧ ᐃᔨᑯᕽ, ᐁᑲᐧ ᐱᓯᐢᑭᐤ ᐁ ᑮᓯ ᐅᐦᐱᑭᓈᐊᐧᓱᐟ, ᑳ ᐊᑎ ᑫᐧᐢᑭᓈᑲᐧᐦᑭ ᐆᐦᐃ ᒪᐢᑭᐦᑭᔭ, ᓂᐱᔭ ᒦᓇ, ᑲ ᓇᓈᐢᑯᒧᔭᕽ ᐁᑲᐧ, ᑮᐦᑖᐧᒼ ᐁᑲᐧ ᐊᐢᑭᐩ ᑲ ᐅᑎᓵᐸᐦᑕᒪᕽ, ᐁᑯᓯ ᐆᐦᐃ ᐁ ᐃᑌᐧᒪᑲᐦᑭ ᐆᐦᐃ ᐁᐧᐱᓈᓯᓇ, ᐯᔭᑲᐧᐣ ᐆᐦᐃ, ᐄᐦ, ᑲ ᒥᔮᐧᓯᐣ ᐁᑯᑕ ᑲ ᐲᐦᑎᑫᐧᒪᑲᐦᑭ ᐆᐦᐃ. ᐁᑯᑕ ᐁᑲᐧ ᑮ ᑳᑮᓯᒧᑐᑕᒥᐦᑭ, ᐁᑯᓂ ᐁᑲᐧ ᐊᐊᐧ ᑫ ᑲᓇᐁᐧᔨᐦᑕᕽ, ᐆᐦᐃ ᐆᑕ ᐅᑕᑐᐢᑫᐦᐋᑲᓇ, ᐯᔭᑲᐧᐣ ᓈᐦᐊ, ᐃᑕ ᐁ ᐱᒧᐦᑕᐦᐋᐟ ᐅᑕᐋᐧᓯᒥᓴ ᐆᓯᓯᒪ, ᐁᑯᓂ ᐁᑲᐧ ᑫ ᑲᓇᐁᐧᔨᐦᑕᕽ. ᐁᐊᐧᑯ ᐊᐊᐧ ᑳ ᐃᑌᐧᔮᐣ ᐁᑲᐧ ᐁᑯᑕ ᑲ ᐲᐦᑎᑫᐧᐤ, ᐁᑯᓂ ᐁᑲᐧ ᑲ ᑲᓅᓯᒧᑐᑕᐋᐧᐟ ᐊᐊᐧ. ᐁᑯᓯ ᐆᒪ, ᐁ ᐃᓯ ᑭᐢᑫᔨᐦᑕᒫᐣ, ᒫᑲ ᐁᑲᐧ ᐋᐊᐧ ᑳ ᐄᐧᐦᑕᒪᐊᐧᐠ ᑫᐦᒋᓈ, ᑫᐦᒋᓈ ᑲ ᑲᑫᐧ ᑳᐦᑎᑎᓇᕽ ᐯᔭᑯᔭᑲᐣ ᒥᓂᓴ, ᑲ ᐱᐦᑎᑫᐧᒪᑲᐦᑭ ᐊᓂᑕ ᒪᑐᑎᓵᓂᕽ.

[20] ᐃᑕ ᑲᐧᔭᐢᐠ ᐊᔨᓯᔨᓂᐤ ᐁ ᐄᐧ ᑑᑕᕽ, ᐆᑌ ᑮᓯᑌᐤ, ᐯᔭᑫᐧᐢᑭᕽ ᐅᓰᐦᑖᐤ, ᒪᐢᑭᐦᑭᐋᐧᐳᐩ, ᐸᐦᑫᐧᓯᑲᐣ, ᐁᑲᐧ ᐁᑲᐧ ᑫᐦᑌ ᐊᔭ – ᑲᐦᑭᔭᐤ ᐆᒪ ᐁ ᐃᑕᐦᑕᐧᐱᔭᕽ ᐁ ᒫᔨᐸᔨᔭᕽ, ᑰᐦᑖᐃᐧᓇᐊᐧᐠ ᑭᒧᓲᒥᓇᐊᐧᐠ, ᐁᑯᓂᐠ ᐊᓂᑭ ᑲ ᓃᒥᓇᒫᐦᒋᐠ, ᑲ ᐲᑭᐢᑫᐧᐢᑕᒫᑯᔭᐦᑭᐠ. ᐁᑯᓯ ᐆᒪ ᐁ ᐃᐢᐸᔨᐠ, ᑳ ᐄᐧ ᐃᓰᐦᒋᑫᐟ ᐊᐊᐧ, ᒪᑐᑎᓵᐣ ᑳ ᐄᐧ ᐅᓰᐦᑖᐟ. ᒫᑲ ᓂᓇᓈᐢᑯᒫᐤ, ᒣᑳᐧᐨ ᐆᑕ ᐁ ᐊᔮᐊᐧᐠ, ᑲ ᑮ ᐄᐧᒨᐦᑲᒪᐊᐧᑭᐠ, ᐁᑯᓯ ᐃᓯ ᐆᒪ.

[21] ᐁᐊᐧᑯ ᐊᓂ ᐱᑯ ᐁ ᐄᐧ ᐄᐧᐦᑕᒫᑕᑯᐠ, ᓂᐋᐧᐦᑰᒫᑲᓂᑎᐠ, ᐊᐦᐹ ᐁᑐᑫᐧ ᑫᑕᐦᑕᐁᐧ ᐯᔭᐠ ᐆᒪ ᑮᑲᐧᐩ ᑳ ᐄᐧᐦᑕᒫᑕᑯᐠ, ᐊᐦᐹ ᐁᑐᑫᐧ ᑭᑲ ᐋᐸᒋᐦᐃᑯᓈᐋᐧᐤ, ᑫᑕᐦᑕᐁᐧ ᐯᔭᐠ ᐁ ᑮᓯᑳᐠ, ᓇᒨᔭ ᑳᑭᑫ ᐆᑕ ᑭᑲ ᐊᔮᓈᓇᐤ ᐊᐢᑮᕽ, ᓇᒨᔭ. ᓇᒨᔭ ᑲ ᑮ ᐃᑌᐧᐤ ᐊᔨᓯᔨᓂᐤ, «ᓂᑎᐯᔨᒥᓱᐣ,» ᑭᑲ ᐃᑌᐧᐟ, ᓇᒨᔭ, ᑰᐦᑖᐃᐧᓇᐤ ᑳ ᑎᐯᔨᒥᑯᔭᕽ. ᐁᐊᐧᑯ ᐊᓂᒪ ᑳ ᐆᐦ ᐄᐧᐦᑕᒫᑕᑯᐠ.

[22] ᑖᓂᐢᐲ ᐁᑐᑫᐧ ᐃᐢᑯ ᐆᒪᑐᐃᐧᕽ ᑲ ᑮ ᐄᐧᑕᐱᒥᑕᑯᐠ, ᑮᑳᐧᐩ ᐁ ᒥᔮᐧᓯᐠ ᑲ ᑮ ᐄᐧᐦᑕᒫᑕᑯᐠ. ᓇᒨᔭ ᐁᑐᑫᐧ ᐆᒪ, ᓂᔭ ᓂᑎᑌᔨᐦᒋᑲᐣ ᐆᒪ ᑳ ᐄᐧᐦᑕᒫᑕᑯᐠ, ᑰᐦᑖᐄᐧᓇᐤ ᐁᑐᑫᐧ ᐅᑭᓭᐋᐧᑎᓯᐃᐧᐣ, ᐃᑕ ᑭᑲ ᐋᐸᒋᐦᐃᑯᓴᐠ ᑮᑳᐧᐩ, ᑳ ᐄᐧᐦᑕᒫᑕᑯᐠ. ᓇᒨᔭ ᒦᓇ ᐁ ᒨᐦᒉᐧᔨᒪᐠ ᐊᔨᓯᔨᓂᐤ, ᑮᑳᐧᐩ ᑳ ᐄᐧᐦᑕᒪᐊᐧᐠ, ᐁ ᑲᑫᐧ ᐄᐧᒎᐦᑲᒪᐊᐧᐠ, ᐁ ᑲᑫᐧ ᐄᐧᒎᐦᑲᒪᐊᐧᐠ ᑮᑳᐧᐩ, ᑭᑲ ᐋᐸᒋᐦᑖᐟ.

[23] "ᐋᐤ, ᐁᑯᓯ ᐱᑯ ᐁ ᐃᓯ ᐄᐧᐦᑕᒫᑕᑯᐠ, ᓅᓯᓯᒥᑎᐠ, ᒫᑲ ᐁᑲᐧ ᐊᐊᐧ ᐅᐢᐹᐧᑲᐣ, ᑫ ᐅᐦᐸᐢᑯᓇᐠ, ᓇᓈᐢᑯᒫᑖᐣ ᑰᐦᑖᐄᐧᓇᐤ ᐁ ᒥᔨᑯᔭᕽ ᐯᔭᐠ ᑮᓯᑳᐤ ᑲ ᐱᒧᐦᑖᑕᒪᕽ, ᐁᐊᐧᑯ ᐊᓂ, ᐁᑯᓯ ᑭᑲ ᐃᓯ ᒫᒥᑐᓀᔨᐦᑌᓈᐊᐧᐤ ᑮᐢᑕᐋᐧᐤ.

4 ᑭᔮᓇᐤ ᐊᓂᒪ ᐁ ᐘᓂᓯᒫᔭᕽ

[1] ᑮᑳᐧᐩ ᐊᓂᒪ, ᐅᐦᑎᑕᐤ ᐆᒪ ᐁ ᐃᐢᐸᔨᐠ ᑲ ᑳᑮᓯᒧᑐᑕᒥᕽ ᐆᒪ ᐚᐢᑲᐦᐃᑲᐣ, ᐃᔨᑯᕽ ᐁ ᑯᓯᑲᐧᕽ ᑭᑕᑐᐢᑫᐃᐧᓂᐋᐧᐤ ᐆᒪ ᑳ ᐊᑐᐢᑳᑕᒣᐠ. ᐅᐦᑎᑕᐤ ᐱᑯ, ᑕ ᓂᑐᑕᒫᐦᐟ ᑰᐦᑖᐄᐧᓇᐤ ᐅᑭᓭᐋᐧᑎᓯᐃᐧᐣ, ᐁᑳ ᑮᑳᐧᐩ ᑲ ᒪᒋᐸᔨᐠ, ᑲᐧᔭᐢᐠ ᑲ ᑲᑫᐧ ᐱᒧᐦᑌᒪᑲᕽ ᐆᒪ ᑭᑕᑐᐢᑫᐃᐧᓂᐋᐧᐤ. ᐁᐊᐧᑯ ᐆᒪ ᐅᐦᒋ ᑳ ᐆᐦ ᐃᓰᐦᒋᑫᕽ, ᐁᑲᐧ ᒦᓇ ᐆᒪ ᐅᐦᒋ ᑳ ᐆᐦ ᐃᓰᐦᒋᑫᕽ ᐅᑖᑯᓯᕽ ᒪᑐᑎᓵᐣ, ᐁᑯᑕ ᐊᓂᒪ ᑮᑳᐧᐩ ᐁ ᒥᔮᐧᓯᐠ, ᑲ ᑳᐦᑎᑎᓇᕽ ᐊᔨᓯᔨᓂᐤ, ᐁ ᒥᔮᐧᓯᐠ ᑮᑳᐧᐩ. ᑖᐱᐢᑰᐨ ᑳ ᐄᐧ ᐃᓰᐦᒋᑫᐟ ᐊᓇ ᓅᓯᓯᒼ, ᐅᑖᓂᓴ ᐊᐊᐧ, ᑳ ᐄᐧ ᐄᐧᐦᑯᐦᑫᐟ, ᒪᐢᑭᐦᑭᔭ ᐊᓂᐦᐃ ᐁ ᐄᐧ ᐄᐧᐦᑯᐦᑲᐦᑕᕽ, ᐆᐦᐃ ᑳ ᓵᑭᑭᐦᑭ. ᐁᑯᓂ ᐁᑲᐧ ᐁᑯᑕ, ᐁ ᐁᐧᐦᒐᓯᐠ ᐁᑯᑕ ᐁᑲᐧ, ᑲ ᓂᑑᐢᑲᕽ ᐊᔨᓯᔨᓂᐤ, ᑮᑳᐧᐩ ᐊᓂᒪ ᐁ ᓂᑕᐁᐧᔨᐦᑕᕽ, ᑮᑳᐧᐩ ᐊᓂᒪ ᐁ ᓂᑕᐁᐧᔨᐦᑕᕽ ᒪᐢᑭᐦᑭᐩ, ᐁᑯᑕ ᐁᑲᐧ ᑲ ᓇᒥᓄᐦᐃᑫᐟ ᐁᑲᐧ. ᒥᐦᒉᑎᐣ ᑮᑳᐧᐩ, ᐁ ᑮ ᒥᔨᑲᐃᐧᔭᕽ ᑲ ᐆᐦ ᐱᒫᑎᓯᔭᕽ ᐁᐊᐧᑯ ᐆᒪ ᑳ ᓵᑭᑭᕽ. ᒫᑲ ᒥᐦᒉᐟ ᓇᒪ ᑮᑳᐧᐩ ᑭᐢᑫᔨᐦᑕᒼ ᐊᔨᓯᔨᓂᐤ ᑖᓂᓯ ᑲ ᐃᓯ ᓂᑑᐢᑲᕽ ᐁᐊᐧᑯ ᐆᒪ ᑮᑳᐧᐩ.

[2] ᑮᑳᐧᐩ ᑳ ᐆᐦ ᐃᐢᐸᔨᐠ, ᑲᔮᐢ ᐁᐧᑎᓇᕽ ᒥᑐᓂ ᑮ ᐱᒥ ᐱᒫᑎᓯᐤ, ᑭᓭᔨᓂᐃᐧ ᐅᐦᐱᑭᐦᐋᑲᐣ ᓂᑲ ᐃᑖᐧᐣ, ᐁ ᐯ ᑲᑫᐢᑭᒥᐦᐟ ᑮᑳᐧᐩ, ᐯᔭᑲᐧᐣ ᐃᐢᑫᐧᐤ, ᑖᓂᓯ ᐁ ᐃᓯ ᓂᑑᐢᑲᕽ ᑮᑳᐧᐩ. ᐊᓄᐦᐨ ᑳ ᑮᓯᑳᐠ, ᐁᐧᐱᓂᑲᑌᐊᐧ ᐁᑯᓂ, ᒋᑫᒨ ᒥᐦᒉᑎᐤ ᒨᓂᔮᐤ ᐅᑕᐋᐧᓯᒥᓴ ᐆᑕ, ᐁ ᐄᐧᑕᐢᑮᐁᐧᒫᔭᕽ. ᐁ ᑭᒧᑑᓴᐟ ᐁᑯᑐᐊᐧᕽ ᐃᐢᑫᐧᐤ, ᒨᓂᔮᐤ ᐅᑕᐋᐧᓯᒥᓴ, ᐁᑲᐧ ᐁᑲᐧ ᐆᑌ ᐃᓯ ᐃᑐᐦᑕᐦᐁᐤ ᑭᑕᐋᐧᓯᒥᓯᓇᐊᐧ, ᐊᐧᓂᓯᓄᐦᑕᐦᐁᐤ ᐅᓀᐦᐃᔮᐃᐧᐃᐧᓂᔨᐤ, ᐁᐊᐧᑯ ᐊᓂᒪ ᑳ ᐆᐦ ᐃᐢᐸᔨᐠ ᐅᐦᒋ.

[3] ᐁᐊᐧᑯ ᐆᒪ ᑳ ᐆᐦ ᐃᑌᐧᔮᐣ, ᐄᐦ, ᒥᐦᒉᑎᐣ ᐁᑯᑕ ᐊᔨᓯᔨᓂᐤ ᑲ ᓂᑑᐢᑲᕽ, ᐋᐧᐄᐧᐢ ᒌ ᐃᐢᑫᐧᐤ ᐁ ᐱᒥ ᐅᐦᐱᑭᓈᐊᐧᓱᐟ, ᑲ ᓂᑑᐢᑲᕽ ᒪᐢᑭᐦᑭᐩ ᐁ ᒥᔮᐧᓯᐠ ᑲ ᐋᐸᒋᐦᑖᕽ, ᐄᐦ. ᐊᐦᐴ ᐆᒪ ᐄᐧᐦᑫᐢ ᑳ ᐃᓯᔩᐦᑳᑌᐠ, ᓇᒨᔭ ᓂᓯᑐᐦᑕᒼ ᒥᓵᐦᑲᒥᐠ ᐊᔨᓯᔨᓂᐤ, ᓃᓱᓵᑊ ᑕᐦᑕᐧᔭᐠ ᐃᑖᐸᑕᐣ ᐁᐊᐧᑯ ᐊᓂᒪ ᒪᐢᑭᐦᑭᐩ. ᐋᑎᐦᐟ ᐊᔨᓯᔨᓂᐤ ᓇᒨᔭ ᐊᐦᐴ ᑭᐢᑫᔨᐦᑕᒼ ᑖᓂᓯ ᐁ ᐃᑕᑭᐦᑌᐠ, ᒫᑲ ᓃᓱᓵᑊ ᑕᐦᑕᐧᔭᐠ ᐁ ᐃᑕᑭᐦᑌᐠ ᐊᓂᒪ, ᑕ ᐋᐸᑕᕽ ᐁᐊᐧᑯ ᒪᐢᑭᐦᑭᐩ. ᐁᐊᐧᑯ ᐅᐦᒋ ᒥᐢᑕᐦᐃ ᑭᐦᒉᔨᐦᑖᑲᐧᐣ ᐁᐊᐧᑯ ᐊᓂᒪ ᒪᐢᑭᐦᑭᐩ, ᐄᐧᐦᑫᐢ ᐆᒪ ᑳ ᐃᓯᔩᐦᑳᑌᐠ,

ᑲᐦᑭᔭᐤ ᑮᑲᐧᐩ ᐃᑕ ᑳ ᐋᓂᓰᐦᑖᐟ ᐁᐊᐧᑯ ᐊᓂᒪ. ᐁᐊᐧᑯ ᐊᓂᒪ ᐅᐦᒋ ᑳ ᐆᐦ ᐃᑌᐧᔮᐣ, ᒥᐢᑕᐦᐃ ᑳ ᓇᓈᐢᑯᒧᔮᕽ ᓅᓯᓯᒼ ᐊᓇ ᑳ ᐄᐧ ᐃᓰᐦᒋᑫᐟ, ᑳ ᐄᐧ ᑮᓯᑌᐳᐟ. ᒥᐢᑕᐦᐃ ᒥᔮᐧᓯᐣ ᑯᑕᐠ ᒦᓇ ᑲ ᐲᐦᑎᑲᐧᑖᐟ ᐁᑯᑕ ᑮᓯᑌᐤ, ᑭᑳᐄᐧᓇᐤ ᐊᐢᑭᐩ, ᐁᑯᑕ ᑮᑲᐧᐩ ᑳ ᐆᐦ ᓵᑭᑭᕽ, ᐁᑯᑕ ᐊᓂᒪ ᑲ ᐆᐦ ᓂᓯᑐᐦᑕᕽ ᐊᔨᓯᔨᓂᐤ.

[4] ᐁᐊᐧᑯ ᐆᒪ ᑳ ᑮ ᐃᑌᐧᒋᐠ ᑭᓭᔨᓂᐊᐧᐠ, ᐃᑕ ᒣᑳᐧᐨ ᑳ ᐊᔮᔭᕽ, ᐁ ᐯ ᑮᐁᐧᒪᑲᕽ ᑮᑲᐧᐩ, ᐆᒥᓯ ᐃᓯ ᐁ ᐯ ᑮᐁᐧᒪᑲᕽ, ᑮᑲᐧᐩ ᐊᓂᒪ ᑲ ᓈᑖᒧᑐᑕᒥᕽ, ᐊᓂᒪ ᑮᑲᐧᐩ ᑳ ᑮ ᒥᔨᑯᔭᕽ ᑰᐦᑖᐄᐧᓇᐤ, ᐅᑭᓭᐋᐧᑎᓯᐃᐧᐣ, ᐁᐊᐧᑯ ᐊᓂᒪ ᑲ ᓈᑖᒧᑐᑕᒥᕽ.

[5] ᐋᓴᐩ ᑭᐄᐧ ᐊᐧᓂᓯᒥᑯᓇᐤ, ᑭᐄᐧ ᐊᐧᓂᓯᒥᑯᓇᐤ ᐋᐧᐱᐢᑭ ᐃᐧᔮᐢ, ᑮ ᐊᔨᒪᐣ ᑲᔮᐢ – ᑳ ᐊᐧᓂᐢᑲᔭᕽ, «ᐦᐋᐤ, ᐆᑕ ᐊᐱᐠ.» ᐁ ᑮ ᐃᑎᑯᔮᕽ ᓅᐦᑖᐃᐧᐩ, ᐁᑯᓯ ᐁ ᐃᓯ ᐊᐱᔮᕽ. ᐆᑕ ᐁ ᐊᐱᐟ, ᐁ ᓇᓈᐢᑯᒫᐟ ᑰᐦᑖᐄᐧᓇᐊᐧ, ᑮᓯᑲᐤ ᐁ ᒥᔨᑯᔮᕽ, ᐃᑕ ᑲ ᐱᒧᐦᑖᑕᒫᕽ ᑮᓯᑲᐤ ᐁ ᒥᔮᐧᓯᐠ. ᐊᓄᐦᐨ ᑭᑕᐋᐧᓯᒥᓯᓇᐤ ᑰᓯᓯᒥᓇᐤ ᑭᐊᐧᓂᓯᒫᓇᐤ, ᓇᒨᔭ ᑭᐋᐧᐸᐦᑌᓈᓇᐤ ᐁ ᐊᐧᓂᓯᒫᔭᕽ. ᐃᔮᔭᐤ ᓀᒪᑐᐊᐧᕽ, ᐄᐦ, ᔫᐦᑌᓇᒪᐁᐧᐊᐧᐠ ᑫᐦᑌ ᐊᔭᐠ, ᓀᒪᑐᐊᐧᕽ, ᐁ ᐊᐧᓂᐢᑳᐟ ᐊᐋᐧᓯᐢ, ᐁᐊᐧᑯ ᐊᓂᒪ ᑭᑖᐸᐦᑕᒼ. ᐆᒪ ᑳ ᓇᓈᐢᑯᒫᐟ ᑰᐦᑖᐄᐧᓇᐊᐧ ᐅᑭᓭᐋᐧᑎᓯᐃᐧᓂᔨᐤ, ᓇᒪ ᑮᑲᐧᐩ, ᐃᔮᔭᐤ ᓀᒪ ᑭᑖᐸᐦᑕᒼ. ᐊᐦᐴ ᐁ ᒨᐦᒍᐃᐧᒋᐠ ᐁᑯᑕ ᐊᔨᓯᔨᓃᐦᑲᓇᐠ ᐁ ᒪᓯᓂᐸᔨᒋᐠ, ᐃᔮᔭᐤ ᐁᐊᐧᑯ ᑭᑖᐸᐦᑕᒼ, ᓇᒨᔭ ᓇᓈᐢᑯᒣᐊᐧᐠ ᑰᐦᑖᐄᐧᓇᐊᐧ, ᑕᐦᑐ ᑮᓯᑲᐤ ᑲ ᐱᒧᐦᑖᑕᕽ, ᐁᑯᑕ ᐋᓴᐩ ᑭᐊᐧᓂᓯᒫᐊᐧᐠ. ᓇᒨᔭ ᑭᑭᐢᑫᔨᐦᑌᓈᓇᐤ, ᑭᔮᓇᐤ ᐁ ᐊᐧᓂᓯᒫᔭᕽ ᑰᓯᓯᒥᓇᐤ ᑭᑕᐋᐧᓯᒥᓯᓇᐤ, ᑭᔮᓇᐤ ᐊᓂᒪ ᐁ ᐊᐧᓂᓯᒫᔭᕽ, ᐁᐊᐧᑯ ᐆᒪ ᐅᐦᒋ ᑳ ᐆᐦ ᐊᐧᓂᓯᒫᔭᕽ. ᐁᑲᐧ ᐃᑕ ᒪᓂᑐᐃᐧ ᑮᓯᑲᐤ ᐁ ᒥᔨᑯᔭᕽ ᑲ ᐅᑎᓵᐸᐦᑕᒪᕽ ᑰᐦᑖᐄᐧᓇᐤ, ᐅᑮᓯᑲᒼ, ᐋᓴᐩ ᒦᓇ ᐁᑯᑕ ᑭᐊᐧᓂᓯᒫᓇᐤ ᑭᑕᐋᐧᓯᒥᓯᓇᐤ, ᓇᒨᔭ ᒦᓇ ᐁᐊᐧᑯ ᑭᑭᐢᑫᔨᐦᑌᓈᓇᐤ.

[6] ᐋᑎᐦᐟ ᑭᓭᔨᓂᐤ ᐁ ᐊᐧᓂᐢᑳᐟ ᓅᑎᑫᐧᐤ ᑳ ᓇᓈᐢᑯᒧᐟ, ᐁ ᒪᐃᐧᐦᑳᑕᒪᐊᐧᐟ ᐅᑭᓭᐋᐧᑎᓯᐃᐧᓂᔨᐤ, ᐅᑮᓯᑲᒼ ᑰᐦᑖᐄᐧᓇᐤ ᐁ ᐅᑎᓵᐸᐦᑕᒪᕽ, ᐁᐊᐧᑯ ᐊᓂᒪ, ᐁᐊᐧᑯ ᓀᐦᐃᔭᐃᐧ ᐄᐧᐦᑕᒪᐊᐧᑲᐣ.

[7] ᑮᑳᐧᐩ ᑳ ᐆᐦ ᐃᑌᐧᔮᐣ ᐃᑕ ᐁ ᐊᐧᓂᓯᒫᔭᕽ ᑭᑖᐊᐧᓯᒥᓯᓇᐤ, ᓀᑌ ᒥᓇᐦᐃᑯᓯᐢ ᒋᒪᓯᐤ, ᐦᐋᐤ, ᐁᑯᑕ ᐁᑲᐧ ᓰᐸ, ᑯᓂᑕ ᐁ ᐱᒪᐢᑌᑭ ᐁ ᑲᐢᑭᐱᑌᑭ ᑮᑳᐧᐩ. ᒪᔭᐤ ᐁ ᐊᐧᓂᐢᑳᐟ ᐊᐋᐧᓯᐢ, ᐃᔮᔭᐤ ᐁᑯᓂ ᐱᒪᑯᒋᐣ, ᓭᐣᑕᑭᕀᐋᐤᓭ ᐃᔮᔭᐤ ᑭᐢᑭᓯᐤ, ᓇᒨᔭ ᑰᐦᑖᐄᐧᓇᐊᐧ, ᐋᓭᐩ ᒦᓇ ᐁᑯᑕ ᐁ ᐊᐧᓂᓯᒫᔭᕽ. ᐱᑕᒫ ᑲ ᑮ ᓇᓈᐢᑯᒧᐟ, ᐅᑮᓯᑳᑦ ᐁ ᐅᑎᓭᐸᐦᑕᒪᕽ, ᑰᐦᑖᐄᐧᓇᐤ, ᐹᒪᐧᓭᐢ ᓀᐦᐃ ᑕᓰᐦᑲᕽ, ᐹᒪᐧᓭᐢ ᒦᓇ ᐆᒪ ᑭᑖᐸᐦᑕᕽ, ᑲ ᑮ ᓇᓈᐢᑯᒧᐟ, ᐁ ᒥᔮᐧᓯᐠ ᑮᓯᑳᐤ ᐃᑕ ᐁ ᒥᔩᐦᐟ ᑕ ᐱᒧᐦᑖᑕᕽ, ᐁᐊᐧᑯ ᐊᓂᒪ ᓇᐊᐧᐨ ᑲ ᑲᑫᐧ ᑭᐢᑭᓄᐦᐊᒪᐋᐧᓭᐠ ᐆᑌ ᐊᑎ ᓃᑳᐣ.

[8] ᐯᔭᐠ ᐁ ᑮᓯᑳᐠ – ᓇᒨᔭ ᐁ ᑲᑫᐧ ᓭᑭᒥᑕᑯᐠ –, ᐯᔭᐠ ᐁ ᑮᓯᑳᐠ ᐁ ᐃᐦᑕᑯᕽ ᑮᑳᐧᐩ ᐁ ᐄᐧ ᒫᑯᐦᐃᑯᔭᕽ. ᐁᑳ ᑮᑳᐧᐩ ᑳ ᓈᑲᑑᐦᑫᐟ ᑮᑳᐧᐩ ᑭᐋᐧᐦᑰᒫᑲᓂᓇᐤ, ᐁᑫᐧᔮᐨ ᐁᑯᑕ ᐁᑲᐧ ᑲ ᐯᑖᒧᐤ, ᑭᓭᔨᓂᐊᐧ ᑲ ᓈᑖᒧᑕᐁᐧᐤ, ᓅᑎᑫᐧᐊᐧ ᑲ ᓈᑖᒧᑕᐁᐧᐤ.

[9] ᑖᐯᐧ, ᑭᓭᐋᐧᑎᓯᐤ ᑰᐦᑯᒥᓇᐤ ᓅᑎᑫᐧᐃᐧ ᐋᑕᔫᐦᑲᐣ ᑳ ᐃᓯᔩᐦᑳᓱᐟ. ᑮᐢᐱᐣ ᐁᑳ ᐁᑯᑐᐊᐧᕽ ᐅᐦᒋ, ᑮᐢᐱᐣ ᐁᑳ ᐃᐢᑫᐧᐤ ᐆᑕ ᑮ ᐸᑭᑎᓂᑯᐃᐧᓯᐟ, ᓇᒨᔭ ᐆᑕ ᑭᑳᐦ ᐊᐱᓈᓇᐤ, ᐊᐄᐧᓇ ᑳᐦ ᓂᐦᑖᐃᐧᑭᐦᑖᐤ ᑭᑕᔨᓯᔨᓃᐃᐧᓂᓇᐤ, ᓇᒪ ᐊᐃᐧᔭᐠ, ᐁᐊᐧᑯ ᐃᐢᑫᐧᐤ ᑳ ᑮ ᒥᔨᐦᐟ ᑭᓭᐋᐧᑎᓯᐃᐧᐣ. ᐁᐊᐧᑯ ᐅᐦᒋ, «ᑭᑎᒫᑫᔨᐦᑐᐠ, ᐃᐢᑫᐧᐊᐧᐠ. ᑭᑎᒫᑫᔨᒥᕽ ᐃᐢᑫᐧᐤ.» ᑳ ᑮ ᐃᑌᐧᒋᐠ ᑫᐦᑌ ᐊᔭᐠ. ᓇᒪ ᓈᓂᑕᐤ ᐃᑖᐸᑕᐣ, ᓇᐯᐤ ᑳ ᐃᓯᔩᐦᑳᓱᐟ ᑲ ᑲᑳᐧᑕᑭᐦᐋᐧᐟ ᐃᐢᑫᐧᐊᐧ, ᐆᑌ ᐊᓇ ᐁ ᐅᐦᒋ ᑭᑖᐸᒥᐦᐟ, ᑳ ᑲᑳᐧᑕᑭᐦᐋᐧᐟ ᐊᓂᐦᐃ ᐃᐢᑫᐧᐊᐧ, ᐃᐧᔭ ᐊᓇ ᐁ ᑭᑎᒪᐦᐃᓱᐟ. ᓇᒨᔭ ᑳᐦ ᐊᔨᓯᔨᓃᐃᐧᐤ ᑮᐢᐱᐣ ᐁᑳ ᐅᐦᒋ ᐃᐢᑫᐧᐊᐧ, ᐁᑲᐧ ᑲ ᑭᑎᒪᐦᐋᐧᐟ ᐁᑯᑐᐊᐧᕽ, ᓇᒨᔭ ᒥᔮᐧᓯᐣ ᐁᐊᐧᑯ ᐊᓂᒪ. ᐁᑲᐧ ᒥᐦᒉᑖᐧᐤ ᓂᐯ ᐄᐧᐦᑌᐣ, ᐁ ᐯ ᐋᐧᐸᐦᑕᒫᐣ ᐁᐊᐧᑯ ᐊᓂᒪ, ᐁ ᐯ ᐅᑎᓇᒫᐣ ᓃᐢᑕ, ᑖᓂᓯ ᐁ ᑮ ᐃᓯ ᐄᐧᐦᑕᒪᐃᐧᐟ ᓅᐦᑖᐃᐧᐩ, «ᐦᐋ. ᐆᑌ ᑫ ᓃᑳᓂᐃᐧᐠ, ᐃᐢᐲ ᑮᓯ ᐊᔨᓯᔨᓃᐃᐧᔭᓂ, ᐄᐧᒉᐊᐧᒋ ᐃᐢᑫᐧᐤ, ᑲᑫᐧ ᑭᑎᒫᑫᔨᐦᑕᒫᓱ.» – ᐁᑯᓯ ᓂᑮ ᐃᑎᐠ ᒫᓇ ᓅᐦᑖᐃᐧᐩ, ᐁᐊᐧᑯ ᒫᓇ ᓂᑭᐢᑭᓯᐣ. ᐁᑳ ᑳ ᓇᐦᐁᔨᐦᑕᒫᐣ, ᓂᐊᐧᔭᐄᐧᐣ, ᓂᑳᑮᓯᒧᑐᑕᐋᐧᐤ ᑰᐦᑖᐄᐧᓇᐤ ᑲ ᐄᐧᒋᐦᐃᐟ, ᑮᑳᐧᐩ ᐁ ᒥᔮᐧᓯᐠ ᑕᒥᔩᐟ ᒥᑐᓀᔩᐦᒋᑲᐣ, ᐁᑯᓯ ᐆᒪ ᐁ ᐃᑕᐦᑲᒥᑭᓯᔭᐣ, ᐊᓯᒋ ᐅᐦᐃ ᐁᐧᐱᓈᓯᓇ

ᐁ ᑲᓇᐍᔨᐦᑕᒫᐣ, ᒪᔭᐤ ᐁ ᐘᓂᐢᑳᔮᐣ, ᐋᓴᐩ ᓂᐘᔭᐄᐧᐣ, ᐁ ᓂᑕᐃᐧ ᓂᑲᒧᔮᐣ ᐁ ᓇᓈᐢᑯᒪᐠ ᑰᐦᑖᐄᐧᓇᐤ, ᐁ ᒥᔮᐧᓯᐠ ᑮᓯᑳᐤ ᐃᑕ ᑲ ᐱᒧᐦᑕᐦᐊᑭᐠ ᓂᑕᐚᐧᓯᒥᓴᐠ. ᒥᐦᒉᑖᐧᐤ ᐊᐊᐧ ᓂᐯᐦᑖᐠ ᐁ ᑲᐯᓯᒧᐢᑕᐊᐧᐠ ᓂᑎᐦᑲᐧᑎᑦ, ᒪᔭᐤ ᐁ ᐯᑯᐸᔨᔮᐣ ᓂᔮᐦᑲᑖᒧᑉ, ᐁ ᓇᓈᐢᑯᒧᔮᐣ ᐊᓂᒪ, ᑮᓯᑳᐤ ᐃᑕ ᐁ ᐚᐸᐦᑕᒫᐣ. ᐁᐊᐧᑯ ᐆᒪ ᑲ ᑲᑫᐧ ᐁᑯᑌ ᐃᑐᐦᑕᐦᐋᔭᕽ ᑭᑕᐚᐧᓯᒥᓯᓇᐤ ᑰᓯᓯᒥᓇᐤ, ᐁᑯᑕ ᐊᓂᒪ ᑫ ᐆᐦ ᑭᑎᒫᑫᔨᐦᑐᐟ. ᐁᑳ ᐁᐊᐧᑯ ᐆᒪ ᑮᑲᐧᐩ ᐄᐧᐦᑕᒪᐚᐧᔭᐦᑯ, ᐋ, ᐁᐊᐧᑯ ᐊᐊᐧ ᑲ ᐊᐧᓂᓯᒥᐦᐟ, ᐊᐚᐧᓯᓴᐠ.

[10] ᐁᐊᐧᑯ ᐅᐦᒋ, ᑭᓭᔨᓂᐤ ᑲᔮᐢ, ᐁ ᐄᐧ ᑭᑐᑎᑯᔮᕽ ᐆᑕ ᑮ ᒋᒪᑖᐤ ᒨᐦᑯᒫᐣ, ᐄᐦ. «ᐦᐋᐤ, ᐆᒪ ᒨᐦᑯᒫᐣ ᑳ ᒋᒪᑖᔮᐣ, ᑭᓰᒥᑖᓂ ᐆᒪ ᑳ ᐄᐧ ᐄᐧᐦᑕᒫᑖᐣ, ᐅᑎᓇᒨᐦᑳᐣ ᐆᒪ ᑖᐦ ᑕᐦᑲᒦᐦᑳᐣ.» – ᐁᑯᓯ ᑮ ᐃᑌᐧᐊᐧᐠ ᑭᓭᔨᓂᐊᐧᐠ. «ᐁᐊᐧᑯ ᐆᒪ ᒨᐦᑯᒫᐣ ᑳ ᒋᒪᑖᔮᐣ, ᐆᑌ ᐆᒪ ᐁ ᒥᔮᐧᓯᐠ ᑮᑲᐧᐩ ᑳ ᐄᐧ ᐄᐧᐦᑕᒫᑖᐣ, ᐁᑳ ᓂᑐᐦᑕᒪᓂ, ᐆᑌ ᐆᒪ ᐁᑳ ᐁ ᒥᔮᐧᓯᐠ, ᐁᐊᐧᑯ ᐆᒪ ᑭᔦ ᐅᑎᓇᒪᐣ,» ᐁᑯᓯ ᐁ ᑮ ᐃᑌᐧᒋᐠ ᑫᐦᑌ ᐊᔭᐠ. ᐁᐊᐧᑯ ᐅᐦᒋ ᑳ ᐆᐦ ᑮ ᓂᑐᐦᑖᐦᐟ ᑫᐦᑌ ᐊᔭ ᑮᑲᐧᐩ ᐁ ᐄᐧᐦᑕᕽ, ᐁᑯᓯ ᐆᒪ ᐁ ᑮ ᐯ ᐃᓯ ᐸᒥᓂᑲᐃᐧᔮᕽ ᓂᔭᓈᐣ. ᑮ ᑭᑎᒫᑲᐣ ᓂᔭᓈᐣ, ᐃᑕ ᑳ ᑮ ᐯ ᐅᐦᐱᑭᔮᕽ. ᐊᓅᐦᐨ ᐅᐢᑳᔭ, ᒥᔮᐧᓯᓂᔨᐤ ᐃᑕ ᒉᑳᐧᐨ ᐁ ᐅᐦᐱᑭᐟ, ᒫᑲ, ᐁᐊᐧᑯ ᐆᒪ ᑳ ᐃᑌᐧᔮᐣ, ᓇᒨᔭ ᐁ ᐄᐧ ᑲᑫᐧ ᓴᑭᒪᐠ ᐊᔨᓯᔨᓂᐤ, ᑭᐄᐧ ᓈᑌᓈᓇᐤ ᐁ ᐄᐧ ᐊᔨᒪᕽ, ᒫᑲ ᓇᒨᔭ ᑭᓄᐧᐢ, ᐁᑯᑕ ᑳ ᐄᐧ ᓅᐦᑌᐦᑲᑌᐟ ᐊᔨᓯᔨᓂᐤ, ᐁᐊᐧᑯ ᐆᒪ ᐁᔮᐱᐨ ᐁ ᐄᐧ ᐚᐸᐦᑕᒪᕽ.

[11] ᒫᑲ, ᐆᑕ ᐊᔮᐤ ᐸᐢᑳᐃᐧ ᒧᐢᑐᐢ, ᒥᓴᑎᑦ ᑳ ᐃᓯᔩᐦᑳᓱᐟ, ᐁᑳᔭ ᐄᐧᐦᑳᐨ ᐸᑭᒌᐠ, ᐁᑳᔭ ᐄᐧᐦᑳᐨ ᐸᑭᒌᐠ. ᐁᐊᐧᑯ ᑳ ᑮ ᒥᔨᑯᔮᕽ ᑰᐦᑖᐄᐧᓇᐤ ᑲ ᐅᐄᐧᒉᐚᐧᑲᓂᔭᕽ, ᒥᓴᑎᑦ ᐊᐊᐧ ᑳ ᐃᓯᔩᐦᑳᓱᐟ. ᐁ ᑭᓴᐚᐧᑎᓯᐟ, ᐁ ᑲᓇᐍᔨᒥᑯᔭᕽ ᐁᐊᐧᑯ ᐁ ᐅᐄᐧᒉᐚᐧᑲᓂᔭᕽ, ᐁᑲᐧ ᐁᐊᐧᑯ ᐊᐊᐧ ᐸᐢᑳᐃᐧ ᒧᐢᑐᐢ, ᐁᔮᐱᐨ ᑲ ᑳᓯᐢᐳᐟ, ᐁᑲᐧ ᐁᐊᐧᑯ ᐁᑲᐧ ᑳ ᐆᐦ ᐱᒫᑎᓯᐟ.

[12] ᐁ ᐄᐧ ᐋᐦᒌᐦᑖᕽ ᐆᒪ ᐊᐢᑭᐩ, ᓇᒨᔭ ᐁ ᐄᐧ ᐴᓂ ᐊᐢᑮᐃᐧᐠ, ᐁ ᐄᐧ ᐋᐦᒌᐦᑖᕽ ᐆᒪ ᐊᐢᑭᐩ, ᐁᑲᐧ ᐆᒪ, ᑭᓅᐦᐃᔮᐃᐧᐃᐧᓂᓇᐤ ᐁ ᐄᐧ ᐯ ᑮᐍᒪᑲᕽ. ᐁᑯᓯ ᐆᒪ ᐁ ᐄᐧ ᐃᓯᓈᑲᐧᕽ, ᓇᒨᔭ ᐁ ᑲᑫᐧ ᓴᑭᒪᐠ

ᐊᔨᓯᔨᓂᐤ, ᒫᑲ ᐁᑯᓯ ᐁ ᐄᐧ ᐃᓯᓈᑲᐧᕽ, ᑮᐦᑳᓈᑲᐧᐣ, ᑖᓂᑕᐦᑕᐧᔭᐠ ᑲ ᐯᐦᑕᐋᐧᐊᐧᐠ, ᐊᐦᐴ ᐊᐋᐧᓯᐢ, ᐋᓴᐩ ᑭᐢᑫᔨᐦᑕᑦ ᐁᐊᐧᑯ, ᐁ ᑭᐢᑫᔨᐦᑕᒨᐦᐃᑯᐃᐧᓯᐟ, ᑲ ᐄᐧᐦᑕᒫᑯᔭᕽ ᐁᐊᐧᑯ ᐆᒪ, ᑖᓂᓯ ᐁ ᐄᐧ ᐃᐢᐸᔨᐠ, ᓇᒧᔭ ᑲ ᑮ ᐄᐧᐦᑌᓈᓇᐤ ᑖᓂᒪ ᐊᓂᒪ ᑮᓯᑳᐤ ᑳ ᐄᐧ ᒫᑯᐦᐃᑯᔭᕽ.

[13] ᒫᒋᑰᑎᑕᐣ, ᓈᐦ ᓈᑲᑐᐋᐧᐸᐦᑕᒧᐠ ᑭᓭᔨᓂᐊᐧᐠ ᐅᐲᑭᐢᑫᐧᐃᐧᓂᐋᐧᐤ. ᓇᒧᔭ ᐁ ᐸᑳᐧᑕᒪᐊᐧᐠ ᐊᔨᓯᔨᓂᐤ, ᐲᑐᐢ ᐆᑭ ᑲ ᐃᓯ ᐊᔭᒥᐦᐋᒋᐠ, ᑲ ᓈᑲᑑᐦᑫᔦᐠ ᐁᐊᐧᑯ ᐆᒪ, ᓀᒪᑐᐊᐧᕽ ᐁ ᔫᐦᑌᓇᒥᕽ, ᑮᑭᓭᐹ ᐋᓴᐩ ᑯᑕᐠ ᒣᐢᑯᒋᑳᐸᐃᐧᐤ ᐁ ᑲᑫᐢᑭᐦᑫᒧᐟ, ᑖᓂᔨᑯᕽ ᐁ ᐅᒋᐱᑖᐟ ᐊᔨᓯᔨᓂᐊᐧ, ᐁᐊᐧᑯ ᐊᓇ ᑳ ᐄᐧ ᐱᑯᓇᕽ ᐆᒪ ᐊᐢᑭᐩ, ᐁᐊᐧᑯ ᑳ ᐄᐧ ᒫᔨᑑᑕᕽ, ᐁᑯᓯ ᐁ ᑮ ᐯ ᐃᑌᐧᒋᐠ ᑭᓭᔨᓂᐊᐧᐠ. ᐁᑯᑐᐊᐧᕽ ᐆᒪ, ᐁ ᐅᓰᐦᑕᒫᓯᐟ ᐊᓇ ᐊᔨᓯᔨᓂᐤ ᐊᔭᒥᐦᐋᐃᐧᐣ, ᓇᒧᔭ ᐁ ᐅᐦᒋ ᒥᔨᑯᐟ ᒫᒪᐃᐧ ᐅᐦᑖᐄᐧᒫᐊᐧ, ᐃᐧᔭ ᐊᓇ ᐁ ᐅᓰᐦᑖᐟ – ᑕᐦᑭ ᐊᔨᐋᐧᐠ ᑲ ᐊᑎ ᒥᐦᒉᑎᐤ ᐁ ᐃᔨᓃᓯᐟ, ᐁᑯᓂᐠ ᐆᑭ ᑳ ᐄᐧ ᑭᓰᐦᑐᒋᐠ, ᐁᑯᑕ ᐆᑭ ᑳ ᐄᐧ ᐅᐦᐱᓇᐦᑭᐠ ᒪᒋ ᑮᑲᐧᐩ, ᐁᑯᓯ ᐁ ᑮ ᐃᑌᐧᒋᐠ ᑭᓭᔨᓂᐊᐧᐠ, ᐁᐊᐧᑯ ᐁᑲᐧ ᓂᐋᐧᐸᐦᑌᐣ ᐁ ᐃᐢᐸᔨᐠ. ᐆᒪᑐᐊᐧᕽ ᑳ ᔫᐦᑌᓇᒥᕽ, ᐋᓴᐩ ᐁᑯᑕ ᑖᓂᔨᑯᕽ ᐁ ᐲᑭᐢᑫᐧᐟ, ᐁᑲᐧ ᐃᔨᑯᕽ ᒥᓵᐦᑲᒥᐠ ᐁ ᐅᒋᐱᑖᐟ ᐊᔨᓯᔨᓂᐊᐧ.

[14] ᒫᑲ ᐋᐦᑲᒣᔨᒧᑖᐣ. ᑮᐢᑕᓇᐤ, ᑳ ᓀᐦᐃᔮᐃᐧᔭᕽ, ᐁ ᒥᔮᐧᓯᐠ ᑮᑲᐧᐩ ᓂᑐᑕᒪᐋᐧᑖᐠ ᑰᐦᑖᐄᐧᓇᐤ, ᑲ ᑭᑎᒫᑭᐦᑖᑯᔭᕽ.

[15] ᑖᓂᓯ ᑎᔫᑕᒪᕽ – ᑭᑕᐋᐧᓯᒥᓯᓇᐤ ᐆᑕ ᐁ ᐯ ᓇᐦᐊᐱᐟ, ᑮᑲᐧᐩ ᐁ ᒥᔮᐧᓯᐠ ᐁ ᓂᑐᑕᒫᑯᔭᕽ, ᑭᓵᑭᐦᑕᒪᐋᐧᓇᐤ, ᓇᒧᔭ ᓴᒫᐠ ᑲ ᒥᔮᓇᐤ. ᐱᓯᐢᐠ ᑲ ᒫᑐᐤ, ᐋᐦᒋ ᐱᑯ ᐊᓂᒪ ᐁ ᓂᑕᐁᐧᔨᐦᑕᕽ. "ᐋ, ᐱᑯ ᐁᑲᐧ ᐁᑯᑕ ᑲ ᒥᔮᔭᕽ, ᐁᑯᓯ ᐊᐊᐧ ᑲ ᐃᑎᐦᑖᑯᓇᐤ ᑰᐦᑖᐄᐧᓇᐤ, ᐁ ᒥᔮᐧᓯᐠ ᑮᑲᐧᐩ ᓂᑐᑕᒪᐋᐧᔭᐦᑯ. ᐁᐊᐧᑯ ᐆᒪ, ᑳ ᐄᐧ ᐅᐦᐸᐢᑯᓇᐠ ᐊᐊᐧ ᐅᐢᐹᐧᑲᐣ, ᒫᒥᑐᓀᔨᐦᑕᒧᐠ ᑮᐢᑕᐋᐧᐤ, ᐁ ᒥᔮᐧᓯᐠ ᑮᑲᐧᐩ ᓂᑐᑕᒫᕽ ᑰᐦᑖᐄᐧᓇᐤ, ᐆᒪ ᐃᑕ ᑳ ᐊᑐᐢᑫᔦᐠ.

[16] "ᐋᐤ, ᐁᐊᐧᑯ ᐆᒪ ᐱᑯ ᑫ ᐱᒧᐦᑕᐦᐃᑯᔭᕽ, "ᐋᐤ, ᐁᑯᓯ ᐱᑯ ᐁ ᐄᐧ ᐃᓯ ᐄᐧᐦᑕᒫᑕᑯᐠ.

5 ᑭᑲ ᐋᒋᒨᒪᑲᐣ ᐅᐢᑭᒋᐩ

[1] ᒣᑳᐧᐨ ᐁ ᐅᑭᒫᐦᑳᓂᐃᐧᐟ, ᐁᐊᐧᑯ ᐊᐊᐧ ᐁ ᑮ ᐄᐧ ᐸᓯᑰᓂᐟ, ᑭᐢᑫᔨᐦᑕᒼ ᑳ ᐊᐱᐟ ᐊᐊᐧ, ᓂᐢᑖᐧᐤ ᐁᑯᑌ ᓂᓂᑕᐃᐧ ᐄᐧᒋᐦᐃᐋᐧᐣ, ᐁ ᓂᑕᐃᐧ ᑳᑮᓯᒧᕽ, ᓂᐱᐩ ᑳ ᐱᑎᐦᑫᐧᐠ, ᐃᑕ ᑳ ᑮ ᐃᐧᔨᐦᒋᑫᐟ ᑭᒧᓰᒥᓇᐤ, ᐁᑯᑕ ᑳ ᑮ ᐋᐸᑕᕽ ᐊᓂᒪ ᐅᐢᑭᒋᐩ, ᐁᐊᐧᑯ ᓀᐦᐃᔭᐊᐧᓯᓇᐦᐃᑲᐣ ᑳ ᑮ ᐅᓰᐦᑖᐟ, ᐁᐊᐧᑯ ᐊᐊᐧ ᓂᒧᓰᒥᓈᐣ ᒐᐢᒐᑭᐢᑫᐧᐢ ᑳ ᑮ ᐃᑎᐦᐟ, ᐁᑯᑕ ᐁᐊᐧᑯ ᑳ ᑮ ᐋᐸᑕᕽ, ᑳ ᑮ ᐃᐧᔨᐦᒋᑫᐟ ᐊᐊᐧ, ᑳ ᑮ ᐱᒧᐦᑌᐢᑕᒫᐧᐟ ᑭᐦᒋ ᐅᑭᒫᐢᑫᐧᐊᐧ ᐆᐦᐃ, ᑳ ᑮ ᐯ ᐊᑖᐁᐧᐟ ᐆᒪ ᐊᐢᑭᐩ, ᐁᑯᑕ ᐊᓂᒪ ᐁᐊᐧᑯ ᐁ ᑮ ᐋᐸᑕᕽ, ᐁᐊᐧᑯ ᐊᓂᒪ ᐅᐦᒋ ᑳ ᐆᐦ ᑮ ᐃᓰᐦᒋᑫᐟ ᐊᐊᐧ, ᒣᑳᐧᐨ ᐆᑕ ᒥᑐᓂ ᐁ ᐅᑭᒫᐦᑳᓂᐃᐧᐟ, ᐁᑯᑕ ᒫᓇ ᐁ ᑮ ᓂᑕᐃᐧ ᑳᑮᓯᒧᕽ, ᐁᑯᑕ ᐅᐦᒋ ᐁ ᑮ ᐄᐧᐦᑕᒫᐦᒋᐠ ᐊᔨᓯᔨᓂᐊᐧᐠ, ᑖᓂᓯ ᐊᓂᒪ ᐁ ᐃᐢᐸᔨᐠ ᑮᑲᐧᐩ.

[2] ᑮ ᐃᑌᐤ ᐁᐊᐧᑯ ᐊᐊᐧ ᐅᑭᒫᐦᑳᐣ, «ᒣᑳᐧᐨ ᐆᑕ ᐁ ᐱᒫᑎᓯᒋᐠ ᑫᐦᑌ ᐊᔭᐠ, ᐯᐦᑕᒧᐃᐧᐣ ᐁ ᑭᐢᑫᔨᐦᑕᐦᑭᐠ, ᐁᐊᐧᑯ ᐆᒪ ᑭᑲ ᐋᒋᒨᒪᑲᐣ ᐅᐢᑭᒋᐩ, ᑖᓂᓯ ᐁ ᑮ ᐃᓯ ᐊᓯᑕᒫᑯᔭᕽ ᐋᐧᐱᐢᑭ ᐄᐧᔮᐢ,» ᑮ ᐃᑌᐤ ᒫᓇ. ᐁᑲᐧ ᒥᐢᑕᐦᐃ ᑳ ᓇᓈᐢᑯᒪᐠ Alec ᐊᐊᐧ, ᐁᐊᐧᑯ ᐆᒪ ᐁᑲᐧ ᑳ ᐄᐧ ᑕᓰᐦᑲᕽ, ᐄᐦ, ᐆᑌ Saskatoon ᐁᐊᐧᑯ ᐊᓂᒪ ᑲ ᐱᐦᑎᑫᐧᒪᑲᕽ, ᑲ ᓀᐦᐃᔭᐊᐧᐢᑌᐠ. ᑖᓂᓯ ᐊᓂᒪ ᐁ ᐯ ᐃᓯ ᑭᐢᑫᔨᐦᑕᕽ ᑫᐦᑌ ᐊᔭ, ᐁᐊᐧᑯ ᐊᓂᒪ ᐁᑲᐧ, ᓀᐦᐃᔭᐃᐧ ᒪᓯᓇᐦᐃᑲᐣ, ᑮᐢᑕᓇᐤ ᐁ ᑮ ᐁᐊᐧᑯ ᐊᓂᒪ ᑕᐦᑯᓇᒨᐦᐃᐦᐟ ᐊᐊᐧ, ᑖᓀᐦᑭ ᑳ ᐆᐦ ᑮ ᑕᐦᑯᓇᒨᐦᐃᐦᐟ ᐁᐊᐧᑯ ᐊᓂᒪ, «ᑭᑕᓯᑕᒫᑯᐃᐧᓂᓇᐤ ᐁᑳᔭ ᐄᐧᐦᑳᐨ ᑲ ᐲᑯᓇᕽ ᐁ ᓃᓰᑳᑌᐟ ᐊᔨᓯᔨᓂᐤ,» ᑮ ᐃᑌᐤ ᐁᓴ, ᑭᑮ ᐊᓯᑕᒫᑯᓇᐤ ᐁᑳᔭ ᐄᐧᐦᑳᐨ ᑲ ᐲᑯᓇᕽ ᐊᐃᐧᔭᐠ, ᐅᑕᓯᑕᒫᑫᐃᐧᐣ ᐊᓂᒪ. ᐁᐊᐧᑯ ᐁᑲᐧ ᑳ ᓈᒋᑳᐸᐃᐧᐢᑕᕽ ᐋᐧᐱᐢᑭ ᐄᐧᔮᐢ, ᐁ ᐄᐧ ᑲᑫᐧ ᐸᑎᑎᓴᐦᐊᒫᑯᔭᕽ. ᐁᐊᐧᑯ ᐅᐦᒋ ᑳ ᐆᐦ ᓇᓈᐢᑯᒧᔭᐣ ᐁᐊᐧᑯ ᐆᒪ ᐁ ᐄᐧ ᐃᓰᐦᒋᑳᑕᒥᕽ, ᑲ ᐊᑎ ᑭᐢᑭᓄᐊᐧᓯᐦᑕᕽ ᐆᒥᓯ ᐃᓯ ᑭᐋᐧᐦᑰᒫᑲᓂᓇᐤ, ᐁᐊᐧᑯ ᐆᒪ ᑖᓂᓯ ᐁ ᐃᑌᐧᒪᑲᕽ, ᐁᐊᐧᑯ ᐆᒪ ᐅᐢᑭᒋᐩ ᑳ ᐃᓯᓰᐦᑳᑌᐠ.

[3] ᐁᑲᐧ ᐊᐊᐧ ᑯᑕᐠ ᐲᓯᒼ, ᑌᐸᑯᐦᐳᓵᑊ ᐊᑭᒥᐦᒋ, ᐆᑌ ᐁᑲᐧ ᑳ ᐄᐧ ᐱᐦᑎᑫᐧᒪᑲᕽ ᒦᓇ, ᐁᑯᓯ ᐁ ᐄᐧ ᐃᓰᐦᒋᑫᒋᐠ ᐆᑭ, Alberta ᑭᐋᐧᐦᑰᒫᑲᓂᓇᐊᐧᐠ. ᒥᐢᑕᐦᐃ ᑲ ᒥᓵᐧᓯᐣ, ᐁᐊᐧᑯ ᐊᓂᒪ ᑳ ᐄᐧ ᐃᓰᐦᒋᑫᕽ, ᐁᐊᐧᑯ ᐆᒪ ᑳ ᐃᓯ ᐯᐦᑕᐊᐧᑭᐠ, ᐆᑕ ᓂᐢᑕᒼ ᑳ ᒫᒥᐢᑰᑕᐦᑭᐠ, ᐆᒥᓯ

ᑲ ᐃᓯ ᐄᐧᑭᕽ, ᐃᑕ ᐆᑭ ᑳ ᐄᐧ ᓂᑐᓇᐦᑭᐠ ᑎᐸᐦᐊᒫᑐᐃᐧᐣ, ᒥᐢᑕᐦᐃ ᑲ ᒥᔮᐧᓯᐣ, ᒫᑕᔭᐠ ᑲ ᑭᐢᑫᔨᐦᑕᐦᑭᐠ ᐁᐊᐧᑯ, ᑭᑕᓱᑕᒫᑯᐃᐧᓂᓇᐤ ᑮᑳᐧᐩ ᑳ ᐊᐢᐱᑐᓈᒧᒋᐠ – ᓇᒧᔭ ᓈᓇᐯᐨ ᐅᒋᐦᒋᐸᔨᑭ, ᑲ ᓈᑖᒧᐢᑕᐦᑭᐠ ᐊᓂᒪ, ᒫᑕᔭᐠ ᑲ ᑭᐢᑫᔨᐦᑕᐦᑭᐠ, ᒣᑳᐧᐨ ᐁ ᐱᒫᑎᓯᒋᐠ ᑫᐦᑌ ᐊᔭᐠ, ᐅᓂᑮᐦᐃᑯᒫᐊᐧᐠ, ᐅᒧᓲᒥᐋᐧᐊᐧ ᐅᑖᒋᒧᐃᐧᓂᔨᐤ, ᐁᑯᑕ ᑭᑕ ᐊᐢᑖᒋᐠ, ᐁᐊᐧᑯ ᐊᓂᒪ ᑳ ᑰᑕᐁᐧᔨᐦᑕᒫᐣ, ᐆᑌ, ᐁᑯᓂᐠ ᐆᑭ ᑳ ᐊᐱᒋᐠ, ᐄᐦ, ᓂᑮ ᑲᑫᐧᒋᒥᑲᐃᐧᐣ Saddle Lake ᐁᐊᐧᑯ ᐆᒪ, ᑖᓂᓯ ᐁ ᐃᐢᐸᔨᐠ ᐆᑕ, ᐁᐊᐧᑯ ᐆᒪ, ᑖᓂᓯ ᐁ ᐃᑌᐧᒪᑲᕽ ᐅᐢᑭᒋᐩ. ᐁᑯᑕ ᓂᑮ ᓂᑐᐦᑖᑲᐧᐠ, ᓂᑮ ᐄᐧᐦᑕᒪᐋᐧᐊᐧᐠ ᐊᓂᑭ, ᑳ ᓃᑳᓂᐢᑕᐦᑭᐠ ᐁᑯᑕ. ᑮ ᓇᓈᐢᑯᒧᐊᐧᐠ, ᐄᐧᐢᑕᐋᐧᐤ ᐊᓂᐠ ᐁ ᐄᐧ ᓈᑖᒧᐢᑕᐦᑭᐠ ᐁᐊᐧᑯ, ᐁᑯᓯ ᐆᒪ ᐁ ᑮ ᐃᓰᐦᒋᑫᕽ ᐁᑯᑌ ᑳ ᒫᒪᐆᐧᐱᕽ, ᐁᑯᓯ ᐆᒪ ᐁᑯᑕ ᑳ ᐄᐧ ᐲᐦᑎᑫᐧᒪᑲᕽ Saskatoon, ᑲ ᒪᓯᓂᐸᔨᐦᑖᕽ ᐊᓂᒪ, ᒫᑲ ᑲ ᓀᐦᐃᔭᐊᐧᐢᑌᐠ ᐊᓂᒪ ᐋᒋᒧᐃᐧᐣ, ᑭᑕᓱᑕᒫᑯᐃᐧᓂᓇᐤ, ᐁᑯᓯ ᐆᒪ ᐁ ᐄᐧ ᐃᓰᐦᒋᑳᑕᒥᕽ ᐊᓂᒪ ᐅᐢᑭᒋᐩ. ᐁᐊᐧᑯ ᐅᐦᒋ ᑳ ᐆᐦ ᓰᐦᑭᒥᑯᔭᕽ ᐅᑖᑯᓯᕽ ᐊᐊᐧ ᓂᑯᓯᐢ, ᐆᑕ David ᑳ ᐹᐦ ᐱᑭᐢᑫᐧᐟ, ᑲ ᒫᒪᐆᐧᐦᑲᒫᑐᔭᕽ, ᑲ ᒫᒪᐆᐧᐦᑲᒫᑐᔭᕽ, «ᐯᔭᐠ ᑲᑕᐋᐧᕽ ᐃᑎᐦᑖᑲᐧᓂᔨᑭ, ᐅᐲᑭᐢᑫᐧᐃᐧᐣ, ᐁᐊᐧᑯ ᐊᓂᒪ ᑫ ᐱᒧᐦᑕᐦᐃᑯᔭᕽ,» ᑳ ᐃᑌᐧᐟ, ᐁᑯᓯ ᐁ ᐃᓯ ᑖᐯᐧᐟ ᐊᓂᒪ ᑳ ᐃᑌᐧᐟ. ᐁᑯᓯ ᐱᑯ ᐁ ᐄᐧ ᐃᓯ ᐄᐧᐦᑕᒫᑕᑯᐠ ᐁᐊᐧᑯ ᐆᒪ.

[4] "ᐋᐤ, ᑕᐦᑖᐧᐤ ᐁ ᑮᓯᑳᐠ ᐋᑕ ᒥᑐᓂ ᐁ ᐋᐦᑲᒣᔨᒧᔮᐣ ᒦᓇ ᓃᐢᑕ ᐁ ᐲᑭᐢᑳᐧᑕᒫᐣ ᑮᑲᐧᐩ, ᐄᐦ, ᓃᐢᑕ ᐁ ᑭᑲᐱᔮᐣ ᐁᐧᐱᓈᓱᓇ ᐁ ᓅᐦᑌ ᑖᐯᐧᔮᐣ, ᐁ ᒫᑫᐧᔨᒧᔮᐣ, ᐁ ᒥᐦᒉᑎᒋᐠ ᓅᓯᓯᒪᐠ ᓂᒫᐹᓇᐠ, ᑖᓂᑌ ᑭᑲ ᐃᑖᒨᐦᐊᑭᐠ. ᐁᐊᐧᑯ ᒫᓇ ᒥᐢᑕᐦᐃ ᓂᒫᒥᑐᓀᔨᐦᑌᐣ. ᐁᑯᓯ ᐆᒪ ᑲ ᑑᑕᒪᕽ, ᓂᐋᐧᐦᑯᒫᑲᓂᑎᐠ, ᐋᐦᑲᒣᔨᒧᑖᐠ, ᒫᒪᐃᐧ ᐄᐧᒉᐦᑐᑖᐠ. ᑲ ᑭᑎᒫᑭᐦᑖᑯᓇᐤ ᐁᑐᑫᐧ ᑰᐦᑖᐄᐧᓇᐤ, ᐃᐧᔭ ᑳ ᐸᒥᐦᑖᐟ ᑮᑲᐧᐩ, ᓇᒧᔭ ᑭᔮᓇᐤ.

[5] ᒋᑫᒨ ᐃᐧᔭ, ᑖᓂᓯ ᐃᑌᔨᐦᑕᐦᑭ, ᐁᐊᐧᑯ ᐊᓂᒪ ᑫ ᐱᒧᐦᑖᑕᒪᕽ ᑮᓯᑳᐤ ᐁ ᒥᔮᐧᓯᐠ. ᐁᑯᓯ ᐱᑯ ᐁ ᐃᑎᑕᑯᐠ, ᒫᑲ, «ᐱᑕᓀ, ᐁᑳ ᑮᑲᐧᐩ ᐹᐢᑖᐦᐆᑐᑕᒫᐣ,» ᓂᑎᑌᔨᐦᑌᐣ ᒫᓇ ᐁᐊᐧᑯ ᐆᒪ ᐋᔨᒨᑕᒫᓂ.

6 ᑮᑲᐧᕀ ᑳ ᐊᐢᐱᑐᓈᒧᔭᕽ

[1] ᐋ, ᐁᐊᐧᑯ ᐆᒪ ᑳ ᐄᐧ ᑖᐦᑰᑕᒫᐣ, ᒪᑖᐧᐣ ᒌ ᑲᐧᔭᐢᐠ ᓂᑲ ᑮ ᐃᓯ ᑖᐦᑰᑌᐣ ᑖᓂᓯ ᐁ ᑮ ᐃᑖᒋᒧᐢᑕᐃᐧᐟ ᑳ ᑮ ᐅᔩᐦᑖᐄᐧᔮᐣ, ᐆᒪ ᐃᑕ ᑳ ᐸᑯᓭᔨᒥᑲᐃᐧᔮᐣ ᑲ ᑮ ᑖᐦᑰᑕᒫᐣ, ᐁᐊᐧᑯ ᐆᒪ ᐅᐢᑭᒋᕀ ᑳ ᐃᓯᔩᐦᑳᑌᐠ, ᐋᑕ ᐊᓂ ᒥᑐᓂ ᑲᐧᔭᐢᐠ ᓂᑮ ᐄᐧᐦᑕᒫᑰᐦ ᒦᓇ ᓅᐦᒑᐄᐧᐢ, ᐃᑕ ᐁ ᑮ ᑲᓇᐁᐧᔩᐦᑕᕽ ᐁᐊᐧᑯ ᐆᒪ, ᐃᑕ ᐅᒧᓰᒪ ᑳ ᑮ ᐅᐦᑕᐢᑲᑕᒥᔨᐟ ᐁᐊᐧᑯ ᐆᒪ ᐅᐢᑭᒋᕀ.

[2] ᐋ, ᒥᐢᑕᐦᐃ ᐃᐧᔭ ᓂᔭ ᓂᓇᓈᐢᑯᒧᐣ, ᑭᑲ ᐅᑑᓂᐦᑳᒋᐠ ᐆᑭ ᐊᓂᑕ ᑳ ᐊᑐᐢᑳᑯᔭᐦᑯᐠ: ᑭᐊᐧᐦᑰᒫᑲᓂᓇᐊᐧᐠ, ᑮᑲᐧᕀ ᐊᓂᒪ ᑭᑕᓯᑕᒫᑯᐃᐧᓂᓇᐤ, ᑳ ᓂᑕᐁᐧᔨᐦᑕᐦᑭᐠ, ᐁ ᐃᓯ ᑭᐢᑫᔨᐦᑕᕽ ᐊᔨᓯᔨᓂᐤ, ᐁ ᐃᓯ ᐯᐦᑕᕽ ᐅᐯᐦᑕᒧᐃᐧᓂᕽ, ᑳ ᐋᑐᑕᕽ ᐁᐊᐧᑯ ᐆᒪ ᐋᒋᒧᐃᐧᐣ. ᐁᐊᐧᑯ ᐆᒪ ᓃᐢᑕ ᐁ ᑮ ᐃᑖᒋᒧᐢᑕᐃᐧᐟ ᒫᓇ ᑳ ᑮ ᐅᔩᐦᑖᐄᐧᔮᐣ, ᑳ ᐄᐧ ᐃᑖᒋᒧᐢᑕᐊᐧᑭᐠ ᐆᑭ. ᒪᑖᐧᐣ ᒌ ᓂᑲ ᑮ ᑌᐱ ᐄᐧᐦᑌᐣ, ᑖᓂᓯ ᐁ ᑮ ᐃᓯ ᐄᐧᐦᑕᒪᐃᐧᐟ ᒫᓇ. ᑰᑕᑌ ᓃᐢᑕ ᐁᑳ ᐁ ᓰᐱ ᑭᐢᑭᓯᔭᐣ, ᒫᑲ ᐁ ᐃᐢᑯ ᑭᐢᑫᔨᐦᑕᒫᐣ ᑮᑲᐧᕀ, ᐁᔨᐁᐧᕽ ᓂᑲ ᑲᑫᐧ ᐋᒋᒧᐢᑕᐋᐧᐊᐧᐠ. ᒫᒋᑲ ᐁᐊᐧᑯ ᐆᒪ, ᓃᑳᐣ ᓂᑲ ᑖᐦᑰᑌᐣ, ᐁᐊᐧᑯ ᐆᒪ ᓂᒧᓰᒥᓈᐣ ᑳ ᑮ ᓇᑲᑕᕽ ᒐᐢᒐᑭᐢᑫᐧᐢ, ᐅᐢᑭᒋᕀ ᐆᒪ.

[3] «ᐁᑯᑕ ᐆᑕ, ᓂᐱᕀ ᑳ ᐱᑎᐦᑫᐧᐠ, ᐁᑯᑕ ᑳ ᒫᐊᐧᒌᐦᐃᑐᕽ ᑳ ᐄᐧ ᐊᑖᐋᐧᑫᕽ ᐊᐢᑭᕀ, ᐁᑯᑕ ᐁ ᑮ ᐋᐸᑕᕽ,» ᑮ ᐃᑌᐤ ᒫᓇ ᑳ ᑮ ᐅᔩᐦᑖᐄᐧᔮᐣ. «ᐋ, ᒥᐢᑕᐦᐃ ᑮ ᐲᑭᐢᑫᐧᒨᐦᐃᑯᓈᓂᐃᐧᐤ ᑮᑲᐧᕀ. ᒥᐢᑕᐦᐃ ᑮ ᐲᑭᐢᑳᐧᑕᒪᐧᐠ, ᑭᓭᔨᓂᐊᐧᐠ, ᐁᐊᐧᑯ ᐆᒪ, ᐁ ᑮ ᒥᐦᑖᑕᐦᑭᐠ, ᐃᑕ ᑰᐦᑖᐄᐧᓇᐤ ᐁ ᑮ ᐸᑭᑎᓂᑯᔭᕽ ᐊᐢᑭᕀ ᑲ ᓂᐦᑖᐃᐧᑮᐢᑕᒪᕽ, ᐁᐊᐧᑯ ᐆᒪ ᐁᑲᐧ ᐁ ᐄᐧ ᐊᑖᐋᐧᑫᐃᐧᐦᐟ, ᐁᐊᐧᑯ ᒥᐢᑕᐦᐃ ᑳ ᑮ ᐲᑭᐢᑳᐧᑕᐦᑭᐠ.» ᐁᑯᓯ ᒫᓇ ᐁᑯᑕ ᑮ ᐃᑌᐤ.

[4] ᐋ, ᐯᔭᐠ ᐊᓇ ᑭᓭᔨᓂᐤ, ᐯᔭᐠ ᐊᓇ ᑭᓭᔨᓂᐤ, ᒥᑐᓂ ᐋᑕ ᑮ ᐄᐧᐦᑕᐨ, ᑖᓂᓯ ᐁ ᐄᐧ ᐃᐢᐸᔩᐠ, ᐁᐊᐧᑯ ᐆᒪ ᐁᑲᐧ, ᐃᑕ ᑳ ᐱᒧᐦᑌᔭᕽ ᒉᑳᐧᐨ, ᐋ, ᒥᑐᓂ ᐃᐧᔭᑳᐨ, ᐁᑳ ᐁ ᒥᐦᒉᑎᒋᐠ, ᒉᑳᐧᐨ ᑭᓭᔨᓂᐊᐧᐠ ᐁ ᐯ ᒥᐦᒉᑎᒋᐠ, ᐁᐊᐧᑯ ᐆᒪ ᑮ ᐊᑐᐢᑳᑕᒥᕽ, ᒥᐢᑕᐦᐃ ᑲ ᑮ ᒥᔭᐧᓯᓅᐸᐣ, ᑲ ᐯᐦᑕᐋᐧᔭᐦᑭᐠ ᐆᒪᑐᐃᐧᕽ ᑲ ᑎᐹᐦᑕᐦᑭᐠ ᐁᐊᐧᑯ ᐆᒪ, ᒫᑲ ᐁᑲᐧ ᐱᑯ, ᑭᐯᐦᑕᒧᐃᐧᓂᓈᕽ ᑮᑲᐧᕀ, ᐋᒋᒧᐃᐧᐣ, ᑖᓂᓯ ᐁ ᑮ ᐃᑖᒋᒧᐢᑖᑲᐃᐧᔭᕽ, ᐁᐊᐧᑯ ᐁᑲᐧ ᐱᑯ ᑲ ᓈᒋᐸᐦᐃᐁᐧᔭᕽ. ᐁᐊᐧᑯ

ᐅᐦᒋ ᑳ ᐆᐦ ᓇᓈᐢᑯᒧᔮᐣ ᓂᔭ, ᐁᐊᐧᑯ ᐆᒪ ᐁ ᐊᑐᐢᑳᑕᐦᑭᐠ, ᐁ ᒫᒥᑐᓀᔨᒫᒋᐠ ᑰᓯᓯᒥᓇᐊᐧ, ᑭᒑᐸᓂᓇᐊᐧ, ᐅᐢᑳᔭ ᐁᑳᔭ ᑮᑲᐧᐩ ᐁ ᓈᑲᑑᐦᑫᐟ, ᑲ ᑲᑫᐧ ᑭᐢᑫᔨᐦᑕᕽ, ᑖᓂᓯ ᐁ ᐃᑖᒋᒨᒪᑲᕽ ᐁᐊᐧᑯ ᐆᒪ, ᐁᑯᓯ ᐆᑭ ᐁᓴ ᐁᑐᑫᐧ ᐁ ᐸᑯᓭᔨᒧᒋᐠ, ᑳ ᐄᐧ ᑲᑫᐧ ᐅᑎᓇᐦᑭᐠ ᐆᒪ ᐋᒋᒧᐃᐧᐣ, ᐁᐊᐧᑯ ᐆᒪ ᒣᑳᐧᐨ ᑳ ᐄᐧ ᐋᑐᑕᒫᐣ ᐁᑲᐧ.

[5] ᐁᐊᐧᑯ ᐊᐊᐧ ᒫᓇ ᑮ ᐃᑌᐧᐤ ᑳ ᑮ ᐅᔩᐦᑖᐄᐧᔮᐣ, «ᐋ, ᐋᑕ ᐊᓂ ᑮ ᐄᐧᐦᑕᑦ, ᑭᓭᔨᓂᐤ ᐯᔭᐠ ᐁ ᐸᓯᑰᐟ, ᐁᑯᑕ ᑮ ᐄᐧᐦᑕᑦ, ᑮᑲᐧᐩ ᐱᑯ ᑲ ᐊᐢᐱᑐᓈᒧᐟ ᐊᔨᓯᔨᓂᐤ, ᑭᑕᔮᓇᓇᐤ ᑮᑲᐧᐩ ᑲ ᐊᐢᐱᑐᓈᒧᔭᕽ ᑳ ᓀᐦᐃᔮᐃᐧᔮᕽ, ᐁᐊᐧᑯ ᐆᒪ ᐅᐢᑭᒥᐩ ᑳ ᐃᓯᔩᐦᑳᑌᐠ, ᐁᐊᐧᑯ ᐱᑯ ᑲ ᑮ ᐊᐢᐱᑐᓈᒧᔭᕽ. ᑳ ᐃᓯ ᐊᓯᑕᒫᑯᔭᕽ ᐊᐊᐧ ᑭᒋᐋᐧᒥᓇᐤ ᐋᐧᐱᐢᑭ ᐃᐧᔮᐢ, ᑭᑕᓯᑕᒫᑯᓇᐤ ᐁᑳᔭ ᐄᐧᐦᑳᐨ ᐆᑕ ᐋᐧᐢᑭᑕᐢᑲᒥᐠ ᐁ ᓂᓰᑳᑌᐟ ᐊᔨᓯᔨᓂᐤ, ᑲ ᑮ ᐲᑯᓇᕽ ᑭᑕᓯᑕᒫᑯᐃᐧᓂᓇᐤ. ᐁᑯᓯ, ᐁᑯᑕ ᑳ ᑮ ᑲᑫᐧᒋᒫᐟ,

ᐁ ᑖᐯᐧᔮᐣ ᒌ ᐆᒪ, ᑳ ᐃᓯ ᐊᓯᑕᒪᐃᐧᔮᐣ, ᐁᑳ ᐄᐧᐦᑳᐨ ᐊᐃᐧᔭᐠ
ᑲ ᑮ ᑲᐢᑭᐦᑖᐟ ᑲ ᑮ ᐲᑯᓇᕽ ᐆᒪ ᑳ ᐃᓯ ᐊᓯᑕᒪᐃᐧᔮᕽ.
ᑭᐯ ᐋᑲᐧᐢᑭᐢᑲᐃᐧᓈᐣ ᐊᔨᐢ, ᑭᐯ ᐋᑲᐧᐢᑭᐢᑲᐋᐧᐤ, ᒫᒪᐃᐧ ᐆᐦᑖᐄᐧᒫᐤ
ᐃᑕ ᐁ ᑮ ᒥᔨᑯᔮᕽ ᑮᑲᐧᐩ ᑲ ᐆᐦ ᐱᒫᑎᓯᔮᕽ, ᑭᐯ ᐋᑲᐧᐢᑭᐢᑲᐋᐧᐤ,
ᑲ ᐯ ᐊᓯᑕᒪᐃᐧᔮᕽ ᐁ ᐄᐧ ᐃᓯ ᐸᒥᐦᐃᔭᕽ, ᐁᐊᐧᑯ ᐆᒪ, ᐁ ᑖᐯᐧᔮᐣ ᒌ
ᐆᒪ ᑳ ᐃᓯ ᐊᓯᑕᒪᐃᐧᔮᕽ, ᐃᑕ ᑲ ᐯ ᐱᒧᐦᑌᐢᑕᒪᐊᐧᐟ ᑭᐦᒋ ᐅᑭᒫᐢᑫᐧᐤ,
ᓇᒨᔭ ᐄᐧᐦᑳᐨ ᒌ ᑲ ᑭᓯᐲᒪᑲᐣ ᐆᒪ ᑳ ᐊᓯᑕᒪᐃᐧᔮᕽ.

ᐋᐧᐸᐦᑕ. ᒫᒋᑰᑎᑕᐣ ᐆᑕ ᐁ ᐃᐢᐱᓯ ᐃᑖᐱᔭᐣ,
ᐁ ᐃᐢᐱᓯ ᐄᐧᐦᑫᐧᐢᑲᒥᑳᐠ, ᐃᔨᑯᕽ ᑳ ᑌᐸᐸᒫᐟ ᐸᐢᑳᐧᐄᐧ ᒨᐢᑐᐢ, ᐁᑯᓂ
ᐆᐦᐃ ᐁ ᑮ ᒥᔨᑯᔮᕽ ᑲ ᐆᐦ ᐱᒫᑎᓯᔮᕽ, ᒫᒪᐃᐧ ᐆᐦᑖᐄᐧᒫᐤ, ᐁᑯᓯ ᒌ
ᑲ ᑮ ᐃᓯ ᐸᒥᐦᐃᓈᐣ, ᐃᐢᑯᔨᑯᕽ ᐆᑕ ᑭᓭ ᐊᐢᑮᐃᐧᐠ.

ᐁᑯᓯ ᑮ ᐃᑌᐤ ᐊᓂᐦᐃ, ᑲ ᑮ ᐯ ᐱᒧᐦᑌᐢᑕᒪᐋᐧᐟ ᐊᐊᐧ ᑭᐦᒋ ᐅᑭᒫᐢᑫᐧᐊᐧ,

ᐁ ᑖᐯᐧᔮᐣ ᒌ ᐆᒪ, ᑳ ᐃᓯ ᐊᓯᑕᒪᐃᐧᔮᕽ, ᐁᑳ ᐄᐧᐦᑳᐨ ᑲ ᑮ ᐲᑯᓇᕽ,
ᐊᔨᓯᔨᓂᐤ ᐁ ᓂᓰᑳᑌᐟ ᑳ ᐃᑌᐧᔮᐣ, ᐁᐊᐧᑯ ᐆᒪ, ᐄᐦ.
ᑳ ᐃᓯ ᐊᓯᑕᒪᐃᐧᔮᕽ. –

ᓇᒨᔭ, ᓇᒨᔭ ᓂᐱᐩ ᑳ ᐊᑖᒥᑖᐣ, ᓇᒨᔭ ᐱᓯᐢᑭᐤ
ᑲ ᐆᐦ ᐱᒫᒋᐦᐅᔭᐣ, ᓇᒨᔭ ᐁᐊᐧᑯ ᑳ ᐊᑖᒥᑖᐣ, ᓇᒨᔭ ᒦᓇ ᑭᓱᓴᐤ,
ᓇᒨᔭ ᒦᓇ ᐁᐊᐧᑯ ᑳ ᐊᑖᒥᑖᐣ, ᒦᓇ ᓇᓈᑐᕽ ᐆᐦᐃ ᒥᓂᓴ
ᑲ ᐆᐦ ᐱᒫᒋᐦᐅᔭᐣ, ᓇᒨᔭ ᐁᑯᓂ ᑳ ᐊᑖᒥᑖᐣ.

ᐁᑯᓯ ᑮ ᐃᑌᐧᐤ, ᐁᐊᐧᑯ ᐊᐊᐧ ᑳ ᑮ ᐯ ᐱᒧᐦᑌᐢᑕᒪᐋᐧᐟ ᑭᐦᒋ ᐅᑭᒫᐢᑫᐧᐊᐧ,»

ᑮ ᐃᑌᐧᐤ ᒫᓇ ᑳ ᑮ ᐅᔫᐦᑖᐄᐧᔭᐣ, ᐊᐩ ᐋᑐᑕᐦᑭ ᐁᐊᐧᑯ ᐆᒪ.

"ᐋᐤ, ᐁ ᑖᐯᐧᔭᐣ ᒌ ᐆᒪ, ᑳᑭᑫ ᐁᑯᓯ ᑲ ᐃᓯ ᐸᒥᐦᐃᔭᐣ.

ᑮ ᐃᑌᐤ ᐊᓂᐦᐃ,

ᑮᐢᐱᐣ ᑭᑖᐸᐧᐣ, ᐁᐊᐧᑯ ᐆᒪ ᑭᑲ ᒥᒋᒥᓀᐣ ᐅᐢᑭᒋᐩ, ᐁ ᑖᐯᐧᔭᐣ ᒌ ᐆᒪ
ᑳ ᐃᓯ ᐊᓯᑕᒪᐃᐧᔮᕽ – ᐁᐦᐋ, ᐋᐦᐴ ᓇᒨᔭ. –
ᐁᐦᐊ.

ᐁ ᐃᑌᐧᔨᐟ, ᐁᑯᑕ ᑳ ᑮ ᑕᐦᑯᓇᒨᐦᐋᒋᐠ, ᐁᐊᐧᑯ ᐆᒪ ᐅᐢᑭᒋᐩ ᐁ ᑮ ᐅᑎᓇᕽ,

"ᐋᐤ. ᓇᒨᔭ ᐊᐃᐧᔭᐠ ᐄᐧᐦᑳᐨ ᑲ ᑲᐢᑭᐦᑖᐤ ᐁ ᓃᓱᑲᑌᐟ ᐊᔨᓯᔨᓂᐤ,
ᑲ ᐲᑯᓈᕽ ᑖᓂᓯ ᐁ ᐃᓯ ᐊᓯᑕᒫᑕᑯᐠ. ᓇᒨᔭ ᐄᐧᐦᑳᐨ
ᑲ ᑌᐱᓀᐦᐊᒫᑎᐣ ᑭᑕᐢᑭᐩ, ᑳᑭᑫ ᑲ ᐱᒥ ᑎᐸᐦᐊᒫᑖᐣ. ᓇᒨᔭ, ᓇᒨᔭ
ᐊᐩ ᐊᑖᒪᐢᑲᒥᐠ ᑳ ᐊᑖᒥᑖᐣ ᐆᒪ ᐊᐢᑭᐩ, ᐯᔭᐠ ᒥᓯᐟ ᐃᑕ
ᑲ ᐅᐦᒋ ᐱᒫᒋᐦᐅᐋᐧᑫᐟ ᐋᐧᐱᐢᑭ ᐃᐧᔮᐢ, ᐁᐊᐧᑯ ᐆᒪ ᑳ ᐊᑖᒥᑖᐣ.
"ᐋᐤ, ᐆᑕ ᐅᐦᒋ, ᑮᑲᐧᐩ ᐊᐩ ᐊᑖᒪᐢᑲᒥᐠ ᐁ ᓲᓂᔮᐃᐧᐠ, ᑲ ᓂᓯᑐᐦᑕᕽ,
ᐁᐊᐧᑯ ᐆᒪ ᐯᔭᐠ ᓀᐦᐃᔭᐤ ᐄᐧᑭ ᐁ ᐱᒥ ᐅᐦᑎᓯᐟ,

ᐁᑯᓯ ᐁᓴ ᑳ ᐃᑌᐧᐟ, ᐁᐊᐧᑯ ᐊᐊᐧ ᑳ ᐯ ᐊᑖᐁᐧᐢᑕᒪᐋᐧᐟ,

ᐁᑲᐧ ᐁᐊᐧᑯ ᐆᒪ, ᑳ ᐃᑕᒫᐣ, ᑳ ᑲᑫᐧᒋᒥᔭᐣ, ᐁᑳᔭ ᐄᐧᐦᑳᐨ
ᑲ ᑮ ᐲᑯᓈᕽ ᐊᐃᐧᔭᐠ, ᑖᐯᐧ. ᑖᐯᐧ. ᓇᒨᔭ ᑲ ᑮ ᐲᑯᓈᑦ. ᐁᐊᐧᑯ
ᐆᒪ ᑳ ᐃᑌᐧᔭᐣ, ᓇᒨᔭ ᓂᐱᐩ, ᓇᒨᔭ ᓵᑲᐦᐃᑲᓇ ᑳ ᐊᑖᒥᑖᐣ, ᓇᒨᔭ
ᑭᓱᓴᐤ, ᑫᑎᐢᐠ ᐱᑯ, ᑲ ᐆᐦ ᐱᒫᒋᐦᐅᐟ ᐆᒪ ᐊᐢᑭᐩ, ᐋᐧᐱᐢᑭ ᐃᐧᔮᐢ.
ᐃᑕ ᐁ ᐅᑎᓇᐢᑫᐟ, ᑭᑲ ᐅᔫᐦᑖᐤ ᒨᓇᐦᐃᐹᐣ, ᐁᐊᐧᑯ ᐊᓂᒪ
ᑫ ᐋᐸᒋᐦᑖᐟ ᓂᐱᐩ. ᐋ, ᐁᐊᐧᑯ ᐅᐦᒋ, ᓇᒨᔭ ᓵᑲᐦᐃᑲᓇ
ᑳ ᐊᑖᒥᑖᐣ, ᑳ ᐃᑎᑖᐣ, ᓇᒨᔭ ᒦᓇ ᐊᓯᓃᐊᐧᒋᐩ ᐆᒪ ᑳ ᐊᑖᒥᑖᐣ,
ᐁᐊᐧᑯ ᐆᒪ ᐱᑯ, ᑳ ᐊᑖᒥᑖᐣ ᐆᒪ, ᐃᑕ ᑲ ᐆᐦ ᐱᒫᒋᐦᐅᐟ
ᐋᐧᐱᐢᑭ ᐃᐧᔮᐢ.

ᐁᑯᓯ ᐁᓴ ᑮ ᐃᓯ ᐊᓱᑕᒫᑲᐧᐠ, ᐁᑯᓂ ᐆᐦᐃ.

[6] ᐁᐊᐧᑯ ᐅᐦᒋ, ᐁᐊᐧᑯ ᑳ ᑮ ᐋᐸᒋᐦᑖᒋᐠ, «ᐆᑌ ᑫ ᓃᑳᓂᐃᐧᐠ, ᒫᒥᐢᑰᒋᑳᑌᑭ, ᐁᐊᐧᑯ ᐆᒪ ᓀᐦᐃᔭᐤ ᐅᒪᓯᓇᐦᐃᑲᐣ, ᑳ ᑕᐦᑯᓇᕽ ᐊᐊᐧ, ᐁ ᓇᐢᑯᑕᕽ, ᐊᓂᒪ ᑳ ᐃᓯ ᐊᓱᑕᒫᑯᔭᕽ, ᐁᑳᔭ ᐄᐧᐦᑳᐨ ᐊᐃᐧᔭᐠ ᑲ ᑮ ᐲᑯᓇᕽ.»
ᐁᑯᓯ ᐁᓴ ᑮ ᐃᑌᐧᐊᐧᐠ ᑭᓭᔨᓂᐊᐧᐠ ᐆᑭ.

"ᐋᐤ, ᐁᑯᓯ ᐁᑲᐧ, ᐁᐊᐧᑯ ᐆᒪ ᑳ ᐃᓯ ᐊᓱᑕᒫᑕᑯᐠ, ᑳᑭᑫ, ᐃᐢᑯᔨᑯᕽ ᐲᓯᒼ ᑲ ᐱᒧᐦᑌᐟ, ᐃᐢᑯᔨᑯᕽ ᓰᐱᐩ ᑲ ᐱᒥᒋᐊᐧᕽ, ᐃᐢᑯᔨᑯᕽ ᒪᐢᑯᓯᔭ ᑫ ᓵᑭᑭᐦᑭ, ᐁᑯᐢᐲ ᐃᐢᑯ ᑲ ᐱᒧᐦᑌᒪᑲᐣ ᐆᒪ ᑳ ᐃᓯ ᐊᓱᑕᒫᑖᐣ,

ᐁᑯᓯ ᐁᓴ ᑳ ᑮ ᐃᑎᐦᒋᐠ ᐆᑭ, ᑭᒧᓲᒥᓇᐊᐧᐠ. – ᐁᐊᐧᑯ ᐆᒪ ᐁᑲᐧ, ᐊᓅᐦᐨ ᐁᑲᐧ, ᐋᐧᐱᐢᑭ ᐃᐧᔮᐢ ᑳ ᒥᑯᐢᑳᒋᐦᑖᐟ, ᐲᑐᐢ ᐁ ᐄᐧ ᑲᑫᐧ ᐃᑕᑭᒥᑯᔭᕽ. –

[7] «"ᐋᐤ, ᐁᑯᑕ ᐁᓴ ᐁᑲᐧ ᒦᓇ ᑳ ᑮ ᐲᑭᐢᑫᐧᐟ ᐁᐊᐧᑯ ᐊᐊᐧ ᑭᓭᔨᓂᐤ,» ᑮ ᐃᑌᐧᐤ ᒫᓇ ᑳ ᑮ ᐅᔫᐦᑖᐄᐧᔮᐣ. «ᐋᑕ ᐊᓂ ᒥᐢᑕᐦᐃ ᓂᒥᐦᑖᑌᐣ, ᓂᒥᐦᑖᑌᐣ ᐆᒪ, ᑭᑕᐢᑮᓇᐤ ᐁ ᑮ ᒥᔨᑯᔭᕽ, ᑰᐦᑖᐄᐧᓇᐤ ᐃᑕ ᑳ ᐆᐦ ᐱᒫᑎᓯᔭᕽ, ᑳ ᐊᑖᐋᐧᑫᕽ ᐆᒪ ᑭᑕᐢᑮᓇᐤ. ᒫᑲ, ᐁᑳ ᐁᑯᓯ ᑫ ᐃᐦᑭᕽ, ᐆᑌ ᐋᐧᐱᐢᑭ ᐃᐧᔮᐢ ᐊᑎ ᓵᑲᐢᑭᓀᒋ, ᐁᑯᑕ ᐆᒪ ᑭᔦ ᐅᐦᒋᐦᐃᑯᔭᕽ ᐊᐢᑭᐩ, ᑮ ᐃᑌᐧᐤ ᐁᓴ ᐁᐊᐧᑯ ᑭᓭᔨᓂᐤ,» ᑮ ᐃᑌᐧᐤ ᒫᓇ ᑳ ᑮ ᐅᔫᐦᑖᐄᐧᔮᐣ. ᐁᐊᐧᑯ ᐆᒪ ᒣᑳᐧᐨ ᐁᑲᐧ.

[8] ᑭᔮᒼ ᐆᑕ ᐊᐊᐧᓵᔨᕽ, ᑫᐧᐢᑲᐦᒑᕽ, ᐆᒪ ᐃᑌ ᐅᓴᐦᒑᕽ ᑫᐧᐢᑳᔨᕽ
ᒪ ᒪᑌᐧᐁᐧᑭ, ᓇᒨᔭ ᐄᐧᐦᑳᐨ ᑲ ᐅᑎᓈᐤ ᓀᐦᐃᔭᐃᐧ ᐊᔨᓯᔨᓂᐤ,
ᓅᑎᓂᑐᐃᐧᓂᕽ ᑲ ᐃᑎᓯᓂᐦᐟ,
ᐁᑯᓯ ᐁᓴ ᒦᓇ ᐁ ᑮ ᐃᓯ ᐊᓱᑕᒫᑫᐟ.

ᐁᑯᓂ ᐆᐦᐃ ᑕᐦᑐ ᑮᑲᐧᐩ ᑳ ᐊᓱᑕᒫᑖᐣ, ᑳᑭᑫ ᐁᐊᐧᑯ ᑲ ᐱᒥᐸᔨᐤ, ᐁᑯᓯ ᐁᓴ ᐁ ᑮ ᐃᓯ ᐊᓱᑕᒫᐦᐟ ᐁᐊᐧᑯ ᐊᐊᐧ ᓀᐦᐃᔭᐤ ᑳ ᑮ ᐊᑖᐋᐧᑫᐟ ᑭᑕᐢᑮᓇᐤ.

[9] ᐋ, ᐁᐊᐧᑯ ᐊᓂᒪ, ᐁᑯᓯ ᐁ ᐃᑖᑐᑕᒫᐣ, ᓃᐢᑕ ᐁ ᑮ ᐃᑖᒋᒧᐢᑕᐃᐧᐟ ᑳ ᑮ ᐅᔫᐦᑖᐄᐧᔮᐣ, ᒪᑖᐧᐣ ᒌ ᑲᐧᔮᐢᐠ ᓂᑖᑐᑌᐣ ᐁᐊᐧᑯ ᐆᒪ, ᑖᓂᓯ

ᐁ ᑮ ᐃᑖᒋᒧᐢᑕᐏᐟ ᒫᓇ, ᐁᐘᑯ ᐆᒪ ᑳ ᐋᒋᒧᐢᑕᐘᑭᐠ ᐆᑭ ᓅᓯᓯᒪᐠ.

[10] ᒫᑲ ᒥᐢᑕᐦᐃ ᑲ ᒥᔮᐧᓯᐣ, ᐁᐘᑯ ᐆᒪ ᑳ ᐑ ᑖᐦᑯᑕᒥᕽ,
ᓂᑯᑖᐧᓯᐠ ᑎᐸᐦᐊᒫᑐᐏᐣ, ᑲ ᐃᐦᑕᑯᐟ ᐁᑯᑕ ᑫᐦᑌ ᐋᔭ, ᐊᐦᐴ ᓅᑎᑫᐧᐤ, ᐄᐧᐢᑕ
ᐁ ᒥᔮᐧᓯᓂᔩᐠ ᑮᑲᐧᐩ ᐁ ᑮ ᐯᑖᐟ, ᐁᑯᑕ ᑲ ᑕᑲᐧᐢᑖᐟ ᐄᐧᐢᑕ ᐆᑖᒋᒧᐏᐣ,
ᑲ ᒫᒥᑐᓀᔩᒫᔭᐦᑯᐠ ᑰᓯᓯᒥᓇᐚᐠ. ᓵᑯᒋᐦᐃᑯᔭᐦᑯ ᐚᐱᐢᑭ ᐏᔮᐢ
ᑳ ᐑ ᐃᑕᔨᐚᑎᑯᔭᕽ, ᒥᐢᑕᐦᐃ ᑭᑲ ᑭᑎᒫᑭᓯᓈᓇᐤ, ᓇᒨᔭ ᐱᑯ ᑫᐦᑌ ᐊᔭ
ᑲ ᑭᑎᒫᑭᓯᐟ, ᐊᐚᓯᓴᐠ ᐆᑭ ᑳ ᐯ ᓇᔭᐘᒋᑭᒋᐠ, ᐁᑯᓂᐠ ᐆᑭ ᑫ ᑭᑎᒫᑭᓯᒋᐠ,
ᐁᑯᓯ ᒫᓇ ᐁ ᐃᑌᔩᐦᑕᒫᐣ ᓂᔭ.

[11] "ᐋᐤ, ᐁᑯᓯ ᐆᒪ ᐁ ᐃᑖᒋᒧᐢᑕᐘᑭᐠ ᐆᑭ, ᑳ ᓂᑕᐍᔩᐦᑕᐦᑭᐠ ᑮᑲᐧᐩ
ᑲ ᐋᒋᒧᐢᑕᐘᑭᐠ. ᒥᐢᑕᐦᐃ ᑲ ᑮ ᒥᔮᐧᓯᓅᐸᐣ, ᑲ ᑮ ᒪᔨᓂᐸᔩᐦᑖᕽ ᐊᓂᒪ ᐆᑕ
ᐅᐢᑭᒋᐩ, ᐃᑕ ᐊᓂᒪ ᑳ ᑮ ᐊᐢᐱᑐᓈᒧᐟ ᑭᓭᔨᓂᐤ.

[12] ᐁᐘᑯ ᐆᒪ ᐃᐢᑫᐧᔮᐨ ᐁ ᐋᐸᑕᕽ, ᐅᐢᑭᒋᐩ, ᐃᑕ ᐁ ᑮ ᓇᑭᐢᑲᒧᐦᑕᑕᒫᐦᐟ
ᐚᐱᐢᑭ ᐏᔮᐢ, ᐁᐘᑯ ᐆᒪ ᐯᐦᐅᓈᓂᕽ ᑳ ᐃᑕᒥᕽ, ᐁᑯᑕ ᑳ ᑮ ᐱᒧᐦᑕᑖᒋᐠ
ᐹᐧᑕᐠ ᐁᐘᑯ ᐆᒪ ᐅᐢᑭᒋᐩ, ᐁᑯᑕ ᐃᐢᑫᐧᔮᐨ ᐁ ᐋᐸᑕᕽ.

[13] "ᐋᐤ, ᐁᑯᓯ ᐱᑯ ᐁ ᐃᓯ ᑭᐢᑫᔩᐦᑕᒫᐣ ᐆᒪ ᑳ ᐃᑖᑐᑕᒫᐣ.

* * *

[14] ᐁᐘᑯ ᐆᒪ, ᑳ ᓂᑕᐍᔩᐦᑕᐦᑭᐠ, ᑲ ᐋᒋᒧᐢᑕᐘᑭᐠ, ᑖᓂᓯ
ᐁ ᑮ ᐃᓯ ᐊᓱᑕᒫᐦᐟ,

ᐁᐘᑯ ᐆᒪ ᑭᐢᑭᓄᐦᐊᒫᑐᐏᑲᒥᐠ ᑳ ᐊᓱᑕᒫᑖᐣ, ᐁᑯᑕ
ᑲ ᑭᐢᑭᓄᐦᐊᒫᐚᐤ, ᑭᑕᐚᓯᒥᐢ ᑰᓯᓯᐡ, ᐁᐘᑯ ᐁᑲᐧ ᑮᓰᐦᑖᒋ,
ᐅᑭᐢᑭᓄᐦᐊᒫᓱᐏᐣ, ᐁᐘᑯ ᐁᑲᐧ ᓂᑯᑖᐧᓱᓵᑊ ᐁ ᐃᑕᐦᑐᐱᐳᓀᐧᒋᐠ, ᐁᑯᑕ
ᐆᒪ ᑫ ᐸᑭᑎᓂᐦᐟ. ᐁᑯᑕ ᐆᒪ ᐁᑲᐧ, ᑫ ᐱᒥ ᐄᐧᒋᐦᐃᐦᐟ,
ᐯᔭᑲᐧᐦᐱᑌᐤ ᒥᓴᑎᒪᐧ ᑲ ᒥᔭᐤ, ᑭᐢᑭᓄᐦᐊᒫᐚᑲᐣ, ᐋᐸᒋᐦᒋᑲᓇ ᐁᑯᑕ

ᐅᐦᒋ ᑲ ᒥᔮᐤ. "ᐋᐤ, ᐆᑕ ᐅᐦᒋ ᒧᐢᑐᓴᐧ ᑲ ᒥᔭᐤ, ᑲ ᐅᐦᐱᑭᐦᑕᒫᓱᐟ,

ᑲ ᐆᐦ ᐱᒫᒋᐦᐅᐟ.

ᐁᑯᓯ ᐁᓴ ᐁᑲᐧ ᐊᓂᒪ ᒦᓇ ᐁ ᑮ ᐃᓯ ᐊᓱᑕᒫᐦᐟ, ᐁᑯᓯ ᐁᐊᐧᑯ ᐁᑲᐧ, ᑳᔮᓴᐢ

ᑳ ᐴᓂᐸᔨᐠ ᐁᐊᐧᑯ ᐆᒪ, ᐁᑯᓯ ᐁ ᑮ ᐃᓯ ᐄᐧᒋᐦᐃᐦᐟ ᐊᔨᓯᔨᓂᐤ.

"ᐋᐤ, ᐁᑲᐧ ᑭᔭ ᐅᑭᒫᐦᑳᐣ, ᑲ ᐸᐹᒥ ᓂᑕᐋᐧᐸᒪᒋᐠ ᑭᑎᔨᓃᒪᐠ,

ᑲ ᒥᔨᑲᐃᐧᐣ ᐯᔭᐠ ᒥᓴᑎᒼ, ᐅᒑᐸᓈᐢᑯᐢ ᑭᑲ ᐋᐸᒋᐦᐊᐟ, ᐁᐊᐧᑯ ᐊᓂ

ᑭᑲ ᐸᐹᒥ ᓂᑕᐋᐧᐸᒪᒋᐠ ᑭᑎᔨᓃᒪᐠ.

ᐅᑭᒫᐦᑳᐣ ᑳ ᐃᓯᔨᐦᑳᓱᐟ, ᐁᑯᓯ ᐁᓴ ᑳ ᐃᓯ ᐊᓱᑕᒫᐦᐟ.

"ᐋᐤ, ᐁᑲᐧ ᐁᐊᐧᑯ ᐆᒪ, ᑳ ᒥᔨᑖᐣ ᑭᐢᑭᓄᐦᐊᒫᑐᐃᐧᑲᒥᐠ ᑳ ᐊᓱᑕᒫᑖᐣ,

ᐁᐊᐧᑯ, ᓇᒨᔭ ᐄᐧᐦᑳᐨ ᑲ ᑭᓯᐲᒪᑲᐣ, ᐁᐊᐧᑯ ᐆᒪ ᒪᐢᑭᐦᑮᐃᐧᐊᐧᒋᐢ

ᑳ ᐊᓱᑕᒫᑖᐣ, ᓇᒨᔭ ᐄᐧᐦᑳᐨ ᑲ ᑎᐸᐦᐁᐣ ᒪᐢᑭᐦᑭᐩ ᐃᑕ

ᑲ ᐆᐦ ᐸᒥᐦᐃᐢᐠ ᒪᐢᑭᐦᑮᐃᐧᔨᓂᐤ.

ᐁᑯᓯ ᐁᓴ ᑳ ᐃᓯ ᐊᓱᑕᒫᐦᐟ ᒦᓇ, ᐁᐊᐧᑯ ᐊᐊᐧ ᑳ ᑮ ᐃᐧᔨᐦᒋᑫᐟ ᑭᒧᓲᒥᓇᐤ.

"ᐋᐤ, ᐁᑲᐧ, ᐁᐊᐧᑯ ᐊᐊᐧ ᑳ ᒥᔨᑖᐣ ᓲᓂᔮᐃᐧᑭᒫᐤ, ᐁᐊᐧᑯ ᐊᐊᐧ

ᑲ ᐄᐧᑕᑐᐢᑫᒪᐟ, ᑮᑲᐧᐩ ᐃᑕ ᐁ ᐊᐧᐋᐧᓀᔩᐦᑕᒥᐦᐃᑯᔭᐣ, ᐁᐊᐧᑯ ᐊᐊᐧ

ᑲ ᑑᑕᒫᐠ.

"ᐋᐤ, ᐁᑲᐧ ᒦᓇ ᐊᐊᐧ ᒪᓯᓇᐦᐃᑫᓰᐢ ᑳ ᒥᔨᑖᐣ, ᐁᐊᐧᑯ ᐁᑲᐧ

ᒦᓇ ᑲ ᐊᑐᐢᑳᐢᐠ, ᑲ ᒪᓯᓇᐦᐃᑫᐢᑕᒫᐢᐠ, ᒪᓯᓇᐦᐃᑲᓇ ᑲ ᐅᓰᐦᑖᐟ,

ᐁᐊᐧᑯ ᒦᓇ ᐊᐊᐧ ᑳ ᒥᔨᑖᐣ.

"ᐋᐤ, ᐁᑲᐧ ᑯᑕᐠ, ᐁᐊᐧᑯ ᐁᑲᐧ ᐅᑭᐢᑎᑫᐃᐧᔨᓂᐤ

ᑳ ᐃᓯᔨᐦᑳᓱᐟ, ᐁᐊᐧᑯ ᐁᑲᐧ ᑲ ᑭᐢᑭᓄᐦᐊᒪᐋᐧᐟ ᑭᑕᐋᐧᓯᒥᓴ ᑯᓯᓯᒪ

ᑖᓂᓯ ᑲ ᐃᓯ ᐱᒫᒋᐦᐅᔨᐟ, ᐁᐊᐧᑯ ᐆᒪ ᑭᐢᑎᑫᐃᐧ ᐱᒫᒋᐦᐅᐃᐧᐣ, ᐁᐊᐧᑯ

ᒦᓇ ᑳ ᒥᔨᑖᐣ.

"ᐋᐤ, ᐁᑲᐧ ᑯᑕᐠ, ᐁᐊᐧᑯ ᐁᑲᐧ, ᐃᐧᔭᐦᐃᓱᐤ ᑲ ᐃᓯᔨᐦᑳᓱᐤ,

ᑮᑲᐧᐩ ᑭᑖᐸᒋᐦᒋᑲᐣ ᐁ ᐲᑯᐸᔨᐠ, ᐃᐧᔭ ᐊᓇ ᐁᑲᐧ ᐁᑯᑕ ᑫ ᑮᔩᐦᑕᒫᐢᐠ,

ᐁᐊᐧᑯ ᐆᒪ ᑲ ᓈᓇᐹᒋᐦᑖᐟ,

ᐁᑯᓯ ᐁᓴ ᑳ ᐃᑎᐦᐟ.

"ᐋᐤ, ᐁᑲᐧ ᐁᐊᐧᑯ ᐆᒪ, ᑭᐸᒥᐦᐃᑯᐃᐧᐣ, ᐊᓴᐦᑐᐃᐧᐣ, ᐋ, ᐁᑯᑕ ᐁᑲᐧ

ᑭᒥᔨᑎᐣ ᒦᓇ ᐅᑕᓴᐦᑫᐤ, ᐁᐊᐧᑯ ᐆᒪ, ᑲ ᐸᒥᐦᐋᐟ ᐊᔨᓯᔨᓂᐊᐧ,

ᑭᑲ ᐊᓴᒫᐟ, ᐁᐊᐧᑯ ᒦᓇ ᐁ ᐊᓱᑕᒫᑖᐣ.

"ᐋᐤ, ᐁᑲᐧ, ᐅᑎᑌᐧᐢᑕᒫᑫᐤ ᒦᓇ ᑭᑕᓱᑕᒫᑎᐣ, ᐃᑕ ᐁ ᐄᐧ ᐄᐧᒋ ᐲᑭᐢᑫᐧᒪᐟ ᐋᐧᐱᐢᑭ ᐃᐧᔮᐢ, ᐁᐊᐧᑯ ᐊᓇ ᑭᓯ ᐃᑌᐧᐢᑕᒫᐢᐠ, ᐁᑯᓯ ᐁᓴ ᒦᓇ ᑳ ᐃᓯ ᐊᓱᑕᒫᐦᐟ.

"ᐋᐤ, ᐁᑲᐧ ᑯᑕᐠ, ᐁᐊᐧᑯ ᐁᑲᐧ ᐊᐊᐧ ᓯᒫᑲᓂᐢ, ᑳ ᒥᔭᑖᐣ, ᑲ ᓈᑲᑑᐦᑫᐟ ᑭᑕᐢᑭᐩ, ᐃᑕ ᑮᑲᐧᐩ ᐁ ᓵᑰᐦᐃᑯᔭᐣ ᐁᑯᑕ ᐁᑲᐧ, ᐃᐧᔭ ᐁᑲᐧ, ᑲ ᓈᑕᒫᐠ ᑮᑲᐧᐩ, ᑲ ᐱᒥᐸᔨᐦᑖᐟ ᐆᒪ ᑭᑕᐢᑮᐦᑳᐣ, ᐁᑯᓯ ᐁᓴ ᒦᓇ ᐁ ᑮ ᐃᓯ ᐊᓱᑕᒫᐦᐟ.

[15] ᐁᐊᐧᑯ ᐆᒪ ᑳ ᓂᑕᐍᔨᐦᑕᐦᑭᐠ ᑲ ᐋᓂᐢᑫ ᐋᑐᑕᒫᐣ, ᐁᑯᓯ ᒫᓇ ᐁ ᑮ ᐃᑖᒋᒧᐢᑕᐏᐟ ᑳ ᑮ ᐆᔩᐦᑖᐄᐧᔮᐣ, ᐁᑯᓂ ᐆᐦᐃ ᐁ ᑮ ᒥᔭᑲᐏᔮᕽ ᑮᑲᐧᐩ ᑭᑲ ᐋᐸᒋᐦᑖᔮᕽ,

ᑭᔭ ᐱᑯ, ᑫ ᐲᑯᓇᒫᓱᔭᐣ, ᑭᑕᓱᑕᒫᑯᐏᐣ.

ᐁᐊᐧᑯ ᐆᒪ ᑳ ᑮ ᐯ ᐄᐧᐦᑕᐦᑭᐠ, ᐁᐊᐧᑯ ᐁᑲᐧ ᒣᑳᐧᐨ ᐆᒪ, ᒥᐢᑕᐦᐃ ᑳ ᐲᑭᐢᑫᐧᒨᐦᐃᑯᔭᕽ.

[16] ᐁᑯᓯ ᐱᑯ ᐁ ᐃᓯ ᑭᐢᑫᔨᐦᑕᒫᐣ, ᐁᐊᐧᑯ ᐆᒪ ᑳ ᓂᑕᐍᔨᐦᑕᐦᑭᐠ ᑲ ᐋᑐᑕᒫᐣ. ᐋ, ᐁᑯᓯ.

7 ᑭᓭᔨᓃᐏ ᐲᑭᐢᑫᐧᐏᐣ

[1] ᐁᐘᑯ ᐆᒪ, ᑳ ᐑ ᑖᐦᑰᑕᒫᐣ, ᑲ ᓂᑕᐍᔨᐦᑕᐦᑭᐠ ᑲ ᑖᐦᑰᑕᒫᐣ, ᑖᓂᓯ ᐊᐘ ᐁ ᐃᑕᑭᓱᐟ ᐊᐘ ᒋᐢᑌᒫᐤ, ᐄᐦ. ᑖᓂᓯ ᐆᒪ ᐁ ᐃᑕᑭᐦᑌᐠ ᐆᒪ ᐍᐱᓈᓱᐣ. ᐁ ᓂᑕᐏ ᑭᐢᑫᔨᐦᑕᕽ ᑮᑲᐧᐩ, ᐅᐢᑳᔭ, ᐊᐦᐴ ᐃᑖᐢᑯᓂᑫᐏᐣ, ᐊᐦᐴ ᑳ ᓂᑕᐏ ᑮᐢᑭᓴᒪᐚᐟ ᑫᐦᑌ ᐊᔭ, ᑳ ᐑ ᓃᒥᓂᑫᐟ ᐆᒪ ᑮᓯᑌᐤ, ᐁᑯᓂ ᐆᐦᐃ ᐁ ᓃᑳᓄᐦᑕᑖᐟ ᐆᐦᐃ, ᑲ ᑭᑎᒫᑭᐦᑖᑯᐟ ᑭᓭᔨᓂᐘ, ᑳ ᓂᑕᐏ ᑮᐢᑭᓴᒪᐚᐟ. ᐁᑲᐧ ᐁᑯᓂ ᐆᐦᐃ, ᑳ ᑮ ᐅᓰᐦᐋᐟ ᑰᐦᑖᐑᓇᐤ, ᒋᐢᑌᒫᐤ ᑲ ᓃᑳᓂᐟ, ᐁ ᑮ ᒪᓂᑐᐘᑭᒫᐟ ᐆᐦᐃ, ᒋᐢᑌᒫᐘ, ᐁᐘᑯ ᐅᐦᒋ ᑳ ᐆᐦ ᓃᑳᓃᐦᐃᐦᐟ ᐊᐘ ᒋᐢᑌᒫᐤ, ᓃᑳᐣ, ᑖᓂᓯ ᐁ ᐃᓯ ᒫᒥᓰᑐᑖᐦᐟ ᑫᐦᑌ ᐊᔭ, ᐊᐦᐴ ᓅᑎᑫᐧᐤ, ᑳ ᐑ ᓈᒋᓀᐦᐊᒪᐚᐟ ᒪᐢᑭᐦᑭᐩ, «ᐁᑯᓂ ᐱᑕ ᐆᐦᐃ ᓃᑳᐣ, ᐁᑯᓂ ᐆᐦᐃ ᐁ ᓃᑳᓄᐦᑌᒪᑲᐦᑭ,» ᑳ ᑮ ᐃᑌᐧᒋᐠ ᑫᐦᑌ ᐊᔭᐠ. ᐁᑯᓯ ᐏᔭ ᐁᐘᑯ, ᐁ ᐃᓯ ᑭᐢᑫᔨᐦᑕᒫᐣ ᐆᒪ.

[2] ᐁᑲᐧ ᐆᒪ ᑯᑕᐠ, ᐁᐘᑯ ᐁᑲᐧ, ᑳ ᓅᐦᑌ ᑭᐢᑫᔨᐦᑕᐦᑭᐠ, ᑖᓂᓯ ᐆᒪ ᐁ ᐃᑌᐧᒪᑲᕽ ᐑᐦᑲᐢᐠ, ᑖᓀᐦᑭ ᐊᓂᒫ ᑳ ᐆᐦ ᐋᐸᑕᕽ ᐑᐦᑲᐢᐠ, ᑖᓀᐦᑭ ᒥᓈ ᑳ ᐆᐦ ᐊᐱᐦᑳᑌᐠ, ᑲ ᓂᐢᑕᐧᐱᐦᑳᑕᒥᕽ, «ᐁ ᓂᐢᑎᓂᔨᑭ ᐁᑯᑕ ᐅᓂᑐᑕᒫᐏᓇ ᐑᐦᑲᐢᑯᔨᓂᐤ,» ᑳ ᑮ ᐃᑌᐧᒋᐠ ᑭᓭᔨᓂᐘᐠ. «ᐦᐋᐤ, ᐁᑯᓂ ᐆᐦᐃ, ᑲ ᐆᐦ ᓴᐍᔨᒥᑎᐣ ᓃᐢᑕ ᐆᒪ, ᑭᔦ ᐃᓯ ᐊᐱᐦᑳᑕᒪᐣ ᐆᒪ ᐑᐦᑲᐢᐠ, ᐁᑯᑕ ᐊᓂ ᑭᔦ ᐊᐱᐦᑳᑕᒪᐘᐟ ᑭᑕᐚᓯᒥᐢ, ᐊᓂᒪ ᐅᐱᒫᑎᓯᐏᐣ ᐊᐚᐢᑲ ᒫᒥᑐᓀᔨᐦᒋᑲᐣ,» ᐁᑯᓯ ᐁᓭ ᐁ ᑮ ᐃᑌᐧᐟ ᐊᐘ ᐑᐦᑲᐢᑯᔨᓂᐤ. «ᐦᐋᐤ, ᑲ ᐅᒋᐦᒋᐢᑳᒪᑲᐣ, ᐃᑌ ᐁ ᐱᒥ ᐚᐦ ᐅᐦᐸᐦᑌᓇᒪᐣ ᑭᐑᐦᑲᐢᑯᐨ, ᐃᑕ ᐁ ᑳᑮᓯᒍᔭᐣ, ᐁᐘᑯ ᐆᒪ ᑭᔦ ᐃᑌᐧᐢᑕᒫᑯᔭᐣ ᐑᐦᑲᐢᐠ, ᐁᐘᑯ ᐅᐦᒋ ᒪᓈᒋᐦᑖ. ᐁ ᒪᓈᒋᐦᑖᔭᐣ ᐆᒪ ᑭᐑᐦᑲᐢᑯᐨ, ᑳ ᐃᓯ ᒥᔮᐧᓯᐠ ᑭᐦᒋ ᐅᑳᐏᒫᐤ ᑳ ᓵᑳᐘᓀᐦᑖᐟ, ᐁᑯᓯ ᐊᓂ ᑭᑲ ᐃᑎᐦᑖᑲᐧᐣ ᑭᓂᑐᑕᒫᐏᐣ,» ᐁᑯᓯ ᐆᒪ ᐁ ᑮ ᐃᑎᐦᒋᐠ ᐁᓭ, ᓂᐢᑕᒣᒫᑲᓇᐠ ᑮᑲᐧᐩ, ᐁᐘᑯ ᐆᒪ ᐑᐦᑲᐢᐠ ᐅᐦᒋ, ᑳ ᐆᐦ ᐋᐸᑕᕽ, ᐁᐘᑯ ᐆᒪ ᑳ ᓅᐦᑌ ᑭᐢᑫᔨᐦᑕᐦᑭᐠ.

[3] ᐦᐋᐤ, ᐁᑲᐧ ᐁᐘᑯ ᐆᒪ, ᑮᑳᐧᔨ ᐊᓂᒪ, ᐄᐘᓂᔩᐦᐃᓱᐏᐣ, ᑲᑳᐧᑕᑭᐦᐅᐏᐣ ᑳ ᐆᐦ ᐋᐸᑕᕽ, ᐁ ᓅᐦᑌ ᑖᐯᐧᐟ ᐊᔨᓯᔨᓂᐤ ᐁ ᓂᑐᑕᒫᐟ, ᐁ ᒫᑯᐦᐃᑯᐟ ᑮᑲᐧᐩ ᐋᐦᑯᓯᐏᐣ, ᐁᑯᑕ ᐁᑲᐧ ᑳ ᑮ ᑲᑳᐧᑕᑭᐦᐃᓱᐟ. ᐁ ᓂᑐᑕᒫᐟ

ᑲ ᑭᑎᒫᑭᐦᑖᑯᐟ ᐋᑕᔫᐦᑲᓇ, ᑮᑲᐧᐩ ᐁ ᓂᑐᑕᒪᐋᐧᐟ, ᑲ ᓂᓯᑕᐃᐧᓇᕽ ᐅᑭᓴᐋᐧᑎᓯᐃᐧᓂᔨᐤ, ᐁᐊᐧᑯ ᐅᐦᒋ ᐊᓂᒪ ᑳ ᐆᐦ ᑲᑳᐧᑕᑭᐦᐃᓱᐟ, ᑖᐱᐢᑰᐨ ᐆᒪ ᑳ ᓂᐹᑫᐧᓯᒧᕽ, ᑳ ᑲᑳᐧᑕᑭᐦᐃᓱᐟ ᐊᔨᓯᔨᓂᐤ, ᐁ ᓂᑕᐃᐧ ᐱᒫᒋᓯᐃᐧᐣ ᓈᑕᕽ, ᑲ ᑭᑎᒫᑭᐦᑖᑯᐟ, ᐃᑕ ᐁ ᐱᒧᐦᑕᐦᐋᐧᐟ ᐅᑕᐋᐧᓯᒥᓴ ᐆᓯᓯᒪ. ᐁᑯᓯ ᐆᒪ ᐁ ᐃᑌᐧᒪᑲᕽ ᐁᐊᐧᑯ.

[4] ᐦᐋᐤ, ᐁᑲᐧ ᐁᐊᐧᑯ ᐆᒪ ᐁᑲᐧ, ᒪᑐᓂᓵᐣ ᐁᑲᐧ ᑳ ᐃᓯᔩᐦᑳᑌᐠ, ᐋ, ᐁᑯᑕ ᐁᑲᐧ ᑳ ᑮ ᐃᐧᔭᑭᒫᐟ ᑭᐢᑌᓯᓇᐤ ᐄᐧᓴᐦᑫᒑᕽ, ᑭᓴ ᓈᐯᐤ ᐊᓯᓂᐩ, «ᐦᐋᐤ, ᑭᔭ ᑭᑲ ᑮᓱᐋᐧᑌᐣ, ᒪᑐᓂᓵᐣ. ᐦᐋᐤ, ᐃᑕ ᐁ ᑳᑮᓯᒧᐟ ᐊᔨᓯᔨᓂᐤ, ᐃᑕ ᐁ ᐸᑐᐋᐧᑕᕽ ᐊᓂᒪ ᐅᑳᑮᓯᒧᐃᐧᐣ, ᐦᐋᐤ, ᑮᓱᐋᐧᑕᒧᕽ. ᑮᓱᐋᐧᑕᒪᐤ, ᑲ ᑖᐯᐧᐤ. ᒫᒋᑯᑎᑕᐣ ᐆᒥᓯ ᐆᒪ ᐄᐧ ᐃᐢᐸᔨᐤ ᐄᐧ ᒣᑕᐋᐧᑳᓂᐃᐧᐤ ᐁᐊᐧᑯ ᐆᒪ, ᐁ ᒧᐢᒋ ᑭᐢᑭᓄᐋᐧᐱᒥᐠ, ᑭᐢᑭᓄᐋᐧᐱᐃᐧᐣ ᑲ ᐋᐸᑕᐣ, ᒫᑲ ᐊᓇ ᐊᔨᓯᔨᓂᐤ ᑫ ᑖᐯᐧᐋᐧᑫᔨᐦᑕᕽ ᑮᓱᐋᐧᑕᒧᕽ ᐅᑳᑮᓯᒧᐃᐧᐣ. ᐁ ᐅᐦᐹᐢᑯᓈᐟ ᐅᐢᐹᐧᑲᓇ, ᒫᐦ ᒦᓈᐧᐢᑯᓇᒪᐤ ᐊᓂᒪ, ᐅᐢᑭᒌᐋᐧᐦᑎᐠ.» ᐁᑯᓯ ᐁᓴ ᑳ ᐃᑌᐧᐟ, «ᑭᑎᒫᑭᐦᑕᐋᐧᐦᑳᐣ, ᒪᑐᓂᓵᓂᕽ ᑮᑲᐧᐩ ᓂᑐᑕᒫᐢᑭ, ᓀᐋᐧᐤ ᐱᒥ ᑖᐦᑳᐸᐋᐧᑖᒋ ᐱᒥ ᐸᑭᑎᓇᒫᐢᑭ ᓰᑲᐦᐊᓯᓈᓈᐳᐩ» – «ᐁᑯᑕ ᐊᓂ ᑫ ᐸᑲᐦᑭᐦᑕᐋᐧᐠ,» ᑮ ᐱᒥ ᐃᓯ ᓇᐢᑫᐧᐋᐧᓯᒧᐤ ᐁᓴ ᐊᐋᐧ, ᑭᓴ ᓈᐯᐤ ᐊᓯᓂᐩ. ᐁᐊᐧᑯ ᐆᒪ ᑳ ᐋᐸᑕᕽ ᑳ ᒪᑐᓂᓯᕽ, ᐱᑯ ᐃᑕ, ᑳ ᓃᑳᓂᐦᐃᐦᐟ. ᓇᓈᑐᕽ ᐁ ᐃᑎᑲᐧᒥᑯᐦᑫᕽ, ᐁ ᓂᐹᑫᐧᓯᒧᕽ ᐁ ᐲᐦᑖᐧᕽ ᐁ ᐱᐦᐁᐃᐧᓯᒧᕽ, ᐋᓴᐩ ᐁᑯᑕ ᑭᓴ ᓈᐯᐤ ᐊᓯᓂᐩ, ᐁᐊᐧᑯ ᐊᓇ ᐁ ᐅᑑᓂᐦᑳᔭᕽ, ᐁ ᐃᑌᐧᐢᑕᒫᑯᔭᕽ. ᐁᐊᐧᑯ ᐊᓂ ᑳ ᓅᐦᑌ ᑭᐢᑫᔨᐦᑕᐦᑭᐠ ᐆᑭ.

[5] ᐦᐋᐤ, ᐁᑯᓯ ᐁᐊᐧᑯ ᐃᐧᔭ ᐁ ᐃᓯ ᑭᐢᑫᔨᐦᑕᒫᐣ ᐆᒪ, ᑳ ᐃᑖᑐᑕᒫᐣ. ᐁᑲᐧ ᐁᐊᐧᑯ ᐊᐊᐧ, ᑳ ᐃᑖᐢᑯᓇᒫᐦᐟ, ᑳ ᐄᐧᐦᑯᒥᐦᐟ ᐆᒪ ᑳ ᐄᐧᐦᑯᐦᑫᐟ ᐊᔨᓯᔨᓂᐤ, ᑮ ᑯᐢᑕᒪᐧᐠ ᑲᔭᐢ ᑭᓴᔨᓂᐊᐧᐠ, ᐁᑳ ᐁᑯᑕ ᑲ ᑲᑫᐹᐦᑲᒥᑭᓯᐟ ᐊᐋᐧᓯᐢ, ᑮ ᑯᐢᑕᒪᐧᐠ, ᐊᓄᐦᐨ ᓇᒪ ᑮᑲᐧᐩ ᐁᐊᐧᑯ, ᐊᐦᐴ ᐁ ᓃᒥᓂᑫᕽ, ᑯᓂᑕ ᐁ ᐋᐧᓴᑳᑎᓴᐦᐅᑐᒋᐠ ᐊᐋᐧᓯᓴᐠ. ᐁᑳ ᑮᑲᐧᐩ ᐁ ᑭᐢᑫᔨᐦᑕᕽ ᐅᓃᑭᐦᐃᑯᒫᐤ, ᒦᓇ ᓅᑎᑫᐧᐊᐧᐠ ᐆᑭ, ᑲ ᐃᓯ ᑭᑕᐦᐊᒪᐋᐧᒋᐠ, ᐅᑕᐋᐧᓯᒥᓯᐋᐧᐊᐧ ᐆᓯᓯᒥᐋᐧᐊᐧ, ᑖᓂᓯ ᐊᓂᒪ ᑮᑲᐧᐩ ᑲ ᐃᓯ ᒪᓈᒋᐦᑖᔨᐟ. ᐁᑯᓯ ᐆᒪ ᒫᓇ ᐁ ᑮ ᐃᓯ ᐄᐧᐦᑕᒫᑲᐃᐧᔭᐣ ᓂᔭ, ᐁᐊᐧᑯ

ᐆᒪ ᑳ ᐋᒋᒧᐢᑕᐊᐧᑭᐠ. ᓇᒪ ᑮᑲᐧᐩ ᐁ ᑭᐢᑫᔨᐦᑕᒫᐣ, ᐁ ᐃᑌᐧᔮᐣ, ᒫᑲ ᑭᓭᔨᓂᐃᐧ ᐲᑭᐢᑫᐧᐃᐧᐣ ᐆᒪ ᑳ ᐋᒋᒧᐢᑕᐊᐧᑭᐠ, ᑖᓂᓯ ᐁ ᐃᐢᐸᔨᐠ.

[6] ᐋ, ᐁᑯᓯ, ᐁᐊᐧᑯ ᐊᓂᒪ ᐁ ᐃᑖᒋᒧᐢᑕᐊᐧᑭᐠ.

* * *

[7] ᑖᐯᐧ ᐊᓇ, ᓇᒨᔭ ᑲᐧᔭᐢᐠ ᐁ ᐃᓯ ᐸᒥᐦᐃᐦᐟ ᐊᐊᐧ ᐅᐢᐹᐧᑲᐣ, ᒥᐦᒉᑖᐧᐤ ᓂᐯ ᐋᐧᐸᒫᐤ, ᐅᑭᐢᑭᓄᐋᐧᐱᐤ ᔮᐦᑭ ᐃᑖᐟ ᑳ ᑭᐢᑭᓄᐦᐊᒫᑫᐟ ᑲ ᐃᓯ ᐸᒥᐦᐃᒥᐦᐟ ᐆᐦᐃ ᐅᐢᐹᐧᑲᓇ.

[8] ᐄᐦ, ᓂᐢᑕᒼ ᐁ ᐯ ᐱᑯ ᐃᐧᔭᑭᒫᐟ ᐆᑕ ᑯᐦᑖᐃᐧᓇᐤ, ᑮᓯᑳᐤ ᐲᓯᒪᐧ ᐆᐦᐃ ᑳ ᑮ ᐸᑭᑎᓇᒪᐋᐧᐟ, ᑲ ᐯ ᓵᑫᐁᐧᑐᑕᕽ ᐆᒪ ᑭᑮᓯᑳᒥᓇᐤ, ᐃᑕ ᐁ ᐱᒧᐦᑖᑕᕽ ᑮᓯᑳᐤ ᐁ ᒥᔦᐧᓯᐠ, ᐁᐊᐧᑯ ᐊᓂᒪ ᑭᓭᐋᐧᑎᓯᐃᐧᐣ ᑳ ᑮ ᒥᔦᐟ, ᐁᑯᑕ ᐅᐦᒋ, ᑯᑕᑲ ᐁ ᑮᓯ ᐃᐧᔭᑭᒫᐟ ᐁᑲᐧ ᐆᑕ ᐋᐱᐦᑖ ᑮᓯᑳᕽ, ᐁᐊᐧᑯ ᐁᑲᐧ ᐱᓭᓯᐤ, ᐃᑕ ᑳ ᐱᒫᐊᐧᐦᐋᐟ ᐅᑕᐋᐧᓯᒥᓴ, ᐁᐊᐧᑯ ᐊᓂᒪ ᑳ ᐱᒥ ᑳᑮᓯᒧᑐᑕᕽ. ᐁᑯᑕ ᐅᐦᒋ ᐆᑌ ᐸᐦᑭᓯᒧᕽ, ᑳ ᐆᐦ ᒥᔦᐦᑳᓱᐦᐟ ᐊᐊᐧ ᐅᐢᐹᐧᑲᐣ, ᐋ, ᐁᐊᐧᑯ ᐁᑲᐧ, ᐁᑯᑕ ᐁ ᐅᓵᐸᐦᑕᕽ, ᐅᑮᓯᑯᐤ, ᑮᓯᑯᕽ ᐅᐦᒋ ᐆᒪ. ᐆᒪ ᐁᑲᐧ ᓇᑕᑳᒼ, ᐁᐊᐧᑯ ᐁᑲᐧ ᐊᐊᐧ ᔩᑎᐣ ᐁᑲᐧ, ᐁᐊᐧᑯ ᐁᑲᐧ, ᐃᐢᑫᐧᔮᐨ ᐆᒥᓯ ᐃᓯ. ᐁᑲᐧ ᐆᒪ ᑳ ᒫᑖᐢᑯᓂᑫᐟ, ᐆᒥᓯ ᑲ ᐃᓯ ᒥᔦᐦᑲᓵᐧᐟ ᐆᐦᐃ ᐅᐢᐹᐧᑲᓇ, ᐆᒥᓯ ᑭᓭ ᐃᓯ ᐋᐧᓴᑳᔮᐢᑯᓈᐟ, ᐆᑌ ᐁᑲᐧ, ᑳ ᒫᑖᐢᑯᓂᑫᐟ, ᐆᑌ ᐋᐱᐦᑖ ᑮᓯᑳᕽ, ᐯᔭᑲᐧᐣ, ᐁᑯᓯ ᑭᓭ ᐃᓯ ᐋᐧᓴᑳᔮᐢᑯᓈᐟ, ᐯᔭᑲᐧᐣ, ᐆᑌ ᒦᓇ, ᐯᔭᑲᐧᐣ ᐊᓂᒪ ᐁᑯᓯ ᑭᓭ ᐃᓯ ᐋᐧᓴᑳᔮᐢᑯᓈᐟ, ᐆᑌ ᐁᑲᐧ ᓇᑕᑳᒼ.

[9] "ᐋᐤ, ᐆᑌ ᐁᑲᐧ ᐁ ᐋᐧᓴᑳᔮᐢᑯᓈᐟ ᐁᑯᑕ ᐁᑲᐧ ᐁᑫᐧᔮᐨ ᑲ ᒥᔦᐟ ᐊᓂᐦᐃ ᑭᓭᔨᓂᐊᐧ, ᐊᓂᐦᐃ ᐅᐢᐹᐧᑲᓇ. ᐁᑯᓯ ᐊᓂᒪ ᑭᑲ ᐃᓯ ᐸᒥᓂᐦᐟ ᐊᐊᐧ ᐅᐢᐹᐧᑲᐣ. ᑖᐱᑕᐃᐧ ᐆᒥᓯ ᐃᓯ, ᐲᓯᒼ ᐊᐊᐧ ᐃᑐᐦᑌᐟ, ᑲ ᐃᓯ ᐋᐧᓴᑳᓇᒫᐣ, ᐁᐊᐧᑯ ᐆᒪ. ᐁᐊᐧᑯ ᑳ ᓅᐦᑌ ᑭᐢᑫᔨᐦᑕᕽ ᐆᒪ, ᐃᑖᐢᑯᓂᑫᐃᐧᐣ.

[10] ᐁᑲᐧ, ᑮᑲᐧᐩ ᐊᓇ ᐅᐢᑳᐯᐃᐧᐢ. ᐁᐊᐧᑯ ᐊᓇ ᐅᐢᐹᐧᑲᓇ ᑳ ᐸᒥᐦᐋᐟ, ᑳ ᐄᐧᐦᑯᐦᑐᕽ, ᓇᓈᑐᕽ ᑳ ᐃᓰᐦᒋᑫᕽ, ᐅᐢᐹᐧᑲᓇ ᐊᓇ ᑳ ᐸᒥᐦᐋᐟ, ᐁᐊᐧᑯ ᐊᓇ ᓃᑳᐣ, ᐁᐊᐧᑯ ᐊᓇ ᓃᑳᐣ ᑭᑲ ᐊᓴᒥᐦᐟ ᐆᒪ ᑮᓯᑌᐤ. ᐁᑯᑕ ᐅᐦᒋ ᐆᑭ ᐅᐢᑳᐯᐃᐧᓴᐠ, ᑖᐱᑕᐤ ᐆᒥᓯ ᑳ ᐃᑐᐦᑌᒋᐠ, ᑳ ᐊᓴᒫᒋᐠ ᐅᐦᐃ ᑮᑲᐧᐩ. ᐁᐊᐧᑯ ᐆᒪ ᑳ ᐃᑕᒫᐣ, ᐁ ᒣᑕᐋᐧᑫᐟ ᐊᓅᐦᐨ ᐊᔨᓯᔨᓂᐤ. ᐆᒥᓯ ᐃᑐᐦᑌᐤ – ᐄᐦ. ᓈᑲᑑᐦᑫᐠ. – ᐊᔨᓯᔨᓂᐤ. ᐁᑲᐧ ᐆᒪ ᓂᐹᑫᐧᓯᒧᐃᐧᐣ ᐁ ᐃᐢᐸᔨᐠ – ᐆᒥᓯ ᐃᓯ ᑳ ᐃᑐᐦᑌᐟ ᐁ ᐸᐹᒥ ᓇᐊᐧᓵᐧᑕᕽ ᓂᐹᑫᐧᓯᒧᐃᐧᓇ ᐆᐦᐃ, ᐁ ᐸᐹ ᐸᑯᓴᔨᒧᐟ ᐊᓂᒪ ᑮᑲᐧᐩ ᑲ ᒥᔨᐦᐟ. ᓇᒨᔭ ᐁᑯᓯ ᐁ ᐆᐦ ᑑᑕᐦᑭᐠ ᑲᔮᐢ ᑭᓴᔨᓂᐊᐧᐠ. ᐁᑯᑕ ᐆᒪ ᑳ ᓂᑕᐃᐧ ᓴᐢᑲᐦᐊᒫᐦᒋᐠ, ᑳ ᐹᐱᒋᒋᐠ, ᐁ ᓂᑕᐃᐧ ᐱᒫᑎᓯᐃᐧᓀᒋᐠ ᐊᓂᒪ, ᐱᒫᑎᓯᐃᐧᐣ ᐁ ᓈᑕᐦᑭᐠ. ᐊᓅᐦᐨ ᐁᑲᐧ, ᓇᓭᐢᑕᐤ ᐸᑭᑎᓈᓱᐃᐧᐣ ᐅᐦᒋ ᑳ ᐆᐦ ᐸᐹᒥᑎᓴᐦᐊᕽ ᐊᔨᓯᔨᓂᐤ, ᓇᒨᔭ ᑖᐯᐧᐊᐧᑫᔨᐦᑕᒼ ᐅᑌᐦᐃᕽ ᑮᑲᐧᐩ ᐅᐦᒋ, ᐁᐊᐧᑯ ᐊᓂᒪ. ᐁᑲᐧ ᐁᐊᐧᑯ ᐆᒪ ᐁᑯᓯ ᐁ ᐃᓰᐦᒋᑫᕽ, ᐁ ᓂᐹᑫᐧᓯᒧᕽ, ᐁᐊᐧᑯ ᐊᐊᐧ ᐅᐢᐹᐧᑲᓇ ᑳ ᐸᒥᐦᐋᐟ, ᐁᐊᐧᑯ ᐊᓇ ᓃᑳᐣ ᑮᑲᐧᐩ ᐁ ᒥᔨᐦᐟ, ᒋᐢᑌᒫᐊᐧ ᐁᐧᐱᓈᓱᐣ, ᐁᑯᑕ ᐅᐦᒋ ᐸᑭᑎᓈᓱᐃᐧᐣ ᐁ ᒥᔨᐦᐟ, ᐱᒫᑎᓯᐃᐧᐣ ᐊᓂᒪ ᑳ ᒥᔨᐦᐟ. ᐁ ᑮᐢᐱᓇᑕᕽ ᐁᐊᐧᑯ, ᐁᐊᐧᑯ ᐅᐢᐹᐧᑲᓇ, ᐁᑯᑕ ᐅᐦᒋ ᐅᐢᑳᐯᐃᐧᓴᐠ, "ᐋᐤ, ᐹᐦ ᐯᔭᐠ ᑮᑲᐧᐩ ᐁ ᒥᔨᐦᒋᐠ, ᐱᒫᑎᓯᐃᐧᐣ ᐊᓂᒪ ᑳ ᒥᔨᐦᒋᐠ, "ᐋᐤ, ᐁᑯᑕ ᐁᑲᐧ ᑫᐦᑌ ᐊᔭᐠ ᐆᑭ, ᐆᑌ ᐆᑭ ᑳ ᐊᐱᒋᐠ, ᐁᑯᓂᐠ ᐁ ᑮ ᓴᐅᐧᐦᑳᑎᐦᒋᐠ, ᐁᑯᓂᐠ ᐁ ᑮ ᓴᐅᐧᐦᑳᑎᐦᒋᐠ, ᐋ, ᐁᑯᑕ ᐁᑲᐧ, ᐁᑳᔭ ᑲ ᐸᑕᐦᐅᐦᑳᑎᐦᐟ ᑮᑲᐧᐩ ᐄᐧᐦᑳᐨ, ᓅᑎᑫᐧᐤ ᑳ ᐃᓯᔩᐦᑳᓱᐟ, ᐁᐊᐧᑯ ᓅᑎᑫᐧᐃᐧ ᐊᑕᔫᐦᑳᐣ. ᐁ ᑖᐯᐧᒪᑲᕽ ᐆᒪ ᓂᐹᑫᐧᓯᒧᐃᐧᐣ, ᑲ ᑭᑖᐸᒫᓭᑯᐠ ᐃᐢᑫᐧᐊᐧᐠ ᐆᑌ ᐁ ᓵᑲᐢᑭᓀᑳᐸᐃᐧᒋᐠ, ᐆᑌ ᑳ ᐃᑖᐱᓭᐠ ᒥᑐᓂ ᐋᐧᐦ ᐋᐧᐦᔭᐤ ᓈᐯᐊᐧ, ᐄᐦ. ᓲᐦᑲᓂᔨᐤ ᐊᐊᐧ ᐃᐢᑫᐧᐤ ᐅᑳᑮᓯᒧᐃᐧᐣ, ᐁᐊᐧᑯ ᐅᐦᒋ ᐁᑳᔭ ᐸᑕᐦᐅᐦᑳᑎᕽ, ᑮᑲᐧᐩ ᑲ ᒥᔮᓭᐠ.

ᑭᓭ ᐃᓯ ᐊᑕᒥᐦᐋᓭᐠ ᐊᓂᒪ ᓅᑎᑫᐧᓯᐤ, ᐁᑯᓯ ᐊᓂᒪ ᑲ ᐃᓯ ᓇᐢᑯᒥᑯᓈᐋᐧᐤ ᑮᑲᐧᐩ, ᐁᑯᓯ ᐆᒪ ᐁ ᑮ ᐃᑌᐧᒋᐠ ᑫᐦᑌ ᐊᔭᐠ. ᐊᓅᐦᐨ ᐁᑲᐧ, ᑳ ᐄᐧ ᐴᔫᕽ, ᑳ ᐄᐧ ᐸᑭᑎᓈᓱᕽ, ᐁᑯᑕ ᐁᑲᐧ ᑕᑳᐧᐊᐧᐦᐃᑐᐊᐧᐠ ᐊᔨᓯᔨᓂᐊᐧᐠ, ᑌᐱᔮᕽ ᐁ ᓈᑕᐦᑭᐠ ᐸᑭᑎᓈᓱᐃᐧᐣ. ᑳ ᑮᓯ ᐸᑭᑎᓈᓱᕽ, ᐊᐢᐱᐣ ᐁᐧᐦᑕᐢᑲᑎᐢᑭᐠ, ᐁᑯᓯ ᐆᒪ ᐁ ᐃᓯ ᓈᑳᐧᕽ ᒣᑳᐧᐨ ᐆᒪ ᐁᑲᐧ ᒪᐃᐧᒧᐢᒋᑫᐃᐧᐣ, ᐁᐊᐧᑯ ᐆᒪ ᑳ ᓅᐦᑌ ᑭᐢᑫᔨᐦᑕᒣᐠ.

[JK:] ᐁᑲᐧ ᐁᑯᓯ ᐃᓯ ᐆᒪ ᐅᐢᑭᓃᑭᐤ, ᑲᔮᐢ ᑮ ᑭᑎᒫᑫᔨᒣᐤ ᐅᒧᓲᒪ – ᒥᐦᑫᑖᐧᐤ ᐁ ᐋᐦ ᐋᔨᒨᒪᐠ ᐊᐊᐧ, ᐁ ᐯᔭᑫᐧᔨᒥᓱᐟ, ᑳ ᑳᐦᒋᑎᓈᐟ ᐃᐢᑫᐧᐊᐧ, ᐃᔮᔭᐤ ᐃᐧᔭ, ᐃᐧᔭ ᐱᑯ.

[TW:] ᐆᑕ ᐆᒪ ᐊᔭ, ᑲ ᑮ ᐋᒋᒧᔭᕽ ᐆᑌ ᐃᐢᐲ, ᑳ ᐃᑐᐦᑌᔮᕽ Winnipeg.

[11] ᐁᑲᐧ ᐁᐊᐧᑯ ᐆᒪ, ᑳ ᐊᐱᐦᑳᑕᒪᐣ ᐆᒪ, ᑳ ᓂᐢᑕᐧᐱᐦᑳᑕᒪᐣ ᐄᐧᐦᑲᐢᑲᐧ, ᐁᐊᐧᑯ ᐊᓂᒪ ᐅᑭᓭᐋᐧᑎᓯᐃᐧᐣ ᑳ ᐊᐱᐦᑳᑕᒪᐧᐟ ᐊᐊᐧ, ᐁᐊᐧᑯ ᐅᐦᒋ, ᑳ ᐆᐦ ᑮ ᒥᔨᐦᐟ ᐊᔨᓯᔨᓂᐤ, ᑭᐋᐧᐸᒫᐤ ᐃᐢᑫᐧᐤ ᐁ ᓭᑭᐸᑖᐧᐟ, ᐁ ᓂᐢᑕᐧᐱᐦᑳᑕᕽ ᐆᐦᐃ. ᒪᔭᐤ ᐁ ᒫᒋ ᐋᐧᐱᐢᑳᔨᐠ ᐅᐢᒋᑳᐧᐣ ᐃᐢᑫᐧᐤ, ᐋᓴᐩ ᐊᓇ ᐁ ᒥᔨᑯᐃᐧᓯᐟ ᐁᑯᑕ – ᐋᑕᔫᐦᑳᐣ, ᐄᐧᐦᑲᐢᐠ ᐊᐊᐧ ᐅᑭᓭᐋᐧᑎᓯᐃᐧᐣ, ᐁᐊᐧᑯ ᐊᓂᒪ ᐅᐦᒋ ᑳ ᐆᐦ ᓂᐢᑕᐧᐱᐦᑳᑕᕽ ᐆᐦᐃ.

[12] ᐁᑯᓯ ᐆᒪ ᓂᑎᑖᐊᐧᐠ ᐆᑌ, ᐆᑭ ᐆᑌ ᐊᔭ, ᑭᑑᑌᒥᓇᐋᐧᐠ ᐁᑳᔭ ᑮᑲᐧᐩ ᐁ ᑭᐢᑫᔨᐦᑕᐦᑭᐠ Saddle Lake, ᑖᓂᔨᑯᕽ ᐁ ᑭᐢᐸᑭ ᒦᐢᑐᐁᐧᑭᐠ, ᓇᒪ ᑮᑲᐧᐩ ᑳ ᑮ ᒥᔨᑯᐃᐧᓯᑭᐠ ᐊᓂᒪ, ᐁᑲᐧ ᐃᐢᑫᐧᐊᐧᐠ ᐆᑭ ᑯᓂᑕ ᐁ ᑎᑎᐸᐁᐧᐦᑲᓴᐦᑭᐠ ᐅᐢᑎᑳᐧᓂᐋᐧᐤ, ᑖᐱᐢᑰᐟ ᐊᐧᒋᐢᑖᐧᐣ, «ᓇᒧᔭ ᐁᐊᐧᑯ ᑳ ᑮ ᒥᔨᑯᐃᐧᓯᔭᐠ,» ᓂᑎᑖᐊᐧᐠ, ᐊᐦᐳ ᒌ ᐆᑭ ᓈᐯᐊᐧᐠ, ᑮᑳᐧᐩ ᐊᓂᒪ ᐁ ᐃᓯ ᐸᐦᐸᑲᐧᑌᔨᐦᑕᐦᑭᐠ, «ᐁ ᐸᓱᓴᐠ ᒌ ᐆᒪ ᑮᑲᐧᐩ, ᑭᒦᐢᑐᐋᐧᓇ,» – ᐋᑕ ᓇᒧᔭ ᒫᒫᔫᐢ ᑮᑲᐧᐩ ᐁ ᐄᐧᐦᑕᒪᐊᐧᑭᐠ, «ᒫᑲ ᐁᑳᔭ ᑲᑫᐧ ᐅᐦᐱᑭᐦᑖᐠ ᑭᒦᐢᑐᐋᐧᓂᐋᐧᐊᐧ.»

* * *

[13] ᒥᐢᑕᐦᐃ ᑲ ᒥᔭᐧᓯᐣ, ᐁᐊᐧᑯ ᐆᒪ ᑮᐢᑕᐋᐧᐤ, ᑲ ᑭᐢᑭᓄᐋᐧᐸᐦᑕᒣᐠ ᐆᒪ ᑳ ᐄᐧ ᐃᓰᐦᒋᑫᔮᕽ, ᐅᐢᑭᓃᑭᐢᑫᐧᐊᐧᐠ, ᑲᐧᔮᐢᐠ, ᐁ ᑮ ᒫᒋ ᒪᓂᑐᐃᐧᐦᐃᐦᐟ ᐊᐊᐧ ᑳ ᒍᐅᐧ ᑎᐱᐢᑳᑭ ᐅᐢᑭᓃᑭᐢᑫᐧᐤ, ᐁᐊᐧᑯ ᐅᐦᒋ, ᑭᐢᑫᔨᐦᑕᐨ ᑭᑳᐃᐧᐩ ᑖᓂᓯ ᐁ ᐃᐢᐸᔨᐠ ᐁᐊᐧᑯ ᐆᒪ, ᐃᐧᔮᑲᓂᐢ ᑮ ᐊᐢᑕᒪᐋᐧᐤ ᐃᑕ ᐁ ᑲᓇᐁᐧᔨᒥᐦᐟ ᐅᐢᑭᓃᑭᐢᑫᐧᐤ, ᐁᑯᑕ ᐁ ᓰᐦᑯᐟ, ᓇᒧᔭ ᒧᐦᒋᕽ. ᑳ ᒍᐅᐧ ᑎᐱᐢᑳᑭ, ᐁᑯᑕ ᐁᑲᐧ ᑳ ᒥᔮᐦᑲᓴᒥᕽ ᐊᓂᒪ. ᓇᓈᑐᕽ ᐁ ᐃᓵᔮᔨᐟ ᐊᔨᓯᔨᓂᐊᐧ, ᐊᐦᐴ ᐁᑳ

ᐁ ᐚᐱᔨᐟ, ᐁ ᐅᐢᑲᓂᓀᔨᐟ, ᑳ ᑭᔭᑲᓭᐟ ᐆᒪ ᐊᐚᓯᐢ, ᐁᑯᑕ ᐁᑲᐧ ᐁ ᑮ ᒥᔨᐦᐟ ᒋᐢᑌᒫᐊᐧ, ᐍᐱᓈᓲᐣ, «ᐦᐋᐤ, ᓇᓈᑕᐃᐧᐦ ᐊᐊᐧ.» ᐁ ᑮ ᐃᑎᐦᐟ ᐅᐢᑭᓃᑭᐢᑫᐧᐤ, ᐁᐊᐧᑯ ᐊᓂᒪ ᐅᐦᒋ ᑳ ᑮ ᓇᓈᑕᐃᐧᐦᐋᐟ. ᐋ, ᒥᐦᒉᑖᐤ ᐁᑯᑕ ᐅᐦᒋ ᐁ ᑮ ᐱᒫᒋᐦᐋᐟ.

[14] ᐁᐊᐧᑯ ᐆᒪ ᐁ ᐋᒋᒨᐢᑕᐊᐧᑭᐠ ᐆᑭ ᐅᓃᑳᓂᐊᐧᐠ, ᒥᑐᓂ ᒥᔦᐧᔨᐦᑕᒪᐧᐠ, ᐁᐊᐧᑯ ᐆᒪ ᑲ ᐆᐦ ᐄᐧ ᐃᓰᐦᒋᑫᒋᐠ, «ᐁᐊᐧᑯ ᐊᓂᒪ ᐁᑲᐧ ᑲ ᑲᑫᐧ ᐱᒥᐸᔨᐠ,» ᐁ ᐃᑌᐧᒋᐠ, ᐁᑯᓯ ᐱᑯ ᐊᔨᐢ ᑮᑳᐧᐩ ᐁ ᐱᒥᐸᔨᐠ. ᒉᑳᐧᐨ ᑮᑳᐧᐩ ᑫᐦᑌ ᐊᔭ ᑭᓭᔨᓂᐤ, ᓅᑎᑫᐧᐤ ᑮᑳᐧᐩ ᐁ ᑭᐢᑫᔨᐦᑕᕽ, ᐁᑯᓯ ᐃᓯ ᑲ ᐄᐧᐦᑕᒫᐊᐧᐟ ᑲ ᑳᓯᐢᐳᐦᑌᒪᑲᕽ ᐁᐊᐧᑯ. ᐁᑳ ᐁᑯᓯ ᑑᑕᒥᐦᑯ, ᒉᐢᑐᐦᑌᑖᐃᐧ ᑫᐦᑌ ᐊᔭᐠ, ᐯᔭᑳᐧᐣ ᐃᐢᑯᑌᐤ ᐁ ᐋᐢᑕᐍᐧᐠ, ᐁᑯᓯ ᐆᒪ ᑲ ᐃᓯ ᑭᑎᒫᑲᐣ ᑭᓀᐦᐃᔭᐃᐧᐃᐧᓂᓇᐤ. ᑲ ᐊᐧᓂᐦᑖᓇᐤ ᑮᑳᐧᐩ ᑯᐦᑖᐃᐧᓈᐤ ᑳ ᑮ ᒥᔨᑯᔭᕽ ᑲ ᐆᐦ ᐱᒫᑎᓯᔭᕽ. ᐁᐊᐧᑯ ᐅᐦᒋ ᒫᓇ ᒥᐢᑕᐦᐃ ᓂᓇᓈᐢᑯᒫᐤ ᐊᔨᓯᔨᓂᐤ ᑳ ᓅᐦᑌ ᑭᐢᑫᔨᐦᑕᕽ.

[15] ᐄᐦ, ᑖᐱᐢᑰᐨ ᐊᐊᐧ John, ᐁ ᓅᐦᑌ ᑭᐢᑫᔨᐦᑕᕽ ᐃᑖᐢᑯᓂᑫᐃᐧᐣ, «ᐁ ᓅᐦᑌ ᑖᐳᐍᔮᐣ ᐆᐦᐃ ᓂᑲᒧᓇ. ᑖᓂᓯ ᑲ ᐃᑑᑕᒫᐣ, ᒉᐢᑐᐦᑌᓴᑯ ᐯ ᒥᔨᑲᐃᐧᔮᓂ ᐍᐱᓈᓲᐣ, ᐯ ᑮᐦᑳᐦᑕᐦᐊᒪᐊᐧᑭ ᐁᑲᐧ ᐋᑕᔫᐦᑲᐣ, ᐃᑎᑲᐃᐧᔮᓂ, ᑯᓂᑕ ᓂᑲ ᑫᐧᑕᑌᔨᑎᐢᑫᐧᔨᐣ, ᒫᑲ ᐄᐧᐦᑕᒪᐃᐧᔮᓂ, ᐋᓴᐩ ᐁᑯᑕ ᓂᑲ ᑭᐢᑭᓱᐸᔨᐣ,» ᑳ ᐃᑌᐧᐟ. ᐁᑯᓯ ᐊᓂᒪ ᐁ ᐃᓯ ᑖᐯᐧᐟ ᐁᐊᐧᑯ.

* * *

[16] ᐁᑲᐧ ᒦᓇ ᐅᐢᑭᓃᑭᐢᑫᐧᐊᐧᐠ ᑲ ᐄᐧᐦᑕᒫᐊᐧᓴᑯᐠ ᐆᑭ, ᐁᑲᐧ ᐆᑌ – ᒪᑖᐧᐣ ᒌ ᐊᐊᐧ ᓂᑮ ᐯᐦᑖᐠ Angus –, Saddle Lake ᐆᑌ ᓂᑮ ᐯ ᑲᑫᐧᒋᒥᐠ ᐯᔭᐠ ᐅᐢᑭᓃᑭᐢᑫᐧᐤ, ᒪᐢᑭᐦᑭᐩ ᐁ ᐯ ᓂᑕᐍᐧᔨᐦᑕᕽ, «ᓀᐅᐧ ᐊᐢᑭᐩ ᐁ ᐄᐧᒉᐊᐧᐠ ᐊᐊᐧ ᓂᓈᐯᒼ,» ᐃᑌᐤ, «ᐁᑳ ᑮᑳᐧᐩ ᐁ ᑮ ᐅᒐᐚᓯᒥᓯᔭᕽ, ᐁ ᓂᑕᐍᔨᐦᑕᒫᐣ ᒪᐢᑭᐦᑭᐩ ᑲ ᒥᔨᔭᐣ,» ᓂᑎᑎᐠ. ᐊᐧᐦᐋᐧ, ᓂᐊᐧᐋᐧᓀᔨᐦᑕᒥᐦᐃᐠ, «ᒉᐢᑲᐧ, ᓅᓯᓴ.» ᓂᑎᑖᐤ, «ᑖᓂᓯᑯᕽ ᒫᑲ ᐆᒪ, ᑭᐃᐧᔭᑭᐦᑕᒪᐃᐧᐣ ᑳ ᐃᓯᔭᐣ.» ᓂᑎᑖᐤ, «ᑖᓂᓯᑯᕽ ᑭᐍᐯᓯᒫᐤ ᓲᓂᔮᐤ.» – «ᐋ, ᑭᔭ, ᓂᒧᓲ. ᐱᑯ ᐃᓯᑯᕽ ᓂᑕᐍᔨᒪᒋ, ᑲ ᒥᔨᑎᐣ.» –

«" ᐋᐤ.» ᓂᑎᑖᐤ, «ᑲᐯᓰ ᐃᐧᑲᒥᐠ ᓂᑕᐃᐧ ᑎᐸᐦᐊ, ᐃᔨᑯᕽ ᐁ ᐁᐧᐯᔨᒪᐟ ᓰᓂᔮᐤ.» ᑯᓂᑕ ᐁ ᓈᓈᒥᐢᑫᐧᔨᐟ, «ᑮ ᑎᐸᐦᐊᒪᓂ, ᐯ ᓈᓰᐦᑲᐣ. ᑲ ᐄᐧᒑᔮᒥᑎᐣ ᐯᔭᐠ ᑎᐱᐢᑳᐤ, ᐊᐋᐧᓯᐢ –.» – «ᓇᒎᔭ ᐁᐊᐧᑯ ᑳ ᑲᑫᐧᒋᒥᑖᐣ, ᓂᒍᓰ.» – «ᐁᐊᐧᑯ ᐱᑯ ᓂᑭᐢᑫᐧᔨᐦᑌᐣ ᒪᐢᑭᐦᑭᐩ,» ᓂᑎᑖᐤ.

8 ᒪ ᒨᐦᒑᐧᑕᔫᐦᑫᐃᐧᐣ

[1] ᐁ ᐄᐧ ᐋᒋᒪᐠ ᐆᑕ ᓂᒧᓲᒼ ᒪᐦᐃᐦᑲᓂᐢ, ᐁ ᐄᐧ ᐋᒋᒧᐢᑕᐊᐧᑭᐠ ᐆᑭ, ᐁᑳ ᑮᑲᐧᐩ ᐁ ᐅᐦᒋ ᑭᐢᑫᔨᐦᑕᕽ, ᐁᑲᐧ ᒥᑐᓂ ᐊᔨ, ᒫᑲ ᐁ ᑮ ᑭᑎᒫᑫᔨᒫᐟ ᐄᐧᒋ ᑮᐦᑳᐊᐧ.

[2] ᐦᐋᐤ, ᑫᑕᐦᑕᐁᐧ ᑳ ᒫᔨᒪᐦᒋᐦᐅᔨᐟ ᐆᐦᐃ ᐄᐧᒋ ᑮᐦᑳᐊᐧ. ᐁᐊᐧᑯ ᐊᐊᐧ ᐁᑲᐧ ᓅᐦᒑᐄᐧᐢ ᐃᐢᐸᐦᑌᐦᐃᑲᐣ ᑳ ᑮ ᐃᑎᐦᐟ ᐁ ᐅᑭᒫᐦᑳᓂᐃᐧᐟ, ᒪᓯᓇᐦᐃᑫᐦᐁᐤ ᐆᐦᐃ ᐄᐧᐢᒑᓴ, ᐁ ᒪᐢᑯᓰᐦᑫᒋᐠ, ᐁ ᐚᐧᐦ ᐄᐧᐢᒌᐦᑫᓯᐟ ᐊᐊᐧ ᓂᒧᓲᒼ. ᑫᑕᐦᑕᐁᐧ ᑳ ᒫᔨᒪᐦᒋᐦᐅᐟ ᐊᐊᐧ ᓅᐦᑯᒥᓈᐣ. ᐋ, ᐁᑲᐧ ᐁ ᐚᐧᐸᕽ, ᐦᐋᐤ, ᑲᐢᑲᐊᐧᓂᐯᐢᑖᐤ ᐁ ᑭᒥᐊᐧᕽ, ᓃᓱ ᑮᓯᑳᐤ ᐋᓴᐩ ᐁᑯᓯ ᐁ ᐃᓵᔮᔨᐠ. «ᐦᐋ, ᑖᓂᓯ ᐊᑕ ᐃᐧᔭ, ᓂᑎᒧᐢ.» – ᑮ ᐊᐧ ᐄᐧᑎᒧᓯᐤ ᐊᓂᐦᐃ ᓅᐦᒑᐄᐧᐢ ᓅᐦᑯᒥᓈᓇ –, «ᑖᓂᓯ ᐊᑕ ᐃᐧᔭ, ᓂᑎᒧᐢ.» – «ᐋ, ᑭᓵᑲᒥᑌᐦᑫᐧᐤ ᐊᓇ ᑮᑭᓭ', ᑎᐱᐢᑯᕽ ᐁ ᑮ ᐲᐦᑖᐸᐊᐧᐦᐊᐠ,»

[LA:] ᒐᐦ. ᐁᑲᐧ.

ᐃᑌᐧᐤ ᐁᓴ ᐊᐊᐧ ᓂᒧᓲᒥᓈᐣ. «ᔫᐦᐆ, ᑮᑳᐧᐩ ᒫᑲ ᐁ ᐋᐸᒋᐦᑖᔭᐣ, ᓂᐢᒑᐢ. ᐄᐧᐦᑳᐧᐢ ᒌ ᐁ ᐊᔮᔭᐣ.» – «ᒪ ᑮᑳᐧᐩ.» – «ᑮᑳᐧᐩ ᒫᑲ ᐁ ᐋᐸᒋᐦᑖᔭᐣ.» – «ᓲᐢᑳᐧᐟ ᐁ ᐹᐦ ᐲᐦᒋ ᓰᑲᑌᐦᑕᒪᐊᐧᐠ, ᐁ ᐲᐦᑖᐸᐊᐧᐦᐊᐠ.»

[to LA:] ᐊᐊᐧᐢ, ᐁᑳᔭ ᑭᔭ ᐹᐦᐱ. ᐁ ᐋᒋᒧᐢᑖᑖᐣ ᐆᒪ.

«ᐋ, ᐁᑲᐧ, ᑭᓵᑲᒥᑌᐦᑫᐧᐤ, ᒥᔫᒪᐦᒋᐦᐅᐤ,» ᐃᑌᐧᐤ. «ᐸᑲᐦᑲᒼ ᑲᐢᑲᐊᐧᓂᐯᐢᑖᐤ,» ᐃᑌᐧᐤ, «ᑭᓰᐯᑭᓂᑫᐤ ᐊᐊᐧ ᓂᒧᓲᒥᓈᐣ ᐁᓴ ᒪᐦᑫᓰᐢ, ᐁᓴ ᐆᒪ ᐅᐱᐦᒐᐁᐧᓵᑲᓂᓯᔩᐤ ᐁ ᐄᐸᒋᐦᑖᔨᐟ. ᒫᑲ ᐁᑯᑕ ᐆᒪ ᐋᓯᐊᐧᐦᐱᑌᐤ ᐲᒥᓈᐦᑳᐧᓂᐢ,» ᐃᑌᐧᐤ, «ᑳ ᓰᓇᕽ ᐆᒪ,» ᐃᑌᐧᐤ. «ᐋ, ᐁᑯᑕ,» ᐃᑌᐧᐤ, «ᐋ, ᓇᒨᔭ ᐁᑐᑫᐧ ᐊᐊᐧ ᑯᓂᑕ ᓂᐢᒑᐢ, ᑳ ᐊᐧᔭᐄᐧᐟ ᐁᑲᐧ ᐁ ᓈᑖᐟ ᐅᑑᐢᐸᐧᑲᓇ, ᐁᐧᐱᓈᓱᐣ,» ᐃᑌᐧᐤ. «ᐋ, ᓂᐢᒑᐢ, ᐊᐊᐧ ᒋᐢᑌᒫᐤ, ᐆᒪ ᐁᐧᐱᓈᓱᐣ – ᐃᑖᐢᑯᓂᑫ ᒪᐦᑎ, ᑭᐄᐧ ᓅᐦᑌᐦᑲᑖᓈᓇᐤ, ᑲ ᑲᑫᐧ ᐋᐢᑌ ᑮᓯᑳᐠ. ᐋᐢᑌ ᑮᓯᑳᑭ ᐁ ᐄᐧ ᒥᓇᐦᐆᔭᐣ, ᐁᑳ ᑲ ᓅᐦᑌᐦᑲᑌᔭᕽ, ᓂᑎᑖᐤ ᓂᐢᒑᐢ,» ᐃᑌᐧᐤ. «ᑖᐯᐧ

ᒫᑲ, ᓃᐢᒑᐢ, ᑖᐯᐧ.» – «ᐋ, ᐁᐊᐧᑯ ᐊᓂ ᓂᒥᔮᐦᑲᓴᒪᐋᐧᐤ,» ᐃᑌᐧᐤ,
«ᐁ ᑮ ᐃᐧᔭᐢᑭᓇᐦᐃᒪᐣ, ᓂᒥᔮᐤ,» ᐃᑌᐧᐤ.

[3] «ᐋᐧᓴᑳᔮᐢᑯᓅᐤ,» ᐃᑌᐧᐤ, «ᐦᐋᐤ, ᐁᐊᐧᑯ ᐊᓇ ᐲᐦᑖᐧᐣ. ᑭᑎᒫᑭᓇᐃᐧᓈᐠ. ᑭᑎᒫᑭᓇᐃᐧᓈᐠ, ᓃᓱᓵᑊ ᑳ ᐃᑕᐦᑎᓂᔨᑭ ᐅᐢᐱᑫᑲᓇ.» – ᑮᑳᐧᔭ ᐁᑲᐧ. – ᐁᓯ ᐆᒪ ᐃᔨᓂᑐ ᒦᑭᐋᐧᐦᑊ ᐁ ᐊᐱᐢᑕᕽ ᐊᐊᐧ, ᓃᓱᓵᑊ ᐋᐸᓱᔭ, ᐁᐊᐧᑯ ᐁᓯ ᐆᒪ ᑳ ᐃᑖᐢᑯᓇᒪᐋᐧᑕᕽ.

[4] «ᐦᐋ, ᑮᐢᑕ ᒦᓇ ᐁᑯᑕ ᐅᐦᒋ, ᐲᐦᑖᐧ, ᑳ ᒫᐦ ᒪᐦᑭᐦᑕᐊᐧᑫᔭᐠ. – ᐁᑲᐧ ᐆᐦᐃ ᐊᐸᐦᑳᐧᓇ, ᐁᑯᓂ ᐁᑲᐧ ᑳ ᐃᑖᐢᑯᓇᒪᐋᐧᐟ, ᐋᐧ, ᑳ ᑫᐧᐢᑳᐢᑯᓈᐟ,» ᐃᑌᐧᐤ.

[5] «ᐋ, ᐁᑲᐧ ᑭᔭ ᐃᑕ ᑳ ᐅᒋᐢᑭᔭᐠ – ᐁᐊᐧᑯ ᐊᓂᒪ ᑭᑎᐢᑯᑌᒥᐋᐧᐤ ᐁᑲᐧ ᐆᒪ,» ᐃᑌᐧᐤ, «ᐦᐋᐤ, ᐆᒪ ᐃᑕ ᑳ ᐅᒋᐢᑭᔭᐠ, ᐁᐊᐧᑯ ᐊᓇ ᐲᐦᑖᐧ. ᐋᐧᓴᑳᔮᐢᑯᓅᐤ, ᐋ, ᓂᐄᐧᑭᒫᑲᐠ ᐅᐲᐦᒐᐁᐧᓵᑳᓂᐢ, ᐁᐊᐧᑯ ᐊᓂᒪ ᒦᓇ,» – ᐁᐩ, ᐁᐊᐧᑯ ᐁ ᑮ ᐸᑲᐧᓇᐊᐧᐦᑖᐟ ᐃᑖᐢᑯᓂᑫᐃᐧᐠ.

[6] ᑕᑲᐦᑭ ᐋᑕᔫᐦᑫᐃᐧᐠ.

[LA:] ᒥᑐᓂ ᒪ ᒨᐦᒑᐧᑕᔫᐦᑫᐃᐧᐠ ᐃᐧᔭ ᐁᐊᐧᑯ.

ana kâ-pimwêwêhahk okakêskihkêmowina

The Counselling Speeches of Jim Kâ-Nîpitêhtêw

1

[1] êwak ôma kîkway, kâ-nitawêyihtahkik ôki ka-wîhtamawakik, êkosi –~ êwak ôma kâ-mâc-îhtâyân ôta, kâ-pôn-âyamihêwi-kîsikâk, k-âyamihêwi-kîsikâk ôta kâ-takohtêyân. kîkwây ohci k-ôh-kî-pê-itohtêyân ôta, êwak ôma kîkway k-âstâhikoyahk, tahtwâw ê-kîsikâk êkâ kîkway kâ-miywâsik. êwakw ânima pêyak kisêyiniw ê-kî-nakiskawak, êwak ôma ê-kî-wîcôhkamawit, tânis ê-itastêyik wîst ôkakêskimâwasowin; êwak ôma kâ-kî-wîhtamawit, kâ-pê-wîhtamawakik ôk ôta.

[2] namôy kinisitohtâkonaw kîkway, kitawâsimisinaw kôsisiminaw pêyâhtik âta kîkway ka-wîhtamawâyahk, môy kinisitohtâkonaw. piko mêmohci ka-nisitohtamôhiht, tânis ê-kî-isi-kakêskimiht kayâs osk-âya, oskinîkiskwêw, oskinîkiw; tânis ê-kî-pê-isi-tâpwêhtahkik kîkway ê-miywâsik kîkway kâ-kî-pê-wîhtamâkocik, onîkihikowâwa ahpô omosômiwâwa ôhkomiwâwa. mistahi kî-nanahihtam oskinîkiskwêw, kîkway kêtâsômikot ôhkoma oti. cikêmô pê-nakacihtâw 'nôtikwêsiw' k-êsiyîhkâsot, kahkiyaw kîkway tânis ê-pê-isi-manâcihtât. êwakw ânima kâ-kî-âsônamawât ôsisima, tânisi kîkway k-êsi-nahêyihtahk, otawâsimisimâw oyôsisimimâw, tânisi k-êsi-nahêyihtamihiht. namôy nânitaw itâpatan, kiyânaw tipiyaw kitawâsimisinaw kôsisiminaw, kiyâm pikoyikohk ka-kisîwêhkahtawâyahk kîkway ê-pakwâtamawâyahk, ka-wîhtamawâyahk. cikêmô, kisaskacihtâkonaw, kîkway anima k-âta-~-kakwê-kitâsômâyahk, êkâ kîkway ka-tôtahk anima, êkâ kîkway ê-miywâsik. kahkiyaw kîkway ati-wêpinam osk-âya anohc, kahkiyaw kîkway ati môy tâpwêwakêyihtam [*sic*]. êwakw âwa kâ-wîhtamawak anohc awa, ôta kâ-wîtapimak awa, misawâc êtokwê kinisitawêyimâwâw, '*Freda*' isiyîhkâsow; êkota ôma wîst ê-atoskêt ôta, tâpiskôc ôm îtê mâna kâ-pê-wîtapimakik ôki, 'nêhiyawi-kiskinohamâtowi-kakêskihkêmowikamik' isiyîhkâtêw.

Counselling the Young

[1] There is something which they want me to tell them in this way –~ this which I began here on Monday, having arrived here on Sunday. Why I had come here is that there is something which is worrying us, the fact that day after day there are things which are not good. I met a certain old man about that, he helped me with it, by the manner in which his own counselling of the young is conducted; what he told me is what I have come to tell them here.

[2] Our children and grandchildren do not understand us in anything, even when we tell them about something quietly, they do not understand us. They have to be made to understand in particular how young people used to be counselled in the old days, young women and young men; how they have always accepted the good things which their parents have been telling them, or their grandfathers and grandmothers. A young woman listened most carefully to the things her grandmother, especially, warned her about. Of course the 'old woman', as she was called, had come to be experienced in always treating everything with respect. That is what she used to pass on to her grandchildren, how the children and grandchildren would have peace of mind, how they would be given peace of mind. For our own children and grandchildren, no matter how much we might yell at them when we disapprove of something for them, it is pointless that we should tell them about it. Of course they are tired of hearing us; even though we try to warn them that they should not do these things because they are not good. Young people today tend to throw everything away, they tend not to believe in anything. I told her this when I was sitting here with her today, I guess you all know her anyway, Freda is her name; she, too, works here, just as I usually come and sit with them over here at the place which is called the 'Indian Cultural College'.

[3] êkotowahk awa wîst ê-atoskâtahk ôta, êwak ôhci k-ôh-nitawêyihtahk apisis kîkway ka-wîhtamawak, tânisi kîkway ê-isi-~ kê-~ kê-~-pê-isi-kiskêyihtamân, tânis ê-kî-pê-isi-wîhtamawit kîkway, kisêyiniw kâ-kî-pê-ohpikihit. piyis êkota ohci kâ-kî-ohtastêk ê-wîtatoskêmakik kisêyiniwak, tahk âyiwâk kîkway nikî-ati-miyikwak ê-miywâsik, kîkwây anima ka-mamisîtotamân tahtwâw ê-kîsikâk. êwak ôhci k-ôh-pê-otihtakik ôk ôta, namôy ê-môhcwêyimakik, namôy mîna nôhtaw ê-itêyimakik tânis ê-ispîhtêyimisoyân, mâk ê-nôhtê-wîcôhkamawakik, kîkwây kik-âpacihikocik, iyikohk ôm ôt[a] ê-kosikwaniyik otatoskêwiniwâw; êwakw ânim ôhci k-ôh-pê-pimohtêyân. êkosi ninanâskomon, wâpahk[i] îskwêyâc ka-wî-~, ôta ka-wîci-pîhtwâmakik, ka-kâkîsimoyahk kîkisêpâ. êkosi mistahi ninahêyihtên, ê-nitohtawicik, êwak ôma ê-nanâskotamwak tânisi wiyawâw ê-isi-nisitohtahkik, mâka miton êkos ê-isi-nisitohtâkocik otôsk-âyimiwâwa (kîkwây ôma mistahi kâ-mâmitonêyihtamihikot awa wîsta otawâsimisa, pêyak âsônê). êwakw ânima mistahi nayêhtâwan, êkos îs êkâ tipiyaw ê-kî-kitotak an[a] ôsk-âya, mâk ê-isi-kaskihtâyân, iyikohk ninitotamâkêstamawâw âta, tahtwâw k-ôhpâskonak ospwâkan. ê-âpahkawiniyik mitonêyihcikan, ka-kakwê-miyikowisit wîsta, ka-kwêski-pimâtisit, tâpiskôc ahcâhko-pimâtisiwinihk itêhkê isi. êwak ôma, âta, k-âhkamêyimototamân, ê-kakwê-isi-wîcôhkamawak; mâka nayêhtâwan, êkâ tipiyaw êkos îsi ê-kî-kitotiht osk-âya awa. mâka kîhtwâm, nahipayiki, ôta takohtêyâni, nika-miywêyihtên, êwakw âwa ka-kitotak osk-âya.

[4] mistahi mâmitonêyihtam, kikiskêyihtênâwâw, kêhtê-aya, otôsk-âyima êkâ kwayask ê-isi-wîcêhtoyit. hâw, mistahi mâmitonêyihcikan êkota miyik, tahtwâw ê-kîsikâk. êkos êwakw ânima, âta kâ-kakwê-wîhtamawakik ôk ôsk-âyak, kika-nanâskomiht kôhtâwînaw, wiya kâ-tipêyihtahk kipimâtisiwininaw, ê-miyikoyahk pêyak-kîsikâw ita ka-pimohtâtamahk kikîsikâminaw, ê-isi-waniskâyahk ka-nanâskomâyahk, ka-nanâskotamwâyahk okisêwâtisiwin.

[3] She, too, is engaged in this work here [at the College], that is why she wants me to tell her a little about what I have come to know, what I have been told by the old man who raised me. Ultimately this was the reason why I worked with the old men, and then they gave me more and more of that which is good, what I might be able to rely upon each day. That is why I have come here to be with them, I do not consider them stupid, I do not think any less of them than I think of myself, but I want to help them with what will sustain them, as their work here is so heavy; that is why I have come here. And so I give thanks, tomorrow I will hold the pipe ceremony here with them for one last time, and chant our morning prayers. Thus I am greatly content that they have listened to me, and I give thanks for it that they, too, understand this, but especially that their young people will understand them (what greatly worries this one here in particular are his children, and more especially one). That is very awkward because I cannot personally speak to that young person, although I will ask on her behalf, to the best of my ability, each time I raise the pipe. That she, too, may be granted a stable mind by the powers, that she may change her life, towards a more spiritual kind of life. I do indeed struggle hard for this, trying to help him in this way; but it is awkward because in this way one cannot personally speak to the young person. But if I come back here another time and it works out, I will be glad to speak to this young person.

[4] The old people worry greatly, you all know that, if their young people do not get along with one another. Indeed, they cause them grievous worry by that, day after day. And I do try to tell that to these young people, that thanks should be given to Our Father, him who rules our lives, that he has granted us another day wherein we might live through our day, as we arise we should give thanks to him, give thanks to him for his grace. And in that way now I do try to help them [the old] in that so that they, too,

êwakw êkw âta k-ôh-kakwê-isi-wîcôhkamawakik ôki, tânisi wîstawâw ka-kî-isi-pîkiskwâtâcik, êkosi wiy êwako ê-isi-pîkiskwâtamân.

[5] êkwa kotak ôma: êwako mâna nôhtâwiy nikî-wîhtamâk, êkwa awa ôtê kisêyiniw kâ-nakiskawak, êwakw êkwa kâ-kiskisômit [*sic*] nôhtâwiy opîkiskwêwin; pêyakwan kâ-kî-isi-wîhtamawit, êkos ê-isi-wîhtamawit awa kisêyiniw, ayinânêwi-mitanaw ayiwâk ayinânêw ê-itahtopiponwêt, "â, ê-pê-wîcôhkamâtân ôma, ê-kiskêyihtamân mistahi ê-kosikwahk kitatoskêwin tahtwâw ê-kîsikâk, mâka êkây pônihtâ! âhkamêyimo!" ê-itwêt êwakw âwa kisêyiniw. êwak ôma kâ-wîhtamawak aw ôta, anohc, ôta ê-pîhtwâyahk, êkosi nitay-âcimostawâw ôm êwak ôpîkiskwêwiniyiw. êkoni ôhi, kî-tâhkômêw nîkân, kâ-kî-oyôhtâwîyân, " 'ayamihêwiyiniw' k-êsiyîhkâsot, akâmaskîhk wî-ohtohtêw wâpiski-wiyâs, 'ayamihêwiyiniw' k-êsiyîhkâsow; mâka, niya, namôy êkotowahk êkosi nitisiyîhkâtâw," nikî-itik kâ-kî-oyôhtâwîyân, "êwakw âwa 'ayamihêwiyiniw' kiyê-isiyîhkâsot, 'onitawahtâw' niya nik-êsiyîhkâtâw; mâcikôtitan ôtê kiy-âti-nîkâniwik, êwakw âwa kahkiyaw êkwa kîkway ka-pê-nôtinam, kâ-kî-miyikoyahk ôma mâmaw-ôhtâwîmâw mawimoscikêwin, êwak ôm ê-wî-pê-nôtinahk. mâka namôya ka-kî-kaskihtâw wîhkâc ka--, êwakw ânima ka-kî-pîkonahk. cikêmô kikî-miyikonaw kôhtâwînaw, kîstanaw kâ-nêhiyâwiyahk, kîkwây ka-nât-- ka-nâtâmototamahk," nikî-itik mâna kâ-kî-oyôhtâwîyân.

[6] cîkâhtaw êkosi k-êsit awa kisêyiniw, mâk êkwa nik-âtotên opîkiskwêwin, k-êsi-wîhtamawak awa kîkway. "pitamâ ôhi mitâtaht kîkway, êkâ ka-tôtaman; êwakw âwa ayamihêwiyiniw kâ-wî-pêtât, wîst ôtayamihâwin wâpiski-wiyâs, êkon ôhi kaskihtâyani mitâtaht êkâ kîkway ka-tôtaman, êkoni 'pâstâhowina' k-êsiyîhkâtahk, hâw, êkota êkwa, kaskihtâyan[i] êkon êkâ ka-tôtaman, êkot[a] êkwa kikâh-kî-wîcêwâw tânis ê-isi-mawimoscikêt. êkosi mâka, ita ê-mawimoscikêt,

might be able to speak to them [the young], that is all I am saying about that.

[5] And another thing: my father used to tell me about this, and then the old man I met over there, he then reminded me of my father's words; this old man who is eighty-eight years old told me the same thing as my father had told me: "Well, I have come to help you, for I know your work is very heavy day after day, but do not cease of it! Persevere!" this old man said. When I told this one here [one of the audience] about that today, here while we held the pipe ceremony, I was repeating his words to him in this way. My late father had discussed this one first: "A White-Man called 'priest' is going to come from overseas, 'priest' he will be called; but, as for me, I will not call that kind by that name," my late father had said to me, "that 'priest', as he will be called, as for me, I will call him 'scout'; there in the future, for instance, that one will come and fight everything, he is going to come and fight the way of worship the All-Father has given us. But he will never succeed, so that he would be able to break that. For of course Our Father has given us, us who are Crees, what we may turn to for help," my late father used to say to me.

[6] What the old man said to me is very close to this, but I will now repeat his words, as I have told them to this one [in the audience]. "First, the ten things which you should not do [*i.e.*, the ten commandments]; that priest is going to bring his own religion, the White-Man's religion, and if you succeed in not doing these ten things, these 'sins' as he calls them, then indeed, if you succeed in not doing these, then you would be able to join him in his way of worship. But where he worships and discusses the All-Father,

mâmaw-ôhtâwîmâwa ê-tâhkômât, nitawi-pakosih, nitawi-nitohtaw! cikêmô wîsta pêyakwan anihi kâ-mamisît, kâ-~ êkoni ôhi. mâka namôy îyawis, ahcâhko-pimâtisiwinihk isi, wî-atoskâtam êwakw âwa. mâcikôtitan ôtê kê-nîkâniwik, nômanak pimâtisiyani, k-âti-wâpahtên, êwakw âwa, 'ayamihêwiyiniw' kiy-êsiyîhkâtiht, êwakw âwa 'onitawahtâw' niya k-êsiyîhkâtak, piyisk an[a] êkotê kik-êspayihow; ka-wâpahtam wîsta, ê-tâpwêmakahk ita kôhtâwînaw ê-kî-miyikoyahk, kîkwây ka-mawimostamahk;" êkosi mâna kî-itwêw awa kisêyiniw, kâ-kî-ohpikihit; êwakw ânima ê-w-~ k-ôh-kiskisômit [*sic*] awa kisêyiniw. mâcik âw ânohc kâ-kitotak, êkon ôhi nikotwâsik kîkway nikakwêcimâw, mahti ka-~ ê-wî-atoskâtahk êkoni, mâcik ôma nistam ê-kakwêcimak, "â, namôy," îtwêw, "môy êwako ê-wî-atoskâtamân," itwêw. êkos ôhpimê ôma nitastân, mwêhci nîsw âsay mîn êkwa kîkway ê-kakwêcimak, "â, namôy," îtwêw, "môy êwako ê-wî-atoskâtamân." mwêhci nisto ê-kakwêcimak, êwako mîna, "â, namôy mîn êwako ê-wî-atoskâtamân," itwêw.

[7] êkon ôhi nikotwâsik, ê-kîsi-kakwêcimak, kahkiyaw môy êkoni wî-atoskâtam – cikêmô namôy êkoni ê-miywâsiki, tânita ka-kî-ohci-nisitohtâkot ôhi wîsta, otawâsimisa ôsisima. êkwa ôhi nêwo k-êskonamân ôhi, kocawâkanisa êkon êkwa nôtinên: "ôh îta, kôhtâwînaw kâ-kî-miyikoyahk, tânisi k-êsi-mawimoscikêyahk, kâ-nêhiyâwiyahk, êwakoyiw [?*sic*] cî kiwî-otinên, kôhtâwînaw okisêwâtisiwin miyo-wîcêhtowin kitimâkêyihtowin, êwakoyiw cî kiwî-otinên," ê-itak, "êha," itwêw; êkosi mistahi ninanâskomâw êwak ôma ê-nanâskotahk [*sic*]. êkosi mâka, taht ôma kê-kitotât êkon ôhi, mistahi nika-nahêyihtên, ka-nanahihtâkot, ka-nitohtâkot, tânis ê-wî-isi-~ kîkway ê-isi-wîhtamawât. cikêmô êkosi piko ka-tôtamahk, kîkway ka-mâmawôhkamâtoyahk ê-miywâsik kôhtâwînaw ka-nitotamawâyahk, ita kîsikâw ê-miyikoyahk, ka-pimohtâtamahk ê-miywâsik kikîsikâminaw; wiy âyisk

go with him and try to benefit, go and listen to him! Of course he, too, relies upon the same one, that one [God]. But this one [the priest] is not going to work exclusively in the direction of a spiritual life. There in the future, for instance, if you live for awhile, you will begin to see it: that 'priest', as he will be called, that 'scout' as I myself call him, ultimately he, too, will move in this direction [towards the Indian way of worship]; he, too, will see that it is fulfilled, the way in which Our Father has given it to us, what we should worship." That is what the old man who had raised me used to say; that is of what this [other] old man reminded me. Today, for example, when I spoke to this one [in the audience], I asked him about these six things, whether he was going to engage in them; and when I asked him the first time, for example, he said, "Well, no, I am not going to engage in that." So I set this one [the first of ten match-sticks] aside, and then, when again already I asked him, about the second one exactly, he said, "Well, no, I am not going to engage in that." When I also asked him about that, the third one exactly, "Well, I am also not going to engage in that," he said.

[7] When I had finished asking him about these six, he would not engage in any of them – of course they are evil, and how would his own children and grandchildren be able to understand him in that. Then I took the four matches I had left over: "These here, which Our Father has given to us, the way in which we who are Crees are to worship, are you going to accept these, Our Father's grace, living in harmony, compassion for one another, are you going to accept these," I said to him, "Yes," he said; thus I am very grateful to him for his response to that. And thus, as many as he will speak to, I will be greatly content that they should pay heed to him and listen to him, to what he is going to tell them. Of course we must do this, we must work together and request of Our Father that he grant us another day, wherein we might live through our beautiful day; for it is he who looks after our lives. That is why the young people are told, "Never say 'I am my own

kâ-pamihtât kipimâtisiwininaw. êwak ôhci, "êkâya wîhkât 'nitipêyimison' itwê!" k-ôh-itihcik osk-âyak; "wiy âna kâ-tipêyihtahk kipimâtisiwininaw. namôy wîhkâc âkaw-âyihk ka-kî-kîkway-tôtênânaw [*sic*], tâpiskôc ôm âyimôhtowin. k-âyimômâyahk kîc-âyisiyinînaw, ahpô ka-pâhpihâyahk ê-kitimâkinâkosit, kiyânaw anima k-âyimômisoyahk;" êkosi kâ-kî-pê-itwêcik kêhtê-ayak. êwak ôhci, kâ-kî-kitahamâcik kêhtê-ayak ôki, kisêyiniwak, cikêmô kî-pê-nisitawinamwak wiyawâw kîkway. "êkây wîhkâc pâhpihihk nôtikwêsiw wâwîs, âtayôhkanakisow ana, nôtikwêsiw, cikêmô awa, wiya kâ-w-~ kâ-pimipayihtât kitayisiyinîwininaw. kîspin êkâ ohc îskwêw, môy kikâh-pimâtisinânaw k-âyisiyinîwiyahk," kâ-kî-itwêcik mâna. êwak ôma, têpiyâhk êkos ê-pê-itâcimostawak aw ôta kâ-wîtapimak awa. êkosi, êkos ê-isi-nanâskomak ôma, ê-nitohtahk ôma kîkway kâ-wîhtamawak. mâka misawâc kîhtwâm takohtêyâni, wêtinahk êkota nik-âcimonân.

[8] êkosi nikâh-miywêyihtên, êwak ôma wî-tâhkôtamahki kîhtwâm, cikêmô kêhtê-aya piko k-âspitonâmoyahk; wiy ôtihtamâsow mâmaw-ôhtâwîmâwa, anima kîkway kâ-kî-isi-miyopitahk, kâ-kî-isi-miyoniskêhkâtahk, êkotê k-ôh-tawâtamâkoyahk, ka-pîkiskwêstamâkoyahk; êkos ê-itêyihtamân mâna, niy ôma. êwak ôhci mistahi ninahêyihtên, k-âspitonâmoyahk kîkway kêhtê-aya, ahpô wêpinâson ahpô kîsitêw. êwak ôhci kâ-nitôskahk awa, "tânis ânima ê-kî-isi-kîkway-waskawîtotahk" – niy ân[a] ê-miskawak [?*sic*] kîkway, ôtê ê-kî-wawânaskêhtât, êkwa kistêsinaw wîsahkêcâhk. â, cikêmô êkonik kahkiyaw kîkway kikî-wawânaskêhtamâkonawak, êwakw âwa kâ-nitawêyihtahk kik-âcimostawak. mâka kîhtwâm takohtêyâni, pîsâkwan ayisk êwako âcimowin, kisêyinîw-âcimowin ôma, êwako piko kik-âpacihtâyân, kik-âcimostawak. êkosi ê-itâcimostawak ana, mâka miton âya, k-âpacihikot ôma kîkway kâ-nitawêyihtahk; êkos ê-isi-~ ti-~ t-êtâcimostawak ana. niya kâ-pîkiskwêyân ôtê ohc *Onion Lake*, kinisitawêyiminâwâw, 'kâ-pimwêwêhahk'

master'!" – "It is he who rules over our lives. We will never be able to do anything and keep it hidden, such as gossiping about one another. When we gossip about our fellow man, or if we were to laugh at someone who looks pitiable, then we are in fact gossiping about ourselves;" that is what the old people always used to say. That is why the old people, the old men, warned them about it, for they, of course, had come to understand things. "Never laugh at an old woman, in particular, for old women are held to be dream-guardians and they, of course, make our life as humans go on. If it were not for women, we who are humans would not be alive," is what they used to say. This is a small part of what I have come to tell him about, as I sit with him here. That is all, and thus I thank him for listening to that about which I have told him. But perhaps I will come back here another time, in any case, then we will take our time telling stories.

[8] Thus I would be glad if we were going to discuss this again another time, for of course we must put our faith in the testimony of the old people; for they have reached the All-Father for themselves, by that which they have accomplished, by the work of their hands, so that they might open the way for us and intercede for us; that is what I, at least, think. That is why I am greatly content that we should put our faith in the testimony of the old people in these things, or on cloth offerings or on ceremonial food. That is why this one [in the audience] seeks to know, "How did they use to carry out these things" – as for me, I have now found [*?sic*] our elder brother Wisahketchahk, leading a peaceful life over there. Well, of course they had created a peaceful life for us in every respect, and this one wants me to tell him stories about it. But perhaps I will come back here another time, for their stories are rich, the stories of the old men, and that is what I will have to use to tell him stories about it. But I am telling him [one of the audience] these stories so that the things he wants to know may sustain him; these are the stories I should tell him. As for me

nititikawin ê-nêhiyaw-wîhikawiyân; êwak ôma niya k-âcimoyân ôta.

[9] êkosi, êwakw ânim êkos ê-itâcimostawak.

who speaks, I am from Onion Lake over there, you all know me, I am called *kâ-pimwêwêhahk* by my Cree name; it is I who am telling stories on here [on the audio-recorder].

[9] That is all, that is the story I am telling him.

2

[1] êwak ôma kâ-wî-wîhtamâtakok, namôy niya kîkway ê-kiskêyihtamân, mâk êtokwê kôhtâwînaw, kâ-tipêyihtahk awa kîkway, êwakw êtok ôm ê-itêyimit, tânisi k-êsi-wîhtamawak kîkway osk-âya, êkâ kinwês ôta ka-kî-wîcêwak ayisiyiniw, êwak ôhci. ê-waniskâyêk ita kîkisêpâ, ka-nanâskomâyêk kôhtâwînaw, ê-miyikoyêk kîsikâw, ê-miywâsik ita ka-pimohtâtamêk, okisêwâtisiwin âhci piko ka-nanâskotamêk; namôy nânitaw itâpatan kîkway, tâpiskôc ôma, îh, iyôtin [*sic*] iyikohk kâ-pimohtêmakahk, êkây wîhkâc sêkisik, êkây wîhkâc mawimok! kiskisik kôhtâwînaw, wiy âna kâ-tipêyihtahk ôma kiwaskawîwininaw; tânis îtêyihtahki, êkosi k-êspayinâwâw. kîspin itêyimikoyahko, kitimâkêyimikoyahko, ka-wîmâskâkonaw ana kâ-pimohtêt iyôtin [*sic*]. êwak ôma, îh, k-ôh-matotisiyâhk, k-ôh-matotisiyâhk, wêpinâson ê-pimi-pakitinamâhk.

[2] tânis ê-itâpatahk, kotakak ôk âskîhkânihk, êkâ kîkway êkotowahk ê-nâtâmostahkik, kâ-tâh-tâwinikocik ôm êwako kîkway. êwak ôma niyanân ê-mamisîyâhk, tahto-nîso-kîsikâw ê-matotisiyâhk, wêpinâsona ê-pakitinamâhk; tânitahtwâw êkwa ê-pimohtêt, niwîmâskâkonân. ê-tâpwêmakahk, kîkway, okisêwâtisiwin ita ê-nitotamâht kôhtâwînaw. môy nânitaw itâpatan ka-mawimoyahk ôta; môy nânitaw, môy kiyânaw kitipêyihtênânaw wiya; wiy îtêyihtahki, kitimâkinâkoyahko, ka-nisitawinênânaw okisêwâtisiwin; êwakw ânima niy ê-âpacihtâyân tahto-kîsikâw. wîhkaskwa k-ôhpahpahtênamân, k-êtwêstamâkoyahk, êkosi wiya niy ê-isi-mamisîyân; êwak ôma, kîstawâw ê-waniskâyêk, nanâskomihk kôhtâwînaw, ê-miyikoyêk kîsikâw ita ka-pimohtâtamêk! âhci piko nitotamâhk okisêwâtisiwin! ka-kitimâkinâkonaw, ê-mâmawôhkamâtohk kîkway, tânis ê-isi-pakosêyimohk, êwakw ânima. namôy nânitaw itâpatan, môy nânitaw itâpatan, ka-wanikiskisiyahk, kôhtâwînaw kîkway ê-kî-~, wiya, ê-tipêyihtahk kiwaskawîwininaw; pikoyikohk, pikw îtê itâmoyahko, pikw îtê mawimoyani, môy nânitaw ka-kî-nâtamâkon, wiy îtêyihtahki,

[1] Of this which I am about to tell you, I myself know nothing, but surely Our Father, he who rules everything, surely it is his will that I should tell these things to the young people in this way, for I will not be able to be amongst the living for long, that is the reason. As you arise in the morning, you should give thanks to Our Father that he has granted you another day wherein you might live through a beautiful day, and despite everything you should give thanks for his grace; anything else is pointless [to rely upon] – for example now, behold, when so many tornadoes go through, never fear, never cry out! Remember Our Father, for it is he who rules our coming and going; whatever is his will, that will happen to you. If it is his will for us, if he thinks of us with pity, this Tornado which is going through will pass around us. This is why, behold, why we have the sweat-lodge, why we hold the sweat-lodge and offer cloth in it.

[2] What is the point [of anything else], other people on reserves, because they do not turn to that kind [the sweat-lodge] for help, that is why these things have been hitting them. As for us, we rely on this, we hold a sweat-lodge every other day, we present cloth offerings; and although it [the Tornado] has gone through now several times, it has passed around us. It is fulfilled, that in which Our Father's grace is requested. It is pointless for us to cry out here; for we ourselves have no control over it, none at all; if it is his will, if he takes pity upon us, we will recognise his grace; as for me, I make use of that every day. When I smudge with sweetgrass and the smoke rises up, that it might speak for us, as for me, that is where I place my reliance; and this holds for you, too, as you arise, do give thanks to Our Father that he has granted you another day wherein you might live through it! Ask him for his grace, despite everything! He will take pity upon us as people work together on something, the things people hope for, all that. It is pointless, it is pointless for us to forget that it is he, Our Father, who rules our coming and going; no matter where we might flee, no matter where you might cry out, it cannot rescue

ka-nâtamâkonaw; êwak ôma kâ-wîhtamawak ayisiyiniw, kâkikê, môy nânitaw itâpatan êwakw ânima, ka-~ ka-mawimot ayisiyiniw. âhci piko kâ-kiskisit kôhtâwînaw ôhi, wiya ka-kitimâkinâkoyahk, ita kâ-kî-pakitinikoyahk ôma, ê-nihtâwikîstamahk askiy. tâpiskôc îh, kahkiyaw kîkway kîs-ôcawâsimisiw, kahkiyaw kîkway, kâ-papâmihât awa, kâ-papâmipahtât ôta askîhk, kahkiyaw kîs-ôtawâsimisiw êwako. pêyakwan ôma maskihkiy, kâ-wîhtamâtân awa, kôhkominaw awa kâ-sâkikihtât ôm âskiy; kahkiyaw êwakw êkwa sâkikin îh. êwak ôhc ânima, ê-ati-kwêskinâkwahk ôm âskiy, êwak ôhci êkâ ka-pônihtât ayisiyiniw, ka-nanâskomot tahto-kîsikâw, ka-kâkîsimototâht êwakw âwa kâ-pimohtêt ôta, wêpinâson ka-miyiht, ka-matotisihk; ka-nitotamâht ê-miywâsik kîkway; êwako piko kiyê-âpacihikoyahk, êwako piko kiyê-âpacihikoyahk.

[3] kiyâm, pikoyikohk ê-iyinîsit ayisiyiniw, mihcêtwâw niwîhtamawâwak okimâhkânak, ê-taswêkinahkik masinahikan; pîtos awa k-ês-âyimihât [*sic*] ayisiyiniw, ê-taswêkinahk masinahikan ê-mamisît, namôy masinahikan ka-kî-nâtamâk; kôhtâwînawa piko ka-nâtamâkot.

[4] ê-kî-isi-wiyakimikoyahk ôta kôhtâwînaw, ôma îh kâ-kî-âpacihtât, ôma [*gesture*] kî-âpacihtâw ômis ê-isiniskêyit [*gesture*], "ê-wî-âyimômiyan ôma, niy ôm ôma," kî-itwêw, ôma ocihciy, "ôhi nêwo, êkoni kâ-miyitân ka-mawimoscikêyan. ôma kwêskinisk, êwak ôma nanâtohk ayimihâwin [*sic*], môniyâw-âyimihâwin [*sic*], namôy êwako kimiyitin," kâ-kî-itât êsa nêhiyawa. "tânita k-ôh-tâpwêhtawiyan, ê-miyitân ôma; kîkway ê-wî-tôtaman, ôma k-ôtinên, îh; êwako kâ-miyitân kisêwâtisiwin." êkos ês ê-kî-itwêt awa kôhtâwînaw ôta, kâ-kî-wîhtamawât kisêyiniwa. êkoni ôhi nêwo mawimoscikêwina, êwak ôm ê-~ nîkânohk matotisân, nipâkwêsimowikamik, pîhtwâwikamik, êk ôma

you, if it is his will, he will rescue us; this is what I tell people all the time, that it is pointless for a person to cry out. When Our Father remembers them despite everything, it is he who will take pity upon us, where he has placed us as we populate the earth. Behold, for example, all creatures have had their young [*i.e.*, in the middle of summer], all creatures, those that fly about and those that run about here on the ground, all of them have had their young. The same is true of the plants, she about whom I have told you, it is Our Grandmother who makes this earth grow forth; behold, now all plants have come out. That is why, as the earth changes colour, that is why people should not cease of it, giving thanks every day, chanting prayers to the one who walks across here [the sun] and for him to be given cloth offerings, and holding a sweat-lodge; that he should be asked for good things; that is the only thing that will sustain us, that is the only thing that will sustain us.

[3] No matter how smart a person may be, many times I have told the chiefs as they open up a book; when a person follows a different religion, opening up a book and relying upon it, a book cannot come to his rescue; only Our Father will rescue him.

[4] As Our Father arranged it for us here, when he used this, he used this [*points to his heart*], behold, as he pointed here [*gestures with his hand*], "You are going to talk about me, it is I," he had said, referring to his hand, "these four, I give you these to worship with. This other hand, this is for all the different religions, for the religions of the Whites, I do not give you that," he had said to the Crees, it is reported. "Wherein you should believe me, I give you this; when you are going to do something, you will take this, behold; this is the grace I am giving you." That is what Our Father had said here, what he told the old men. These are the four ways of worship, the sweat-lodge in the first place, the sun-dance, the pipe-lodge, and also this ghost-dance; these were given

wâsakâmêsimowin ôma; êkon ôhi kâ-kî-miyiht ayisiyiniw, ka-kâkîsimwâkêt. tâpiskôt pêyakwan ôma kâ-kîsitêpoyan, kâ-nîminamawat kêhtê-aya, âsay êkota k-ôh-kitâpamikowisin, êkos ânima ê-kî-itakihtahk êwak ôma. êwak ôhc ôma, k-ôh-kî-itwêcik kisêyiniwak, "kahkiyaw kîkway ê-kîsi-nihtâwikik, ê-nihtâwikinâwasot kahkiyaw pisiskiw, mâcikôtitan wayawî! miton îtê ê-kanâtahcâk, êkota nahapi! ômis îsi [*gesture*] pâskina maskosiya! ka-wâpamâw êkot[a] ê-pimâhtawît manicôs, ê-askôs--, êwakw ân[a] ê-askîwiskahk askiy, êwak ôhci kitimâkêyimihk! wâwîs awa -- piyêsîsa, êkon ê-kihcêyimât kôhtâwînaw, ê-ocawâsimisit ê-wâpamâyêk, êkâya wîhkâc pisiskêyimihk ana!" kî-itwêwak mâna kisêyiniwak, êwak ôhci k-ôh-manâcihtâhk kîkway. wiy âna ê-kitimâkêyimât êkoni. tâpiskôc îh, pêpîsis kimiyikawin, ka-kitimâkêyimat an[a] êwako, ka-kitimâkêyimat.

[5] anohc kâ-kîsikâk kipihcipôhikonaw wâpiski-wiyâs, ita ôma kâ-pimohtêyahk. kîhkânâkwan ât[a] êwako, mâka namôy, âsay kiwanisimikonaw wâpiski-wiyâs, wanisimêw kitawâsimisinawa. mâcikôtitan, tânita k-ôh-tâpwêhtahk ayisiyiniw, 'misatim' awa k-êsiyîhkâsot nik-ôtinâw, nika-sakahpitâw ôta, nika-sîkihtatamawâw kistikâna, iyâyaw êkoni ka-pimakocin; êkosi mwêhci ê-tôtâhcik ôki, kitawâsimisinawak kôsisiminawak, tahto-nîsw-âyamihêwi-kîsikâw ê-miyihcik ka-mîcisocik kîkway, êkoni mêtawâkêwak; wanisimikwak âsay êkota môniyâwa. itê niyanân kâ-kî-pê-ohpikiyâhk, nikî-nitonênân kîkway ka-pimâcihwâkêyâhk, nikî-atoskânân; nama kîkway êkwa anohc, êkota âsay ê-wanisimikoyahk. k-- êwak ôhc êkâ k-ôh-tâpwêwakêyihtahk nêhiyawi-mawimoscikêwin, osk-âya ana. nama kîkway, ôtê, nâway ahêw kêhtê-aya, nôtikwêwa ôtê ahêw; "niya nawat nitiyinîsin," ê-itêyihtahk; ê-wanisimikot anihi môniyâwa. êkos ôma ê-isinâkwahk, mêkwât ita kâ-pimohtêyahk; êwak ôm ôhci, osk-âya, namôy mîna nânitaw ê-itâpatahk ka-kisîkitotat kitawâsimis, kôsisim mîna; môy nânitaw itâpatan ka-kisîwêhkahtawat kîkway ê-kitahamawat; môy ka-kî-âpacihik,

to the people with which to chant their prayers. The same is true, for example, when you cook a feast, when you offer food to the old people, on those grounds alone you will be looked upon with favour by the powers, that is the value he had put on that. That is why the old men used to say, "When all the plants have come out and all the creatures have had their young, just see, go outside! Sit down where the ground is really clean! Open the blades of grass up like this [*gesture*]! There you will see an insect crawling along, populating the earth, therefore think of it with compassion! Especially the birds, Our Father thinks highly of them, and when you see a bird with its young, never bother it!" the old men used to say, that is why one should treat things with respect. He himself thinks of them with pity. For example, behold, you have been given a baby so that you might think of that one with compassion, you are to think of it with compassion.

[5] Today the Whites have poisoned us, and the place where we live. That is obvious indeed, but no [*i.e.*, it is too late], already the Whites have led us astray, they have led our children astray. As an illustration, so that people might thereby believe it, I will take the 'horse' as he is called, I will tie him here, I will pour him some grain, and before anything else he will go for that; this is exactly what is being done to our children and grandchildren, every two weeks they are simply given things to eat, and they play with that; in that already they have been led astray by the Whites. At the time when we ourselves were growing up, we used to look for something with which to make our living, we used to work; there is none of that today; in that already they have lead us astray. That is why the young do not believe in the Cree way of worship. They do not believe in anything, they have put the old people over there in the background, they have put the old women over there; "I am smarter myself," they think; they have been led astray by the Whites. This is what it looks like, the situation in which we live at present; that is also why it is pointless for you to scold your children and also your grandchildren; it is pointless for you to

pêyâhtik kitos! pêyâhtik kitos! nisitohtamôh ôma! tânis ê-ispayik, kitimâkêyihtowin, tâpiskôc ôki, îh, k-êtapicik, kitimâkêyihtowin êtokwê, ê-owîcisânihtocik, êwako kâ-kî-miyikoyahk kôhtâwînaw, ka-kitimâkêyihtoyahk. kiyâm pikoyikohk ê-kitimâkisit kisêyiniw, nôtikwêsiw ê-kitimâkisit, ka-kitimâkêyimiht; âsay ôtê kikitâpamikawin. wâwîs cî ê-kîwâtisit awâsis, ê-kicimâkisit, ka-wîcôhkamawâyêk; âsay ôtê kikitâpamikawin, kîkway ê-kîspinataman. îh, nêwosâp ê-at-îtahtopiponwêyân ê-ohc-âtoskawak kisêyiniw, nama kîkway nôh-wâpahtên ka-kîspinatamân; anohc kâ-kîsikâk mâna ninanâskomon, ê-mihcêticik nôsisimak, pêyakosâp ihtasiwak nôsisimak, mihcêtiwak nitâniskotâpânak; êkonik êcik ôki ê-kîspinatamawakik, iyikohk ê-kî-pê-kakwâtakihoyân, êwako mâna ninanâskomon êyâpic. êwak ôhc îtê tiyêpwâtikawiyâni, niwî-kakwê-takohtân, kîkway ê-miywâsik ka-kakwê-wîcôhkamawak ayisiyiniw. namôy ôta [*gesture*] ê-otinamân, môy ê-iyinîsiyân, ê-itwêyân, mâka kôhtâwînaw êtokwê ê-itêyimit, ka-kî-wîcôhkamawak ayisiyiniw. êwak ôhci mâna nimiywêyihtên ka-wîhtamawak kîkway ê-miywâsik ayisiyiniw. misawâc ôta, ispî mêht-~ [*sic*] mêstohtêtwâwi, tâpiskôc ôma kiyânaw kâ-kêhtê-ayiwiyahk, nakatamahk[i] ôm âskiy, êkâ kîkway wîhtamawâyahk[i] ôsk-âya, tânis êkwa kê-tôtahk?

[6] êwak ôm ôhci, nawac ê-miywâsik kîkway ka-nakatamahk, k-âpacihtât, tâpiskôc ômatowihk [*gesture*] ka-nitohtahk, êkota k-ôh-kiskisôhtot osk-âya. namôy nânitaw ê-itâpatahk ôta ayisiyiniw k-âyimôhtot, wâwîs ê-ot-~ ê-owîcisânihtot. nânitaw ê-wî-itwêt ayisiyiniw, ahpô niya tipiyaw, nânitaw ê-isit ayisiyiniw, niyîkatêhtân, namôy ninôhtê-nitohtawâw, môy nânitaw itâpatan ayisk ka-nitohtawak, konita ka-naskwêwasimak; nawac anima, êkâ ka-nitohtawak, êkos ê-kî-isi-wîhtamâkawiyân niya; êwak ôhci kik-âpacihikonâwâw

raise your voice and scold them when you are warning them about something; it cannot benefit them, speak to them quietly! Speak to them quietly! Make them understand it! How it works to love one another, just like these, behold, as they sit here and seem to love one another like siblings, that is what Our Father has given us, that we should love one another. No matter how poor an old man may be, how poor an old woman may be, one must look upon them with compassion; already you are looked upon with favour from over there. Especially a child that is orphaned, that poor little thing, you all should help him; already you are looked upon with favour from over there, you have your reward. Behold, since I was going on fourteen years of age I worked for an old man, and I did not see anything by way of reward; today I always give thanks that I have many grandchildren, my grandchildren number eleven, and my great-grandchildren are many; they, of course, are my reward for having made myself suffer over the years, and I still always give thanks for that. Because of that I try to go wherever they call me from, so that I might try to help people with good things. I do not take it from here [*gesture*], I am not saying that I am smart, but it must be Our Father's will for me that I should be able to help people. For that reason I always like telling people good things. In any case, when all those here will have died, just like us ourselves, once we who are old will have departed this earth, if we do not tell the young about this, what will they do then?

[6] That is why it is better that we should leave behind good things for them to use, for example, that they might listen on this kind [*points to the audio-recorder*] and that the young might thereby remind one another. It is pointless for people here to gossip about one another, especially as they are siblings. When a person is going to say something negative, even to me personally, when a person says something negative to me, I simply walk away, I do not want to listen to him, for it is pointless for me to listen to him, and it is in vain for me to respond to him; it is

ê-isi-owîcisânihtoyêk, ê-isi-otawâsimisiyêk kôsisimak, ka-kitimâkêyimiskik, mêkwâc ê-wîcêwacik, êwakw ânima piko kê-pimohtahikocik; êkosi ê-kî-isi-wîhtamâkawiyân niya. êk ôm ânohc k-ôh-miywêyihtamân ka-wîhtamawak kîkway ê-miywâsik, kîkway.

[7] kîkwây ohci k-ôh-wîhtamân, maskihkiy ôma k-ôtinamân, ê-miywâsik ê-kî-nakatamâkawiyân, ayisiyiniw êwako ê-âpacihtamôhak mihcêt, ê-ohci-miyw-âyât êkota ohci. pêyakwan kâkîsimowin, wêpinâsona kâ-pîkiskwâtamân, ê-nisitawinahk ayisiyiniw, ninanâskomon mân êwako. namôya, môy kîkway ê-mâyêyihtamân ka-tôtamân, mâka, kîkway kâ-mamisîwâtikawiyân, tâpwê nitêhihk ninitotamân kîkway ê-miywâsik ka-nisitawinamân; êkos ôma ê-ispayik êwak ôma. [*to FA:*] êwak ôhci mîna, ôma wâhyaw kâ-wî-itohtêyan ôma, êkây wîhkâc wanikiskisi kitawâsimisak ôtê ê-nakatacik! kôhtâwînaw nitotamaw, ka-kanawêyihtamâsk! – êwakw ânima piko kê-âpacihikoyan.

[8] hâw, êkosi piko ê-isi-wîhtamâtakok, k-âpacihikoyêk ôma kîkway.

better that I should not even listen to him, that is what I myself was told and that [rule] will benefit you as the siblings you are to one another, and as the parents and grandparents you are, so that they might love you while you are here on earth with them, that is the only thing that will guide them through life; that is what I myself was told; that is why today I like to tell them good things.

[7] The reason why I tell this is that the medicine which I collect is good medicine which has been left behind for me, and that I have used it for the benefit of many people and they have gotten well from it. The same is true of the chanting of prayers, when I speak a prayer over cloth offerings, people recognise it [as good], and I always give thanks for that. No, I do not venture out to do things, but when someone relies on me for something, then I truly ask from my heart for the good things that I might recognise; this is how it works. [*to FA:*] And for that reason you, too, when you are going to travel far away, never forget that you are leaving your children behind over here! Ask Our Father to keep them for you! – That is the only thing that will sustain you.

[8] Indeed, that is all I am telling you, about things that will sustain you.

3

[1] êwak ôma kêhcinâ, ê-nôhtê-ati-pîkiskwâtak *Alec* awa, êwak ôhci k-ôh-kî-pê-sêwêpitamawak, ôtê ê-ohtohtêyân ôma, itê kâ-kî-pê-nâtitisahokawiyân; mâka, pitamâ êwakw ê-wî-âcimostâtakok, wîsta êtokwê ê-itêyimikot mâmaw-ôhtâwîmâwa, ê-wî-nakatahk askiy, êkota kâ-kî-pîkiskwâtât ayisiyiniwa. "tânêhk êtokwê," nititêyihtên, "ê-kitimâkisiyân niya, êkâ kîkway ê-kiskêyihtamân, itê wâhyaw k-ôh-pê-nâtitisahokawiyân, ka-nitawi-nitohtawak an[a] ê-wî-pîkiskwêt;" – ê-kiskêyihtahk ê-wî-nakatahk askiy. êwakw ânima, môy kakêtihk nikî-mâmitonêyihtên êkotê ê-takohtêyân, ê-wâpamak, ê-âspatisihk ômis îsi [*gesture*], "matwân cî awa tâpwê ê-wî-nakatahk askiy," nititêyihtên, namôy mitoni nitâpwêwakêyihtên ê-wî-nakatahk askiy, kâ-wî-pîkiskwêt ôma.

[2] hâw, êkwa ospwâkan ê-kî-miyikawiyân, ê-kîsi-pîhtwâyân nimâmitonêyihtên, "tâpwê, tâpwê, wiya kôhtâwînaw kâ-tipêyihtahk kipimâtisiwininaw, tâpwê êtokw âwa ê-kiskêyihtamôhikowisit kîkway ka-wîhtamawât ayisiyiniwa," nititêyihtên.

[3] êkos êkwa, êwak ôm ê-mâmitonêyimak mêkwâc ê-apit, "â, mitoni tâpwê, kwayask kimâmitonêyihtên ôma k-êsi-mâmitonêyihtaman," k-êsit, "mâka, kiya nîkân ôma ê-wî-kitotitân," nititik. "âha!" nititâw, "tâpwê mistahi ka-miywâsin kîkway ê-miywâsik ka-wîhtamawiyan," nititâw.

[4] "hâw! ôma k-êtahkamikisiyan, êkây wîhkât nânitaw itêyihta! êkây wîhkât nânitaw itêyihta! anohc mistahi kimâmitonêyihtên ita k-âpiyan," nititik. "êha," nititâw; "kitâpwân; nîso-kîkway ôma mistah ê-mâmitonêyihtamân," nititâw; "kiy ôma ê-mâmitonêyimitân," nititâw. "êkwa ôm îta k-âpiyân," nititâw, "wâhyaw ôma k-ôhtohtêyân," nititâw; "êkwa ôm îta k-âpiyân, mâka namôy nânitaw êyâpic ê-itêyihtamân," nititâw, "êkos ôm

[1] This is for certain that I wanted to speak to Alec [Greyeyes], that is why I had phoned him here, coming from over there where they had sent for me; but first I am going to tell you that story, that it must have been the will of the All-Father for this one [a certain old man], too, as he was about to depart this world, to have spoken to the people at that time. "I wonder why," I thought, "as for me, since I am poor and do not know anything, why they had sent for me far away over there so that I might go and listen to the one who was about to speak;" – he knew he was about to depart this world. I thought about that a great deal as I arrived over there and saw him lying back like this [*gesture:* propped up], "I wonder if he is truly about to die," I thought, I did not really believe that he was about to depart this world, he who was about to speak.

[2] Indeed, now I was given the pipe, and when I had finishing smoking, I thought about it, "It is true, it is true, for it is Our Father who rules our lives, it must be true that he [the old man] has been given some spiritual knowledge so that he might tell the people about it," I thought.

[3] So then I was thinking this of him while he sat there, "Well, it is really true, you think about it properly, this what you are thinking about," he said to me, "but it is you [rather than the people at large] whom I am about to address first," he said to me. "Yes!" I said to him, "It will truly be very good that you will tell me good things," I said to him.

[4] "Indeed! The work you do, never complain about it in your thoughts! Never complain about it in your thoughts! At this time, as you sit here, you think about it a great deal," he said to me. "Yes," I said to him; "you tell the truth; I am thinking a great deal about two things," I said to him; "it is you I am thinking about," I said to him. "Now as I sit here," I said to him, "for I have come from far away," I said to him; "now as I sit here, I am still not

ôta ê-micimôhoyân," nititâw, "ôta ôma kâ-wâpamiyan ê-apiyân, katisk ôma nipimohtêwin ôt[a] ê-takohtêyân ê-têpipayiyân; êwak ôma mîna kâ-mâmitonêyihtamân," nititâw; "mâka, kôhtâwînaw itêyihtahk[i] êtokwê, kâwi nika-wâyonîn ôta ohci," nititâw, "wiy âyisk, kîkway kâ-pimipayihtât," nititâw.

[5] êwak ôhci, namôy wîhkât nânitaw nititêyihtên, ayisk nikî-isi-wîhtamâk kisêyiniw. " 'ita kîkway ê-wawânêyihtaman, ahpô misatimwak ê-âpacihacik ê-pimitâpâsoyan, kîkway ê-pîkopayik, êkây wîhkâc ka-kisiwâhik kôhtâwînaw, wiy âna, ê-itêyihtahk ê-kotêyimisk, mahti tânis ê-itastêk kimitonêyihcikan;' êkosi mâna nikî-itik nôhtâwiy," nititâw, "mêkwâc ê-pimâtisit," nititâw. "êwako mâna nikiskisopayin," nititâw, "itê kâ-micimôhoyân, môy nânitaw nititêyihtên; âhci piko ninitotamawâw kôhtâwînaw okisêwâtisiwin. êkos ôma, k-ôh-nanâskomoyân tahtwâw ê-waniskâyân, tahtwâw ê-kîsikâk ninanâskomâw kôhtâwînaw. ê-nanâskomak, ê-wîcihak ayisiyiniw, ê-mihcêticik nôsisimak; pêyakosâp ê-ihtasicik nôsisimak, nitâniskotâpânak ê-mihcêticik. 'êwako êcik ôma ê-kîspinatamân,' nititêyihtên mâna, êwako mâna k-ôh-nanâskomak." êkosi nitisi-kitotâw awa. "tâpwê kwayask kimâmitonêyihtên. mâk ôma, kâ-tasîhkaman, êkây pônihtâ!" nititik. matotisân ôma, êwak ôma piko ka-pimohtahikoyêk ôtê nîkân, êkwa êkoni ôhi (îh! k-êtastêki ôhi wêpinâsona), êkâya konita pîhtikwêtotamok matotisân! êkon ôhi êkota ka-pîhtikwêmakanwa.

[6] êkoni ôhi kîsi-pîkiskwâtamêko, êkon ôhi kê-kanawêyimikoyêk, 'wêpinâsona' k-êsiyîhkâtêki; êwak ôhci, k-ôh-kî-pê-miyawâkâtinikêt kisêyiniw, kîkway ê-nâtâmostahk, ê-nâcinêhikêhk ôhi. kôhtâwînaw otôskinîkîma okisêwâtisiwin ê-nitôskamâmiht, êkon ôhi k-êtastêki, îh, kiwâpahtênâwâw êkon ôhi. tâpiskôc aw êwakw âwa kâ-wîhtamawak otâkosihk, mistahi nimiywêyihtên ôm ît[a] ê-kikastêk ôma. êkotowahk

complaining in my thoughts," I said to him, "and now I am stuck here," I said to him; "as you see me sit here, I had barely enough for my travel in coming here; I am also thinking of that," I said to him; "but, I suppose if it is Our Father's will, I will again return from here," I said to him, "for it is he who runs things," I said to him.

[5] For that reason I never complain in my thoughts, for the old man had told me this. " 'Whenever you are worried about something, even when you are using horses and driving along and something breaks, never let yourself get angry at Our Father, for it is he, it is his will, and he is trying your patience, to see how your mind is set;' that is what my father used to tell me," I said to him, "while he was alive," I said to him. "This often comes to my mind," I said to him, "when I am stuck, I do not complain in my thoughts; despite everything I ask Our Father for his grace. Thus I give thanks each time I arise, as each new day breaks I give thanks to Our Father. I give thanks to him that I am able to help people and that I have many grandchildren; my grandchildren number eleven, and my great-grandchildren are many. 'Evidently this is the reward I have earned,' I often think, and for that I always give him thanks." In this way I spoke to this one [the old man]. "You truly think about it properly. But this in which you are engaged, do not cease of it!" he said to me. The sweat-lodge, that is the only thing which will guide you there in the future, and these (behold! how these cloth offerings are arranged here), do not enter the sweat-lodge without them! Let these go in there.

[6] When you have finished offering them in prayer, these will keep you, 'the cloth offerings' as they are called; that is why the old men always used to be so particular in their ceremonies, when they were turning to something for help, when one is seeking to obtain help with these [cloth offerings]. Our Father's grace is requested from his servants with these cloth offerings as they are arranged here, behold, you all see them [these piles of cloth] here.

ôta ka-kî-astêk, mâka namôya nânitaw; pêyakwan ôma [*gesture*]kikâwînaw ôma, k-êtakihtêk ôma wêpinâson, mwêhci niyânan êwak ôma. cikêmô, wiya, ôta k-ôh-âpiyahk, kikâwînaw askiy awa, êkota ê-kî-pakitinât kôhtâwînaw; askiy ôma, ita k-ôhpikihitoyahk.

[7] êwak ôhci, nistam ê-kîsakimât ayisiyiniwa ôta kâ-kî-kitotât ('nâpêw' k-êsiyîhkâsot), êkoni kâ-kî-kitotât. "kiwâpahtên cî ôhi" (ômisi [*gesture*] k-êsiniskêyit), "kiwâpahtên cî ôhi ê-itwêmakahki?" – "namôya, namôya." – "kika-wîhtamâtin, tânis ê-itwêmakahk."

[8] ôm ôt[a] ê-itahtwapiyahk, awîn ôma mitoni nêhiyaw-~ ê-nêhiyâwit t-êtêyihtahk, ôm ôta ê-itahtwapiyêk? kîkwây nêhiyâwiwin mitoni ka-kiskêyihtahk, kisêyiniwak kâ-kî-pê-nakatahkik? môy êkâ êtokwê awiyak ohci-wîhtamawâw – mâcikôtitan kitâpahtamok nêma [*gesture*] kâ-masinahikâtêk, nêma. nêma watihkwan kâ-nâtwâpayik, îh, piyêsiw anima ê-kî-tôtahk, êwakw ânima. êkos ê-isi-wâpahtamêk, kâ-nâtwâwêpahahk ôma, ê-na-~ ê-otinamihk anima, otinikâtêw, ê-kî-itôtahkik kêhtê-ayak, êkwa êwakw ânima ê-kanawêyihtahkik. mêton ôma kâ-nîpihk, kâ-misi-mâyi-kîsikâyik, capasis kâ-kitocik, ê-kî-macostêhahkik anima. ispahkêkocin aw êwako kâ-kitot. êkos ânim ê-kî-itâpacihtâcik êwakw ânima. êkwa mîna pîtos kî-itâpacihtâwak, mêtoni kâ-wî-~ kâ-wî-nipahikot wîpita ôm âyisiyiniw, êkota mîna êkot[a] ânim ê-kî-astâcik – pîkwatowanw[a] ânihi mîpita; êkos ôma ê-kî-itâpacihtâcik nêma.

It is as I told this one yesterday, I am very pleased that this one [*i.e.*, a cloth printed with a pattern, rather than in solid colour] is included here amongst them. That kind [*i.e.*, printed pattern] should be included here, but no matter if it is not [for it counts as green, and there is already a green cloth amongst the solid ones]; for Our Mother, this cloth [*points to solid green*] counts the same [as the printed pattern], this makes exactly five cloth offerings. For she is the cause, of course, why we sit here upon her, here upon this earth Our Mother has Our Father placed us; upon this earth, where we are to multiply.

[7] For this reason, when first he had completed his charge to the people, here he had spoken to him ('man' as he is called), he had spoken to that one. "Do you see these" (pointing in this direction [*gesture*] with his hand), "do you see these, what they stand for?" – "No, no." – "I will tell you what they stand for."

[8] As many of us as are sitting here, who then is really Cree – who thinks that he is really Cree, as many of you as are sitting here? That he would really know what Creeness is, what the old men have been leaving behind for us? No doubt **someone** must have been told about it – wait, you all look at that painting over yonder [*points to the framed picture of a tree with a broken branch*], that one over yonder. That broken branch over yonder, behold, the Thunderbird has done that, that very thing. And as you all see, when he has broken it off and thrown it down, they take it, it is taken, that is what the old people used to do, and they kept it. Then, in midsummer in a severe thunderstorm, with the thunderclaps low to the ground, they used to throw it into the fire. That Thunderer rises up high. That is how they made use of that one [the branch]. And they also used it for something else, when a person had a terrible toothache, they also used to place that [*i.e.*, a piece of the branch] on there; those teeth then rot [*i.e.*, and fall out]; thus did they made use of that one yonder.

[9] êwak ôhci, mayaw ê-wâpahtahkik êkotowahk, kî-otinamwak kisêyiniwak, ê-kanawêyihtahkik êwako. êwakw ânima kâ-kakwêcimitakok, îh, môy âhpô awiyak êtok ôh-pê-nâkatôhkêw êwako.

[10] êkwa anima capasis, ana kâ-pimohtêt ana, tâpiskôt piyêsîs k-êsinâkosit – awîn ânihi kâh-kî-wîhêw, ka-nêhiyawêt, tânisi k-êsiyîhkâtât êkoni? kîspin kî-pêhtam, tânis ê-isiyîhkâsot êwakw âna? kipêhtawâwâw êwako k-êkwaskwahk [*sic*], ômatowihk [*gesture*] ê-pê-~ ê-pêhtâkosit ispimihk, ômis [*gesture*] ê-isi-tapahcipayihot ê-kitot, êwakw ân[a] âna kâ-masinahikâsot. êkwa, k-êkwaskwahk [*sic*] ôma kâ-pêhtâkosit, ahpô k-ât[i]-âstê-kîsikâk, âsay êkota pêhtâkosiw, ômis [*gesture*] ê-isi-tâh-tapahcipayihot ê-ât-~. êwako ê-nêhiyawêhk 'opacaskahasîs' isiyîhkâsow; ôm ê-~, tâpiskôc askiy ê-~ ê-kitâpahtahk êkwa kîsik; êwakw ânima k-ôh-isiyîhkâsot, 'opacaskahasîs'; tâpiskôt ôma kîsik êkwa askiy, êwakw ânima k-ôh-tapahcipayihot; êwakw ân[a] âna kâ-masinahikâsot. êwakw ânima, kâ-itamân, môy kinitawi-kiskêyihtênânaw tânisi kîkway ê-pê-ispayik ôma, kâ-nêhiyawi-wîhtamohk.

[11] êwak ôhci, mistahi k-ôh-nanâskomoyân, mêkwâc ôta ê-pimâtisiyân kîkway ka-wîhtamawak ayisiyiniw. namôy wiyê kîkway ê-kiskêyihtamân, mâka, kîkwây anoht k-âpacihikot, êwako kâ-nôhtê-wîhtamawak ayisiyiniw. êwak ôhc îh, mayaw kâ-takohtêyân nêtê, nitaskîhk, âsay êkota wêpinâson ê-astêk, cistêmâw ê-apit, "hâw, êkotê ê-nitomikawiyan!" hâ, tânisi kê-kî-tôtamân – piyisk mân ôsiskêpayiw tânis ê-isi-pimohtêyân. êwako kâ-itamân, môy wîhkâc nimihtâtên, ka-nitawi-wîcôhkamawak nawac ayisiyiniw, mêkwâc ôta ê-pimâtisiyân.

[12] êkâ êkosi tôtahki kêhtê-aya, mihcêt kêhtê-aya kipê-wâpamâwâw mâcikôtitan, nama kîkway ê-miywâsik

[9] For this reason the old men used to take it, as soon as they saw that kind, and they kept it. That is what I ask you, behold, I am sure no one has ever even paid attention to that.

[10] And that one below, the one who walks along, the one who looks like a bird – who could name that one, in Cree, what does he call that one? If he has heard his name, what is the name of that one? You have all heard his cry when it is cloudy, he can be heard in this place [*gesture*], high in the sky, he gives this cry as he comes swooping down like this [*gesture*], that is the one depicted in the painting. And it is when it is cloudy that he can be heard, even when the storm is beginning to subside, then already he can be heard, as he comes swooping down like this [*gesture*]. In Cree that one is called *opacaskahasîs*; it is as if he were looking at the earth and the sky; that is why he is called that, *opacaskahasîs*; it is like the sky and the earth, that is why he swoops down low; that is the one depicted in the painting. That is what I meant, we do not usually go and find out how it has come about, when one uses the Cree name for something.

[11] That is why I greatly give thanks that I might tell people something while I am still alive here on earth. Of course I do not know anything, but whatever might be of benefit to people now, that is what I want to tell them. For that reason, behold, as soon as I arrive back yonder over there, on my own reserve, there is already a cloth offering waiting there, and tobacco waiting, "Indeed, you are invited over there!" Well, to the best of my ability – at last things usually fall into place with respect to my travel arrangements [*i.e.*, gas money, a driver]. That is what I meant, I never regret it [the work I do], it is better that I should go and help people as long as I am still alive here on earth.

[12] If the old people do not do this, and you have seen many old people, lo, they have not left behind anything good for you,

kinakatamâkowâw, ma kîkway. kîkwây anim îta ka-kî-ohci-pimohtahât otawâsimisa ôsisima, ma kîkway nakatam.

[13] êwak ôma, piko kêhtê-aya êkosi ka-tôtahk, ka-nakatamawât osk-âya kîkway ê-miywâsik, tâpiskôc aw ôspwâkan, îh, tânisi kik-êsi-paminiht; piko ka-nakatamawât êwako (awa mîna, îh!); piko ka-nakatamawât – tânêhk âwa, k-ôh-ihtakot ôta? namôy âyisiyiniw ôh ê-ohc-ôsîhât ôhi, ôta kâ-kî-ihtakot awa. kîsikâwi-pîsim ôhi, ê-kî-osîhât, ôhi, awa kâ-pê-sâkohtêt ôta [*gesture*] kâ-pimohtâtahk ôma. êwak ôhci, mwayês âpatisit, miyawâkâc-pîhtikwahiht matotisânihk, ê-kâkîsimototâht. hâw, ê-kîsîhât ôh ômisi kî-itêw: "hâw, kiya! ka-têpwâtamawâw ayisiyiniw, nistam matotisânihk pîhtikwahikawiyani, sîpwêpinam-~ sêwêpinikawiyani, pêtwêwêhtamawâhkan ôkisêwâtisiwin [*sic*] ayisiyiniw!" êkos êkwa kî-itik awa, "hâw! kîhtwâm isi-wêpinikawiyani, êkwa êkota okisêwâtisiwin ka-pêtwêwêhtamawâw ayisiyiniw. mwêhci nistwâw isi-wêpinikawiyani, pimâtisiwin êkota ka-pêtwêwêhtamawâw, k-ôh-ohpikinâwasot kîkway. mwêhci nêwâw isi-wêpinikawiyani – 'kîkway k-âstâhikoyân êkâ ê-miywâsik, êkw êkwa ka-mîtâkwêwiyan [*?sic*];' " – êkos âw ê-kî-itakimiht awa os-~ sîsîkwan awa. mihcêt namôy kiskêyihtam konita (kâ-nipâkwêsimohk, mihcêtwâw niwîhtên êkota ê-apiyân; ômatowahk ê-âpacihât kisêyiniw ê-pê-kîhkâtahahk, ê-kîsi-nikamot ôtê k-êsi-wêpinât, mistikwaskihkwa ê-otinât); namôy kiskêyihtam êkota ê-kisipipayiyik onitotamâwin; êwakw âwa, konit ê-mêtawâkêhk awa sîsîkwan, êwakw ânima; môy mâk ê-kiskêyihtahk, konit ê-mamacikastêt, mistikwaskihkwa otinêw, êkon êkwa ê-matwêhwât; êk ôh âsênêw.

nothing. Whatever they could have used with which to guide their children and grandchildren, they did not leave anything behind.

[13] It is this, that the old people have to do that, to leave something good behind for the young people, like the pipe, behold, how it is to be treated; they have to leave that knowledge behind for them (and with respect to this one [*i.e.*, a new rattle], too, behold!); they have to leave it behind for them – why does this one here [the rattle] exist? Man did not make it, he who has been in existence here. It is the Sun that has made it, the one who comes moving into view here [*gesture*] and passes through its course. For that reason, before it is used and taken into the sweat-lodge with special care, a prayer is chanted for it. Indeed, in finishing the rattle, the Sun spoke to it thus: "Indeed, as for you! You will call out [as an advocate] for people, when first you are taken into the sweat-lodge, when you are made to ring out, do you then pray for his [God's] grace to come to the people!" And then it [the rattle] was told thus [by the Sun]: "Indeed! When next you are shaken, you will then pray for his grace to come to the people. Exactly the third time you are shaken, then you will pray for life for him with which he might raise his children. Exactly the fourth time you are shaken – 'When something worries me because it is not good, may you then deliver me from it [?*sic*];' " – thus this rattle was charged. Many people do not know this and [use it] without preparation (during a sun-dance, I tell about this many times as I sit there; using this kind [the rattle], an old man makes its clear sound ring out, then finishes his singing and throws it aside over there, taking the drum); he does not know that this is the end of his request; as for this one, it means that people are fooling around with the rattle without purpose; but he does not know that he is showing off without purpose, he takes the drum and drums on that; and he has rejected this one [the rattle].

[14] pêyakwan ayisiyiniw kâ-miyiht kanôsimon k-âpacihtât, êkâ ê-tâpwêwakêyihtahk k-âsênahk, ê-asênahk anima kôhtâwînaw okisêwâtisiwin, ana kâ-kî-osîhtât kanôsimon. kiyîkatênên ayis, êkot[a] êkwa kisipipayiw kinitotamâwin; êwako kâ-kî-kostahkik kisêyiniwak. êwak ôm ôhci, mistahi nimiywêyihtên ka-wîhtamawak ayisiyiniw mêkwâc ôta ê-pimâtisiyân; nikiskêyihtên ôtê, môy kinwês ayisiyiniw kîkway ka-kî-wîhtamawak, môy mîna kîkway niy[a] ê-kiskêyihtamân ê-itwêyân, tânis ê-kî-pê-isi-nakatamawit nôhtâwiy, êwak ôm ôpîkiskwêwin k-âpacihtâyân. tânita ka-kî-ohci-tâpwêwakêyimiht kâ-kî-oyôhtâwîyân, îh, nêwo-kîsikâw ê-kî-nakatahk askiy – êwak ôma kikiskêyihtênâwâw, ê-nêhiyawêhk 'wâwâskêsiwacîs' isiyîhkâtêw, mâk ê-âkayâsîmohk '*White Elk Hills*' [*?sic*] isiyîhkâtêw; anim ôcênâs k-âyâk, pê-sipwêmon mêskanaw, môy wâhyaw ê-pê-itamok, ôta minahikoskâw, ôta osêhcâw, êkota ê-wîkiyâhk ê-miyoskamik, êkota kâ-kî-nakatahk askiy. anima sâkahikan ôtê itakâm ê-ispatinâk, êkota kâ-kî-nitaw-âkotiht. "hâw!" itwêw, ê-wî-nakatahk askiy, "mahti kêyiwêhk, kî-nêwo-tipiskâki, awiyak ka-pê-nitawâpênikêw; mâka misatimwayân, ômatowahk, êkotowihk ka-wêwêkahpisinâwâw," kî-itwêw. êkosi kî-isi-pamihâw.

[15] mêkwât nistês ê-pimâtisit êkospî, ana mâna kâ-kî-kosâpahtahk; ê-kî-nêwo-tipiskâk êkwa, kanâtanohk kâ-mânokêcik mîkiwâhp, ê-miyâhkasikêcik êkota. "hâ, mahti kêyiwêhk, niya nika-nitawâpênikân nôhtâwiy!" – kâ-sakâpêkipahât misatimwa. êkot[a] êkw ê-âh-apihk êkwa, niyânan mîkiwâhp-~, papakiwayânikamikwa êkot[a] ê-cimatêki, ê-miyoskamik ôm ê-nôcihcikêhk, ômis [*gesture*] ê-itapicik ayisiyiniwak, ê-asawâpi-~ – kêtahtawê kâ-pê-nôkosicik, kî-pê-nîsiwak; ôt[a] ê-takopayicik, êkota kâ-pê-wîcihiwêt nôhtâwiy awa. îh, êkota anim ê-kî-wâh-~-pê-kîs-îtâskonikêt, êwak ôma ê-kî-wîhtahk ôma, kîkway ê-kî-wîhtamawit, tânis-~,

[14] In the same way, when people are given a protective talisman to use, when they reject it because they do not believe in it, they actually reject the grace of Our Father, of the one who made the protective talisman. For you set it aside, and this is the end of your request; that is what the old men feared. For this reason I am very pleased to tell people about it while I am still alive here on earth; I know that it is not for long that I will be able to tell people about things, and I am also not saying that I myself know anything, I use my father's words as he had left them behind for me. The reason that my late father should be believed, behold, it had been four days after he had departed this world – you all know the place, in Cree it is called *wâwâskêsiwacîs* but in English it is called 'White Elk Hills' [*?sic*]; where that little town is, there a road starts towards here, and it does not run far towards here when there is a spruce bluff, when there is a ravine, there we were living early in the spring and there he departed this world. There is a hill on the hither side of that lake, and there they had gone to place him on a burial scaffold. "Indeed!" he said, as he was about to depart this world, "After four nights will have passed, just in case, let someone come here and check up; but in a horsehide blanket, this kind, you will wrap me up in that kind," he had said. Thus he had been looked after.

[15] My older brother was still alive at that time, the one who used to hold the shaking-lodge ceremony; and now, after four nights had passed, they built a lodge in a clean place, smudging everything there. "Well, just in case, I, I will check up on my father!" – he [my brother] led a horse. And then the people sat there in groups, there were five tents standing there, it was trapping-time in the spring, the people were seated like this [*gesture*], waiting and watching – suddenly they could be seen approaching, there were two approaching; as they rode into the camp, then one of them was my father. Behold, then, when he [my father] had come and finished pointing the pipestem, then

tânisi k-êspayik, "hâw! nômanak kiwî-pimâtisin, nikosis! ê-miywâsik kîkway nakatamawâhkan ayisiyiniw! namôy kika-kî-kiki-sipwêhtân kîkway, namôy kika-kî-kiki-sipwêhtân ispî nakataman[i] âskiy; ê-miywâsik kîkway nakatamawâhkan. êwakw âni piko ka-kiskinowâpahtahk oskayisiyiniw [*sic*]. ayisiyiniw ômis îsi [*gesture*] k-âyimômat, kîc-âyisiyiniw, ôta kik-âpiw kitawâsimis, ôta kik-âpiw kôsisim, êwakw ânima êkây ê-miywâsik kîkway, ka-kiskinowâsohtahk. mâk ê-waniskâyan, kôhtâwînaw nanâskom! ê-miywâsik kîkway nitotamaw! ka-kiskinowâsohtahk awa kitawâsimis, tânis ô-~ kik-êsi-kitimâkêyihtot ayisiyiniw;" êkosi mâna nikî-itik; "â, êwako, êkâya wîhkâc kisiwâhihk ayisiyiniw!"

[16] êkwa, êkot[a] êkwa kâ-kî-ati-pîkiskwâsit nikâwiy, "â, nikosis! ê-miywâsik kîkway kiwîhtamâkawin, kakwê-kanawêyiht[a] ôma kâ-wîhtamâkawiyan! mâk êkwa niya kâ-wî-wîhtamâtân, êkon ôhi maskihkiya kâ-nakatamâtân, ê-pimâtisiwinowiki ôhi, kitimâkihtawin, êkoni otina! ôma maskihkiy awiyak wî-miyiski, êkây ê-miywakihtêk, êkâya wîhkâc otina, êkâya wîhkâc otina! nama nânitaw kik-êtohtahikon ôma, ka-kî-ohci-pimâcihat ayisiyiniw;" nikî-itik êwako nikâwiy. "mâcikôtitan, êwak ôma, kanawêyihta kâ-wîhtamâtân! ôma niya k-êspîhtisiyân, ê-kî-miyikowisiyân mîkwan kâ-kanawêyimit tahtwâw ê-kîsikâk. hâw, awa mîkwan kinakatamâtin, kiwî-kêhtê-ayiwin ôma, kanawêyim awa mîkwan!" nikî-itik mâna. îh, kayâs kâ-nakasit nikâwiy, êyâpic nikanawêyimâw ana mîkwan. opîkiskwêwina êkwa, kêhtê-aya ê-âpaciht-~, "êwak ôm ôtinamani, maskihkiy êkây ê-miywâsik – maskihkiy kîkway kik-âpacihikoyan kâ-nakatamâtân, êwakw âni piko âpacihtâ! mayaw otinaman[i] êkây ê-miywâsik maskihkiy, namôy nânitaw kik-êtâpacihikon ôma maskihkiy;" êkosi mâna nikî-itik. êwak ôhci mistahi nimiywêyihtên ayisiyiniw êkotowahk ê-nitôskahk.

he told about that, then he told me what would come to pass, "Indeed! You are going to live for quite a while, my son! Do then leave good things behind for people! You will not be able to take anything along, you will not be able to take anything with you when you depart this world; do then leave good things behind for them! That will be the only thing for the young people to watch and learn from. When you gossip about your fellow people in this fashion [*gesture*], your children will sit here, your grandchildren will sit here, to hear and learn that which is not good. But when you arise, give thanks to Our Father! Ask him for good things! So that your children may hear and learn how people should love one another;" thus he used to tell me; "Well, it is that, never anger a person!"

[16] And then also my mother began to speak to me, "Well, my son! You have been told good things, try to keep that which you have been told! But as for me, what I am about to tell you now, these medicines which I am leaving behind for you, they have life, listen to me with care and accept them! If someone is about to give you medicine that is not counted as good, never take it! It will not take you where you might be able to give life to people," this my mother said to me. "Lo, keep this about which I have told you! I, as long as I have lived, I have had a feather given to me by the powers which has kept me each day. Indeed, I leave this feather behind for you, you are going to be old, keep this feather!" she used to say to me. Behold, it was long ago when my mother left me, and I still keep that feather. Her words now, the elders use-~, "If you take that medicine that is not good – I am leaving you some medicine which will be of benefit to you, use only that! As soon as you accept medicine which is not good, then this medicine [which I leave you] will not be of any benefit to you;" thus she used to say to me. For this reason I am very pleased that people are searching for that kind.

[17] anohc kâ-kîsikâk, niwâhkômâkanitik, kikiskêyihtênâwâw (tâpiskôc awa nôsisim awa *Ted*, ê-nîkânîstahk ôta, êkwa mîn âwa, ôm ôta k-âtoskêyêk, kîkwây kâ-nîkânîstamêk), ôt[a] âna ê-osâpamikoyêk ayisiyiniw, ôtê k-ôh-osâpamikowâw. hâ, m'ahti kê-kî-tôtâskik, âsay êkota ê-kotêyihtahk ôma maskihkiy. namôy âna kiyawâw ê-kitimahikoyêk, namwâ [*sic*]; wiy ân[a] ê-kitimahisot. wî-nakatahk[i] âskiy, ôt[a] ân[a] êkwa kê-kakwâtakihtâw [*sic*] êwako, môy wîhkâc ka-kî-pihkohêw ocahcâhkwa.

[18] êwako kisêyinîwi-pîkiskwêwin ê-wîhtamâtakok, ayisiyiniw k-âyimômât wîc-âyisiyiniwa, kâ-~, ahpô otawâsimisa nânitaw ê-itimiht, kâ-nâtamâwasot, môy nânitaw k-êtohtahik, môy nânitaw k-êtohtahik; ôt[a] an[a] êkwa kê-kakwâtakihtât ôta askîhk. êwak ôma tahto-kîsikâw nanâskomâyahki kôhtâwînaw, ispî têpwâtikoyahki ka-nakatamahk ôm âskiy, tâpiskôc ê-tawâk, itê kik-êtohtêyahk. "nistinwa ôhi iskwâhtêma," kâ-kî-itwêcik kisêyiniwak; "kwayask pimâtisiyani, ka-tawâw kitiskwâhtêm; êkâ kwayask pimâtisiyani, môy ka-kî-tawâw kitiskwâhtêm; mwêhci nist[o] ôma kitiskwâhtêm, kikiskêyihtên cî tânêhk ôma nisto kitiskwâhtêm?" – "namôya, namôya nikiskêyihtên." – "êwak ôm îskwêyâc kitiskwâhtêm ôma, wâtihkân ê-kîsîhtamâkawiyan ê-pakitinamâkawiyan, mwêhci nisto kitiskwâhtêma, êkota anima kiyê-tasi-kakwâtakihtâyan, êkâ katawâhk ê-is-âyisiyinîwiyani;" êkosi mân ê-kî-itwêt nôhtâwiy; êwak ôma mâna nimâmitonêyihtên.

[19] mistahi nimiywêyihtên anohc, ê-isi-pêhtamân otâkosihk, êwakw âwa k-âpit, îh, kâ-wî-pasikônahk anohc kâ-kîsikâk, ê-wî-nanâskomot, matotisân ôma kâ-wî-osîhtât. kiwâpahtênâwâw kahkiyaw êkw îyikohk [?*sic*], êkwa pisiskiw ê-kîs-ôhpikinâwasot, k-âti-kwêskinâkwahki ôhi maskihkiya, nipiya mîna, ka-nanâskomoyahk êkwa, kîhtwâm êkwa askiy k-ôtisâpahtamahk; êkos ôhi ê-itwêmakahki ôhi wêpinâsona,

[17] Today, my relatives, you all know (for example my grandson here, Ted [Whitecalf], he is the head here, and also this one [Freda Ahenakew], those of you who work here, whatever you head up), that some people are [jealously] watching you here, that they are [jealously] watching you from over there. Well, let's see what they can do to you [with bad medicine], already they are challenging this [my] medicine. As for you all, they do not harm you, not at all; they are only harming themselves. When they are about to depart this world, then they will suffer here, they will never be able to free their soul.

[18] I am telling you this word of the old men, when people gossip about their fellow people, or when something is said to someone's children and she takes up for her children, it will not lead her anywhere, it will not lead her anywhere; that one will suffer, then, here on earth. It is this, if we give thanks to Our Father each day, when the time comes and he calls us to depart this world, it will seem like an opening for us to go to. "There are three doors," as the old men used to say; "if you do live properly, your door will be open; if you do not live properly, your door cannot be open; the third door of yours, exactly, do you know why that third one is your door?" – "No, I do not know." – "This last door is your door, where a hole has been finished for you and arranged for you, exactly the third one of your doors, that is where you will spend your time suffering, if you do not live like a proper human;" thus my father used to say; I often think about this.

[19] I am very pleased today about what I heard yesterday, that this one who sits here [John Cuthand], behold, and is about to raise it today, that he is about to give thanks, the one who is about to make a sweat-lodge. You all have now seen so much of this, now that the animals have finished raising their young, when the plants are about to change their colours, and also the leaves, that we should give thanks now, that we might live to see

pêyakwan ôhi, îh, ka-miywâsin êkota ka-pîhtikwêmakahki ôhi. êkot[a] êkwa kî-kâkîsimototamihki, êkon êkwa awa kê-kanawêyihtahk, ôh ôta otatoskêhâkana, pêyakwan nâha, ita ê-pimohtahât otawâsimisa ôsisima, êkon êkwa kê-kanawêyihtahk. êwakw âwa k-êtwêyân êkw êkota ka-pîhtikwêw, êkon êkwa ka-kanôsimototawât awa. êkos ôma, ê-isi-kiskêyihtamân, mâk êkw âwa kâ-wîhtamawak kêhcinâ, kêhcinâ ka-kakwê-kâhtitinahk pêyakoyâkan mînisa, ka-pîhtikwêmakahki anita matotisânihk.

[20] ita kwayask ayisiyiniw ê-wî-tôtahk, ôtê kîsitêw, pêyakwêskihk osîhtâw, maskihkiwâpoy [*sic*], pahkwêsikan; êkw êkwa kêhtê-aya – kahkiyaw ôm ê-itahtwapiyahk ê-mâyipayiyahk, kôhtâwînawak kimosôminawak, êkonik aniki ka-nîminamâhcik, ka-pîkiskwêstamâkoyahkik. êkos ôma ê-ispayik, kâ-wî-isîhcikêt awa, matotisân kâ-wî-osîhtât. mâka ninanâskomâw; mêkwâc ôta ê-ayâwak, ka-kî-wîcôhkamawakik, êkos îs ôma.

[21] êwakw âni piko ê-wî-wîhtamâtakok, niwâhkômâkanitik; ahpô êtokwê kêtahtawê pêyak ôma kîkway kâ-wîhtamâtakok, ahpô êtokwê kik-âpacihikonâwâw, kêtahtawê pêyak ê-kîsikâk; môy kâkikê ôta kik-âyânânaw askîhk, namôya. môy ka-kî-itwêw ayisiyiniw, "nitipêyimison," kik-êtwêt, namôya; kôhtâwînaw kâ-tipêyimikoyahk. êwakw ânima k-ôh-wîhtamâtakok.

[22] tânispî êtokwê isko ômatowihk ka-kî-wîtapimitakok, kîkway ê-miywâsik ka-kî-wîhtamâtakok. namôy êtok ôma, niya nititêyihcikan ôma kâ-wîhtamâtakok, kôhtâwînaw êtokwê okisêwâtisiwin, ita kik-âpacihikoyêk kîkway, kâ-wîhtamâtakok. namôya mîn ê-môhcwêyimak ayisiyiniw, kîkway

another year; that is the meaning of these cloth offerings, the same as these, behold, it will be good that they should go inside there [the sweat-lodge]. And once prayers have been chanted over them, then this one [Ted Whitecalf] will keep them for all the people who work for him here; the same with that one yonder [Freda Ahenakew], she will keep them [the cloth offerings] as she guides her children and grandchildren along. And that one [the rattle], as I said, will now go inside there, and then she will use it for protection. This is what I know, but this one [John Cuthand] now is the one to whom I am telling this especially, that he should make a special effort to get a dish of berries that they might go inside there into the sweat-lodge.

[20] When a person is going to do it properly, there will be cooked food over here and he makes one pot of tea, then bannock; and then for the old people – all of us, as many of us as are sitting here have been bereaved, of our fathers and grandfathers, they are the ones to whom the cooked food is to be offered so that they might intercede for us. This is what goes on, the ceremony which he is about to perform, the one who is making a sweat-lodge. But I give thanks to him; so that I might be able to help them while I am still here with him, that is how it will be.

[21] That is all I am going to tell you about, my relatives; perhaps someday one of the things which I am telling you may be of benefit to you, on some future day; we will not always be here on earth, no. People should not say, "I am my own master," no; it is Our Father who has power over us. That is why I tell you this.

[22] I do not know how long I might sit with you in this place and tell you good things. It cannot be that I tell you about my own thinking, it must be Our Father's grace, where something will be of benefit to you of that which I am telling you. I also do not consider people stupid when I tell them something; I am trying to

kâ-wîhtamawak; ê-kakwê-wîcôhkamawak, ê-kakwê-wîcôhkamawak kîkway, kik-âpacihtât.

[23] hâw, êkosi piko ê-isi-wîhtamâtakok, nôsisimitik, mâk êkwa aw ôspwâkan, kê-ohpâskonahk [*sic*]; nanâskomâtân kôhtâwînaw ê-miyikoyahk pêyak-kîsikâw ka-pimohtâtamahk; êwakw âni, êkosi kik-êsi-mâmitonêyihtênâwâw kîstawâw.

help them, I am trying to help them with something they might use.

[23] Indeed, that is all I am telling you, my grandchildren, but now I will raise this pipe; let us give thanks to Our Father that he has granted us another day to live through; it is that, and you, too, will think about that.

4

[1] kîkwây anima, ohtitaw ôm ê-ispayik ka-kâkîsimototamihk ôma wâskahikan, iyikohk ê-kosikwahk kitatoskêwiniwâw ôma k-âtoskâtamêk. ohtitaw piko, ta-nitotamâht kôhtâwînaw okisêwâtisiwin, êkâ kîkway ka-macipayik, kwayask ka-kakwê-pimohtêmakahk ôma kitatoskêwiniwâw. êwak ôm ôhci k-ôh-isîhcikêhk, êkwa mîn ôm ôhci k-ôh-isîhcikêhk otâkosihk matotisân; êkota anima kîkway ê-miywâsik, ka-kâhtitinahk ayisiyiniw, ê-miywâsik kîkway. tâpiskôc kâ-wî-isîhcikêt ana nôsisim, otânisa awa, kâ-wî-wîhkohkêt; maskihkiy[a] ânihi ê-wî-wîhkohkahtahk, ôhi kâ-sâkikihki. êkon êkw êkota, ê-wêhcasik êkot[a] êkwa, ka-nitôskahk ayisiyiniw, kîkwây anima ê-nitawêyihtahk; kîkwây anima ê-nitawêyihtahk maskihkiy, êkot[a] êkwa ka-nâcinêhikêt êkwa. mihcêtin kîkway, ê-kî-miyikawiyahk k-ôh-pimâtisiyahk êwak ôma kâ-sâkikihk. mâka mihcêt nama kîkway kiskêyihtam ayisiyiniw tânisi k-êsi-nitôskahk êwak ôma kîkway.

[2] kîkwây k-ôh-ispayik, kayâs wêtinahk mitoni kî-pimi-pimâtisiw, 'kisêyinîw-ôhpikihâkan' nik-êtwân, ê-pê-kakêskimiht kîkway, pêyakwan iskwêw, tânis ê-isi-nitôskahk kîkway. anohc kâ-kîsikâk, wêpinikâtêwa êkoni, cikêmô mihcêtiw môniyâw otawâsimisa ôta, ê-wîtaskîwêmâyahk. ê-kimotôsêt êkotowahk iskwêw, môniyâw otawâsimisa, êkw êkwa ôtê isi itohtahêw kitawâsimisinawa, wanisinohtahêw onêhiyâwiwiniyiw; êwakw ânima k-ôh-ispayik ohci [*sic*].

[3] êwak ôma k-ôh-itwêyân, îh, mihcêtin êkota ayisiyiniw ka-nitôskahk, wâwîs cî iskwêw ê-pim-ôhpikinâwasot, ka-na-~ ka-nitôskahk maskihkiy ê-miywâsik k-âpacihtâhk, îh. ahpô ôma 'wîhkês' k-êsiyîhkâtêk, namôy nisitohtam misâhkamik ayisiyiniw, nîsosâp tahtwayak itâpatan êwakw ânima maskihkiy.

[1] What is that, it is the proper thing to take place that one should chant prayers for this building, for this your work upon which you are engaged is so heavy. It is only proper that Our Father should be asked for his grace, so that nothing bad will happen, so that with divine protection your work might proceed properly. This is the reason why this ceremony is being held, and also the reason why the sweat-lodge ceremony was held yesterday; so that people might obtain something good from it, good things. This grandchild of mine, for example, this one's [Eli Bear's] daughter, she is about to perform a ceremony, she is about to hold a feast; she is about to hold a feast for the medicinal herbs, these which are emerging from the earth. Now with these, it is easy with these now for people to make a request [of a medicine man] for what they want; for what medicine they want, that they might go there and pay for it. They are plentiful, and they have been given to us so that we should have life through them, through these that emerge from the earth. But many people do not know anything about the manner of making a request for them.

[2] Why this happens is that long ago people led a quiet life, 'raised by the old men', I will say, they were constantly counselled about things, and young women the same, about the manner of making a request for something. Today now these things have been cast aside, of course the Whites and their children are numerous here, and we live in peace with them on this earth. Women have illegitimate childen with that kind, the Whites and their children, and then they take our children over there [to the city], they lead them to lose their Creeness; that is why this happens.

[3] This is why I say this, behold, the medicines are plentiful for people to make requests, especially for women in the course of raising their children, that they might request good medicine to use, behold. Many people do not even understand the 'ratroot' as it is called, that medicine has twelve distinct uses. Some people

âtiht ayisiyiniw môy âhpô kiskêyihtam tânis ê-itakihtêk, mâka nîsosâp tahtwayak ê-itakihtêk anima, t-âpatahk êwako maskihkiy. êwak ôhci mistahi kihcêyihtâkwan êwakw ânima maskihkiy, 'wîhkês' ôma k-êsiyîhkâtêk, kahkiyaw kîkway ita k-ânisîhtât êwakw ânima. êwakw ânim ôhci k-ôh-itwêyân, mistahi kâ-nanâskomoyâhk nôsisim ana kâ-wî-isîhcikêt, kâ-wî-kîsitêpot. mistahi miywâsin kotak mîna ka-pîhtikwatât êkota kîsitêw, kikâwînaw askiy, êkota kîkway k-ôh-sâkikihk, êkot[a] ânima k-ôh-nisitohtahk ayisiyiniw.

[4] êwak ôma kâ-kî-itwêcik kisêyiniwak, ita mêkwâc k-âyâyahk, ê-pê-kîwêmakahk kîkway, ômis îsi [*gesture*] ê-pê-kîwêmakahk, kîkway anima ka-nâtâmototamihk; anima kîkway kâ-kî-miyikoyahk kôhtâwînaw, okisêwâtisiwin, êwakw ânima ka-nâtâmototamihk.

[5] âsay kiwî-wanisimikonaw, kiwî-wanisimikonaw wâpiski-wiyâs; kî-âyiman kayâs – kâ-waniskâyâhk, "hâw, ôta apik!" ê-kî-itikoyâhk nôhtâwiy, êkos ê-is-âpiyâhk. ôta ê-apit, ê-nanâskomât kôhtâwînawa, kîsikâw ê-miyikoyâhk, ita ka-pimohtâtamâhk kîsikâw ê-miywâsik. anohc kitawâsimisinaw kôsisiminaw kiwanisimânaw; môy kiwâpahtênânaw ê-wanisimâyahk. iyâyaw nêmatowahk, îh, yôhtênamawêwak kêhtê-ayak, nêmatowahk; ê-waniskât awâsis, êwakw ânima kitâpahtam. ôma k-ôh-- kâ-nanâskomât kôhtâwînawa okisêwâtisiwiniyiw, nama kîkway; iyâyaw nêma kitâpahtam. ahpô ê-môhcowicik êkota ayisiyinîhkânak ê-masinipayicik, iyâyaw êwako kitâpahtam, môy nanâskomêwak kôhtâwînawa, tahto-kîsikâw ka-pimohtâtahk; êkota âsay kiwanisimâwak. môy kikiskêyihtênânaw, kiyânaw ê-wanisimâyahk kôsisiminaw kitawâsimisinaw, kiyânaw anim ê-wanisimâyahk, êwak ôm ôhci k-ôh-wanisimâyahk. êkwa ita manitowi-kîsikâw ê-miyikoyahk k-ôtisâpahtamahk kôhtâwînaw, okîsikâm, âsay mîn êkota kiwanisimânaw kitawâsimisinaw; môy mîn êwako kikiskêyihtênânaw.

do not even know its value, but this medicine has twelve distinct values in which it may be used. For this reason that medicine is highly thought of, this 'ratroot' as it is called, since it works as an antidote against everything. That is why I say we greatly give thanks that this my grandchild is about to hold a ceremony, that she is about to cook a feast. It is also another very good thing for her to bring in ceremonial food for Our Mother the Earth, whence things emerge, so that people might thereby understand it.

[4] That is what the old men used to say, where we find ourselves at this time, things are coming back, things like this [*gesture; i.e.*, ceremonies] are coming back, so that one might turn to these things for help; that one might turn for help to this which Our Father had given us, his grace.

[5] The Whites are leading us astray already, they are leading us astray; long ago it used to be arduous – when we got up, my father used to say to us, "Indeed, you sit down here!", and thus we sat down. He sat down here, giving thanks to Our Father that he had granted us another day wherein we might live through a beautiful day. Today we are leading our children and grandchildren astray; we do not see that we are leading them astray. Instead we turn to that kind over there [a television set], behold, the old people turn it on for them, that kind over there; as the children get up, they look at that. As for giving thanks to Our Father for his grace, there is none of it; instead they look at that over there. They even have crazed mannikins [*i.e.*, cartoon figures] shown on there, and they would rather look at that, they do not give thanks to Our Father that they might live through each day; in that we have already led them astray. We do not realise that we ourselves are leading our children and grandchildren astray, that we ourselves are leading them astray, that we are leading them astray with that. And where Our Father grants it to us that we might live to see Christmas day,

[6] âtiht kisêyiniw ê-waniskât nôtikwêw kâ-nanâskomot, ê-mawihkâtamawât okisêwâtisiwiniyiw, okîsikâm kôhtâwînaw ê-otisâpahtamahk; êwakw ânima, êwako nêhiyawi-wîhtamawâkan.

[7] kîkwây k-ôh-itwêyân it[a] ê-wanisimâyahk kitawâsimisinaw, nêtê minahikosis cimasiw, hâw, êkota êkwa sîpâ, konita ê-pimastêki ê-kaskipitêki kîkway. mayaw ê-waniskât awâsis, iyâyaw êkoni pimakocin; santakilâwsa [*sic*] iyâyaw kiskisiw, môy kôhtâwînawa kis--, âsay mîn êkot[a] ê-wanisimâyahk. pitamâ ka-kî-nanâskomot, okîsikâm ê-otisâpahtamahk, kôhtâwînaw, pâmwayês nêhi tasîhkahk; pâmwayês mîna ôma kitâpahtahk, ka-kî-nanâskomot, ê-miywâsik kîsikâw ita ê-miyiht ta-pimohtâtahk; êwakw ânima nawac ka-kakwê-kiskinohamawâyêk ôtê ati nîkân.

[8] pêyak ê-kîsikâk (môy ê-kakwê-sêkimitakok), pêyak ê-kîsikâk ê-ihtakohk kîkway ê-wî-mâkohikoyahk. êkâ kîkway kâ-nâkatôhkêt kîkway kiwâhkômâkaninaw, êkwêyâc êkot[a] êkwa ka-pêtâmow, kisêyiniwa ka-nâtâmototawêw, nôtikwêwa ka-nâtâmototawêw.

[9] tâpwê, kisêwâtisiw kôhkominaw 'nôtikwêw-âtayôhkan' k-êsiyîhkâsot. kîspin êkâ êkotowahk ohci, kîspin êkâ iskwêw êko-~ ọta kî-pakitinikowisit, namôy ôta kikâh-apinânaw; awîna kâh-nihtâwikihtâw kitayisiyinîwininaw, nam âwiyak; êwako iskwêw kâ-kî-miyiht kisêwâtisiwin. êwak ôhci, "kitimâkêyihtok, iskwêwak! kitimâkêyimihk iskwêw!" kâ-kî-itwêcik kêhtê-ayak. nama nânitaw itâpatan, 'nâpêw' k-êsiyîhkâsot ka-kakwâtakihât iskwêwa; ôtê ana ê-ohci-kitâpamiht, kâ-kakwâtakihât anih îskwêwa, wiy ân[a] ê-kitimahisot. namôya kâh-ayisiyinîwiw

his day, again we have already led our children astray; and we do not even realise it.

[6] Some old men and old women, as they arise, they give thanks, crying out to him for his grace, because we have lived to see Our Father's [Christmas] day; that is a Cree teaching.

[7] Why I say that we are leading our children astray in this, indeed, over there stands a little tree, and beneath that now there is a row of wrapped parcels. Just as soon as the children get up, they rush over to them instead. They remember Santa Claus instead, and not Our Father, and again already we have led them astray. They should be giving thanks first that we have lived to see his day, Our Father's day, before they trifle with those things over there; and also before they look at this [television set], they should be giving thanks that it has been granted to them to live through a beautiful day; and that is what you had better try to teach them there in the future.

[8] One day (and I am not trying to scare you), one day it will come to pass that something will throw us into crisis. For our relatives do not pay attention to anything [*i.e.*, ceremonies], and only then will they come fleeing to them, they will turn to the old men for help, they will turn to the old women for help.

[9] Truly, Our Grandmother is kind, 'Old-Woman-Spirit' as she is called. If it were not for that kind, if women had not been put here on earth by the powers, we would not be sitting here; who would give birth to our existence as humans? – no one; that grace [*i.e.*, to bear children] was given to women. That is why the old people used to say, "Think of one another with compassion, you women! You all, think of the women with compassion!" There is no excuse for 'man' as he is called to be abusive to women; he is watched from over there, and when he is abusive to a woman,

kîspin êkâ ohc îskwêwa, êkwa ka-kitimahât êkotowahk, môy miywâsin êwakw ânima. êkwa mihcêtwâw nipê-wîhtên, ê-pê-wâpahtamân êwakw ânima, ê-pê-otinamân nîsta, tânis ê-kî-isi-wîhtamawit nôhtâwiy: "hâ! ôtê kê-nîkâniwik [*sic*], ispî kîs-âyisiyinîwiyani, wîcêwac[i] îskwêw, kakwê-kitimâkêyihtamâso!" – êkosi nikî-itik mâna nôhtâwiy; êwako mâna nikiskisin. êkâ kâ-nahêyihtamân, niwayawîn, nikâkîsimototawâw kôhtâwînaw ka-wîcihit, kîkway ê-miywâsik ta-miyit mitonêyihcikan; êkos ôm ê-itahkamikisiyân; asici ôhi wêpinâsona ê-kanawêyihtamân, mayaw ê-waniskâyân, âsay niwayawîn; ê-nitawi-nikamoyân ê-nanâskomak kôhtâwînaw, ê-miywâsik kîsikâw ita ka-pimohtahakik nitawâsimisak. mihcêtwâw awa nipêhtâk ê-kapêsimostawak nitihkwatim, mayaw ê-pêkopayiyân niyâhkatâmon; ê-nanâskomoyân anima, kîsikâw it[a] ê-wâpahtamân. êwak ôma ka-kakwê-êkotê-itohtahâyahk [*sic*] kitawâsimisinaw kôsisiminaw, êkot[a] ânima kê-ôh-kitimâkêyihtot. êkâ êwak ôma kîkway wîhtamawâyahko, â, êwakw âwa ka-wanisimiht, awâsisak [*sic*].

[10] êwak ôhci, kisêyiniw kayâs, ê-wî-kitotikoyâhk ôta kî-cimatâw môhkomân, îh. "hâw, ôma môhkomân kâ-cimatâyân, kisîmitân[i] ôma kâ-wî-wîhtamâtân, otinamôhkan ôma tâh-tahkamîhkan!" – êkosi kî-itwêwak kisêyiniwak. "êwak ôma môhkomân kâ-cimatâyân, ôtê ôm ê-miywâsik kîkway kâ-wî-wîhtamâtân, êkâ nitohtaman[i], ôtê ôm êkâ ê-miywâsik, êwak ôma kiyê-otinaman;" êkosi ê-kî-itwêcik kêhtê-ayak. êwak ôhci k-ôh-kî-nitohtâht kêhtê-aya kîkway ê-wîhtahk; êkos ôm ê-kî-pê-isi-paminikawiyâhk niyanân. kî-kitimâkan niyanân, ita kâ-kî-pê-ohpikiyâhk. anohc osk-âya, miywâsiniyiw ita mêkwâc ê-ohpikit; mâka, êwak ôma k-êtwêyân, namôy ê-wî-kakwê-sêkimak ayisiyiniw, kiwî-nâtênânaw ê-wî-âyimahk, mâka namôy kinwês, êkota kâ-wî-nôhtêhkatêt ayisiyiniw; êwak ôma êyâpic ê-wî-wâpahtamahk.

he is being mean to himself. He would not exist as a human being if it were not for a woman, and for him to be mean to that kind, that is not good. And I have told this many times that I have constantly seen that and that I have accepted it myself, too, what my father had told me: "Well! There in the future, when you have become an adult and marry a woman, try to think of her with compassion for your own sake!" – thus my father used to say to me; I always remember that. When I am upset, I go out and chant prayers to Our Father that he might help me, that he should give me something good to think about; this is what I do; I also keep these cloth offerings, and as soon as I arise, I go out without delay; I go and sing and give thanks to Our Father so that I might guide my children through a beautiful day. Many times my nephew [Eli Bear] has heard me when I stayed overnight at his place, as soon as I wake up I start singing out; I give thanks for the moment when I see another day. That is where we should try to lead our children and grandchildren, so that they might learn from that to think of one another with compassion. If we do not tell them these things, well, then these children will be led astray.

[10] For this reason did the old men long ago, when they were about to address us, plant a knife into the ground here, behold. "Indeed, this knife which I have planted into the ground, if I anger you by what I am about to tell you, take then this knife and stab me over and over!" – thus the old men used to say. "This knife which I have planted here into the ground, if you do not listen to the good things over there which I am about to tell you, then you will accept the evil things over there;" thus the old people used to say. That is why the old people used to be listened to when they told something; as for us, this is how we were always treated long ago. For us, it was a hard life where we grew up. For today's young, it is good where they are growing up at the present time; but, this is what I said, and I am not trying to scare anyone, we are about to head into hard times, but it will not be

[11] mâka, ôta ayâw paskwâwi-mostos, 'misatim' k-êsiyîhkâsot, êkây wîhkâc pakicîk, êkâya wîhkâc pakicîk! êwako kâ-kî-miyikoyahk kôhtâwînaw k-ôwîcêwâkaniyahk, 'misatim' awa k-êsiyîhkâsot. ê-kisêwâtisit, ê-kanawêyimikoyahk êwako ê-owîcêwâkaniyahk [?*sic*]; êkw êwakw âwa paskwâwi-mostos, êyâpic ka-kâsispôt, êkw êwakw êkwa k-ôh-pimâtisit.

[12] ê-wî-âhcîhtâhk ôm âskiy, namôya ê-wî-pôn-âskîwik, ê-wî-âhcîhtâhk ôm âskiy; êkwa ôma, kinêhiyâwiwininaw ê-wî-pê-kîwêmakahk. êkos ôm ê-wî-isinâkwahk, môy ê-kakwê-sêkimak ayisiyiniw, mâk êkos ê-wî-isinâkwahk, kîhkânâkwan, tânitahtwayak ka-pêhtawâwak; ahpô awâsis, âsay kiskêyihtam êwako, ê-kiskêyihtamôhikowisit, ka-wîhtamâkoyahk êwak ôma, tânis ê-wî-ispayik; namôy ka-kî-wîhtênânaw tânim ânima kîsikâw kâ-wî-mâkohikoyahk.

[13] mâcikôtitan, nâh-nâkatowâpahtamok kisêyiniwak opîkiskwêwiniwâw! namôy ê-pakwâtamawak ayisiyiniw, pîtos ôki k-ês-âyamihâcik; ka-nâkatôhkêyêk êwak ôma, nêmatowahk ê-yôhtênamihk, kîkisêpâ âsay kotak mêskocikâpawiw ê-kakêskihkêmot, tâniyikohk ê-ocipitât ayisiyiniwa, êwakw âna kâ-wî-pîkonahk ôm âskiy, êwako kâ-wî-mâyitôtahk; êkosi ê-kî-pê-itwêcik kisêyiniwak. êkotowahk ôma, ê-osîhtamâsot an[a] âyisiyiniw ayamihâwin, namôy ê-ohci-miyikot mâmaw-ôhtâwîmâwa, wiy ân[a] ê-osîhtât – tahk âyiwâk k-âti-mihcêtiw ê-iyinîsit; êkonik ôki kâ-wî-kisîhtocik, êkot[a] ôki kâ-wî-ohpinahkik maci-kîkway; êkos ê-kî-itwêcik kisêyiniwak, êwakw êkwa niwâpahtên ê-ispayik. ômatowahk kâ-yôhtênamihk, âsay êkota tâniyikohk ê-pîkiskwêt, êkwa iyikohk misâhkamik ê-ocipitât ayisiyiniwa.

long now that people are going to go hungry; we are going to see this yet.

[11] But there are still buffalo here and 'horses' as they are called, never let go, never let go! This one Our Father gave us to have as a companion, the 'horse' as he is called. He is kind, he keeps us and we have him as our companion; and the buffalo, too, will still go on into another generation, and from that he will survive.

[12] This earth is about to be changed, it will not be the end of the world but this earth is about to be changed; and our Creeness is about to come back. That is how it will look, I am not trying to scare people, but that is how it will look, it is clearly visible, you will hear them in a number of places; even children already know it, it is made known to them by the powers, for them to tell us what is going to happen; we will not be able to tell the day which will throw us into crisis.

[13] Lo, take note of the old men's words. I do not disapprove of it for people that they should follow different religions; but you must take note of this, in turning on that kind over there [a television set], in the morning already one after another person taking turns and preaching, pulling in so many people, they are the ones who are about to break the earth, they are the ones who will cause serious trouble; that is what the old men used to say. It is that kind, these people make up their own religions, they did not have it given to them by the All-Father, they have made it up themselves – there will be more and more smart people; they are the ones who will anger one another by what they say, and with that they create evil; that is what the old men used to speak about, and I see that happen now. When you turn on this kind [the television set], already they talk so much, and they pull in a great many people.

[14] mâk âhkamêyimotân! kîstanaw, kâ-nêhiyâwiyahk, ê-miywâsik kîkway nitotamawâtâk kôhtâwînaw, ka-kitimâkihtâkoyahk.

[15] tânisi tiyôtamahk – kitawâsimisinaw ôt[a] ê-pê-nahapit, kîkway ê-miywâsik ê-nitotamâkoyahk, kisâkihtamawânaw, môy sêmâk ka-miyânaw. piyisk ka-mâtow, âhci pikw ânima ê-nitawêyihtahk. hâ, pikw êkw êkota ka-miyâyahk, êkos âwa k-êtihtâkonaw kôhtâwînaw, ê-miywâsik kîkway nitotamawâyahko. êwak ôma, kâ-wî-ohpâskonak aw ôspwâkan, mâmitonêyihtamok kîstawâw, ê-miywâsik kîkway nitotamâhk kôhtâwînaw, ôm îta k-âtoskêyêk!

[16] hâw, êwak ôma piko kê-pimohtahikoyahk; hâw, êkosi piko ê-wî-isi-wîhtamâtakok.

[14] But let us persevere! We, we who are Cree, let us ask Our Father for good things, that he may hear us and take pity upon us.

[15] What are we to do – when our children come and sit down here beside us, asking us for something good, we hold it back from them, we will not give it to them right away. At last they will cry, they want it nonetheless. Well, then we must give it to them, and in the same way Our Father will hear us when we ask him for something good. It is this, I am about to raise up this pipe, you all think about it, too, and ask Our Father for good things here where you work!

[16] Indeed, this is the only thing that will guide us; indeed, that is all I am going to tell you.

5

[1] mêkwâc ê-okimâhkâniwit, êwakw âwa ê-kî-wî-pasikônit; kiskêyihtam k-âpit awa, nistwâw êkotê ninitawi-wîcihiwân, ê-nitawi-kâkîsimohk, nipiy kâ-pitihkwêk, ita kâ-kî-wiyihcikêt kimosôminaw; êkota kâ-kî-âpatahk anim ôskiciy, êwako nêhiyawasinahikan kâ-kî-osîhtât, êwakw âwa nimosôminân 'cascakiskwês' kâ-kî-itiht, êkot[a] êwako kâ-kî-âpatahk, kâ-kî-wiyihcikêt awa, kâ-kî-pimohtêstamawât kihc-ôkimâskwêwa ôhi, kâ-kî-pê-atâwêt ôm âskiy; êkota anim êwako ê-kî-âpatahk, êwakw ânim ôhci k-ôh-kî-isîhcikêt awa, mêkwâc ôta mitoni ê-okimâhkâniwit, êkota mân ê-kî-nitawi-kâkîsimohk; êkota ohc ê-kî-wîhtamâhcik ayisiyiniwak, tânis ânim ê-ispayik kîkway.

[2] kî-itwêw êwakw âw ôkimâhkân, "mêkwâc ôta ê-pimâtisicik kêhtê-ayak, pêhtamowin ê-kiskêyihtahkik, êwak ôma kik-âcimômakan oskiciy, tânis ê-kî-is-âsotamâkoyahk wâpiski-wiyâs," kî-itwêw mâna. êkwa mistahi kâ-nanâskomak *Alec* awa, êwak ôm êkwa kâ-wî-tasîhkahk, îh, ôtê *Saskatoon* êwakw ânima ka-pîhtikwêmakahk, ka-nêhiyawastêk! tânis ânima ê-pê-isi-kiskêyihtahk kêhtê-aya, êwakw ânim êkwa, nêhiyawi-~ nêhiyawi-masinahikan, kîstanaw ê-kî-êwakw-ânima-tahkonamôhiht awa, tânêhki k-ôh-kî-tahkonamôhiht êwakw ânima, "kitasotamâkowininaw êkây wîhkâc ka-pîkonahk ê-nîsokâtêt ayisiyiniw," kî-itwêw êsa; kikî-asotamâkonaw êkây wîhkâc ka-pîkonahk awiyak, otasotamâkêwin anima. êwakw êkwa kâ-nâcikâpawistahk [*sic*] wâpiski-wiyâs, ê-wî-kakwê-patitisahamâkoyahk. êwak ôhci k-ôh-nanâskomoyân êwak ôma ê-wî-isîhcikâtamihk, k-âti-kiskinowâsohtahk ômis îsi kiwâhkômâkaninaw, êwak ôma tânis ê-itwêmakahk, êwak ôma 'oskiciy' k-êsiyîhkâtêk.

[3] êkwa awa kotak pîsim, têpakohposâp akimihci, ôtê êkwa kâ-wî-pîhtikwêmakahk mîna, êkos ê-wî-isîhcikêcik ôki, *Alberta*

The Testimony of the Pipestem

[1] While he was chief, this one [David Ahenakew] had raised me up [amongst the elders at the Saskatchewan Indian Cultural College]; he knows it, the one who sits here, I went to join them over there three times, when one went there to chant prayers, there at *nipiy kâ-pitihkwêk* where our grandfather had concluded the treaty; that was the time when the pipestem was used, he was the one who made it into the Cree document of the treaty, it was our grandfather *cascakiskwês* as he was called, that was the time when it was used, when the one who represented the Queen in concluding the treaty had come to buy this land; that was the time when it was used, that is why this one here [David Ahenakew] had arranged, while he was grand chief, for people to go there and chant prayers; and for people to be told through that how things came to pass.

[2] This chief used to say, "While the old people are still living amongst us and know what was heard, this pipestem will tell the story of the promises which the Whites had made to us," he used to say. Now I am very grateful to Alec [Greyeyes], who is going to do deal with this, behold, so that this will be kept at the College over there in Saskatoon and that it will be written down in Cree! What the old people have known by tradition, now that Cree document is for us, too: that he was made to hold this one [the pipestem], and why he was made to hold it, "So that no human walking on two legs would ever break the promises made to us," he [the Queen's representative] had said, it is reported; he had promised us that no one would ever break that which he had promised. That is the point towards which the Whites are now moving, they are about to try to wreck it for us. That is why I give thanks that this [audio-recording] is being arranged, so that our relatives might learn by hearing about it in this way what this 'pipestem', as it is called, means.

[3] Now this next month, on the seventeenth, it [the pipestem] is also about to go into an assembly over there, our relatives in

kiwâhkômâkaninawak. mistahi ka-miywâsin, êwakw ânima kâ-wî-isîhcikêhk; êwak ôma k-êsi-pêhtawakik, ôta nistam kâ-mâmiskôtahkik, ômisi [*gesture*] k-êsi-wîkihk, ita ôki kâ-wî-nitonahkik tipahamâtowin; mistahi ka-miywâsin, mâtayak ka-kiskêyihtahkik êwako, kitasotamâkowininaw kîkwây k-âspitonâmocik – namôy nânapêc ocihcipayiki [*sic*], ka-nâtâmostahkik anima; mâtayak ka-kiskêyihtahkik, mêkwâc ê-pimâtisicik kêhtê-ayak, onîkihikomâwak, omosômiwâwa otâcimowiniyiw, êkota kit-âstâcik; êwakw ânima kâ-kôtawêyihtamân, ôtê, êkonik ôki k-âpicik, îh, nikî-kakwêcimikawin *Saddle Lake* êwak ôma, tânis ê-ispayik ôta, êwak ôma, tânis ê-itwêmakahk oskiciy. êkota nikî-nitohtâkwak, nikî-wîhtamawâwak aniki, kâ-nîkânistahkik [*sic*] êkota. kî-nanâskomowak, wîstawâw anik ê-wî-nâtâmostahkik êwako; êkos ôm ê-kî-isîhcikêhk êkotê kâ-mâmawôpihk, êkos ôm êkota kâ-wî-pîhtikwêmakahk *Saskatoon*, ka-masinipayihtâhk anima, mâka ka-nêhiyawastêk anim âcimowin, kitasotamâkowininaw, êkos ôma ê-wî-isîhcikâtamihk anima oskiciy. êwak ôhci k-ôh-sîhkimikoyahk otâkosihk awa nikosis, ôta *David* kâ-pâh-pîkiskwêt, ka-mâmawôhkamâtoyahk, ka-mâmawôhkamâtoyahk; "pêyak katawâhk itihtâkwaniyiki, opîkiskwêwin, êwakw ânima kê-pimohtahikoyahk," k-êtwêt, êkos ê-isi-tâpwêt anima k-êht-~ k-êtwêt. êkosi piko ê-wî-isi-wîhtamâtakok êwak ôma.

[4] hâw, tahtwâw ê-kîsikâk âta miton ê-âhkamêyimoyân mîna nîsta ê-pîkiskwâtamân kîkway; îh, nîsta ê-kikapiyân wêpinâsona ê-nôhtê-tâpwêyân; ê-mâkwêyimoyân, ê-mihcêticik nôsisimak nicâpânak, tânitê kik-êtâmôhakik? êwako mâna mistahi nimâmitonêyihtên. êkos ôma ka-tôtamahk, niwâhkômâkanitik, âhkamêyimotâk, mâmawo-wîcêhtotâk! ka-kitimâkihtâkonaw êtokwê kôhtâwînaw; wiya kâ-pamihtât kîkway, môy kiyânaw, ka-kî-wîh-pêht-~.

Alberta are about to arrange this. It will be very good when that is arranged; this is what I heard them say when first they were talking about it, that they would live like this [*gesture; i.e.*, in a circle of lodges] where they are going to investigate the making of the treaty; it will be very good that they should know this ahead of time, what they [our grandfathers at the signing of the treaty] had relied upon as testimony of the promises that were made to us – not to wait until the last moment, when the time comes for them to turn to that [the pipestem] for help; so that they should know their grandfather's story ahead of time, while the old people are still alive, and that the parents should place it there [at the College]; that is what I miss over there, look at these who sit here, I was asked about this at Saddle Lake, about what is happening here, about what the pipestem means. They listened to me there, I told the leaders there. They were grateful, and they too are going to turn to it [the pipestem] for help; that was arranged over there at the meeting, and in this way it [the pipestem] is going to be kept right at the College in Saskatoon, so that it will be photographed, but that this story will be written down in Cree, the promises that were made to us, that is being arranged for the pipestem. That is the reason why my nephew David [Ahenakew] here was urging us yesterday, when he was speaking here, that we should work together, that we should work together; "If the words of a certain elder are properly heard, they will be the ones to guide us," he said, and thus he spoke the truth when he said that. That is all I am going to tell you about that.

[4] Indeed, each day I, too, also greatly persevere in praying for things; behold, I, too, sit with cloth offerings wanting for the prayers to be fulfilled; I am worried since my grandchildren and great-grandchildren are many, where will I direct them to turn for help? I think about that all the time. This is what we should do, my relatives, let us persevere, let us all join in together! Surely Our Father will take pity upon us; it is he who looks after things, not us, that we might be able to hear –~.

[5] cikêmô wiya, tânis îtêyihtahki, êwakw ânima kê-pimohtâtamahk kîsikâw ê-miywâsik. êkosi piko ê-ititakok, mâka, "pitanê, êkâ kîkway pâstâhôtotamân," nititêyihtên mân êwak ôm âyimôtamâni.

[5] Of course it is up to him, whatever his will may be, that we might live through that beautiful day. That is all I say to you, but, "I wish that I might not commit any sacrilege," I usually think when I talk about this.

6

[1] â, êwak ôma kâ-wî-tâhkôtamân, matwân cî kwayask nika-kî-isi-tâhkôtên tânis ê-kî-itâcimostawit kâ-kî-oyôhtâwîyân, ôm îta kâ-pakosêyimikawiyân ka-kî-tâhkôtamân, êwak ôm 'ôskiciy' k-êsiyîhkâtêk; ât[a] âni mitoni kwayask nikî-wîhtamâkoh mîna nôhcâwîs, ita ê-kî-kanawêyihtahk êwak ôma, ita omosôma kâ-kî-ohtaskatamiyit êwak ôm ôskiciy.

[2] â, mistahi wiya niya ninanâskomon, kik-ôtônihkâcik ôk ânita k-âtoskâkoyahkok kiwâhkômâkaninawak, kîkwây anima kitasotamâkowininaw; kâ-nitawêyihtahkik, ê-isi-kiskêyihtahk ayisiyiniw, ê-isi-pêhtahk opêhtamowinihk, k-âtotahk êwak ôma âcimowin. êwak ôma nîsta ê-kî-itâcimostawit mâna kâ-kî-oyôhtâwîyân, kâ-wî-itâcimostawakik ôki. matwân cî nika-kî-têpi-wîhtên, tânisi ê-kî-isi-wîhtamawit mâna. kôtatê nîst êkâ ê-sîpi-kiskisiyân, mâk ê-isko-kiskêyihtamân kîkway, êyiwêhk nika-kakwê-âcimostawâwak. mâcik êwak ôma, nîkân nika-tâhkôtên, êwak ôma nimosôminân kâ-kî-nakatahk cascakiskwês, oskiciy ôma.

[3] "êkota ôta, nipiy kâ-pitihkwêk, êkota kâ-mâwacîhitohk kâ-wî-atâwâkêhk askiy, êkot[a] ê-kî-âpatahk," kî-itwêw mâna kâ-kî-oyôhtâwîyân. "â, mistahi kî-pîkiskwêmôhikonâniwiw kîkway. mistahi kî-pîkiskwâtamwak, kisêyiniwak, êwak ôma, ê-kî-mihtâtahkik, ita kôhtâwînaw ê-kî-pakitinikoyahk askiy ka-nihtâwikîstamahk, êwak ôm êkwa ê-wî-atâwâkêwiht, êwako mistahi kâ-kî-pîkiskwâtahkik." êkosi mân êkota kî-itwêw.

[4] â, pêyak ana kisêyiniw, pêyak ana kisêyiniw, miton âta kî-wîhtam, tânis ê-wî-ispayik, êwak ôm êkwa, ita kâ-pimohtêyahk mêkwâc; â, mitoni wiyakâc, êkâ ê-mihcêticik,

The Pipestem and the Making of Treaty Six

[INTRODUCTION]

[1] Well, this which I am about to discuss, I wonder if I will be able to discuss it with proper faithfulness, just as my late father had told me the story about it, here [at the Saskatchewan Indian Languages Institute] where they wish that I should be able to discuss it, this pipestem as it is called; although I had most properly been told about it also by my father's brother, where he had kept this, where his grandfather had left this pipestem behind.

[2] Well, I am very grateful of course that these our relatives who work for us in this place [at the Saskatchewan Indian Languages Institute] will have it [the pipestem] as their witness of what these promises are which have been made to us; that they want for a person [*i.e.*, me] to tell about this story, just as he knows it, just as he heard it in his own hearing. Just as I myself used to be told the story by my late father, that is how I am going to tell it to them. I wonder if I will be able to tell it exactly, just as he used to tell it to me. It cannot be helped that my memory, too, lapses, but to the extent that I know this story, I will nevertheless try to tell it to them. This, for instance, I will discuss first, this which our grandfather *cascakiskwês* has left behind, the pipestem.

[PART I]

[3] "At that time, when they gathered here at *nipiy kâ-pitihkwêk*, where they were going to sell the land, at that time it was used," my late father used to say. "Well, the situation had everyone speaking with great concern. The old men spoke about this with great concern, they were full of regret that where Our Father had put us down on this earth that we should populate it, that this was going to be sold in their name, that was what they spoke about with great concern." That he used to say at that time.

[4] Well, a certain old man, one old man, had in fact foretold what was going to happen, the situation in which we find ourselves at present; well, it is sad indeed that the old men are

ki-~ mêkwâc kisêyiniwak ê-pê-mihcêticik, êwak ôma kî-atoskâtamihk, mistahi ka-kî-miywâsinôpan, ka-pêhtawâyahkik ômatowihk ka-tipôtahkik êwak ôma; mâk êkwa piko, kipêhtamowininâhk kîkway, âcimowin, tânis ê-kî-itâcimostâkawiyahk, êwakw êkwa piko ka-nâcipahiwêyahk. êwak ôhci k-ôh-nanâskomoyân niya, êwak ôma ê-atoskâtahkik, ê-mâmitonêyimâcik kôsisiminawa, kicâpâninawa, osk-âya êkâya kîkway ê-nâkatôhkêt, ka-kakwê-kiskêyihtahk, tânis ê-itâcimômakahk êwak ôma, êkos ôk ês êtokwê ê-pakosêyimocik, kâ-wî-kakwê-otinahkik ôm âcimowin, êwak ôma mêkwâc kâ-wî-âtotamân êkwa.

[5] êwakw âwa mâna kî-itwêw kâ-kî-oyôhtâwîyân, "â, ât[a] âni kî-wîhtam, kisêyiniw pêyak ê-pasikôt; êkota kî-wîhtam: 'kîkway piko k-âspitonâmot ayisiyiniw, kitayânânaw kîkway k-âspitonâmoyahk kâ-nêhiyâwiyahk; êwak ôma 'oskiciy' k-êsiyîhkâtêk, êwako piko ka-kî-aspitonâmoyahk. k-ês-âsotamâkoyahk awa kimôn-~ kiciwâminaw wâpiski-wiyâs, kitasotamâkonaw êkây wîhkâc ôta waskitaskamik ê-nîsokâtêt ayisiyiniw, ka-kî-pîkonahk kitasotamâkowininaw. êkosi, êkota kâ-kî-kakwêcimât:

> *«ê-tâpwêyan cî ôma, k-ês-âsotamawiyan, êkâ wîhkâc awiyak ka-kî-kaskihtât ka-kî-pîkonahk ôma k-ês-âsotamawiyâhk. kipê-âkwaskiskawinân ayis, kipê-âkwaskiskawâw, mâmaw-ôhtâwîmâw ita ê-kî-miyikoyâhk kîkway k-ôh-pimâtisiyâhk, kipê-âkwaskiskawâw; kâ-pê-asotamawiyâhk ê-wî-isi-pamihiyâhk, êwak ôma, k-~ ê-tâpwêyan cî ôma k-ês-âsotamawiyâhk; ita kâ-pê-pimohtêstamawat kihc-ôkimâskwêw, namôy wîhkâc cî ka-kisipîmakan ôma kitasota-~ k-âsotamawiyâhk.*
>
> *wâpahta! mâcikôtitan ôta ê-ispis-îtâpiyan, ê-ispisi-wîhkwêskamikâk, iyikohk kâ-têpâpamat paskwâwi-mostos, êkon ôhi ê-kî-miyikoyâhk k-ôh-pimâtisiyâhk, mâmaw-ôhtâwîmâw; êkosi cî ka-kî-isi-pamihinân, iskoyikohk ôta kiy-âskîwik.»*

not many, it would have been very good if one had worked on this earlier, while they were numerous, so that we would hear them discussing this with their authority on that kind [the audio-recorder]; but now the story is only something from our hearing, how the story had been told to us, now that is all we have to fall back upon. That is why I for one am grateful that they are working on this, that they are thinking of our grandchildren and great-grandchildren, because young people do not pay any attention to trying to learn about it, how the story is told about this, and this then must be the wish of those who are going to try to record this story, now this is what I am going to tell about at present.

[5] He, my late father, used to say this, "Well, a certain old man had in fact foretold it, rising from his seat; then he had foretold it: 'The people must have something to rely upon as testimony, and we who are Crees do have something to rely upon as testimony; that which is called the pipestem, that is all upon which we can rely as testimony. When he, our brother the White-Man, made these promises to us, he did promise us that no human walking on two legs upon the surface of the earth would ever be able to break the promises made to us. Thus, it was then that he had asked him:

> *«Do you speak the truth in this which you have promised me, that no one will ever be in a position to be able to break the promises which you have made to us? For you have come between us, you have come between the All-Father and us, where he has given us the sustenance upon which we live, you have come between him and us; in coming to promise us that you are going to look after us, do you speak the truth in this which you have promised us; here where you have come representing the Queen, will it never end, that which you have promised us?*
>
> *Behold it! Lo, here as far as you can see, as far as the corners of the earth reach, as many buffalo as your eyes can grasp, the All-Father has given us all these to live upon; will you be able to provide for us to the same extent so long as this world shall exist?»*

êkosi kî-itêw anihi, kâ-kî-pê-pimohtêstamawât awa kihc-ôkimâskwêwa;

«ê-tâpwêyan cî ôma, k-ês-âsotamawiyâhk, êkâ wîhkâc ka-kî-pîkonahk, 'ayisiyiniw ê-nîsokâtêt' k-êtwêyan, êwak ôma, îh! k-ês-âsotamawiyâhk.» –

«namôya, namôya nipiy k-âtâmitân, namôya pisiskiw k-ôh-pimâcihoyan, namôy êwako k-âtâmitân; namôya mîna kinosêw, môya mîn êwako k-âtâmitân; mîna nanâtohk ôhi mînisa k-ôh-pimâcihoyan, namôy êkoni k-âtâmitân.»

êkosi kî-itwêw, êwakw âwa kâ-kî-pê-pimohtêstamawât kihc-ôkimâskwêwa,' " kî-itwêw mâna kâ-kî-oyôhtâwîyân, ay-âtotahki êwak ôma;

«hâw, ê-tâpwêyan cî ôma, kâkikê êkosi k-êsi-pamihiyan?»

kî-itêw anihi;

«kîspin kitâpwân, êwak ôma ka-~ kika-miciminên oskiciy; ê-tâpwêyan cî ôma k-ês-âsotamawiyâhk – êhâ, ahpô namôya?» –

«êha!»

ê-itwêyit, êkota kâ-kî-tahkonamôhâcik, êwak ôm ôskiciy ê-kî-otinahk,

«hâw! môy âwiyak wîhkâc ka-kaskihtâw ê-nîsokâtêt ayisiyiniw, ka-pîkonahk tânis ê-is-âsotamâtakok. môy wîhkâc ka-têpinêhamâtin kitaskiy, kâkikê ka-pimi-tipahamâtân. namôya, namôya ay-atâmaskamik k-âtâmitân ôm âskiy, pêyak-misit ita k-ôhci-pimâcihwâkêt wâpiski-wiyâs, êwak ôma k-âtâmitân. hâw, ôta ohci, kîkway ay-atâmaskamik ê-sôniyâwik, ka-nisitohtahk, êwak ôma pêyak nêhiyaw wîk[i] ê-pim-ôhtisit;»

êkos êsa kâ-itwêt, êwakw âwa kâ-pê-atâwêstamawât;

«êkwa êwak ôma, kâ-itamân, kâ-kakwêcimiyan, êkây wîhkâc ka-kî-pîkonahk awiyak, tâpwê! tâpwê! namôy ka-kî-pîkonam. êwak ôma k-êtwêyân, namôya nipiy, namôya sâkahikana k-âtâmitân, namôya kinosêw; kêtisk piko, k-ôh-pimâcihot ôm âskiy, wâpiski-wiyâs. ita ê-otinaskêt, kik-ôsîhtâw mônahipân, êwakw ânima kê-âpacihtât nipiy. â, êwak ôhci, môy

Thus he spoke to him, to the one who had come representing the Queen;

«Do you speak the truth in this which you have promised us, that no 'human walking on two legs', as you put it, will ever be able to break that, look, which you have promised us.» –

«No, I have not bought the water from you, nor the animals upon which you live, I have not bought them from you; also not the fish, I have not bought that either; and the various kinds of berries upon which you live, I also have not bought those.»

Thus he spoke, the one who had come representing the Queen,' " my late father used to say when telling about this;

[PART II]

«Indeed, do you speak the truth in that you will forever look after me to this extent?»

he had said to that one;

«If you speak the truth, hold then this pipestem; do you speak the truth in this which you have promised us – Yes, or no?» –

«Yes!»

he said, and when they had made him hold the pipestem, then he had taken this pipestem,

«Indeed! No human walking on two legs will ever be able to break what I am hereby promising you. I will never pay you in full for your land, I will forever make continuous payments to you for it. No, I do not buy from you what is deep beneath this land, only one foot deep whence the White-Man makes his living, that is what I buy from you. Indeed, from here on, any monies drawn from beneath the ground, let people understand that this is one benefit which the Crees will continue to be paid from their homeland;»

thus then he spoke, the one who had come to make the purchase for them;

«Now that which I said, what you ask me about, that no one will ever be able to break it, it is true! it is true! no one will be able to break it. This is what I said, I do not buy the water, nor the lakes, from you, nor the fish; only enough land [i.e.,

sâkahikana k-âtâmitân, k-êtitân, namôy mîn âsinîwaciy ôma k-âtâmitân; êwak ôma piko, k-âtâmitân ôma, ita k-ôh-pimâcihot wâpiski-wiyâs.»
êkos êsa kî-is-âsotamâkwak, êkon ôhi.

[6] êwak ôhci, kâ-~ êwako kâ-kî-âpacihtâcik, "ôtê kê-nîkâniwik, mâmiskôcikâtêki, êwak ôma nêhiyaw omasinahikan, kâ-tahkonahk awa, ê-naskotahk, anima k-ês-âsotamâkoyahk, êkây wîhkâc awiyak ka-kî-pîkonahk;" êkos êsa kî-itwêwak kisêyiniwak ôki.

«hâw, êkos êkwa, êwak ôma k-ês-âsotamâtakok, ka-~ kâkikê, iskoyikohk pîsim ka-pimohtêt, iskoyikohk sîpiy ka-pimiciwahk, iskoyikohk maskosiya kê-sâkikihki, êkospî isko ka-pimohtêmakan ôma k-ês-âsotamâtân;»
êkos êsa kâ-kî-itihcik ôki, kimosôminawak. (êwak ôm êkwa, anohc êkwa, wâpiski-wiyâs kâ-mikoskâcihtât, pîtos ê-wî-kakwê-itakimikoyahk.)

[7] "hâw, êkota ês êkwa mîna kâ-kî-pîkiskwêt êwakw âwa kisêyiniw," kî-itwêw mâna kâ-kî-oyôhtâwîyân. " 'ât[a] âni mistahi nimihtâtên, nimihtâtên ôma, kitaskînaw ê-kî-miyikoyahk w-~, kôhtâwînaw ita k-ôh-pimâtisiyahk, k-âtâwâkêhk ôma kitaskînaw. mâka, êkâ êkosi kê-ihkihk, ôtê wâpiski-wiyâs ati-sâkaskinêci, êkot[a] ôma kiyê-ohcihikoyahk askiy-~ askiy,' kî-itwêw ês êwako kisêyiniw," kî-itwêw mâna kâ-kî-oyôhtâwîyân. êwako ôma mêkwâc êkwa.

one foot deep] *for the White-Man to make his living. Where he homesteads, he will make a well, and that is the water he will use. Well, that is why I said to you that I am not buying the lakes from you, and I am also not buying the Rocky Mountains; I am only buying this whence the White-Man will make his living.»*

Thus then they had these promises made to them, by that one.

[PART III]

[6] That is why they had used that [the pipestem], "In the future, when these things are discussed, this is the bible of the Cree which he held, swearing upon it in response that no one would ever be able to break the promises he had made to us;" thus then spoke these old men.

«Indeed, thus now the promises which I have made to you, forever, so long as the sun shall cross the sky, so long as the rivers shall run, so long as the grass shall grow, that is how long these promises I have made to you will last;»

thus then our grandfathers had been told. (And that is what the White-Man is now tampering with, trying to change our status.)

[PART IV]

[7] "Indeed, there then again this old man had spoken," my late father used to say. " 'I do regret it greatly, I regret it, since Our Father has given us this our land upon which to live, that this our land should have been sold. But, if that does not happen [*i.e.*, if we do not accept the treaty], if the Whites then increasingly crowd the land, it will be then that they will fight us over the land,' that old man had then said," my late father used to say. And that is what is before us at the present time.

[8] *"kiyâm ôta awas-âyihk -~ kwêskahcâhk, ôm îtê osêhcâhk kwêsk-âyihk ma-matwêwêki, namôy wîhkâc k-ôtinâw nêhiyaw-âyisiyiniw, nôtinitowinihk k-âpati-~ k-êtisiniht;"*
êkos êsa mîna ê-kî-is-âsotamâkêt.
"êkon ôhi tahto-kîkway k-âsotamâtân, kâkikê êwako ka-pimipayiw;"
êkos ês ê-kî-is-âsotamâht êwakw âwa nêhiyaw kâ-kî-atâwâkêt kitaskînaw.

[9] â, êwakw ânima, êkos ê-itâtotamân, nîsta ê-kî-itâcimostawit kâ-kî-oyôhtâwîyân; matwân cî k-~ kwayask nitâtotên êwak ôma, tânis ê-kî-itâcimostawit mâna, êwak ôma k-âcimostawakik ôki nôsisimak.

[10] mâka mistahi ka-miywâsin, êwak ôma kâ-wî-tâhkôtamihk, nikotwâsik-tipahamâtowin, k-êhtakot êkota kêhtê-âya, ahpô nôtikwêw, wîst ê-miywâsiniyik kîkway ê-kî-pêtât, êkota ka-takwastât wîst ôtâcimowin, ka-mâmitonêyimâyahkok kôsisiminawak. sâkôcihikoyahko wâpiski-wiyâs kâ-wî-itasiwâtikoyahk, mistahi kika-kitimâkisinânaw; môy piko kêhtê-aya ka-kitimâkisit, awâsisak ôki kâ-pê-nayawacikicik, êkonik ôki kê-kitimâkisicik, êkosi mân ê-itêyihtamân niya.

[11] hâw, êkos ôma ê-itâcimostawakik ôki, kâ-nitawêyihtahkik kîkway k-âcimostawakik. mistahi ka-kî-miywâsinôpan, ka-kî-masinipayihtâhk anim ôta oskiciy, ita anima kâ-kî-aspitonâmot kisêyiniw.

[12] êwak ôm îskwêyâc ê-âpatahk, oskiciy, ita ê-kî-nakiskamohtatamâht wâpiski-wiyâs, êwak ôma 'pêhonânihk' k-êtamihk, êkota kâ-kî-pimohtatâcik pwâtak êwak ôm ôskiciy; êkota iskwêyâc ê-âpatahk.

[SUPPLEMENT]

[8] *"Assuming there were here on the other side -- on the other side of a hill, if there on a hillside on the other side there were gunshots heard, the Cree Indians will never be conscripted to be handed over into military service;"*

thus then he had also promised.

"These promises, as many as I have made to you, all this will hold forever;"

thus then had the promises been made to that Cree who had sold our land.

[CONCLUSION]

[9] Well, as I tell this story, just so I, too, had it told to me by my late father; I wonder if I tell this properly, just as he used to tell me this story, it is this that I have told to these my grandchildren.

[10] But it will be very good when one is going to discuss Treaty Six, that there should be an old person, or an old woman, with her, too, bringing along something valuable, there to add her own story, so that we might think of our grandchildren. If the Whites overpower us when they are going to make laws for us, we will live in great misery; not only will the old people live in misery, but the children, too, who are coming after us in their various ages will live in misery, thus, as for me, I usually think.

[11] Indeed, this is the story I am telling those who want me to tell them the story about it. It would have been very good to have photographed this pipestem here, the one upon which the old man had relied as testimony.

[12] That was the last time it was used, the pipestem, where one first used it with the Whites, it was here at *pêhonânihk* as it is called, that is where the Sioux had brought along that pipestem; that was the last time it was used.

[13] hâw, êkosi piko ê-isi-kiskêyihtamân ôma k-êtâtotamân.

[*some conversation at very low volume*]

[14] êwak ôma, kâ-nitawêyihtahkik, k-âcimostawakik, tânis ê-kî-is-âsotamâht:

"êwak ôma kiskinohamâtowikamik k-âsotamâtân, êkota ka-kiskinohamawâw, kitawâsimis kôsisim; êwakw êkwa kîsîhtâci, okiskinohamâsowin, êwakw êkwa nikotwâsosâp ê-itahtopiponwêcik, êkot[a] ôma kê-pakitiniht. êkota ôm êkwa, kê-pimi-wîcihiht, pêyakwahpitêw misatimwa ka-miyâw, kiskinohamawâkan, âpacihcikana êkota ohci ka-miyâw. hâw, ôta ohci mostoswa ka-miyâw, k-ôhpikihtamâsot, k-ôh-pimâcihot."

êkos ês êkwa anima mîn ê-kî-is-âsotamâht; êkos êwakw êkwa, kayâsês kâ-pônipayik êwak ôma, êkos ê-kî-isi-wîcihiht ayisiyiniw.

"hâw, êkwa kiya okimâhkân: ka-papâmi-nitawâpamacik kitiyinîmak, ka-miyikawin pêyak misatim, ocâpânâskos kik-âpacihat, êwakw âni kika-papâmi-nitawâpamacik kitiyinîmak."

'okimâhkân' k-êsiyîhkâsot, êkos êsa kâ-is-âsotamâht.

"hâw, êkwa êwak ôma, kâ-miyitân kiskinohamâtowikamik k-âsotamâtân, êwako, môy wîhkâc ka-kisipîmakan, êwak ôma maskihkîwiwacis k-âsotamâtân, môy wîhkâc ka-tipahên maskihkiy ita k-ôh-pamihisk maskihkîwiyiniw."

êkos êsa kâ-is-âsotamâht mîna, êwakw âwa kâ-kî-wiyihcikêt kimosôminaw.

"hâw, êkwa, êwakw âwa kâ-miyitân sôniyâwikimâw, êwakw âwa ka-wîtatoskêmat; kîkway ita ê-wawânêyihtamihikoyan, êwakw âwa ka-tôtamâk.

hâw, êkwa mîn âwa omasinahikêsîs kâ-miyitân, êwako êkwa mîna k-âtoskâsk, ka-masinahikêstamâsk, masinahikana k-ôsîhtât; êwako mîn âwa kâ-miyitân.

hâw, êkwa kotak, êwakw êkwa 'okistikêwiyiniw'

[13] Indeed, this is all I know of the story as I have been told it.

[*some conversation at very low volume*]

[APPENDIX]

[14] This is what they want that I should tell them the story about, what had been promised to him:

> *"It is this school house which I have promised you, there your children and grandchildren will be taught; and then when they have finished their schooling, then when they are sixteen years old, then they will be released, and then they will continue to receive help, the students will be given a team of horses, and they will also be given implements from there* [by the government]. *Indeed, they will be given cattle from here* [by the government] *to raise for themselves, with which to make their living."*

Thus this also had been promised to him; and this stopped quite a long time ago, that people received this kind of help.

> *"Indeed, now for you, the chief: you will be given one horse, for you to go around and visit your people, a buggy for you to use, for you to go around and visit your people with that."*

This then had been promised to the 'chief', as he was called.

> *"Indeed, now this which I have given you, the school house which I have promised you, that will never end, and this medicine-chest which I have promised you, you will never pay for medicine with which the doctor treats you."*

This then he had also been promised, that grandfather of ours who concluded the treaty.

> *"Indeed, now, I have given you this agent to work with you; when something worries you, he will deal with it for you.*
>
> *Indeed, now I have also given you this clerk, for that one also to work for you, to write things for you, to make written records; this one I have also given you.*
>
> *Indeed, now another, now this farm instructor as he is called, for this one to teach your children and grandchildren*

k-êsiyîhkâsot, êwakw êkwa ka-kiskinohamawât kitawâsimisa kôsisima tânisi k-êsi-pimâcihoyit, êwak ôma kistikêwi-pimâcihowin; êwako mîna kâ-miyitân.

hâw, êkwa kotak, êwako êkwa, 'wiyahisow' k-êsiyîhkâsow; kîkway kitâpacihcikan ê-pîkopayik, wiy ân[a] êkwa êkota kê-kîsîhtamâsk, êwak ôma ka-nânapâcihtât,"

êkos êsa kâ-itiht.

"hâw, êkwa êwak ôma, kipamihikowin, asahtowin, â, êkota êkwa kimiyitin mîn ôtasahkêw, êwak ôma, ka-pamihât ayisiyiniwa, kik-âsamât, êwako mîna ê-asotamâtân.

hâw, êkwa, otitwêstamâkêw mîna kitasotamâtin; ita ê-wî-wîci-pîkiskwêmat wâpiski-wiyâs, êwakw âna ki-~kiy-êtwêstamâsk;"

êkos êsa mîna kâ-is-âsotamâht.

"hâw, êkwa kotak, êwakw êkw âwa simâkanis, kâ-miyitân, ka-nâkatôhkêt kitaskiy, ita kîkway ê-sâkôhikoyan êkota êkwa, wiy êkwa, ka-nâtamâk kîkway, ka-pimipayihtât ôma kitaskîhkân;"

êkos êsa mîna ê-kî-is-âsotamâht.

[15] êwak ôma kâ-nitawêyihtahkik k-âniskê-âtotamân, êkosi mân ê-kî-itâcimostawit kâ-kî-oyôhtâwîyân, êkon ôhi ê-kî-miyikawiyahk kîkway kik-âpacihtâyahk,

"kiya piko, kê-pîkonamâsoyan, kitasotamâkowin."

êwak ôma kâ-kî-pê-wîhtahkik, êwakw êkwa mêkwâc ôma, mistahi kâ-pîkiskwêmôhikoyahk.

[16] êkosi piko ê-isi-kiskêyihtamân, êwak ôma kâ-nitawêyihtahkik k-âtotamân. â, êkosi.

how to make their living, that farm economy; this one I have also given you.

Indeed, now another, now this one will be called blacksmith; when your implements break, then for that one to repair them for you, to fix them,"

thus then he was told.

"Indeed, now that, your welfare, rations, well, in that respect now I give you a rations agent, that too, to look after people, to provide them with food, that I promise you also.

Indeed, now I also promise you an interpreter; where you are going to speak to the Whites, for that one to interpret for you;"

this then also had been promised to him.

"Indeed, now another, now for the policeman I have given you to pay attention to your reserve, where something turns out to be too difficult for you in that respect, he now will take up for you in these things, in running your reserve;"

this then also had been promised to him.

[15] This is what they want that I should tell about in order to continue the oral tradition, thus my late father used to tell me the story, that these things were given to us to use,

"Only you yourself will be able to break the promises made to you."

That is what they had always foretold, and this is what has us speaking with great concern at the present time.

[16] This is all I know about this which they wanted that I should tell about. Well, that is all.

7

[1] êwak ôma, kâ-wî-tâhkôtamân, kâ-nitawêyihtahkik ka-tâhkôtamân, tânis âw ê-itakisot awa cistêmâw, îh! tânis ôma ê-itakihtêk ôma wêpinâson. ê-nitawi-kiskêyihtahk kîkway, osk-âya, ahpô itâskonikêwin, ahpô kâ-nitawi-kîskisamawât kêhtê-aya, kâ-wî-nîminikêt ôma kîsitêw, êkon ôhi ê-nîkânohtatât ôhi, ka-kitimâkihtâkot kisêyiniwa, kâ-nitawi-kîskisamawât. êkwa êkoni ôhi, kâ-kî-osîhât kôhtâwînaw, cistêmâw ka-nîkânît, ê-kî-manitowakimât ôhi, cistêmâwa, êwak ôhci k-ôh-nîkânîhiht awa cistêmâw, nîkân, tânis ê-isi-mamisîtotâht kêhtê-aya, ahpô nôtikwêw, kâ-wî-nâcinêhamawat maskihkiy, "êkoni pit[a] ôhi nîkân, êkon ôh ê-nîkânohtêmakahki," kâ-kî-itwêcik kêhtê-ayak. êkosi wiy êwako, ê-isi-kiskêyihtamân ôma.

[2] êkwa ôma kîk-~, kotak, êwakw êkwa, kâ-nôhtê-kiskêyihtahkik, tânis ôm ê-itwêmakahk wîhkask, tânêhk ânima k-ôh-âpatahk wîhkask; tânêhki mîna k-ôh-apihkâtêk, kâ-nistwapihkâtamihk, "ê-nistiniyiki êkota onitotamâwina wîhkaskoyiniw," kâ-kî-itwêcik kisêyiniwak. "hâw, êkoni ôhi, k-ôh-sawêyimitin nîst ôma, kiy-ês-âpihkâtaman ôma wîhkask, êkot[a] âni kiy-~ kiy-âpihkâtamawat kitawâsimis, anima opimâtisiwin awâska-mâmitonêyihcikan [?*sic*]," êkosi êsa ê-kî-itwêt awa wîhkaskoyiniw. "hâw, k-ôcihciskâmakan, itê ê-pimi-wâh-ohpahtênaman kiwîhkaskom, it[a] ê-kâkîsimoyan, êwak ôma kiy-êtwêstamâkoyan wîhkask; êwak ôhci manâcihtâ! ê-manâcihtâyan ôma kiwîhkaskom, k-êsi-miywâsik kihc-ôkâwîmâw kâ-sâkâwanêhtât, êkos âni kik-êtihtâkwan kinitotamâwin;" êkos ôma ê-kî-itihcik êsa, nistamêmâkanak kîkway; êwak ôma wîhkask ohci, k-ôh-âpatahk; êwak ôma kâ-nôhtê-kiskêyihtahkik.

[3] hâw, êkwa êwak ôma, kîkwây ânima, îwanisîhisowin, kakwâtakihowin k-ôh-âpatahk, ê-nôhtê-tâpwêt ayisiyiniw

[1] This which I am going to discuss, what they want that I should discuss, what is the rôle of the tobacco, behold! what is the rôle of the cloth. When a young person goes in search of knowledge about something, either about [something secret like] the pipe ceremony, or when he cuts off tobacco for an elder, when he is going to offer up the food, he places these two [tobacco and cloth] first so that the old man will hear and take pity upon the one who goes to cut off tobacco for him. Now amongst these which Our Father has made, for tobacco to be the foremost, he endowed the tobacco with supernatural powers, that is why the tobacco is given the foremost position, the first place, in the way in which one places one's reliance for something upon an elder, or upon an old woman, when you are going to buy medicine from them, "These will be first for now, these occupy the foremost place," that is what the elders used to say. That is all I know about this.

[2] And another thing now which they want to know about, what is the meaning of the sweetgrass, why is that sweetgrass used; also why is it braided, when one braids it in three strands, "Three are the requests made there of the Sweetgrass-Old-Man," that is what the old men used to say. "Indeed, with these I myself will bless you, as you will braid the sweetgrass thus [*i.e.*, in three strands], as you will braid it for your child, then, for his life and for a stable mind," that then the Sweetgrass-Old-Man had reportedly said. 'Indeed, it will come to pass where you are raising the wafts of your sweetgrass smoke, where you are chanting your prayers, that this sweetgrass will speak for you; for that reason respect it! When you respect your sweetgrass, just as it is beautiful when the Great Mother pushes it up through the ground, that is how your requests will be listened to;" that is what they were reportedly told, the first ones; this is why sweetgrass is used; this is what they want to know.

[3] Indeed, and now for this, what is that, fasting, why is use made of making oneself suffer; wanting a favourable answer and

ê-nitotamât, ê-mâkohikot kîkway âhkosiwin, êkota êkwa kâ-kî-kakwâtakihisot. ê-nitotamât ka-kitimâkihtâkot âtayôhkana, kîkway ê-nitotamawât, ka-nisitawinahk okisêwâtisiwiniyiw; êwak ôhc ânima k-ôh-kakwâtakihisot, tâpiskôc ôma kâ-nipâkwêsimohk, kâ-kakwâtakihisot ayisiyiniw; ê-nitawi-pimâcisiwin-nâtahk [*sic*], ka-kitimâkihtâkot, ita ê-pimohtahât otawâsimisa ôsisima. êkos ôma ê-itwêmakahk êwako.

[4] hâw, êkwa êwak ôm êkwa, 'matotisân' êkwa k-êsiyîhkâtêk, â, êkot[a] êkwa kâ-kî-wiyakimât kistêsinaw wîsahkêcâhk, kisê-nâpêw-asiniy: "hâw, kiya kika-kîsowâtên, matotisân. hâw, ita ê-kâkîsimot ayisiyiniw, ita ê-patowâtahk anima okâkîsimowin, hâw, kîsi-~ kîsowâtamohk! kîsowâtamaw, ka-tâpwêw! mâcikôtitan ômis ôma wî-ispayiw wî-mêtawâkâniwiw êwak ôma, ê-mosci-kiskinowâpicik, kiskinowâpiwin k-âpatan; mâk ân[a] âyisiyiniw kê-tâpwêwakêyihtahk kîsowâtamohk okâkîsimowin! ê-ohpâskonât ospwâkana, mâh-mînwâskonamaw anima, oskicîwâhtik!" êkos êsa kâ-itwêt; "kitimâkihtawâhkan, matotisânihk kîkway nitotamâski, nêwâw pimi-tâhkâpâwatâci pimi-pakitinamâski sîkahasinânâpoy" – "êkot[a] âni kê-pakahkihtawak," kî-pim-îsi-naskwêwasimow ês âwa, kisê-nâpêw-asiniy. êwak ôma k-âpatahk kâ-matotisihk, pikw îta, kâ-nîkânîhiht. nanâtohk ê-itikwamikohkêhk, ê-nipâkwêsimohk ê-pîhtwâhk ê-pihêwisimohk, âsay êkota kisê-nâpêw-asiniy; êwakw ân[a] ê-otônihkâyahk, ê-itwêstamâkoyahk. êwakw âni kâ-nôhtê-kiskêyihtahkik ôki.

[5] hâw, êkos êwako wiy ê-isi-kiskêyihtamân ôma, k-êtât-~ k-êtâtotamân. êkwa êwakw âwa, kâ-naka-~ k-êtâskonamâht,

making a request, when troubled by some illness, that is when a person used to make himself suffer. Requesting that the dream spirit should listen to him with pity and that he would see recognisable signs of his grace when asking for something of him; that is why he makes himself suffer, for example in the sun-dance, when a person makes himself suffer; he seeks to obtain life, so that he [the dream spirit] should listen to him with pity, as he takes his children and grandchildren along in his prayers. This is the meaning of that.

[4] Indeed, and now for this, the sweat-lodge, as it is called, well, it was then that our elder brother Wisahketchahk charged the Kind-Man-Rock: "You, indeed, you will complete the prayer for the sweat-lodge. Indeed, where a person is chanting his prayers, where he makes a mistake in chanting his prayer, indeed, you all complete his prayer! You complete the prayer for him, let him obtain a favourable answer! Lo, this is going to happen and people are going to play around with this, learning merely by imitation [rather than by instruction], learning by imitation will be used; but for a person who believes in it, you all complete his chanting prayer! As he raises the pipe, help him to point it the right way, the pipestem," that is what he reportedly said; "then listen to him with pity when he requests something from you in the sweat-lodge, as four times he gradually cools the rock with water, as he gradually pours the rock-sprinkling-water for you." – "It is then that I will hear him clearly," thus reportedly spoke in response, all along, Kind-Man-Rock. This is what is used in the sweat-lodge, everywhere where he [Kind-Man-Rock] is placed in the foremost position. Various lodges are made, the sun-dance, the pipe-lodge, the prairie-chicken dance, already he is there [in first position], Kind-Man-Rock; we make him our advocate and he speaks for us. This is what they want to know.

[5] Indeed, for about this I know in this way, in the way I am telling about it. Now the one for whom the pipe is being pointed,

kâ-wîhkomiht ôma kâ-wîhkohkêt ayisiyiniw, kî-kostamwak kayâs kisêyiniwak, êkâ êkota ka-kakêpâhkamikisit awâsis; kî-kostamwak, anohc nama kîkway êwako, ahpô ê-nîminikêhk, konit ê-wâsakâtisahotocik awâsisak. êkâ kîkway ê-kiskêyihtahk onîkihikomâw, mîna nôtikwêwak ôki, k-êsi-kitahamawâcik, otawâsimisiwâwa ôsisimiwâwa, tânis ânima kîkway k-êsi-manâcihtâyit. êkos ôma mân ê-kî-isi-wîhtamâkawiyân niya, êwak ôma k-âcimostawakik. nama kîkway ê-kiskêyihtamân, ê-itwêyân, mâka kisêyinîwi-pîkiskwêwin ôma k-âcimostawakik, tânis ê-ispayik.

[6] â, êkosi, êwakw ânima ê-itâcimostawakik.

[*external break*]

[7] [*conversation: ...*] ~– paminihk! tâpwê ana, namôy kwayask ê-isi-pamihiht aw ôspwâkan, mihcêtwâw nipê-wâpamâw, okiskinowâpiw yâhk-îtâp kâ-kiskinohamâkêt k-êsi-pamihimiht ôh ôspwâkana.

[8] îh, nistam ê-pê-piko-~-wiyakimât ôta [*gesture*] kôhtâwînaw, kîsikâw-pîsimwa ôhi kâ-kî-pakitinamawât, ka-pê-sâkêwêtotahk ôma kikîsikâminaw; it[a] ê-pimohtâtahk kîsikâw ê-miywâsik, êwakw ânima kisêwâtisiwin kâ-kî-miyât; êkota ohci, ê-kî-~, kotaka ê-kîsi-wiyakimât êkwa ôta âpihtâ-kîsikâhk, êwakw êkwa piyêsiw, ita kâ-pimâwahât otawâsimisa, êwakw ânima kâ-pimi-~-kâkîsimototahk. êkota ohc ôtê âpiht-~ pahkisimohk, k-ôh-miyâhkasoht aw ôspwâkan, â, êwakw êkwa, êkota ê-osâpahtahk, okîsikow, kîsikohk ohc ôma. ôm êkwa nâtakâm, êwakw êkwa awa yôtin êkwa, êwakw êkwa, iskwêyâc ômis îsi [*gesture*]. êk ôma kâ-mâtâskonikêt, ômisi k-êsi-miyâhkaswât ôhi ospwâkana, ômisi kiy-êsi-wâsakâyâskonât; ôtê êkwa, kâ-mâtâskonikêt, ôtê âpihtâ-kîsikâhk, pêyakwan; êkosi

the one who is invited when people make a feast, in the old days the old men used to fear it that children should be getting in the way; they used to fear it, but today there is none of that, even when one makes the offering of the food, the children blithely chase one another around. For the parents, of course, do not know anything, the old women also, about how to caution their children and grandchildren about it, how they should hold this in respect. That is how I myself used to be told about the story which I am telling them. I do not know anything, I say, but I am telling them the story of what the old men spoke, how things are done.

[6] Well, in that way I am telling them the story of that.

[*external break*]

[7] [*conversation: ...*] –– treat it! When the pipe is not handled with proper respect, it is true of those who have learnt by [mere] imitation that I have many times seen them teach it as if they knew how one should treat the pipe.

[8] Behold, first Our Father came to charge the Sun here [*gesture*], when he had arranged for him to rise upon our day; wherein he passes through the beautiful day, that grace he gave him; next from there he had completed charging the other here in the south, that was the Thunderbird, where he leads his children and goes along chanting about that. Next from there, over there to the west, that is from where one smudges the pipe, well, now that one, the Sky-Spirit, looks down from there, from the sky. Now the north, and now it is the Wind, and now, the last one is like this [*points the pipe*]. Now when he starts pointing the pipestem, in order to smudge the pipe in this way, then he will turn it around in this way; now starting to point the pipestem over here to the south, the same; that is how he will turn it

kiy-êsi-wâsakâyâskonât, pêyakwan; ôtê mîna, pêyakwan anima êkosi kiy-êsi-wâsakâyâskonât, ôtê êkwa nâtakâm.

[9] hâw, ôtê êkwa ê-wâsakâyâskonât êkota êkwa êkwêyâc ka-miyât anihi kisêyiniwa, anih ôspwâkana. êkos ânima kik-êsi-paminiht aw ôspwâkan. tâpitawi ômis îsi, pîsim aw êtohtêt [*sic*], k-êsi-wâsakânaman, êwak ôma. êwako kâ-nôhtê-kiskêyihtahk ôma, itâskonikêwin.

[10] êkwa, kîkwây an[a] ôskâpêwis? êwakw âna ospwâkana kâ-pamihât, kâ-wîhkohtohk, nanâtohk k-êsîhcikêhk, ospwâkan[a] âna kâ-pamihât, êwakw âna nîkân, êwakw âna nîkân kik-âsamiht ôma kîsitêw. êkota ohc ôk ôskâpêwisak, tâpitaw ômisi [*gesture*] k-êtohtêcik, k-âsamâcik ôhi kîkway. êwak ôma kâ-itamân, ê-mêtawâkêt anohc ayisiyiniw. ômis [*gesture*] îtohtêw (îh! nâkatôhkêk!) ayisiyiniw. êk ôma nipâkwêsimowin ê-ispayik – ômis îsi k-êtohtêt ê-papâmi-nawaswâtahk nipâkwêsimowina ôhi, ê-papâ-pakosêyimot anima kîkway ka-miyiht. namôy êkosi ê-ôh-tôtahkik kayâs kisêyiniwak. êkota ôma kâ-nitawi-saskahamâhcik, kâ-pâpicicik, ê-nitawi-pimâtisiwinêcik anima, pimâtisiwin ê-nâtahkik. anohc êkwa, nayêstaw pakitinâsowin ohci k-ôh-papâmitisahahk ayisiyiniw; namôy tâpwêwakêyihtam otêhihk kîkway ohci, êwakw ânima. êkwa êwak ôma êkos ê-isîhcikêhk, ê-nipâkwêsimohk, êwakw âwa ospwâkana kâ-pamihât, êwakw âna nîkân kîkway ê-miyiht, cistêmâwa wêpinâson, êkota ohci pakitinâsowin ê-miyiht; pimâtisiwin anima kâ-miyiht. ê-kîspinatahk êwako, êwako ospwâkana kâ-~, êkota ohc ôskâpêwisak, hâw, pâh-pêyak kîkway ê-miyihcik, pimâtisiwin anima kâ-miyihcik; hâw, êkot[a] êkwa kêhtê-ayak ôki, ôtê ôki k-âpicik, êkonik ê-kî-sawohkâtihcik, êkonik ê-kî-sawohkâtihcik, â, êkot[a] êkwa, êkâya ka-patahohkâtiht kîkway wîhkâc, 'nôtikwêw' k-êsiyîhkâsot, êwako nôtikwêw-âtayôhkan. ê-tâpwêmakahk ôma nipâkwêsimowin, ka-kitâpamâyêkok iskwêwak ôtê ê-sâkaskinêkâpawicik, ôtê k-êtâpiyêk mitoni wâh-wâhyaw

around, the same; and also over here, he will turn it around in the same way, now over there to the north.

[9] Indeed, now that he turns the pipe around over there, only then now to give it for the first time to the old man, that pipe. That is how the pipe is to be handled. Always in this way, as the sun goes, so you turn that one, the stem. This is what they wanted to know, the pointing of the pipestem.

[10] Now, what is the Server? He takes care of the pipe, when there is a feast, when various ceremonies are performed, he takes care of the pipe, that one [the Server] is first, that one is the first to be fed the food. Thereafter the Servers always walk in this way [*gesture; i.e.*, in the direction of the sun] when serving something to the people. This is what I meant, people play around with it today. People walk like this [*gesture; i.e.*, opposite to the direction of the sun] (look, you pay attention)! Now this is what happens with the sun-dance – they go like this chasing these sun-dances, going around wishing that they might be given something [at the give-away]. The old men did not use to do that in the old days. At that time, when one went and lit a pipe for them, they would come with their camps, in the pursuit of life, seeking life. Today now, people are chasing around only because of the give-away. They do not believe things in their heart, it is that. And this is the way in which the ceremonies are performed in a sun-dance, the one who takes care of the pipe, he is first given something, tobacco and cloth, and after that he is given the give-away; it is life that he is given. He has earned that, he who takes care of the pipe, and after that the Servers, indeed, each of them in turn is given something, it is life that they are given; indeed, it is then that the old people, those sitting over there, used to receive the blessing, they used to receive the blessing, well, and then there she is, never to be overlooked, the Old Woman as she is called, that Old Woman dream-spirit. The sun-dance is powerful, for you to watch these women standing crowded over there [on their side

nâpêwa; îh! sôhkaniyiw aw îskwêw okâkîsimowin, êwak ôhci êkây patahohkâtihk, kîkway ka-miyâyêk! kiy-ês-âtamihâyêk anima nôtikwêsiw, êkos ânima k-êsi-naskomikonâwâw kîkway; êkos ôma ê-kî-itwêcik kêhtê-ayak. anohc êkwa, kâ-wî-pôyohk; kâ-wî-pakitinâsohk, êkot[a] êkwa takwâwahitowak ayisiyiniwak, têpiyâhk ê-nâtahkik pakitinâsowin. kâ-kîsi-pakitinâsohk, aspin wêhtaskatiskik; êkos ôma ê-isi-nâkwahk mêkwâc ôm êkwa mawimoscikêwin; êwak ôma kâ-nôhtê-kiskêyihtamêk.

[JK:] êkwa êkos îs ôma oskinîkiw, kayâs kî-kitimâkêyimêw omosôma – mihcêtwâw ê-âh-âyimômak awa, ê-pêyakwêyimisot;

[AE:] [*laughs*]

[JK:] kâ-kâhcitinât iskwêwa, iyâyaw wiya, wiya piko.

[TW:] ôta ôm âya, ka-kî-âcimoyahk ôtê ispî, k-êtohtêyâhk *Winnipeg*.

[JK:] [*laughs*]

[11] êkwa êwak ôma, k-âpihkâtaman ôma, kâ-nistwapihkâtaman wîhkaskwa, êwakw ânima okisêwâtisiwin k-âpihkâtamwat awa, êwak ôhci, k-ôh-kî-miyiht ayisiyiniw, kiwâpamâw iskwêw ê-sêkipatwât, ê-nistwapihkâtahk ôhi. mayaw ê-mâci-wâpiskâyik oscikwân iskwêw, âsay an[a] ê-miyikowisit êkota – âtayôhkan, wîhkask awa okisêwâtisiwin, êwakw ânim ôhci k-ôh-nistwapihkâtahk ôhi.

[12] êkos ôma nititâwak ôtê ô-~, ôk ôtê aya, kitôtêminawak êkây kîkway ê-kiskêyihtahkik *Saddle Lake*, tâniyikohk ê-kispaki-mîstowêcik, nama kîkway kâ-kî-miyikowisicik anima, êkwa iskwêwak ôki konit ê-titipawêhkasahkik ostikwâniwâw,

of the lodge] as you look over here where the men are few and far between; behold, the women's chanting is strong, therefore never overlook them, you should always give them something! With that you will make the Old-Woman-Spirit grateful so that she will answer your prayers with something; this is what the old people used to say. Today now, towards the end, when it is time for the give-away, then the people come there in droves, they only come for the give-away. When the give-away is over, they are gone and leave you behind, this is what worship looks like at present; this is what you want to know.

[JK:] Now in this way did a young man in the old days care for his grandfather – many times do I complain about this one [Angus Esperance], that he only thinks of himself;

[AE:] [*laughs*]

[JK:] when he finds himself a woman, of himself first, only of himself.

[TW:] We should tell the story here about our trip to Winnipeg at that time.

[JK:] [*laughs*]

[11] Now when you braid this, when you braid sweetgrass in three strands, you are braiding that grace of the Sweetgrass-Spirit with respect to her [the Old-Woman-Spirit], that is why people used to have it given to them, you see a woman with braids, she braids them in three strands. As soon as a woman's head begins to turn white, then she is already given a gift by the powers – the grace of a dream-spirit, of Sweetgrass, that is why she braids it in three strands.

[12] This is what I said to them over there, because these over there, our friends in Saddle Lake, do not know anything, they have such heavy beards, and that is not part of what they were given, and the women simply put perms in their hair, just like

tâpiskôt wacistwan, "namôy êwako kâ-kî-miyikowisiyêk," nititâwak; ahpô cî ôki nâpêwak, kîkwây anim ê-isi-pâhpakwatêyihtahkik, "ê-pasoyêk cî ôma kîkway, kimîstow-- [*laughs*]," – âta namôy mâmâsîs kîkway ê-wîhtamawakik [*laughter*]; "mâk êkây kakwê-ohpikihtâk kimîstowâniwâwa [*laughter*]."

[*some conversation at very low volume*]

[13] mistahi ka-miywâsin, êwak ôma kîstawâw, ka-kiskinowâpahtamêk ôma kâ-wî-isîhcikêyâhk, oskinîkiskwêwak, kwayask; ê-kî-mâci-manitowihiht awa kâ-nêwo-tipiskâk[i] ôskinîkiskwêw, êwak ôhci, kiskêyihtam kikâwiy tânis ê-ispayik êwak ôma: wiyâkanis kî-astamawâw ita ê-kanawêyimiht oskinîkiskwêw, êkota ê-sîhkot, namôy mohcihk. kâ-nêwo-tipiskâki, êkot[a] êkwa kâ-miyâhkasamihk anima. nanâtohk ê-is-âyâyit ayisiyiniwa, ahpô êkâ ê-wâpiyit, ê-oskaninêyit, kâ-kiyakasêt ôm âwâsis, êkota êkwa ê-kî-miyiht cistêmâwa, wêpinâson; "hâw, nanâtawih awa!" ê-kî-itiht oskinîkiskwêw; êwakw ânim ôhci kâ-kî-nanâtawihât. â, mihcêtwâw êkota ohci ê-kî-pimâcihât.

[14] êwak ôm ê-âcimostawakik ôk ônîkâniwak, mêtoni miywêyihtamwak, êwak ôma k-ôh-wî-isîhcikêcik, "êwakw ânim êkwa ka-kakwê-pimipayik," ê-itwêcik; êkosi pikw âyis t-êsi-- kîkway ê-pimipayik. mêkwâc kîkway kêhtê-aya kisêyiniw, nôtikwêw kîkway ê-kiskêyihtahk, êkos îsi ka-wîhtamawât ka-kâsispohtêmakahk êwako. êkâ êkosi tôtamihko, mêstohtêtwâwi kêhtê-ayak, pêyakwan iskotêw ê-âstawêk, êkos ôma k-êsi-kitimâkan kinêhiyâwiwininaw. ka-wanihtânaw kîkway kôhtâwînaw kâ-kî-miyikoyahk k-ôh-pimâtisiyahk. êwak ôhci mâna mistahi ninanâskomâw ayisiyiniw kâ-nôhtê-kiskêyihtahk.

a nest, "This is not what you were given," I said to them; or else the men, what amusement do they get out of it, 'Do you smell something, your beards [*laughs*]?" – I did not spare them with words to tell them [*laughter*]; "but try not to grow your beards [*laughter*]!"

[*some conversation at very low volume*]

[13] It will be very good, for you, too, the young women, to watch what we are going to do and learn from it, properly; the young woman used to have powers first given to her after four nights, that is why, your mother knows how that works: one used to put a cup for the young girl where she was kept, and she spat into that, not on the ground. After four nights, that is when they smudged it [the saliva]. No matter what illness a person has, even if he is blind, or arthritic, or when a child has eczema, now then she [the young girl] was given tobacco and cloth; "Indeed, doctor this one," the young girl was told; and it was with that saliva that she was able to doctor them. Well, many times she used to restore someone to life with that.

[14] When I told this story to the leaders, they were very glad, that is why they are going to hold this recording session, "This is what should happen now," they said, for that is the only way things will happen. While the elders, the old men and the old women, still know something, they should tell them [the young] about it so that it might be handed down. If this is not done, then our Cree culture will be miserable once the old people are all gone, like a fire that has gone out. We will lose the things which Our Father had given us that we might live upon them. I am very grateful, therefore, when a person wants to know.

[15] îh, tâpiskôc awa *John*; ê-nôhtê-kiskêyihtahk itâskonikêwin, "ê-nôhtê-tâpowêyân [*sic*] ôhi nikamona. tânisi k-êtôtamân, mêstohtêyêko pê-miyikawiyâni wêpinâson, pê-kîhkâtahamawak[i] êkwa âtayôhkan, itikawiyâni, konita nika-kwêtatêyitiskwêyin; mâka wîhtamawiyani, âsay êkota nika-kiskisopayin," k-êtwêt. êkos ânima ê-isi-tâpwêt êwako.

[*some conversation at very low volume*]

[16] êkwa mîn ôskinîkiskwêwak ka-wîhtamawâyêkok ôki, êk ôtê ê-kî-~ (matwân cî awa nikî-pêhtâk *Angus*), *Saddle Lake* ôtê nikî-pê-kakwêcimik pêyak oskinîkiskwêw, maskihkiy ê-pê-nitawêyihtahk: "nêw-âskiy ê-wîcêwak awa ninâpêm," itwêw, "êkâ kîkway ê-kî-ocawâsimisiyâhk, ê-nitawêyihtamân maskihkiy ka-miyiyan," nititik. wahwâ, niwawânêyihtamihik, "cêskwa, nôsisê!" nititâw, "tâniyikohk mâk ôma, kiwiyakihtamawin k-êsiyan?" nititâw, "tâniyikohk kiwêpêyimâw sôniyâw." – "â, kiya, nimosô! pikw îyikohk nitawêyimaci, ka-miyitin." – "hâw!" nititâw, "kapêsîwikamik nitawi-tipaha, iyikohk ê-wêpêyimat sôniyâw!" konita ê-nânâmiskwêyit, "kî-tipahamani, pê-nâsîhkan! ka-wîc-âyâmitin pêyak-tipiskâw, awâsis ka-pê-~." – "namôy êwako kâ-kakwêcimitân, nimosô [*laughs*]!" – "êwako piko nikiskêyihtên maskihkiy," nititâw.

[15] Look, for example John [Cuthand], he wants to know the pointing of the pipestem, "I want to learn to sing these songs correctly, what will I do when you are all gone if someone comes and gives me cloth and then tells me if I would sing clearly to the spirit, and I will simply be at a loss as to where to turn; but if you tell me, I will always then remember right away," is what he said. And he speaks the truth in this.

[*some conversation at very low volume*]

[16] And you also should tell these young girls, and over there (I wonder if Angus [Esperance] here heard me), over there in Saddle Lake one young woman came up to me and asked me, wanting medicine: "I have been married to my husband for four years," she said, "I want you to give me medicine, because we have not been able to have any children," she said to me. Oh my, she put me in a quandary by what she said, "Wait, my grandchild!" I said to her, "but how much – are you willing to pay me for what you have asked me," I said to her, "how much money do you want to throw away?" – "Well, it's up to you, grandfather! No matter how much money you want, I will give it to you." – "Indeed!" I said to her, "go and pay for a hotel room, for as much money as you want to throw away!" She just nodded, "When you have paid for it, come and get me! For one night I will stay with you, with a child to come –" – "That is not what I asked of you, grandfather [*laughs*]!" – "This is the only medicine I know," I said to her.

8

[1] ê-wî-âcimak ôta nimosôm mahihkanis, ê-wî-âcimostawakik ôki, êkâ kîkway ê-ohci-kiskêyihtahk, êkwa miton âyi, mâk ê-kî-kitimâkêyimât wîci-kîhkâwa.

[2] hâw, kêtahtawê kâ-mâyimahcihoyit ôhi wîci-kîhkâwa. êwakw âw êkwa nôhcâwîs 'ispâhtêhikan' kâ-kî-itiht ê-okimâhkâniwit, masinahikêhêw ôhi wîscâsa; ê-maskosîhkêcik, ê-wâh-wîscîhkêsit awa nimosôm. kêtahtawê kâ-mâyimahcihot awa nôhkominân. â, êkwa ê-wâpahk, hâw, kaskawanipêstâw ê-kimiwahk, nîso-kîsikâw âsay êkos ê-is-âyâyik. "hâ, tânis âta wiya, nîtimos?" (kî-wa-wîtimosiw anihi nôhcâwîs nôhkominâna), "tânis âta wiya, nîtimos?" – "â, kisâkamitêhkwêw ana kîkisêp, tipiskohk ê-kî-pîhtâpâwahak [*laughter*],"

[LA:] cah! êkwa!

itwêw ês âwa nimosôminân. "yôhô, kîkwây mâka ê-âpacihtâyan, nîscâs? wîhkwâs cî ê-ayâyan?" – "ma kîkway!" – "kîkwây mâk ê-âpacihtâyan?" – "sôskwât ê-pâh-pîhci-sîkatêhtamawak, ê-pîhtâpâwahak [*laughter*]."

[*aside to LA:*] awas, êkây kiya pâhpi! ê-âcimostâtân ôma [*laughter*].

"â, êkwa, kisâkamitêhkwêw, miyomahcihow," itwêw. "pakahkam kaskawanipêstâw," itwêw, "kisîpêkinikêw awa nimosômim-~, nimosôminân êsa mahkêsîs, ês ôm ôpîhcawêsâkânisiyiw ê-îpâcihtâyit [*sic*]. mâk êkota ôm âsowahpitêw pîminâhkwânis," itwêw, "kâ-sînahk ôm," îtwêw. "â, êkota," itwêw, "â, namôy êtokw âwa konita nîscâs, kâ-wayawît êkwa ê-nâtât otôspwâkana, wêpinâson," itwêw. " 'â, nîscâs, awa cistêmâw, ôma wêpinâson – itâskonikê mahti, kiwî-nôhtêhkatânânaw, ka-kakwê-âstê-kîsikâk!

[1] I am going to tell a story here [on the audio-recorder] about my grandfather *mahihkanis*, and I am going to tell it to these, for my grandfather did not know anything but he cared greatly for his old companion, his wife.

[2] Indeed, one time his old companion felt sick. Now this one, my father's brother, *ispâhtêhikan* he used to be called and he was chief, he had hired his cousin [*i.e.*, my grandfather]; they were haying, and my grandfather was making little hay coils. All of a sudden our grandmother felt sick. Well, then in the morning, indeed, now it was drizzling, it was raining, it had been like this for two days already. "Well, how are you doing, my cousin?" [my uncle asked my grandmother] (our grandmother was my uncle's cross-cousin), "Well, how are you doing, my cousin?" – "Well, she has had a hot drink this morning, and last night I had given her an enema [*laughter*],"

> [LA:] Ho! Now what!

said our grandfather. "Oh, but what did you use, my cousin? Did you have a bird's craw?" – "I had nothing!" – "But what did you use?" – "I simply kept spitting it into her, giving her an enema [*laughter*]."

> [*aside to LA:*] Go on, you, don't you laugh! I am telling you a story [*laughter*].

"Well, now, she has had a hot drink and she feels better," he said. "I think it was drizzling," he said [*i.e.*, the original narrator, evidently *ispâhtêhikan*], "and our grandfather *mahihkanis* did the laundry as she had soiled her undershirt. But there was a line strung across," he said, "when he had wrung it out," he said. "Well, there," he said, "Well, my cousin had not gone out for nothing, it seems, now he went to get his pipe and a cloth offering," he said. " 'Well, my cousin, here is some tobacco, here

âstê-kîsikâki ê-wî-minahoyân, êkâ ka-nôhtêhkatêyahk,' nititâw nîscâs," itwêw. "tâpwê mâka, nîscâs, tâpwê." – "â, êwakw âni nimiyâhkasamawâw," itwêw, "ê-kî-wiyaskinahimak, nimiyâw," itwêw.

[3] "wâsakâyâskonêw," itwêw, " 'hâw, êwakw âna pîhtwâk! kitimâkinawinân! kitimâkinawinân, nîsosâp k-êtahtiniyiki ospikêkana!' " [*laughter*] – kîkwâya êkwa? – ês ôm îyinito-mîkiwâhp ê-apistahk [*sic*] awa, nîsosâp âpasoya ê-pa-~, êwakw ês ôma k-êtâskonamawâtahk [*laughter*].

[4] " 'hâ, kîsta mîn êkota ohci, pîhtwâ, kâ-mâh-mahkihtawakêyan!' – êkwa ôhi k-~ âpahkwâna [*sic*], êkon êkwa k-êtâskonamawât; wâ, kâ-kwêskâskonât," itwêw.

[5] " 'â, êkwa kiy îta k-ôtiskiyan [*sic*]' – êwakw ânima kitiskotêmiwâw êk ôm," îtwêw, " 'hâw, ôm îta k-ôciskiyan [*sic*], êwakw âna pîhtwâ!'. wâsakâyâskonêw, 'â, niwîkimâkan opîhcawêsâkânis, êwakw ânima mîna [*laughter*],' " – êy, êwako ê-kî-pakwanawahtât itâskonikêwin [*laughs*].

[6] takahk-âtayôhkêwin [*laughter*].

[LA:] mitoni ma-môhcw-âtayôhkêwin wiy êwako.

is a cloth offering – please point the pipestem, we are going to go hungry, so that the rain might stop. Once it stops raining, I am going to kill an animal, lest we go hungry,' I said to my cousin," he said. " 'Agreed then, my cousin, agreed.' – Well, I smudged the pipe for him," he said, "I had filled the pipe and I gave it to him," he said.

[3] "He turned the pipestem around in a circle," he said, " 'Indeed, you all smoke this pipe! You all have pity upon us! You all have pity upon us, you ribs who are twelve in number!' " [*laughter*] – Now what were they? – living in an ordinary tipi, this old man was pointing the pipestem towards the twelve poles [*laughter*]!

[4] " 'Indeed, next also for you, too, you smoke it, you with the big ears!' – now the tent-flap, he was pointing the pipestem towards this one [the one with the big ears]; well, he randomly turned the pipe," he said.

[5] " 'Well, now you, where you have your rectum,' – and that is where you all have your hearth-fire," he said, " 'Indeed, there where you have your rectum, you smoke this pipe!' – He turned the pipestem around in a circle, 'Well, my wife's undershirt, that one, too [*laughter*],' " – hey, that one didn't have a clue about pointing the pipestem [*laughs*].

[6] A fine sacred story [*laughter*].

[LA:] That one really is a crazy sacred story.

Commentary and Notes

H.C. Wolfart

Commentary

Spoken texts, especially when devoted to transcendental topics and delivered in an elevated register, presuppose fluency in the language and culture of which they are a salient part; in playing on the literary and aesthetic properties of formal prose and in the light they throw on the more arcane realms of historical and ritual knowledge, they permit and demand a heightened sense of language and text.

This essay, selective and tentative at once, is an attempt to explicate at least some of the features of the texts presented in this volume; the notes range from the identity of individual sounds and the shape of particular words or fragments of words to the cultural and historiographical background.

Parts and Chapters

The editorial arrangement of the texts, which mostly belong to the genre of *kakêskihkêmowina* or 'counselling discourses', reflects their form and content rather than the order in which they were performed. While they are all suffused with the issues and the language of theology, the first four display their homiletic character most plainly. These four, for instance, begin with an *apologia* declaring that the speaker speaks neither at his own initiative nor on his own authority but at the urging of those who called on him and as instructed by others older and wiser than him.

In proclaiming the importance of preaching to the young and persevering in one's lectures, 'Counselling the Young' (1) includes references to several founding members of the Saskatchewan Indian Languages Institute and specifically mentions both Freda Ahenakew and the College; in closing, the speaker identifies himself by name and place, thereby emphasising the exordial quality of this speech. The lamentations of 'Spiritual Help' (2) begin and end with reference to specific events – the tornadoes of the summer of 1989 and the perennial travels of Freda Ahenakew – but otherwise expound in general terms the paradox of active submission faced by those seeking the consolations of theology. 'Leaving a Legacy' (3) elaborates on the authority invoked by the speaker, relating the visionary experience of his father's return from the dead, and offers guidance in the proper approach to Cree ritual. While focussing on the ravages of industrial culture, 'Leading our Children Astray' (4) also treats the collection of medicinal plants, the proper behaviour of men towards women and the ritual form of counselling young men. Like that in chapter 3, the text in chapter 4 is preparatory to a pipe ceremony; in the latter case, the text both begins and ends with an explicit reference to the Saskatchewan Indian Languages Institute whose work it was delivered to inaugurate.

The second half of this collection is primarily narrative and documentary. While personal encounters and exploits predominate in earlier publications, these texts represent the cumulative memory of communal experience and the collective knowledge of the proper conduct of ritual. Both the historical accounts and the presentation of various rituals are interspersed with contemplative and exhortative passages, and chapter 6, the outstanding piece in this collection, once more includes the double *apologia* of having been commissioned and of being spoken on ulterior authority.

In 'The Testimony of the Pipestem' (5) the surpassing significance of the pipestem as warrant of the faithfully executed treaty is reviewed in a general fashion. 'The Pipestem and the Making of Treaty Six' (6) records a *verbatim* recitation of certain key parts of both the process and the product. Throughout this text, the issue of authenticity is paramount. 'The Meaning of Rituals' (7) presents a series of objects and ceremonies, beginning with a declaration of the primacy of tobacco and culminating in increasingly detailed accounts of proper behaviour. Chapter 7 ends with a contrary example, foreshadowed by two jocular interludes (the first in dialogue, aside); this paedagogical form is taken to a pointed conclusion in chapter 8, 'Profaning the Sacred.' In a didactic reversal of classical proportions, the speaker tells the tale of a would-be ritualist and his inadvertent improprieties, all in the literary form of a factual narrative.

Linguistic Form

Among the linguistic properties of these discourses and the rhetorical patterns found in them, lexical sets of several types are the most common.

The subject matter of a text is only in the rarest cases covered by a single term. Instead, we tend to find a rich choice of verbs and nouns denoting and evoking various aspects of the issue under discussion.

Word Families

Choosing the right word in Cree often is a matter of varying only one of the constituents of the stem while keeping the other (or others) stable.

In these texts, for example, the speaker uses four primary stems built on the final morpheme *-ôt-:*

mâmiskôt– VTI 'discuss s.t., expound s.t.'
tâhkôt– VTI 'discuss s.t., discourse upon s.t.'
tipôt– VTI 'discuss s.t. with authority'
âyimôt– VTI 'discuss s.t., speak of s.t.; gossip about s.t.'

In addition to these four basic stems, he uses the matching VTA stem, built on *-ôm-*, for two of them:

tâhkôm– VTA 'discuss s.o., discourse upon s.o.'
âyimôm– VTA 'discuss s.o., speak of s.o.; gossip about s.o.'

He also exploits the further derivatives; in the case of *mâmiskôt–*, the derived stem *mâmiskôcikâtê–* VII 'be discussed, be expounded'

is passive in meaning, with the agent suppressed. In the case of *âyimôm–*, the text exemplifies both the reflexive stem,

âyimômiso– VAI 'discuss oneself; speak unguardedly about oneself, gossip about oneself',

and the reciprocal stem,

âyimôhto– VAI 'discuss one another; gossip about one another'.

The abstract noun

âyimôhtowin– NI 'discussing one another; gossiping about one another, gossip',

finally, is further derived from the reciprocal verb stem.

Semantic Domains

While the stems cited in the preceding section constitute a single set, with each member sharing at least some of the morphological material, lexical sets may also be semantically defined; in this case, the stems which constitute the set are built upon morphological material without demonstrable etymological relationships.

In the homiletic texts of the present volume, for example, the semantic domain of reliance and refuge is prominent. The classical term of reliance,

mamisî– VAI 'rely on (it/him)',

is here complemented by the much more elaborate and formal term

> *aspitonâmo–* VAI 'flee to rely on spoken words, rely on (it) as a formal confirmation of the spoken word'.

While *mamisî–* is, for all practically purposes, etymologically opaque, the structure of *aspitonâmo–* is overtly bipartite, with *-âmo-* 'flee, seek refuge' as the final, stem-forming constituent. The initial constituent in turn consists of the root *asp-* 'rely on, find support upon' and the medial *-(i)ton-* 'mouth, speech'.

The texts also provide instances of the final *-âmo-* construed with the roots *pêt-* 'hither' and *it-* 'thither, thus' as the initial constituents:

> *pêtâmo–* VAI 'flee hither'
> *itâmo–* VAI 'flee thus or there, seek such refuge'

Many of these stems also appear in further derivations. Besides the basic stem *mamisî–*, for example, which belongs to the VAI class, there is also a parallel VTI stem,

> *mamisîtot–* VTI 'rely on s.t.',

which more explicitly specifies the object upon which reliance is placed. In addition, we find the applicative VTA stem

> *mamisîwât–* VTA 'rely on s.o. for (it/him)'.

The simple intransitive stem *itâmo–* similarly gives rise to the causative stem

> *itâmôh–* VTA 'make s.o. flee thus or there, direct s.o. to seek such refuge'.

Conversely, the texts contain several instances of derived stems based on an unattested base stem *nâtâmo–* VAI; there are, in fact, two transitive stems with identical glosses,

nâtâmost– VTI 'flee to s.t., turn to s.t. for help, seek refuge in s.t.'
nâtâmotot– VTI 'flee to s.t., turn to s.t. for help, seek refuge in s.t.'

as well as the parallel VTA stem

nâtâmototaw– VTA 'flee to s.o., turn to s.o. for help, seek refuge with s.o.'

The semantic range of these stems is not limited to the primary domain of placing reliance and seeking refuge, as in this example:

[...], *cikêmô kêhtê-aya piko k-âspitonâmoyahk;* (1-8)
'[...], for of course we must put our faith in the words of the old people;'.

In addition, the stem also has a narrower meaning, which is prominent in chapter 6; e.g.,

[...], *êwako piko ka-kî-aspitonâmoyahk.* (6-5)
'[...], that is all upon which we can rely as testimony.'

In both uses, the stem *aspitonâmo–* with its medial *-(i)ton-* 'mouth, speech' (note the short *-o-*) overlaps with another fairly rare stem based on the corresponding initial constituent *otôn-* 'mouth' (note the long *-ô-*):

otônihkâ– VAI 'use (it/him) as one's mouthpiece, make (it/him) one's advocate'.

While this stem belongs to the VAI class, it may be construed either with an animate or an inanimate patient noun:

êwakw ân[a] ê-otônihkâyahk, ê-itwêstamâkoyahk. (7-4)
'we make him our advocate and he speaks for us.'

[...], *kik-ôtônihkâcik* [...], *kîkwây anima kitasotamâkowininaw;* (6-2)
'[...], that they should have it as their witness [...], of what these promises are which have been made to us;'

Finally, the same semantic field also includes another term used in a highly specialised fashion. The inverse forms of

nâtamaw– VTA 'fetch (it/him) for s.o.; take up for s.o.'

are used in the sense of 'be rescued by s.o./s.t.', e.g.,

[...], *môy nânitaw ka-kî-nâtamâkon, wiy îtêyihtahki, ka-nâtamâkonaw;* (2-2)
'[...], it cannot rescue you, if it is his will, he will rescue us;'

in the above example, the first instance has an inanimate agent, while that of the second is animate.

Pragmatic Sets

In view of the theological and homiletic nature of these sermons, it is not surprising that a number of verbs are used with inanimate nouns such as *oskiciy–* NI 'pipestem' as their subject; e.g.,

ka-pimohtêmakan (6-6)
'[what I have promised to you] shall last'

ka-kakwê-pimohtêmakahk (4-1)
'so that [your work] might proceed'

ê-nîkânohtêmakahki (7-1)
'as these [tobacco] occupy the foremost place'
ê-pê-kîwêmakahk (4-4)
'as [something] is coming back'

ka-kâsispohtêmakahk (7-14)
'so that [this knowledge] will be handed down'
ê-tâpwêmakahk (1-6, 2-2)
'that it is fulfilled'

This grammatical and stylistic pattern is especially striking with verbs of saying, which usually occur with an animate (indeed, human) agent:

tânis ôm ê-itwêmakahk wîhkask (7-2)
'what is the meaning of sweetgrass'
êkos ôma ê-itwêmakahk êwako. (7-3)
'This is the meaning of that.'

kik-âcimômakan (5-2)
'[this pipestem] will tell the story'
tânis ê-itâcimômakahk êwak ôma (6-4)
'how this story is told'

In this special usage, as illustrated by *itwê–* VAI 'say thus, call (it) thus; have such a meaning' and its counterpart *itwêmakan–* VII 'say thus, have such a meaning', a subtle shift of meaning seems symptomatic of those *verba dicendi* used with an inanimate agent (which are also given separate entries in the glossary).

Agent- and Patient-centred Nouns

The texts in this volume also illustrate the perspectival opposition of abstract nouns indicating either the agent or the patient as the more salient.

These nouns, which may be derived from verb stems of various types, mostly occur as possessed forms, e.g.,

> *nipimohtêwin* (3-4) 'my travelling'
> cf. *pimohtê–* VAI 'go along, walk along; travel along'

> *kinitotamâwin* (3-14, 7-3) 'request made by you'
> cf. *nitotamâ–* VAI 'ask for (it), pray for (it), make a request for (it)'

> *kipêhtamowininâhk* (6-4) 'in what we have heard'
> cf. *pêht–* VTI 'hear s.t.'

The above examples are all agent-centred; the following, by contrast, is patient-centred and derived, not from the stem *pamih–* VTA 'tend to s.o., look after s.o.', but from the abstract underlying theme *pamihiko-*:

> *kipamihikowin* (6-14)
> 'the fact that you are looked after'.

In the most striking illustration of this perspectival opposition, two derived abstract nouns differ only by a single vowel:

> *asotamâkêwin–* NI 'promise'
> *asotamâkowin–* NI 'promise, promise made'

While the English gloss 'promise' is ambiguous, the first of these abstract nouns is derived from the stem *asotamâkê–* VAI 'make a promise' (which in turn is derived from the stem *asotamaw–* VTA 'promise (it) to s.o.'), and the second from the theme *asotamâko-*, corresponding to the same VTA stem but not normally attested as a stem.

Thus, the narrator exploits the minimal contrast between the agent-centred

> *otasotamâkêwin* (5-2)
> 'his promise: what he has promised'

and the patient-centred

> *kitasotamâkowininaw* (5-2)
> 'our promise: what has been promised to us'

to striking effect:

> *"kitasotamâkowininaw êkây wîhkâc ka-pîkonahk ê-nîsokâtêt ayisiyiniw," kî-itwêw êsa; kikî-asotamâkonaw êkây wîhkâc ka-pîkonahk awiyak, otasotamâkêwin anima.* (5-2)
> ' "So that no human walking on two legs would ever break the promises made to us," he [the Queen's representative] had said, it is reported; he had promised us that no one would ever break that which he had promised.'

Literary Form

The formal speeches which make up much of the present volume are instances of the *kakêskihkêmowin* 'counselling discourse'. While this genre is not explicitly flagged, within the text, by a technical term (as is typical, above all, for the *âcimowin* 'factual account' and *âtayôhkêwin* 'sacred story'; cf. Wolfart 1982:78-80), such texts tend to be characterised, at the beginning, the end or both, by declarations approving of the ritualist endeavours of a particular apprentice – or, as the case may be, deploring the lack of interest shown by the succeeding generation.

The formal quality of these texts also finds expression in a dense texture of rhetorical devices going beyond lexical patterns and etymological figures.

Generic Singular

The stylistic effect of using the unmarked member of a grammatical opposition is well known, for example from the "historical present" of Latin and many other languages. Similarly, many languages use a "generic singular" with reference to a large number of individuals.

The most common occurrence of the generic singular is with nouns, and the text contains literally dozens of instances (beginning at the start of section 1-2) of nouns like *kitawâsimis* 'your children' [literally 'your child' – this being the closest English usage might come in approaching this prominent feature of Cree] or *kôsisiminaw* 'our grandchildren' [literally 'our grandchild'] which in the original appear in the singular.

The literary use of the generic singular is found even with quantifier particles like *mihcêt* 'many', e.g.,

> *mihcêt namôy kiskêyihtam* [...] (3-13)
> 'Many people do not know this [...]'

Explicit quantifiers such as *mihcêt* offer no scope for referential ambiguity.

In Cree, the effect of the generic singular seems especially dramatic when it is used with stems which are inherently reciprocal and marked as such by their derivational form:

> *êwak ôma ka-kakwê-êkotê-itohtahâyahk* [sic] *kitawâsimisinaw kôsisiminaw, êkot*[*a*] *ânima kê-ôh-kitimâkêyihtot.* (4-9)
> 'That is where we should try to lead our children and grandchildren, so that they might learn from that to think of one another with compassion.'

ka-kiskinowâsohtahk awa kitawâsimis, tânis ô-~ kik-êsi-kitimâkêyihtot ayisiyiniw; (3-15)
'So that your children may hear and learn how people should love one another;'.

In both these examples, the verb stem *kitimâkêyihto–* VAI 'feel pity towards one another, love one another, think of one another with compassion' occurs in a context where the nouns denoting children or grandchildren are also used in the generic singular. In the second example above, the same is true of the noun construed with this verb within the same clause, *ayisiyiniw* 'person, human being' (what a few years ago might have been rendered as the generic *man* of *Man is mortal*).

This pattern recurs throughout the book, e.g.,

namôy nânitaw ê-itâpatahk ôta ayisiyiniw k-âyimôhtot, wâwîs ê-ot-~ ê-owîcisânihtot. (2-6)
'It is pointless for people here to gossip about one another, especially as they are siblings.'

A more elevated translation, in a slightly archaic form of English, might attempt to replicate the generic singular: 'It is idle for Man here on earth to gossip' – and succeed with the generic singular of nouns in English; but the attempt will break down when we reach the verb (which is why the translation of these sentences into English has to be fairly free), for reciprocal verbs in English simply cannot be put in the singular.

In such cases, the English translation, unfortunately, is only a weak echo of the highly elevated tone of the Cree original.

In the following example, finally, the stylistic effect of the generic singular as expressed in both noun and verb is heightened further by two additional features:

[...], *cikêmô mihcêtiw môniyâw otawâsimisa ôta,* [...] (4-2)
'[...], of course the Whites and their children are numerous here, [...]'

First, the comitative construction which allows the proximate noun *môniyâw* 'whiteman' and the possessed noun *otawâsimisa* 'his children' be construed as a single nominal phrase (as the subject of the singular verb form *mihcêtiw*). Second, the choice of the stem *mihcêti–* VAI 'be numerous, be plentiful' for the singular verb form *mihcêtiw* 'he/she is numerous'.

Negative Irrealis

Even in formal texts marked by high rhetoric, few constructions stand out as sharply as the negative irrealis conditional.

The more common type employs a verbless prodosis, e.g.,

kîspin êkâ ohc îskwêw, [...] (1-7)
'If it were not for women, [...]'

kîspin êkâ êkotowahk ohci, [...] (4-9)
'If it were not for that kind, [...]'

The verb, if it occurs, is in the simple conjunct, e.g.,

[...], *kîspin êkâ iskwêw êko-~ ôta kî-pakitinikowisit,* [...] (4-9)
'[...], if women had not been put here on earth, [...]'

The apodosis exhibits the preverb *kâh* with strong devoicing to indicate the hypothetical (cf. Wolfart 1989*a*):

[...], *môy kikâh-pimâtisinânaw k-âyisiyinîwiyahk;* (1-7)
'[...], we who are humans would not be alive;'

Note that the same preverb also occurs in positive declarative sentences, e.g.,

> *êkosi nikâh-miywêyihtên,* [...] (1-8)
> 'Thus I would be glad [...]'

and in positive rhetorical questions, e.g.,

> *awîn ânihi kâh-kî-wîhêw,* [...] (3-10)
> 'who could name that one, [...]',

but especially those with an irrealis element, e.g.,

> *awîna kâh-nihtâwikihtâw kitayisiyinîwininaw,* [...] (4-9)
> 'who would give birth to our existence as humans, [...]'

In negative irrealis conditionals, the volitional force of the negator *êkâ* (cf. Wolfart 1996:396, 405), in contrast with the declarative character of *namôya* (represented by *môy*, *namôy* in these examples), is sharply highlighted:

> *kîspin êkâ ohc îskwêw, môy kikâh-pimâtisinânaw k-âyisiyinîwiyahk;* (1-7)
> 'If it were not for women, we who are humans would not be alive;'

> *kîspin êkâ êkotowahk ohci, kîspin êkâ iskwêw êko-~ ôta kî-pakitinikowisit, namôy ôta kikâh-apinânaw;* (4-9)
> 'If it were not for that kind, if women had not been put here on earth, we would not be sitting here;'

The order of the clauses is not fixed, and the apodosis may precede the prodosis:

namôya kâh-ayisiyinîwiw kîspin êkâ ohc îskwêwa, [...]' (4-9)
'He would not exist as a human being if it were not for a woman, [...]'

Finally, these texts also illustrate another type of irrealis (cf. Wolfart 1973:sec. 5.32), which exhibits no devoicing in the preverb but instead relies on the combination of the preverb complex *ka-kî* with the preterite ending *-pan* (with a lengthening effect on the preceding vowel, overt or covert) to mark a perfective irrealis conditional:

mistahi ka-kî-miywâsinôpan, ka-kî-masinipayihtâhk anim ôta oskiciy, [...] (6-11)
'It would have been very good to have photographed this pipestem here, [...]'

[...], *êwak ôma kî-atoskâtamihk, mistahi ka-kî-miywâsinôpan,* [...] (6-4)
'[...], it would have been been very good if one had worked on this earlier, [...]'

While such constructions are reasonably common in other Cree dialects (and occur occasionally in texts recorded in 1925), they are rare in modern Plains Cree and occur only in the most elevated registers.

Repetition

Cree literary style exploits repetition and subtle variation in contexts ranging from the seemingly simple to the saliently elevated.

Even relatively ordinary phrases that happen to recur on more than one occasion often show such variation; for example, when the speaker repeats himself in discussing the same topic on different days.

In the case of chapters 2 and 3, recorded almost a year apart (on 1 August 1989 and 8 September 1988), the speaker uses almost identical phrases to refer to the large number of grandchildren and great-grandchildren with which he has been blessed:

> *anohc kâ-kîsikâk mâna ninanâskomon, ê-mihcêticik nôsisimak, pêyakosâp ihtasiwak nôsisimak, mihcêtiwak nitâniskotâpânak;* (2-5)
> 'today I always give thanks that I have many grandchildren, my grandchildren number eleven, and my great-grandchildren are many;'

> *ê-nanâskomak, ê-wîcihak ayisiyiniw, ê-mihcêticik nôsisimak; pêyakosâp ê-ihtasicik nôsisimak, nitâniskotâpânak ê-mihcêticik.* (3-5)
> 'I give thanks to him that I am able to help people and that I have many grandchildren; my grandchildren number eleven, and my great-grandchildren are many.'

In both instances he gives thanks, using the root in an intransitive stem in the first example and in a transitive in the second, and in both he continues (after the passage quoted) with the stem *kîspinat–* VTI 'earn s.t. as one's reward'; in short, these are clearly theological declarations as much as the joyful pronouncements of a proud grandfather and great-grandfather.

From a grammatical perspective, however, it is remarkable that the speaker varies the choice of inflectional category in the verbs specifying what it is for which he gives thanks. In both examples, the first clause is in the conjunct order; in fact, the two clauses are identical:

> *ê-mihcêticik nôsisimak.*

But the second and third clauses differ. In those of chapter 2 (1989), the verbs are inflected for the independent order:

pêyakosâp ihtasiwak nôsisimak,
mihcêtiwak nitâniskotâpânak;

In chapter 3 (1988), they are inflected for the conjunct order:

pêyakosâp ê-ihtasicik nôsisimak,
nitâniskotâpânak ê-mihcêticik.

The word order in the third clause is reversed, but the translations are referentially indistinguishable. (In terms of syntactic and stylistic analysis, morever, these two examples suggest that the choice of inflectional order – independent or conjunct – in such sentences is either immaterial or too subtle to have been caught in the analytical net.)

There is, in fact, a third parallel, recorded on a third date (26 April 1989), which uses a slightly different construction:

ê-mâkwêyimoyân, ê-mihcêticik nôsisimak nicâpânak,
tânitê kik-êtâmôhakik? (5-4)
'I am worried, since my grandchildren and great-grandchildren are many, where will I direct them to turn for help?'

But the context is different as well, and the key phrase is isolated and not embedded in thanksgiving and the theological conclusion of just rewards.

A more complex instance of parallel text passages also shows the speaker using both verbal orders, independent and conjunct, on different occasions – but in the case of the indefinite agent forms, the two are strikingly different.

In the first case, the superordinate clause, *êwakw ânima* 'it is the case, it means', is non-verbal and follows the subordinate clause, which appears in the conjunct:

> *êwakw âwa, konit ê-mêtawâkêhk awa sîsîkwan, êwakw ânima;* (3-13)
> 'as for this one, it means that people are playing around with the rattle without purpose;'

In the second instance, the key verb is in the independent, with a highly marked, secondarily derived suffix *-niwiw* following the *-â-* variant of the VAI *ê*-stem *mêtawâkê–:*

> *mâcikôtitan ômis ôma wî-ispayiw wî-mêtawâkâniwiw êwak ôma, ê-mosci-kiskinowâpicik, kiskinowâpiwin k-âpatan;* (7-4)
> 'Lo, this is going to happen and people are going to play around with this, learning merely by imitation [rather than by instruction], learning by imitation will be used;'

It is remarkable that the speaker continues with a plural verb.

There is also a third instance, where neither variant of the indefinite agent form is used; instead, the speaker uses the generic singular of the noun *ayisiyiniw–* NA 'person, human being',

> *êwak ôma kâ-itamân, ê-mêtawâkêt anohc ayisiyiniw.* (7-10)
> 'This is what I meant, people play around with it today.'

in a construction reminiscent of the English use of *people* to correspond to the non-specific *on* of French.

WHILE INADVERTENT repetitions cannot be replicably distinguished from their more deliberate exploitation as artistic devices, parallel constructions offer the most obvious instances of the latter.

Conventionally paired terms such as *kitawâsimisinaw kôsisiminaw* 'our children, our grandchildren' (1-2) or *otawâsimisimâw oyôsisimimâw* 'the children, the grandchildren' (1-2) provide one type of limiting case, with the simple repetition of a phrase, e.g., *pêyâhtik kitos! pêyâhtik kitos!* 'speak to them quietly! speak to them quietly!' (2-5) constituting another basic pattern.

Slight variations tend to heighten the repetitive effect, as in

> [...], *tânis âw ê-itakisot awa cistêmâw,*
> *îh! tânis ôma ê-itakihtêk ôma wêpinâson.* (7-1)
> '[...], what is the rôle of the tobacco,
> behold! what is the rôle of the cloth.'

and, at the beginning of the subsequent paragraph,

> [...], *tânis ôm ê-itwêmakahk wîhkask,*
> *tânêhk ânima k-ôh-âpatahk wîhkask;* (7-2)
> '[...], what is the meaning of the sweetgrass,
> why is that sweetgrass used;'

(For a brief grammatical review of these examples see the note to 7-1.)

Much more complex permutations of grammatical elements are employed in the formulaic incantation found repeatedly in chapters 1 to 4 (and again in chapters 5 and 7); e.g.,

> [...], *kika-nanâskomiht kôhtâwînaw,* [...],
> *ê-miyikoyahk pêyak-kîsikâw ita ka-pimohtâtamahk*
> *kikîsikâminaw,* [...] (1-4)
> '[...], that thanks should be given to Our Father, [...],
> that he has granted us another day wherein we might
> live through this day of our life, [...]'

[...], *ka-nanâskomâyêk kôhtâwînaw,*
ê-miyikoyêk kîsikâw, ê-miywâsik ita ka-pimohtâtamêk, [...]
(2-1)
'[...], you should give thanks to Our Father
that he has granted you another beautiful day wherein
to live through it, [...]'

(The major grammatical structures used in these formulae are reviewed, along with further examples, in the notes to 1-4 and 2-2.)

Another dimension of verbal art is invoked in the litany formed by the seven repetitions (supplemented by two of the conjunct order counterpart, *ê-itâpatahk*) of

namôy nânitaw itâpatan
'it is of no avail'

in chapter 2 (especially 2-2, but also 2-5, 2-6; for isolated instances cf. 1-2, 4-9) and concluded (at the end of 2-2) by another, identically repeated phrase:

êwako piko kiyê-âpacihikoyahk,
êwako piko kiyê-âpacihikoyahk. (2-2)
'that is the only thing that will sustain us,
that is the only thing that will sustain us.'

Simple enough in themselves, the fundamental patterns of repetition combine and re-combine to yield a rich and complex texture – thereby ultimately accounting, as Haiman (1998:26) argues, not just for style and rhythm but also for order and rules, norms and exaggeration.

Parallelism

The most elaborate instance of parallel structures occurs in the questions which the Cree spokesman puts to the Queen's representative in the treaty text (chapter 6). He speaks four times (which in itself may or may not be significant), and each of his brief orations is dominated by the demand for affirmation:

> *ê-tâpwêyan cî ôma,* [...] (6-5)
> 'Do you speak the truth in this [...]'

This is the formulaic opening of the first three speeches; the fourth begins with a conditional and a sacramental injunction (cf. pp. 192-197, below),

> *kîspin kitâpwân, êwak ôma ka-~ kika-miciminên oskiciy;* (6-5)
> 'If you speak the truth, hold then this pipestem;'

before the speaker returns to the standard question. (The four questions are schematically outlined on page 162.)

The content clauses which follow the interrogative in each case seem to fall into pairs. The first two are relatively complex, while the latter two are very brief.

With the exception of C3, all these questions include a second level at which the validity of the treaty is being tested: besides openly questioning the veracity of the Queen's representative, the speaker explicitly refers to the promises which have been made. In the very first instance, he speaks of promises 'you have made to me' but throughout the rest of this passage (again with the exception of C3), the transitive first person singular patient ending *-iyan* 'you – me' is replaced by its plural counterpart, *-iyâhk* 'you – us'.

The first two orations in the present set exhibit a further parallel: in both, the phrase *k-ês-âsotamawiyâhk* 'what you have thus promised us' (or, in the very first case, *k-ês-âsotamawiyan* 'what you have thus promised me') is repeated after the content clause. In the first instance (C1), the repetition is preceded simply by the demonstrative *ôma* 'this'; in the second (C2), it is

DEMAND FOR AFFIRMATION	PROMISE	CONTENT	BACKGROUND
[C1]			
ê-tâpwêyan cî ôma,			
	k-ês-âsotamawiyan,		
		êkâ wîhkâc awiyak	
		ka-kî-kaskihtât ka-kî-pîkonahk	
	ôma k-ês-âsotamawiyâhk.		
[EXCURSUS]			
			kipê-âkwaskiskawinân ...
			... pê-âkwaskiskawâw;
	kâ-pê-asotamawiyâhk		
		ê-wî-isi-pamihiyâhk,	
	êwak ôma, k-~		
ê-tâpwêyan cî ôma			
	k-ês-âsotamawiyâhk;		
		ita kâ-pê-pimohtêstamawat	
		kihc-ôkimâskwêw, namoy	
		wîhkâc cî ka-kisipîmakan	
	ôma kitasota-~ k-âsotamawiyâhk.		
			wâpahta! ...
			... mâmaw-ôhtâwîmâw;
		êkosi cî ka-kî-isi-pamihinân,	
		iskoyikohk ôta kiy-âskîwik.	
[C2]			
ê-tâpwêyan cî ôma,			
	k-ês-âsotamawiyâhk,		
		êkâ wîhkâc ka-kî-pîkonahk,	
		'ayisiyiniw ê-nîsokâtêt' k-êtwêyan,	
	êwak ôma, îh! k-ês-âsotamawiyâhk.		
[C3]			
hâw, ê-tâpwêyan cî ôma,			
		kâkikê êkosi k-êsi-pamihiyan?	
[C4]			
kîspin kitâpwân,			
		êwak ôma ka-~ kika-miciminên oskiciy;	
ê-tâpwêyan cî ôma			
	k-ês-âsotamawiyâhk		
		– êhâ, ahpô namôya?	

the resumptive demonstrative phrase *êwak ôma* 'this very one', followed by the evocative interjection *îh!* 'behold!'

The same phrase, *k-ês-âsotamawiyâhk*, also appears with yet another instance of the primary question, *ê-tâpwêyan cî ôma*, this time in the context of a digression.

IN PRESENTING background information, the digression inserted between the parallel core constituents of C1 and C2 relies on two declarative passages directly holding the Queen's representative responsible for the interference which has played havoc with the livelihood of the Crees. The first of these comprises three instances of a single verb, *âkwaskiskaw–* VTA 'head s.o. off, get in s.o.'s way', all three in the most fully declarative form (the independent); the first is inflected for 'you – us', the second and the third, which are inflected for 'you (singular) – him', actually accuse the Queen's representative of getting in God's way:

> [...], *mâmaw-ôhtâwîmâw ita ê-kî-miyikoyâhk kîkway k-ôh-pimâtisiyâhk,* [...] (6-5)
> '[...], where the All-Father has given us the sustenance upon which we live, [...]'

The second, exhortative as well as declamatory, begins with an appeal to the abundance of buffalo and then repeats the key clause of the first in a slightly varied form:

> [...], *êkon ôhi ê-kî-miyikoyâhk k-ôh-pimâtisiyâhk, mâmaw-ôhtâwîmâw;* (6-5)
> '[...], the All-Father has given us all these [buffalo] to live upon;'

The key part of the excursus presenting this background follows the first declarative statement and precedes the second. At its core it consists of the affirmatory and promissory constituents of the standard question, but they in turn are framed by two more variants of the promissory clause: it is foreshadowed by an opening which localises the scene by means of the preverb *pê* 'hither, thence' (and without the otherwise ubiquitous preverb *isi* 'thus'): *kâ-pê-asotamawiyâhk* 'you, in coming to promise us that [...]'. And the closing echo, which elaborates on the localisation by means of the deictic *ita* 'there', uses the plain verb stem (i.e., without the preverb *isi*, which except for these two appears in all instances of the stem in these speeches): *ôma k-âsotamawiyâhk* 'what you have promised us'; note that this final instance corrects a noun fragment *kitasota-~* (*sc. kitasotamâkêwin* 'your promise, what you have promised').

THERE ARE TWO other stock elements which appear twice each in these supplementary questions: the verb forms *ê-wî-isi-pamihiyâhk* (conjunct) and *ka-kî-isi-pamihinân* (independent), with the stem *pamih–* VTA 'tend to s.o., look after s.o.' in both cases inflected for 'you – us' and the timeless validity of the promises expressed in complementary terms:

> [...], *namôy wîhkâc cî ka-kisipîmakan* [...] (6-5)
> '[...], will it never come to an end [...]'

> *êkosi cî ka-kî-isi-pamihinân, iskoyikohk ôta kiy-âskîwik.* (6-5)
> 'will you be able to provide for us to the same extent [as the All-Father] so long as this world shall exist?'

The inviolability, indeed sanctity, of the promises made is also the ultimate content of the doubly posed and doubly framed questions in C1 and C2:

> [...], *êkâ wîhkâc awiyak ka-kî-kaskihtât ka-kî-pîkonahk* [...] (6-5)
> '[...], that no one will ever be in a position to be able to break them [...]'

[...], *êkâ wîhkâc ka-kî-pîkonahk, 'ayisiyiniw ê-nîsokâtêt' k-êtwêyan,* [...] (6-5)
'[...], that no 'human walking on two legs', as you put it, will ever be able to break it, [...]'

(For a discussion of the affirmatory formula itself, cf. pages 190-192, below.)

Amongst the content clauses, C3 stands out by being sharply focussed on the alimentary obligation itself and its timeless quality:

[...], *kâkikê êkosi k-êsi-pamihiyan?* (6-5)
'[...], that you will forever look after me to this extent?'

All the others mediate the ultimate content by another clause invoking the promises that have been made before specifying the content of these promises. But in the content clause of C3, the verb form based on the stem *pamih–* recalls the overriding concern with the necessities of life which is the topic of the background section.

In C3, the content verb is inflected for a singular patient and thus formally echoes the promissory verb form of the very first question in C1, but there is a referential difference. While the singular patient of the earlier instance might conceivably denote the Cree spokesman rather than the collective leadership, in C3 the *kâkikê* 'forever' alone ensures the interpretation of the verb form as a generic singular, referring to all Crees present and future.

In the fourth and last repetition of the question (C4), finally, the content is left unmentioned. Only the promise matters, and the question is simply, yes or no.

Documentary Form

While most of the texts in this collection are homiletic in genre and essentially linear in structure, chapter 6 stands apart by presenting a documentary account of the speeches preceding the conclusion of Treaty Six.

This is not the place to review once again the value of oral documents – an issue brought to the notice of historians no later than 1961, when Vansina's codification of ethnographic practice first appeared in print, and which finally began to attract legal and public attention with the *Delgamuukw* decision of the Supreme Court of Canada (1997, notably paragraphs 87, 92-99, 106-108) – but to explicate and illustrate the structure of a particular document of rare prominence in the history of western Canada.

The representatives of the Crown recorded their positions not only in official reports but also in popular publications which were practically contemporary. As literary gentlemen of the Victorian age, they presumably also left private papers and correspondence which might elucidate their views, and similar records were probably produced by the various observers, many of them members of the clergy. The reminiscences of the interpreters (above all Erasmus 1976 [1920/1928]) by the very essence of their ambiguous position present problems of another order entirely. As for the Cree side of the story, the printed record is almost wholly silent.

This text, by contrast, presents part of the Cree record of the negotiations, such as they were, which took place in the late summer of 1876 on the North Saskatchewan. Preserved in accordance with the canons of the oral tradition, this record takes the form of a narrative which has been transmitted from its original narrator to *kâ-pimwêwêhahk*'s father and thence to the speaker himself, and the chain of transmission forms part of the report.

Parts of the Discourse

For all its internal complexity, the report which *kâ-pimwêwêhahk* has recorded of the speeches leading to the signing of Treaty Six is remarkable for the transparency of the overall discourse structure.

The four parts which make up the main body of the text are preceded by an introduction and followed first by a supplement, which is part of the main body, and a conclusion, and then by an appendix:

- INTRODUCTION
- MAIN BODY
  - PART I
  - PART II
  - PART III
  - PART IV
  - SUPPLEMENT
- CONCLUSION
- APPENDIX

These are the constituent parts of the discourse, presumably inherent structures of the text but only made explicit by philological analysis. (For ease of reference they are flagged in the translation by editorial 'stage directions' printed in small caps and enclosed in square brackets.)

Even though they frequently coincide, the discourse constituents and the paragraphs are independent of one another. The paragraphs into which the printed text is divided are text units, largely identifiable on the basis of prosodic features (e.g., pause, pitch, volume) or stylistic markers (ranging from discourse particles like the introductory *â* 'well' or the hortatory *hâw* 'now then' to shifts in inflectional order typical of concluding quotative verbs) or even by the form of comments which, depending on whether they fall at the end of one paragraph or the beginning of the next, may be taken as either summative or resumptive.

THE INTRODUCTION exhibits the classical traits of a formal Cree discourse.

It begins with the twin issues of authenticity and authority, tempered by deference. The speaker refers with some formality to those, usually members of the audience, who have commissioned him to speak. He declares his intention to report the text as faithfully as his limited powers permit. And he attributes the text itself to his late father, with corroboration by his father's late brother.

Having made these points in the first paragraph, he elaborates upon all three in the second before finally introducing the keeper of the pipestem by his personal name.

THE MAIN BODY of the text falls into four distinct main parts.

In PART I, the three layers of reported speech are separately identified on various occasions, and the outermost, that spoken by *kâ-pimwêwêhahk*'s father, is fully specified both at the beginning (at the start of 6-3) and at the end (in the middle of 6-5, following the first response of the Queen's representative). In 6-4 the speaker also recapitulates his concern with fidelity, expressed most fully in the introduction.

In PART II, the two outer layers are taken for granted and marked neither prosodically nor segmentally. The quotative verbs identify only the two protagonists:

kî-itêw anihi; (6-5)
'he [C] had thus said to that one [Q];'

ê-itwêyit, [...] (6-5)
'he [Q] thus said, [...]'

êkos êsa kâ-itwêt, [...] (6-5)
'Thus then he [Q] spoke, [...]'

Only at the very end does the focus shift to the collectivity of Cree leaders:

êkos êsa kî-is-âsotamâkwak, êkon ôhi. (6-5)
'Thus then they had these promises made to them, by that one [Q].'

The Queen's representative is identified by a noun phrase, *êkon ôhi* 'that one'; the Cree leaders are understood, the verb indicating a third person plural as its patient.

PART III maintains the focus on the Cree leaders, their collectivity reflected in the plural agent of the first verb (*kâ-kî-âpacihtâcik* 'they had used it') and in the two quotative verbs, both of which are construed with explicit noun phrases:

êkos êsa kî-itwêwak kisêyiniwak ôki. (6-6)
'Thus then spoke these old men.'

êkos êsa kâ-kî-itihcik ôki, kimosôminawak. (6-6)
'Thus then our grandfathers had been told.'

In this second example, which follows the ringing declaration of the Queen's representative, the verb of saying is inagentive but inflected for a third person plural patient. (This part of the text closes with a parenthetical comment about the situation of today.)

PART IV contains the conclusion of the main text; in formal literary terms, this is evident from the renewed identification of the primary authority for the authenticity of the text: *kâ-pimwêwêhahk*'s father is explicitly mentioned both at the beginning and at the end of the main text, with the words of the witness quoted as part of his report. The final mention of this primary authority is followed by a concluding remark which is clearly evaluative in tone:

êwako ôma mêkwâc êkwa. (6-7)
'And that is what is before us at the present time.'

The SUPPLEMENT which follows this concluding remark takes the form of an afterthought, consisting of two direct quotations from the speech of the Queen's representative and explicitly identified as contract prose by the two quotative phrases which follow them:

êkos êsa mîna ê-kî-is-âsotamâkêt. (6-8)
'Thus then he had also promised.'

êkos ês ê-kî-is-âsotamâht êwakw âwa nêhiyaw [...] (6-8)
'Thus then had the promises been made to that Cree [...]'

The verb form in the first of these highlights the speaker; in the second the verb is inagentive and only identifies the patient.

THE CONCLUSION consists of five very brief paragraphs. The first (6-9), despite its self-deprecatory tone, re-asserts the unbroken continuity of the oral tradition. The second (6-10) expands on the utility and value of the enterprise, and the third (6-11) resumes the self-deprecation. The fourth (6-12) adds a confirmatory conclusion, and the last (6-13) provides the standard closing formula.

THE APPENDIX is externally defined by the break in the recording, which confirms the concluding quality of the paragraphs which precede it. The sentence which follows the break plainly reflects the entreaties which caused the speaker to resume his report and to quote additional parts of the treaty in the form of an appendix.

The quoted passages evidently represent the commitments made by the Queen's representative, but in the subsidiary form of an appendix they merely echo the structure of the main text.

They lack the formal embedding in the speech of the witness and of *kâ-pimwêwêhahk*'s father, neither of whom are mentioned (except at the very end).

Thus, while the appendix is distinct in literary and documentary form from the main text, this is most striking at the beginning; at the end, the speaker returns to the traditional form in the self-effacing phrases and by one last mention of his father, on whose authority he has complied with the wishes of his audience.

Quoted Speech

In the traditional form of texts told at a remove (cf. Wolfart 1982, 1992:362-363, 1998), the current speaker opens the reported discourse with an explicitly marked quotation but continues in the voice and persona of the original narrator.

After setting the stage and formally stressing his concern with authenticity, *kâ-pimwêwêhahk* begins by quoting his father directly:

> *"êkota ôta,* [...], *êkot*[*a*] *ê-kî-âpatahk," kî-itwêw mâna kâ-kî-oyôhtâwîyân.* (6-3)
> ' "At that time, [...], at that time it was used," my late father used to say.'

This example illustrates the most common form of direct quotation in Cree, with the quotative verb following the quoted material. Much less frequently, a verb of saying may also precede the reported speech.

At the beginning of the crucial section of the text (6-5), the salient information is the identity of the primary speaker being quoted (*kâ-pimwêwêhahk*'s father), especially since *kisêyiniw pêyak* 'a certain old man' is introduced as another, second-level speaker (and re-introduced as a dramatis persona, having made his first appearance at the beginning of 6-4) in the very next clause – and a third, the Cree spokesman, shortly thereafter.

Of the three speakers whose speech is being reported, only the first two are identified by noun phrases, but all three speeches have their beginnings flagged by a verb of saying. The report of *kâ-pimwêwêhahk*'s father is introduced by the unmarked term *kî-itwêw* 'thus he had said'. For the old man who is cited as a direct witness of these events, a more formal term is used repeatedly (6-4, 6-5) and in a specialised sense: *kî-wîhtam* 'he had foretold it'. And the key question of the Cree spokesman, quoted *in extenso* and repeatedly, is introduced by the most specific term:

> *êkosi, êkota kâ-kî-kakwêcimât:* (6-5)
> 'Thus, it was then that he had asked him:'

At the end of the first major set of quotations (i.e., the end of part I), while *kâ-pimwêwêhahk*'s father is again fully identified, the other speakers are not.

Thus, three layers need to be distinguished in this nested discourse:

LAYER	TYPOGRAPHICAL REPRESENTATION	SPEAKER
1	"..." (double)	*kâ-pimwêwêhahk*'s father
2	'...' (single)	a certain old man, the witness
3	«...» (guillemets)	the Cree spokesman (C) and the Queen's representative (Q)

The inherent asymmetry of quoted material preceding the quotative verb typically results in situations where the levels of embedding are conflated at the beginning of a quotation but kept distinct at its end. The clearest example of this pattern is found at the end of the main body:

> " '[...],' *kî-itwêw ês êwako kisêyiniw," kî-itwêw mâna kâ-kî-oyôhtâwîyân.* (6-7)
> ' " '[...],' that old man had then said," my late father used to say.'

In the purely prosodic marking of the beginning of a direct quotation, the two layers are conflated, as shown in print by the juxtaposition of primary (here, double) and secondary (here, single) opening quotation marks. (In the citation format used here, this holds only for the Cree original; for the English translation, the standard convention calls for another layer of single quotation marks to enclose the entire block.)

The above examples illustrate the fully explicit pattern, where each layer is separately identified. In a running text, however, layers are often conflated even at the end of the quotation, for example at the end of the first speech of the Queen's representative:

> " [...] '[...] «[...].»
> *êkosi kî-itwêw, êwakw âwa kâ-kî-pê-pimohtêstamawât kihc-ôkimâskwêwa,' " kî-itwêw mâna kâ-kî-oyôhtâwîyân, ay-âtotahki êwak ôma;* (6-5)
> ' " [...] '[...] «[...].»
> Thus he spoke, the one who had come representing the Queen,' " my late father used to say when telling about this;'

Where the context and the content of the reported speech are unambiguous, the specification of the speaker is often omitted. After the first long speech of the Cree spokesman, for example, the two protagonists (both at the third level of reported speech) are fully identified:

êkosi kî-itêw anihi, kâ-kî-pê-pimohtêstamawât awa kihc-ôkimâskwêwa; (6-5)
'Thus he spoke to him, to the one who had come representing the Queen;'

The same speaker then recapitulates his key question and his interlocutor replies to it – but the switch between two speakers on the same level of embedding is marked by prosodic means exclusively and there is no trace of overt quotative markers (normally a quotative verb). In terms of content and other linguistic structures, of course, the switch is also marked by the transition from an interrogative sentence posed to a second person to a ringing declarative featuring the first.

Only at the conclusion of the answer do we find another quotative verb:

" [...] '[...] «[...].»
êkosi kî-itwêw, êwakw âwa kâ-kî-pê-pimohtêstamawât kihc-ôkimâskwêwa, [...]' " (6-5)
' " [...] '[...] «[...].»
Thus he spoke, the one who had come representing the Queen, [...]' " '

Unlike most of the other quotation frames in this text, the present one includes a full relative clause to match the preceding frame.

THE CHOICE of full noun phrases to identify the speaker either at the beginning or at the end of the quoted speech, the use of full verbs to introduce a quoted speech, and the various patterns of conflating the multiple layers of quotation do not exhaust the expressive repertoire at the disposal of a Cree narrator wishing to delimit the constituent parts of a text. In a documentary text, in particular, the quotative verbs themselves and the choice of inflected forms in which they may appear add a further dimension.

It is a standard feature of Cree texts that the quotative verb follows the material being quoted. In the case of the most common verbs of saying, those based on the root *it-* 'thither, thus', this pattern is the textual reflection of a syntactic property: verb stems like *it–* VTA 'say thus to s.o.' or *itwê–* VAI 'say thus' require an antecedent. In the case of other verbs of saying, notably the verbs of promise which appear with high frequency in chapter 6, this feature is taken as stylistic.

The passages quoted for the Cree spokesman and the Queen's representative (marked C and Q, respectively, and numbered consecutively in the table below) exhibit a fairly clearcut pattern. The dialogue between the two contracting parties is quoted by means of the unmarked verbs of saying, *it–* VTA and *itwê–* VAI. The recital of the contractual provisions, on the other hand, is dominated by the use of the stem *asotamaw–* VTA 'promise (it/him) to s.o.' (and its secondary derivative *asotamâkê–* VAI 'make a promise'):

" '[...]. *êkosi, êkota kâ-kî-kakwêcimât:*
' " '[...]. Thus, it was then that he had asked him:'
« [C1]. »
êkosi kî-itêw anihi, kâ-kî-pê-pimohtêstamawât awa kihc-ôkimâskwêwa;
'Thus he spoke to him, to the one who had come representing the Queen;'
« [C2]. »
« [Q1]. »
êkosi kî-itwêw, êwakw âwa kâ-kî-pê-pimohtêstamawât kihc-ôkimâskwêwa,' " [...]
'Thus he spoke, the one who had come representing the Queen,' " [...]'
« [C3]? »

kî-itêw anihi;
'he had said to that one;'

« [C4]? »

« [Q2]! »

ê-itwêyit, [...],
'he said, [...],'

« [Q3]; »

êkos êsa kâ-itwêt, êwakw âwa kâ-pê-atâwêstamawât;
'thus then he spoke, the one who had come to make the purchase for them;

« [Q4]. »

êkos êsa kî-is-âsotamâkwak, êkon ôhi.
'Thus then they had these promises made to them, by that one.'

« [Q5]; »

êkos êsa kâ-kî-itihcik ôki, kimosôminawak.
'thus then they, our grandfathers, had been told.'

« [Q6]; »

êkos êsa mîna ê-kî-is-âsotamâkêt.
'thus then he had also promised.'

« [Q7]; »

êkos ês ê-kî-is-âsotamâht êwakw âwa nêhiyaw kâ-kî-atâwâkêt kitaskînaw.
'thus then had the promises been made to the Cree who had sold our land.'

[APPENDIX:]

[...], *tânis ê-kî-is-âsotamâht:*
'[...], what had been promised to him:'

« [Q8]. »

êkos ês êkwa anima mîn ê-kî-is-âsotamâht;
'Thus this also had been promised to him;'

« [Q9]. »

[...], *êkos êsa kâ-is-âsotamâht.*
'This then had been promised to him [the chief].'

« [Q10]. »
êkos êsa kâ-is-âsotamâht mîna, êwakw âwa kâ-kî-wiyihcikêt kimosôminaw.
'This then had also been promised to him, to that grandfather of ours who had concluded the treaty.'
« [Q11], »
êkos êsa kâ-itiht.
'thus then he was told.'
« [Q12]. »
êkos êsa mîna kâ-is-âsotamâht.
'This then also had been promised to him.'
« [Q13]; »
êkos êsa mîna ê-kî-is-âsotamâht.
'This then also had been promised to him.'

With minor exceptions, the choice of quotative verbs also corresponds to the distinction between the primary parts (I-IV) of the text, containing all C-quotations and Q1-Q5, and, secondarily, the supplement (Q6-Q7) taken together with the appendix (Q8-Q13).

Within the main body of the text, a further distinction is evident between the central portion (parts I-II), where the bulk of the quoted material is found, and the marginal sections (parts III-IV) together with the supplement. In the central portion, the quotative verbs are almost all unmarked verbs of saying, with the VTA forms belonging exclusively to the direct subset (cf. Wolfart 1973:sec. 2.5, 1996:409-415). In short, these are invariably the least marked stems appearing in their least marked inflected forms.

The only exception to this overall pattern comes at the very end of part II (following Q4), where the final quotative verb is in fact the inverse form *kî-is-âsotamâkwak*, inflected for an obviative (3') agent and a proximate third person plural (3p) patient.

At the end of part III (following Q5), the stem *it–* VTA appears in the indefinite agent form, ***kâ-kî-itihcik***, also with a third person plural (3p) patient.

In their recital of contract prose, the supplement and the appendix are indistinguishable. Except for the unique VAI form *ê-kî-is-âsotamâkêt* (following Q6) and the single occurrence of the stem *it–* VTA for Q11, all of these verbs take an inagentive form with a third person singular (3) patient – 'had been promised to him' – and that includes the *it–* for Q11 as well as the introductory verb which launches the appendix.

THE STYLISTIC DISTINCTION between the treaty dialogue and the list of contractual provisions is corroborated by another documentary pattern closely linked to the choice of quotative stems and their forms: the use of the evidential particle *êsa*.

With the gloss 'reportedly' (or 'I understand') little more than a rough label, *êsa* indicates that the speaker did not personally experience the event in question. It belongs to a set of evidential markers amongst which it and *êtokwê* 'apparently; I suppose' (which corresponds in form and function to the dubitative paradigm of verbs; cf. Wolfart 1973:sec. 5.311) are by far the most common.

The evidential force of *êsa* varies greatly with the genre of the text and even from one speaker to the next; it is remarkable, for instance, how infrequently both *êsa* and *êtokwê* are found in the present volume. The evidential force is almost always weakened when *êsa* occurs as part of the particle phrase *êkos êsa*, conventionally glossed 'thus then'.

This is the only form, in fact, in which *êsa* appears in the present set of quotative frames; yet the particle phrase *êkos êsa* is found in every one of the quotative clauses in the supplement and the appendix – i.e., exactly in those parts of the text which are no longer explicitly marked as part of the primary report of *kâ-pimwêwêhahk*'s father. Only as the narration becomes less direct – and this evidently may happen in part III already, with transitional instances occurring as early as the frames following Q3 and Q4 – does the immediacy give way to a more distant reportage.

Significantly, there is no attenuation in the truth value of the report, whether it relies on quotative *it–* or *itwê–* or on *êsa*. But there is a difference – and it emerges very sharply in this text – in the strategy employed in the transmission of reported speech.

Fidelity of Transmission

When Cree texts (irrespective of genre) are told at a remove, the current performer speaks on the authority of the original narrator. In such texts it is not uncommon to find the current speaker expressing concern for the integrity of the text entrusted to him or her:

> *â, êwak ôma kâ-wî-tâhkôtamân,*
> *matwân cî kwayask nika-kî-isi-tâhkôtên*
> *tânis ê-kî-itâcimostawit kâ-kî-oyôhtâwîyân,* [...] (6-1)
> 'Well, this which I am about to discuss,
> I wonder if I will be able to discuss it with proper faithfulness,
> just as my late father had told me the story about it, [...]'

In placing this statement at the very opening of the text and by his use of the polar dubitative particle *matwân cî* 'I wonder whether or not', *kâ-pimwêwêhahk* appears to give it the additional force of an invocation.

From the first to the last, *kâ-pimwêwêhahk* repeatedly breaks away from the text itself to a meta-text of protestations of fidelity. After touching on the issue once more in the opening sentence, he returns to it (and its twin, deference to those who want him to speak) in a slightly different form in the second paragraph:

kâ-nitawêyihtahkik,
ê-isi-kiskêyihtahk ayisiyiniw,
ê-isi-pêhtahk opêhtamowinihk,
k-âtotahk êwak ôma âcimowin. (6-2)
'[I give thanks] that they want for a person [*i.e.*, me],
just as he knows it,
just as he heard it in his own hearing.
to tell this story.'

He then expands the exordial invocation into two distinct parts, and this also is the form of the echo which appears at the conclusion, substituting a new set of lexical items but retaining the syntactic structure of the first instance:

êwak ôma nîsta ê-kî-itâcimostawit mâna kâ-kî-oyôhtâwîyân,
kâ-wî-itâcimostawakik ôki. (6-2)
'Just as I myself used to be told this story by my late father,
that is how I am going to tell it to them.'

matwân cî nika-kî-têpi-wîhtên,
tânisi ê-kî-isi-wîhtamawit mâna. (6-2)
'I wonder if I will be able to tell it exactly,
just as he used to tell it to me.'

Finally, he elaborates the point even further, explicitly adverting to the frailties of his age:

kôtatê nîst êkâ ê-sîpi-kiskisiyân,
mâk ê-isko-kiskêyihtamân kîkway,
êyiwêhk nika-kakwê-âcimostawâwak. (6-2)
'It cannot be helped that my memory, too, lapses,
but to the extent that I know the story,
I will nevertheless try to tell it to them.'

As the main body of the text draws to an end, the speaker returns to this issue once more, still mindful, even with his task accomplished, of human fallibility:

â, êwakw ânima, êkos ê-itâtotamân,
nîsta ê-kî-itâcimostawit kâ-kî-oyôhtâwîyân;
matwân cî k-~ kwayask nitâtotên êwak ôma,
tânis ê-kî-itâcimostawit mâna,
êwak ôma k-âcimostawakik ôki nôsisimak. (6-9)

'Well, as I tell this story,
just so I, too, had it told to me by my late father;
I wonder if I tell this properly,
just as he used to tell me this story,
it is this that I have told to these my grandchildren.'

At the end of the appendix, the issue of fidelity is resumed one last time:

êwak ôma kâ-nitawêyihtahkik
k-âniskê-âtotamân,
êkosi mân ê-kî-itâcimostawit kâ-kî-oyôhtâwîyân, [...]
(6-15)

'This is what they want
that I should tell about to continue the oral tradition,
thus my late father used to tell me the story, [...]'

In stressing his concern as often and as elaborately as he does, *kâ-pimwêwêhahk* does not merely attend to an issue of historical accuracy. That he is at least equally worried about ritual propriety is suggested by the repeated use of the term *kwayask* 'properly' (twice in 6-1 and again in 6-9). The nature of this worry is made explicit by the choice of the verb stem *pâstâhôtot–* VTI in the concluding remark of chapter 5:

"pitanê, êkâ kîkway pâstâhôtotamân," nititêyihtên mân êwak ôm âyimôtamani. (5-5)
' "I wish that I might not commit any sacrilege," I usually think when I talk about this.'

The impact of such a transgression would go well beyond history; to make a mistake in speaking about the pipestem would constitute a serious offence against the sacred.

Lectio difficilior

Obscure elements of a text, whether they be phonological, grammatical, semantic or pragmatic, hold a prominent position in the philological discipline of textual criticism. Having survived the scribe's or speaker's tendency to smooth over unexpected, out-of-place or incomprehensible material, such 'more difficult readings' are taken to indicate the earlier of two texts or, with only somewhat diminished force, to mark a text as belonging to an independent tradition.

The treaty text in chapter 6 includes one provision which stands out from all the others:

"kiyâm ôta awas-âyihk --~ kwêskahcâhk, ôm îtê osêhcâhk kwêsk-âyihk ma-matwêwêki, namôy wîhkâc k-ôtinâw nêhiyaw-âyisiyiniw, nôtinitowinihk k-âpati-~ k-êtisiniht;" (6-8)
' "Assuming there were here on the other side --~ on the other side of a hill, if there on a hillside on the other side there were gunshots heard, the Cree Indians will never be conscripted to be handed over into military service;" '

When read within the limited context of the particular text (which is, after all, often the only context available), this passage is wholly unexpected and opaque.

Not only does this sentence, with its two false starts and several locatives stacked one upon the other, present grammatical problems. It is also semantically difficult because it consists largely of technical terms. As is often the case with technical terms in Cree, whether for post-contact institutions, as in this passage, or not (cf. the medical terms in Wolfart 1989*b*), general terms are extended and used polysemously in their new, narrow sense. *otin–* VTA, for example, the first verb of the main clause, is a perfectly ordinary, commonplace stem meaning 'take s.o., choose s.o.', e.g., *mistikwaskihkwa ê-otinât* 'as he takes the drum' (3-13). It is also used in the more specialised sense 'steal s.o.', but here it is further extended to include the technical sense 'force s.o. into military service, conscript s.o.'. Much the same holds for the other verb in the main clause: *itisin–* VTA by itself normally means 'thus hold (it/him) for s.o., thus hand (it/him) over to s.o.' but here, in construction with *nôtinitowinihk*, the locative form of the normal noun for 'fighting one another, fighting', it takes on the modern, highly specialised meaning 'thus press s.o. into military service'. The only unambiguous verb in this sentence is *matwêwê–* VII 'be heard as gunshot, be the report of a gun', with the light reduplication (cf. Ahenakew and Wolfart 1983) imparting a sense of continuity.

Short as it is, then, this passage presents considerable difficulties of a purely linguistic nature. Yet even they pale beside the pragmatic problems – why should the Cree seek, or the government offer, exemption from military service a full forty years before the conscription crisis of 1916?

As it turns out, a corresponding provision appears in all the English reports of the treaty proceedings. Jackes (1876:215) and Erasmus (1976 [1920/1928]:253) both have it as part of a list of requests compiled for the chiefs at Carlton by "the interpreter" (i.e., Peter Erasmus) and read out early on 23 August 1876:

> *Lastly in case of war occurring in the country, we do not want to be liable to serve in it.* (Jackes 1876:215)

To which «Tee-tee-quay-say» (presumably *opitihkwahâkêw*; cf. Ahenakew and Wolfart 1987:x) added: "When we look back to the past we do not see where the Cree nation has ever watered the ground with the white man's blood, [...]" (Jackes 1876:215). While these records offer little to elucidate the *realia*, they come as welcome confirmation of our linguistic analysis.

Nor is the pragmatic context made any clearer by the reply of Morris (as cited by Jackes 1876:218), granting exemption from military service in High Victorian terms. Morris's personal aside (1876:183) adds only a morsel of background: "I had ascertained that the Indian mind was oppressed with vague fears; [that] they dreaded the treaty; [that] they had been made to believe [...] that in time of war, they would be placed in the front and made to fight."

The solution to this conundrum is not revealed until we turn to Morris's opening speech at Fort Pitt on 7 September 1876 (Jackes 1876:234): "[...] you will never be asked to fight against your will; and I trust the time will never come of war between the Queen and the great country near us." The larger context in which this passage and the entire conscription issue is no longer inexplicable is the massacre by Americans of an Assiniboine camp in the Cypress Hills – now compellingly retold by Guy Vanderhaeghe, and with unparalleled artifice, in *The Englishman's Boy* – and the subsequent establishment of the N.W.M.P., both mentioned by Morris just before his reference to the U.S.

Without this pragmatic context, the conscription clause constitutes a 'foreign body' in what is otherwise a normal Cree text. (As there can be no legal or political motivation, morever, for introducing this provision into the discussions of the late 20th century, it further constitutes a solid argument against the surmise that the oral record might have been contaminated by the printed report.)

Not admitting of reasonable interpretation, this obscure object illustrates one of the key corollaries of the principle of *lectio difficilior*: that it should have been carried along as part of the text for well over a century, despite its opacity, underscores the reliability of the record.

Contractual and Sacramental Form

The authenticity of *kâ-pimwêwêhahk*'s report – today's spoken record of words first spoken more than a century earlier – is a function of the linguistic, textual and historiographic form of the document.

The contractual validity of the treaty itself is a distinct issue, various aspects of which are addressed either in the particular provisions of the treaty or in the accounts of its conclusion. In their separate attempts to assert – and assay – the validity of the treaty, the contracting parties refer variously to truthfulness, the natural environment, the human condition and the supernatural order.

Truth

The fundamental question of truthfulness is addressed quite differently by the two parties, but with equal directness.

In his opening speech at Fort Carlton, for example, Morris is cited (Jackes 1876) as follows:

> [...], *I always keep my promises;* (199)
> [...] *I did not forget my word,* [...] (199)
> [...] *the words are true.* (200)
> *when I say yes, I mean it,*
> *and when I say no, I mean it too.* (201)

Throughout his speeches, moreover, Morris makes much of the fact that the treaty is being discussed and, ultimately, signed in public (rather than, as must have been customary, behind closed doors), repeatedly stressing that the proceedings are taking place "before the whole people" or "in the face of the people" (Jackes 1876:199, 208, 221).

By the same token, the government's intentions, the veracity of the Queen's representative and the validity of the treaty itself are tested overtly and repeatedly:

ê-tâpwêyan cî ôma, k-ês-âsotamawiyan, [...] (6-5)
'Do you speak the truth in this which you have promised me, [...]'

[...], *êwak ôma, k-~ ê-tâpwêyan cî ôma k-ês-âsotamawiyâhk;* (6-5)
'[...], do you speak the truth in this which you have promised us;'

ê-tâpwêyan cî ôma, k-ês-âsotamawiyâhk, [...] (6-5)
'Do you speak the truth in this which you have promised us, [...]'

ê-tâpwêyan cî ôma k-ês-âsotamawiyâhk – êhâ, ahpô namôya? (6-5)
'Do you speak the truth in this which you have promised us – Yes, or no?'

Rather than questioning the treaty commitments as a whole, the initial part of the formula may also be used to specify a particular provision:

hâw, ê-tâpwêyan cî ôma, kâkikê êkosi k-êsi-pamihiyan? (6-5)
'Indeed, do you speak the truth in that you will forever look after me to this extent?'

None of the above examples, of course, reveals any detail of the concept of truth being tested, which might range from the personal honesty of Alexander Morris to the extent of his authority to make commitments, and from the legalistic interpretation of the particulars to the term during which the contract would be valid.

That these are vital issues, on the other hand, is not in doubt. The fourfold repetition – and in short order – of the key phrase is ultimately followed by another variant in the form of a conditional prodosis:

> *kîspin kitâpwân, êwak ôma ka-~ kika-miciminên oskiciy;* (6-5)
> 'If you speak the truth, hold then this pipestem;'

By this reduced form of the formula, the Queen's representative is invited, indeed challenged, to submit himself and the treaty to the most powerful test of veracity and validity.

Nature

The temporal validity of the treaty is confirmed to be without limit in the words of the widely repeated formula:

> [...], *kâkikê,*
> *iskoyikohk pîsim ka-pimohtêt,*
> *iskoyikohk sîpiy ka-pimiciwahk,*
> *iskoyikohk maskosiya kê-sâkikihki,*
> *êkospî isko ka-pimohtêmakan ôma k-ês-âsotamâtân;* (6-6)
> '[...], forever,
> so long as the sun shall cross the sky,
> so long as the rivers shall run,
> so long as the grass shall grow,
> that is how long these promises I have made to you will last;'

In the published account of the Secretary to the Treaty Commission, A.G. Jackes M.D., we see a consistent pattern reported for the two successive sets of speeches. At Fort Carlton first and subsequently at Fort Pitt, the formula is initially used by Morris (twice in the case of Carlton, on the first and second day of the proceedings) and then echoed by the Cree respondents.

Jackes's careful record preserves several subtle variations, some of which may well be significant. At Fort Carlton, Morris is twice reported to have used the verb *flow*, and that is the verb recorded for both responses at Fort Pitt, while both responses at Fort Carlton (as also the response at the supplementary meeting of 28 August) and Morris's own use at Fort Pitt are recorded with the verb *run*. (Though no doubt by the speaker's and the reporter's inadvertence, this pattern is none the less chiastic.)

Other discrepancies seem more important. Speaking at Fort Pitt, *wîhkasko-kisêyin* is cited with two non-standard variants. In one of these, a truncated version of the formula appears in a somewhat unusual context:

> [...] *that [they]* [...] *can stand together*
> *as long as the sun shines.* (Jackes 1876:237)

In the other, the initial part of the parallel is replaced:

> [...] *as long as this earth stands*
> *and the river flows.* (Jackes 1876:236)

The non-standard phrase presupposes a distinctly apocalyptic image, but this is the phrase also found in *kâ-pimwêwêhahk*'s text:

> *êkosi cî ka-kî-isi-pamihinân,*
> *iskoyikohk ôta kiy-âskîwik.* (6-5)
> 'will you be able to provide for us to the same extent
> so long as this world shall exist?'

It can hardly have escaped Jackes that *opîhtokahânapiwiyin*, without modifying the formula itself, mocks not only the docility of the chiefs but also Morris's High Victorian rhetoric:

> *From what I can hear and see now, I cannot understand*
> *that I shall be able to clothe my children and feed them*
> *as long as sun shines* [sic]
> *and water runs* [sic]. (Jackes 1876:219-220)

Whatever the significance of the reduced formula may be, the question as a whole drips with bitter irony.

In the version reported for 'Little Hunter' (Jackes 1876:238), the sun *moves* – presumably an English reflexion of the much more idiomatic Cree phrase, *iskoyikohk pîsim ka-pimohtêt* 'so long as the sun shall move along' (6-6); cf. the verb stems similarly built on the morpheme *-ohtê-* 'walk' in the phrase *pîsim aw êtohtêt* 'as the sun goes' (7-9) and, especially, in:

> [...], *awa kâ-pê-sâkohtêt ôta* [gesture] *kâ-pimohtâtahk ôma.* (3-13)
> '[...], the one who comes moving into view here [*gesture*] and passes through its course.'

The most remarkable deviation from the formulaic use of this well-worn topos is the very first instance, on 18 August 1876, when Jackes records Morris as using the specific demonstratives *that* and *yonder*:

> *what I will promise,* [...], *is to last*
> *as long as that sun shines*
> *and yonder river flows.* (Jackes 1876:202)

(The second, on 19 August, is given in the form of indirect, reported speech.)

While the affirmatory topos itself belongs to a familiar set (cf. Gill 1987), the variation found in Jackes's record offers a basis for fuller philological analysis. The unpublished papers of the prolific diarists and correspondents (including assorted clergy) who attended as observers may well provide further, independent records of the formula as it was used at Fort Carlton and Fort Pitt.

Humanity

An even more powerful phrase is used to affirm the immunity of the treaty from human interference:

> [...], *kitasotamâkonaw*
> *êkây wîhkâc ôta waskitaskamik ê-nîsokâtêt ayisiyiniw,*
> *ka-kî-pîkonahk kitasotamâkowininaw.* (6-5)
> '[...], he did promise us
> that no human walking on two legs upon the surface of the earth
> would ever be able to break the promises made to us.'

While the key noun phrase recalls some of the many names of the bear, e.g., *nêwokâtêwayisiyiniw* [*sic*] 'four-legged person' (SW), the text includes an explicit attribution of the phrase to the Queen's representative:

> *ê-tâpwêyan cî ôma,* [...],
> *êkâ wîhkâc ka-kî-pîkonahk,*
> *'ayisiyiniw ê-nîsokâtêt' k-êtwêyan,*
> *êwak ôma, îh! k-ês-âsotamawiyâhk.* (6-5)
> 'Do you speak the truth in this [...],
> that no 'human walking on two legs', as you put it,
> will ever be able to break that,
> look, which you have promised us.'

In fact, although no trace of it could be found in the reports of Jackes and Morris, this formula, too, appears exclusively in the speeches of the Queen's representative, either quoted directly:

> *hâw! môy âwiyak wîhkâc ka-kaskihtâw ê-nîsokâtêt ayisiyiniw, ka-pîkonahk tânis ê-is-âsotamâtakok.* (6-5)
> 'Indeed! No human walking on two legs will ever be able to break what I am hereby promising you.'

or indirectly, in reported speech:

> *kitasotamâkowininaw*
> *êkây wîhkâc ka-pîkonahk ê-nîsokâtêt ayisiyiniw;* (5-2)
> 'So that no human walking on two legs would ever break the promises made to us;'

(For the English original one would have to search the papers and letters of the various clerical observers at these proceedings; with respect to Morris's opening speech at Fort Pitt, for example, John McDougall writes [1970 (c. 1912):59]: "Very carefully and minutely I went over my notes of yesterday [...]")

Much the same form of words is also found without the key noun phrase. In the following example, in fact, it occurs twice, first as an embedded question and then as a proclamation, with the verb inflected in the independent order:

> *êkwa êwak ôma, kâ-itamân, kâ-kakwêcimiyan,*
> *êkây wîhkâc ka-kî-pîkonahk awiyak,*
> *tâpwê! tâpwê!*
> *namôy ka-kî-pîkonam.* (6-5)
> 'Now that which I said, what you ask me about,
> that no one will ever be able to break it,
> it is true! it is true!
> no one will be able to break it.'

Even in the absence of the formula, the power to abrogate the treaty is declared to rest solely with the Cree side:

> *kiya piko, kê-pîkonamâsoyan, kitasotamâkowin.* (6-15)
> 'Only you yourself will be able to break the promises made to you.'

While various attenuated versions are cited throughout, the full form occurs no fewer than four times, all in the central body of treaty speeches.

It is astounding that this key term, which is evidently of the greatest weight in Cree historiography, has left no reflexion at all in the English records of Jackes, Morris or Erasmus.

Divine Authority

The various affirmatory formulae notwithstanding, it may not have seemed sufficient for a contract to be read out and signed without reference to divine authority and sanction.

Such appeals, ubiquitous in Anglo-Norman legal practice, are especially common in courtroom testimony, where the truth of a statement is affirmed by swearing on a bible. The rôle of the pipestem under roughly similar circumstances is sketched, as cursorily as that of the bible in the preceding remark, by Mandelbaum (1940). Each in its own culture, these sacramental objects offer an ultimate guarantee – public and sacred at once – of faithfulness.

They differ fundamentally, however, in the nature of their respective force. The bible as the repository of God's word and wrath is a symbol of divine retribution upon those who would mock it. The pipestem, by contrast, offers reassurance to all:

> [...], *êwak ôma kik-âcimômakan oskiciy,*
> *tânis ê-kî-is-âsotamâkoyahk wâpiski-wiyâs,* [...] (5-2)

'[...], this pipestem will tell the story
of the promises which the Whites had made to us, [...]'

Breaches which result in retribution are very much part of Cree morality; cf. the use of the standard term *pâstâhowin* in Whitecalf 1993:sec. 13 and the discussion of the more specialised James Bay Cree term *pâstâmowin* 'tale of requital for blasphemy' in Ellis 1989:19-20. In fact, *kâ-pimwêwêhahk* himself expresses concern lest he commit a breach of the natural order merely by misspeaking in his account of the pipestem:

> *"pitanê, êkâ kîkway pâstâhôtotamân," nititêyihtên mân* [...] (5-5)
> ' "I wish that I might not commit any sacrilege," I usually think [...]'

But there is no mention anywhere in this volume of sanctions to be visited upon those who would break a commitment made while holding the pipestem. The awesome quality of the pipestem seems to rest in itself.

Instead of threatening sanctions, in fact, the pipestem is spoken of with confidence as a source of support, a refuge:

> [...], *wîstawâw anik ê-wî-nâtâmostahkik êwako;* (5-3)
> '[...], and they too are going to turn to it [the pipestem] for help;'

It also constitutes the ultimate record of what is true:

> [...], *kitasotamâkowininaw kîkwây k-âspitonâmocik* – (5-3)
> '[...], what they [our grandfathers at the signing of the treaty] had relied upon as testimony of the promises that were made to us – '

kîkway piko k-âspitonâmot ayisiyiniw,
kitayânânaw kîkway k-âspitonâmoyahk kâ-nêhiyâwiyahk;
êwak ôma 'oskiciy' k-êsiyîhkâtêk,
êwako piko ka-kî-aspitonâmoyahk. (6-5)
'The people must have something to rely upon as testimony,
and we who are Crees do have something to rely upon as
testimony;
that which is called the pipestem,
that is all upon which we can rely as testimony.'

Indeed, as the above examples illustrate, the meaning of the stem *aspitonâmo–* reflects its complex morphological structure by including confirmation and refuge at once.

The pipestem is a "sacrosanct object," and Mandelbaum goes to some lengths to evoke "its peculiar potency" (1940:230-231, 259-260): "Very few men dare tamper with anything as highly charged with supernatural power as is the Sacred Pipestem bundle, [...]" (It may well be a reflexion of the "awe in which the stem was held" that the term *oskiciy* does not seem to occur in any of the texts published by Bloomfield.)

In the presence of the pipestem, above all, there could be neither quarrel nor hostility, and "when peace was to be made with a hostile tribe, the Pipestem Bearer led the way."

It is well within the scope of the doctrine outlined by Mandelbaum that the proceedings at Fort Carlton and Fort Pitt each began with "the dance of the 'pipe stem' " or "stem dance" (Morris 1876:183, 190), later grandiosely (but misleadingly) called "the national stem or pipe dance" (Morris 1880:179).

Jackes gives a much more detailed and reliable account of both events, describing "a large and gorgeously adorned pipe stem" at Carlton (1876:198) and reporting the use of four pipestems at Fort Pitt (1876:230). Like Morris, he recounts the stroking of the pipestem, "in token of good feeling and amity" (at Fort Pitt, 1876:230), adding that at Carlton Morris "stroked it several times," thereby "accepting the friendship of the tribe"

(1876:198). Morris's own understanding is confirmed by this passage (Jackes 1876:234) from his opening speech at Fort Pitt: "Now I have stroked the pipe with your brothers at Carlton as with you." Could this casual "stroking of the pipe" correspond to the sacramental *holding* of the stem related by *kâ-pimwêwêhahk*?

In his report from Fort Pitt, too, Jackes (1876:230) adds a valuable detail: "The stems, which were finely decorated, were placed with great solemnity on the table in front of the Governor [Morris], to be covered for the bearers with blue cloth."

At Fort Carlton, on the other hand, there seems to have been only a single pipestem. Jackes seems to have recognised that the bearer of the stem is a most important figure, as he even records his name (1876:198, 203, 215): *wâwikanihk-kâ-otâmahoht* 'the man you strike on the back' (otherwise known as 'Strike-Him-on-the-Back'; cf. Mandelbaum 1940:242) "of the River Indians."

kâ-pimwêwêhahk cursorily mentions the Sioux as having brought the pipestem at the heart of his account to Carlton (6-12; cf. the notes to chapter 6) with them. More significantly, he points out that the making of Treaty Six marks the first occasion for the pipestem to be used in formal dealings with the colonial power and, at the same time, the last public exercise of its sacramental faculty.

To the assembled Crees and all who are told about it, the sacramental act of holding the pipestem is the most powerful part of the proceedings:

> *kîspin kitâpwân, êwak ôma ka-~ kika-miciminên oskiciy; ê-tâpwêyan cî ôma k-ês-âsotamawiyâhk – êhâ, ahpô namôya?* (6-5)
>
> 'If you speak the truth, hold then this pipestem; do you speak the truth in this which you have promised us – Yes, or no?'

It is equated with swearing on the bible as the guarantee of an inviolable commitment:

[...], *êwak ôma nêhiyaw omasinahikan, kâ-tahkonahk awa, ê-naskotahk,* [...] (6-6)
'[...], this is the bible of the Cree which he held, swearing upon it in response, [...]'

In reviewing the force of the treaty on another occasion (chapter 5), *kâ-pimwêwêhahk* makes the equivalence fully explicit:

êkota kâ-kî-âpatahk anim ôskiciy,
êwako nêhiyawasinahikan kâ-kî-osîhtât, [...] (5-1)
'that was the time when the pipestem was used,
he was the one who made it into the Cree document of the treaty, [...]'

In repeating the point, he singles out the sacramental importance of holding the pipestem:

tânis ânima ê-pê-isi-kiskêyihtahk kêhtê-aya,
êwakw ânim êkwa, nêhiyawi-~ nêhiyawi-masinahikan,
kîstanaw ê-kî-êwakw-ânima-tahkonamôhiht awa,
tânêhki k-ôh-kî-tahkonamôhiht êwakw ânima, [...] (5-2)
'What the old people have known by tradition,
now that Cree document is for us, too:
that he was made to hold this one [the pipestem],
and why he was made to hold it, [...]'

Neither of the government's official record-keepers makes even the least reference to the declarative rôle of the pipestem, nor to any closing rite other than the affixing of marks in ink. (While it is hardly surprising that the significance of the pipestem would have escaped the notice of Morris and Jackes, it is remarkable that it also rates no mention in the recollections of Peter Erasmus.)

From the perspective of the Crees, on the other hand, nothing could have been more awe-inspiring than this holiest of holies, the "tribal palladium" (as Mandelbaum 1940:259 calls it) of the Sacred Pipestem.

Notes

Most of the texts included in this volume were delivered at the Saskatchewan Indian Languages Institute in Saskatoon; chapters 5 and 8 were recorded in the course of a retreat held by the Saskatchewan Indian Cultural College at Thunderchild Reserve.

The Speaker's Names

The speaker's personal name, *kâ-pimwêwêhahk*, is perhaps best glossed as 'Goes-Along-Drumming'; a fuller rendition might be 'Heard-Going-Along-With-A-Drumming-Sound'.

The family name *kâ-nîpitêhtêw* (also spelt «Kahneepotaytayo», «Ka-ne-pe-ta-ta», «Canepotatoe», etc., and sometimes even anglicised as if read *can-o'-potato*) may be glossed as 'Walks-Abreast'. This is the personal name by which *kâ-pimwêwêhahk*'s father was known (cf. the notes to 1-8 and to chapter 6).

Text Presentation

The editorial conventions in general follow the practice of other recent text editions (Vandall and Douquette 1987, Bear et al. 1992, Whitecalf 1993). In preserving the variation between the full form of words and preverbs and their reduced variants (with word-final vowels elided), we specifically adopt the conventions of Minde 1997; cf. Wolfart 1992:32-27, 351-356. (In the syllabic printing, by contrast, all sandhi effects have been removed.)

The distinction between the text itself and the editorial apparatus needs to be maintained at all times. All queries and comments are marked by being enclosed in square brackets. The chapter and section numbers and the chapter titles printed as part of the English translation (and subsequently translated into Cree, for design reasons, to be printed in syllabics) are also editorial additions.

When the spoken text includes occasional words or brief stretches in English, these are printed *in italics*; the same rule applies to English proper names. (In the translation, conversely, proper names or technical terms which retain their original Cree form are also printed in italics.) Terms being cited or defined, including proper names, are enclosed in single quotation marks.

Fragmentary words are mainly due to the speaker interrupting himself while searching for the right word, or catching himself in a slip of the tongue. In normal speech, however, not all slips of the tongue are corrected, and audio-recordings in any language include sentences which an author might well rewrite in revising a written text for publication; such sentences have not been modified in this edition but left as originally spoken.

The manual and facial gestures which are part of most narrative events are documented only at a minimal level. Where their linguistic and pragmatic traces can be recovered in the text as recorded, they are identified by the standard notation [*gesture*] and, occasionally, some further detail.

Amongst other non-linguistic features, only those audible responses which can be subsumed under the category of laughter have been included. While the notation [*laughs*] refer to the speaker, [*laughter*] mark the response of the audience (but may, of course, also include the speaker).

In addition to the speaker himself, three others are identified as participants in the discourse: Freda Ahenakew [FA], Lizette Ahenakew [LA], and Angus Esperance [AE].

TYPOGRAPHICAL CONVENTIONS AND SPECIAL SYMBOLS

xxxx	[text in roman type] primary language (Cree in the text, English in the translation)
xxxx	[text in italic type] secondary language (English in the text, Cree in the translation)
"xxxx"	[double quotation marks] quoted speech
'xxxx'	[single quotation marks] [1] quoted speech (if embedded within quoted speech) [2] cited word
«xxxx»	[guillemets] quoted speech embedded within two outer layers of quoted speech
–	[long hyphen] syntactic or rhetorical break (usually sharper than those marked by comma or semicolon) within a sentence
( )	[parentheses] parenthetical insertion (usually spoken at lower pitch or volume)

-~-	[wave-hyphen within the word] fragmentary word, resumed
-~	[wave-hyphen at the end of the word] fragmentary word

—~ [long hyphen and wave-hyphen following the word]
fragmentary sentence

[a] [roman type enclosed in square brackets]
editorially supplied word-final vowel (elided under the rules of vowel combination and restored on the basis of vocalic, prosodic or syntactic evidence)

[*xxxx*] [italic type enclosed in square brackets]
editorial comment (including such standard comments as [*laughs*], [*gesture*], etc.)

[*sic*] ['indeed']
confirmation that the preceding word is correctly printed (usually in the case of an uncommon or otherwise remarkable form, e.g., minor idiosyncracies, dialect discrepancies, slips of the tongue)

[*sc.*] ['that is']
proposed emendation or completion of a fragment; explication or elaboration
(in the English translation, *i.e.* is used instead of the more technical *sc.*; it, in turn, is omitted where an editorial insertion, marked by square brackets, simply blends into an English sentence)

[*?sic*] ['really?']
caution that the identification of the preceding word remains in doubt

(Note that the glosses and translations given in the Commentary and Notes may be more literal than those found in the running translation of the texts.)

Notes to Chapter 1

[Counselling the Young / kakêskimâwasowin]

This lecture on a topic of perennial concern to Cree grandparents was recorded on 16 September 1988 (an alternative notation gives the year as 1987) at an Elders' Workshop, with direct reference throughout to the staff of the Saskatchewan Indian Languages Institute. It very much has the character of an opening lecture.

1-1 *ati môy tâpwêwakêyihtam* [sic]

While it is rare for the preverb *ati* to be found "floating" outside the verbal complex, such sentences show several distinct patterns. For example, the preverb may precede a conjunct verb with the subordinating preverb *ê*, as in *at*[*i*] *ê-kî-sâsâkihtiyâhk mâna.* 'And we could still go barefoot.' (GB 8-4 in Bear et al. 1992).

It may also follow the verbal complex, e.g., [...] *kâ-tâh-tahkâyâk ati.* '[...] when it begins to get cold.' (GB 5-6 in Bear et al. 1992; cf. Wolfart 1992:375); cf. also the note to 4-7 and, for traces of a similar pattern in a distant dialect of Cree, Ellis 1995, especially note 4 to text 52 and note 6 to text 53.

The present example, however, is remarkable for its parallelism, with both instances of *ati* – one within, the other outside the verbal complex – immediately following the clause-initial patient phrase *kahkiyaw kîkway* 'something, anything'.

1-2 kinisitawêyimâwâw, 'Freda' *isiyîhkâsow* 'you all know her, Freda is her name'

This formal introduction, by name, is echoed in 3-17. In the remainder of the chapter, all other references to members of the audience are by means of the demonstrative pronouns *awa* 'this one' or deictic phrases such as *aw ôta* 'this one here'; cf. also *nâha* 'that one yonder' (3-19), *k-âpit awa* 'the one who sits here' (5-1) and *êwakw âwa k-âpit* 'that one who sits here' (3-19).

A more formal style of reference employs one of the kin terms (which may of course be used in an extended or even metaphorical sense), e.g., *awa* [...] *nitihkwatim* 'this [...] my nephew [i.e., cross-nephew]' (4-9) or *awa nikosis, ôta* David 'this my nephew [i.e., parallel nephew], David here' (5-3).

Nor is this style of reference limited to kin terms proper; cf. *awa niwîcêwâkanis* 'my partner here', *awa ôtê kiwîcêwâkaninaw* 'our [inclusive] partner over there', or the comitative use of the first person exclusive verb form, e.g., *ôma ôtê kâ-itapiyâhk* 'when we [she and I] sit [as Elders] over there', in Sarah Whitecalf's lectures (1993:secs. 18, 16, 1).

1-4 *ka-pimohtâtamahk kikîsikâminaw* 'for us to live through our day'

The noun *kikîsikâminaw* illustrates a highly specialised use of possessive theme formation. Derived from the stem *kîsikâw–* NI 'day, daylight' by means of the thematic suffix *-im-* (cf. Wolfart 1973:sec. 3.21), the possessed theme *–kîsikâm–* has a meaning which goes well beyond the general attribution found, for example, in *okîsikâm kôhtâwînaw* 'Our Father's Day, Christmas Day' (6-6; for further examples see the note to 4-5).

In the present context, the possessed theme seems to emphasise the agentive (indeed, creative) nexus between the possessor and the day lived by him or her. With its semantic force recalling that of a *life lived* in English and countless instances of *figura etymologica* (now 'cognate object constructions') in other Indoeuropean languages (cf. the note to 2-4), the term might best be rendered with some formality as 'the days of one's life'.

The literary effect is heightened by collocation with the elevated and highly marked verb stem *pimohtât–* VTI 'pass through s.t. (e.g., the sun through its course; cf. 3-13), live through s.t., live s.t.', which takes the possessed noun as its patient (cf. also the note to 2-2).

Much the same phrase recurs a few paragraphs later, but with the possessed noun modified by a participle: [...], *ka-pimohtâtamahk ê-miywâsik kikîsikâminaw;* '[...] for us to live through our beautiful day;' (1-7).

The same construction is also attested with the demonstrative pronoun *ôma* (albeit with another verb stem): [...], *ka-pê-sâkêwêtotahk ôma kikîsikâminaw;* '[...] for him [the sun] to come and rise upon this our day;' (7-8).

1-5 *nôhtâwiy nikî-wîhtamâk* 'my father used to tell me about this'

The culturally salient fact that the speaker's father is no longer alive at the time of speaking is marked by the perfective preverb *kî*; both the verb and the nominal phrase are marked by *kî* in clauses such as *nikî-itik kâ-kî-oyôhtâwîyân* 'thus my late father had said to me' (1-5), with the participial literally denoting 'the one whom I used to have as father'.

This volume does not contain a single instance of a noun with the preterital suffix *-pan*; cf. *nicâhkosipan* 'my late sister-in-law', *nimosômipan* 'my late grandfather', *omosômipaniwâwa* 'their late grandfathers' (MF 4-1, 4-6, JF 3-9 in Bear et al. 1992; cf. also Wolfart 1992:373, 405-406).

1-5 *kâ-kiskisômit* [sic]

Cf. *kiskisom–* VTA with short *-o-* (e.g., FA, AL in Bear et al. 1992); both variants are recorded in Minde 1997.

1-5 *mâmaw-ôhtâwîmâw* 'All-Father'

Common throughout, this formal compound (which

echoes the usage of Emma Minde, e.g., 1997:sec. 9) is still much less frequent (by a factor of seven in this volume) than the metaphorical use of the kin term *kôhtâwînaw* 'our father; [*fig.*] Our Father'.

There is also a single instance of *kihc-ôkâwîmâw* 'Great Mother' (7-2) along with several of the kin term *kikâwînaw* 'our mother; [*fig.*] Our Mother'; note especially the explicit parataxis of the latter with the noun *askiy–* 'earth' (cf. Gill 1987), e.g., *kikâwînaw askiy awa* (3-6) 'this Our Mother the earth', which in this case may well have to be interpreted as animate.

The above terms, which give the appearance of neologisms in either form or function (and sometimes both), occur side by side with such seemingly archaic counterparts as *kôhkominaw* 'our grandmother' (e.g., 4-9). For a more general discussion of religious syncretism and theological nomenclature cf. Wolfart 1992:27-28, 31, 375-376; 1997.

1-6 *k-ôh-kiskisômit* [sic]

See the note to 1-5.

1-7 *êwakoyiw* [?sic]

Recording not clear; the whole phrase, including an unambiguous rendition of *êwakoyiw*, recurs later in the same sentence.

1-7 *ê-nanâskotahk* [sic]

sc. *ê-naskotahk*; cf. *naskot–* VTI 'respond to s.t.; swear upon s.t. in response' in contrast to *nanâskot–* VTI 'be grateful for s.t., give thanks for s.t.'

1-7 *ka-kî-kîkway-tôtênânaw* [sic]

The pronoun *kîkway* 'something, anything' is included within the verbal complex (cf. Wolfart 1973:sec. 6.52).

1-8 *ê-miskawak* [?sic]

Recording not clear; ?sc. *ê-misawak*.

1-8 *kistêsinaw wîsahkêcâhk* 'our elder brother Wisahketchahk'

The hierological implications of this reference are obscure; the same phrase is employed in 7-4.

1-8 *kâ-pimwêwêhahk* [man's name]

This name illustrates the use of a fully inflected conjunct verb, to be glossed literally as 'the one who goes along drumming'; cf. *pimwêwêh–* VTI.

In the alternative pattern, exemplified in the family name *kâ-nîpitêhtêw*, literally 'the one who walks abreast', the same preverb *kâ* appears with the stem exhibiting the inflectional suffix of the independent order; cf. *nîpitêhtê–* VAI. This construction is restricted to personal names.

While the grammatically marked pattern tends to be the preferred choice for personal names, both are documented, for instance, amongst the signatories to Treaty Six, e.g., *kâ-mîhyistowêsit*, *kâ-papâmahcâhkwêw* (cf. «Kah-mee-yis-too-way-sit», «Kah-pah-pah-mah-chahk-nay» [*sic*] for 'Beardy', 'Wandering Spirit' in Morris 1880:358, 357), and also amongst the men and women of Sweet Grass reserve whose texts Leonard Bloomfield recorded in 1925, e.g., *kâ-wîhkaskosahk*, literally 'the one who burns it [sweet-grass] as incense', *kâ-kîsikâw-pîhtokêw*, conventionally rendered as 'Coming-Day'.

Notes to Chapter 2

[Spiritual Help / kîkway ka-âpacihikoyêk]

In outlining the consolations of theology, this sermon (which was recorded on 1 August 1989) also expounds a variety of moral imperatives.

2-1 *iyôtin* [sic]

Both instances exhibit primary stress on the antepenult; cf. the disyllabic variant *yôtin* (7-8) with final stress.

In a topical allusion to the *realia* of prairie life, the shift back and forth between *iyôtin–* NI 'wind, high wind, tornado' and the personified spirit of the wind, *iyôtin–* NA 'Wind, Tornado', adds a dramatic element.

2-2 *k-ôhpahpahtênamân*

sc. *k[â]-[o]hpahpahtênamân.*

2-2 *nanâskomihk kôhtâwînaw, ê-miyikoyêk kîsikâw ita ka-pimohtâtamêk* 'do give thanks to Our Father that he has granted you another day to live through'

This is the simplest version of a formulaic exhortation which appears in complex variations through this volume.

The verb *pimohtât–* VTI (cf. the note to 1-4) usually appears in a purposive clause with the preverbs *ka*, *ta* or *kê* and introduced by the particle *ita* 'therein; wherein'; but it may also occur without *ita*, e.g., [...], *êwakw ânima kê-pimohtâtamahk kîsikâw ê-miywâsik.* '[...], for us to live through that beautiful day.' (5-5).

It is almost always construed with a full patient noun phrase, either the possessed theme *kikîsikâminaw* 'the day of our life' or simply *kîsikâw* 'a day', or also with the particle *pêyak-kîsikâw*, literally 'one day's worth'; e.g., [...] *ê-miyikoyahk pêyak-kîsikâw ka-pimohtâtamahk;* '[...] that he has granted us to live through another day;' (3-23). (In an alternative reading of such passages, *pêyak* might be taken as a free-standing numeral, and *kîsikâw* as the noun.)

Both the possessed theme *–kîsikâm–* and the simple noun *kîsikâw–* may appear freely with the participial phrase *ê-miywâsik* 'being beautiful'. In all cases where the context includes a proximate third person, the verb might have been expected to show obviative inflection, as in the following instance: [...], *wîst ê-miywâsiniyik kîkway ê-kî-pêtât,* [...] '[...], with her, too, having brought along something valuable, [...]' (6-10).

In this volume, however, the vast majority of cases shows the participial phrase inflected for the proximate even where the absence of prosodic boundaries, the presence of a proximate noun phrase – usually *kôhtâwînaw* 'Our Father' – or both would lead one to expect the obviative, e.g., [...], *ka-kî-nanâskomot, ê-miywâsik kîsikâw ita ê-miyiht ta-pimohtâtahk;* '[...], they [literally 'the young person'] should be giving thanks that it has been granted to them [singular] to live through a beautiful day;' (4-7); [...] *ê-nanâskomak kôhtâwînaw, ê-miywâsik kîsikâw ita ka-pimohtahakik nitawâsimisak.* '[...] I give thanks to Our Father that he might guide my children through a beautiful day.' (4-9); *it[a] ê-pimohtâtahk kîsikâw ê-miywâsik,* [...] 'wherein he passes through the beautiful day, [...]' (7-8).

2-3 *k-ês-âyimihât* [sic]
cf. *ayamihâ–* passim.

2-4 *ayimihâwin* [sic], *môniyâw-âyimihâwin* [sic]
cf. *ayamihâwin–* passim.

2-4 *k-ôh-kitâpamikowisin*
sc. *k[a]-ôh-kitâpamikowisin.*

2-4 *ê-askîwiskahk askiy* 'populating the earth'

The homiletic tenor of this text is expressed in a number of contexts where *askiy–* NI 'earth, land' is construed as the patient of a highly transitive VTI stem. e.g., *ê-nihtâwikîstamahk askiy* 'as we people the earth' (2-2), *kâ-sâkikihtât ôm âskiy* 'who makes this earth grow forth' (2-2).

With the stem *askîwisk–* VTI, the above clause stands out as a classical instance of the 'cognate object construction' (cf. English *sing a song*) known in rhetoric as *figura etymologica.*

2-4 *k-ôh-manâcihtâhk*

sc. *k[a]-ôh-manâcihtâhk.*

2-5 *ôtê, nâway ahêw kêhtê-aya, nôtikwêwa ôtê ahêw* 'they have put the old people over there in the background, they have put the old women over there'

The common pattern of a general term referring to males primarily (or even exclusively) often becomes manifest only when it is followed, in the form of an afterthought, by a specific mention of women; another typical example omits the general term altogether and then highlights the inclusion of women, e.g., *pêyakwan iskwêw* 'and the same with respect to women' (4-2). In an especially emphatic example, the noun *nôtikwêw* 'old woman' is in turn followed by two instances of *wista* 'she, too': [...], *k-êhtakot êkota kêhtê-âya, ahpô nôtikwêw, wîst* [...], [...] *wîst ôtâcimowin,* [...] '[...], that there should be an old person, or an old woman, with her, too, [...], [...] her own story, [...]' (6-10); cf. also the similar passage in 7-1.

Of course the texts also contain many examples of conventionally balanced pairs, e.g., [...] *osk-âya, oskinîkiskwêw, oskinîkiw;* '[...] young people, young women and young men;' (1-2), and also more elaborate instances of parallelism, e.g., [...], *kisêyiniwa ka-nâtâmototawêw, nôtikwêwa ka-nâtâmototawêw.* '[...], they will turn to the old men, they will turn to the old women.' (4-8).

While chiastic structures are rare in this volume, the initial example with its reversal of word order is followed, in the same paragraph, by another instance: *kiyâm pikoyikohk ê-kitimâkisit kisêyiniw, nôtikwêsiw ê-kitimâkisit,* [...] 'No matter how poor an old man may be, how poor an old woman may be, [...]' (2-5).

2-5 *mêht-~* [sic] *mêstohtêtwâwi*

Correction of *mêht-* to *mêst-*; cf. Wolfart 1978:233, 1984:75.

2-6 *k-âyimôhtot*

sc. *k[â]-âyimôhtot.*

Notes to Chapter 3

[Leaving a Legacy / nakatamawâhkan]

This discourse about the duties of those who have been entrusted with understanding and a long life was recorded on 8 September 1988, preceding a pipe ceremony. It ranges over a number of ritual subjects, notably cloth offerings and the rattle, and culminates in the visionary experience of the speaker's father returning from the dead.

3-6 *k-ôhpikihitoyahk*

sc. *k[a]-[o]hpikihitoyahk.*

3-8 *capasis kâ-kitocik* 'with the thunder low to the ground'

The stem *kito–*, which is usually reduplicated when referring to thunder, and nominalised, appears here as a plain verb, presumably with reference to an individual thunderclap.

3-9 *môy âhpô awiyak êtok ôh-pê-nâkatôhkêw êwako* 'I am sure no one has ever even paid attention to that'

It is relatively rare for the perfective preverb *ôh* to be found in initial position.

3-10 *k-êsiyîhkâtât*

sc. *k[â]-[i]siyîhkâtât.*

3-10 *k-êkwaskwahk* [sic]

In both instances the sandhi vowel *-ê-*, which would normally represent the vowel of the preverb *kâ* followed by a stem beginning in *-i-*, is here interpreted as reflecting the stem in the form *îkwaskwan–* (cf. *yîkwaskwan–* and the discussion in Wolfart 1992:377); an alternative reading, *k-êyîkwaskwahk* (based on a presumed variant shape of the stem, *iyîkwaskwan–*), is not supported by the syllable and stress patterns. Cf. also the note to 8-2.

3-10 *opacaskahasîs* [name of a certain bird]

Despite the apparent transparency of this bird-name, the etymology suggested in the text remains opaque. Nor has the identity of the bird been established, even though Freda Ahenakew queried a number of elderly Cree speakers about this term.

The same interpretation of the bird's flight pattern is implied, on the other hand, by the gloss 'Weather Bird' which the modern editor provides (on the authority, apparently, of Stan Cuthand) for the personal name «Pacaskahas» (presumably *opacaskahasis* or *opacaskahasîs*), repeatedly recorded (in syllabics) by Robert Terrill Rundle in his journals for 1845-48 (1977:173 et passim).

The term appears to be an agent noun derived from the diminutive *pacaskahasi–* of a VTI stem *pataskah–* (identified and documented by D.H. Pentland, p.c.); in Atikamikw, Béland (1978) glosses it as 'to stick, spear, prick, sting it' but the corresponding evidence in Ojibwe (cited from Nichols and Nyholm 1995) illustrates a wider semantic range: besides *badaka'igan–* NI 'fork', *badakin–* VTA 'stick s.o. in, plant s.o. in', etc., a term such as *badakizo–* VAI 'stand up from a surface, be planted in' emphasises the vertical dimension against a flat ground. The diminutive may reflect the small size of the bird; whether the verb stem refers to the sharp angle of its descent or the appearance of piercing the earth (or, of course, both at once) has to remain open.

The behaviour of the bird as represented in the text is compatible, as Pentland suggests, with that of the chimney swift, described by Godfrey (1966:228) as "foraging in the air, often at considerable heights in fair weather but tending to fly lower during threatening or rainy weather" and with its voice "a far-carrying, sharp, staccato;" and, again, "in cloudy weather they fly low."

3-13 *pêtwêwêhtamawâhkan ôkisêwâtisiwin* [sic] *ayisiyiniw*

The verb ending *-âhkan* specifies a proximate patient, and the stem itself (*pêtwêwêhtamaw–* VTA 'come audibly bringing (it/him) for s.o.') as well as the pragmatic context identify the noun *ayisiyiniw* as the primary object; thus, the possessor of the secondary object might have been expected to be inflected for an obviative possessor, *okisêwâtisiwiniyiw*. Note also the unexplained lengthening of the personal prefix *o-*.

3-13 *ka-mîtâkwêwiyan* [?sic]

Neither the recording nor the form are clear; cf. the derived stem found in the standard translation of the Lord's Prayer, *mîtâkwênamawinân nimacihtawininâna* 'and forgive us our trespasses', literally 'ward them off for us'.

3-14 *White Elk Hills* [?sic]

Recording not clear; the topographic reference has not been established either for the Cree place-name *wâwâskêsiwacîs* or its English counterpart.

The locale appears to be southeast of Onion Lake, where Smith Atimoyoo (p.c.) has identified *anim ôcênâs* 'that little town' as Paradise Hill (situated on Glenbogie Creek, just north of the North Saskatchewan River, i.e., on the road from Turtleford to Onion Lake).

3-15 *ê-asawâpi-~*

sc. *ê-asawâpicik* 'as they were lying in wait'.

3-15 *oskayisiyiniw* [sic]

In contrast to the more common pattern, e.g., *kîc-âyisiyiniw* 'your fellow-person' (in the following sentence) or *osk-âya* 'young person' (3-13 et passim), the short *-a-* shows that this is not a compound but a unit stem; cf. the note to 5-1.

3-17 *namwâ* [sic]

cf. *namwâc* (e.g., FA; RL in Bear et al. 1992); both variants are recorded for JF in Bear et al. 1992.

3-17 *kê-kakwâtakihtâw* [sic]

?sc. *kê-kakwâtakihtât*; the construction with the independent order ending is uncommon.

3-18 *kisêyinîwi-pîkiskwêwin* 'old men's saying'

This compound recurs at the end of 7-5; the corresponding possessive construction, *kisêyiniwak opîkiskwêwiniwâw* 'the old men's words' (4-13) is remarkable for showing the possessor in the plural and the possessed in the generic singular. For another instance of compound and possessive phrase occurring side by side cf. the note to 5-1.

3-19 *êkw îyikohk* [?sic]

Recording not clear; ?sc. *êkoyikohk*.

3-20 *maskihkiwâpoy* [sic]

cf. *maskihkîwâpoy–* (e.g., FA; GB, MW in Bear et al. 1992).

3-23 *kê-ohpâskonahk* [sic]

sc. *kê-ohpâskonak* 'I will raise it [the pipe]', reflecting the stem *ohpâskon–* VTA 'raise s.o. (e.g., pipe)'; but cf. also the parallel stem *ohpâskon–* VTI 'raise s.t. (e.g., pipestem)', which does not, however, occur elsewhere in this volume.

Notes to Chapter 4

[Leading Our Children Astray / kiyânaw anima ê-wanisimâyahk]

Recorded on 6 May 1987, introducing the pipe ceremony at the inauguration of the Saskatchewan Indian Languages Institute.

4-2 *êwakw ânima k-ôh-ispayik ohci* [sic].

The postverbal position of *ohci* and the discontinuous status of the phrase *êwakw ânim ôhci* is not uncommon; but cf. also *êwakw ânim ôhci k-ôh-itwêyân,* [...] 'that is why I say, [...]' (4-3).

4-3 *k-ânisîhtât*

sc. *k[â]-ânisîhtât.*

4-3 *k-ôh-sâkikihk,* [...] *k-ôh-nisitohtahk*

sc. *k[â]-ôh-sâkikihk, k[a]-ôh-nisitohtahk.*

4-4 *k-âyâyahk*

sc. *k[â]-[a]yâyahk.*

4-5 *k-ôtisâpahtamahk*

sc. *k[a]-[o]tisâpahtamahk.*

4-5 *k-ôtisâpahtamahk kôhtâwînaw, okîsikâm* 'that we might live to see Christmas Day'

Much the same phrase, with the two nouns to be translated literally as 'Our Father's Day', recurs three times, the first expanding and, presumably, elaborating upon the compound *manitowi-kîsikâw–* NI 'Christmas Day'.

The other two instances follow in rapid succession: *okîsikâm kôhtâwînaw ê-otisâpahtamahk* (4-6), *okîsikâm ê-otisâpahtamahk, kôhtâwînaw* 'that we have lived to see

Christmas Day' (4-7). Irrespective of the variation in word order, two of the three cases show a prosodic break within the possessive phrase.

Context aside, the formation and syntax of the verb are far from neologistic; cf. *namwâc* [...] *nôhci-otisâpahtên* 'I am not old enough to have seen it' (JF 3-8 in Bear et al. 1992) and also the parallel stem *otisâpam–* VTA 'have lived long enough to have seen s.o.' (PO in Wolfart 1982). For other instances of the possessed theme *–kîsikâm–* see the note to 1-4.

4-6 *nêhiyawi-wîhtamawâkan* 'Cree pronouncement'

While this is not the only patient noun derived from a benefactive stem to occur in these texts (cf. *kiskinohamawâkan–* NA 'student', literally 'one to whom it is being taught'), it is noteworthy both semantically and syntactically. In this case it is not the animate recipient which is at the centre of the nominalisation but the inanimate subject matter which is being declared. Correspondingly, the noun is inanimate, as demonstrated by the agreement with the pronominal phrase *êwakw ânima*.

Patient nouns in *-âkan* are commonly animate and derived from highly transitive stems (cf. Wolfart 1980); besides dependent kin terms such as *–wîkimâkan–* NDA 'spouse', nouns based on causative stems, e.g., *atoskêhâkan–* NA 'employee' or *kisêyinîw-ôhpikihâkan–* NA 'old man's raisling' are especially transparent (but cf. also such more opaque instances as *nistamêmâkan–* NA 'the first one, the original one' in 7-2).

4-7 *santakilâwsa* [sic]

The use of *-l-* marks this as a recent loan (cf. *nâpwên* 'frying pan', borrowed from the French noun phrase *la* *poêle*, etc.), and the stress pattern, with primary stress on the epenthetic *-i-*, suggests that no short vowels have been elided between *-n-* and *-t-* and between *-w-* and *-s-*.

4-7 *ôtê ati nîkân* 'there in the future'

Although the distinction between the "floating" preverb *ati* (cf. the note to 1-2) and a particle phrase like *ati nîkân* 'in the future' may not always be clearcut, the latter appears to recur as a (lexicalised) phrase, either simply in the form found here (and as also used by GB in Bear et al. 1992) or in more complex particle phrases such as *mwêstas ati ôtê nîkân* 'later there in the future' or *mwêstas at[i] ôtê* 'later in what lies ahead' (both GB in Bear et al. 1992).

4-9 *kîspin êkâ* [...] *kî-pakitinikowisit* 'if she had not been put down [...] by the powers'

Simple conjunct used in the prodosis of an irrealis conditional (cf. Wolfart 1973:sec. 5.32).

4-9 *kê-nîkâniwik* [sic]

cf. *nîkânîwi-* VII (e.g., FA; Vandall and Douquette 1987).

4-9 *ka-kakwê-êkotê-itohtahâyahk* [sic]

The locative deictic *êkotê* 'over there', which serves as the antecedent of the relative root *it-*, is included between the last preverb and the stem (cf. Wolfart 1973:sec. 6.52).

4-9 *êwakw âwa ka-wanisimiht, awâsisak* [sic].

The plural noun phrase *awâsisak* is added in the form of an afterthought to elaborate the singular pronoun phrase *êwakw âwa*, which shows agreement with the verb form.

4-10 *kî-cimatâw môhkomân* 'he planted a knife upright in the ground'

The formal counselling protocol, as defined by a knife

planted in the earth, is reported in fuller detail (including the verbal form of the ritual challenge) in the concluding section of Whitecalf 1993.

Sarah Whitecalf specifically mentions that this ritual admonition was administered to young men; this limitation is omitted in the current passage with its autobiographical perspective.

4-11 *ê-kisêwâtisit, ê-kanawêyimikoyahk êwako ê-owîcêwâkaniyahk* [?sic];

Recording not clear; the pragmatic context might suggest an alternative reading with a third-person agent, *ê-owîcêwâkanit* 'he has (us as) a companion' rather than 'we have (him as) a companion'.

Notes to Chapter 5

[The Testimony of the Pipestem / kika-âcimômakan oskiciy]

As a commentary on the key issues of contractual validity, this text serves as a welcome introduction to the documentary account of chapter 6. Recorded on 26 April 1989, following the recording of chapter 8.

5-1 *nipiy kâ-pitihkwêk* [place-name]

See the note to 6-3.

5-1 *nêhiyawasinahikan* 'Cree bible'

This is one of three variants of a term to be glossed literally as 'Cree book'; the other two are *nêhiyawi-masinahikan* in 5-2 and *nêhiyaw omasinahikan* in 6-6.

The variant used here is a unit stem (cf. Wolfart 1973:sec. 6.5), with *-asinahikan-* marked as the non-initial alternant by the absence of the morpheme-initial *-m-*; cf. also *oskayisiyiniw* and the note to 3-15.

In the corresponding compound stem, written with a hyphen, the stem is *masinahikan–* in its full, initial form; it is preceded by a prenoun particle in *-i-* but without the lengthening of the penultimate vowel which is heard, for example, in *kisêyinîwi-pîkiskwêwin* (3-18) or, in the context before a consonant-initial stem, the vowel sandhi which is obvious when the stem itself begins in a vowel: *kisêyinîw-ôhpikihâkan* (4-2), *nêhiyaw-âyisiyiniw* (6-8).

The third variant is a possessive phrase.

5-1 *cascakiskwês* [man's name]

See the note to 6-2.

5-2 *kâ-nâcikâpawistahk* [sic]

cf. *nâcikâpawîst-* VTI (e.g., FA); cf. also *nihtâwikîst-* VTI in 2-3, 6-3.

5-2 *k-âti-kiskinowâsohtahk*

sc. *k[a]-[a]ti-kiskinowâsohtahk.*

5-3 *k-êsi-wîkihk*

sc. *k[a]-[i]si-wîkihk.*

5-3 *ocihcipayiki* [sic]

?sc. *ocihcipayiyiki*; the presence of a third-person verb in the main clause might lead one to expect an obviative form.

5-3 *kâ-nîkânistahkik* [sic]

cf. *kâ-nîkânîstamêk* in 3-17; cf. also *nîkânîst-* VTI (e.g., FA).

Notes to Chapter 6

[The Pipestem and the Making of Treaty Six / kîkway ka-aspitonâmoyahk]

This text with its elaborate repetitions and the equally ornate variations exhibited by these repetitions constitutes a rare and especially valuable example of the indigenous record of the treaty proceedings. It was recorded on 2 May 1989.

The Anglo-Canadian view of the occasion was published within four years of the events (in Morris 1880).

With respect to the site where the speeches here reported were made, the text is contradictory. The topographical reference of *nipiy kâ-pitihkwêk* remains to be identified, but the evidence of the deictics discussed in the note to 6-3 and the summary mention of *pêhonânihk* in 6-12 seem to favour Carlton, as does the fact that Jackes (1876:198) reports a single bearer of the pipestem for Carlton (and even identifies him by name). Fort Pitt, on the other hand, appears to be indicated by the presence of *cascakiskwês*. In view of the evidence here assembled, then, it seems likely that, as in so many English accounts, Treaty Six is in fact treated as a unit, with the successive signings at and near Fort Carlton (on 23 and 28 August) and Fort Pitt (on 9 September) effectively conflated into one.

The text also offers a hint of the relative chronology of the exchange reported here. The pessimistic predictions of the old man related in 6-4 and 6-5 indicate that the formal attempt to forestall breach of contract fell between Morris's initial presentation of the treaty and the signing. Unless the promises cited in 6-5 were based on reports received at Fort Pitt of the proceedings at Fort Carlton, this passage suggests that the events reported here took place after the opening speeches of 7 September (Jackes 1876:230-235) and before the speeches by Morris, *kihiwin*, *wîhkasko-kisêyin* and Morris again which (according to Jackes 1876:235-238) preceded the signing on

9 September. Nor can we exclude the possibility that they followed the signing and were part of the subsequent speeches by six other chiefs, including «Tus-tuk-ee-skuais», related by Jackes (1876:238-239), or indeed the complex further exchanges on the occasion of the farewell speeches of 13 September (Jackes 1876: 239-242).

6-1 *nikî-wîhtamâkoh* 'he had been telling me about it'

While the perfective preverb *kî* indicates that the agent of the verb is no longer alive at the time of speaking, the use of the h-preterite (not otherwise found in this volume) emphasises the durative or repetitive aspect.

6-1 *nôhcâwîs* 'my father's brother'

While the term *nimosôminân* 'our grandfather' in this chapter (6-2) and in chapter 5 (5-1) serves both as a kin term and as the general honorific for all old men, *nôhcâwîs* is restricted to use as a kin term, specifying a brother of the speaker's father. It is not clear from the text whether the form *omosôma* 'his grandfather' at the end of the paragraph is used as a kin term or general honorific, nor whether or not it refers to *cascakiskwês*.

kâ-pimwêwêhahk's father, whose Christian name was Joseph, is usually referred to exclusively as *kâ-nîpitêhtêw*. A ceremonial leader whose importance as early as 1885 is evident in the eye-witness account of Cameron 1926 (especially chapters 16 and 29, the latter including a photograph taken in 1925), he is described as a "nephew" of 'Little Poplar'. His mother was a daughter of *apiscaskos* or 'Little Bear' (Chief 1985). He also appears in the reminiscences of Joe Dion's mother, who had arrived at Frog Lake shortly after the climactic events of 1885, while "buildings were still burning" and "a big dance was going on" (Dion 1976:95). She particularly recalls "a young man called *Kanipitetew* wearing the long cloak which is commonly used by the priests at evening vespers."

6-2 *cascakiskwês* [man's name]

Cited by name both here and at the beginning of chapter 5, *cascakiskwês* is presumably identical to the «Chaschakiskways» 'Head-Held-Back' who was chief at Frog Lake in 1885 (Edward Ahenakew 1976 [1951]:357), a "Bush Indian" shortly afterwards succeeded by his son *onîpawîhêw* 'Makes-Him-Stand', by whose name the band is often identified in 19th-century records.

In a consistently garbled spelling, «Tus-tusk-ee-skwais», his name appears twice on the list of signatories to Treaty Six at Fort Pitt (Morris 1880:358-359), and Jackes (1876:238) also mentions him – characteristically in a more accurate rendition, «Tus-tuk-ee-skuais» – as one of those who spoke after the signing of the treaty on 9 September 1876.

6-3 *nipiy kâ-pitihkwêk* [place-name]

It appears from the text in chapters 5 and 6 that *nipiy kâ-pitihkwêk* (which may literally be rendered as 'where the water makes a thudding sound', typically that of rushing waters) is situated in the proximity of Fort Carlton, i.e., on or near the North Saskatchewan River, and this interpretation seems consistent with the reports of Morris 1876, 1880 and Jackes 1876. (All other arguments aside, *kâ-pimwêwêhahk* uses the proximal deictic phrase *êkota ôta* 'at that place here' (6-3) when speaking at Saskatoon, i.e., not far from Carlton, but its distal counterpart *êkotê* 'over there' (5-1) when speaking at a place much closer to Fort Pitt than Saskatoon or Carlton.)

Unfortunately, no occasion was found to ask the narrator himself to clarify this point, and although Freda

Ahenakew subsequently questioned a number of elderly Cree speakers who might have been expected to be familiar with the name, the exact location could not be ascertained.

A search of the records written in English has also been unrewarding. Deanna Christensen and David Meyer (p.c.) have suggested that this text refers not to the primary signings of Treaty Six (at and near Fort Carlton on 23 and 28 August 1876 and at Fort Pitt on 9 September 1876) but to a later adhesion. This suggestion depends on the identification (which they credit to Barry Ahenakew) of *nipiy kâ-pitihkwêk* as 'Sounding Lake' (in east-central Alberta, southwest of Macklin, Saskatchewan). The hypothesis of a secondary signing, however, would conflict not only with the explicit reference to *pêhonânihk* 'at Carlton' (6-12), which may be a minor matter, but also with the presence of *cascakiskwês*, who is listed among the signatories (Morris 1880:358-359) and the speakers (Jackes 1876:238) at Fort Pitt on 9 September 1876.

6-4 *êwak ôma kî-atoskâtamihk* 'if one had worked on this'

The prodosis of an irrealis conditional exhibits the simple conjunct (cf. pages 153-155 in the Commentary and also Wolfart 1973:sec. 5.32). The perfective preverb *kî* indicates a past that need not be temporally remote but is irretrievably gone.

6-7 *askiy-~ askiy*

sc. *askiy[a]*, with primary stress on the first vowel, identifying it as the antepenult and implying the plural ending *-a*; thus, correction of *áskiy[a]* to *askíy*.

6-10 *k-êhtakot*

sc. *k[a]-[i]htakot.*

6-12 *pêhonânihk* [place-name]

This is the standard term for Fort Carlton in contemporary Cree usage (e.g., Vandall and Douquette 1987:92-93); literally 'at the waiting place', the term may originally have referred more narrowly to the point on the North Saskatchewan River below which Carlton House was built and which is known in the fur-trade records as *La Montée* or *The Crossing Place* (cf. Johnston 1967:xxx, 10*n*; Henry 1897.2:490-491).

The same place-name, it appears, has also been applied (whether successively or not – perhaps even inclusively?) to one of the locales at or near Fort à la Corne, one of the major "rendezvous centres" identified by Meyer and Thistle (1995), where «Payoenan» (Henry 1897.2:483*n*; modern *Peonan*) Creek flows into the Saskatchewan River (and further to a peninsula in Lake Manitoba). The name *Carlton House*, too, had been used for a post in this location (by James Bird in 1795-96; cf. Johnston 1967:9*n*, 53*n*) before being transferred to the more strategic site upriver.

Notes to Chapter 7

[The Meaning of Rituals / kisêyinîwi-pîkiskwêwin]

In response to a series of rhetorical questions, this text (recorded on 2 May 1989, immediately following the recording of chapter 6) surveys a wide range of ritual topics: tobacco and sweetgrass, fasting and the sweat-lodge, proper conduct in the presence of the pipe and the pointing of the pipestem, the rôle of Servers, the braids of old women and the saliva of pubescent girls.

7-1 *tânis âw ê-itakisot awa cistêmâw* 'what is the rôle of the tobacco'

Many of the divisions of this text are headed by formal questions. The initial heading comes in two parallel parts, reflecting the gender difference between *cistêmâw–* NA 'tobacco' and *wêpinâson–* NI 'cloth' and the corresponding distinction between the verb stems *itakiso–* VAI and *itakihtê–* VII 'be counted thus, be held in such esteem'.

The second heading (7-2) also shows a parallel structure, with slight variation in the demonstrative pronouns and distinct interrogatives and verbs. Later sections are introduced by such direct questions as *kîkwây an[a] ôskâpêwis?* 'what is that Server?' (7-10).

7-2 *awâska-mâmitonêyihcikan* [?sic]

Recording and analysis not clear; the structure of the putative prenoun has not been established.

7-2 *ôma kiwîhkaskom* 'this your sweetgrass'

The interplay between the plain stem *wîhkaskw–* and the possessed theme formed by means of the suffix *-im-* echoes that of *kîsikâw–* and *–kîsikâm–*; cf. the notes to 1-4 and 4-5.

7-2 *nistamêmâkanak* 'the original ones'

See the note to 4-6.

7-3 *ê-nitawi-pimâcisiwin-nâtahk* [sic]

The noun *pimâcisiwin* 'life' is included within the verbal complex, immediately preceding the stem (cf. Wolfart 1973:sec. 6.52).

7-9 *pîsim aw êtohtêt* [sic]

The prosodic pattern unambiguously indicates initial change; constrast *ê-itohtêt.*

In view of the elevated register of these texts, it is remarkable that instances of initial change directly affecting the stem are relatively rare; but note *kêtâsômikot* (1-2), cf. *kitâsôm–* VTA; *tiyêpwâtikawiyâni* (2-5), cf. *têpwât–* VTA; *tiyôtamahk* (4-15), cf. *tôt–* VTI.

7-10 [dialogue]

The light banter of this brief interlude is typical of a more general pattern of sacred discourse being tempered by ludic profanity; cf. also sections 7-12, 7-16 and the whole of chapter 8.

7-11 *kâ-nistwapihkâtaman* 'when she braids it in three strands'

This section resumes the discussion of section 7-2 and the analogy between braiding sweetgrass and braiding women's hair, and concludes with a causal claim: [...], *êwakw ânim ôhci k-ôh-nistwapihkâtahk ôhi.* '[...], that is why she braids it in three strands.'

The reference to the number three is coincidental in other passages, e.g., *mwêhci nistwâw isi-wêpinikawiyani,* [...] *mwêhci nêwâw isi-wêpinikawiyani –* 'Exactly the third time you are shaken, [...] Exactly the fourth time you are shaken –' (3-13), where it is simply part of a count from one to four. There are, however, also some passages, e.g., *nistinwa ôhi iskwâhtêma* 'There are three doors' (3-18), which give every sign of religious syncretism.

7-12 *kimîstow-~*

sc. *kimîstowâna* 'your [singular] beards'. Under the guise of casual joking, these remarks are presumably intended to be censorious.

7-13 *ita ê-kanawêyimiht oskinîkiskwêw* 'where the young girl was kept'

This section deals with puberty rites and the healing power possessed by the saliva of girls at menarche; there is no mention of this complex in Mandelbaum's account (1940) of Plains Cree life cycles.

7-15 *ê-nôhtê-tâpowêyân* [sic]

cf. *ê-nôhtê-tâpwêyân* 'I want it to come true, I want it to be fulfilled' (5-4) and the more ordinary phrase *ê-tâpwêyan cî ôma* 'do you speak the truth in this' (6-5). The prosodic difference between the two stems *tâpowê-* VAI 'recite one's prayers correctly' and *tâpwê-* VAI 'speak true' is subtle but distinctive. The stems *kîsowât-* VTI 'complete one's words, complete one's prayers' and *patowât-* VTI 'misspeak s.t.' reflect the same morpheme *-owê-*.

7-16 [story]

This anecdote is a classical instance of a sacred discourse abruptly lapsing into profanity; cf. also sections 7-10, 7-12 and the whole of chapter 8.

Notes to Chapter 8

[Profaning the Sacred / ma-môhcw-âtayôhkêwin]

This briefest of texts, recorded on 26 April 1989 shortly before the recording of chapter 5, constitutes a defining illustration of the proximity of the sacred and the profane. Without even exploring its specific import, we readily recognise it as part of a more general pattern of carnivalistic reversals, described most forcefully in recent years for the ritual blasphemies of Christian Europe in the late middle ages and the early modern period; cf., for example, Le Roy Ladurie 1979.

8-1 *nimosôm mahihkanis* 'my grandfather *mahihkanis*'

It cannot be established on the basis of the text whether 'my grandfather *mahihkanis*' (to be glossed 'Little-Wolf') and the *nôhcâwîs 'ispâhtêhikan' kâ-kî-itiht* 'my father's brother, called *ispâhtêhikan*' (presumably to be glossed 'Pole-to-Hold-up-Tentflap') are real kinsmen with real names or merely fictitious individuals with courtesy kin terms.

8-2 *nôhcâwîs 'ispâhtêhikan' kâ-kî-itiht* 'my father's brother, *ispâhtêhikan* he used to be called'

cf. the note to 8-1; this name, presumably to be glossed 'Pole-to-Hold-up-Tentflap', is based on an inanimate noun.

8-2 *ê-îpâcihtâyit* [sic]

cf. such common variants of this root as *yî-*, *iyî-* and *wî-*; cf. also the discussion in Wolfart 1992:377 and the note to 3-10.

8-3 *ê-apistahk* [sic]

cf. *apîst–* VTI (e.g., FA; RL in Bear 1992).

8-4 *âpahkwâna* [sic]

sc. *apahkwâna*, literally 'roof covering, tent covers'.

8-5 *k-ôtiskiyan* [sic]

cf. *k-ôciskiyan* [sic] in the following sentence; the form with *-t-* may constitute a hypercorrection.

8-5 *kitiskotêmiwâw* 'your [plural] fire'

The pragmatic reference appears to be to the opening at the centre of the lodge, where the smoke escapes, rather than to the fire itself.

For the use of the possessive suffix *-im-*, cf. *kikîsikâminaw*, *kiwîhkaskom* and the notes to 1-4 and 7-2.

8-6 *takahk-âtayôhkêwin* 'a fine sacred story'

The mocking stance assumed by the narrator both in this summative evaluation and in the scolding aside in 8-2 gives no indication whether the extraordinary mishandling of the pipe related in this text is merely an occasion for merriment or also a didactic device – even if the morale of such interludes (cf. also sections 7-12, 7-16) remains obscure to outsiders.

In terms of literary treatment, the loving care with which the protagonist looks after his old spouse provides a striking contrast to his ineptitude in ritual matters.

References

Ahenakew, Edward

1976 Sixty-five years ago [1951]. Stuart Hughes, ed., *The Frog Lake "Massacre": Personal Perspectives on Ethnic Conflict*, pp. 352-359. Toronto: McClelland and Stewart.

Ahenakew, Freda, and H.C. Wolfart

1983 Productive reduplication in Plains Cree. William Cowan, réd., *Actes du Quatorzième Congrès des Algonquinistes*, pp. 369-377.

1987 The story-tellers and their stories. Freda Ahenakew, ed., *wâskahikaniwiyiniw-âcimowina / Stories of the House People, Told by Peter Vandall and Joe Douquette*, pp. x-xiv. Winnipeg: University of Manitoba Press.

Bear, Glecia, et al.

1992 *kôhkominawak otâcimowiniwâwa / Our Grandmothers' Lives as Told in Their Own Words*, Told by Glecia Bear et al. Edited and translated by Freda Ahenakew and H.C. Wolfart. Saskatoon: Fifth House Publishers.

Béland, Jean-Pierre

1978 *Atikamekw Morphology and Lexicon.* Ph.D. thesis, University of California, Berkeley.

Bloomfield, Leonard

1930 *Sacred Stories of the Sweet Grass Cree.* National Museum of Canada Bulletins, 60. Ottawa.

1934 *Plains Cree Texts.* American Ethnological Society Publications, 16. New York.

Cameron, William Blaisdell
1926 *The War Trail of Big Bear.* Toronto: Ryerson Press.

Chief, Jimmy
1985 Story told by Jimmy Chief [ed. by J.G. MacDonald and Edgar Mapletoft]. Edgar Mapletoft et al., *Fort Pitt History Unfolding, 1829-1985*, pp. 99-104. Frenchman Butte, Saskatchewan: Fort Pitt Historical Society.

Delgamuukw
1997 Delgamuukw *v.* British Columbia, [1997] 3 S.C.R. 1010.

Dion, Joseph F.
1979 *My Tribe the Crees.* Edited by Hugh A. Dempsey. Calgary: Glenbow Museum.

Ellis, C. Douglas
1989 *"Now then, still another story –" Literature of the Western James Bay Cree: Content and Structure.* The 1988 Belcourt Lecture. Winnipeg: Voices of Rupert's Land.

1995 *âtalôhkâna nêsta tipâcimôwina / Cree Legends and Narratives from the West Coast of James Bay, Told by Simeon Scott et al.: Text and Translation.* Edited and with a glossary by C. Douglas Ellis. Publications of the Algonquian Text Society. Winnipeg: University of Manitoba Press.

Erasmus, Peter
1976 *Buffalo Days and Nights, As Told to Henry Thompson* [1920/1920]. Edited by Irene Spry. Calgary: Glenbow-Alberta Institute.

Gill, Sam D.
1987 *Mother Earth: An American Story*. Chicago: University of Chicago Press.

Godfrey, W. Earl
1066 *The Birds of Canada.* National Museums of Canada Bulletins, 203. Ottawa.

Haiman, John
1998 *Talk is Cheap: Sarcasm, Alienation and the Evolution of Language.* New York: Oxford University Press.

Henry, Alexander [the younger]
1897 *New Light on the Early History of the Greater Northwest: The Manuscript Journals of Alexander Henry* [...] *and of David Thompson* [...] *1799-1814.* Edited by Elliott Coues. New York: Francis P. Harper.

Jackes, A.G.
1876 Narrative of the proceedings connected with the effecting of the treaties at Forts Carlton and Pitt, in the year 1876, together with a report of the speeches of the Indians and Commissioners. Alexander Morris, *The Treaties of Canada with the Indians of Manitoba and the North-West Territories*, pp. 196-244. Toronto: Belfords, Clark & Co.

Johnson, Alice M., ed.
1967 *Saskatchewan Journals and Correspondence: Edmonton House 1795-1800, Chesterfield House 1800-1802.* Publications of the Hudson's Bay Record Society, 26. London.

Le Roy Ladurie, Emmanuel
1979 *Carnaval de Romans.* Paris: Gallimard.

Mandelbaum, David G.
1940 *The Plains Cree.* American Museum of Natural History, Anthropological Papers, vol. 37, part 2. New York.

McDougall, John
1970 *Opening the Great West: Experiences of a Missionary 1875-76* [c. 1912]. Edited by Hugh A. Dempsey, with an introduction by J. Ernest Nix. Calgary: Glenbow-Alberta Institute.

Meyer, David, and Paul C. Thistle
1995 Saskatchewan River rendezvous centers and trading posts: Continuity in a Cree social geography. *Ethnohistory* 42:403-444.

Minde, Emma
1997 *kwayask ê-kî-pê-kiskinowâpahtihicik / Their Example Showed Me the Way: A Cree Woman's Life Shaped by Two Cultures*, Told by Emma Minde, edited, translated and with a glossary by Freda Ahenakew and H.C. Wolfart. Edmonton: University of Alberta Press.

Morris, Alexander
1876 [Despatch ... giving an account of the journey and of the negotations attending the treaty, 4 December 1876]. Alexander Morris, *The Treaties of Canada with the Indians of Manitoba and the North-West Territories*, pp. 180-196. Toronto: Belfords, Clark & Co.

1880 *The Treaties of Canada with the Indians of Manitoba and the North-West Territories, Including the Negotiations on which they were Based and other Information Related thereto.* Toronto: Belfords, Clark & Co.

Nichols, John D., and Earl Nyholm
1995 *A Concise Dictionary of Minnesota Ojibwe.* Minneapolis and London: University of Minnesota Press.

Rundle, Robert Terrill
1977 *The Rundle Journals, 1840-1848.* Edited by Hugh A. Dempsey, with an introduction and notes by Gerald M. Hutchinson. Calgary: Alberta Records Publications Board, Historical Society of Alberta and Glenbow-Alberta Institute.

Vandall, Peter, and Joe Douquette
1987 *wâskahikaniwiyiniw-âcimowina / Stories of the House People.* Told by Peter Vandall and Joe Douquette. Edited, translated and with a glossary by Freda Ahenakew. Publications of the Algonquian Text Society. Winnipeg: University of Manitoba Press.

Vanderhaeghe, Guy
1996 *The Englishman's Boy.* Toronto: McClelland and Stewart.

Vansina, Jan
1961 *De la tradition orale: Essai de méthode historique.* Annales du Musée Royal de l'Afrique centrale, Sciences humaines, no. 36. Tervuren.

Whitecalf, Sarah
1993 *kinêhiyâwiwininaw nêhiyawêwin / The Cree Language is Our Identity: The La Ronge Lectures of Sarah Whitecalf.* Edited, translated and with a glossary by H.C. Wolfart and Freda Ahenakew. Publications of the Algonquian Text Society. Winnipeg: University of Manitoba Press.

Wolfart, H.C.

1973 *Plains Cree: A Grammatical Study*. Transaction of the American Philosophical Society, new series, vol. 63, part 2. Philadelphia.

1978 Proto-Algonquian ?c. *International Journal of American Linguistics* 44:232-235.

1980 Marked terms for marginal kin. William Cowan, ed., *Papers of the Eleventh Algonquian Conference*, pp. 283-293.

1982 Empirische Untersuchungen zur mündlichen Literatur-Überlieferung. Eberhard Lämmert, ed., *Erzählforschung*, pp. 74-97. Stuttgart: Metzler.

1984 Notes on the Cree texts in Petitot's 'Traditions indiennes du Canada Nord-Ouest'. H.C. Wolfart, ed., *Essays in Algonquian Bibliography in Honour of V. M. Dechene*, pp. 47-78. Algonquian and Iroquoian Linguistics, Memoir 1.

1989*a* Prosodische Grenzsignale im Plains Cree. *Folia Linguistica* 23:327-334.

1989*b* Cree midwifery: Linguistic and literary observations. William Cowan, réd., *Actes du Vingtième Congrès des Algonquinistes*, pp. 326-342.

1992 Introduction to the Texts; Notes. Freda Ahenakew and H.C. Wolfart, eds., *kôhkominawak otâcimowiniwâwa / Our Grandmothers' Lives as Told in Their Own Words, Told by Glecia Bear et al.*, pp. 17-37; 351-408. Saskatoon: Fifth House Publishers.

1996 Sketch of Cree, an Algonquian language. Ives Goddard, ed., *Languages*, pp. 390-439. William C. Sturtevant, gen. ed., *Handbook of North American Indians*, vol. 17. Washington, D.C.: Smithsonian Institution.

1997 The education of a Cree woman. Freda Ahenakew and H.C. Wolfart, eds., *kwayask ê-kî-pê-kiskinowâpahtihicik / Their Example Showed Me the Way: A Cree Woman's Life Shaped by Two Cultures, Told by Emma Minde*, pp. ix-xliv. Edmonton: University of Alberta Press.

1998 Authenticity and *aggiornamento* in spoken texts and their critical edition. Lisa Philips Valentine and Regna Darnell, eds., *Theorising the Americanist Tradition*. Toronto: University of Toronto Press. [*in press*]

Cree-English Glossary

STEM-CLASS CODES

NA	animate noun
NI	inanimate noun
NDA	animate noun, dependent
NDI	inanimate noun, dependent
VAI	verb of type AI (animate actor, usually intransitive)
VII	verb of type II (inanimate actor, intransitive)
VTA	verb of type TA (animate goal, transitive)
VTI	verb of type TI (inanimate goal, usually transitive)
PR	pronoun
IPC	indeclinable particle
IPV	indeclinable preverb particle
IPN	indeclinable prenoun particle
INM	indeclinable nominal

ALL NOUN AND VERB ENTRIES in this glossary end in a long hyphen, indicating that the form given in the glossary is a stem.

Only some stems are identical to words; most Cree words consist of stems combined with inflectional endings. In the case of noun stems in post-consonantal *-w-*, the stem-final *-w-* does not appear in the singular form of the word.

Dependent noun stems have a long hyphen both at the end and at the beginning: such stems also require a personal prefix.

FOR TRANSITIVE STEMS of the VTA and VTI types, the primary goal (or object) for which the verb is inflected is indicated by the notations *s.o.* and *s.t.*, to be read 'someone' and 'something', respectively:

tipêyim– *VTA* own s.o., control s.o.
tipêyiht– *VTI* own s.t., control s.t.

The secondary goal (or object), which is not specified by inflection, is conventionally indicated by the notation *(it/him)*:

nakatamaw– *VTA* leave (it/him) behind for s.o.
(*cf.* **nakat–** *VTI* leave s.t. behind)

For transitive stems of the VAI type, the corresponding notation is *(it)*:

manâcihtâ– *VAI* treat (it) with respect

(For a fuller survey of verb types and their syntactic relations see Wolfart 1996:402-404.)

LEXICAL ENTRIES appearing exclusively in the interventions of speakers other than *kâ-pimwêwêhahk* are marked by an asterisk.

Glossary

–awâsimis– *NDA* child [*e.g.*, kitawâsimisinaw]
–âniskotâpân– *NDA* great-grandchild [*e.g.*, nitâniskotâpânak]
–câpân– *NDA* great-grandchild [*e.g.*, nicâpânak]
–cihciy– *NDI* hand [*e.g.*, ocihciy]
–ciwâm– *NDA* male parallel cousin (man speaking); [*fig.*] brother, male of the same generation (man speaking) [*e.g.*, kiciwâminaw]
–iyinîm– *NDA* people, followers [*usually plural; e.g.*, kitiyinîmak]
–îc-âyisiyiniw– *NDA* fellow human [*e.g.*, kîc-âyisiyinînaw]
–îci-kîhkâw– *NDA* aged spouse, fellow old person, fellow oldster, companion of one's old age [*e.g.*, wîci-kîhkâwa]
–îk– *NDI* house, dwelling, home [*e.g.*, wîki]
–îpit– *NDI* tooth [*e.g.*, wîpita]
–îscâs– *NDA* male cross-cousin (man speaking) [*diminutive; e.g.*, wîscâsa]
–îtimos– *NDA* cross-cousin of the opposite sex [*e.g.*, nîtimos]
–kâwiy– *NDA* mother; [*fig.*] Our Mother [*e.g.*, nikâwiy; kikâwînaw]
–kîsikâm– *NDI* day, day of one's life; [*fig.*] [Our Father's] day, Christmas Day [*e.g.*, kikîsikâminaw; kôhtâwînaw okîsikâm]
–kosis– *NDA* son; parallel nephew; [*fig.*] younger man [*e.g.*, nikosis; *vocative:* nikosis]
–mosôm– *NDA* grandfather; [*fig.*] old man [*e.g.*, kimosôminaw; *vocative:* nimosô]
–nâpêm– *NDA* husband [*e.g.*, ninâpêm]
–nîkihikw– *NDA* parent [*e.g.*, onîkihikowâwa]
–osk-âyim– *NDA* young people, children, the young [*e.g.*, otôsk-âyima]
–oskinîkîm– *NDA* young man, follower; [*fig.*] servant [*e.g.*, otôskinîkîma]
–ôhcâwîs– *NDA* father's brother [*e.g.*, nôhcâwîs]
–ôhkom– *NDA* grandmother, grandmother's sister, great-aunt; [*fig.*] old woman; Our Grandmother [*e.g.*, nôhkominân; kôhkominaw]
–ôhtâwiy– *NDA* father, father's brother; [*fig.*] Our Father [*e.g.*, kôhtâwînawak; kôhtâwînaw]
–ôsisim– *NDA* grandchild; [*fig.*] young person [*e.g.*, kôsisiminaw; *vocative:* nôsisê]
–scikwân– *NDI* head [*diminutive; e.g.*, oscikwân]
–spikêkan– *NDI* rib [*e.g.*, ospikêkana]

–stês– *NDA* older brother [*e.g.*, kistêsinaw]
–stikwân– *NDI* head; head of hair [*e.g.*, ostikwâniwâw]
–stim– *NDA* cross-niece; daughter-in-law [*e.g.*, ostima]
–tânis– *NDA* daughter [*e.g.*, otânisa]
–têh– *NDI* heart; [*fig.*] heart, soul [*e.g.*, otêhihk]
–tihkwatim– *NDA* cross-nephew; son-in-law [*e.g.*, nitihkwatim]
–tôtêm– *NDA* kinsman; friend [*e.g.*, kitôtêminawak]
–wâhkômâkan– *NDA* relative [*e.g.*, kiwâhkômâkaninaw]
–wîkimâkan– *NDA* spouse, housemate [*e.g.*, niwîkimâkan]
aciyaw *IPC* for a little while [*]
ah *IPC* ho! [*exclamatory*]
ah– *VTA* place s.o.
ahâw *IPC* now indeed [*]
ahcâhko-pimâtisiwin– *NI* spiritual life
ahcâhkw– *NA* soul
ahpô *IPC* even, possibly; or
ahpô cî *IPC* or else
akâmaskîhk *IPC* across the water, overseas
akim– *VTA* count s.o.
akot– *VTA* hang s.o. up; place s.o. on a burial scaffold
ana *PR* that [*demonstrative; e.g.*, ana, aniki, anihi; anima, anihi]
ani *IPC* [*enclitic:*] then [*emphatic; enclitic*]
anima *IPC* it is that; the fact that [*factive; also predicative*]
anita *IPC* there
anohc *IPC* today [*also* anoht]
apahkwân– *NI* roof [*sic:* NI]
apasoy– *NI* tentpole
api– *VAI* sit, be present
apihkât– *VTI* braid s.t.
apihkâtamaw– *VTA* braid (it/him) for s.o.
apihkâtê– *VII* be braided
apisis *IPC* a little
apist– *VTI* sit by s.t., live in s.t. (e.g., lodge) [*sic:* -i-]
asahtowin– *NI* feeding one another, rations
asam– *VTA* feed s.o.; hand out rations to s.o.
asawâpi– *VAI* look out, be on watch
asên– *VTA* reject s.o., turn s.o. back
asên– *VTI* reject s.t., turn s.t. back

asici *IPC* also, additionally
asinîwaciy– *NI* the Rocky Mountains [*usually sg.*]
askiy– *NI* earth, land, country; world
askîhkân– *NI* reserve
askîwi– *VII* be the earth, exist as world
askîwisk– *VTI* subject the earth to oneself, populate the earth, make the earth live
asotamaw– *VTA* promise (it) to s.o.
asotamâkê– *VAI* make a promise
asotamâkêwin– *NI* promise [*sc. 'agent-centred' noun; e.g.,* otasotamâkêwin 'what he has promised']
asotamâkowin– *NI* promise, promise made [*sc. 'patient-centred' noun; e.g.,* kitasotamâkowininaw 'what has been promised to us']
aspatisin– *VII* lie leaning upon something, lie back upon something, lie propped up
aspin *IPC* off, away; the last I knew
aspitonâmo– *VAI* flee to rely on spoken words, rely on (it) as a formal confirmation of the spoken word
astamaw– *VTA* put (it/him) for s.o.
astâ– *VAI* place (it)
astâh– *VTA* frighten s.o.; [*especially in inverse:*] cause s.o. to be wary, worry s.o.
astê– *VII* be placed
atamih– *VTA* make s.o. grateful, make s.o. indebted, please s.o.
atâm– *VTA* buy (it/him) from s.o.
atâwâkê– *VAI* sell (it/him)
atâwê– *VAI* buy (it)
atâwêstamaw– *VTA* buy (it/him) for s.o.
ati *IPV* progressively, proceed to
ati nîkân *IPC* in the future
atoskaw– *VTA* work for s.o.
atoskât– *VTI* work at s.t.
atoskê– *VAI* work
atoskêhâkan– *NA* employee
atoskêwin– *NI* work
awa *PR* this [*demonstrative; e.g.,* awa, ôki, ôhi; ôma, ôhi]
awas *IPC* go away! away with you! [*]

awas-âyihk *IPC* on the other side, on the far side
awâsis– *NA* child
awâska-mâmitonêyihcikan– *NI* stable mind, steady mind, balanced mind [*?sic*]
awiyak *PR* someone; [*in negative clause:*] anyone [*indefinite; e.g.*, awiyak]
awîna *PR* who [*interrogative; e.g.*, awîna]
ay-atâmaskamik *IPC* inside the earth, below the ground [*reduplicated*]
ayamihâ– *VAI* pray, hold a church service; follow a religion [*also* ayimihâ–]
ayamihâwin– *NI* praying, church service; religion [*also* ayimihâwin–]
ayamihêwi-kîsikâ– *VII* be Sunday
ayamihêwiyiniw– *NA* priest; minister
ayâ– *VAI* be there, live there; exist
ayâ– *VII* be there, exist
ayi *IPC* ah [*hesitatory*]
ayinânêw *IPC* eight
ayinânêwi-mitanaw *IPC* eighty
ayis *IPC* for, because [*causal conjunction; also* ayisk]
ayisiyiniw– *NA* person, human being
ayisiyinîhkân– *NA* doll, mannikin; cartoon figure
ayisiyinîwi– *VAI* be a person, be a human being
ayisiyinîwin– *NI* being human, human existence
ayiwâk *IPC* more; [*in numeral phrases:*] plus
â *IPC* well [*introductory; cf.* hâ, wâ]
âcim– *VTA* tell about s.o.
âcimo– *VAI* tell, tell a story, give an account
âcimostaw– *VTA* tell s.o. about (it/him), give s.o. an account
âcimowin– *NI* story, account, report
âha *IPC* yes [*affirmative; cf.* êha]
âhci piko *IPC* still, nevertheless, despite everything [*adversative*]
âhcîhtâ– *VAI* make (it) over, make (it) different, change (it)
âhkamêyimo– *VAI* persist in one's will, persevere
âhkamêyimotot– *VTI* persists in s.t., persevere in s.t.
âhkosiwin– *NI* illness
âkaw-âyihk *IPC* in a hidden place, behind an obstacle to vision

âkayâsîmo– *VAI* speak English
âkwaskiskaw– *VTA* head s.o. off, get in s.o.'s way
ânisîhtâ– *VAI* alleviate the effect of (it), be an antidote to (it)
âniskê *IPV* successively, one joining the other, surviving
âpacih– *VTA* use s.o., find s.o. useful; [*especially in inverse:*] be helped by s.o.
âpacihcikan– *NI* tool; appliance, machine
âpacihtamôh– *VTA* make s.o. use (it/him), give (it/him) to s.o. to use; use (it/him) for s.o.
âpacihtâ– *VAI* use (it), make use of (it)
âpahkawin– *VII* be level-headed, be sensible, be conscious
âpatan– *VII* be used, be useful
âpatisi– *VAI* be used, be useful
âpihtâ-kîsikâhk *IPC* in the south, to the south
âsay *IPC* already; without delay [*also aspectual*]
âsowahpitê– *VII* be stretched across, be strung across
âsônamaw– *VTA* pass (it/him) on to s.o.
âsônê *IPC* especially, in particular
âstawê– *VII* be without fire, be extinct (e.g., fire)
âstê-kîsikâ– *VII* cease being stormy weather, be better weather
âta *IPC* although; on the other hand [*concessive conjunction*]
âtayôhkan– *NA* spirit being, dream guardian
âtayôhkanakiso– *VAI* be held to be a spirit being, a dream guardian
âtayôhkêwin– *NI* sacred story
âtiht *IPC* some
âtot– *VTI* tell about s.t., give an account of s.t.
âyiman– *VII* be difficult
âyimôhto– *VAI* discuss one another; gossip about one another
âyimôhtowin– *NI* discussing one another; gossiping about one another, gossip
âyimôm– *VTA* discuss s.o.; gossip about s.o.
âyimômiso– *VAI* discuss oneself; speak unguardedly about oneself, gossip about oneself
âyimôt– *VTI* speak of s.t., discuss s.t.; gossip about s.t.
cah *IPC* gosh! [*; *exclamatory*]
capasis *IPC* down low

cascakiskwês– *NA* [*man's name*] [*literally:* Head-Thrown-Back, Head-Held-Back]

cêskwa *IPC* wait; [*in negative clause:*] not yet

cikêmô *IPC* of course, obviously, as might be expected [*weak concessive; cf.* cikêmâ]

cimasi– *VAI* stand upright, stand erect

cimatâ– *VAI* place (it) upright, plant (it) upright

cimatê– *VII* stand upright, stand erect

cistêmâw– *NA* tobacco

cî *IPC* [*interrogative; enclitic*]

cîkâhtaw *IPC* close, nearby, in the area

cîki *IPC* close, close by

êcika *IPC* what is this! [*exclamatory; preclitic, usually with demonstrative pronoun*]

êha *IPC* yes [*affirmative; also* êhâ, hêha, âha]

êkâ *IPC* not [*negator in volitional clauses; also* êkâya]

êkos êsa *IPC* thus then

êkos îsi *IPC* thus, in that way; that is how it is

êkosi *IPC* thus, in that way; that is all

êkospî *IPC* then, at that time

êkota *IPC* there

êkotê *IPC* over there

êkotowahk *IPC* of that kind

êkotowihk *IPC* in that place

êkwa *IPC* then, now; and

êkwêyâc *IPC* only then

êsa *IPC* reportedly

êtokwê *IPC* presumably, I guess

êwako *PR* that one [*resumptive demonstrative; e.g.*, êwako, êkonik, êkoni; êwako, êkoni, êwakoyiw]

êy *IPC* hey [*introductory, also exclamatory*]

êyâpic *IPC* still

êyiwêhk *IPC* just in case, nevertheless; despite shortcomings [*also* kêyiwêhk]

hâ *IPC* well [*introductory; cf.* â]

hâw *IPC* now then [*hortatory, indicating readiness or impatience*]

ihkin– *VII* occur, take place

ihtako– *VAI* exist

ihtakon– *VII* exist [*e.g.*, ê-ihtakohk]
ihtasi– *VAI* be so many, be as many
ihtâ– *VAI* be there, exist
is-âyâ– *VAI* be thus in health; be unwell, be in poor health
isi *IPC* thus, there [*also* IPV]
isinâkosi– *VAI* look thus
isinâkwan– *VII* look thus, give such an appearance
isiniskêyi– *VAI* move one's arm thus or there, point in that direction with one's arm
isiyîhkâso– *VAI* be called thus, have such a name
isiyîhkât– *VTA* call s.o. thus, use such a name for s.o.
isiyîhkât– *VTI* call s.t. thus, use such a name for s.t.
isiyîhkâtê– *VII* be called thus, have such a name
isîhcikât– *VTI* do things thus for s.t., proceed thus for s.t.
isîhcikê– *VAI* do things thus, proceed thus, perform such a ritual
isko *IPC* to such an extent, thus far [*also* IPV]
iskon– *VTI* have so much left over of s.t.
iskotêw– *NI* fire, hearth-fire
iskoyikohk *IPC* to such an extent, to such a degree
iskwâhtêm– *NI* door
iskwêw– *NA* woman
iskwêyâc *IPC* at last, at the end
ispatinâ– *VII* be a hill
ispayi– *VAI* be thus affected; be thus afflicted
ispayi– *VII* take place thus, occur thus; have passed (e.g., days, years) [*e.g.*, ispayiw, ê-ispayik]
ispayiho– *VAI* throw oneself thus or there, move thus or there
ispâhkêkocin– *VII* rise high up, be high in the air
ispâhtêhikan– *NA* [*man's name*] [*literally:* ispâhtêhikan– NI 'pole holding up tent-flap to allow air in']
ispimihk *IPC* high up, up above
ispisi *IPV* to such an extent, so far
ispî *IPC* at such a time, then
ispîhtêyimiso– *VAI* think thus highly of oneself
ispîhtisî– *VAI* be of such an age
it– *VTA* say thus to s.o.
it– *VTI* say thus of s.t., say thus about s.t.
ita *IPC* there; there where

itahkamikisi– *VAI* do things thus

itahtin– *VII* be so many

itahtopiponwê– *VAI* be so many years old

itahtwapi– *VAI* sit as so many, be present as so many

itakâm *IPC* on the hither side of a body of water, on the near side of a body of water

itakiht– *VTI* count s.t. thus, value s.t. thus, hold s.t. in such esteem

itakihtê– *VII* be counted thus, cost so much; be held in such esteem

itakim– *VTA* count s.o. thus, value s.o. thus, hold s.o. in such esteem

itakiso– *VAI* be counted thus; be held in such esteem, have such a function

itamon– *VII* run thus or there as a path

itapi– *VAI* sit thus or there, be present thus or there

itasiwât– *VTA* give s.o. such a command, impose such laws on s.o.

itasiwê– *VAI* give such a command, impose such laws [*]

itastê– *VII* be placed thus; be written thus

itâcimostaw– *VTA* tell s.o. thus about (it), tell s.o. such a story

itâcimômakan– *VII* tell thus about (it), tell such a story

itâmo– *VAI* flee thus or there, seek such refuge

itâmôh– *VTA* make s.o. flee thus or there, direct s.o. to seek such refuge

itâpacih– *VTA* use s.o. thus, find s.o. useful thus; [*especially in inverse:*] be thus helped by s.o.

itâpacihtâ– *VAI* use (it) thus, use such (things)

itâpatan– *VII* be thus used, be of such use

itâpi– *VAI* look thus or there

itâskonamaw– *VTA* thus point the pipe for s.o., thus point the pipe at s.o.

itâskonamawât– *VTI* thus point the pipe at s.t.

itâskonikê– *VAI* thus point the pipe or pipestem; thus hold a pipe ceremony

itâskonikêwin– *NI* thus pointing the pipe or pipestem; such a pipe ceremony

itâtot– *VTI* tell about s.t. thus, give such an account of s.t.

itê *IPC* there, thither

itêhkê isi *IPC* in that direction, in the thither direction
itêyihcikan– *NI* thinking thus; such thought
itêyiht– *VTI* think thus of s.t.
itêyim– *VTA* think thus of s.o.
itihtaw– *VTA* hear s.o. thus
itihtâkwan– *VII* be thus heard
itikwamikohkê– *VAI* hold such a lodge, hold such a ceremony
itisin– *VTA* thus hold (it/him) for s.o., thus hand (it/him) over to s.o.
itohtah– *VTA* take s.o. thus or there
itohtê– *VAI* go there or thus
itôt– *VTI* do s.t. thus [*cf.* tôt-]
itwê– *VAI* say thus, call (it) thus; have such a meaning
itwêmakan– *VII* say thus, have such a meaning
itwêmakisi– *VAI* say thus, have such a meaning [*]
itwêstamaw– *VTA* say thus for s.o.; speak for s.o.; interpret for s.o.
iyaw *IPC* well now [**; introductory, also exclamatory*]
iyawis *IPC* fully, entirely; [*in negative clause:*] only partially, not exclusively
iyâyaw *IPC* eagerly, intently; by preference, rather
iyikohk *IPC* so much, to such a degree, to such an extent
iyinito *IPN* plain, ordinary
iyinîsi– *VAI* be clever
iyôtin– *NA* [*spirit's name:*] Wind
iyôtin– *NI* high wind, tornado [*also* yôtin–]
îh *IPC* look! behold! [*exclamatory*]
îkwaskwan– *VII* be cloudy [*sic:* î-; *cf.* yî-]
îpâcihtâ– *VAI* make (it) dirty, soil (it) [*sic:* î-; *cf.* wiyî-]
îwanisîhisowin– *NI* fasting, denying oneself food [*usually but not always restricted to food*]
kahkiyaw *IPC* all
kakêpâhkamikisi– *VAI* fool around, get in the way
kakêskihkêmo– *VAI* counsel people, preach at people
kakêskim– *VTA* counsel s.o., lecture s.o.
kakêskimâwasowin– *NI* counselling the young
kakwâtakih– *VTA* make s.o. suffer, be mean to s.o., be abusive to s.o.

kakwâtakihiso– *VAI* make oneself suffer; torture oneself, deny oneself food and drink

kakwâtakiho– *VAI* make oneself suffer; torture oneself, deny oneself food and drink

kakwâtakihowin– *NI* making oneself suffer; denying oneself food and drink

kakwâtakihtâ– *VAI* suffer (it), suffer

kakwê *IPV* try to; circumstances permitting, by divine grace

kakwêcim– *VTA* ask s.o.; make a request of s.o.; ask s.o. about (it/him)

kanawêyiht– *VTI* look after s.t., take care of s.t.

kanawêyihtamaw– *VTA* look after (it/him) for s.o., take care of (it/him) for s.o.

kanawêyim– *VTA* keep s.o., guard s.o. closely

kanâtahcâ– *VII* be clean ground, be clean land

kanâtanohk *IPC* in a clean place

kanôsimon– *NI* protective talisman (usually worn around the neck, wrapped in leather)

kanôsimototaw– *VTA* have s.o. (e.g., rattle) as protection

kapêsimostaw– *VTA* stay overnight with s.o., stay overnight at s.o.'s place

kapêsîwikamikw– *NI* inn, hotel

kaskawanipêstâ– *VII* be drizzle, be rainy

kaskihtâ– *VAI* be able to do (it), be competent at (it)

kaskipitê– *VII* be tied up, be wrapped up

katawâhk *IPC* properly, in seemly manner

katisk *IPC* just now, exactly; [*in negative clause:*] not merely

kayâs *IPC* long ago, in earlier days; previously

kayâsês *IPC* quite a long time ago

kâ-nîpitêhtêw *INM* [*man's name*] [*; *literally:* Walks-Abreast]

kâ-pimwêwêhahk *INM* [*man's name:*] Jim Kâ-Nîpitêhtêw [*literally:* Goes-Along-Drumming]

kâhcitin– *VTA* catch s.o. [*also* kâhtitin–]

kâkikê *IPC* always, forever

kâkîsimo– *VAI* pray, plead, chant prayers

kâkîsimotot– *VTI* chant prayers for s.t.; chant prayers over s.t.

kâkîsimototaw– *VTA* chant prayers for s.o.; chant prayers over s.o.

kâkîsimowin– *NI* chanting prayers
kâkîsimwâkê– *VAI* chant prayers with things
kâsispô– *VAI* survive into another generation
kâsispôhtêmakan– *VII* go on from one generation to another, survive into another generation
kâwi *IPC* again
kêhcinâ *IPC* surely, for certain
kêhtê-ay– *NA* old person, the old; elder
kêhtê-ayiwi– *VAI* be an old person; be an elder
kêtahtawê *IPC* suddenly; at one time
kêtastotinê– *VAI* put one's hat on [*]
kêtisk *IPC* just barely, to exact measure
kêyiwêhk *IPC* just in case, nevertheless; despite shortcomings [*also* êyiwêhk]
kicimâkisi– *VAI* be pitiable, be miserable [*diminutive*]
kihc-ôkâwîmâw– *NA* [*fig.*] Great Mother, Mother Earth
kihc-ôkimâskwêw– *NA* Queen
kihcêyihtâkwan– *VII* be respected; be held sacred
kihcêyim– *VTA* think highly of s.o., hold s.o. sacred
kikapi– *VAI* sit along with something
kikastê– *VII* be placed along with something
kiki *IPV* along with
kimiwan– *VII* rain, be rain
kimotôsê– *VAI* bear an illegitimate child
kinosêw– *NA* fish
kinwês *IPC* for a long time
kisâkamitêhkwê– *VAI* drink a hot liquid, have a hot drink
kisê-nâpêw-asiniy– *NA* [*spirit's name:*] Kind-Man-Rock
kisêwâtisi– *VAI* be kind, be of compassionate disposition; [*fig.*] be full of grace
kisêwâtisiwin– *NI* kindness, compassion; [*fig.*] grace
kisêyiniw– *NA* old man
kisêyinîw-âcimowin– *NI* old man's story, report of the old men
kisêyinîw-ôhpikihâkan– *NA* old man's pupil, ward of the old men
kisêyinîwi-pîkiskwêwin– *NI* old man's word, word of the old men
kisipipayi– *VII* come to an end, reach the end

kisipîmakan– *VII* come to an end, have an end
kisiwâh– *VTA* anger s.o.
kisîhto– *VAI* anger one another by speech
kisîkitot– *VTA* speak to s.o. in anger [*sic:* -î-]
kisîm– *VTA* anger s.o. by speech
kisîpêkinikê– *VAI* wash things, do the laundry
kisîwê– *VII* be loud, speak loudly (e.g., audio-recorder) [*]
kisîwêhkahtaw– *VTA* speak loudly to s.o.
kiskêyiht– *VTI* know s.t.; have knowledge
kiskêyihtamôhikowisi– *VAI* be granted knowledge by the powers
kiskinohamaw– *VTA* teach s.o., teach (it) to s.o.
kiskinohamawâkan– *NA* student
kiskinohamâkê– *VAI* teach (it) to people
kiskinohamâsowin– *NI* schooling, education [*sc. 'patient-centred' noun; e.g.,* okiskinohamâsowin 'his schooling']
kiskinohamâtowikamikw– *NI* school, school-house
kiskinowâpaht– *VTI* learn merely by watching s.t.
kiskinowâpiwin– *NI* learning merely by watching
kiskinowâsoht– *VTI* learn merely by listening to s.t.
kiskisi– *VAI* remember, remember (it)
kiskisopayi– *VAI* think of something, suddenly remember
kiskisôhto– *VAI* remind one another
kiskisôm– *VTA* remind s.o. [*sic:* -ô-]
kispaki *IPV* thickly
kistikân– *NA* grain, seed; sheaf of grain
kistikêwi-pimâcihowin– *NI* agricultural way of life, farm economy
kitahamaw– *VTA* advise s.o. against (it/him)
kitâpaht– *VTI* look at s.t.
kitâpam– *VTA* look at s.o.
kitâpamikowisi– *VAI* be looked upon by the powers
kitâsôm– *VTA* warn s.o. about (it/him)
kitimah– *VTA* be mean to s.o., treat s.o. badly
kitimahiso– *VAI* be mean to oneself, hurt oneself
kitimâkan– *VII* be pitiable, be miserable
kitimâkêyihtamâso– *VAI* think of (it/him) with compassion for one's own sake

kitimâkêyihto– *VAI* feel pity towards one another, love one another, think of one another with compassion

kitimâkêyihtowin– *NI* feeling pity towards one another, loving one another, thinking of one another with compassion

kitimâkêyim– *VTA* take pity upon s.o., think of s.o. with compassion

kitimâkihtaw– *VTA* listen to s.o. with pity, listen to s.o. with compassion

kitimâkinaw– *VTA* look with pity upon s.o., look with compassion upon s.o.; regard s.o. with respect

kitimâkinâkosi– *VAI* look pitiable, look miserable, look poor

kitimâkisi– *VAI* be pitiable, be miserable, be poor

kito– *VAI* make noises (e.g., animal); produce a thunderclap

kitot– *VTA* address s.o., speak to s.o., lecture s.o.

kiya *PR* you (sg.)

kiyakasê– *VAI* have itchy skin, suffer from eczema

kiyawâw *PR* you (pl.)

kiyâm *IPC* let it be, let there be no further delay; please

kiyânaw *PR* we-and-you (incl.)

kî *IPV* able to

kî *IPV* complete, past

kîhkânâkwan– *VII* be clearly visible

kîhkâtah– *VTI* make the sound of (it) sing out clearly

kîhkâtahamaw– *VTA* make the sound of (it) sing out clearly to s.o.

kîhtwâm *IPC* again

kîkisêp *IPC* early in the morning [*sic; cf.* kîkisêpâ]

kîkisêpâ *IPC* early in the morning [*also* kîkisêp]

kîkway *PR* something, thing; [*in negative clause:*] anything, any [*indefinite; e.g.*, kîkway]

kîkwây *PR* what [*interrogative; e.g.*, kîkwây(i), kîkwaya]

kîsakim– *VTA* finish counting s.o.; finish giving orders to s.o., complete one's charge to s.o.

kîsi *IPV* completely, to completion

kîsikâ– *VII* be day, be daylight

kîsikâwi-pîsimw– *NA* sun [*sc. as opposed to moon*]

kîsikw– *NI* sky

kîsitêpo– *VAI* cook; cook a feast, cook ceremonial food

kîsitêw– *NI* food, ceremonial food
kîsîh– *VTA* complete s.o. (e.g., rattle)
kîsîhtamaw– *VTA* complete (it/him) for s.o.
kîsîhtâ– *VAI* finish (it), complete (it)
kîskisamaw– *VTA* cut (it/him) off for s.o.; offer tobacco to s.o.
kîsowât– *VTI* complete one's words, complete one's prayers
kîsowâtamaw– *VTA* complete words for s.o., complete prayers for s.o.
kîspin *IPC* if [*conditional conjunction*]
kîspin êkâ ohci *IPC* if it were not for [*irrealis conditional, usually with noun phrase or simple conjunct*]
kîspinat– *VTI* earn enough to buy s.t.; earn s.t. as reward, earn one's reward
kîspinatamaw– *VTA* earn one's reward in s.o., earn s.o. as one's reward
kîsta *PR* you, too; you, by contrast; you yourself
kîstanaw *PR* we-and-you (incl.), too; we-and-you (incl.) by contrast
kîstawâw *PR* you (pl.), too; you (pl.) by contrast; you yourselves
kîwâtisi– *VAI* be orphaned, be an orphan
kîwêmakan– *VII* return home, come back
kocawâkanis– *NI* match, match-stick [*diminutive*]
kocihtâ– *VAI* try (it), try to do (it) [*]
konita *IPC* in vain, without reason, without purpose; without further ado
kosâpaht– *VTI* hold a shaking-lodge, hold the shaking-lodge ceremony
kosikwan– *VII* be heavy
kost– *VTI* fear s.t.
kotak *PR* other, another [*e.g.*, kotaka]
kotêyiht– *VTI* try s.t. in one's mind, think strenuously about s.t., test s.t.; challenge s.t.
kotêyim– *VTA* try s.o., test s.o., put s.o.'s mind to the test; challenge s.o.
kôtatê *IPC* at a loss; due to limitations beyond one's control [*also predicative:* 'it cannot be helped'; *cf.* kwêtatêyitiskwêyi–]
kôtawêyiht– *VTI* be at a loss for s.t., miss s.t.
kwayask *IPC* properly, by rights
kwêsk-âyihk *IPC* on the opposite side

kwêskahcâhk *IPC* on the opposite side of a rise in the land
kwêskâskon– *VTA* turn s.o. (e.g., pipe) to the opposite side
kwêski *IPV* turned around, turned to the opposite side
kwêskinâkwan– *VII* look changed, look turned around to the opposite
kwêskinisk *IPC* the other hand, changing one's hand
kwêtatêyitiskwêyi– *VAI* be at a loss as to where to turn one's head; be at a loss for a response [*cf.* kôtatê]
ma-môhcw-âtayôhkêwin– *NI* stupid sacred story, crazy sacred story [*; *reduplicated*]
maci-kîkway– *NI* something bad, bad things
macipayi– *VII* go badly
macostêh– *VTI* throw s.t. into the fire
mahihkanis– *NA* [*man's name*] [*literally:* Little-Wolf]
mahkêsîs– *NA* [*man's name*] [*literally:* Fox]
mahkihtawâkê– *VAI* have a big ear [*usually reduplicated:* mâh-mahkihtawâkê– 'have big ears']
mahti *IPC* let's see [*hortatory, often jussive*]
mamacikastê– *VAI* show off
mamisî– *VAI* rely on (it/him)
mamisîtot– *VTI* rely on s.t.
mamisîwât– *VTA* rely on s.o. for (it/him)
manâcihtâ– *VAI* treat (it) with respect
manicôs– *NA* insect, bug
manitowakim– *VTA* endow s.o. (e.g., tobacco) with supernatural powers
manitowi-kîsikâw– *NI* Christmas Day
manitowih– *VTA* grant s.o. supernatural powers
masinahikan– *NI* book; written document; bible
masinahikâso– *VAI* be pictured, be depicted
masinahikâtê– *VII* be pictured, be depicted; have marks, have writing; be written
masinahikêh– *VTA* hire s.o., employ s.o.
masinahikêstamaw– *VTA* write things for s.o., write things down for s.o.
masinipayi– *VAI* be depicted as moving (e.g., on film)
masinipayihtâ– *VAI* depict (it) (e.g., on film)
maskihkiwâpoy– *NI* tea [*sic:* -i-]

maskihkiy– *NI* herb, plant; medicine
maskihkîwiwacis– *NI* medicine chest
maskihkîwiyiniw– *NA* doctor, physician
maskosiy– *NI* grass, hay
maskosîhkê– *VAI* make hay
matotisân– *NI* sweat-lodge
matotisi– *VAI* hold a sweat-lodge
matwân cî *IPC* I wonder [*polar dubitative*]
matwêhw– *VTA* sound a beat upon s.o. (e.g., drum), drum on s.o.
matwêwê– *VII* be heard as a gunshot, be the report of a gun
mawihkâtamaw– *VTA* cry out in prayer to s.o., wail to s.o.
mawimo– *VAI* cry out; cry out in prayer, wail
mawimoscikê– *VAI* cry out in prayer, wail; worship with (it)
mawimoscikêwin– *NI* crying out in prayer, wailing; form of worship, ceremony
mawimost– *VTI* cry out in prayer to s.t., wail to s.t.
mayaw *IPC* as soon as [*temporal conjunction*]
mâci *IPV* begin; initially
mâcika *IPC* for instance [*weak concessive*]
mâcikôtitan *IPC* wait and see! lo! [*exlamatory; sic:* -â-, -ô-, -a-]
mâka *IPC* but [*concessive*]
mâkoh– *VTA* worry s.o., trouble s.o.; oppress s.o., throw s.o. into crisis
mâkwêyimo– *VAI* be worried, be troubled
mâmaw-ôhtâwîmâw– *NA* [*fig.*] All-Father
mâmawi *IPV* collectively, jointly
mâmawôhkamâto– *VAI* work together at (it/him) as a group, help one another
mâmawôpi– *VAI* sit together, hold a meeting
mâmâsîs *IPC* sparingly, delicately; quickly, roughly, without care
mâmiskôcikâtê– *VII* be discussed, be expounded
mâmiskôt– *VTI* discuss s.t., expound s.t.
mâmitonêyihcikan– *NI* mind; troubled mind
mâmitonêyiht– *VTI* think about s.t., worry about s.t.
mâmitonêyihtamih– *VTA* cause s.o. to think about (it/him), cause s.o. to worry about (it/him)
mâmitonêyim– *VTA* think about s.o., have s.o. on one's mind
mâna *IPC* habitually, usually

mânokê– *VAI* build a lodge, set up a tent
mâtayak *IPC* beforehand, in advance
mâtâskonikê– *VAI* begin to point the pipe
mâto– *VAI* cry, wail
mâwacîhito– *VAI* collect one another, gather
mâyêyiht– *VTI* consider s.t. challenging; be willing to tackle a difficult task, venture out
mâyi-kîsikâ– *VII* be stormy weather, be foul weather
mâyimahciho– *VAI* feel poorly, feel in ill health
mâyipayi– *VAI* suffer ill; be bereaved
mâyitôt– *VTI* do bad things, cause serious trouble
mêkwâc *IPC* while, in the course of
mêmohci *IPC* in particular, above all; exactly, precisely
mêskanaw– *NI* path, trail, road
mêskocikâpawi– *VAI* stand up instead [*sic:* -ê-]
mêstohtê– *VAI* die off, become extinct
mêtawâkâniwi– *VII* be general playing around
mêtawâkê– *VAI* play around with things, fool around with things
micimin– *VTI* hold on to s.t.
micimôho– *VAI* be held fast, be stuck [*sic:* -h-]
mihcêt *IPC* many
mihcêti– *VAI* be numerous, be plentiful
mihcêtin– *VII* be numerous, be plentiful
mihcêtwâw *IPC* many times
mihtât– *VTI* regret s.t.
mikoskâcihtâ– *VAI* trifle with (it), tamper with (it)
minahikosis– *NI* spruce [*diminutive*]
minahikoskâ– *VII* be a spruce thicket, be an abundance of spruce
minaho– *VAI* kill an animal, make a kill
misatimw– *NA* horse
misatimwayân– *NA* horse-hide
misawâc *IPC* in any case, whatever might be thought
misâhkamik *IPC* in great number
misi *IPV* greatly
miskaw– *VTA* find s.o.
mistahi *IPC* greatly, very much so [*also* IPV]
mistikwaskihkw– *NA* drum
mitâtaht *IPC* ten

mitonêyihcikan– *NI* mind
mitoni *IPC* intensively, really [*also* IPV]
miy– *VTA* give (it/him) to s.o.
miyawâkâc *IPV* with particular care
miyawâkâtinikê– *VAI* be particularly careful in handling things (e.g., ceremonial objects)
miyâhkas– *VTI* cense s.t., smudge s.t. with sweetgrass
miyâhkasamaw– *VTA* cense (it/him) for s.o., smudge (it/him) with sweetgrass for s.o.
miyâhkasikê– *VAI* cense things, smudge things with sweetgrass
miyâhkasw– *VTA* cense s.o. (e.g., pipe), smudge s.o. (e.g., pipe) with sweetgrass
miyikowisi– *VAI* be given (it/him) by the powers
miyo *IPV* good, well, beautiful, valuable
miyomahciho– *VAI* feel well, feel healthy; feel pleased
miyoniskêhkât– *VTI* accomplish s.t. by the work of one's hands
miyopayin– *VII* work well, run well [*]
miyopit– *VTI* carry s.t. off well, accomplish s.t.
miyoskamin– *VII* be early spring
miyw-âyâ– *VAI* be well, be in good health
miywakihtê– *VII* be considered good; [*in negative clause:*] be considered bad, be considered evil
miywâsin– *VII* be good, be valuable; [*in negative clause:*] be bad, be evil
miywêyiht– *VTI* be glad, be pleased; like s.t.
mîciso– *VAI* eat, have a meal
mîkiwâhp– *NI* lodge, tipi
mîkwan– *NA* feather
mîna *IPC* also, and also
mînis– *NI* berry
mînwâskonamaw– *VTA* straighten (it/him) for s.o.
mîstowân– *NI* beard [*sic:* -î-; *cf.* -îhi-]
mîstowê– *VAI* be bearded, wear a beard [*sic:* -î-; *cf.* -îhi-]
mîtâkwêwi– *VAI* ward (it/him) off for s.o. [*?sic*]
mohcihk *IPC* on the bare ground
moskâcih– *VTA* bother s.o., trouble s.o., hurt s.o.
mostosw– *NA* cattle, cow
môhcowi– *VAI* be stupid, be silly; be mad, be crazy

môhcwêyim– *VTA* consider s.o. stupid
môhkomân– *NI* knife
mônahipân– *NI* source, well
môniyâw– *NA* White-Man, White
môniyâw-âyamihâwin– *NI* White religion
môy êkâ êtokwê *IPC* without any doubt, of necessity [*usually with independent indicative*]
môy kakêtihk *IPC* a great many
môya *IPC* not [*cf.* namôya]
mwayês *IPC* before [*temporal conjunction; cf.* pâmwayês]
mwêhci *IPC* exactly
nahapi– *VAI* sit down in one's place, be properly seated
nahêyiht– *VTI* be satisfied with s.t.; have peace of mind
nahêyihtamih– *VTA* cause s.o. to be satisfied with (it/him); grant s.o. peace of mind
nahipayi– *VII* be convenient, fall into place
nakacihtâ– *VAI* be familiar with doing (it), be practised at (it)
nakat– *VTA* leave s.o. behind
nakat– *VTI* leave s.t. behind
nakatamaw– *VTA* leave (it/him) behind for s.o.
nakiskamohtatamaw– *VTA* take (it/him) to meet s.o., meet s.o. with (it/him); introduce (it/him) to s.o.
nakiskaw– *VTA* encounter s.o., meet s.o.
nama *IPC* not [*negator in nominal phrases*]
namôya *IPC* not; no [*negator in independent and non-volitional conjunct clauses*]
namwâ *IPC* not; no [*sic; cf.* namwâc*; emphatic negator in independent and non-volitional conjunct clauses*]
nanahiht– *VTI* listen obediently to s.t.; obey s.t.
nanahihtaw– *VTA* listen well to s.o., obey s.o.
nanâskom– *VTA* be grateful to s.o., give thanks to s.o.
nanâskomo– *VAI* be grateful, give thanks
nanâskot– *VTI* be grateful for s.t., give thanks for s.t.
nanâtawih– *VTA* doctor s.o., heal s.o.
nanâtohk *IPC* variously, of various kinds
naskom– *VTA* respond to s.o. with (it/him), answer s.o.'s prayer with (it/him)
naskot– *VTI* respond to s.t.; swear upon s.t. in response

naskwêwasim– *VTA* speak to s.o. in response, respond to s.o. by speech
naskwêwasimo– *VAI* speak in response, respond by speech
nawac *IPC* more, better, rather
nawaswât– *VTI* pursue s.t., chase after s.t.
nayawaciki– *VAI* grow up to reach various ages, be variously grown up [*usually plural*]
nayêhtâwan– *VII* be difficult, be troublesome
nayêstaw *IPC* only; it is only that [*often predicative*]
nâcikâpawist– *VTI* seek to shift one's position to s.t. [*sic:* -i-]
nâcinêhamaw– *VTA* obtain (it/him) from s.o. by payment, seek to buy medicine from s.o.
nâcinêhikê– *VAI* obtain things by payment, seek to buy medicine
nâcipahiwê– *VAI* go to fetch things, run to fetch things
nâha *PR* that one yonder [*demonstrative; e.g.*, nâha, nêhi; nêma]
nâkatowâpaht– *VTI* pay attention in looking at s.t.
nâkatôhkê– *VAI* pay attention, take notice
nânapâcihtâ– *VAI* fix (it) up, repair (it)
nânapêc *IPC* late, at the last moment, barely in time (e.g., when it should have been done previously); [*in negative clause:*] too late
nânâmiskwêyi– *VAI* nod one's head
nânitaw *IPC* simply; something, anything; something bad, anything bad; somewhere; approximately [*usually with pejorative presupposition*]
nâpêw– *NA* man, male, adult male
nât– *VTA* fetch s.o.
nât– *VTI* fetch s.t.
nâtakâm *IPC* in the north, to the north
nâtamaw– *VTA* fetch (it/him) for s.o.; take up for s.o.
nâtamâwaso– *VAI* take up for one's children
nâtâmost– *VTI* flee to s.t., turn to s.t. for help, seek refuge in s.t.
nâtâmotot– *VTI* flee to s.t., turn to s.t. for help, seek refuge in s.t.
nâtâmototaw– *VTA* flee to s.o., turn to s.o. for help, seek refuge with s.o.
nâtitisahw– *VTA* send for s.o.
nâtwâpayi– *VII* break off (e.g., branch)
nâtwâwêpah– *VTI* break s.t. off and throw it down
nâway *IPC* behind, at the rear

nêhiyaw– *NA* Cree, Indian
nêhiyawi-masinahikan– *NI* Cree book; Cree bible
nêhiyawasinahikan– *NI* Cree book; Cree bible
nêhiyawastê– *VII* be written in Cree; be written in syllabics
nêhiyawê– *VAI* speak Cree
nêhiyawi *IPN* Cree, Indian
nêhiyawi-kiskinohamâtowi-kakêskihkêmowikamikw– *NI* Saskatchewan Indian Cultural College [*literally:* counselling building for Cree (or Indian) teaching]
nêhiyawi-wîh– *VTA* use s.o.'s Cree name, call s.o. by a Cree name
nêhiyawi-wîhtamawâkan– *NI* Cree etymology; Cree teaching
nêhiyawi-wîht– *VTI* use the Cree name of s.t., call s.t. by a Cree name
nêhiyâwi– *VAI* be Cree
nêhiyâwiwin– *NI* being Cree, Cree identity, Creeness
nêmatowahk *IPC* of that kind yonder
nêtê *IPC* over yonder
nêw-âskiy *IPC* four years
nêwâw *IPC* four times
nêwo-kîsikâw *IPC* four days
nêwo-tipiskâ– *VII* be four nights, be the fourth night
nêwosâp *IPC* fourteen
nihtâwikihtâ– *VAI* give birth to (it), bring (it) forth
nihtâwikin– *VII* grow forth (e.g., plant), come forth
nihtâwikinâwaso– *VAI* give birth to a child, bring forth a child, bring forth a young one (of the species)
nihtâwikîst– *VTI* populate s.t. (e.g., the earth) [*sic:* -î-]
nikamo– *VAI* sing, sing a ritual song
nikamon– *NI* song, ritual song
nikotwâsik *IPC* six
nikotwâsik-tipahamâtowin– *NI* Treaty Six
nikotwâsosâp *IPC* sixteen
nipah– *VTA* kill s.o.
nipâkwêsimo– *VAI* attend a sundance, participate in a sundance
nipâkwêsimowikamikw– *NI* sundance-lodge, sundance ceremony
nipâkwêsimowin– *NI* sundance
nipiy kâ-pitihkwêk *INM* [*place-name*] [*literally:* Thundering-Water; *most likely near Fort Carlton, Saskatchewan*]

nipiy– *NI* water
nisitawêyim– *VTA* recognise s.o.
nisitawin– *VTI* recognise s.t.
nisitoht– *VTI* understand s.t.
nisitohtamôh– *VTA* make s.o. understand (it/him)
nisitohtaw– *VTA* understand s.o.
nistam *IPC* for the first time, initially, originally
nistamêmâkan– *NA* the first one, the original one [*sic*]
nistin– *VII* be three
nisto *IPC* three
nistwapihkât– *VTI* braid s.t. in three
nistwâw *IPC* three times
nitawâpam– *VTA* go and see s.o.
nitawâpênikê– *VAI* check up on people, check up on things
nitawêyiht– *VTI* want s.t.
nitawêyim– *VTA* want s.o., want (it/him) of s.o.
nitawi *IPV* go to, go and
nitoht– *VTI* listen to s.t.
nitohtaw– *VTA* listen to s.o.
nitom– *VTA* invite s.o.
niton– *VTI* look for s.t.
nitotamaw– *VTA* ask s.o. for (it/him)
nitotamâ– *VAI* ask for (it), pray for (it), make a request for (it)
nitotamâkêstamaw– *VTA* make a request for s.o., on s.o.'s behalf
nitotamâwin– *NI* request [*sc. 'agent-centred' noun; e.g.,* kinitotamâwin 'request made by you']
nitôsk– *VTI* seek s.t.; make a request for s.t. (e.g., medicine)
nitôskamaw– *VTA* seek (it/him) of s.o., make a request for (it/him) of s.o.
niya *PR* I
niyanân *PR* we (excl.)
niyânan *IPC* five
nîkân *IPC* first, at the head
nîkâni– *VAI* be at the lead (e.g., tobacco)
nîkânist– *VTI* be at the head of s.t., lead s.t. [*sic:* -i-*; cf.* nîkânîst–]
nîkâniwi– *VII* be ahead, be the future; lie in the future [*sic:* -i-]
nîkânîh– *VTA* place s.o. (e.g., tobacco) at the lead
nîkânîst– *VTI* be at the head of s.t., lead s.t. [*also* nîkânist–]

nîkânohk *IPC* in the lead position
nîkânohtatâ– *VAI* be in the lead with (it), carry (it) in the lead
nîkânohtêmakan– *VII* be in the lead, proceed in the lead position
nîminamaw– *VTA* hold (it/him) aloft for s.o., offer (it/him) up for s.o.
nîminikê– *VAI* hold things aloft, offer things up
nîpin– *VII* be summer
nîsi– *VAI* be two in number
nîso *IPC* two
nîso-kîsikâw *IPC* two days
nîsokâtê– *VAI* have two legs, be two-legged
nîsosâp *IPC* twelve
nîsta *PR* I, too; I by contrast; I myself
nîswâw *IPC* twice
nôcihcikê– *VAI* trap things
nôhtaw *IPC* less; minus
nôhtê *IPV* want to
nôhtêhkatê– *VAI* be hungry, want food
nôkosi– *VAI* be visible; be born
nômanak *IPC* a while
nôtikwêsiw– *NA* old woman [*diminutive*]
nôtikwêw– *NA* old woman
nôtin– *VTI* fight s.t., fight with s.t.
nôtinitowin– *NI* fighting one another, fighting
ocawâsimisi– *VAI* have a child, have (her/him) as one's child
ocâpânâskos– *NI* cart; small wagon, small sled [*diminutive*]
ocihcipayi– *VII* come to pass
ocihciskâmakan– *VII* come to pass, take place [*literally:* by foot or body movement]
ocipit– *VTA* pull s.o. along, pull s.o. in
ociski– *VAI* have a rectum, have (it) as one's rectum
ohci *IPC* with, by means of; because of; from then [*enclitic; also* IPV]
ohci *IPV* thence, from there; [*in negative clause:*] past [*cf.* ôh]
ohcih– *VTA* fight s.o. over something; hold s.o. off
ohpahpahtên– *VTI* raise up the smoke of s.t. [*?sic*]
ohpahtên– *VTI* raise up the smoke of s.t.
ohpâskon– *VTA* raise s.o. (e.g., pipe)

ohpâskon– *VTI* raise s.t. (e.g., pipestem)
ohpiki– *VAI* grow up
ohpikih– *VTA* make s.o. grow up, raise s.o.
ohpikihito– *VAI* make one another grow up, raise one another
ohpikihtamâso– *VAI* make (it) grow for oneself
ohpikihtâ– *VAI* make (it) grow
ohpikinâwaso– *VAI* make one's children grow up, raise one's children
ohpimê *IPC* off, away, to the side
ohpin– *VTI* raise s.t., create s.t.
ohtaskat– *VTI* leave s.t. suddenly thereby or there
ohtastê– *VII* be placed thereby or there
ohtisi– *VAI* obtain payment thereby or therefrom
ohtitaw *IPC* expressly, specifically; it is requisite, it is meet indeed
ohtohtê– *VAI* come from there
okimâhkân– *NA* chief, elected chief
okimâhkâniwi– *VAI* be chief, serve as elected chief
okiskinowâpiw– *NA* one who learns merely by watching
okistikêwiyiniw– *NA* farm instructor
okîsikow– *NA* [*spirit's name:*] Sky-Spirit
omasinahikêsîs– *NA* scribe, clerk
onitawahtâw– *NA* scout, explorer, spy
onîkânîw– *NA* leader
onîkihikomâw– *NA* parent
opacaskahasîs– *NA* [*bird-name*]
osâm *IPC* because; for [*causal conjunction*]
osâpaht– *VTI* look at s.t. from there
osâpam– *VTA* look at s.o. from there
osêhcâw– *NI* rise in the land, gentle hill
osiskêpayi– *VII* fall into place, work itself out, be practicable
osîh– *VTA* prepare s.o. (e.g., rattle), make s.o.
osîhtamâso– *VAI* make (it/him) for oneself
osîhtâ– *VAI* prepare (it), make (it)
osk-ây– *NA* young person, the young
oskaninê– *VAI* suffer from arthritis
oskayisiyiniw– *NA* young person [*sic:* -a-]
oskâpêwis– *NA* server, servitor (e.g., in ritual)

oskiciy– *NI* pipestem
oskicîwâhtikw– *NI* wood of pipestem
oskinîkiskwêw– *NA* young woman
oskinîkiw– *NA* young man, youth
ospwâkan– *NA* pipe
otasahkêw– *NA* one who distributes rations; Indian agent
otawâsimisi– *VAI* have a child [*sic:* -t-; *cf.* ocawâsimisi–]
otawâsimisimâw– *NA* child [*sic:* -t-]
otâkosihk *IPC* yesterday
otiht– *VTA* reach s.o.
otihtamâso– *VAI* reach (it/him) for oneself
otin– *VTA* take s.o., choose s.o.
otin– *VTI* take s.t., choose s.t.
otinaskê– *VAI* take land, settle the land, homestead
otinikâtê– *VII* be taken, be chosen
otisâpaht– *VTI* have lived long enough to see s.t.
otitwêstamâkêw– *NA* interpreter; advocate
otônihkâ– *VAI* use (it/him) as one's mouthpiece, make (it/him) one's advocate
owîcêwâkani– *VAI* have a companion or partner, have (her/him) as companion or partner
owîcisânihto– *VAI* have one another as siblings
oyôhtâwî– *VAI* have a father, have (him) as one's father
oyôsisimimâw– *NA* grandchild
ôcênâs– *NI* small town [*diminutive*]
ôh *IPV* from there; [*in negative clause:*] past [*cf.* ohci]
ôma *IPC* it is this; the fact that [*factive; also predicative*]
ômatowahk *IPC* of this kind
ômatowihk *IPC* in this place
ômis îsi *IPC* in this way; that is how it is
ômisi *IPC* in this way
ôta *IPC* here
ôtê *IPC* there
pahkisimohk *IPC* in the west, to the west
pahkwêsikan– *NA* bannock, bread; flour
pahpakwatêyiht– *VTI* enjoy s.t., be amused by s.t.
pakahkam *IPC* I believe
pakahkihtaw– *VTA* hear s.o. clearly

pakicî– *VAI* release (him), let go of (him)
pakitin– *VTA* let s.o. go, give permission to s.o.
pakitin– *VTI* let s.t. go, release s.t., give s.t. up
pakitinamaw– *VTA* release (it/him) for s.o., arrange (it) for s.o.
pakitinâso– *VAI* hold a give-away ceremony
pakitinâsowin– *NI* give-away ceremony
pakitinikowisi– *VAI* be permitted by the powers
pakosêyim– *VTA* wish for (it/him) of s.o., expect (it/him) of s.o.
pakosêyimo– *VAI* wish for (it), have an expectation
pakosih– *VTA* beg from s.o.; be a hanger-on to s.o., go with s.o., be part of s.o.
pakwanawahtâ– *VAI* go on with (it) at random, know nothing about (it), be clueless about (it)
pakwâtamaw– *VTA* hate (it/him) for s.o., dislike (it/him) for s.o., disapprove of (it/him) for s.o.
pamih– *VTA* tend to s.o., look after s.o.
pamihikowin– *NI* being looked after, welfare [*sc. 'patient-centred' noun; e.g.,* kipamihikowin 'the fact that you are looked after']
pamihtâ– *VAI* look after (it)
pamin– *VTA* tend to s.o., look after s.o.
papakiwayânikamikw– *NI* tent
papâ *IPV* go about
papâmi *IPV* about, around, here and there
papâmihâ– *VAI* fly about
papâmipahtâ– *VAI* run about
papâmitisah– *VTI* chase s.t. about
pasikô– *VAI* arise (from sitting)
pasikôn– *VTA* raise s.o. (e.g., to a position of leadership)
pasikôn– *VTI* raise s.t. (e.g., lodge)
paskwâwi-mostosw– *NA* bison, buffalo
paso– *VAI* smell (it)
patahohkât– *VTA* overlook s.o., ignore s.o.
patitisahamaw– *VTA* drive (it/him) off the path for s.o., send (it/him) awry for s.o., spoil (it/him) for s.o.
patowât– *VTI* misspeak s.t., commit an error in one's prayers
pâh-pêyak *IPC* singly, one at a time; each individually
pâhpi– *VAI* laugh
pâhpih– *VTA* laugh at s.o., deride s.o.

pâmwayês *IPC* before [*temporal conjunction; cf.* mwayês]
pâpici– *VAI* move one's camp hither
pâskin– *VTI* open s.t. up, take the cover off s.t.; fold s.t. (e.g., book) open
pâstâhowin– *NI* transgression, breach of the natural order; sin
pâstâhôtot– *VTI* commit a transgression in s.t., commit sacrilege in s.t.
pê *IPV* thence, from there on down
pêhonânihk *INM* [*place-name:*] at Fort Carlton [*literally:* at the Waiting-Place]
pêht– *VTI* hear s.t.
pêhtamowin– *NI* what is heard [*sc. 'agent-centred' noun; e.g.,* kipêhtamowininâhk 'in what we have heard']
pêhtaw– *VTA* hear s.o.
pêhtâkosi– *VAI* be heard, make oneself heard
pêhtâkwan– *VII* be heard [*]
pêkopayi– *VAI* awake, wake up
pêpîsis– *NA* baby [*diminutive*]
pêtâ– *VAI* bring (it) hither
pêtâmo– *VAI* flee hither
pêtwêwêhtamaw– *VTA* come audibly bringing (it/him) for s.o.
pêyak *IPC* one, a single; the only one
pêyak-kîsikâw *IPC* one day
pêyak-misit *IPC* one foot (measure)
pêyak-tipiskâw *IPC* one night
pêyakosâp *IPC* eleven
pêyakoyâkan *IPC* one dish (measure)
pêyakwahpitêw *IPC* one team (of two horses)
pêyakwan *IPC* the same
pêyakwêskihk *IPC* one kettle (measure)
pêyakwêyimiso– *VAI* think solely of oneself
pêyâhtik *IPC* quietly, softly, slowly [*sic:* -i-]
pihcipôh– *VTA* poison s.o.
pihêwisimo– *VAI* dance the prairie-chicken dance
pihkoh– *VTA* free s.o., release s.o.
piko *IPC* only [*enclitic*]
piko *IPC* must, have to [*clause-initial predicative*]

pikoyikohk *IPC* no matter how much, to any extent [*also* pikw îyikohk]
pikw îta *IPC* no matter where, in any place
pikw îtê *IPC* no matter whither, to any place
pikw îyikohk *IPC* no matter how much, to any extent [*cf.* pikoyikohk]
pimakocin– *VII* make a rush in linear fashion, charge headlong
pimastê– *VII* be placed in linear fashion, run along
pimâcih– *VTA* make s.o. live, give life to s.o.; make a living for s.o.
pimâciho– *VAI* make a life for oneself, make one's living; live
pimâcihwâkê– *VAI* make one's living with things
pimâhtawî– *VAI* crawl along
pimâtisi– *VAI* live, be alive
pimâtisiwin– *NI* life [*also* pimâcisiwin–]
pimâtisiwinê– *VAI* have life, seek life
pimâtisiwinowi– *VII* have life, provide life
pimâwah– *VTA* lead s.o. along as a group, pull s.o. along
pimi *IPV* along, in linear progression; while moving in linear progression
pimiciwan– *VII* flow along
pimipayi– *VII* take place
pimipayihtâ– *VAI* run (it), keep (it) up, exercise (it)
pimitâpâso– *VAI* move along in a conveyance
pimohtah– *VTA* carry s.o. along, guide s.o. along
pimohtatâ– *VAI* carry (it) along, travel with (it)
pimohtât– *VTI* live s.t. (e.g., day), live through s.t.
pimohtê– *VAI* go along, walk along
pimohtêmakan– *VII* go along, move along; be in effect (e.g., treaty)
pimohtêstamaw– *VTA* go along for s.o., represent s.o.
pimohtêwin– *NI* travel [*sc. 'agent-centred' noun; e.g.,* nipimohtêwin 'my travelling']
pisiskêyim– *VTA* pay attention to s.o., tend s.o.; bother s.o., harrass s.o.
pisiskiw– *NA* animal
pita *IPC* first, for a while [*cf.* pitamâ]
pitamâ *IPC* first, for a while [*cf.* pita]
pitanê *IPC* wish that [*with simple conjunct*]

piyêsiw– *NA* [*spirit's name:*] Thunderbird
piyêsîs– *NA* bird
piyisk *IPC* finally, at last
pîhcawêsâkânis– *NI* undershirt, slip [*diminutive*]
pîhci *IPV* in between, inside
pîhtâpâwah– *VTA* pour liquid into s.o., give s.o. an enema
pîhtikwah– *VTA* enter with s.o., take s.o. inside
pîhtikwatâ– *VAI* enter with (it), take (it) inside
pîhtikwê– *VAI* enter, go inside
pîhtikwêmakan– *VII* enter, go inside
pîhtikwêtot– *VTI* enter s.t. (e.g., sweat-lodge)
pîhtwâ– *VAI* smoke, use the pipe; smoke (him) (e.g., pipe)
pîhtwâwikamikw– *NI* pipe-lodge ceremony
pîkiskwât– *VTA* speak to s.o.
pîkiskwât– *VTI* speak about s.t., speak about s.t. with concern; speak a prayer over s.t.
pîkiskwê– *VAI* use words, speak
pîkiskwêmohtâ– *VAI* cause (it) to speak; make an audio-recording [*]
pîkiskwêmôh– *VTA* cause s.o. to speak with concern
pîkiskwêstamaw– *VTA* speak for s.o., speak on s.o.'s behalf
pîkiskwêwin– *NI* word, expression, phrase; speech, language
pîkon– *VTI* break s.t.
pîkonamâso– *VAI* break (it) for oneself, break it oneself
pîkopayi– *VII* break down, be broken
pîkwatowan– *VII* be rotten (e.g., tooth)
pîminâhkwânis– *NI* string, rope [*diminutive*]
pîsâkwan– *VII* contain plenty, offer lots of room; be plentiful, be rich [*sic:* -â-]
pîsimw– *NA* sun [*cf.* kîsikâwi-pîsimw–]
pîtos *IPC* strangely, differently
pôn-âyamihêwi-kîsikâ– *VII* be Monday
pôni *IPV* cease
pônihtâ– *VAI* cease of (it)
pônipayi– *VII* cease, stop, come to an end
pôyo– *VAI* cease, quit
pwât– *NA* Sioux [*e.g.*, pwâtak]
sakahpit– *VTA* tie s.o. (e.g., horse) up

sakâpêkipah– *VTA* lead s.o. (e.g., horse) by a rope
santakilâws– *NA* Santa Claus
saskacihtaw– *VTA* be tired of hearing s.o., be fed up with hearing s.o.
saskahamaw– *VTA* light (it/him) for s.o.; light the pipe for s.o.
sawêyim– *VTA* be generous towards s.o., bless s.o.
sawohkât– *VTA* bestow a palpable blessing upon s.o. [*?sic*]
sâkahikan– *NI* lake
sâkaskinê– *VAI* crowd in, fill a place
sâkaskinêkâpawi– *VAI* stand crowded in, stand to fill a place
sâkâwanêhtâ– *VAI* push (it) to emerge from the ground, make (it) come forth
sâkêwêtot– *VTI* come out upon s.t., rise (e.g., sun) upon s.t.
sâkihtamaw– *VTA* hold on to (it/him) for s.o.; hold (it/him) back from s.o.
sâkikihtâ– *VAI* make (it) (e.g., earth) bring forth plants
sâkikin– *VII* grow forth, emerge from the ground
sâkohtê– *VAI* walk into view, move into view
sâkôcih– *VTA* overcome s.o., beat s.o.
sâkôh– *VTA* overcome s.o., overwhelm s.o.
sêkim– *VTA* frighten s.o. by speech
sêkipatwâ– *VAI* braid one's hair, have braided hair
sêkisi– *VAI* be afraid
sêmâk *IPC* immediately, right away
sêwêpin– *VTA* make s.o. (e.g., rattle) ring out
sêwêpitamaw– *VTA* make (it) ring out for s.o.; call s.o. by telephone
sihko– *VAI* spit, spit out
simâkanis– *NA* policeman
sipwêhtê– *VAI* leave, depart
sipwêmon– *VII* leave as path, trail, road; begin as path, trail, road
sîhkim– *VTA* urge s.o. by speech
sîkahasinânâpoy– *NI* rock-sprinkling water (in sweat-lodge)
sîkatêhtamaw– *VTA* spit (it/him) out for s.o.
sîkihtatamaw– *VTA* pour (it) for s.o.
sîn– *VTI* wring s.t. out
sîpâ *IPC* beneath, underneath

sîpi *IPV* stretching far back
sîpiy– *NI* river
sîsîkwan– *NA* rattle
sôhkan– *VII* be powerful
sôniyâw– *NA* gold, silver; money
sôniyâwi– *VII* be precious metal; be money
sôniyâwikimâw– *NA* Indian agent
sôskwât *IPC* simply, without further ado
tahk âyiwâk *IPC* increasingly, more and more
tahkam– *VTA* stab s.o. [*reduplicated:* tâh-tahkam–]
tahkâpâwat– *VTA* pour water to cool s.o. (e.g., rock), cool s.o. (e.g., rock) with water (in sweat-lodge)
tahkon– *VTI* carry s.t., hold s.t.
tahkonamôh– *VTA* make s.o. carry (it/him), make s.o. hold (it/him)
tahto *IPC* so many, as many
tahto-kîkway *IPC* so many things, as many things
tahto-kîsikâw *IPC* every day, daily
tahto-nîso-kîsikâw *IPC* every second day, every other day
tahto-nîsw-âyamihêwi-kîsikâw *IPC* every second week, fortnightly
tahtwayak *IPC* in so many places, in so many ways
tahtwâw *IPC* so many times
takahki *IPN* nice, good, beautiful
takohtê– *VAI* arrive walking
takopayi– *VAI* arrive on horseback, arrive by conveyance
takwastâ– *VAI* add (it) in
takwâwahito– *VAI* arrive pulling one another along, arrive as a crowd
tapahcipayiho– *VAI* swoop down, swoop low
tasi *IPV* for such a time, for the duration
tasihtamaw– *VTA* discuss (it/him) with s.o. [*]
tasîhk– *VTI* bother with s.t., trifle with s.t.; be engaged in s.t.
taswêkin– *VTI* open s.t. (e.g., book) up flat
tawâ– *VII* be open, have room
tawâtamaw– *VTA* open (it) up for s.o.; clear the way for s.o.
tâhkôm– *VTA* discuss s.o., discourse upon s.o.
tâhkôt– *VTI* discuss s.t., discourse upon s.t.

tânêhki *IPC* why
tânima *PR* which one
tânisi *IPC* how, in what way
tânispî *IPC* when, at what time
tânita *IPC* where
tânitahtwayak *IPC* in how many places; in so many places
tânitahtwâw *IPC* how many times; so many times
tânitê *IPC* where, whither
tâniyikohk *IPC* to what extent; to such an extent
tâpiskôc *IPC* it seems, seemingly, apparently; as if
tâpitawi *IPC* all the time
tâpowê- *VAI* speak correctly; recite one's prayer correctly
tâpwê *IPC* truly, indeed
tâpwê- *VAI* speak true, speak the truth
tâpwêht- *VTI* agree with s.t., believe s.t.
tâpwêhtaw- *VTA* agree with s.o., believe s.o.
tâpwêmakan- *VII* come true; [*fig.*] be fulfilled
tâpwêwakêyiht- *VTI* believe in s.t.
tâpwêwakêyim- *VTA* believe in s.o.
tâwin- *VTA* encounter s.o., bump into s.o., hit s.o.
têpakohposâp *IPC* seventeen
têpâpam- *VTA* see plenty of s.o., see s.o. fully
têpi *IPV* fully, sufficiently
têpinêhamaw- *VTA* make full payment for (it/him) to s.o.
têpipayi- *VAI* have the full amount, have enough
têpiyâhk *IPC* the only thing; the most (if any)
têpwât- *VTA* call out to s.o., yell at s.o.
têpwâtamaw- *VTA* call out for s.o., be an advocate for s.o.
tipah- *VTI* measure s.t.; pay s.t., pay for s.t.
tipahamaw- *VTA* pay s.o. for (it/him), repay a debt to s.o.
tipahamâtowin- *NI* treaty
tipêyiht- *VTI* own s.t., control s.t.
tipêyim- *VTA* own s.o., control s.o.
tipêyimiso- *VAI* control oneself, govern oneself
tipiskohk *IPC* last night
tipiyaw *IPC* personally, really
tipôt- *VTI* discuss s.t. with authority

titipawêhkas– *VTI* curl s.t. (e.g., head of hair) by heat; have a perm
tôt– *VTI* do s.t. thus [*cf.* itôt-]
tôtamaw– *VTA* do (it) thus for s.o.
tôtaw– *VTA* do thus to s.o.
wacistwan– *NI* nest
wahwâ *IPC* oh my! [*exclamatory*]
wanihtâ– *VAI* lose (it); get relief from (it)
wanikiskisi– *VAI* forget (it)
wanisim– *VTA* cause s.o. to get lost, lead s.o. astray
wanisinohtah– *VTA* lead s.o. to lose (it/him)
waniskâ– *VAI* arise (from lying down or sleep)
waskawîtot– *VTI* carry on with s.t.
waskawîwin– *NI* being active, enterprise
waskitaskamik *IPC* on the face of the earth
watihkwan– *NI* branch
wawânaskêhtamaw– *VTA* create a peaceful life for s.o.
wawânaskêhtâ– *VAI* live a peaceful life
wawânêyiht– *VTI* worry about s.t., be worried
wawânêyihtamih– *VTA* cause s.o. to worry about (it/him)
wayawî– *VAI* go outside
wâ *IPC* well [*introductory; cf.* â]
wâh-wâhyaw *IPC* in far places [*reduplicated*]
wâhyaw *IPC* far
wâpahki *IPC* tomorrow
wâpaht– *VTI* see s.t., witness s.t.
wâpam– *VTA* see s.o., witness s.o.
wâpan– *VII* be dawn, be early morning
wâpi– *VAI* be sighted, have vision; [*in negative clause:*] be blind
wâpiskâ– *VII* be white
wâpiski-wiyâs– *NA* White-Man, White
wâsakâmêsimowin– *NI* ghost-dance
wâsakân– *VTI* turn s.t. around a circle
wâsakâtisahoto– *VAI* chase one another around a circle
wâsakâyâskon– *VTA* point s.o. (e.g., pipe) right around (full circle)
wâskahikan– *NI* house
wâtihkân– *NI* hole, cellar

wâwâskêsiwacîs– *NI* [*place-name*] [*diminutive; literally:* Elk-Hill, Red-Deer-Hill]
wâwîs *IPC* especially
wâwîs cî *IPC* especially, all the more so
wâyonî– *VAI* turn back, return
wêhcasin– *VII* be easy
wêpêyim– *VTA* be inclined to throw s.o. (e.g., money) away
wêpin– *VTA* throw s.o. away; abandon s.o. (e.g., child)
wêpin– *VTI* throw s.t. away
wêpinâson– *NI* draped cloth, flag, cloth offering
wêpinikâtê– *VII* be thrown away, be abandoned, be discarded
wêtinahk *IPC* quietly
wêwêkahpit– *VTA* wrap and tie s.o. up
wiya *IPC* for, because [*also* wiyê*; clause-initial causal conjunction*]
wiya *PR* he, she
wiyahisow– *NA* blacksmith
wiyakâc *IPC* it is regrettable [*predicative*]
wiyakihtamaw– *VTA* set a price on (it/him) for s.o., charge s.o. for (it/him)
wiyakim– *VTA* set a price on s.o. (e.g., bread); arrange (it) for s.o.; decide on s.o.; give orders to s.o.
wiyaskinah– *VTA* fill s.o. (e.g., pipe)
wiyawâw *PR* they
wiyâkanis– *NI* small dish, small bowl [*diminutive*]
wiyihcikê– *VAI* arrange things, conduct negotiations, conclude a treaty
wî *IPV* intend to
wîc-âyâm– *VTA* be with s.o., live with s.o.
wîcêhto– *VAI* live with one another, join with one another; get along with one another
wîcêhtowin– *NI* living with one another; getting along with one another, living in harmony with one another
wîcêw– *VTA* accompany s.o., join s.o.
wîci-pîhtwâm– *VTA* smoke together with s.o.
wîci-pîkiskwêm– *VTA* speak together with s.o.
wîcih– *VTA* help s.o.
wîcihiwê– *VAI* be along, be part of a group, join in
wîcôhkamaw– *VTA* help s.o. by action

wîh– *VTA* name s.o., mention s.o. by name
wîhcêkaskosîwi-sâkahikanihk *INM* [*place-name:*] at Onion Lake
wîhkaskoyiniw– *NA* [*spirit's name:*] Sweetgrass-Old-Man
wîhkaskw– *NI* sweetgrass
wîhkâc *IPC* ever; [*in negative clause:*] never
wîhkês– *NI* ratroot
wîhkohkât– *VTI* hold a feast for s.t. (e.g., medicinal herbs)
wîhkohkê– *VAI* hold a feast
wîhkohto– *VAI* invite one another to a feast
wîhkom– *VTA* invite s.o. to a feast
wîhkwâs– *NI* craw, first stomach of fowl
wîhkwêskamikâ– *VII* be the corners of the earth
wîht– *VTI* tell about s.t., report s.t.; decree s.t.
wîhtamaw– *VTA* tell s.o. about (it/him)
wîki– *VAI* live, dwell, have one's abode
wîmâskaw– *VTA* pass around s.o., pass s.o. by
wîsahkêcâhkw– *NA* Wisahketchahk
wîscihkêsi– *VAI* pile hay into small heaps [*diminutive*]
wîsta *PR* he, too; she, too; he by contrast, she by contrast
wîstawâw *PR* they, too; they, by contrast; they themselves
wîtapim– *VTA* sit with s.o., be present with s.o.; work together with s.o.
wîtaskîwêm– *VTA* live together with s.o.; live in the same country with s.o., live in peace with s.o.
wîtatoskêm– *VTA* work together with s.o.
wîtimosi– *VAI* have a cross-cousin of the opposite sex, have (him/her) as cross-cousin of the opposite sex
yahkatâmo– *VAI* sing out vigorously
yâhk îtâp *IPC* as if, pretendingly
yîkatêhtê– *VAI* walk off to the side
yîkatên– *VTI* set s.t. aside
yôhô *IPC* oh! [*exclamatory*]
yôhtên– *VTI* open s.t.; turn s.t. (e.g., television set) on
yôhtênamaw– *VTA* open (it/him) for s.o.; turn (it/him) (e.g., television set) on for s.o.
yôtin– *NA* [*spirit's name:*] Wind [*cf.* iyôtin–]

English Index to the Glossary

This is a *selective* index of the English glosses which correspond to each Cree stem. Thus it is merely a rough guide to the entries in the glossary and should not be confused with the English-Cree part of a bilingual dictionary.

It often takes several English words or phrases to capture the meaning of a single Cree stem, e.g.,

> **itakihtê-** *VII* be counted thus, cost so much; be held in such esteem.

In its literal sense, this stem appears under COUNT and COST (while no effort has been made also to include stems of this type under headwords like THUS, SO, SUCH); in its transferred sense, it is indexed under ESTEEM. A single Cree stem may thus give rise to several entries in the English index.

Conversely, the entries listed under a single headword are arranged simply in alphabetical order; no attempt has been made to group them semantically (e.g., 'sound a beat upon s.o. (e.g., drum)' vs 'beat s.o., overcome s.o.' under BEAT) or syntactically (e.g., under DOCTOR, the noun for 'doctor, physician' vs the verb glossed 'doctor s.o., heal s.o.').

Although the headwords themselves may be ambiguous, the individual entries which are listed under them are fully identified by stem, stem-class code and an explicit gloss. The distinction between headword and cited entry emphasises the fact that this is not a dictionary but merely an index.

Index

ABANDON

wêpin– *VTA* throw s.o. away; abandon s.o. (e.g., child)

wêpinikâtê– *VII* be thrown away, be abandoned, be discarded

ABLE

kaskihtâ– *VAI* be able to do (it), be competent at (it)

kî *IPV* able to

ABODE

wîki– *VAI* live, dwell, have one's abode

ABOUT

papâ *IPV* go about

papâmi *IPV* about, around, here and there

papâmihâ– *VAI* fly about

papâmipahtâ– *VAI* run about

papâmitisah– *VTI* chase s.t. about

ABOVE

ispimihk *IPC* high up, up above

ABOVE ALL

mêmohci *IPC* in particular, above all; exactly, precisely

ABUNDANCE

minahikoskâ– *VII* be a spruce thicket, be an abundance of spruce

ABUSIVE

kakwâtakih– *VTA* make s.o. suffer, be mean to s.o., be abusive to s.o.

ACCOMPANY

wîcêw– *VTA* accompany s.o., join s.o.

ACCOMPLISH

miyoniskêhkât– *VTI* accomplish s.t. by the work of one's hands

miyopit– *VTI* carry s.t. off well, accomplish s.t.

ACCOUNT

âcimo– *VAI* tell, tell a story, give an account

âcimostaw– *VTA* tell s.o. about (it/him), give s.o. an account

âcimowin– *NI* story, account, report

âtot– *VTI* tell about s.t., give an account of s.t.

itâtot– *VTI* tell about s.t. thus, give such an account of s.t.

ACROSS

akâmaskîhk *IPC* across the water, overseas

âsowahpitê– *VII* be stretched across, be strung across

ACTIVE

waskawîwin– *NI* being active, enterprise

ADD

takwastâ– *VAI* add (it) in

ADDITIONALLY

asici *IPC* also, additionally

ADDRESS

kitot– *VTA* address s.o., speak to s.o., lecture s.o.

ADULT

nâpêw– *NA* man, male, adult male

ADVISE AGAINST

kitahamaw– *VTA* advise s.o. against (it/him)

ADVOCATE

otitwêstamâkêw– *NA* interpreter; advocate

otônihkâ– *VAI* use (it/him) as one's mouthpiece, make (it/him) one's advocate

têpwâtamaw– *VTA* call out for s.o., be an advocate for s.o.

AFFECTED

ispayi– *VAI* be thus affected; be thus afflicted

AFFLICTED

ispayi– *VAI* be thus affected; be thus afflicted

AFRAID

sêkisi– *VAI* be afraid

AGAIN

kâwi *IPC* again

kîhtwâm *IPC* again

AGE

ispîhtisî– *VAI* be of such an age

nayawaciki– *VAI* grow up to reach various ages, be variously grown up [*usually plural*]

AGED

–îci-kîhkâw– *NDA* aged spouse, fellow old person, fellow oldster, companion of one's old age [*e.g.*, wîci-kîhkâwa]

AGENT

otasahkêw– *NA* one who distributes rations; Indian agent

sôniyâwikimâw– *NA* Indian agent

AGO

kayâs *IPC* long ago, in earlier days; previously

kayâsês *IPC* quite a long time ago

AGREE

tâpwêht– *VTI* agree with s.t., believe s.t.

tâpwêhtaw– *VTA* agree with s.o., believe s.o.

AGRICULTURAL

kistikêwi-pimâcihowin– *NI* agricultural way of life, farm economy

AH

ayi *IPC* ah [*hesitatory*]

AHEAD

nîkâniwi– *VII* be ahead, be the future; lie in the future [*sic:* -i-]

ALIVE

pimâtisi– *VAI* live, be alive

ALL

êkosi *IPC* thus, in that way; that is all

kahkiyaw *IPC* all

tâpitawi *IPC* all the time

ALL-FATHER

mâmaw-ôhtâwîmâw– *NA* [*fig.*] All-Father

ALLEVIATE

ânisîhtâ– *VAI* alleviate the effect of (it), be an antidote to (it)

ALOFT

nîminamaw– *VTA* hold (it/him) aloft for s.o., offer (it/him) up for s.o.

nîminikê– *VAI* hold things aloft, offer things up

ALONG

ocipit– *VTA* pull s.o. along, pull s.o. in

pimastê– *VII* be placed in linear fashion, run along

pimâhtawî– *VAI* crawl along

pimâwah– *VTA* lead s.o. along as a group, pull s.o. along

pimi *IPV* along, in linear progression; while moving in linear progression

pimiciwan– *VII* flow along

pimitâpâso– *VAI* move along in a conveyance

pimohtah– *VTA* carry s.o. along, guide s.o. along

pimohtatâ– *VAI* carry (it) along, travel with (it)

pimohtê– *VAI* go along, walk along

pimohtêmakan– *VII* go along, move along; be in effect (e.g., treaty)

pimohtêstamaw– *VTA* go along for s.o., represent s.o.

takwâwahito– *VAI* arrive pulling one another along, arrive as a crowd

ALONG WITH

kikapi– *VAI* sit along with something

kikastê– *VII* be placed along with something

kiki *IPV* along with

ALREADY

âsay *IPC* already; without delay [*also aspectual*]

ALSO

asici *IPC* also, additionally

mîna *IPC* also, and also

ALTHOUGH

âta *IPC* although; on the other hand [*concessive conjunction*]

ALWAYS

kâkikê *IPC* always, forever

AMOUNT

têpipayi– *VAI* have the full amount, have enough

AMUSED

pahpakwatêyiht– *VTI* enjoy s.t., be amused by s.t.

AND

êkwa *IPC* then, now; and

mîna *IPC* also, and also

ANGER

kisiwâh– *VTA* anger s.o.

kisîhto– *VAI* anger one another by speech

kisîkitot– *VTA* speak to s.o. in anger [*sic:* -î-]

kisîm– *VTA* anger s.o. by speech

ANIMAL

pisiskiw– *NA* animal

ANOTHER

kotak *PR* other, another [*e.g.*, kotaka]

ANSWER

naskom– *VTA* respond to s.o. with (it/him), answer s.o.'s prayer with (it/him)

ANTIDOTE

ânisîhtâ– *VAI* alleviate the effect of (it), be an antidote to (it)

ANY

kîkway *PR* something, thing; [*in negative clause:*] anything, any [*indefinite; e.g.*, kîkway]

misawâc *IPC* in any case, whatever might be thought

môy êkâ êtokwê *IPC* without any doubt, of necessity [*usually with independent indicative*]

pikoyikohk *IPC* no matter how much, to any extent [*also* pikw îyikohk]

pikw îta *IPC* no matter where, in any place

pikw îtê *IPC* no matter whither, to any place

pikw îyikohk *IPC* no matter how much, to any extent [*cf.* pikoyikohk]

ANYONE

awiyak *PR* someone; [*in negative clause:*] anyone [*indefinite; e.g.*, awiyak]

ANYTHING

kîkway *PR* something, thing; [*in negative clause:*] anything, any [*indefinite; e.g.*, kîkway]

nânitaw *IPC* simply; something, anything; something bad, anything bad; somewhere; approximately [*usually with pejorative presupposition*]

APPARENTLY

tâpiskôc *IPC* it seems, seemingly, apparently; as if

APPLIANCE

âpacihcikan– *NI* tool; appliance, machine

APPROXIMATELY

nânitaw *IPC* simply; something, anything; something bad, anything bad; somewhere; approximately [*usually with pejorative presupposition*]

ARISE

pasikô– *VAI* arise (from sitting)

waniskâ– *VAI* arise (from lying down or sleep)

ARM

isiniskêyi– *VAI* move one's arm thus or there, point in that direction with one's arm

AROUND

kwêski *IPV* turned around, turned to the opposite side

kwêskinâkwan– *VII* look changed, look turned around to the opposite

papâmi *IPV* about, around, here and there

wâsakân– *VTI* turn s.t. around a circle

wâsakâtisahoto– *VAI* chase one another around a circle

wâsakâyâskon– *VTA* point s.o. (e.g., pipe) right around (full circle)

wîmâskaw– *VTA* pass around s.o., pass s.o. by

ARRANGE

pakitinamaw– *VTA* release (it/him) for s.o., arrange (it) for s.o.

wiyakim– *VTA* set a price on s.o. (e.g., bread); arrange (it) for s.o.; decide on s.o.; give orders to s.o.

wiyihcikê– *VAI* arrange things, conduct negotiations, conclude a treaty

ARRIVE

takohtê– *VAI* arrive walking

takopayi– *VAI* arrive on horseback, arrive by conveyance

takwâwahito– *VAI* arrive pulling one another along, arrive as a crowd

ARTHRITIS

oskaninê– *VAI* suffer from arthritis

AS IF

tâpiskôc *IPC* it seems, seemingly, apparently; as if

yâhk îtâp *IPC* as if, pretendingly

AS MANY

tahto *IPC* so many, as many

tahto-kîkway *IPC* so many things, as many things

AS SOON

mayaw *IPC* as soon as [*temporal conjunction*]

ASIDE

yîkatên– *VTI* set s.t. aside

ASK

kakwêcim– *VTA* ask s.o.; make a request of s.o.; ask s.o. about (it/him)

nitotamaw– *VTA* ask s.o. for (it/him)

nitotamâ– *VAI* ask for (it), pray for (it), make a request for (it)

ASTRAY

wanisim– *VTA* cause s.o. to get lost, lead s.o. astray

AT

êkospî *IPC* then, at that time

iskwêyâc *IPC* at last, at the end

ispî *IPC* at such a time, then

itâskonamaw– *VTA* thus point the pipe for s.o., thus point the pipe at s.o.

itâskonamawât– *VTI* thus point the pipe at s.t.

kêtahtawê *IPC* suddenly; at one time

kitâpaht– *VTI* look at s.t.

kitâpam– *VTA* look at s.o.

nânapêc *IPC* late, at the last moment, barely in time (e.g., when it should have been done previously); [*in negative clause:*] too late

nâway *IPC* behind, at the rear

nîkân *IPC* first, at the head

nîkâni– *VAI* be at the lead (e.g., tobacco)

nîkânist– *VTI* be at the head of s.t., lead s.t. [*sic:* -i-; *cf.* nîkânîst–]

nîkânîh– *VTA* place s.o. (e.g., tobacco) at the lead

piyisk *IPC* finally, at last

tânispî *IPC* when, at what time

ATTENTION

nâkatowâpaht– *VTI* pay attention in looking at s.t.

nâkatôhkê– *VAI* pay attention, take notice

pisiskêyim– *VTA* pay attention to s.o., tend s.o.; bother s.o., harrass s.o.

AUDIBLY

pêtwêwêhtamaw– *VTA* come audibly bringing (it/him) for s.o.

AUDIO-RECORDING

pîkiskwêmohtâ– *VAI* cause (it) to speak; make an audio-recording [*]

AUTHORITY

tipôt– *VTI* discuss s.t. with authority

AWAKE

pêkopayi– *VAI* awake, wake up

AWAY

aspin *IPC* off, away; the last I knew

awas *IPC* go away! away with you! [*]

ohpimê *IPC* off, away, to the side

wêpêyim– *VTA* be inclined to throw s.o. (e.g., money) away

wêpin– *VTA* throw s.o. away; abandon s.o. (e.g., child)

wêpin– *VTI* throw s.t. away

wêpinikâtê– *VII* be thrown away, be abandoned, be discarded

AWRY

patitisahamaw– *VTA* drive (it/him) off the path for s.o., send (it/him) awry for s.o., spoil (it/him) for s.o.

BABY

pêpîsis– *NA* baby [*diminutive*]

BACK

asên– *VTA* reject s.o., turn s.o. back

asên– *VTI* reject s.t., turn s.t. back

kîwêmakan– *VII* return home, come back

wâyonî– *VAI* turn back, return

BAD

kitimah– *VTA* be mean to s.o., treat s.o. badly

maci-kîkway– *NI* something bad, bad things

macipayi– *VII* go badly

mâyitôt– *VTI* do bad things, cause serious trouble

miywakihtê– *VII* be considered good; [*in negative clause:*] be considered bad, be considered evil

miywâsin– *VII* be good, be valuable; [*in negative clause:*] be bad, be evil

nânitaw *IPC* simply; something, anything; something bad, anything bad; somewhere; approximately [*usually with pejorative presupposition*]

BALANCED

awâska-mâmitonêyihcikan– *NI* stable mind, steady mind, balanced mind [*?sic*]

BANNOCK

pahkwêsikan– *NA* bannock, bread; flour

BARE

mohcihk *IPC* on the bare ground

BARELY

kêtisk *IPC* just barely, to exact measure

nânapêc *IPC* late, at the last moment, barely in time (e.g., when it should have been done previously); [*in negative clause:*] too late

BEAR

kimotôsê– *VAI* bear an illegitimate child

BEARD

mîstowân– *NI* beard [*sic:* -î-; *cf.* -îhi-]

mîstowê– *VAI* be bearded, wear a beard [*sic:* -î-; *cf.* -îhi-]

BEAT

matwêhw– *VTA* sound a beat upon s.o. (e.g., drum), drum on s.o.

sâkôcih– *VTA* overcome s.o., beat s.o.

BEAUTIFUL

miyo *IPV* good, well, beautiful, valuable

takahki *IPN* nice, good, beautiful

BECAUSE

ayis *IPC* for, because [*causal conjunction; also* ayisk]

ohci *IPC* with, by means of; because of; from then [*enclitic; also* IPV]

osâm *IPC* because; for [*causal conjunction*]

wiya *IPC* for, because [*also* wiyê; *clause-initial causal conjunction*]

BEFORE

mwayês *IPC* before [*temporal conjunction; cf.* pâmwayês]

pâmwayês *IPC* before [*temporal conjunction; cf.* mwayês]

BEFOREHAND

mâtayak *IPC* beforehand, in advance

BEG

pakosih– *VTA* beg from s.o.; be a hanger-on to s.o., go with s.o., be part of s.o.

BEGIN

mâci *IPV* begin; initially

mâtâskonikê– *VAI* begin to point the pipe

sipwêmon– *VII* leave as path, trail, road; begin as path, trail, road

BEHALF

nitotamâkêstamaw– *VTA* make a request for s.o., on s.o.'s behalf

pîkiskwêstamaw– *VTA* speak for s.o., speak on s.o.'s behalf

BEHIND

âkaw-âyihk *IPC* in a hidden place, behind an obstacle to vision

nakat– *VTA* leave s.o. behind

nakat– *VTI* leave s.t. behind

nakatamaw– *VTA* leave (it/him) behind for s.o.

nâway *IPC* behind, at the rear

BEHOLD

îh *IPC* look! behold! [*exclamatory*]

BELIEVE

pakahkam *IPC* I believe

tâpwêht– *VTI* agree with s.t., believe s.t.

tâpwêhtaw– *VTA* agree with s.o., believe s.o.

tâpwêwakêyiht– *VTI* believe in s.t.

tâpwêwakêyim– *VTA* believe in s.o.

BELOW

ay-atâmaskamik *IPC* inside the earth, below the ground [*reduplicated*]

BENEATH

sîpâ *IPC* beneath, underneath

BEREAVED

mâyipayi– *VAI* suffer ill; be bereaved

BERRY

mînis– *NI* berry

BESTOW

sawohkât– *VTA* bestow a palpable blessing upon s.o. [*?sic*]

BETTER

âstê-kîsikâ– *VII* cease being stormy weather, be better weather

nawac *IPC* more, better, rather

BETWEEN

pîhci *IPV* in between, inside

BEYOND

kôtatê *IPC* at a loss; due to limitations beyond one's control [*also predicative:* 'it cannot be helped'*; cf.* kwêtatêyitiskwêyi–]

BIBLE

masinahikan– *NI* book; written document; bible

nêhiyawasinahikan– *NI* Cree book; Cree bible

nêhiyawi-masinahikan– *NI* Cree book; Cree bible

BIG

mahkihtawâkê– *VAI* have a big ear [*usually reduplicated:* mâh-mahkihtawâkê– 'have big ears']

BIRD

piyêsîs– *NA* bird

BIRTH

nihtâwikihtâ– *VAI* give birth to (it), bring (it) forth

nihtâwikinâwaso– *VAI* give birth to a child, bring forth a child, bring forth a young one (of the species)

BISON

paskwâwi-mostosw– *NA* bison, buffalo

BLACKSMITH

wiyahisow– *NA* blacksmith

BLESS

sawêyim– *VTA* be generous towards s.o., bless s.o.

sawohkât– *VTA* bestow a palpable blessing upon s.o. [*?sic*]

BLIND

wâpi– *VAI* be sighted, have vision; [*in negative clause:*] be blind

BODY

itakâm *IPC* on the hither side of a body of water, on the near side of a body of water

BOOK

masinahikan– *NI* book; written document; bible

nêhiyawasinahikan– *NI* Cree book; Cree bible

nêhiyawi-masinahikan– *NI* Cree book; Cree bible

BORN

nôkosi– *VAI* be visible; be born

BOTHER

moskâcih– *VTA* bother s.o., trouble s.o., hurt s.o.

pisiskêyim– *VTA* pay attention to s.o., tend s.o.; bother s.o., harrass s.o.

tasîhk– *VTI* bother with s.t., trifle with s.t.; be engaged in s.t.

BOWL

wiyâkanis– *NI* small dish, small bowl [*diminutive*]

BRAID

apihkât– *VTI* braid s.t.

apihkâtamaw– *VTA* braid (it/him) for s.o.

apihkâtê– *VII* be braided

nistwapihkât– *VTI* braid s.t. in three

sêkipatwâ– *VAI* braid one's hair, have braided hair

BRANCH

watihkwan– *NI* branch

BREACH

pâstâhowin– *NI* transgression, breach of the natural order; sin

BREAD

pahkwêsikan– *NA* bannock, bread; flour

BREAK

nâtwâpayi– *VII* break off (e.g., branch)

nâtwâwêpah– *VTI* break s.t. off and throw it down

pîkon– *VTI* break s.t.

pîkonamâso– *VAI* break (it) for oneself, break it oneself

pîkopayi– *VII* break down, be broken

BRING

nihtâwikihtâ– *VAI* give birth to (it), bring (it) forth

nihtâwikinâwaso– *VAI* give birth to a child, bring forth a child, bring forth a young one (of the species)

pêtâ– *VAI* bring (it) hither

pêtwêwêhtamaw– *VTA* come audibly bringing (it/him) for s.o.

sâkikihtâ– *VAI* make (it) (e.g., earth) bring forth plants

BROKEN

pîkopayi– *VII* break down, be broken

BROTHER

–ciwâm– *NDA* male parallel cousin (man speaking); [*fig.*] brother, male of the same generation (man speaking) [*e.g.*, kiciwâminaw]

–ôhcâwîs– *NDA* father's brother [*e.g.*, nôhcâwîs]

–ôhtâwiy– *NDA* father, father's brother; [*fig.*] Our Father [*e.g.*, kôhtâwînawak; kôhtâwînaw]

–stês– *NDA* older brother [*e.g.*, kistêsinaw]

BUFFALO

paskwâwi-mostosw– *NA* bison, buffalo

BUG

manicôs– *NA* insect, bug

BUILD

mânokê– *VAI* build a lodge, set up a tent

BUMP INTO

tâwin– *VTA* encounter s.o., bump into s.o., hit s.o.

BURIAL

akot– *VTA* hang s.o. up; place s.o. on a burial scaffold

BUT

mâka *IPC* but [*concessive*]

BUY

atâm– *VTA* buy (it/him) from s.o.

atâwê– *VAI* buy (it)

atâwêstamaw– *VTA* buy (it/him) for s.o.

kîspinat– *VTI* earn enough to buy s.t.; earn s.t. as reward, earn one's reward

nâcinêhamaw– *VTA* obtain (it/him) from s.o. by payment, seek to buy medicine from s.o.

nâcinêhikê– *VAI* obtain things by payment, seek to buy medicine

BY

cîki *IPC* close, close by

CALL

isiyîhkâso– *VAI* be called thus, have such a name

isiyîhkât– *VTA* call s.o. thus, use such a name for s.o.

isiyîhkât– *VTI* call s.t. thus, use such a name for s.t.

isiyîhkâtê– *VII* be called thus, have such a name

itwê– *VAI* say thus, call (it) thus; have such a meaning

nêhiyawi-wîh– *VTA* use s.o.'s Cree name, call s.o. by a Cree name

nêhiyawi-wîht– *VTI* use the Cree name of s.t., call s.t. by a Cree name

sêwêpitamaw– *VTA* make (it) ring out for s.o.; call s.o. by telephone

têpwât– *VTA* call out to s.o., yell at s.o.

têpwâtamaw– *VTA* call out for s.o., be an advocate for s.o.

CAMP

pâpici– *VAI* move one's camp hither

CARE

mâmâsîs *IPC* sparingly, delicately; quickly, roughly, without care

miyawâkâc *IPV* with particular care

CAREFUL

miyawâkâtinikê– *VAI* be particularly careful in handling things (e.g., ceremonial objects)

CARRY

nîkânohtatâ– *VAI* be in the lead with (it), carry (it) in the lead

pimohtah– *VTA* carry s.o. along, guide s.o. along

pimohtatâ– *VAI* carry (it) along, travel with (it)

tahkon– *VTI* carry s.t., hold s.t.

tahkonamôh– *VTA* make s.o. carry (it/him), make s.o. hold (it/him)

CARRY OFF

miyopit– *VTI* carry s.t. off well, accomplish s.t.

CARRY ON

waskawîtot– *VTI* carry on with s.t.

CART

ocâpânâskos– *NI* cart; small wagon, small sled [*diminutive*]

CARTOON

ayisiyinîhkân– *NA* doll, mannikin; cartoon figure

CATCH

kâhcitin– *VTA* catch s.o. [*also* kâhtitin–]

CATTLE

mostosw– *NA* cattle, cow

CAUSE

astâh– *VTA* frighten s.o.; [*especially in inverse:*] cause s.o. to be wary, worry s.o.

mâmitonêyihtamih– *VTA* cause s.o. to think about (it/him), cause s.o. to worry about (it/him)

mâyitôt– *VTI* do bad things, cause serious trouble

nahêyihtamih– *VTA* cause s.o. to be satisfied with (it/him); grant s.o. peace of mind
pîkiskwêmohtâ– *VAI* cause (it) to speak; make an audio-recording [*]
pîkiskwêmôh– *VTA* cause s.o. to speak with concern
wanisim– *VTA* cause s.o. to get lost, lead s.o. astray
wawânêyihtamih– *VTA* cause s.o. to worry about (it/him)

CEASE
âstê-kîsikâ– *VII* cease being stormy weather, be better weather
pôni *IPV* cease
pônihtâ– *VAI* cease of (it)
pônipayi– *VII* cease, stop, come to an end
pôyo– *VAI* cease, quit

CELLAR
wâtihkân– *NI* hole, cellar

CENSE
miyâhkas– *VTI* cense s.t., smudge s.t. with sweetgrass
miyâhkasamaw– *VTA* cense (it/him) for s.o., smudge (it/him) with sweetgrass for s.o.
miyâhkasikê– *VAI* cense things, smudge things with sweetgrass
miyâhkasw– *VTA* cense s.o. (e.g., pipe), smudge s.o. (e.g., pipe) with sweetgrass

CEREMONIAL
kîsitêpo– *VAI* cook; cook a feast, cook ceremonial food
kîsitêw– *NI* food, ceremonial food

CEREMONY
itâskonikê– *VAI* thus point the pipe or pipestem; thus hold a pipe ceremony
itâskonikêwin– *NI* thus pointing the pipe or pipestem; such a pipe ceremony
itikwamikohkê– *VAI* hold such a lodge, hold such a ceremony
kosâpaht– *VTI* hold a shaking-lodge, hold the shaking-lodge ceremony
mawimoscikêwin– *NI* crying out in prayer, wailing; form of worship, ceremony
nipâkwêsimowikamikw– *NI* sundance-lodge, sundance ceremony
pakitinâso– *VAI* hold a give-away ceremony
pakitinâsowin– *NI* give-away ceremony

pîhtwâwikamikw– *NI* pipe-lodge ceremony

CERTAIN

kêhcinâ *IPC* surely, for certain

CHALLENGE

kotêyiht– *VTI* try s.t. in one's mind, think strenuously about s.t., test s.t.; challenge s.t.

kotêyim– *VTA* try s.o., test s.o., put s.o.'s mind to the test; challenge s.o.

mâyêyiht– *VTI* consider s.t. challenging; be willing to tackle a difficult task, venture out

CHANGE

âhcîhtâ– *VAI* make (it) over, make (it) different, change (it)

kwêskinâkwan– *VII* look changed, look turned around to the opposite

kwêskinisk *IPC* the other hand, changing one's hand

CHANT

kâkîsimo– *VAI* pray, plead, chant prayers

kâkîsimotot– *VTI* chant prayers for s.t.; chant prayers over s.t.

kâkîsimototaw– *VTA* chant prayers for s.o.; chant prayers over s.o.

kâkîsimwâkê– *VAI* chant prayers with things

CHANTING

kâkîsimowin– *NI* chanting prayers

CHARGE

kîsakim– *VTA* finish counting s.o.; finish giving orders to s.o., complete one's charge to s.o.

pimakocin– *VII* make a rush in linear fashion, charge headlong

wiyakihtamaw– *VTA* set a price on (it/him) for s.o., charge s.o. for (it/him)

CHASE

nawaswât– *VTI* pursue s.t., chase after s.t.

papâmitisah– *VTI* chase s.t. about

wâsakâtisahoto– *VAI* chase one another around a circle

CHECK

nitawâpênikê– *VAI* check up on people, check up on things

CHEST

maskihkîwiwacis– *NI* medicine chest

CHIEF

okimâhkân– *NA* chief, elected chief

okimâhkâniwi– *VAI* be chief, serve as elected chief

CHILD

–awâsimis– *NDA* child [*e.g.*, kitawâsimisinaw]

–osk-âyim– *NDA* young people, children, the young [*e.g.*, otôsk-âyima]

awâsis– *NA* child

kimotôsê– *VAI* bear an illegitimate child

nâtamâwaso– *VAI* take up for one's children

ocawâsimisi– *VAI* have a child, have (her/him) as one's child

ohpikinâwaso– *VAI* make one's children grow up, raise one's children

otawâsimisi– *VAI* have a child [*sic:* -t-; *cf.* ocawâsimisi–]

otawâsimisimâw– *NA* child [*sic:* -t-]

CHOOSE

otin– *VTA* take s.o., choose s.o.

otin– *VTI* take s.t., choose s.t.

otinikâtê– *VII* be taken, be chosen

CHRISTMAS

–kîsikâm– *NDI* day, day of one's life; [*fig.*] [Our Father's] day, Christmas Day [*e.g.*, kikîsikâminaw; kôhtâwînaw okîsikâm]

manitowi-kîsikâw– *NI* Christmas Day

CHURCH

ayamihâ– *VAI* pray, hold a church service; follow a religion [*also* ayimihâ–]

ayamihâwin– *NI* praying, church service; religion [*also* ayimihâwin–]

CIRCLE

wâsakân– *VTI* turn s.t. around a circle

wâsakâtisahoto– *VAI* chase one another around a circle

CLEAN

kanâtahcâ– *VII* be clean ground, be clean land

kanâtanohk *IPC* in a clean place

CLEAR

tawâtamaw– *VTA* open (it) up for s.o.; clear the way for s.o.

CLEARLY

kîhkânâkwan– *VII* be clearly visible

kîhkâtah– *VTI* make the sound of (it) sing out clearly

kîhkâtahamaw– *VTA* make the sound of (it) sing out clearly to s.o.

pakahkihtaw– *VTA* hear s.o. clearly

CLERK

omasinahikêsîs– *NA* scribe, clerk

CLEVER

iyinîsi– *VAI* be clever

CLOSE

cîkâhtaw *IPC* close, nearby, in the area

cîki *IPC* close, close by

CLOSELY

kanawêyim– *VTA* keep s.o., guard s.o. closely

CLOTH

wêpinâson– *NI* draped cloth, flag, cloth offering

CLOUDY

îkwaskwan– *VII* be cloudy [*sic:* î-; *cf.* yî-]

CLUELESS

pakwanawahtâ– *VAI* go on with (it) at random, know nothing about (it), be clueless about (it)

COLLECT

mâwacîhito– *VAI* collect one another, gather

COLLECTIVELY

mâmawi *IPV* collectively, jointly

COME

kîwêmakan– *VII* return home, come back

nihtâwikin– *VII* grow forth (e.g., plant), come forth

ohtohtê– *VAI* come from there

pêtwêwêhtamaw– *VTA* come audibly bringing (it/him) for s.o.

sâkâwanêhtâ– *VAI* push (it) to emerge from the ground, make (it) come forth

sâkêwêtot– *VTI* come out upon s.t., rise (e.g., sun) upon s.t.

COMMAND

itasiwât– *VTA* give s.o. such a command, impose such laws on s.o.

itasiwê– *VAI* give such a command, impose such laws [*]

COMMIT

patowât– *VTI* misspeak s.t., commit an error in one's prayers

pâstâhôtot– *VTI* commit a transgression in s.t., commit sacrilege in s.t.

COMPANION

–îci-kîhkâw– *NDA* aged spouse, fellow old person, fellow oldster, companion of one's old age [*e.g.*, wîci-kîhkâwa]

owîcêwâkani– *VAI* have a companion or partner, have (her/him) as companion or partner

COMPASSION

kisêwâtisiwin– *NI* kindness, compassion; [*fig.*] grace

kitimâkêyihtamâso– *VAI* think of (it/him) with compassion for one's own sake

kitimâkêyihto– *VAI* feel pity towards one another, love one another, think of one another with compassion

kitimâkêyihtowin– *NI* feeling pity towards one another, loving one another, thinking of one another with compassion

kitimâkêyim– *VTA* take pity upon s.o., think of s.o. with compassion

kitimâkihtaw– *VTA* listen to s.o. with pity, listen to s.o. with compassion

kitimâkinaw– *VTA* look with pity upon s.o., look with compassion upon s.o.; regard s.o. with respect

COMPASSIONATE

kisêwâtisi– *VAI* be kind, be of compassionate disposition; [*fig.*] be full of grace

COMPETENT

kaskihtâ– *VAI* be able to do (it), be competent at (it)

COMPLETE

kî *IPV* complete, past

kîsakim– *VTA* finish counting s.o.; finish giving orders to s.o., complete one's charge to s.o.

kîsîh– *VTA* complete s.o. (e.g., rattle)

kîsîhtamaw– *VTA* complete (it/him) for s.o.

kîsîhtâ– *VAI* finish (it), complete (it)

kîsowât– *VTI* complete one's words, complete one's prayers

kîsowâtamaw– *VTA* complete words for s.o., complete prayers for s.o.

COMPLETELY

kîsi *IPV* completely, to completion

CONCERN

pîkiskwât– *VTI* speak about s.t., speak about s.t. with concern; speak a prayer over s.t.

pîkiskwêmôh– *VTA* cause s.o. to speak with concern

CONCLUDE

wiyihcikê– *VAI* arrange things, conduct negotiations, conclude a treaty

CONDUCT

wiyihcikê– *VAI* arrange things, conduct negotiations, conclude a treaty

CONFIRMATION

aspitonâmo– *VAI* flee to rely on spoken words, rely on (it) as a formal confirmation of the spoken word

CONSCIOUS

âpahkawin– *VII* be level-headed, be sensible, be conscious

CONSIDER

mâyêyiht– *VTI* consider s.t. challenging; be willing to tackle a difficult task, venture out

miywakihtê– *VII* be considered good; [*in negative clause:*] be considered bad, be considered evil

môhcwêyim– *VTA* consider s.o. stupid

CONTAIN

pîsâkwan– *VII* contain plenty, offer lots of room; be plentiful, be rich [*sic:* -â-]

CONTROL

tipêyiht– *VTI* own s.t., control s.t.

tipêyim– *VTA* own s.o., control s.o.

tipêyimiso– *VAI* control oneself, govern oneself

CONVENIENT

nahipayi– *VII* be convenient, fall into place

CONVEYANCE

pimitâpâso– *VAI* move along in a conveyance

takopayi– *VAI* arrive on horseback, arrive by conveyance

COOK

kîsitêpo– *VAI* cook; cook a feast, cook ceremonial food

COOL

tahkâpâwat– *VTA* pour water to cool s.o. (e.g., rock), cool s.o. (e.g., rock) with water (in sweat-lodge)

CORNERS

wîhkwêskamikâ– *VII* be the corners of the earth

CORRECTLY

tâpowê– *VAI* speak correctly; recite one's prayer correctly

COST

itakihtê– *VII* be counted thus, cost so much; be held in such esteem

COUNSEL

kakêskihkêmo– *VAI* counsel people, preach at people

kakêskim– *VTA* counsel s.o., lecture s.o.

COUNSELLING

kakêskimâwasowin– *NI* counselling the young

COUNT

akim– *VTA* count s.o.

itakiht– *VTI* count s.t. thus, value s.t. thus, hold s.t. in such esteem

itakihtê– *VII* be counted thus, cost so much; be held in such esteem

itakim– *VTA* count s.o. thus, value s.o. thus, hold s.o. in such esteem

itakiso– *VAI* be counted thus; be held in such esteem, have such a function

kîsakim– *VTA* finish counting s.o.; finish giving orders to s.o., complete one's charge to s.o.

COUNTRY

askiy– *NI* earth, land, country; world

wîtaskîwêm– *VTA* live together with s.o.; live in the same country with s.o., live in peace with s.o.

COURSE

mêkwâc *IPC* while, in the course of

COUSIN

–ciwâm– *NDA* male parallel cousin (man speaking); [*fig.*] brother, male of the same generation (man speaking) [*e.g.*, kiciwâminaw]

–îscâs– *NDA* male cross-cousin (man speaking) [*diminutive; e.g.*, wîscâsa]

–îtimos– *NDA* cross-cousin of the opposite sex [*e.g.*, nîtimos]

wîtimosi– *VAI* have a cross-cousin of the opposite sex, have (him/her) as cross-cousin of the opposite sex

COVER

pâskin– *VTI* open s.t. up, take the cover off s.t.; fold s.t. (e.g., book) open

COW

mostosw– *NA* cattle, cow

CRAW

wîhkwâs– *NI* craw, first stomach of fowl

CRAWL

pimâhtawî– *VAI* crawl along

CRAZY

ma-môhcw-âtayôhkêwin– *NI* stupid sacred story, crazy sacred story [*; *reduplicated*]

môhcowi– *VAI* be stupid, be silly; be mad, be crazy

CREATE

ohpin– *VTI* raise s.t., create s.t.

wawânaskêhtamaw– *VTA* create a peaceful life for s.o.

CREE

nêhiyaw– *NA* Cree, Indian

nêhiyawasinahikan– *NI* Cree book; Cree bible

nêhiyawastê– *VII* be written in Cree; be written in syllabics

nêhiyawê– *VAI* speak Cree

nêhiyawi *IPN* Cree, Indian

nêhiyawi-masinahikan– *NI* Cree book; Cree bible

nêhiyawi-wîh– *VTA* use s.o.'s Cree name, call s.o. by a Cree name

nêhiyawi-wîht– *VTI* use the Cree name of s.t., call s.t. by a Cree name

nêhiyawi-wîhtamawâkan– *NI* Cree etymology; Cree teaching

nêhiyâwi– *VAI* be Cree

nêhiyâwiwin– *NI* being Cree, Cree identity, Creeness

CRISIS

mâkoh– *VTA* worry s.o., trouble s.o.; oppress s.o., throw s.o. into crisis

CROSS-COUSIN

–îscâs– *NDA* male cross-cousin (man speaking) [*diminutive; e.g.*, wîscâsa]

–îtimos– *NDA* cross-cousin of the opposite sex [*e.g.*, nîtimos]

wîtimosi– *VAI* have a cross-cousin of the opposite sex, have (him/her) as cross-cousin of the opposite sex

CROSS-NEPHEW

–tihkwatim– *NDA* cross-nephew; son-in-law [*e.g.*, nitihkwatim]

CROSS-NIECE

–stim– *NDA* cross-niece; daughter-in-law [*e.g.*, ostima]

CROWD

sâkaskinê– *VAI* crowd in, fill a place

sâkaskinêkâpawi– *VAI* stand crowded in, stand to fill a place

takwâwahito– *VAI* arrive pulling one another along, arrive as a crowd

CRY

mawihkâtamaw– *VTA* cry out in prayer to s.o., wail to s.o.

mawimo– *VAI* cry out; cry out in prayer, wail

mawimoscikê– *VAI* cry out in prayer, wail; worship with (it)

mawimost– *VTI* cry out in prayer to s.t., wail to s.t.

mâto– *VAI* cry, wail

CRYING

mawimoscikêwin– *NI* crying out in prayer, wailing; form of worship, ceremony

CURL

titipawêhkas– *VTI* curl s.t. (e.g., head of hair) by heat; have a perm

CUT

kîskisamaw– *VTA* cut (it/him) off for s.o.; offer tobacco to s.o.

DAILY

tahto-kîsikâw *IPC* every day, daily

DANCE

pihêwisimo– *VAI* dance the prairie-chicken dance

DAUGHTER

–tânis– *NDA* daughter [*e.g.*, otânisa]

DAUGHTER-IN-LAW

–stim– *NDA* cross-niece; daughter-in-law [*e.g.*, ostima]

DAWN

wâpan– *VII* be dawn, be early morning

DAY

–kîsikâm– *NDI* day, day of one's life; [*fig.*] [Our Father's] day, Christmas Day [*e.g.*, kikîsikâminaw; kôhtâwînaw okîsikâm]

kîsikâ– *VII* be day, be daylight

manitowi-kîsikâw– *NI* Christmas Day

nêwo-kîsikâw *IPC* four days

nîso-kîsikâw *IPC* two days

pêyak-kîsikâw *IPC* one day

tahto-kîsikâw *IPC* every day, daily

tahto-nîso-kîsikâw *IPC* every second day, every other day

DAYLIGHT

kîsikâ– *VII* be day, be daylight

DAYS

kayâs *IPC* long ago, in earlier days; previously

DEBT

tipahamaw– *VTA* pay s.o. for (it/him), repay a debt to s.o.

DECIDE

wiyakim– *VTA* set a price on s.o. (e.g., bread); arrange (it) for s.o.; decide on s.o.; give orders to s.o.

DECREE

wîht– *VTI* tell about s.t., report s.t.; decree s.t.

DEGREE

iskoyikohk *IPC* to such an extent, to such a degree

iyikohk *IPC* so much, to such a degree, to such an extent

DELAY

âsay *IPC* already; without delay [*also aspectual*]

kiyâm *IPC* let it be, let there be no further delay; please

DELICATELY

mâmâsîs *IPC* sparingly, delicately; quickly, roughly, without care

DENY

kakwâtakihiso– *VAI* make oneself suffer; torture oneself, deny oneself food and drink

kakwâtakiho– *VAI* make oneself suffer; torture oneself, deny oneself food and drink

DENYING

îwanisîhisowin– *NI* fasting, denying oneself food [*usually but not always restricted to food*]

kakwâtakihowin– *NI* making oneself suffer; denying oneself food and drink

DEPART

sipwêhtê– *VAI* leave, depart

DEPICT

masinahikâso– *VAI* be pictured, be depicted

masinahikâtê– *VII* be pictured, be depicted; have marks, have writing; be written

masinipayi– *VAI* be depicted as moving (e.g., on film)

masinipayihtâ– *VAI* depict (it) (e.g., on film)

DERIDE

pâhpih– *VTA* laugh at s.o., deride s.o.

DESPITE

âhci piko *IPC* still, nevertheless, despite everything [*adversative*]

êyiwêhk *IPC* just in case, nevertheless; despite shortcomings [*also* kêyiwêhk]

kêyiwêhk *IPC* just in case, nevertheless; despite shortcomings [*also* êyiwêhk]

DIE

mêstohtê– *VAI* die off, become extinct

DIFFERENT

âhcîhtâ– *VAI* make (it) over, make (it) different, change (it)

DIFFERENTLY

pîtos *IPC* strangely, differently

DIFFICULT

âyiman– *VII* be difficult

mâyêyiht– *VTI* consider s.t. challenging; be willing to tackle a difficult task, venture out

nayêhtâwan– *VII* be difficult, be troublesome

DIRECT

itâmôh– *VTA* make s.o. flee thus or there, direct s.o. to seek such refuge

DIRECTION

isiniskêyi– *VAI* move one's arm thus or there, point in that direction with one's arm

itêhkê isi *IPC* in that direction, in the thither direction

DIRTY

îpâcihtâ– *VAI* make (it) dirty, soil (it) [*sic:* î-; *cf.* wiyî-]

DISAPPROVE

pakwâtamaw– *VTA* hate (it/him) for s.o., dislike (it/him) for s.o., disapprove of (it/him) for s.o.

DISCARDED

wêpinikâtê– *VII* be thrown away, be abandoned, be discarded

DISCOURSE

tâhkôm– *VTA* discuss s.o., discourse upon s.o.

tâhkôt– *VTI* discuss s.t., discourse upon s.t.

DISCUSS

âyimôhto– *VAI* discuss one another; gossip about one another

âyimôm– *VTA* discuss s.o.; gossip about s.o.

âyimômiso– *VAI* discuss oneself; speak unguardedly about oneself, gossip about oneself

âyimôt– *VTI* speak of s.t., discuss s.t.; gossip about s.t.

mâmiskôcikâtê– *VII* be discussed, be expounded

mâmiskôt– *VTI* discuss s.t., expound s.t.

tasihtamaw– *VTA* discuss (it/him) with s.o. [*]

tâhkôm– *VTA* discuss s.o., discourse upon s.o.

tâhkôt– *VTI* discuss s.t., discourse upon s.t.

tipôt– *VTI* discuss s.t. with authority

DISCUSSING

âyimôhtowin– *NI* discussing one another; gossiping about one another, gossip

DISH

pêyakoyâkan *IPC* one dish (measure)

wiyâkanis– *NI* small dish, small bowl [*diminutive*]

DISLIKE

pakwâtamaw– *VTA* hate (it/him) for s.o., dislike (it/him) for s.o., disapprove of (it/him) for s.o.

DISPOSITION

kisêwâtisi– *VAI* be kind, be of compassionate disposition; [*fig.*] be full of grace

DISTRIBUTE

otasahkêw– *NA* one who distributes rations; Indian agent

DO

isîhcikât– *VTI* do things thus for s.t., proceed thus for s.t.

isîhcikê– *VAI* do things thus, proceed thus, perform such a ritual

itahkamikisi– *VAI* do things thus

itôt– *VTI* do s.t. thus [*cf.* tôt-]

kaskihtâ– *VAI* be able to do (it), be competent at (it)

kocihtâ– *VAI* try (it), try to do (it) [*]

mâyitôt– *VTI* do bad things, cause serious trouble

nakacihtâ– *VAI* be familiar with doing (it), be practised at (it)

tôt– *VTI* do s.t. thus [*cf.* itôt-]

tôtamaw– *VTA* do (it) thus for s.o.

tôtaw– *VTA* do thus to s.o.

DOCTOR

maskihkîwiyiniw– *NA* doctor, physician

nanâtawih– *VTA* doctor s.o., heal s.o.

DOCUMENT

masinahikan– *NI* book; written document; bible

DOLL

ayisiyinîhkân– *NA* doll, mannikin; cartoon figure

DOOR

iskwâhtêm– *NI* door

DOUBT

môy êkâ êtokwê *IPC* without any doubt, of necessity [*usually with independent indicative*]

DOWN

capasis *IPC* down low

nâtwâwêpah– *VTI* break s.t. off and throw it down
tapahcipayiho– *VAI* swoop down, swoop low

DRAPED
wêpinâson– *NI* draped cloth, flag, cloth offering

DREAM
âtayôhkan– *NA* spirit being, dream guardian
âtayôhkanakiso– *VAI* be held to be a spirit being, a dream guardian

DRINK
kakwâtakihiso– *VAI* make oneself suffer; torture oneself, deny oneself food and drink
kakwâtakiho– *VAI* make oneself suffer; torture oneself, deny oneself food and drink
kakwâtakihowin– *NI* making oneself suffer; denying oneself food and drink
kisâkamitêhkwê– *VAI* drink a hot liquid, have a hot drink

DRIVE
patitisahamaw– *VTA* drive (it/him) off the path for s.o., send (it/him) awry for s.o., spoil (it/him) for s.o.

DRIZZLE
kaskawanipêstâ– *VII* be drizzle, be rainy

DRUM
matwêhw– *VTA* sound a beat upon s.o. (e.g., drum), drum on s.o.
mistikwaskihkw– *NA* drum

DURATION
tasi *IPV* for such a time, for the duration

DWELL
wîki– *VAI* live, dwell, have one's abode

DWELLING
–îk– *NDI* house, dwelling, home [*e.g.*, wîki]

EACH
pâh-pêyak *IPC* singly, one at a time; each individually

EAGERLY
iyâyaw *IPC* eagerly, intently; by preference, rather

EAR
mahkihtawâkê– *VAI* have a big ear [*usually reduplicated:* mâh-mahkihtawâkê– 'have big ears']

EARLIER
kayâs *IPC* long ago, in earlier days; previously

EARLY

kîkisêp *IPC* early in the morning [*sic; cf.* kîkisêpâ]

kîkisêpâ *IPC* early in the morning [*also* kîkisêp]

miyoskamin– *VII* be early spring

wâpan– *VII* be dawn, be early morning

EARN

kîspinat– *VTI* earn enough to buy s.t.; earn s.t. as reward, earn one's reward

kîspinatamaw– *VTA* earn one's reward in s.o., earn s.o. as one's reward

EARTH

askiy– *NI* earth, land, country; world

askîwi– *VII* be the earth, exist as world

askîwisk– *VTI* subject the earth to oneself, populate the earth, make the earth live

ay-atâmaskamik *IPC* inside the earth, below the ground [*reduplicated*]

kihc-ôkâwîmâw– *NA* [*fig.*] Great Mother, Mother Earth

waskitaskamik *IPC* on the face of the earth

wîhkwêskamikâ– *VII* be the corners of the earth

EASY

wêhcasin– *VII* be easy

EAT

mîciso– *VAI* eat, have a meal

ECONOMY

kistikêwi-pimâcihowin– *NI* agricultural way of life, farm economy

ECZEMA

kiyakasê– *VAI* have itchy skin, suffer from eczema

EDUCATION

kiskinohamâsowin– *NI* schooling, education [*sc. 'patient-centred' noun; e.g.,* okiskinohamâsowin 'his schooling']

EFFECT

ânisîhtâ– *VAI* alleviate the effect of (it), be an antidote to (it)

pimohtêmakan– *VII* go along, move along; be in effect (e.g., treaty)

EIGHT

ayinânêw *IPC* eight

EIGHTY

ayinânêwi-mitanaw *IPC* eighty

ELDER

kêhtê-ay– *NA* old person, the old; elder

kêhtê-ayiwi– *VAI* be an old person; be an elder

ELECTED

okimâhkân– *NA* chief, elected chief

okimâhkâniwi– *VAI* be chief, serve as elected chief

ELEVEN

pêyakosâp *IPC* eleven

ELSE

ahpô cî *IPC* or else

EMERGE

sâkâwanêhtâ– *VAI* push (it) to emerge from the ground, make (it) come forth

sâkikin– *VII* grow forth, emerge from the ground

EMPLOY

masinahikêh– *VTA* hire s.o., employ s.o.

EMPLOYEE

atoskêhâkan– *NA* employee

ENCOUNTER

nakiskaw– *VTA* encounter s.o., meet s.o.

tâwin– *VTA* encounter s.o., bump into s.o., hit s.o.

END

iskwêyâc *IPC* at last, at the end

kisipipayi– *VII* come to an end, reach the end

kisipîmakan– *VII* come to an end, have an end

pônipayi– *VII* cease, stop, come to an end

ENDOW

manitowakim– *VTA* endow s.o. (e.g., tobacco) with supernatural powers

ENEMA

pîhtâpâwah– *VTA* pour liquid into s.o., give s.o. an enema

ENGAGED

tasîhk– *VTI* bother with s.t., trifle with s.t.; be engaged in s.t.

ENGLISH

âkayâsîmo– *VAI* speak English

ENJOY

pahpakwatêyiht– *VTI* enjoy s.t., be amused by s.t.

ENOUGH

kîspinat– *VTI* earn enough to buy s.t.; earn s.t. as reward, earn one's reward

otisâpaht– *VTI* have lived long enough to see s.t.
têpipayi– *VAI* have the full amount, have enough

ENTER

pîhtikwah– *VTA* enter with s.o., take s.o. inside
pîhtikwatâ– *VAI* enter with (it), take (it) inside
pîhtikwê– *VAI* enter, go inside
pîhtikwêmakan– *VII* enter, go inside
pîhtikwêtot– *VTI* enter s.t. (e.g., sweat-lodge)

ENTERPRISE

waskawîwin– *NI* being active, enterprise

ENTIRELY

iyawis *IPC* fully, entirely; [*in negative clause:*] only partially, not exclusively

ERECT

cimasi– *VAI* stand upright, stand erect
cimatê– *VII* stand upright, stand erect

ERROR

patowât– *VTI* misspeak s.t., commit an error in one's prayers

ESPECIALLY

âsônê *IPC* especially, in particular
wâwîs *IPC* especially
wâwîs cî *IPC* especially, all the more so

ESTEEM

itakiht– *VTI* count s.t. thus, value s.t. thus, hold s.t. in such esteem
itakihtê– *VII* be counted thus, cost so much; be held in such esteem
itakim– *VTA* count s.o. thus, value s.o. thus, hold s.o. in such esteem
itakiso– *VAI* be counted thus; be held in such esteem, have such a function

ETYMOLOGY

nêhiyawi-wîhtamawâkan– *NI* Cree etymology; Cree teaching

EVEN

ahpô *IPC* even, possibly; or

EVER

wîhkâc *IPC* ever; [*in negative clause:*] never

EVERY

tahto-kîsikâw *IPC* every day, daily
tahto-nîso-kîsikâw *IPC* every second day, every other day

tahto-nîsw-âyamihêwi-kîsikâw *IPC* every second week, fortnightly

EVERYTHING

âhci piko *IPC* still, nevertheless, despite everything [*adversative*]

EVIL

miywakihtê– *VII* be considered good; [*in negative clause:*] be considered bad, be considered evil

miywâsin– *VII* be good, be valuable; [*in negative clause:*] be bad, be evil

EXACT

kêtisk *IPC* just barely, to exact measure

EXACTLY

katisk *IPC* just now, exactly; [*in negative clause:*] not merely

mêmohci *IPC* in particular, above all; exactly, precisely

mwêhci *IPC* exactly

EXCLUSIVELY

iyawis *IPC* fully, entirely; [*in negative clause:*] only partially, not exclusively

EXERCISE

pimipayihtâ– *VAI* run (it), keep (it) up, exercise (it)

EXIST

askîwi– *VII* be the earth, exist as world

ayâ– *VAI* be there, live there; exist

ayâ– *VII* be there, exist

ihtako– *VAI* exist

ihtakon– *VII* exist [*e.g.,* ê-ihtakohk]

ihtâ– *VAI* be there, exist

EXISTENCE

ayisiyinîwin– *NI* being human, human existence

EXPECT

pakosêyim– *VTA* wish for (it/him) of s.o., expect (it/him) of s.o.

EXPECTATION

pakosêyimo– *VAI* wish for (it), have an expectation

EXPECTED

cikêmô *IPC* of course, obviously, as might be expected [*weak concessive; cf.* cikêmâ]

EXPLORER

onitawahtâw– *NA* scout, explorer, spy

EXPOUND

mâmiskôcikâtê– *VII* be discussed, be expounded

mâmiskôt– *VTI* discuss s.t., expound s.t.

EXPRESSION

pîkiskwêwin– *NI* word, expression, phrase; speech, language

EXPRESSLY

ohtitaw *IPC* expressly, specifically; it is requisite, it is meet indeed

EXTENT

isko *IPC* to such an extent, thus far [*also* IPV]

iskoyikohk *IPC* to such an extent, to such a degree

ispisi *IPV* to such an extent, so far

iyikohk *IPC* so much, to such a degree, to such an extent

pikoyikohk *IPC* no matter how much, to any extent [*also* pikw îyikohk]

pikw îyikohk *IPC* no matter how much, to any extent [*cf.* pikoyikohk]

tâniyikohk *IPC* to what extent; to such an extent

EXTINCT

âstawê– *VII* be without fire, be extinct (e.g., fire)

mêstohtê– *VAI* die off, become extinct

FACE

waskitaskamik *IPC* on the face of the earth

FACT

anima *IPC* it is that; the fact that [*factive; also predicative*]

ôma *IPC* it is this; the fact that [*factive; also predicative*]

FALL

nahipayi– *VII* be convenient, fall into place

osiskêpayi– *VII* fall into place, work itself out, be practicable

FAMILIAR

nakacihtâ– *VAI* be familiar with doing (it), be practised at (it)

FAR

awas-âyihk *IPC* on the other side, on the far side

isko *IPC* to such an extent, thus far [*also* IPV]

ispisi *IPV* to such an extent, so far

sîpi *IPV* stretching far back

wâh-wâhyaw *IPC* in far places [*reduplicated*]

wâhyaw *IPC* far

FARM

kistikêwi-pimâcihowin– *NI* agricultural way of life, farm economy

okistikêwiyiniw– *NA* farm instructor

FASHION

pimakocin– *VII* make a rush in linear fashion, charge headlong

pimastê– *VII* be placed in linear fashion, run along

FAST

micimôho– *VAI* be held fast, be stuck [*sic:* -h-]

FASTING

îwanisîhisowin– *NI* fasting, denying oneself food [*usually but not always restricted to food*]

FATHER

–ôhtâwiy– *NDA* father, father's brother; [*fig.*] Our Father [*e.g.*, kôhtâwînawak; kôhtâwînaw]

oyôhtâwî– *VAI* have a father, have (him) as one's father

FEAR

kost– *VTI* fear s.t.

FEAST

kîsitêpo– *VAI* cook; cook a feast, cook ceremonial food

wîhkohkât– *VTI* hold a feast for s.t. (e.g., medicinal herbs)

wîhkohkê– *VAI* hold a feast

wîhkohto– *VAI* invite one another to a feast

wîhkom– *VTA* invite s.o. to a feast

FEATHER

mîkwan– *NA* feather

FED UP

saskacihtaw– *VTA* be tired of hearing s.o., be fed up with hearing s.o.

FEED

asam– *VTA* feed s.o.; hand out rations to s.o.

FEEDING

asahtowin– *NI* feeding one another, rations

FEEL

kitimâkêyihto– *VAI* feel pity towards one another, love one another, think of one another with compassion

mâyimahciho– *VAI* feel poorly, feel in ill health

miyomahciho– *VAI* feel well, feel healthy; feel pleased

FEELING

kitimâkêyihtowin– *NI* feeling pity towards one another, loving one another, thinking of one another with compassion

FELLOW

–îc-âyisiyiniw– *NDA* fellow human [*e.g.*, kîc-âyisiyinînaw]

–îci-kîhkâw– *NDA* aged spouse, fellow old person, fellow oldster, companion of one's old age [*e.g.*, wîci-kîhkâwa]

FETCH

nâcipahiwê– *VAI* go to fetch things, run to fetch things

nât– *VTA* fetch s.o.

nât– *VTI* fetch s.t.

nâtamaw– *VTA* fetch (it/him) for s.o.; take up for s.o.

FIGHT

nôtin– *VTI* fight s.t., fight with s.t.

ohcih– *VTA* fight s.o. over something; hold s.o. off

FIGHTING

nôtinitowin– *NI* fighting one another, fighting

FIGURE

ayisiyinîhkân– *NA* doll, mannikin; cartoon figure

FILL

sâkaskinê– *VAI* crowd in, fill a place

sâkaskinêkâpawi– *VAI* stand crowded in, stand to fill a place

wiyaskinah– *VTA* fill s.o. (e.g., pipe)

FINALLY

piyisk *IPC* finally, at last

FIND

miskaw– *VTA* find s.o.

FINISH

kîsakim– *VTA* finish counting s.o.; finish giving orders to s.o., complete one's charge to s.o.

kîsîhtâ– *VAI* finish (it), complete (it)

FIRE

âstawê– *VII* be without fire, be extinct (e.g., fire)

iskotêw– *NI* fire, hearth-fire

macostêh– *VTI* throw s.t. into the fire

FIRST

nistam *IPC* for the first time, initially, originally

nistamêmâkan– *NA* the first one, the original one [*sic*]

nîkân *IPC* first, at the head

pita *IPC* first, for a while [*cf.* pitamâ]

pitamâ *IPC* first, for a while [*cf.* pita]

FISH

kinosêw– *NA* fish

FIVE

niyânan *IPC* five

FIX

nânapâcihtâ– *VAI* fix (it) up, repair (it)

FLAG

wêpinâson– *NI* draped cloth, flag, cloth offering

FLAT

taswêkin– *VTI* open s.t. (e.g., book) up flat

FLEE

aspitonâmo– *VAI* flee to rely on spoken words, rely on (it) as a formal confirmation of the spoken word

itâmo– *VAI* flee thus or there, seek such refuge

itâmôh– *VTA* make s.o. flee thus or there, direct s.o. to seek such refuge

nâtâmost– *VTI* flee to s.t., turn to s.t. for help, seek refuge in s.t.

nâtâmotot– *VTI* flee to s.t., turn to s.t. for help, seek refuge in s.t.

nâtâmototaw– *VTA* flee to s.o., turn to s.o. for help, seek refuge with s.o.

pêtâmo– *VAI* flee hither

FLOUR

pahkwêsikan– *NA* bannock, bread; flour

FLOW

pimiciwan– *VII* flow along

FLY

papâmihâ– *VAI* fly about

FOLD

pâskin– *VTI* open s.t. up, take the cover off s.t.; fold s.t. (e.g., book) open

FOLLOW

ayamihâ– *VAI* pray, hold a church service; follow a religion [*also* ayimihâ–]

FOLLOWER

–iyinîm– *NDA* people, followers [*usually plural; e.g.*, kitiyinîmak]

–oskinîkîm– *NDA* young man, follower; [*fig.*] servant [*e.g.*, otôskinîkîma]

FOOD

îwanisîhisowin– *NI* fasting, denying oneself food [*usually but not always restricted to food*]

kakwâtakihiso– *VAI* make oneself suffer; torture oneself, deny oneself food and drink

kakwâtakiho– *VAI* make oneself suffer; torture oneself, deny oneself food and drink

kakwâtakihowin– *NI* making oneself suffer; denying oneself food and drink
kîsitêpo– *VAI* cook; cook a feast, cook ceremonial food
kîsitêw– *NI* food, ceremonial food
nôhtêhkatê– *VAI* be hungry, want food

FOOL

kakêpâhkamikisi– *VAI* fool around, get in the way
mêtawâkê– *VAI* play around with things, fool around with things

FOOT

pêyak-misit *IPC* one foot (measure)

FOR

ayis *IPC* for, because [*causal conjunction; also* ayisk]
kîspin êkâ ohci *IPC* if it were not for [*irrealis conditional, usually with noun phrase or simple conjunct*]
osâm *IPC* because; for [*causal conjunction*]
pita *IPC* first, for a while [*cf.* pitamâ]
tasi *IPV* for such a time, for the duration
wiya *IPC* for, because [*also* wiyê; *clause-initial causal conjunction*]

FOREVER

kâkikê *IPC* always, forever

FORGET

wanikiskisi– *VAI* forget (it)

FORM

mawimoscikêwin– *NI* crying out in prayer, wailing; form of worship, ceremony

FORMAL

aspitonâmo– *VAI* flee to rely on spoken words, rely on (it) as a formal confirmation of the spoken word

FORT CARLTON

pêhonânihk *INM* [*place-name:*] at Fort Carlton [*literally:* at the Waiting-Place]

FORTH

nihtâwikihtâ– *VAI* give birth to (it), bring (it) forth
nihtâwikin– *VII* grow forth (e.g., plant), come forth
nihtâwikinâwaso– *VAI* give birth to a child, bring forth a child, bring forth a young one (of the species)
sâkâwanêhtâ– *VAI* push (it) to emerge from the ground, make (it) come forth
sâkikihtâ– *VAI* make (it) (e.g., earth) bring forth plants

sâkikin– *VII* grow forth, emerge from the ground

FORTNIGHTLY

tahto-nîsw-âyamihêwi-kîsikâw *IPC* every second week, fortnightly

FOUL

mâyi-kîsikâ– *VII* be stormy weather, be foul weather

FOUR

nêw-âskiy *IPC* four years

nêwâw *IPC* four times

nêwo-kîsikâw *IPC* four days

nêwo-tipiskâ– *VII* be four nights, be the fourth night

FOURTEEN

nêwosâp *IPC* fourteen

FREE

pihkoh– *VTA* free s.o., release s.o.

FRIEND

–tôtêm– *NDA* kinsman; friend [*e.g.*, kitôtêminawak]

FRIGHTEN

astâh– *VTA* frighten s.o.; [*especially in inverse:*] cause s.o. to be wary, worry s.o.

sêkim– *VTA* frighten s.o. by speech

FROM

ohci *IPC* with, by means of; because of; from then [*enclitic; also* IPV]

ohci *IPV* thence, from there; [*in negative clause:*] past [*cf.* ôh]

ohtohtê– *VAI* come from there

osâpaht– *VTI* look at s.t. from there

osâpam– *VTA* look at s.o. from there

ôh *IPV* from there; [*in negative clause:*] past [*cf.* ohci]

pê *IPV* thence, from there on down

FULFILLED

tâpwêmakan– *VII* come true; [*fig.*] be fulfilled

FULL

kisêwâtisi– *VAI* be kind, be of compassionate disposition; [*fig.*] be full of grace

têpinêhamaw– *VTA* make full payment for (it/him) to s.o.

têpipayi– *VAI* have the full amount, have enough

FULLY

iyawis *IPC* fully, entirely; [*in negative clause:*] only partially, not exclusively

têpâpam– *VTA* see plenty of s.o., see s.o. fully
têpi *IPV* fully, sufficiently
FUNCTION
itakiso– *VAI* be counted thus; be held in such esteem, have such a function
FURTHER
kiyâm *IPC* let it be, let there be no further delay; please
konita *IPC* in vain, without reason, without purpose; without further ado
sôskwât *IPC* simply, without further ado
FUTURE
ati nîkân *IPC* in the future
nîkâniwi– *VII* be ahead, be the future; lie in the future [*sic:* -i-]
GATHER
mâwacîhito– *VAI* collect one another, gather
GENERAL
mêtawâkâniwi– *VII* be general playing around
GENERATION
kâsispô– *VAI* survive into another generation
kâsispôhtêmakan– *VII* go on from one generation to another, survive into another generation
GENEROUS
sawêyim– *VTA* be generous towards s.o., bless s.o.
GENTLE
osêhcâw– *NI* rise in the land, gentle hill
GET ALONG
wîcêhto– *VAI* live with one another, join with one another; get along with one another
GETTING ALONG
wîcêhtowin– *NI* living with one another; getting along with one another, living in harmony with one another
GHOST-DANCE
wâsakâmêsimowin– *NI* ghost-dance
GIVE
âcimo– *VAI* tell, tell a story, give an account
âcimostaw– *VTA* tell s.o. about (it/him), give s.o. an account
âpacihtamôh– *VTA* make s.o. use (it/him), give (it/him) to s.o. to use; use (it/him) for s.o.
âtot– *VTI* tell about s.t., give an account of s.t.
itasiwât– *VTA* give s.o. such a command, impose such laws on s.o.

itasiwê– *VAI* give such a command, impose such laws [*]
itâtot– *VTI* tell about s.t. thus, give such an account of s.t.
miy– *VTA* give (it/him) to s.o.
miyikowisi– *VAI* be given (it/him) by the powers
nanâskom– *VTA* be grateful to s.o., give thanks to s.o.
nanâskomo– *VAI* be grateful, give thanks
nanâskot– *VTI* be grateful for s.t., give thanks for s.t.
nihtâwikihtâ– *VAI* give birth to (it), bring (it) forth
nihtâwikinâwaso– *VAI* give birth to a child, bring forth a child, bring forth a young one (of the species)
pimâcih– *VTA* make s.o. live, give life to s.o.; make a living for s.o.

GIVE-AWAY

pakitinâso– *VAI* hold a give-away ceremony
pakitinâsowin– *NI* give-away ceremony

GLAD

miywêyiht– *VTI* be glad, be pleased; like s.t.

GO

awas *IPC* go away! away with you! [*]
itohtê– *VAI* go there or thus
kâsispôhtêmakan– *VII* go on from one generation to another, survive into another generation
macipayi– *VII* go badly
nâcipahiwê– *VAI* go to fetch things, run to fetch things
nitawâpam– *VTA* go and see s.o.
nitawi *IPV* go to, go and
pakicî– *VAI* release (him), let go of (him)
pakitin– *VTA* let s.o. go, give permission to s.o.
pakitin– *VTI* let s.t. go, release s.t., give s.t. up
pakosih– *VTA* beg from s.o.; be a hanger-on to s.o., go with s.o., be part of s.o.
pakwanawahtâ– *VAI* go on with (it) at random, know nothing about (it), be clueless about (it)
papâ *IPV* go about
pimohtê– *VAI* go along, walk along
pimohtêmakan– *VII* go along, move along; be in effect (e.g., treaty)
pimohtêstamaw– *VTA* go along for s.o., represent s.o.

pîhtikwê– *VAI* enter, go inside
pîhtikwêmakan– *VII* enter, go inside
wayawî– *VAI* go outside

GOLD
sôniyâw– *NA* gold, silver; money

GOOD
miyo *IPV* good, well, beautiful, valuable
miyw-âyâ– *VAI* be well, be in good health
miywakihtê– *VII* be considered good; [*in negative clause:*] be considered bad, be considered evil
miywâsin– *VII* be good, be valuable; [*in negative clause:*] be bad, be evil
takahki *IPN* nice, good, beautiful

GOSH
cah *IPC* gosh! [*; *exclamatory*]

GOSSIP
âyimôhto– *VAI* discuss one another; gossip about one another
âyimôhtowin– *NI* discussing one another; gossiping about one another, gossip
âyimôm– *VTA* discuss s.o.; gossip about s.o.
âyimômiso– *VAI* discuss oneself; speak unguardedly about oneself, gossip about oneself
âyimôt– *VTI* speak of s.t., discuss s.t.; gossip about s.t.

GOSSIPING
âyimôhtowin– *NI* discussing one another; gossiping about one another, gossip

GOVERN
tipêyimiso– *VAI* control oneself, govern oneself

GRACE
kakwê *IPV* try to; circumstances permitting, by divine grace
kisêwâtisi– *VAI* be kind, be of compassionate disposition; [*fig.*] be full of grace
kisêwâtisiwin– *NI* kindness, compassion; [*fig.*] grace

GRAIN
kistikân– *NA* grain, seed; sheaf of grain

GRANDCHILD
–ôsisim– *NDA* grandchild; [*fig.*] young person [*e.g.*, kôsisiminaw; *vocative:* nôsisê]
oyôsisimimâw– *NA* grandchild

GRANDFATHER

–mosôm– *NDA* grandfather; [*fig.*] old man [*e.g.*, kimosôminaw; *vocative:* nimosô]

GRANDMOTHER

–ôhkom– *NDA* grandmother, grandmother's sister, great-aunt; [*fig.*] old woman; Our Grandmother [*e.g.*, nôhkominân; kôhkominaw]

GRANT

kiskêyihtamôhikowisi– *VAI* be granted knowledge by the powers

manitowih– *VTA* grant s.o. supernatural powers

nahêyihtamih– *VTA* cause s.o. to be satisfied with (it/him); grant s.o. peace of mind

GRASS

maskosiy– *NI* grass, hay

GRATEFUL

atamih– *VTA* make s.o. grateful, make s.o. indebted, please s.o.

nanâskom– *VTA* be grateful to s.o., give thanks to s.o.

nanâskomo– *VAI* be grateful, give thanks

nanâskot– *VTI* be grateful for s.t., give thanks for s.t.

GREAT

kihc-ôkâwîmâw– *NA* [*fig.*] Great Mother, Mother Earth

misâhkamik *IPC* in great number

môy kakêtihk *IPC* a great many

GREAT-AUNT

–ôhkom– *NDA* grandmother, grandmother's sister, great-aunt; [*fig.*] old woman; Our Grandmother [*e.g.*, nôhkominân; kôhkominaw]

GREAT-GRANDCHILD

–âniskotâpân– *NDA* great-grandchild [*e.g.*, nitâniskotâpânak]

–câpân– *NDA* great-grandchild [*e.g.*, nicâpânak]

GREATLY

misi *IPV* greatly

mistahi *IPC* greatly, very much so [*also* IPV]

GROUND

ay-atâmaskamik *IPC* inside the earth, below the ground [*reduplicated*]

kanâtahcâ– *VII* be clean ground, be clean land

mohcihk *IPC* on the bare ground

sâkâwanêhtâ– *VAI* push (it) to emerge from the ground, make (it) come forth

sâkikin– *VII* grow forth, emerge from the ground

GROUP

mâmawôhkamâto– *VAI* work together at (it/him) as a group, help one another

pimâwah– *VTA* lead s.o. along as a group, pull s.o. along

wîcihiwê– *VAI* be along, be part of a group, join in

GROW

nayawaciki– *VAI* grow up to reach various ages, be variously grown up [*usually plural*]

nihtâwikin– *VII* grow forth (e.g., plant), come forth

ohpiki– *VAI* grow up

ohpikih– *VTA* make s.o. grow up, raise s.o.

ohpikihito– *VAI* make one another grow up, raise one another

ohpikihtamâso– *VAI* make (it) grow for oneself

ohpikihtâ– *VAI* make (it) grow

ohpikinâwaso– *VAI* make one's children grow up, raise one's children

sâkikin– *VII* grow forth, emerge from the ground

GUARD

kanawêyim– *VTA* keep s.o., guard s.o. closely

GUARDIAN

âtayôhkan– *NA* spirit being, dream guardian

âtayôhkanakiso– *VAI* be held to be a spirit being, a dream guardian

GUESS

êtokwê *IPC* presumably, I guess

GUIDE

pimohtah– *VTA* carry s.o. along, guide s.o. along

GUNSHOT

matwêwê– *VII* be heard as a gunshot, be the report of a gun

HABITUALLY

mâna *IPC* habitually, usually

HAIR

–stikwân– *NDI* head; head of hair [*e.g.*, ostikwâniwâw]

sêkipatwâ– *VAI* braid one's hair, have braided hair

HAND

–cihciy– *NDI* hand [*e.g.*, ocihciy]

itisin– *VTA* thus hold (it/him) for s.o., thus hand (it/him) over to s.o.

kwêskinisk *IPC* the other hand, changing one's hand

miyoniskêhkât– *VTI* accomplish s.t. by the work of one's hands

HANDLING

miyawâkâtinikê– *VAI* be particularly careful in handling things (e.g., ceremonial objects)

HANG

akot– *VTA* hang s.o. up; place s.o. on a burial scaffold

HANGER-ON

pakosih– *VTA* beg from s.o.; be a hanger-on to s.o., go with s.o., be part of s.o.

HARMONY

wîcêhtowin– *NI* living with one another; getting along with one another, living in harmony with one another

HARRASS

pisiskêyim– *VTA* pay attention to s.o., tend s.o.; bother s.o., harrass s.o.

HAT

kêtastotinê– *VAI* put one's hat on [*]

HATE

pakwâtamaw– *VTA* hate (it/him) for s.o., dislike (it/him) for s.o., disapprove of (it/him) for s.o.

HAVE

iskon– *VTI* have so much left over of s.t.

kanôsimototaw– *VTA* have s.o. (e.g., rattle) as protection

piko *IPC* must, have to [*clause-initial predicative*]

têpipayi– *VAI* have the full amount, have enough

HAY

maskosiy– *NI* grass, hay

maskosîhkê– *VAI* make hay

wîscihkêsi– *VAI* pile hay into small heaps [*diminutive*]

HE

wiya *PR* he, she

wîsta *PR* he, too; she, too; he by contrast, she by contrast

HEAD

–scikwân– *NDI* head [*diminutive; e.g.*, oscikwân]

–stikwân– *NDI* head; head of hair [*e.g.*, ostikwâniwâw]

âkwaskiskaw– *VTA* head s.o. off, get in s.o.'s way

nânâmiskwêyi– *VAI* nod one's head

nîkân *IPC* first, at the head

nîkânist– *VTI* be at the head of s.t., lead s.t. [*sic:* -i-; *cf.* nîkânîst–]

nîkânîst– *VTI* be at the head of s.t., lead s.t. [*also* nîkânist–]

HEADLONG

pimakocin– *VII* make a rush in linear fashion, charge headlong

HEAL

nanâtawih– *VTA* doctor s.o., heal s.o.

HEALTH

is-âyâ– *VAI* be thus in health; be unwell, be in poor health

mâyimahciho– *VAI* feel poorly, feel in ill health

miyw-âyâ– *VAI* be well, be in good health

HEALTHY

miyomahciho– *VAI* feel well, feel healthy; feel pleased

HEAR

itihtaw– *VTA* hear s.o. thus

itihtâkwan– *VII* be thus heard

matwêwê– *VII* be heard as a gunshot, be the report of a gun

pakahkihtaw– *VTA* hear s.o. clearly

pêht– *VTI* hear s.t.

pêhtamowin– *NI* what is heard [*sc. 'agent-centred' noun; e.g.*, kipêhtamowininâhk 'in what we have heard']

pêhtaw– *VTA* hear s.o.

pêhtâkosi– *VAI* be heard, make oneself heard

pêhtâkwan– *VII* be heard [*]

saskacihtaw– *VTA* be tired of hearing s.o., be fed up with hearing s.o.

HEART

–têh– *NDI* heart; [*fig.*] heart, soul [*e.g.*, otêhihk]

HEARTH-FIRE

iskotêw– *NI* fire, hearth-fire

HEAT

titipawêhkas– *VTI* curl s.t. (e.g., head of hair) by heat; have a perm

HEAVY

kosikwan– *VII* be heavy

HELD

micimôho– *VAI* be held fast, be stuck [*sic:* -h-]

HELP

âpacih– *VTA* use s.o., find s.o. useful; [*especially in inverse:*] be helped by s.o.

itâpacih– *VTA* use s.o. thus, find s.o. useful thus; [*especially in inverse:*] be thus helped by s.o.

mâmawôhkamâto– *VAI* work together at (it/him) as a group, help one another

nâtâmost– *VTI* flee to s.t., turn to s.t. for help, seek refuge in s.t.

nâtâmotot– *VTI* flee to s.t., turn to s.t. for help, seek refuge in s.t.

nâtâmototaw– *VTA* flee to s.o., turn to s.o. for help, seek refuge with s.o.

wîcih– *VTA* help s.o.

wîcôhkamaw– *VTA* help s.o. by action

HERB

maskihkiy– *NI* herb, plant; medicine

HERE

ôta *IPC* here

papâmi *IPV* about, around, here and there

HEY

êy *IPC* hey [*introductory, also exclamatory*]

HIDDEN

âkaw-âyihk *IPC* in a hidden place, behind an obstacle to vision

HIGH

ispâhkêkocin– *VII* rise high up, be high in the air

ispimihk *IPC* high up, up above

iyôtin– *NI* high wind, tornado [*also* yôtin–]

HIGHLY

ispîhtêyimiso– *VAI* think thus highly of oneself

kihcêyim– *VTA* think highly of s.o., hold s.o. sacred

HILL

ispatinâ– *VII* be a hill

osêhcâw– *NI* rise in the land, gentle hill

HIRE

masinahikêh– *VTA* hire s.o., employ s.o.

HIT

tâwin– *VTA* encounter s.o., bump into s.o., hit s.o.

HITHER

itakâm *IPC* on the hither side of a body of water, on the near side of a body of water

pâpici– *VAI* move one's camp hither

pêtâ– *VAI* bring (it) hither

pêtâmo– *VAI* flee hither

HO

ah *IPC* ho! [*exclamatory*]

HOLD

itâskonikê– *VAI* thus point the pipe or pipestem; thus hold a pipe ceremony

itikwamikohkê– *VAI* hold such a lodge, hold such a ceremony

itisin– *VTA* thus hold (it/him) for s.o., thus hand (it/him) over to s.o.

kosâpaht– *VTI* hold a shaking-lodge, hold the shaking-lodge ceremony

matotisi– *VAI* hold a sweat-lodge

mâmawôpi– *VAI* sit together, hold a meeting

micimin– *VTI* hold on to s.t.

nîminamaw– *VTA* hold (it/him) aloft for s.o., offer (it/him) up for s.o.

nîminikê– *VAI* hold things aloft, offer things up

pakitinâso– *VAI* hold a give-away ceremony

sâkihtamaw– *VTA* hold on to (it/him) for s.o.; hold (it/him) back from s.o.

tahkon– *VTI* carry s.t., hold s.t.

tahkonamôh– *VTA* make s.o. carry (it/him), make s.o. hold (it/him)

wîhkohkât– *VTI* hold a feast for s.t. (e.g., medicinal herbs)

wîhkohkê– *VAI* hold a feast

HOLE

wâtihkân– *NI* hole, cellar

HOME

–îk– *NDI* house, dwelling, home [*e.g.*, wîki]

kîwêmakan– *VII* return home, come back

HOMESTEAD

otinaskê– *VAI* take land, settle the land, homestead

HORSE

misatimw– *NA* horse

pêyakwahpitêw *IPC* one team (of two horses)

HORSE-HIDE

misatimwayân– *NA* horse-hide

HORSEBACK

takopayi– *VAI* arrive on horseback, arrive by conveyance

HOT

kisâkamitêhkwê– *VAI* drink a hot liquid, have a hot drink

HOTEL

kapêsîwikamikw– *NI* inn, hotel

HOUSE

–îk– *NDI* house, dwelling, home [*e.g.*, wîki]

wâskahikan– *NI* house

HOUSEMATE

–wîkimâkan– *NDA* spouse, housemate [*e.g.*, niwîkimâkan]

HOW

êkos îsi *IPC* thus, in that way; that is how it is

ômis îsi *IPC* in this way; that is how it is

pikoyikohk *IPC* no matter how much, to any extent [*also* pikw îyikohk]

pikw îyikohk *IPC* no matter how much, to any extent [*cf.* pikoyikohk]

tânisi *IPC* how, in what way

tânitahtwayak *IPC* in how many places; in so many places

tânitahtwâw *IPC* how many times; so many times

HUMAN

–îc-âyisiyiniw– *NDA* fellow human [*e.g.*, kîc-âyisiyinînaw]

ayisiyiniw– *NA* person, human being

ayisiyinîwi– *VAI* be a person, be a human being

ayisiyinîwin– *NI* being human, human existence

HUNGRY

nôhtêhkatê– *VAI* be hungry, want food

HURT

kitimahiso– *VAI* be mean to oneself, hurt oneself

moskâcih– *VTA* bother s.o., trouble s.o., hurt s.o.

HUSBAND

–nâpêm– *NDA* husband [*e.g.*, ninâpêm]

I

niya *PR* I

nîsta *PR* I, too; I by contrast; I myself

IDENTITY

nêhiyâwiwin– *NI* being Cree, Cree identity, Creeness

IF

kîspin *IPC* if [*conditional conjunction*]

kîspin êkâ ohci *IPC* if it were not for [*irrealis conditional, usually with noun phrase or simple conjunct*]

IGNORE

patahohkât– *VTA* overlook s.o., ignore s.o.

ILL

mâyimahciho– *VAI* feel poorly, feel in ill health

mâyipayi– *VAI* suffer ill; be bereaved

ILLEGITIMATE

kimotôsê– *VAI* bear an illegitimate child

ILLNESS

âhkosiwin– *NI* illness

IMMEDIATELY

sêmâk *IPC* immediately, right away

IMPOSE

itasiwât– *VTA* give s.o. such a command, impose such laws on s.o.

itasiwê– *VAI* give such a command, impose such laws [*]

IN

êkotowihk *IPC* in that place

ômatowihk *IPC* in this place

pikw îta *IPC* no matter where, in any place

pîhci *IPV* in between, inside

tahtwayak *IPC* in so many places, in so many ways

tânitahtwayak *IPC* in how many places; in so many places

wâh-wâhyaw *IPC* in far places [*reduplicated*]

IN CASE

êyiwêhk *IPC* just in case, nevertheless; despite shortcomings [*also* kêyiwêhk]

kêyiwêhk *IPC* just in case, nevertheless; despite shortcomings [*also* êyiwêhk]

misawâc *IPC* in any case, whatever might be thought

IN VAIN

konita *IPC* in vain, without reason, without purpose; without further ado

INCLINED

wêpêyim– *VTA* be inclined to throw s.o. (e.g., money) away

INCREASINGLY

tahk âyiwâk *IPC* increasingly, more and more

INDEBTED

atamih– *VTA* make s.o. grateful, make s.o. indebted, please s.o.

INDEED

ahâw *IPC* now indeed [*]

ohtitaw *IPC* expressly, specifically; it is requisite, it is meet indeed

tâpwê *IPC* truly, indeed

INDIAN

nêhiyaw– *NA* Cree, Indian

nêhiyawi *IPN* Cree, Indian

nêhiyawi-kiskinohamâtowi-kakêskihkêmowikamikw– *NI* Saskatchewan Indian Cultural College [*literally:* counselling building for Cree (or Indian) teaching]

otasahkêw– *NA* one who distributes rations; Indian agent

sôniyâwikimâw– *NA* Indian agent

INDIVIDUALLY

pâh-pêyak *IPC* singly, one at a time; each individually

INITIALLY

mâci *IPV* begin; initially

nistam *IPC* for the first time, initially, originally

INN

kapêsîwikamikw– *NI* inn, hotel

INSECT

manicôs– *NA* insect, bug

INSIDE

ay-atâmaskamik *IPC* inside the earth, below the ground [*reduplicated*]

pîhci *IPV* in between, inside

pîhtikwah– *VTA* enter with s.o., take s.o. inside

pîhtikwatâ– *VAI* enter with (it), take (it) inside

pîhtikwê– *VAI* enter, go inside

pîhtikwêmakan– *VII* enter, go inside

INSTANCE

mâcika *IPC* for instance [*weak concessive*]

INSTEAD

mêskocikâpawi– *VAI* stand up instead [*sic:* -ê-]

INSTRUCTOR

okistikêwiyiniw– *NA* farm instructor

INTEND

wî *IPV* intend to

INTENSIVELY

mitoni *IPC* intensively, really [*also* IPV]

INTENTLY

iyâyaw *IPC* eagerly, intently; by preference, rather

INTERPRET

itwêstamaw– *VTA* say thus for s.o.; speak for s.o.; interpret for s.o.

INTERPRETER

otitwêstamâkêw– *NA* interpreter; advocate

INTO

pîhtâpâwah– *VTA* pour liquid into s.o., give s.o. an enema

sâkohtê– *VAI* walk into view, move into view

INTRODUCE

nakiskamohtatamaw– *VTA* take (it/him) to meet s.o., meet s.o. with (it/him); introduce (it/him) to s.o.

INVITE

nitom– *VTA* invite s.o.

wîhkohto– *VAI* invite one another to a feast

wîhkom– *VTA* invite s.o. to a feast

ITCHY

kiyakasê– *VAI* have itchy skin, suffer from eczema

JOIN

wîcêhto– *VAI* live with one another, join with one another; get along with one another

wîcêw– *VTA* accompany s.o., join s.o.

wîcihiwê– *VAI* be along, be part of a group, join in

JOINING

âniskê *IPV* successively, one joining the other, surviving

JOINTLY

mâmawi *IPV* collectively, jointly

JUST

êyiwêhk *IPC* just in case, nevertheless; despite shortcomings [*also* kêyiwêhk]

katisk *IPC* just now, exactly; [*in negative clause:*] not merely

kêtisk *IPC* just barely, to exact measure

kêyiwêhk *IPC* just in case, nevertheless; despite shortcomings [*also* êyiwêhk]

KEEP

kanawêyim– *VTA* keep s.o., guard s.o. closely

pimipayihtâ– *VAI* run (it), keep (it) up, exercise (it)

KETTLE

pêyakwêskihk *IPC* one kettle (measure)

KILL

minaho– *VAI* kill an animal, make a kill

nipah– *VTA* kill s.o.

KIND

êkotowahk *IPC* of that kind

kisê-nâpêw-asiniy– *NA* [*spirit's name:*] Kind-Man-Rock

kisêwâtisi– *VAI* be kind, be of compassionate disposition; [*fig.*] be full of grace

nanâtohk *IPC* variously, of various kinds

nêmatowahk *IPC* of that kind yonder

ômatowahk *IPC* of this kind

KINDNESS

kisêwâtisiwin– *NI* kindness, compassion; [*fig.*] grace

KINSMAN

–tôtêm– *NDA* kinsman; friend [*e.g.*, kitôtêminawak]

KNIFE

môhkomân– *NI* knife

KNOW

kiskêyiht– *VTI* know s.t.; have knowledge

pakwanawahtâ– *VAI* go on with (it) at random, know nothing about (it), be clueless about (it)

KNOWLEDGE

kiskêyiht– *VTI* know s.t.; have knowledge

kiskêyihtamôhikowisi– *VAI* be granted knowledge by the powers

LAKE

sâkahikan– *NI* lake

wîhcêkaskosîwi-sâkahikanihk *INM* [*place-name:*] at Onion Lake

LAND

askiy– *NI* earth, land, country; world

kanâtahcâ– *VII* be clean ground, be clean land

kwêskahcâhk *IPC* on the opposite side of a rise in the land

osêhcâw– *NI* rise in the land, gentle hill

otinaskê– *VAI* take land, settle the land, homestead

LANGUAGE

pîkiskwêwin– *NI* word, expression, phrase; speech, language

LAST

aspin *IPC* off, away; the last I knew

iskwêyâc *IPC* at last, at the end

nânapêc *IPC* late, at the last moment, barely in time (e.g., when it should have been done previously); [*in negative clause:*] too late

piyisk *IPC* finally, at last

tipiskohk *IPC* last night

LATE

nânapêc *IPC* late, at the last moment, barely in time (e.g., when it should have been done previously); [*in negative clause:*] too late

LAUGH

pâhpi– *VAI* laugh

pâhpih– *VTA* laugh at s.o., deride s.o.

LAUNDRY

kisîpêkinikê– *VAI* wash things, do the laundry

LAWS

itasiwât– *VTA* give s.o. such a command, impose such laws on s.o.

itasiwê– *VAI* give such a command, impose such laws [*]

LEAD

nîkâni– *VAI* be at the lead (e.g., tobacco)

nîkânist– *VTI* be at the head of s.t., lead s.t. [*sic:* -i-; *cf.* nîkânîst–]

nîkânîh– *VTA* place s.o. (e.g., tobacco) at the lead

nîkânîst– *VTI* be at the head of s.t., lead s.t. [*also* nîkânist–]

nîkânohk *IPC* in the lead position

nîkânohtatâ– *VAI* be in the lead with (it), carry (it) in the lead

nîkânohtêmakan– *VII* be in the lead, proceed in the lead position

pimâwah– *VTA* lead s.o. along as a group, pull s.o. along

sakâpêkipah– *VTA* lead s.o. (e.g., horse) by a rope

wanisim– *VTA* cause s.o. to get lost, lead s.o. astray

wanisinohtah– *VTA* lead s.o. to lose (it/him)

LEADER

onîkânîw– *NA* leader

LEANING

aspatisin– *VII* lie leaning upon something, lie back upon something, lie propped up

LEARN

kiskinowâpaht– *VTI* learn merely by watching s.t.

kiskinowâsoht– *VTI* learn merely by listening to s.t.

okiskinowâpiw– *NA* one who learns merely by watching

LEARNING

kiskinowâpiwin– *NI* learning merely by watching

LEAVE

nakat– *VTA* leave s.o. behind

nakat– *VTI* leave s.t. behind

nakatamaw– *VTA* leave (it/him) behind for s.o.

ohtaskat– *VTI* leave s.t. suddenly thereby or there
sipwêhtê– *VAI* leave, depart
sipwêmon– *VII* leave as path, trail, road; begin as path, trail, road

LECTURE
kakêskim– *VTA* counsel s.o., lecture s.o.
kitot– *VTA* address s.o., speak to s.o., lecture s.o.

LEFT OVER
iskon– *VTI* have so much left over of s.t.

LEG
nîsokâtê– *VAI* have two legs, be two-legged

LESS
nôhtaw *IPC* less; minus

LET
kiyâm *IPC* let it be, let there be no further delay; please
mahti *IPC* let's see [*hortatory, often jussive*]
pakicî– *VAI* release (him), let go of (him)
pakitin– *VTA* let s.o. go, give permission to s.o.
pakitin– *VTI* let s.t. go, release s.t., give s.t. up

LEVEL-HEADED
âpahkawin– *VII* be level-headed, be sensible, be conscious

LIE
aspatisin– *VII* lie leaning upon something, lie back upon something, lie propped up
nîkâniwi– *VII* be ahead, be the future; lie in the future [*sic:* -i-]

LIFE
ahcâhko-pimâtisiwin– *NI* spiritual life
kistikêwi-pimâcihowin– *NI* agricultural way of life, farm economy
pimâcih– *VTA* make s.o. live, give life to s.o.; make a living for s.o.
pimâciho– *VAI* make a life for oneself, make one's living; live
pimâtisiwin– *NI* life [*also* pimâcisiwin–]
pimâtisiwinê– *VAI* have life, seek life
pimâtisiwinowi– *VII* have life, provide life
wawânaskêhtamaw– *VTA* create a peaceful life for s.o.
wawânaskêhtâ– *VAI* live a peaceful life

LIGHT
saskahamaw– *VTA* light (it/him) for s.o.; light the pipe for s.o.

LIKE

miywêyiht– *VTI* be glad, be pleased; like s.t.

LIMITATIONS

kôtatê *IPC* at a loss; due to limitations beyond one's control [*also predicative:* 'it cannot be helped'; *cf.* kwêtatêyitiskwêyi–]

LINEAR

pimakocin– *VII* make a rush in linear fashion, charge headlong

pimastê– *VII* be placed in linear fashion, run along

pimi *IPV* along, in linear progression; while moving in linear progression

LIQUID

kisâkamitêhkwê– *VAI* drink a hot liquid, have a hot drink

pîhtâpâwah– *VTA* pour liquid into s.o., give s.o. an enema

LISTEN

kiskinowâsoht– *VTI* learn merely by listening to s.t.

kitimâkihtaw– *VTA* listen to s.o. with pity, listen to s.o. with compassion

nanahiht– *VTI* listen obediently to s.t.; obey s.t.

nanahihtaw– *VTA* listen well to s.o., obey s.o.

nitoht– *VTI* listen to s.t.

nitohtaw– *VTA* listen to s.o.

LITTLE

aciyaw *IPC* for a little while [*]

apisis *IPC* a little

LIVE

apist– *VTI* sit by s.t., live in s.t. (e.g., lodge) [*sic:* -i-]

askîwisk– *VTI* subject the earth to oneself, populate the earth, make the earth live

ayâ– *VAI* be there, live there; exist

otisâpaht– *VTI* have lived long enough to see s.t.

pimâcih– *VTA* make s.o. live, give life to s.o.; make a living for s.o.

pimâciho– *VAI* make a life for oneself, make one's living; live

pimâtisi– *VAI* live, be alive

pimohtât– *VTI* live s.t. (e.g., day), live through s.t.

wawânaskêhtâ– *VAI* live a peaceful life

wîc-âyâm– *VTA* be with s.o., live with s.o.

wîcêhto– *VAI* live with one another, join with one another; get along with one another

wîki– *VAI* live, dwell, have one's abode
wîtaskîwêm– *VTA* live together with s.o.; live in the same country with s.o., live in peace with s.o.

LIVING

pimâcih– *VTA* make s.o. live, give life to s.o.; make a living for s.o.
pimâciho– *VAI* make a life for oneself, make one's living; live
pimâcihwâkê– *VAI* make one's living with things
wîcêhtowin– *NI* living with one another; getting along with one another, living in harmony with one another

LO

mâcikôtitan *IPC* wait and see! lo! [*exlamatory; sic:* -â-, -ô-, -a-]

LODGE

itikwamikohkê– *VAI* hold such a lodge, hold such a ceremony
mânokê– *VAI* build a lodge, set up a tent
mîkiwâhp– *NI* lodge, tipi

LONG

kayâs *IPC* long ago, in earlier days; previously
kayâsês *IPC* quite a long time ago
kinwês *IPC* for a long time
otisâpaht– *VTI* have lived long enough to see s.t.

LOOK

asawâpi– *VAI* look out, be on watch
isinâkosi– *VAI* look thus
isinâkwan– *VII* look thus, give such an appearance
itâpi– *VAI* look thus or there
îh *IPC* look! behold! [*exclamatory*]
kitâpaht– *VTI* look at s.t.
kitâpam– *VTA* look at s.o.
kitâpamikowisi– *VAI* be looked upon by the powers
kitimâkinaw– *VTA* look with pity upon s.o., look with compassion upon s.o.; regard s.o. with respect
kitimâkinâkosi– *VAI* look pitiable, look miserable, look poor
kwêskinâkwan– *VII* look changed, look turned around to the opposite
nâkatowâpaht– *VTI* pay attention in looking at s.t.
niton– *VTI* look for s.t.
osâpaht– *VTI* look at s.t. from there
osâpam– *VTA* look at s.o. from there

LOOK AFTER

kanawêyiht– *VTI* look after s.t., take care of s.t.

kanawêyihtamaw– *VTA* look after (it/him) for s.o., take care of (it/him) for s.o.

pamih– *VTA* tend to s.o., look after s.o.

pamihikowin– *NI* being looked after, welfare [*sc. 'patient-centred' noun; e.g.,* kipamihikowin 'the fact that you are looked after']

pamihtâ– *VAI* look after (it)

pamin– *VTA* tend to s.o., look after s.o.

LOSE

wanihtâ– *VAI* lose (it); get relief from (it)

wanisim– *VTA* cause s.o. to get lost, lead s.o. astray

wanisinohtah– *VTA* lead s.o. to lose (it/him)

LOSS

kôtatê *IPC* at a loss; due to limitations beyond one's control [*also predicative:* 'it cannot be helped'*; cf.* kwêtatêyitiskwêyi–]

kôtawêyiht– *VTI* be at a loss for s.t., miss s.t.

kwêtatêyitiskwêyi– *VAI* be at a loss as to where to turn one's head; be at a loss for a response [*cf.* kôtatê]

LOTS

pîsâkwan– *VII* contain plenty, offer lots of room; be plentiful, be rich [*sic:* -â-]

LOUD

kisîwê– *VII* be loud, speak loudly (e.g., audio-recorder) [*]

LOUDLY

kisîwê– *VII* be loud, speak loudly (e.g., audio-recorder) [*]

kisîwêhkahtaw– *VTA* speak loudly to s.o.

LOVE

kitimâkêyihto– *VAI* feel pity towards one another, love one another, think of one another with compassion

LOVING

kitimâkêyihtowin– *NI* feeling pity towards one another, loving one another, thinking of one another with compassion

LOW

capasis *IPC* down low

tapahcipayiho– *VAI* swoop down, swoop low

MACHINE

âpacihcikan– *NI* tool; appliance, machine

MAD

môhcowi– *VAI* be stupid, be silly; be mad, be crazy

MAKE

osîh– *VTA* prepare s.o. (e.g., rattle), make s.o.

osîhtamâso– *VAI* make (it/him) for oneself

osîhtâ– *VAI* prepare (it), make (it)

MALE

–ciwâm– *NDA* male parallel cousin (man speaking); [*fig.*] brother, male of the same generation (man speaking) [*e.g.*, kiciwâminaw]

–îscâs– *NDA* male cross-cousin (man speaking) [*diminutive; e.g.*, wîscâsa]

nâpêw– *NA* man, male, adult male

MAN

–kosis– *NDA* son; parallel nephew; [*fig.*] younger man [*e.g.*, nikosis; *vocative:* nikosis]

–mosôm– *NDA* grandfather; [*fig.*] old man [*e.g.*, kimosôminaw; *vocative:* nimosô]

–oskinîkîm– *NDA* young man, follower; [*fig.*] servant [*e.g.*, otôskinîkîma]

kisêyiniw– *NA* old man

nâpêw– *NA* man, male, adult male

oskinîkiw– *NA* young man, youth

MANNER

katawâhk *IPC* properly, in seemly manner

MANNIKIN

ayisiyinîhkân– *NA* doll, mannikin; cartoon figure

MANY

ihtasi– *VAI* be so many, be as many

itahtin– *VII* be so many

itahtopiponwê– *VAI* be so many years old

itahtwapi– *VAI* sit as so many, be present as so many

mihcêt *IPC* many

mihcêtwâw *IPC* many times

môy kakêtihk *IPC* a great many

tahto *IPC* so many, as many

tahto-kîkway *IPC* so many things, as many things

tahtwayak *IPC* in so many places, in so many ways

tahtwâw *IPC* so many times

tânitahtwayak *IPC* in how many places; in so many places

tânitahtwâw *IPC* how many times; so many times

MARK

masinahikâtê– *VII* be pictured, be depicted; have marks, have writing; be written

MATCH

kocawâkanis– *NI* match, match-stick [*diminutive*]

MATCH-STICK

kocawâkanis– *NI* match, match-stick [*diminutive*]

MATTER

pikoyikohk *IPC* no matter how much, to any extent [*also* pikw îyikohk]

pikw îta *IPC* no matter where, in any place

pikw îtê *IPC* no matter whither, to any place

pikw îyikohk *IPC* no matter how much, to any extent [*cf.* pikoyikohk]

MEAL

mîciso– *VAI* eat, have a meal

MEAN

kakwâtakih– *VTA* make s.o. suffer, be mean to s.o., be abusive to s.o.

kitimah– *VTA* be mean to s.o., treat s.o. badly

kitimahiso– *VAI* be mean to oneself, hurt oneself

MEANING

itwê– *VAI* say thus, call (it) thus; have such a meaning

itwêmakan– *VII* say thus, have such a meaning

itwêmakisi– *VAI* say thus, have such a meaning [*]

MEANS

ohci *IPC* with, by means of; because of; from then [*enclitic; also* IPV]

MEASURE

kêtisk *IPC* just barely, to exact measure

tipah– *VTI* measure s.t.; pay s.t., pay for s.t.

MEDICINAL

wîhkohkât– *VTI* hold a feast for s.t. (e.g., medicinal herbs)

MEDICINE

maskihkiy– *NI* herb, plant; medicine

maskihkîwiwacis– *NI* medicine chest

nâcinêhamaw– *VTA* obtain (it/him) from s.o. by payment, seek to buy medicine from s.o.

nâcinêhikê– *VAI* obtain things by payment, seek to buy medicine

MEET

nakiskamohtatamaw– *VTA* take (it/him) to meet s.o., meet s.o. with (it/him); introduce (it/him) to s.o.

nakiskaw– *VTA* encounter s.o., meet s.o.

ohtitaw *IPC* expressly, specifically; it is requisite, it is meet indeed

MEETING

mâmawôpi– *VAI* sit together, hold a meeting

MENTION

wîh– *VTA* name s.o., mention s.o. by name

MERELY

katisk *IPC* just now, exactly; [*in negative clause:*] not merely

kiskinowâpaht– *VTI* learn merely by watching s.t.

kiskinowâpiwin– *NI* learning merely by watching

kiskinowâsoht– *VTI* learn merely by listening to s.t.

okiskinowâpiw– *NA* one who learns merely by watching

METAL

sôniyâwi– *VII* be precious metal; be money

MIND

awâska-mâmitonêyihcikan– *NI* stable mind, steady mind, balanced mind [*?sic*]

kotêyiht– *VTI* try s.t. in one's mind, think strenuously about s.t., test s.t.; challenge s.t.

kotêyim– *VTA* try s.o., test s.o., put s.o.'s mind to the test; challenge s.o.

mâmitonêyihcikan– *NI* mind; troubled mind

mâmitonêyim– *VTA* think about s.o., have s.o. on one's mind

mitonêyihcikan– *NI* mind

nahêyiht– *VTI* be satisfied with s.t.; have peace of mind

nahêyihtamih– *VTA* cause s.o. to be satisfied with (it/him); grant s.o. peace of mind

MINISTER

ayamihêwiyiniw– *NA* priest; minister

MINUS

nôhtaw *IPC* less; minus

MISERABLE

kicimâkisi– *VAI* be pitiable, be miserable [*diminutive*]

kitimâkan– *VII* be pitiable, be miserable

kitimâkinâkosi– *VAI* look pitiable, look miserable, look poor

kitimâkisi– *VAI* be pitiable, be miserable, be poor

MISS

kôtawêyiht– *VTI* be at a loss for s.t., miss s.t.

MISSPEAK

patowât– *VTI* misspeak s.t., commit an error in one's prayers

MOMENT

nânapêc *IPC* late, at the last moment, barely in time (e.g., when it should have been done previously); [*in negative clause:*] too late

MONDAY

pôn-âyamihêwi-kîsikâ– *VII* be Monday

MONEY

sôniyâw– *NA* gold, silver; money

sôniyâwi– *VII* be precious metal; be money

MORE

ayiwâk *IPC* more; [*in numeral phrases:*] plus

nawac *IPC* more, better, rather

tahk âyiwâk *IPC* increasingly, more and more

wâwîs cî *IPC* especially, all the more so

MORNING

kîkisêp *IPC* early in the morning [*sic; cf.* kîkisêpâ]

kîkisêpâ *IPC* early in the morning [*also* kîkisêp]

wâpan– *VII* be dawn, be early morning

MOST

têpiyâhk *IPC* the only thing; the most (if any)

MOTHER

-kâwiy– *NDA* mother; [*fig.*] Our Mother [*e.g.*, nikâwiy; kikâwînaw]

kihc-ôkâwîmâw– *NA* [*fig.*] Great Mother, Mother Earth

MOUNTAIN

asiniîwaciy– *NI* the Rocky Mountains [*usually sg.*]

MOUTHPIECE

otônihkâ– *VAI* use (it/him) as one's mouthpiece, make (it/him) one's advocate

MOVE

isiniskêyi– *VAI* move one's arm thus or there, point in that direction with one's arm

ispayiho– *VAI* throw oneself thus or there, move thus or there

masinipayi– *VAI* be depicted as moving (e.g., on film)

pâpici– *VAI* move one's camp hither

pimi *IPV* along, in linear progression; while moving in linear progression

pimitâpâso– *VAI* move along in a conveyance

pimohtêmakan– *VII* go along, move along; be in effect (e.g., treaty)

sâkohtê– *VAI* walk into view, move into view

MUCH

iskon– *VTI* have so much left over of s.t.

itakihtê– *VII* be counted thus, cost so much; be held in such esteem

iyikohk *IPC* so much, to such a degree, to such an extent

mistahi *IPC* greatly, very much so [*also* IPV]

pikoyikohk *IPC* no matter how much, to any extent [*also* pikw îyikohk]

pikw îyikohk *IPC* no matter how much, to any extent [*cf.* pikoyikohk]

MUST

piko *IPC* must, have to [*clause-initial predicative*]

MY

wahwâ *IPC* oh my! [*exclamatory*]

NAME

isiyîhkâso– *VAI* be called thus, have such a name

isiyîhkât– *VTA* call s.o. thus, use such a name for s.o.

isiyîhkât– *VTI* call s.t. thus, use such a name for s.t.

isiyîhkâtê– *VII* be called thus, have such a name

nêhiyawi-wîh– *VTA* use s.o.'s Cree name, call s.o. by a Cree name

nêhiyawi-wîht– *VTI* use the Cree name of s.t., call s.t. by a Cree name

wîh– *VTA* name s.o., mention s.o. by name

NATURAL

pâstâhowin– *NI* transgression, breach of the natural order; sin

NEAR

itakâm *IPC* on the hither side of a body of water, on the near side of a body of water

NEARBY

cîkâhtaw *IPC* close, nearby, in the area

NECESSITY

môy êkâ êtokwê *IPC* without any doubt, of necessity [*usually with independent indicative*]

NEGOTIATIONS

wiyihcikê– *VAI* arrange things, conduct negotiations, conclude a treaty

NEPHEW

–kosis– *NDA* son; parallel nephew; [*fig.*] younger man [*e.g.*, nikosis; *vocative:* nikosis]

–tihkwatim– *NDA* cross-nephew; son-in-law [*e.g.*, nitihkwatim]

NEST

wacistwan– *NI* nest

NEVER

wîhkâc *IPC* ever; [*in negative clause:*] never

NEVERTHELESS

âhci piko *IPC* still, nevertheless, despite everything [*adversative*]

êyiwêhk *IPC* just in case, nevertheless; despite shortcomings [*also* kêyiwêhk]

kêyiwêhk *IPC* just in case, nevertheless; despite shortcomings [*also* êyiwêhk]

NICE

takahki *IPN* nice, good, beautiful

NIECE

–stim– *NDA* cross-niece; daughter-in-law [*e.g.*, ostima]

NIGHT

nêwo-tipiskâ– *VII* be four nights, be the fourth night

pêyak-tipiskâw *IPC* one night

tipiskohk *IPC* last night

NO

namôya *IPC* not; no [*negator in independent and non-volitional conjunct clauses*]

namwâ *IPC* not; no [*sic; cf.* namwâc; *emphatic negator in independent and non-volitional conjunct clauses*]

NOD

nânâmiskwêyi– *VAI* nod one's head

NOISE

kito– *VAI* make noises (e.g., animal); produce a thunderclap

NORTH

nâtakâm *IPC* in the north, to the north

NOT

cêskwa *IPC* wait; [*in negative clause:*] not yet

êkâ *IPC* not [*negator in volitional clauses; also* êkâya]

iyawis *IPC* fully, entirely; [*in negative clause:*] only partially, not exclusively

katisk *IPC* just now, exactly; [*in negative clause:*] not merely

kîspin êkâ ohci *IPC* if it were not for [*irrealis conditional, usually with noun phrase or simple conjunct*]

môya *IPC* not [*cf.* namôya]

nama *IPC* not [*negator in nominal phrases*]

namôya *IPC* not; no [*negator in independent and non-volitional conjunct clauses*]

namwâ *IPC* not; no [*sic; cf.* namwâc; *emphatic negator in independent and non-volitional conjunct clauses*]

NOTHING

pakwanawahtâ– *VAI* go on with (it) at random, know nothing about (it), be clueless about (it)

NOTICE

nâkatôhkê– *VAI* pay attention, take notice

NOW

ahâw *IPC* now indeed [*]

êkwa *IPC* then, now; and

hâw *IPC* now then [*hortatory, indicating readiness or impatience*]

iyaw *IPC* well now [*; *introductory, also exclamatory*]

katisk *IPC* just now, exactly; [*in negative clause:*] not merely

NUMBER

misâhkamik *IPC* in great number

nîsi– *VAI* be two in number

NUMEROUS

mihcêti– *VAI* be numerous, be plentiful

mihcêtin– *VII* be numerous, be plentiful

OBEDIENTLY

nanahiht– *VTI* listen obediently to s.t.; obey s.t.

OBEY

nanahiht– *VTI* listen obediently to s.t.; obey s.t.

nanahihtaw– *VTA* listen well to s.o., obey s.o.

OBSTACLE

âkaw-âyihk *IPC* in a hidden place, behind an obstacle to vision

OBTAIN

nâcinêhamaw– *VTA* obtain (it/him) from s.o. by payment, seek to buy medicine from s.o.

nâcinêhikê– *VAI* obtain things by payment, seek to buy medicine

ohtisi– *VAI* obtain payment thereby or therefrom

OBVIOUSLY

cikêmô *IPC* of course, obviously, as might be expected [*weak concessive; cf.* cikêmâ]

OCCUR

ihkin– *VII* occur, take place

ispayi– *VII* take place thus, occur thus; have passed (e.g., days, years) [*e.g.*, ispayiw, ê-ispayik]

OF COURSE

cikêmô *IPC* of course, obviously, as might be expected [*weak concessive; cf.* cikêmâ]

OFF

aspin *IPC* off, away; the last I knew

kîskisamaw– *VTA* cut (it/him) off for s.o.; offer tobacco to s.o.

nâtwâpayi– *VII* break off (e.g., branch)

nâtwâwêpah– *VTI* break s.t. off and throw it down

ohpimê *IPC* off, away, to the side

patitisahamaw– *VTA* drive (it/him) off the path for s.o., send (it/him) awry for s.o., spoil (it/him) for s.o.

pâskin– *VTI* open s.t. up, take the cover off s.t.; fold s.t. (e.g., book) open

yîkatêhtê– *VAI* walk off to the side

OFFER

kîskisamaw– *VTA* cut (it/him) off for s.o.; offer tobacco to s.o.

nîminamaw– *VTA* hold (it/him) aloft for s.o., offer (it/him) up for s.o.

nîminikê– *VAI* hold things aloft, offer things up

pîsâkwan– *VII* contain plenty, offer lots of room; be plentiful, be rich [*sic:* -â-]

OFFERING

wêpinâson– *NI* draped cloth, flag, cloth offering

OH

wahwâ *IPC* oh my! [*exclamatory*]

yôhô *IPC* oh! [*exclamatory*]

OLD

–îci-kîhkâw– *NDA* aged spouse, fellow old person, fellow oldster, companion of one's old age [*e.g.*, wîci-kîhkâwa]

–mosôm– *NDA* grandfather; [*fig.*] old man [*e.g.*, kimosôminaw; *vocative:* nimosô]

–ôhkom– *NDA* grandmother, grandmother's sister, great-aunt; [*fig.*] old woman; Our Grandmother [*e.g.*, nôhkominân; kôhkominaw]

itahtopiponwê– *VAI* be so many years old

kêhtê-ay– *NA* old person, the old; elder

kêhtê-ayiwi– *VAI* be an old person; be an elder

kisêyiniw– *NA* old man

kisêyinîw-âcimowin– *NI* old man's story, report of the old men

kisêyinîw-ôhpikihâkan– *NA* old man's pupil, ward of the old men

kisêyinîwi-pîkiskwêwin– *NI* old man's word, word of the old men

nôtikwêsiw– *NA* old woman [*diminutive*]

nôtikwêw– *NA* old woman

OLDER

–stês– *NDA* older brother [*e.g.*, kistêsinaw]

OLDSTER

–îci-kîhkâw– *NDA* aged spouse, fellow old person, fellow oldster, companion of one's old age [*e.g.*, wîci-kîhkâwa]

ONE

êwako *PR* that one [*resumptive demonstrative; e.g.*, êwako, êkonik, êkoni; êwako, êkoni, êwakoyiw]

kêtahtawê *IPC* suddenly; at one time

nâha *PR* that one yonder [*demonstrative; e.g.*, nâha, nêhi; nêma]

pâh-pêyak *IPC* singly, one at a time; each individually

pêyak *IPC* one, a single; the only one

pêyak-kîsikâw *IPC* one day

pêyak-misit *IPC* one foot (measure)

pêyak-tipiskâw *IPC* one night

pêyakoyâkan *IPC* one dish (measure)

pêyakwahpitêw *IPC* one team (of two horses)

pêyakwêskihk *IPC* one kettle (measure)

tânima *PR* which one

ONION LAKE

wîhcêkaskosîwi-sâkahikanihk *INM* [*place-name:*] at Onion Lake

ONLY

êkwêyâc *IPC* only then

iyawis *IPC* fully, entirely; [*in negative clause:*] only partially, not exclusively

nayêstaw *IPC* only; it is only that [*often predicative*]

pêyak *IPC* one, a single; the only one

piko *IPC* only [*enclitic*]

têpiyâhk *IPC* the only thing; the most (if any)

OPEN

pâskin– *VTI* open s.t. up, take the cover off s.t.; fold s.t. (e.g., book) open

taswêkin– *VTI* open s.t. (e.g., book) up flat

tawâ– *VII* be open, have room

tawâtamaw– *VTA* open (it) up for s.o.; clear the way for s.o.

yôhtên– *VTI* open s.t.; turn s.t. (e.g., television set) on

yôhtênamaw– *VTA* open (it/him) for s.o.; turn (it/him) (e.g., television set) on for s.o.

OPPOSITE

kwêsk-âyihk *IPC* on the opposite side

kwêskahcâhk *IPC* on the opposite side of a rise in the land

kwêskâskon– *VTA* turn s.o. (e.g., pipe) to the opposite side

kwêski *IPV* turned around, turned to the opposite side

kwêskinâkwan– *VII* look changed, look turned around to the opposite

OPPRESS

mâkoh– *VTA* worry s.o., trouble s.o.; oppress s.o., throw s.o. into crisis

OR

ahpô *IPC* even, possibly; or

ahpô cî *IPC* or else

ORDER

kîsakim– *VTA* finish counting s.o.; finish giving orders to s.o., complete one's charge to s.o.

pâstâhowin– *NI* transgression, breach of the natural order; sin

wiyakim– *VTA* set a price on s.o. (e.g., bread); arrange (it) for s.o.; decide on s.o.; give orders to s.o.

ORDINARY

iyinito *IPN* plain, ordinary

ORIGINAL

nistamêmâkan– *NA* the first one, the original one [*sic*]

ORIGINALLY

nistam *IPC* for the first time, initially, originally

ORPHAN

kîwâtisi– *VAI* be orphaned, be an orphan

OTHER

awas-âyihk *IPC* on the other side, on the far side

âta *IPC* although; on the other hand [*concessive conjunction*]

kotak *PR* other, another [*e.g.*, kotaka]

kwêskinisk *IPC* the other hand, changing one's hand

tahto-nîso-kîsikâw *IPC* every second day, every other day

OUT

sâkêwêtot– *VTI* come out upon s.t., rise (e.g., sun) upon s.t.

sihko– *VAI* spit, spit out

sîkatêhtamaw– *VTA* spit (it/him) out for s.o.

OUTSIDE

wayawî– *VAI* go outside

OVER

êkotê *IPC* over there

nêtê *IPC* over yonder

OVERCOME

sâkôcih– *VTA* overcome s.o., beat s.o.

sâkôh– *VTA* overcome s.o., overwhelm s.o.

OVERLOOK

patahohkât– *VTA* overlook s.o., ignore s.o.

OVERNIGHT

kapêsimostaw– *VTA* stay overnight with s.o., stay overnight at s.o.'s place

OVERSEAS

akâmaskîhk *IPC* across the water, overseas

OVERWHELM

sâkôh– *VTA* overcome s.o., overwhelm s.o.

OWN

tipêyiht– *VTI* own s.t., control s.t.

tipêyim– *VTA* own s.o., control s.o.

PALPABLE

sawohkât– *VTA* bestow a palpable blessing upon s.o. [*?sic*]

PARENT

–nîkihikw– *NDA* parent [*e.g.*, onîkihikowâwa]

onîkihikomâw– *NA* parent

PART

pakosih– *VTA* beg from s.o.; be a hanger-on to s.o., go with s.o., be part of s.o.

wîcihiwê– *VAI* be along, be part of a group, join in

PARTIALLY

iyawis *IPC* fully, entirely; [*in negative clause:*] only partially, not exclusively

PARTICULAR

âsônê *IPC* especially, in particular

mêmohci *IPC* in particular, above all; exactly, precisely

miyawâkâc *IPV* with particular care

PARTICULARLY

miyawâkâtinikê– *VAI* be particularly careful in handling things (e.g., ceremonial objects)

PARTNER

owîcêwâkani– *VAI* have a companion or partner, have (her/him) as companion or partner

PASS

âsônamaw– *VTA* pass (it/him) on to s.o.

ispayi– *VII* take place thus, occur thus; have passed (e.g., days, years) [*e.g.,* ispayiw, ê-ispayik]

ocihcipayi– *VII* come to pass

ocihciskâmakan– *VII* come to pass, take place [*literally:* by foot or body movement]

wîmâskaw– *VTA* pass around s.o., pass s.o. by

PAST

kî *IPV* complete, past

ohci *IPV* thence, from there; [*in negative clause:*] past [*cf.* ôh]

ôh *IPV* from there; [*in negative clause:*] past [*cf.* ohci]

PATH

itamon– *VII* run thus or there as a path

mêskanaw– *NI* path, trail, road

patitisahamaw– *VTA* drive (it/him) off the path for s.o., send (it/him) awry for s.o., spoil (it/him) for s.o.

sipwêmon– *VII* leave as path, trail, road; begin as path, trail, road

PAY

tipah– *VTI* measure s.t.; pay s.t., pay for s.t.

tipahamaw– *VTA* pay s.o. for (it/him), repay a debt to s.o.

PAYMENT

nâcinêhamaw– *VTA* obtain (it/him) from s.o. by payment, seek to buy medicine from s.o.

nâcinêhikê– *VAI* obtain things by payment, seek to buy medicine

ohtisi– *VAI* obtain payment thereby or therefrom

têpinêhamaw– *VTA* make full payment for (it/him) to s.o.

PEACE

nahêyiht– *VTI* be satisfied with s.t.; have peace of mind

nahêyihtamih– *VTA* cause s.o. to be satisfied with (it/him); grant s.o. peace of mind

wîtaskîwêm– *VTA* live together with s.o.; live in the same country with s.o., live in peace with s.o.

PEACEFUL

wawânaskêhtamaw– *VTA* create a peaceful life for s.o.

wawânaskêhtâ– *VAI* live a peaceful life

PEOPLE

–iyinîm– *NDA* people, followers [*usually plural; e.g.*, kitiyinîmak]

–osk-âyim– *NDA* young people, children, the young [*e.g.*, otôsk-âyima]

PERFORM

isîhcikê– *VAI* do things thus, proceed thus, perform such a ritual

PERM

titipawêhkas– *VTI* curl s.t. (e.g., head of hair) by heat; have a perm

PERMISSION

pakitin– *VTA* let s.o. go, give permission to s.o.

PERMIT

kakwê *IPV* try to; circumstances permitting, by divine grace

pakitinikowisi– *VAI* be permitted by the powers

PERSEVERE

âhkamêyimo– *VAI* persist in one's will, persevere

âhkamêyimotot– *VTI* persists in s.t., persevere in s.t.

PERSIST

âhkamêyimo– *VAI* persist in one's will, persevere

âhkamêyimotot– *VTI* persists in s.t., persevere in s.t.

PERSON

–îci-kîhkâw– *NDA* aged spouse, fellow old person, fellow oldster, companion of one's old age [*e.g.*, wîci-kîhkâwa]

–ôsisim– *NDA* grandchild; [*fig.*] young person [*e.g.*, kôsisiminaw; *vocative:* nôsisê]

ayisiyiniw– *NA* person, human being
ayisiyinîwi– *VAI* be a person, be a human being
kêhtê-ay– *NA* old person, the old; elder
kêhtê-ayiwi– *VAI* be an old person; be an elder
osk-ây– *NA* young person, the young
oskayisiyiniw– *NA* young person [*sic:* -a-]

PERSONALLY
tipiyaw *IPC* personally, really

PHRASE
pîkiskwêwin– *NI* word, expression, phrase; speech, language

PHYSICIAN
maskihkîwiyiniw– *NA* doctor, physician

PICTURE
masinahikâso– *VAI* be pictured, be depicted
masinahikâtê– *VII* be pictured, be depicted; have marks, have writing; be written

PILE
wîscihkêsi– *VAI* pile hay into small heaps [*diminutive*]

PIPE
itâskonamaw– *VTA* thus point the pipe for s.o., thus point the pipe at s.o.
itâskonamawât– *VTI* thus point the pipe at s.t.
itâskonikê– *VAI* thus point the pipe or pipestem; thus hold a pipe ceremony
itâskonikêwin– *NI* thus pointing the pipe or pipestem; such a pipe ceremony
mâtâskonikê– *VAI* begin to point the pipe
ospwâkan– *NA* pipe
pîhtwâ– *VAI* smoke, use the pipe; smoke (him) (e.g., pipe)
saskahamaw– *VTA* light (it/him) for s.o.; light the pipe for s.o.

PIPE-LODGE
pîhtwâwikamikw– *NI* pipe-lodge ceremony

PIPESTEM
itâskonikê– *VAI* thus point the pipe or pipestem; thus hold a pipe ceremony
itâskonikêwin– *NI* thus pointing the pipe or pipestem; such a pipe ceremony
oskiciy– *NI* pipestem
oskicîwâhtikw– *NI* wood of pipestem

PITIABLE

kicimâkisi– *VAI* be pitiable, be miserable [*diminutive*]

kitimâkan– *VII* be pitiable, be miserable

kitimâkinâkosi– *VAI* look pitiable, look miserable, look poor

kitimâkisi– *VAI* be pitiable, be miserable, be poor

PITY

kitimâkêyihto– *VAI* feel pity towards one another, love one another, think of one another with compassion

kitimâkêyihtowin– *NI* feeling pity towards one another, loving one another, thinking of one another with compassion

kitimâkêyim– *VTA* take pity upon s.o., think of s.o. with compassion

kitimâkihtaw– *VTA* listen to s.o. with pity, listen to s.o. with compassion

kitimâkinaw– *VTA* look with pity upon s.o., look with compassion upon s.o.; regard s.o. with respect

PLACE

ah– *VTA* place s.o.

akot– *VTA* hang s.o. up; place s.o. on a burial scaffold

astâ– *VAI* place (it)

astê– *VII* be placed

âkaw-âyihk *IPC* in a hidden place, behind an obstacle to vision

cimatâ– *VAI* place (it) upright, plant (it) upright

êkotowihk *IPC* in that place

itastê– *VII* be placed thus; be written thus

kanâtanohk *IPC* in a clean place

kikastê– *VII* be placed along with something

nahapi– *VAI* sit down in one's place, be properly seated

nahipayi– *VII* be convenient, fall into place

nîkânîh– *VTA* place s.o. (e.g., tobacco) at the lead

ohtastê– *VII* be placed thereby or there

ômatowihk *IPC* in this place

pikw îta *IPC* no matter where, in any place

pikw îtê *IPC* no matter whither, to any place

pimastê– *VII* be placed in linear fashion, run along

tahtwayak *IPC* in so many places, in so many ways

tânitahtwayak *IPC* in how many places; in so many places

wâh-wâhyaw *IPC* in far places [*reduplicated*]

PLAIN

iyinito *IPN* plain, ordinary

PLANT

cimatâ– *VAI* place (it) upright, plant (it) upright

maskihkiy– *NI* herb, plant; medicine

sâkikihtâ– *VAI* make (it) (e.g., earth) bring forth plants

PLAY

mêtawâkâniwi– *VII* be general playing around

mêtawâkê– *VAI* play around with things, fool around with things

PLEAD

kâkîsimo– *VAI* pray, plead, chant prayers

PLEASE

atamih– *VTA* make s.o. grateful, make s.o. indebted, please s.o.

kiyâm *IPC* let it be, let there be no further delay; please

miyomahciho– *VAI* feel well, feel healthy; feel pleased

miywêyiht– *VTI* be glad, be pleased; like s.t.

PLENTIFUL

mihcêti– *VAI* be numerous, be plentiful

mihcêtin– *VII* be numerous, be plentiful

pîsâkwan– *VII* contain plenty, offer lots of room; be plentiful, be rich [*sic:* -â-]

PLENTY

pîsâkwan– *VII* contain plenty, offer lots of room; be plentiful, be rich [*sic:* -â-]

têpâpam– *VTA* see plenty of s.o., see s.o. fully

PLUS

ayiwâk *IPC* more; [*in numeral phrases:*] plus

POINT

isiniskêyi– *VAI* move one's arm thus or there, point in that direction with one's arm

itâskonamaw– *VTA* thus point the pipe for s.o., thus point the pipe at s.o.

itâskonamawât– *VTI* thus point the pipe at s.t.

itâskonikê– *VAI* thus point the pipe or pipestem; thus hold a pipe ceremony

mâtâskonikê– *VAI* begin to point the pipe

wâsakâyâskon– *VTA* point s.o. (e.g., pipe) right around (full circle)

POINTING

itâskonikêwin– *NI* thus pointing the pipe or pipestem; such a pipe ceremony

POISON

pihcipôh– *VTA* poison s.o.

POLICEMAN

simâkanis– *NA* policeman

POOR

is-âyâ– *VAI* be thus in health; be unwell, be in poor health

kitimâkinâkosi– *VAI* look pitiable, look miserable, look poor

kitimâkisi– *VAI* be pitiable, be miserable, be poor

mâyimahciho– *VAI* feel poorly, feel in ill health

POPULATE

askîwisk– *VTI* subject the earth to oneself, populate the earth, make the earth live

nihtâwikîst– *VTI* populate s.t. (e.g., the earth) [*sic:* -î-]

POSITION

nâcikâpawist– *VTI* seek to shift one's position to s.t. [*sic:* -i-]

nîkânohk *IPC* in the lead position

nîkânohtêmakan– *VII* be in the lead, proceed in the lead position

POSSIBLY

ahpô *IPC* even, possibly; or

POUR

pîhtâpâwah– *VTA* pour liquid into s.o., give s.o. an enema

sîkihtatamaw– *VTA* pour (it) for s.o.

tahkâpâwat– *VTA* pour water to cool s.o. (e.g., rock), cool s.o. (e.g., rock) with water (in sweat-lodge)

POWERFUL

sôhkan– *VII* be powerful

POWERS

kiskêyihtamôhikowisi– *VAI* be granted knowledge by the powers

kitâpamikowisi– *VAI* be looked upon by the powers

manitowakim– *VTA* endow s.o. (e.g., tobacco) with supernatural powers

manitowih– *VTA* grant s.o. supernatural powers

miyikowisi– *VAI* be given (it/him) by the powers

pakitinikowisi– *VAI* be permitted by the powers

PRACTICABLE

osiskêpayi– *VII* fall into place, work itself out, be practicable

PRACTISED

nakacihtâ– *VAI* be familiar with doing (it), be practised at (it)

PRAIRIE-CHICKEN

pihêwisimo– *VAI* dance the prairie-chicken dance

PRAY

ayamihâ– *VAI* pray, hold a church service; follow a religion [*also* ayimihâ–]

kâkîsimo– *VAI* pray, plead, chant prayers

nitotamâ– *VAI* ask for (it), pray for (it), make a request for (it)

PRAYER

kâkîsimotot– *VTI* chant prayers for s.t.; chant prayers over s.t.

kâkîsimototaw– *VTA* chant prayers for s.o.; chant prayers over s.o.

kâkîsimowin– *NI* chanting prayers

kâkîsimwâkê– *VAI* chant prayers with things

kîsowât– *VTI* complete one's words, complete one's prayers

kîsowâtamaw– *VTA* complete words for s.o., complete prayers for s.o.

mawihkâtamaw– *VTA* cry out in prayer to s.o., wail to s.o.

mawimo– *VAI* cry out; cry out in prayer, wail

mawimoscikê– *VAI* cry out in prayer, wail; worship with (it)

mawimoscikêwin– *NI* crying out in prayer, wailing; form of worship, ceremony

mawimost– *VTI* cry out in prayer to s.t., wail to s.t.

naskom– *VTA* respond to s.o. with (it/him), answer s.o.'s prayer with (it/him)

patowât– *VTI* misspeak s.t., commit an error in one's prayers

pîkiskwât– *VTI* speak about s.t., speak about s.t. with concern; speak a prayer over s.t.

tâpowê– *VAI* speak correctly; recite one's prayer correctly

PRAYING

ayamihâwin– *NI* praying, church service; religion [*also* ayimihâwin–]

PREACH

kakêskihkêmo– *VAI* counsel people, preach at people

PRECIOUS

sôniyâwi– *VII* be precious metal; be money

PRECISELY

mêmohci *IPC* in particular, above all; exactly, precisely

PREFERENCE

iyâyaw *IPC* eagerly, intently; by preference, rather

PREPARE

osîh– *VTA* prepare s.o. (e.g., rattle), make s.o.

osîhtâ– *VAI* prepare (it), make (it)

PRESENT

api– *VAI* sit, be present

itahtwapi– *VAI* sit as so many, be present as so many

itapi– *VAI* sit thus or there, be present thus or there

wîtapim– *VTA* sit with s.o., be present with s.o.; work together with s.o.

PRESUMABLY

êtokwê *IPC* presumably, I guess

PRETENDINGLY

yâhk îtâp *IPC* as if, pretendingly

PREVIOUSLY

kayâs *IPC* long ago, in earlier days; previously

PRICE

wiyakihtamaw– *VTA* set a price on (it/him) for s.o., charge s.o. for (it/him)

wiyakim– *VTA* set a price on s.o. (e.g., bread); arrange (it) for s.o.; decide on s.o.; give orders to s.o.

PRIEST

ayamihêwiyiniw– *NA* priest; minister

PROCEED

ati *IPV* progressively, proceed to

isîhcikât– *VTI* do things thus for s.t., proceed thus for s.t.

isîhcikê– *VAI* do things thus, proceed thus, perform such a ritual

nîkânohtêmakan– *VII* be in the lead, proceed in the lead position

PROGRESSION

pimi *IPV* along, in linear progression; while moving in linear progression

PROGRESSIVELY

ati *IPV* progressively, proceed to

PROMISE

asotamaw– *VTA* promise (it) to s.o.

asotamâkê– *VAI* make a promise

asotamâkêwin– *NI* promise [*sc. 'agent-centred' noun; e.g.*, otasotamâkêwin 'what he has promised']

asotamâkowin– *NI* promise, promise made [*sc. 'patient-centred' noun; e.g.*, kitasotamâkowininaw 'what has been promised to us']

PROPERLY

katawâhk *IPC* properly, in seemly manner

kwayask *IPC* properly, by rights

nahapi– *VAI* sit down in one's place, be properly seated

PROPPED UP

aspatisin– *VII* lie leaning upon something, lie back upon something, lie propped up

PROTECTION

kanôsimototaw– *VTA* have s.o. (e.g., rattle) as protection

PROTECTIVE

kanôsimon– *NI* protective talisman (usually worn around the neck, wrapped in leather)

PULL

ocipit– *VTA* pull s.o. along, pull s.o. in

pimâwah– *VTA* lead s.o. along as a group, pull s.o. along

takwâwahito– *VAI* arrive pulling one another along, arrive as a crowd

PUPIL

kisêyinîw-ôhpikihâkan– *NA* old man's pupil, ward of the old men

PURPOSE

konita *IPC* in vain, without reason, without purpose; without further ado

PURSUE

nawaswât– *VTI* pursue s.t., chase after s.t.

PUSH

sâkâwanêhtâ– *VAI* push (it) to emerge from the ground, make (it) come forth

PUT

astamaw– *VTA* put (it/him) for s.o.

kêtastotinê– *VAI* put one's hat on [*]

QUEEN

kihc-ôkimâskwêw– *NA* Queen

QUICKLY

mâmâsîs *IPC* sparingly, delicately; quickly, roughly, without care

QUIETLY

pêyâhtik *IPC* quietly, softly, slowly [*sic:* -i-]

wêtinahk *IPC* quietly

QUIT

pôyo– *VAI* cease, quit

RAIN

kimiwan– *VII* rain, be rain

RAINY

kaskawanipêstâ– *VII* be drizzle, be rainy

RAISE

ohpahpahtên– *VTI* raise up the smoke of s.t. [*?sic*]

ohpahtên– *VTI* raise up the smoke of s.t.

ohpâskon– *VTA* raise s.o. (e.g., pipe)

ohpâskon– *VTI* raise s.t. (e.g., pipestem)

ohpikih– *VTA* make s.o. grow up, raise s.o.

ohpikihito– *VAI* make one another grow up, raise one another

ohpikinâwaso– *VAI* make one's children grow up, raise one's children

ohpin– *VTI* raise s.t., create s.t.

pasikôn– *VTA* raise s.o. (e.g., to a position of leadership)

pasikôn– *VTI* raise s.t. (e.g., lodge)

RANDOM

pakwanawahtâ– *VAI* go on with (it) at random, know nothing about (it), be clueless about (it)

RATHER

iyâyaw *IPC* eagerly, intently; by preference, rather

nawac *IPC* more, better, rather

RATIONS

asahtowin– *NI* feeding one another, rations

asam– *VTA* feed s.o.; hand out rations to s.o.

otasahkêw– *NA* one who distributes rations; Indian agent

RATROOT

wîhkês– *NI* ratroot

RATTLE

sîsîkwan– *NA* rattle

REACH

kisipipayi– *VII* come to an end, reach the end

nayawaciki– *VAI* grow up to reach various ages, be variously grown up [*usually plural*]

otiht– *VTA* reach s.o.

otihtamâso– *VAI* reach (it/him) for oneself

REALLY

mitoni *IPC* intensively, really [*also* IPV]

tipiyaw *IPC* personally, really

REAR

nâway *IPC* behind, at the rear

REASON

konita *IPC* in vain, without reason, without purpose; without further ado

RECITE

tâpowê– *VAI* speak correctly; recite one's prayer correctly

RECOGNISE

nisitawêyim– *VTA* recognise s.o.

nisitawin– *VTI* recognise s.t.

RECTUM

ociski– *VAI* have a rectum, have (it) as one's rectum

REFUGE

itâmo– *VAI* flee thus or there, seek such refuge

itâmôh– *VTA* make s.o. flee thus or there, direct s.o. to seek such refuge

nâtâmost– *VTI* flee to s.t., turn to s.t. for help, seek refuge in s.t.

nâtâmotot– *VTI* flee to s.t., turn to s.t. for help, seek refuge in s.t.

nâtâmototaw– *VTA* flee to s.o., turn to s.o. for help, seek refuge with s.o.

REGARD

kitimâkinaw– *VTA* look with pity upon s.o., look with compassion upon s.o.; regard s.o. with respect

REGRET

mihtât– *VTI* regret s.t.

REGRETTABLE

wiyakâc *IPC* it is regrettable [*predicative*]

REJECT

asên– *VTA* reject s.o., turn s.o. back

asên– *VTI* reject s.t., turn s.t. back

RELATIVE

–wâhkômâkan– *NDA* relative [*e.g.*, kiwâhkômâkaninaw]

RELEASE

pakicî– *VAI* release (him), let go of (him)

pakitin– *VTI* let s.t. go, release s.t., give s.t. up

pakitinamaw– *VTA* release (it/him) for s.o., arrange (it) for s.o.

pihkoh– *VTA* free s.o., release s.o.

RELIEF

wanihtâ– *VAI* lose (it); get relief from (it)

RELIGION

ayamihâ– *VAI* pray, hold a church service; follow a religion [*also* ayimihâ–]

ayamihâwin– *NI* praying, church service; religion [*also* ayimihâwin–]

môniyâw-âyamihâwin– *NI* White religion

RELY

aspitonâmo– *VAI* flee to rely on spoken words, rely on (it) as a formal confirmation of the spoken word

mamisî– *VAI* rely on (it/him)

mamisîtot– *VTI* rely on s.t.

mamisîwât– *VTA* rely on s.o. for (it/him)

REMEMBER

kiskisi– *VAI* remember, remember (it)

kiskisopayi– *VAI* think of something, suddenly remember

REMIND

kiskisôhto– *VAI* remind one another

kiskisôm– *VTA* remind s.o. [*sic:* -ô-]

REPAIR

nânapâcihtâ– *VAI* fix (it) up, repair (it)

REPAY

tipahamaw– *VTA* pay s.o. for (it/him), repay a debt to s.o.

REPORT

âcimowin– *NI* story, account, report

kisêyiniîw-âcimowin– *NI* old man's story, report of the old men

matwêwê– *VII* be heard as a gunshot, be the report of a gun

wîht– *VTI* tell about s.t., report s.t.; decree s.t.

REPORTEDLY

êsa *IPC* reportedly

REPRESENT

pimohtêstamaw– *VTA* go along for s.o., represent s.o.

REQUEST

kakwêcim– *VTA* ask s.o.; make a request of s.o.; ask s.o. about (it/him)

nitotamâ– *VAI* ask for (it), pray for (it), make a request for (it)

nitotamâkêstamaw– *VTA* make a request for s.o., on s.o.'s behalf

nitotamâwin– *NI* request [*sc. 'agent-centred' noun; e.g.*, kinitotamâwin 'request made by you']

nitôsk– *VTI* seek s.t.; make a request for s.t. (e.g., medicine)

nitôskamaw– *VTA* seek (it/him) of s.o., make a request for (it/him) of s.o.

REQUISITE

ohtitaw *IPC* expressly, specifically; it is requisite, it is meet indeed

RESERVE

askîhkân– *NI* reserve

RESPECT

kihcêyihtâkwan– *VII* be respected; be held sacred

kitimâkinaw– *VTA* look with pity upon s.o., look with compassion upon s.o.; regard s.o. with respect

manâcihtâ– *VAI* treat (it) with respect

RESPOND

naskom– *VTA* respond to s.o. with (it/him), answer s.o.'s prayer with (it/him)

naskot– *VTI* respond to s.t.; swear upon s.t. in response

naskwêwasim– *VTA* speak to s.o. in response, respond to s.o. by speech

naskwêwasimo– *VAI* speak in response, respond by speech

RESPONSE

kwêtatêyitiskwêyi– *VAI* be at a loss as to where to turn one's head; be at a loss for a response [*cf.* kôtatê]

naskot– *VTI* respond to s.t.; swear upon s.t. in response

naskwêwasim– *VTA* speak to s.o. in response, respond to s.o. by speech

naskwêwasimo– *VAI* speak in response, respond by speech

RETURN

kîwêmakan– *VII* return home, come back

wâyonî– *VAI* turn back, return

REWARD

kîspinat– *VTI* earn enough to buy s.t.; earn s.t. as reward, earn one's reward

kîspinatamaw– *VTA* earn one's reward in s.o., earn s.o. as one's reward

RIB

–spikêkan– *NDI* rib [*e.g.*, ospikêkana]

RICH

pîsâkwan– *VII* contain plenty, offer lots of room; be plentiful, be rich [*sic:* -â-]

RING

sêwêpin– *VTA* make s.o. (e.g., rattle) ring out

sêwêpitamaw– *VTA* make (it) ring out for s.o.; call s.o. by telephone

RISE

ispâhkêkocin– *VII* rise high up, be high in the air

kwêskahcâhk *IPC* on the opposite side of a rise in the land

osêhcâw– *NI* rise in the land, gentle hill

sâkêwêtot– *VTI* come out upon s.t., rise (e.g., sun) upon s.t.

RITUAL

isîhcikê– *VAI* do things thus, proceed thus, perform such a ritual

nikamo– *VAI* sing, sing a ritual song

nikamon– *NI* song, ritual song

RIVER

sîpiy– *NI* river

ROAD

mêskanaw– *NI* path, trail, road

sipwêmon– *VII* leave as path, trail, road; begin as path, trail, road

ROCK-SPRINKLING

sîkahasinânâpoy– *NI* rock-sprinkling water (in sweat-lodge)

ROCKY MOUNTAINS

asinîwaciy– *NI* the Rocky Mountains [*usually sg.*]

ROOF

apahkwân– *NI* roof [*sic:* NI]

ROOM

pîsâkwan– *VII* contain plenty, offer lots of room; be plentiful, be rich [*sic:* -â-]

tawâ– *VII* be open, have room

ROPE

pîminâhkwânis– *NI* string, rope [*diminutive*]

sakâpêkipah– *VTA* lead s.o. (e.g., horse) by a rope

ROTTEN

pîkwatowan– *VII* be rotten (e.g., tooth)

ROUGHLY

mâmâsîs *IPC* sparingly, delicately; quickly, roughly, without care

RUN

itamon– *VII* run thus or there as a path

miyopayin– *VII* work well, run well [*]

nâcipahiwê– *VAI* go to fetch things, run to fetch things

papâmipahtâ– *VAI* run about

pimastê– *VII* be placed in linear fashion, run along

pimipayihtâ– *VAI* run (it), keep (it) up, exercise (it)

RUSH

pimakocin– *VII* make a rush in linear fashion, charge headlong

SACRED

âtayôhkêwin– *NI* sacred story

kihcêyihtâkwan– *VII* be respected; be held sacred

kihcêyim– *VTA* think highly of s.o., hold s.o. sacred

ma-môhcw-âtayôhkêwin– *NI* stupid sacred story, crazy sacred story [*; *reduplicated*]

SACRILEGE

pâstâhôtot– *VTI* commit a transgression in s.t., commit sacrilege in s.t.

SAME

pêyakwan *IPC* the same

wîtaskîwêm– *VTA* live together with s.o.; live in the same country with s.o., live in peace with s.o.

SATISFIED

nahêyiht– *VTI* be satisfied with s.t.; have peace of mind

nahêyihtamih– *VTA* cause s.o. to be satisfied with (it/him); grant s.o. peace of mind

SAY

it– *VTA* say thus to s.o.

it– *VTI* say thus of s.t., say thus about s.t.

itwê– *VAI* say thus, call (it) thus; have such a meaning

itwêmakan– *VII* say thus, have such a meaning

itwêmakisi– *VAI* say thus, have such a meaning [*]

itwêstamaw– *VTA* say thus for s.o.; speak for s.o.; interpret for s.o.

SCAFFOLD

akot– *VTA* hang s.o. up; place s.o. on a burial scaffold

SCHOOL

kiskinohamâtowikamikw– *NI* school, school-house

SCHOOL-HOUSE

kiskinohamâtowikamikw– *NI* school, school-house

SCHOOLING

kiskinohamâsowin– *NI* schooling, education [*sc. 'patient-centred' noun; e.g.,* okiskinohamâsowin 'his schooling']

SCOUT

onitawahtâw– *NA* scout, explorer, spy

SCRIBE

omasinahikêsîs– *NA* scribe, clerk

SEATED

nahapi– *VAI* sit down in one's place, be properly seated

SECOND

tahto-nîso-kîsikâw *IPC* every second day, every other day

tahto-nîsw-âyamihêwi-kîsikâw *IPC* every second week, fortnightly

SEE

mahti *IPC* let's see [*hortatory, often jussive*]

mâcikôtitan *IPC* wait and see! lo! [*exlamatory; sic:* -â-, -ô-, -a-]

nitawâpam– *VTA* go and see s.o.

otisâpaht– *VTI* have lived long enough to see s.t.

têpâpam– *VTA* see plenty of s.o., see s.o. fully

wâpaht– *VTI* see s.t., witness s.t.

wâpam– *VTA* see s.o., witness s.o.

SEED

kistikân– *NA* grain, seed; sheaf of grain

SEEK

itâmo– *VAI* flee thus or there, seek such refuge

itâmôh– *VTA* make s.o. flee thus or there, direct s.o. to seek such refuge

nâcikâpawist– *VTI* seek to shift one's position to s.t. [*sic:* -i-]

nâcinêhamaw– *VTA* obtain (it/him) from s.o. by payment, seek to buy medicine from s.o.

nâcinêhikê– *VAI* obtain things by payment, seek to buy medicine

nâtâmost– *VTI* flee to s.t., turn to s.t. for help, seek refuge in s.t.

nâtâmotot– *VTI* flee to s.t., turn to s.t. for help, seek refuge in s.t.

nâtâmototaw– *VTA* flee to s.o., turn to s.o. for help, seek refuge with s.o.

nitôsk– *VTI* seek s.t.; make a request for s.t. (e.g., medicine)

nitôskamaw– *VTA* seek (it/him) of s.o., make a request for (it/him) of s.o.

pimâtisiwinê– *VAI* have life, seek life

SEEM

tâpiskôc *IPC* it seems, seemingly, apparently; as if

SEEMINGLY

tâpiskôc *IPC* it seems, seemingly, apparently; as if

SEEMLY

katawâhk *IPC* properly, in seemly manner

SELL

atâwâkê– *VAI* sell (it/him)

SEND

nâtitisahw– *VTA* send for s.o.

patitisahamaw– *VTA* drive (it/him) off the path for s.o., send (it/him) awry for s.o., spoil (it/him) for s.o.

SENSIBLE

âpahkawin– *VII* be level-headed, be sensible, be conscious

SERIOUS

mâyitôt– *VTI* do bad things, cause serious trouble

SERVANT

–oskinîkîm– *NDA* young man, follower; [*fig.*] servant [*e.g.*, otôskinîkîma]

SERVE

okimâhkâniwi– *VAI* be chief, serve as elected chief

SERVER

oskâpêwis– *NA* server, servitor (e.g., in ritual)

SERVICE

ayamihâ– *VAI* pray, hold a church service; follow a religion [*also* ayimihâ–]

ayamihâwin– *NI* praying, church service; religion [*also* ayimihâwin–]

SERVITOR

oskâpêwis– *NA* server, servitor (e.g., in ritual)

SET

wiyakihtamaw– *VTA* set a price on (it/him) for s.o., charge s.o. for (it/him)

wiyakim– *VTA* set a price on s.o. (e.g., bread); arrange (it) for s.o.; decide on s.o.; give orders to s.o.

yîkatên– *VTI* set s.t. aside

SETTLE

otinaskê– *VAI* take land, settle the land, homestead

SEVENTEEN

têpakohposâp *IPC* seventeen

SHAKING-LODGE

kosâpaht– *VTI* hold a shaking-lodge, hold the shaking-lodge ceremony

SHE

wiya *PR* he, she

wîsta *PR* he, too; she, too; he by contrast, she by contrast

SHEAF

kistikân– *NA* grain, seed; sheaf of grain

SHIFT

nâcikâpawist– *VTI* seek to shift one's position to s.t. [*sic:* -i-]

SHORTCOMINGS

êyiwêhk *IPC* just in case, nevertheless; despite shortcomings [*also* kêyiwêhk]

kêyiwêhk *IPC* just in case, nevertheless; despite shortcomings [*also* êyiwêhk]

SHOW OFF

mamacikastê– *VAI* show off

SIBLINGS

owîcisânihto– *VAI* have one another as siblings

SIDE

awas-âyihk *IPC* on the other side, on the far side

itakâm *IPC* on the hither side of a body of water, on the near side of a body of water

kwêsk-âyihk *IPC* on the opposite side

kwêskahcâhk *IPC* on the opposite side of a rise in the land

kwêskâskon– *VTA* turn s.o. (e.g., pipe) to the opposite side

kwêski *IPV* turned around, turned to the opposite side

ohpimê *IPC* off, away, to the side

yîkatêhtê– *VAI* walk off to the side

SIGHTED

wâpi– *VAI* be sighted, have vision; [*in negative clause:*] be blind

SILLY

môhcowi– *VAI* be stupid, be silly; be mad, be crazy

SILVER

sôniyâw– *NA* gold, silver; money

SIMPLY

nânitaw *IPC* simply; something, anything; something bad, anything bad; somewhere; approximately [*usually with pejorative presupposition*]

sôskwât *IPC* simply, without further ado

SIN

pâstâhowin– *NI* transgression, breach of the natural order; sin

SING

kîhkâtah– *VTI* make the sound of (it) sing out clearly

kîhkâtahamaw– *VTA* make the sound of (it) sing out clearly to s.o.

nikamo– *VAI* sing, sing a ritual song

yahkatâmo– *VAI* sing out vigorously

SINGLE

pêyak *IPC* one, a single; the only one

SINGLY

pâh-pêyak *IPC* singly, one at a time; each individually

SIOUX

pwât– *NA* Sioux [*e.g.*, pwâtak]

SISTER

–ôhkom– *NDA* grandmother, grandmother's sister, great-aunt; [*fig.*] old woman; Our Grandmother [*e.g.*, nôhkominân; kôhkominaw]

SIT

api– *VAI* sit, be present

apist– *VTI* sit by s.t., live in s.t. (e.g., lodge) [*sic:* -i-]

itahtwapi– *VAI* sit as so many, be present as so many

itapi– *VAI* sit thus or there, be present thus or there

kikapi– *VAI* sit along with something

mâmawôpi– *VAI* sit together, hold a meeting

nahapi– *VAI* sit down in one's place, be properly seated

wîtapim– *VTA* sit with s.o., be present with s.o.; work together with s.o.

SIX

nikotwâsik *IPC* six

nikotwâsik-tipahamâtowin– *NI* Treaty Six

SIXTEEN

nikotwâsosâp *IPC* sixteen

SKIN

kiyakasê– *VAI* have itchy skin, suffer from eczema

SKY

kîsikw– *NI* sky

SKY-SPIRIT

okîsikow– *NA* [*spirit's name:*] Sky-Spirit

SLED

ocâpânâskos– *NI* cart; small wagon, small sled [*diminutive*]

SLIP

pîhcawêsâkânis– *NI* undershirt, slip [*diminutive*]

SLOWLY

pêyâhtik *IPC* quietly, softly, slowly [*sic:* -i-]

SMALL

ocâpânâskos– *NI* cart; small wagon, small sled [*diminutive*]

ôcênâs– *NI* small town [*diminutive*]

wiyâkanis– *NI* small dish, small bowl [*diminutive*]

wîscihkêsi– *VAI* pile hay into small heaps [*diminutive*]

SMELL

paso– *VAI* smell (it)

SMOKE

ohpahpahtên– *VTI* raise up the smoke of s.t. [*?sic*]

ohpahtên– *VTI* raise up the smoke of s.t.

pîhtwâ– *VAI* smoke, use the pipe; smoke (him) (e.g., pipe)

wîci-pîhtwâm– *VTA* smoke together with s.o.

SMUDGE

miyâhkas– *VTI* cense s.t., smudge s.t. with sweetgrass

miyâhkasamaw– *VTA* cense (it/him) for s.o., smudge (it/him) with sweetgrass for s.o.

miyâhkasikê– *VAI* cense things, smudge things with sweetgrass

miyâhkasw– *VTA* cense s.o. (e.g., pipe), smudge s.o. (e.g., pipe) with sweetgrass

SO

mistahi *IPC* greatly, very much so [*also* IPV]

wâwîs cî *IPC* especially, all the more so

SOFTLY

pêyâhtik *IPC* quietly, softly, slowly [*sic:* -i-]

SOIL

îpâcihtâ– *VAI* make (it) dirty, soil (it) [*sic:* î-; *cf.* wiyî-]

SOLELY

pêyakwêyimiso– *VAI* think solely of oneself

SOME

âtiht *IPC* some

SOMEONE

awiyak *PR* someone; [*in negative clause:*] anyone [*indefinite; e.g.*, awiyak]

SOMETHING

kîkway *PR* something, thing; [*in negative clause:*] anything, any [*indefinite; e.g.*, kîkway]

maci-kîkway– *NI* something bad, bad things

nânitaw *IPC* simply; something, anything; something bad, anything bad; somewhere; approximately [*usually with pejorative presupposition*]

SOMEWHERE

nânitaw *IPC* simply; something, anything; something bad, anything bad; somewhere; approximately [*usually with pejorative presupposition*]

SON

–kosis– *NDA* son; parallel nephew; [*fig.*] younger man [*e.g.*, nikosis; *vocative:* nikosis]

SON-IN-LAW

–tihkwatim– *NDA* cross-nephew; son-in-law [*e.g.*, nitihkwatim]

SONG

nikamo– *VAI* sing, sing a ritual song

nikamon– *NI* song, ritual song

SOON

mayaw *IPC* as soon as [*temporal conjunction*]

SOUL

–têh– *NDI* heart; [*fig.*] heart, soul [*e.g.*, otêhihk]

ahcâhkw– *NA* soul

SOUND

kîhkâtah– *VTI* make the sound of (it) sing out clearly

kîhkâtahamaw– *VTA* make the sound of (it) sing out clearly to s.o.

matwêhw– *VTA* sound a beat upon s.o. (e.g., drum), drum on s.o.

SOURCE

mônahipân– *NI* source, well

SOUTH

âpihtâ-kîsikâhk *IPC* in the south, to the south

SPARINGLY

mâmâsîs *IPC* sparingly, delicately; quickly, roughly, without care

SPEAK

âkayâsîmo– *VAI* speak English

âyimômiso– *VAI* discuss oneself; speak unguardedly about oneself, gossip about oneself

âyimôt– *VTI* speak of s.t., discuss s.t.; gossip about s.t.

itwêstamaw– *VTA* say thus for s.o.; speak for s.o.; interpret for s.o.

kisîkitot– *VTA* speak to s.o. in anger [*sic:* -î-]

kisîwê– *VII* be loud, speak loudly (e.g., audio-recorder) [*]

kisîwêhkahtaw– *VTA* speak loudly to s.o.

kitot– *VTA* address s.o., speak to s.o., lecture s.o.

naskwêwasim– *VTA* speak to s.o. in response, respond to s.o. by speech

naskwêwasimo– *VAI* speak in response, respond by speech

nêhiyawê– *VAI* speak Cree

pîkiskwât– *VTA* speak to s.o.

pîkiskwât– *VTI* speak about s.t., speak about s.t. with concern; speak a prayer over s.t.

pîkiskwê– *VAI* use words, speak

pîkiskwêmohtâ– *VAI* cause (it) to speak; make an audio-recording [*]

pîkiskwêmôh– *VTA* cause s.o. to speak with concern

pîkiskwêstamaw– *VTA* speak for s.o., speak on s.o.'s behalf

tâpowê– *VAI* speak correctly; recite one's prayer correctly

tâpwê– *VAI* speak true, speak the truth

wîci-pîkiskwêm– *VTA* speak together with s.o.

SPECIFICALLY

ohtitaw *IPC* expressly, specifically; it is requisite, it is meet indeed

SPEECH

kisîhto– *VAI* anger one another by speech

kisîm– *VTA* anger s.o. by speech

naskwêwasim– *VTA* speak to s.o. in response, respond to s.o. by speech

naskwêwasimo– *VAI* speak in response, respond by speech

pîkiskwêwin– *NI* word, expression, phrase; speech, language

sêkim– *VTA* frighten s.o. by speech

sîhkim– *VTA* urge s.o. by speech

SPIRIT

âtayôhkan– *NA* spirit being, dream guardian

âtayôhkanakiso– *VAI* be held to be a spirit being, a dream guardian

SPIRITUAL

ahcâhko-pimâtisiwin– *NI* spiritual life

SPIT

sihko– *VAI* spit, spit out

sîkatêhtamaw– *VTA* spit (it/him) out for s.o.

SPOIL

patitisahamaw– *VTA* drive (it/him) off the path for s.o., send (it/him) awry for s.o., spoil (it/him) for s.o.

SPOKEN

aspitonâmo– *VAI* flee to rely on spoken words, rely on (it) as a formal confirmation of the spoken word

SPOUSE

–îci-kîhkâw– *NDA* aged spouse, fellow old person, fellow oldster, companion of one's old age [*e.g.*, wîci-kîhkâwa]

–wîkimâkan– *NDA* spouse, housemate [*e.g.*, niwîkimâkan]

SPRING

miyoskamin– *VII* be early spring

SPRUCE

minahikosis– *NI* spruce [*diminutive*]

minahikoskâ– *VII* be a spruce thicket, be an abundance of spruce

SPY

onitawahtâw– *NA* scout, explorer, spy

STAB

tahkam– *VTA* stab s.o. [*reduplicated:* tâh-tahkam–]

STABLE

awâska-mâmitonêyihcikan– *NI* stable mind, steady mind, balanced mind [*?sic*]

STAND

cimasi– *VAI* stand upright, stand erect

cimatê– *VII* stand upright, stand erect

mêskocikâpawi– *VAI* stand up instead [*sic:* -ê-]

sâkaskinêkâpawi– *VAI* stand crowded in, stand to fill a place

STAY

kapêsimostaw– *VTA* stay overnight with s.o., stay overnight at s.o.'s place

STEADY

awâska-mâmitonêyihcikan– *NI* stable mind, steady mind, balanced mind [*?sic*]

STILL

âhci piko *IPC* still, nevertheless, despite everything [*adversative*]

êyâpic *IPC* still

STOMACH

wîhkwâs– *NI* craw, first stomach of fowl

STOP

pônipayi– *VII* cease, stop, come to an end

STORMY

âstê-kîsikâ– *VII* cease being stormy weather, be better weather

mâyi-kîsikâ– *VII* be stormy weather, be foul weather

STORY

âcimo– *VAI* tell, tell a story, give an account

âcimowin– *NI* story, account, report

âtayôhkêwin– *NI* sacred story

itâcimostaw– *VTA* tell s.o. thus about (it), tell s.o. such a story

itâcimômakan– *VII* tell thus about (it), tell such a story

kisêyiniw-âcimowin– *NI* old man's story, report of the old men

ma-môhcw-âtayôhkêwin– *NI* stupid sacred story, crazy sacred story [*; *reduplicated*]

STRAIGHTEN

mînwâskonamaw– *VTA* straighten (it/him) for s.o.

STRANGELY

pîtos *IPC* strangely, differently

STRENUOUSLY

kotêyiht– *VTI* try s.t. in one's mind, think strenuously about s.t., test s.t.; challenge s.t.

STRETCH

âsowahpitê– *VII* be stretched across, be strung across

sîpi *IPV* stretching far back

STRING

pîminâhkwânis– *NI* string, rope [*diminutive*]

STRUNG

âsowahpitê– *VII* be stretched across, be strung across

STUCK

micimôho– *VAI* be held fast, be stuck [*sic:* -h-]

STUDENT

kiskinohamawâkan– *NA* student

STUPID

ma-môhcw-âtayôhkêwin– *NI* stupid sacred story, crazy sacred story [*; *reduplicated*]

môhcowi– *VAI* be stupid, be silly; be mad, be crazy
môhcwêyim– *VTA* consider s.o. stupid

SUBJECT
askîwisk– *VTI* subject the earth to oneself, populate the earth, make the earth live

SUCCESSIVELY
âniskê *IPV* successively, one joining the other, surviving

SUCH
isko *IPC* to such an extent, thus far [*also* IPV]
iskoyikohk *IPC* to such an extent, to such a degree
ispisi *IPV* to such an extent, so far
ispî *IPC* at such a time, then
ispîhtisî– *VAI* be of such an age
iyikohk *IPC* so much, to such a degree, to such an extent
tasi *IPV* for such a time, for the duration
tâniyikohk *IPC* to what extent; to such an extent

SUDDENLY
kêtahtawê *IPC* suddenly; at one time
kiskisopayi– *VAI* think of something, suddenly remember
ohtaskat– *VTI* leave s.t. suddenly thereby or there

SUFFER
kakwâtakih– *VTA* make s.o. suffer, be mean to s.o., be abusive to s.o.
kakwâtakihiso– *VAI* make oneself suffer; torture oneself, deny oneself food and drink
kakwâtakiho– *VAI* make oneself suffer; torture oneself, deny oneself food and drink
kakwâtakihowin– *NI* making oneself suffer; denying oneself food and drink
kakwâtakihtâ– *VAI* suffer (it), suffer
kiyakasê– *VAI* have itchy skin, suffer from eczema
mâyipayi– *VAI* suffer ill; be bereaved
oskaninê– *VAI* suffer from arthritis

SUFFICIENTLY
têpi *IPV* fully, sufficiently

SUMMER
nîpin– *VII* be summer

SUN
kîsikâwi-pîsimw– *NA* sun [*sc. as opposed to moon*]

pîsimw– *NA* sun [*cf.* kîsikâwi-pîsimw–]

SUNDANCE

nipâkwêsimo– *VAI* attend a sundance, participate in a sundance

nipâkwêsimowikamikw– *NI* sundance-lodge, sundance ceremony

nipâkwêsimowin– *NI* sundance

SUNDANCE-LODGE

nipâkwêsimowikamikw– *NI* sundance-lodge, sundance ceremony

SUNDAY

ayamihêwi-kîsikâ– *VII* be Sunday

SUPERNATURAL

manitowakim– *VTA* endow s.o. (e.g., tobacco) with supernatural powers

manitowih– *VTA* grant s.o. supernatural powers

SURELY

kêhcinâ *IPC* surely, for certain

SURVIVE

âniskê *IPV* successively, one joining the other, surviving

kâsispô– *VAI* survive into another generation

kâsispôhtêmakan– *VII* go on from one generation to another, survive into another generation

SWEAR

naskot– *VTI* respond to s.t.; swear upon s.t. in response

SWEAT-LODGE

matotisân– *NI* sweat-lodge

matotisi– *VAI* hold a sweat-lodge

SWEETGRASS

miyâhkas– *VTI* cense s.t., smudge s.t. with sweetgrass

miyâhkasamaw– *VTA* cense (it/him) for s.o., smudge (it/him) with sweetgrass for s.o.

miyâhkasikê– *VAI* cense things, smudge things with sweetgrass

miyâhkasw– *VTA* cense s.o. (e.g., pipe), smudge s.o. (e.g., pipe) with sweetgrass

wîhkaskoyiniw– *NA* [*spirit's name:*] Sweetgrass-Old-Man

wîhkaskw– *NI* sweetgrass

SWOOP

tapahcipayiho– *VAI* swoop down, swoop low

SYLLABICS

nêhiyawastê– *VII* be written in Cree; be written in syllabics

TACKLE

mâyêyiht– *VTI* consider s.t. challenging; be willing to tackle a difficult task, venture out

TAKE

itohtah– *VTA* take s.o. thus or there

nakiskamohtatamaw– *VTA* take (it/him) to meet s.o., meet s.o. with (it/him); introduce (it/him) to s.o.

otin– *VTA* take s.o., choose s.o.

otin– *VTI* take s.t., choose s.t.

otinaskê– *VAI* take land, settle the land, homestead

otinikâtê– *VII* be taken, be chosen

pîhtikwah– *VTA* enter with s.o., take s.o. inside

pîhtikwatâ– *VAI* enter with (it), take (it) inside

TAKE CARE OF

kanawêyiht– *VTI* look after s.t., take care of s.t.

kanawêyihtamaw– *VTA* look after (it/him) for s.o., take care of (it/him) for s.o.

TAKE UP FOR

nâtamaw– *VTA* fetch (it/him) for s.o.; take up for s.o.

nâtamâwaso– *VAI* take up for one's children

TALISMAN

kanôsimon– *NI* protective talisman (usually worn around the neck, wrapped in leather)

TAMPER WITH

mikoskâcihtâ– *VAI* trifle with (it), tamper with (it)

TASK

mâyêyiht– *VTI* consider s.t. challenging; be willing to tackle a difficult task, venture out

TEA

maskihkiwâpoy– *NI* tea [*sic:* -i-]

TEACH

kiskinohamaw– *VTA* teach s.o., teach (it) to s.o.

kiskinohamâkê– *VAI* teach (it) to people

TEACHING

nêhiyawi-wîhtamawâkan– *NI* Cree etymology; Cree teaching

TEAM

pêyakwahpitêw *IPC* one team (of two horses)

TELEPHONE

sêwêpitamaw– *VTA* make (it) ring out for s.o.; call s.o. by telephone

TELEVISION

yôhtên– *VTI* open s.t.; turn s.t. (e.g., television set) on

yôhtênamaw– *VTA* open (it/him) for s.o.; turn (it/him) (e.g., television set) on for s.o.

TELL

âcim– *VTA* tell about s.o.

âcimo– *VAI* tell, tell a story, give an account

âcimostaw– *VTA* tell s.o. about (it/him), give s.o. an account

âtot– *VTI* tell about s.t., give an account of s.t.

itâcimostaw– *VTA* tell s.o. thus about (it), tell s.o. such a story

itâcimômakan– *VII* tell thus about (it), tell such a story

itâtot– *VTI* tell about s.t. thus, give such an account of s.t.

wîht– *VTI* tell about s.t., report s.t.; decree s.t.

wîhtamaw– *VTA* tell s.o. about (it/him)

TEN

mitâtaht *IPC* ten

TEND

pamih– *VTA* tend to s.o., look after s.o.

pamin– *VTA* tend to s.o., look after s.o.

pisiskêyim– *VTA* pay attention to s.o., tend s.o.; bother s.o., harrass s.o.

TENT

mânokê– *VAI* build a lodge, set up a tent

papakiwayânikamikw– *NI* tent

TENTPOLE

apasoy– *NI* tentpole

TEST

kotêyiht– *VTI* try s.t. in one's mind, think strenuously about s.t., test s.t.; challenge s.t.

kotêyim– *VTA* try s.o., test s.o., put s.o.'s mind to the test; challenge s.o.

THANK

nanâskom– *VTA* be grateful to s.o., give thanks to s.o.

nanâskomo– *VAI* be grateful, give thanks

nanâskot– *VTI* be grateful for s.t., give thanks for s.t.

THAT

ana *PR* that [*demonstrative; e.g.*, ana, aniki, anihi; anima, anihi]

anima *IPC* it is that; the fact that [*factive; also predicative*]

êkos îsi *IPC* thus, in that way; that is how it is

êkosi *IPC* thus, in that way; that is all

êkospî *IPC* then, at that time

êkotowahk *IPC* of that kind

êkotowihk *IPC* in that place

êwako *PR* that one [*resumptive demonstrative; e.g.*, êwako, êkonik, êkoni; êwako, êkoni, êwakoyiw]

itêhkê isi *IPC* in that direction, in the thither direction

nayêstaw *IPC* only; it is only that [*often predicative*]

nâha *PR* that one yonder [*demonstrative; e.g.*, nâha, nêhi; nêma]

nêmatowahk *IPC* of that kind yonder

ôma *IPC* it is this; the fact that [*factive; also predicative*]

ômis îsi *IPC* in this way; that is how it is

THEN

ani *IPC* [*enclitic:*] then [*emphatic; enclitic*]

êkos êsa *IPC* thus then

êkospî *IPC* then, at that time

êkwa *IPC* then, now; and

êkwêyâc *IPC* only then

hâw *IPC* now then [*hortatory, indicating readiness or impatience*]

ispî *IPC* at such a time, then

ohci *IPC* with, by means of; because of; from then [*enclitic; also* IPV]

THENCE

ohci *IPV* thence, from there; [*in negative clause:*] past [*cf.* ôh]

pê *IPV* thence, from there on down

THERE

anita *IPC* there

ayâ– *VAI* be there, live there; exist

ayâ– *VII* be there, exist

êkota *IPC* there

êkotê *IPC* over there

ihtâ– *VAI* be there, exist

isi *IPC* thus, there [*also* IPV]

isiniskêyi– *VAI* move one's arm thus or there, point in that direction with one's arm

ispayiho– *VAI* throw oneself thus or there, move thus or there

ita *IPC* there; there where

itamon– *VII* run thus or there as a path

itapi– *VAI* sit thus or there, be present thus or there
itâmo– *VAI* flee thus or there, seek such refuge
itâmôh– *VTA* make s.o. flee thus or there, direct s.o. to seek such refuge
itâpi– *VAI* look thus or there
itê *IPC* there, thither
itohtah– *VTA* take s.o. thus or there
itohtê– *VAI* go there or thus
kiyâm *IPC* let it be, let there be no further delay; please
ohci *IPV* thence, from there; [*in negative clause:*] past [*cf.* ôh]
ohtaskat– *VTI* leave s.t. suddenly thereby or there
ohtastê– *VII* be placed thereby or there
ohtohtê– *VAI* come from there
osâpaht– *VTI* look at s.t. from there
osâpam– *VTA* look at s.o. from there
ôh *IPV* from there; [*in negative clause:*] past [*cf.* ohci]
ôtê *IPC* there
pê *IPV* thence, from there on down

THEREBY
ohtaskat– *VTI* leave s.t. suddenly thereby or there
ohtastê– *VII* be placed thereby or there
ohtisi– *VAI* obtain payment thereby or therefrom

THEREFROM
ohtisi– *VAI* obtain payment thereby or therefrom

THEY
wiyawâw *PR* they
wîstawâw *PR* they, too; they, by contrast; they themselves

THICKET
minahikoskâ– *VII* be a spruce thicket, be an abundance of spruce

THICKLY
kispaki *IPV* thickly

THING
kîkway *PR* something, thing; [*in negative clause:*] anything, any [*indefinite; e.g.*, kîkway]
têpiyâhk *IPC* the only thing; the most (if any)

THINGS
maci-kîkway– *NI* something bad, bad things
tahto-kîkway *IPC* so many things, as many things

THINK

ispîhtêyimiso– *VAI* think thus highly of oneself

itêyiht– *VTI* think thus of s.t.

itêyim– *VTA* think thus of s.o.

kihcêyim– *VTA* think highly of s.o., hold s.o. sacred

kiskisopayi– *VAI* think of something, suddenly remember

kitimâkêyihtamâso– *VAI* think of (it/him) with compassion for one's own sake

kitimâkêyihto– *VAI* feel pity towards one another, love one another, think of one another with compassion

kitimâkêyim– *VTA* take pity upon s.o., think of s.o. with compassion

kotêyiht– *VTI* try s.t. in one's mind, think strenuously about s.t., test s.t.; challenge s.t.

mâmitonêyiht– *VTI* think about s.t., worry about s.t.

mâmitonêyihtamih– *VTA* cause s.o. to think about (it/him), cause s.o. to worry about (it/him)

mâmitonêyim– *VTA* think about s.o., have s.o. on one's mind

misawâc *IPC* in any case, whatever might be thought

pêyakwêyimiso– *VAI* think solely of oneself

THINKING

itêyihcikan– *NI* thinking thus; such thought

kitimâkêyihtowin– *NI* feeling pity towards one another, loving one another, thinking of one another with compassion

THIS

awa *PR* this [*demonstrative; e.g.*, awa, ôki, ôhi; ôma, ôhi]

êcika *IPC* what is this! [*exclamatory; preclitic, usually with demonstrative pronoun*]

ôma *IPC* it is this; the fact that [*factive; also predicative*]

ômatowahk *IPC* of this kind

ômatowihk *IPC* in this place

ômis îsi *IPC* in this way; that is how it is

ômisi *IPC* in this way

THITHER

itê *IPC* there, thither

itêhkê isi *IPC* in that direction, in the thither direction

THREE

nistin– *VII* be three

nisto *IPC* three

nistwapihkât– *VTI* braid s.t. in three

nistwâw *IPC* three times

THROUGH

pimohtât– *VTI* live s.t. (e.g., day), live through s.t.

THROW

ispayiho– *VAI* throw oneself thus or there, move thus or there

macostêh– *VTI* throw s.t. into the fire

mâkoh– *VTA* worry s.o., trouble s.o.; oppress s.o., throw s.o. into crisis

nâtwâwêpah– *VTI* break s.t. off and throw it down

wêpêyim– *VTA* be inclined to throw s.o. (e.g., money) away

wêpin– *VTA* throw s.o. away; abandon s.o. (e.g., child)

wêpin– *VTI* throw s.t. away

wêpinikâtê– *VII* be thrown away, be abandoned, be discarded

THUNDERBIRD

piyêsiw– *NA* [*spirit's name:*] Thunderbird

THUNDERCLAP

kito– *VAI* make noises (e.g., animal); produce a thunderclap

THUS

êkos êsa *IPC* thus then

êkos îsi *IPC* thus, in that way; that is how it is

êkosi *IPC* thus, in that way; that is all

isi *IPC* thus, there [*also* IPV]

isko *IPC* to such an extent, thus far [*also* IPV]

TIE

kaskipitê– *VII* be tied up, be wrapped up

sakahpit– *VTA* tie s.o. (e.g., horse) up

wêwêkahpit– *VTA* wrap and tie s.o. up

TIME

êkospî *IPC* then, at that time

ispî *IPC* at such a time, then

kayâsês *IPC* quite a long time ago

kêtahtawê *IPC* suddenly; at one time

kinwês *IPC* for a long time

nânapêc *IPC* late, at the last moment, barely in time (e.g., when it should have been done previously); [*in negative clause:*] too late

nistam *IPC* for the first time, initially, originally

pâh-pêyak *IPC* singly, one at a time; each individually

tasi *IPV* for such a time, for the duration
tânispî *IPC* when, at what time
tâpitawi *IPC* all the time

TIMES
mihcêtwâw *IPC* many times
nêwâw *IPC* four times
nistwâw *IPC* three times
tahtwâw *IPC* so many times
tânitahtwâw *IPC* how many times; so many times

TIPI
mîkiwâhp– *NI* lodge, tipi

TIRED
saskacihtaw– *VTA* be tired of hearing s.o., be fed up with hearing s.o.

TOBACCO
cistêmâw– *NA* tobacco
kîskisamaw– *VTA* cut (it/him) off for s.o.; offer tobacco to s.o.

TODAY
anohc *IPC* today [*also* anoht]

TOGETHER
mâmawôhkamâto– *VAI* work together at (it/him) as a group, help one another
mâmawôpi– *VAI* sit together, hold a meeting
wîci-pîhtwâm– *VTA* smoke together with s.o.
wîci-pîkiskwêm– *VTA* speak together with s.o.
wîtapim– *VTA* sit with s.o., be present with s.o.; work together with s.o.
wîtaskîwêm– *VTA* live together with s.o.; live in the same country with s.o., live in peace with s.o.
wîtatoskêm– *VTA* work together with s.o.

TOMORROW
wâpahki *IPC* tomorrow

TOO
kîsta *PR* you, too; you, by contrast; you yourself
kîstanaw *PR* we-and-you (incl.), too; we-and-you (incl.) by contrast
kîstawâw *PR* you (pl.), too; you (pl.) by contrast; you yourselves

nânapêc *IPC* late, at the last moment, barely in time (e.g., when it should have been done previously); [*in negative clause:*] too late

nîsta *PR* I, too; I by contrast; I myself

wîsta *PR* he, too; she, too; he by contrast, she by contrast

wîstawâw *PR* they, too; they, by contrast; they themselves

TOOL

âpacihcikan– *NI* tool; appliance, machine

TOOTH

–îpit– *NDI* tooth [*e.g.*, wîpita]

TORNADO

iyôtin– *NI* high wind, tornado [*also* yôtin–]

TORTURE

kakwâtakihiso– *VAI* make oneself suffer; torture oneself, deny oneself food and drink

kakwâtakiho– *VAI* make oneself suffer; torture oneself, deny oneself food and drink

TOWARDS

kitimâkêyihto– *VAI* feel pity towards one another, love one another, think of one another with compassion

kitimâkêyihtowin– *NI* feeling pity towards one another, loving one another, thinking of one another with compassion

sawêyim– *VTA* be generous towards s.o., bless s.o.

TOWN

ôcênâs– *NI* small town [*diminutive*]

TRAIL

mêskanaw– *NI* path, trail, road

sipwêmon– *VII* leave as path, trail, road; begin as path, trail, road

TRANSGRESSION

pâstâhowin– *NI* transgression, breach of the natural order; sin

pâstâhôtot– *VTI* commit a transgression in s.t., commit sacrilege in s.t.

TRAP

nôcihcikê– *VAI* trap things

TRAVEL

pimohtatâ– *VAI* carry (it) along, travel with (it)

pimohtêwin– *NI* travel [*sc. 'agent-centred' noun; e.g.,* nipimohtêwin 'my travelling']

TREAT

kitimah- *VTA* be mean to s.o., treat s.o. badly

manâcihtâ- *VAI* treat (it) with respect

TREATY

nikotwâsik-tipahamâtowin- *NI* Treaty Six

tipahamâtowin- *NI* treaty

wiyihcikê- *VAI* arrange things, conduct negotiations, conclude a treaty

TRIFLE

mikoskâcihtâ- *VAI* trifle with (it), tamper with (it)

tasîhk- *VTI* bother with s.t., trifle with s.t.; be engaged in s.t.

TROUBLE

mâkoh- *VTA* worry s.o., trouble s.o.; oppress s.o., throw s.o. into crisis

mâyitôt- *VTI* do bad things, cause serious trouble

moskâcih- *VTA* bother s.o., trouble s.o., hurt s.o.

TROUBLED

mâkwêyimo- *VAI* be worried, be troubled

mâmitonêyihcikan- *NI* mind; troubled mind

TROUBLESOME

nayêhtâwan- *VII* be difficult, be troublesome

TRUE

tâpwê- *VAI* speak true, speak the truth

tâpwêmakan- *VII* come true; [*fig.*] be fulfilled

TRULY

tâpwê *IPC* truly, indeed

TRUTH

tâpwê- *VAI* speak true, speak the truth

TRY

kakwê *IPV* try to; circumstances permitting, by divine grace

kocihtâ- *VAI* try (it), try to do (it) [*]

kotêyiht- *VTI* try s.t. in one's mind, think strenuously about s.t., test s.t.; challenge s.t.

kotêyim- *VTA* try s.o., test s.o., put s.o.'s mind to the test; challenge s.o.

TURN

asên- *VTA* reject s.o., turn s.o. back

asên- *VTI* reject s.t., turn s.t. back

kwêskâskon- *VTA* turn s.o. (e.g., pipe) to the opposite side

kwêski *IPV* turned around, turned to the opposite side

kwêskinâkwan– *VII* look changed, look turned around to the opposite

kwêtatêyitiskwêyi– *VAI* be at a loss as to where to turn one's head; be at a loss for a response [*cf.* kôtatê]

nâtâmost– *VTI* flee to s.t., turn to s.t. for help, seek refuge in s.t.

nâtâmotot– *VTI* flee to s.t., turn to s.t. for help, seek refuge in s.t.

nâtâmototaw– *VTA* flee to s.o., turn to s.o. for help, seek refuge with s.o.

wâsakân– *VTI* turn s.t. around a circle

wâyonî– *VAI* turn back, return

yôhtên– *VTI* open s.t.; turn s.t. (e.g., television set) on

yôhtênamaw– *VTA* open (it/him) for s.o.; turn (it/him) (e.g., television set) on for s.o.

TWELVE

nîsosâp *IPC* twelve

TWICE

nîswâw *IPC* twice

TWO

nîsi– *VAI* be two in number

nîso *IPC* two

nîso-kîsikâw *IPC* two days

nîsokâtê– *VAI* have two legs, be two-legged

TWO-LEGGED

nîsokâtê– *VAI* have two legs, be two-legged

UNDERNEATH

sîpâ *IPC* beneath, underneath

UNDERSHIRT

pîhcawêsâkânis– *NI* undershirt, slip [*diminutive*]

UNDERSTAND

nisitoht– *VTI* understand s.t.

nisitohtamôh– *VTA* make s.o. understand (it/him)

nisitohtaw– *VTA* understand s.o.

UNGUARDEDLY

âyimômiso– *VAI* discuss oneself; speak unguardedly about oneself, gossip about oneself

UNWELL

is-âyâ– *VAI* be thus in health; be unwell, be in poor health

UP

akot– *VTA* hang s.o. up; place s.o. on a burial scaffold

ispâhkêkocin– *VII* rise high up, be high in the air
ispimihk *IPC* high up, up above
nayawaciki– *VAI* grow up to reach various ages, be variously grown up [*usually plural*]
nîminamaw– *VTA* hold (it/him) aloft for s.o., offer (it/him) up for s.o.
nîminikê– *VAI* hold things aloft, offer things up
ohpahpahtên– *VTI* raise up the smoke of s.t. [*?sic*]
ohpahtên– *VTI* raise up the smoke of s.t.
ohpiki– *VAI* grow up
ohpikih– *VTA* make s.o. grow up, raise s.o.
ohpikihito– *VAI* make one another grow up, raise one another
ohpikinâwaso– *VAI* make one's children grow up, raise one's children

UPON

aspatisin– *VII* lie leaning upon something, lie back upon something, lie propped up
matwêhw– *VTA* sound a beat upon s.o. (e.g., drum), drum on s.o.
naskot– *VTI* respond to s.t.; swear upon s.t. in response
sâkêwêtot– *VTI* come out upon s.t., rise (e.g., sun) upon s.t.

UPRIGHT

cimasi– *VAI* stand upright, stand erect
cimatâ– *VAI* place (it) upright, plant (it) upright
cimatê– *VII* stand upright, stand erect

URGE

sîhkim– *VTA* urge s.o. by speech

USE

âpacih– *VTA* use s.o., find s.o. useful; [*especially in inverse:*] be helped by s.o.
âpacihtamôh– *VTA* make s.o. use (it/him), give (it/him) to s.o. to use; use (it/him) for s.o.
âpacihtâ– *VAI* use (it), make use of (it)
âpatan– *VII* be used, be useful
âpatisi– *VAI* be used, be useful
itâpacih– *VTA* use s.o. thus, find s.o. useful thus; [*especially in inverse:*] be thus helped by s.o.
itâpacihtâ– *VAI* use (it) thus, use such (things)
itâpatan– *VII* be thus used, be of such use

otônihkâ– *VAI* use (it/him) as one's mouthpiece, make (it/him) one's advocate

USEFUL

âpacih– *VTA* use s.o., find s.o. useful; [*especially in inverse:*] be helped by s.o.

âpatan– *VII* be used, be useful

âpatisi– *VAI* be used, be useful

itâpacih– *VTA* use s.o. thus, find s.o. useful thus; [*especially in inverse:*] be thus helped by s.o.

USUALLY

mâna *IPC* habitually, usually

VALUABLE

miyo *IPV* good, well, beautiful, valuable

miywâsin– *VII* be good, be valuable; [*in negative clause:*] be bad, be evil

VALUE

itakiht– *VTI* count s.t. thus, value s.t. thus, hold s.t. in such esteem

itakim– *VTA* count s.o. thus, value s.o. thus, hold s.o. in such esteem

VARIOUS

nanâtohk *IPC* variously, of various kinds

nayawaciki– *VAI* grow up to reach various ages, be variously grown up [*usually plural*]

VARIOUSLY

nanâtohk *IPC* variously, of various kinds

nayawaciki– *VAI* grow up to reach various ages, be variously grown up [*usually plural*]

VENTURE

mâyêyiht– *VTI* consider s.t. challenging; be willing to tackle a difficult task, venture out

VERY

mistahi *IPC* greatly, very much so [*also* IPV]

VIEW

sâkohtê– *VAI* walk into view, move into view

VIGOROUSLY

yahkatâmo– *VAI* sing out vigorously

VISIBLE

kîhkânâkwan– *VII* be clearly visible

nôkosi– *VAI* be visible; be born

VISION

âkaw-âyihk *IPC* in a hidden place, behind an obstacle to vision

wâpi– *VAI* be sighted, have vision; [*in negative clause:*] be blind

WAGON

ocâpânâskos– *NI* cart; small wagon, small sled [*diminutive*]

WAIL

mawihkâtamaw– *VTA* cry out in prayer to s.o., wail to s.o.

mawimo– *VAI* cry out; cry out in prayer, wail

mawimoscikê– *VAI* cry out in prayer, wail; worship with (it)

mawimost– *VTI* cry out in prayer to s.t., wail to s.t.

mâto– *VAI* cry, wail

WAILING

mawimoscikêwin– *NI* crying out in prayer, wailing; form of worship, ceremony

WAIT

cêskwa *IPC* wait; [*in negative clause:*] not yet

mâcikôtitan *IPC* wait and see! lo! [*exlamatory; sic:* -â-, -ô-, -a-]

WAKE UP

pêkopayi– *VAI* awake, wake up

WALK

pimohtê– *VAI* go along, walk along

sâkohtê– *VAI* walk into view, move into view

takohtê– *VAI* arrive walking

yîkatêhtê– *VAI* walk off to the side

WANT

nitawêyiht– *VTI* want s.t.

nitawêyim– *VTA* want s.o., want (it/him) of s.o.

nôhtê *IPV* want to

nôhtêhkatê– *VAI* be hungry, want food

WARD

kisêyinîw-ôhpikihâkan– *NA* old man's pupil, ward of the old men

mîtâkwêwi– *VAI* ward (it/him) off for s.o. [*?sic*]

WARN

kitâsôm– *VTA* warn s.o. about (it/him)

WARY

astâh– *VTA* frighten s.o.; [*especially in inverse:*] cause s.o. to be wary, worry s.o.

WASH

kisîpêkinikê– *VAI* wash things, do the laundry

WATCH

asawâpi– *VAI* look out, be on watch

kiskinowâpaht– *VTI* learn merely by watching s.t.

kiskinowâpiwin– *NI* learning merely by watching

okiskinowâpiw– *NA* one who learns merely by watching

WATER

akâmaskîhk *IPC* across the water, overseas

itakâm *IPC* on the hither side of a body of water, on the near side of a body of water

nipiy– *NI* water

sîkahasinânâpoy– *NI* rock-sprinkling water (in sweat-lodge)

tahkâpâwat– *VTA* pour water to cool s.o. (e.g., rock), cool s.o. (e.g., rock) with water (in sweat-lodge)

WAY

âkwaskiskaw– *VTA* head s.o. off, get in s.o.'s way

êkos îsi *IPC* thus, in that way; that is how it is

êkosi *IPC* thus, in that way; that is all

kakêpâhkamikisi– *VAI* fool around, get in the way

ômis îsi *IPC* in this way; that is how it is

ômisi *IPC* in this way

tahtwayak *IPC* in so many places, in so many ways

tawâtamaw– *VTA* open (it) up for s.o.; clear the way for s.o.

tânisi *IPC* how, in what way

WE

niyanân *PR* we (excl.)

WE-AND-YOU

kiyânaw *PR* we-and-you (incl.)

kîstanaw *PR* we-and-you (incl.), too; we-and-you (incl.) by contrast

WEAR

mîstowê– *VAI* be bearded, wear a beard [*sic:* -î-; *cf.* -îhi-]

WEATHER

âstê-kîsikâ– *VII* cease being stormy weather, be better weather

mâyi-kîsikâ– *VII* be stormy weather, be foul weather

WEEK

tahto-nîsw-âyamihêwi-kîsikâw *IPC* every second week, fortnightly

WELFARE

pamihikowin– *NI* being looked after, welfare [*sc. 'patient-centred' noun; e.g.,* kipamihikowin 'the fact that you are looked after']

WELL

â *IPC* well [*introductory; cf.* hâ, wâ]

hâ *IPC* well [*introductory; cf.* â]

iyaw *IPC* well now [*; *introductory, also exclamatory*]

miyo *IPV* good, well, beautiful, valuable

miyomahciho– *VAI* feel well, feel healthy; feel pleased

miyopayin– *VII* work well, run well [*]

miyopit– *VTI* carry s.t. off well, accomplish s.t.

miyw-âyâ– *VAI* be well, be in good health

mônahipân– *NI* source, well

nanahihtaw– *VTA* listen well to s.o., obey s.o.

wâ *IPC* well [*introductory; cf.* â]

WERE

kîspin êkâ ohci *IPC* if it were not for [*irrealis conditional, usually with noun phrase or simple conjunct*]

WEST

pahkisimohk *IPC* in the west, to the west

WHAT

êcika *IPC* what is this! [*exclamatory; preclitic, usually with demonstrative pronoun*]

kîkwây *PR* what [*interrogative; e.g.,* kîkwây(i), kîkwaya]

tânisi *IPC* how, in what way

tânispî *IPC* when, at what time

tâniyikohk *IPC* to what extent; to such an extent

WHATEVER

misawâc *IPC* in any case, whatever might be thought

WHEN

tânispî *IPC* when, at what time

WHERE

ita *IPC* there; there where

pikw îta *IPC* no matter where, in any place

tânita *IPC* where

tânitê *IPC* where, whither

WHICH

tânima *PR* which one

WHILE

aciyaw *IPC* for a little while [*]

mêkwâc *IPC* while, in the course of

nômanak *IPC* a while

pita *IPC* first, for a while [*cf.* pitamâ]

pitamâ *IPC* first, for a while [*cf.* pita]

WHITE

môniyâw– *NA* White-Man, White

môniyâw-âyamihâwin– *NI* White religion

wâpiskâ– *VII* be white

wâpiski-wiyâs– *NA* White-Man, White

WHITHER

pikw îtê *IPC* no matter whither, to any place

tânitê *IPC* where, whither

WHO

awîna *PR* who [*interrogative; e.g.*, awîna]

WHY

tânêhki *IPC* why

WILL

âhkamêyimo– *VAI* persist in one's will, persevere

mâyêyiht– *VTI* consider s.t. challenging; be willing to tackle a difficult task, venture out

WIND

iyôtin– *NA* [*spirit's name:*] Wind

iyôtin– *NI* high wind, tornado [*also* yôtin–]

yôtin– *NA* [*spirit's name:*] Wind [*cf.* iyôtin–]

WISAHKETCHAHK

wîsahkêcâhkw– *NA* Wisahketchahk

WISH

pakosêyim– *VTA* wish for (it/him) of s.o., expect (it/him) of s.o.

pakosêyimo– *VAI* wish for (it), have an expectation

pitanê *IPC* wish that [*with simple conjunct*]

WITH

kâkîsimwâkê– *VAI* chant prayers with things

kikapi– *VAI* sit along with something

kikastê– *VII* be placed along with something

kiki *IPV* along with

mawimoscikê– *VAI* cry out in prayer, wail; worship with (it)

mêtawâkê– *VAI* play around with things, fool around with things

miyawâkâc *IPV* with particular care

nakiskamohtatamaw– *VTA* take (it/him) to meet s.o., meet s.o. with (it/him); introduce (it/him) to s.o.

nîkânohtatâ– *VAI* be in the lead with (it), carry (it) in the lead

ohci *IPC* with, by means of; because of; from then [*enclitic; also* IPV]

pakosih– *VTA* beg from s.o.; be a hanger-on to s.o., go with s.o., be part of s.o.

pimâcihwâkê– *VAI* make one's living with things

pimohtatâ– *VAI* carry (it) along, travel with (it)

pîhtikwah– *VTA* enter with s.o., take s.o. inside

pîhtikwatâ– *VAI* enter with (it), take (it) inside

wîc-âyâm– *VTA* be with s.o., live with s.o.

wîcêhtowin– *NI* living with one another; getting along with one another, living in harmony with one another

wîci-pîhtwâm– *VTA* smoke together with s.o.

wîci-pîkiskwêm– *VTA* speak together with s.o.

wîtapim– *VTA* sit with s.o., be present with s.o.; work together with s.o.

wîtaskîwêm– *VTA* live together with s.o.; live in the same country with s.o., live in peace with s.o.

wîtatoskêm– *VTA* work together with s.o.

WITHOUT

âstawê– *VII* be without fire, be extinct (e.g., fire)

konita *IPC* in vain, without reason, without purpose; without further ado

mâmâsîs *IPC* sparingly, delicately; quickly, roughly, without care

môy êkâ êtokwê *IPC* without any doubt, of necessity [*usually with independent indicative*]

sôskwât *IPC* simply, without further ado

WITNESS

wâpaht– *VTI* see s.t., witness s.t.

wâpam– *VTA* see s.o., witness s.o.

WOMAN

–ôhkom– *NDA* grandmother, grandmother's sister, great-aunt; [*fig.*] old woman; Our Grandmother [*e.g.*, nôhkominân; kôhkominaw]

iskwêw– *NA* woman

nôtikwêsiw– *NA* old woman [*diminutive*]

nôtikwêw– *NA* old woman

oskinîkiskwêw– *NA* young woman

WONDER

matwân cî *IPC* I wonder [*polar dubitative*]

WOOD

oskicîwâhtikw– *NI* wood of pipestem

WORD

aspitonâmo– *VAI* flee to rely on spoken words, rely on (it) as a formal confirmation of the spoken word

kisêyinîwi-pîkiskwêwin– *NI* old man's word, word of the old men

kîsowât– *VTI* complete one's words, complete one's prayers

kîsowâtamaw– *VTA* complete words for s.o., complete prayers for s.o.

pîkiskwê– *VAI* use words, speak

pîkiskwêwin– *NI* word, expression, phrase; speech, language

WORK

atoskaw– *VTA* work for s.o.

atoskât– *VTI* work at s.t.

atoskê– *VAI* work

atoskêwin– *NI* work

mâmawôhkamâto– *VAI* work together at (it/him) as a group, help one another

miyoniskêhkât– *VTI* accomplish s.t. by the work of one's hands

miyopayin– *VII* work well, run well [*]

wîtapim– *VTA* sit with s.o., be present with s.o.; work together with s.o.

wîtatoskêm– *VTA* work together with s.o.

WORLD

askiy– *NI* earth, land, country; world

askîwi– *VII* be the earth, exist as world

WORRY

astâh– *VTA* frighten s.o.; [*especially in inverse:*] cause s.o. to be wary, worry s.o.

mâkoh– *VTA* worry s.o., trouble s.o.; oppress s.o., throw s.o. into crisis

mâkwêyimo– *VAI* be worried, be troubled

mâmitonêyiht– *VTI* think about s.t., worry about s.t.